STREET CULTURE

seleen saleh

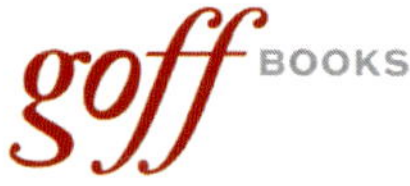

Published by Goff Books, an Imprint of ORO Editions.
Executive publisher: Gordon Goff.

www.goffbooks.com
info@goffbooks.com

Images: Hannan Saleh
Graphic Design: Sumana Ghosh-Witherspoon *shoemona.myportfolio.com*
Goff Books Project Coordinator: Kirby Anderson

10 9 8 7 6 5 4 3 2 1 First Edition

Library of Congress data available upon request. World Rights: available.

ISBN: 978-1-943532-59-9

Color separations and printing: ORO Group Ltd.Printed in China.

International distribution: www.goffbooks.com/distribution

ORO Editions makes a continuous effort to minimize the overall carbon footprint of its publications. As part of this goal, ORO Editions, in association with Global ReLeaf, arranges to plant trees to replace those used in the manufacturing of the paper produced for its books. Global ReLeaf is an international campaign run by American Forests, one of the world's oldest nonprofit conservation organizations. Global ReLeaf is American Forests' education and action program that helps individuals, organizations, agencies, and corporations improve the local and global environment by planting and caring for trees.

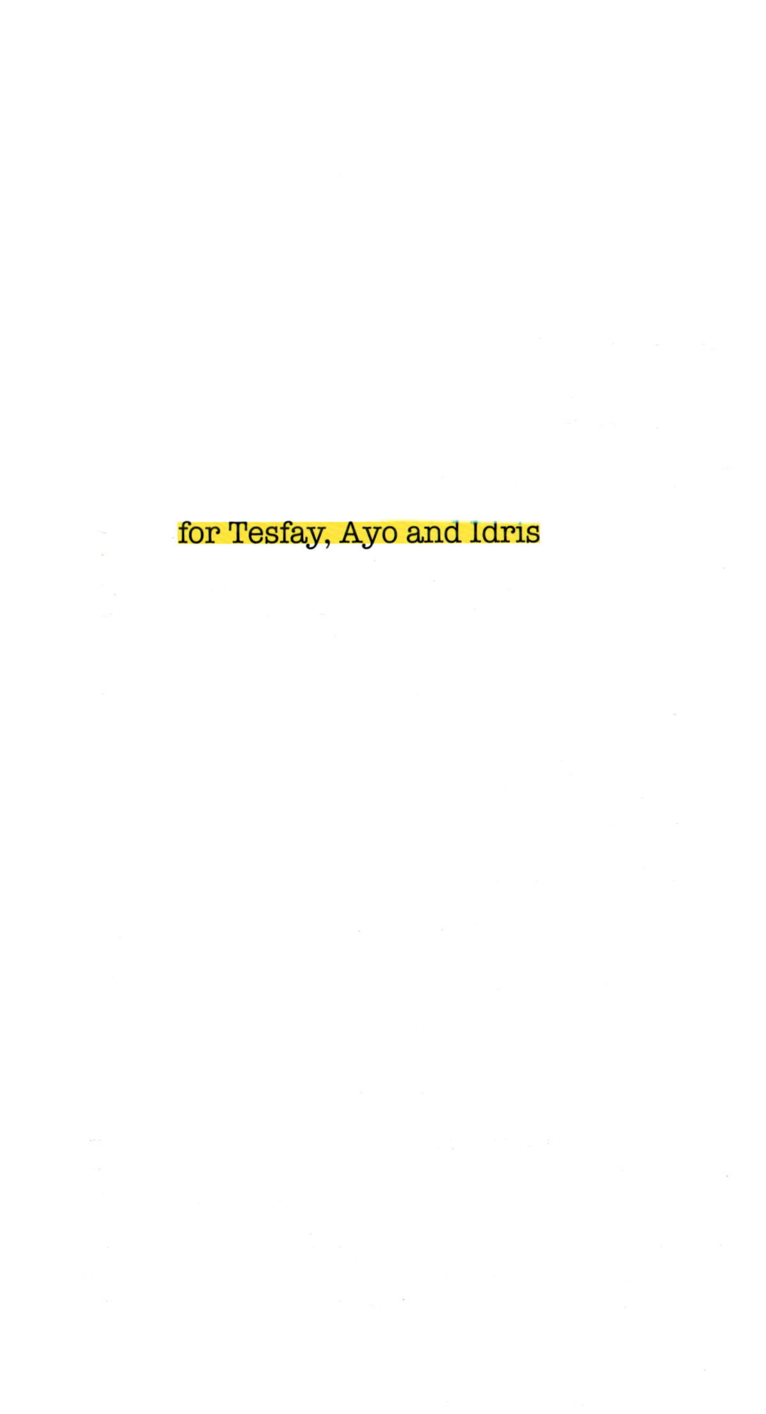

for Tesfay, Ayo and Idris

FOREWARD

It was my last day on set as a fashion model, many years ago when I decided I had enough of the fashion industry that consumed my life for over a decade. I was scouted off the s treets of New York immediately after high school, little did I know my life would drastically change in a direction I never imagined for myself. As a young woman I was excited to submerge in the industry, entering into this new chapter of my life, but as a woman of color my excitement quickly deteriorated when I found out what it entailed; a forced acceptance of beauty and fashion, that was not relatable or realistic. Quite frankly breaking down the foundation of what I thought beauty and fashion really was: an inclusive platform of creativity and diversity.

The misconceived, stereotypical and limited ideologies of beauty and style regarding women of color, bombarded upon me daily, was in a sense the unwavering 10 commandments of the fashion industry. Any who dare dispute those warped standards, standing against the grain, would quickly find themselves banished.

After many, many years of feeling depleted and defeated I had enough, and summoned the strength to decide how I wanted to be defined, how I wanted the world to see me; Street Culture is the ultimate source, an everlasting imprint in defining how we want the world to see us, not how the world many times wants to define you.

It was a beautiful, sunny but brisk day when I met Seleen Saleh at a coffee shop in the meatpacking district of New York, almost eight years ago. We spoke of how in her childhood she would find herself in the library browsing through magazines, admiring women in fashion. One of her most memorable recollections is of British *Vogue's* January 1990 issue, featuring four of the biggest supermodels, one a woman of color: Naomi Campbell. Seeing Naomi on the cover brought retrospection to Seleen's inspiration, of wanting to create a space for people of color to express themselves, beyond the limited accepted standards.

As a photographer Seleen is a notable recurring face within the industry, under the umbrella of one of the top fashion publications. She gives recognition, etching monumental space in the street style arena to influencers, professionals, models, style-enthusiasts of color when a majority of major publications lacked representation, whether it be consciously or unconsciously. There is a constant unfed and unrepresented market within the industry, yet Seleen's body of work brings much needed nourishment to that starving audience.

Times are now changing, diversity is an influential driving force; yet inclusivity, a table of our own where diversity is always at the forefront and not an afterthought to fill a quota, is presently a reality that is inconsistent. A space where who you are, designer labels, the number of social media followers, or color of your skin is not a determining factor, rather the essence, creativity, talent, or authenticity of style is–the true unadulterated culture of the streets. Every single page is a breathtaking multifaceted beacon of representation. In its totality *Street Culture* provides not just a seat but a seat for everyone at the table of Seleen's creation, in an undeniably irresistible and magnetizing way.

In the pages before you, we see style for what it genuinely is; derived from culture in an uninhibited, original, bold yet naturally flawless depiction. Free of stereotypical societal norms of what qualifies as street-style, but instead showcasing style beyond aesthetics, a style enriched in culture from our vision, our world, our streets.

I hope you are as captivated by Seleen's photography as much as I was–this book is a physical testament to the courageous beauty of defining how you wish the world to see you.

"Define how you want the world to see you, not how the world wants to define you."

—Cipriana Quann

“

Seleen is one of the first people in the industry to capture street style authenticely...I am looking forward to seeing all the beautiful people showing their own personal style and representing how we influence culture at large.

”

—Jerome Lamaar

“

What is “street style” without a great street and great style? I’ve always seen Seleen as someone who has that unique eye for capturing that brief moment before we end up at the party or after the event, knowing what street to be on and what angle to center people around that also matches with the environment. This work reminds me that Instant shooting with organic lighting isn’t easy, leave it to the street legends!

”

—Young Paris

“

Seleen has that eye that catches
the intricacies of style; she notices
the subtle details that make
one coat stand out from another;
she understands why the loud
prints aren’t just cacophony but a
great tune which you won’t get
out of your head. To be seen
by Seleen’s lens is to be celebrated.
And I for one, am grateful
for the continuous celebration!

”

—Bozoma Saint John

“

I am so glad that someone
with the eye and appreciation for
personal style exists to
reflect social society in the way
Seleen Saleh has...

”

—Bethann Hardison

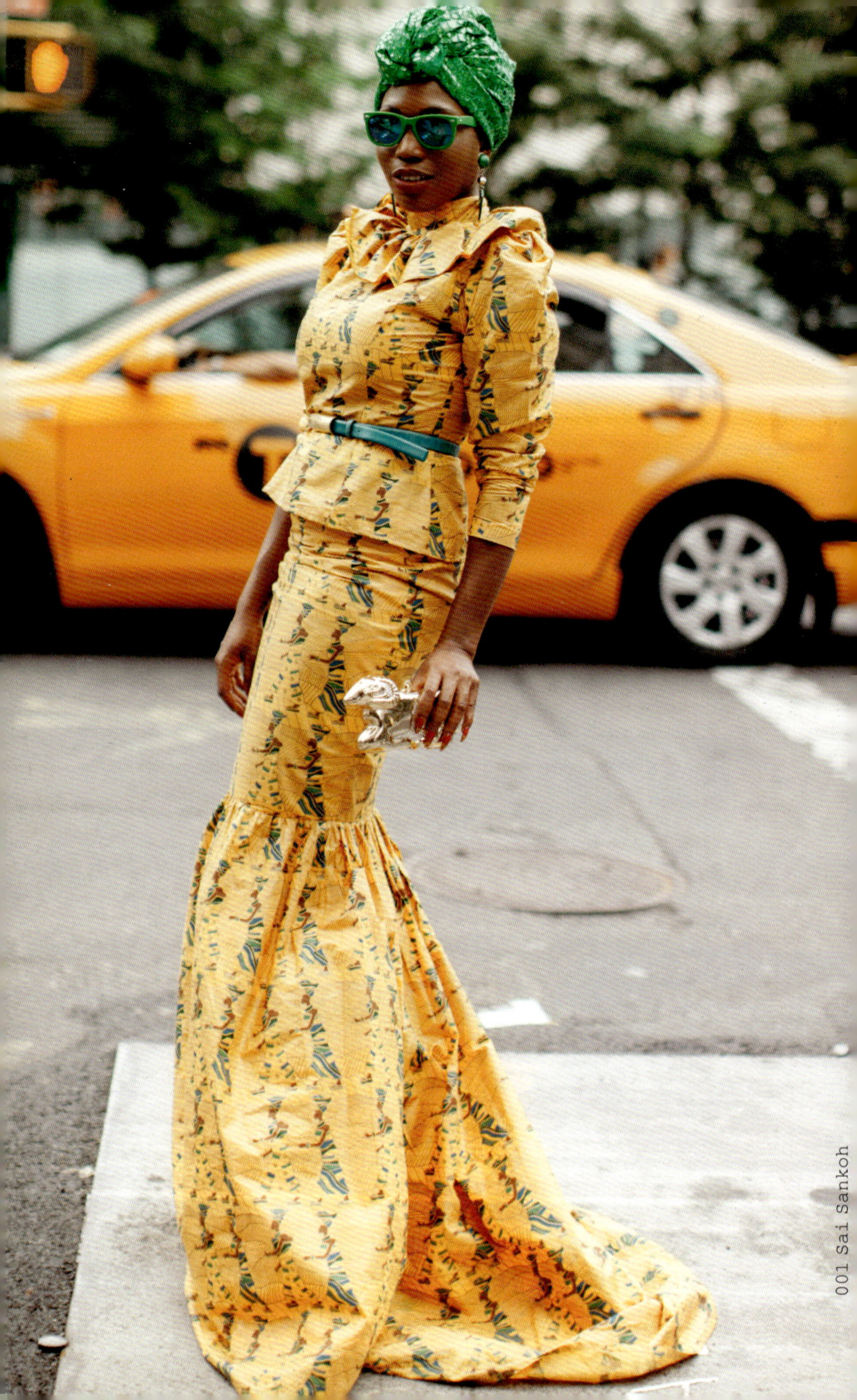

001 Sai Sankoh

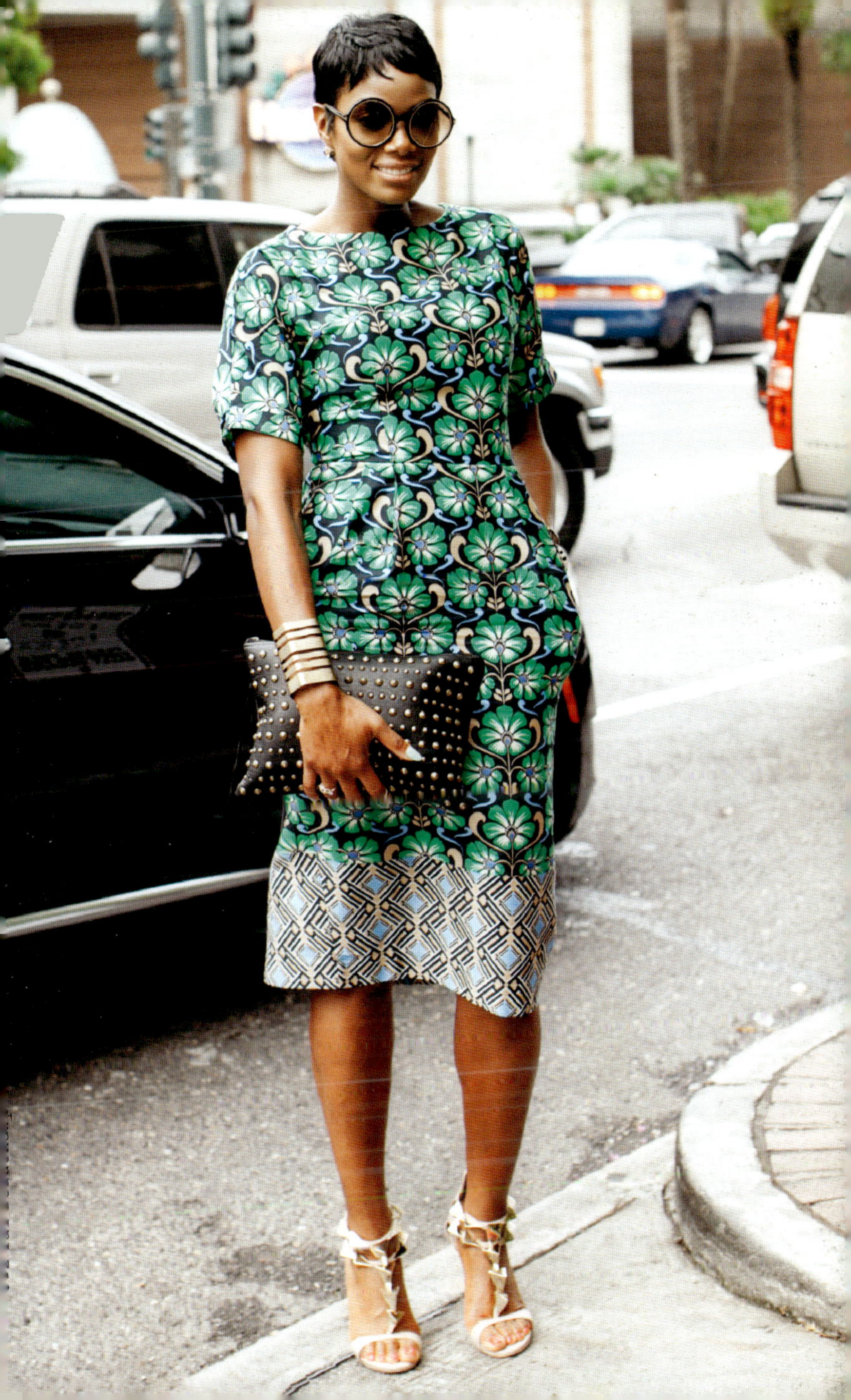

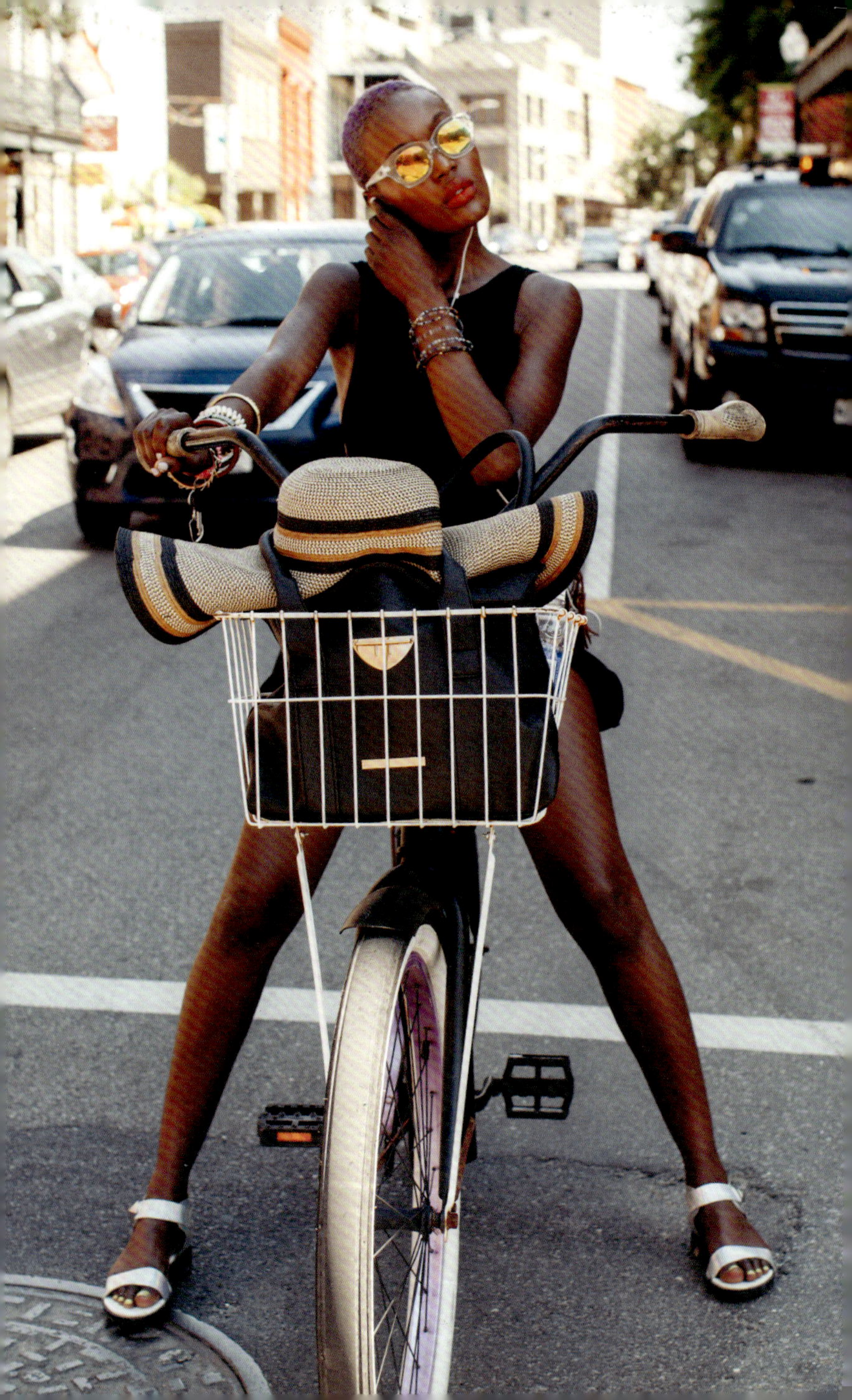

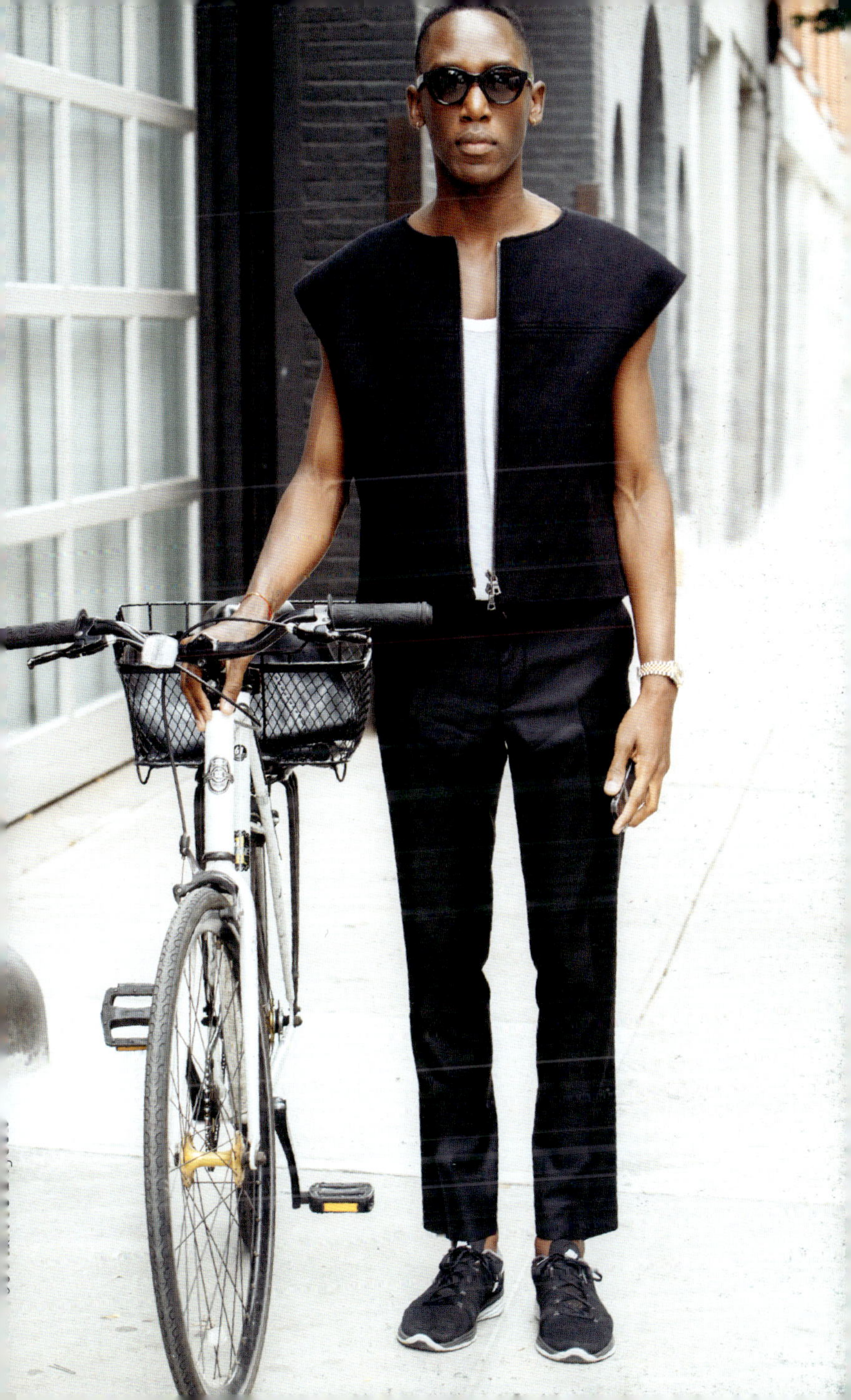

"Living in New York has modified my style a lot. I wear what works between morning and evening."

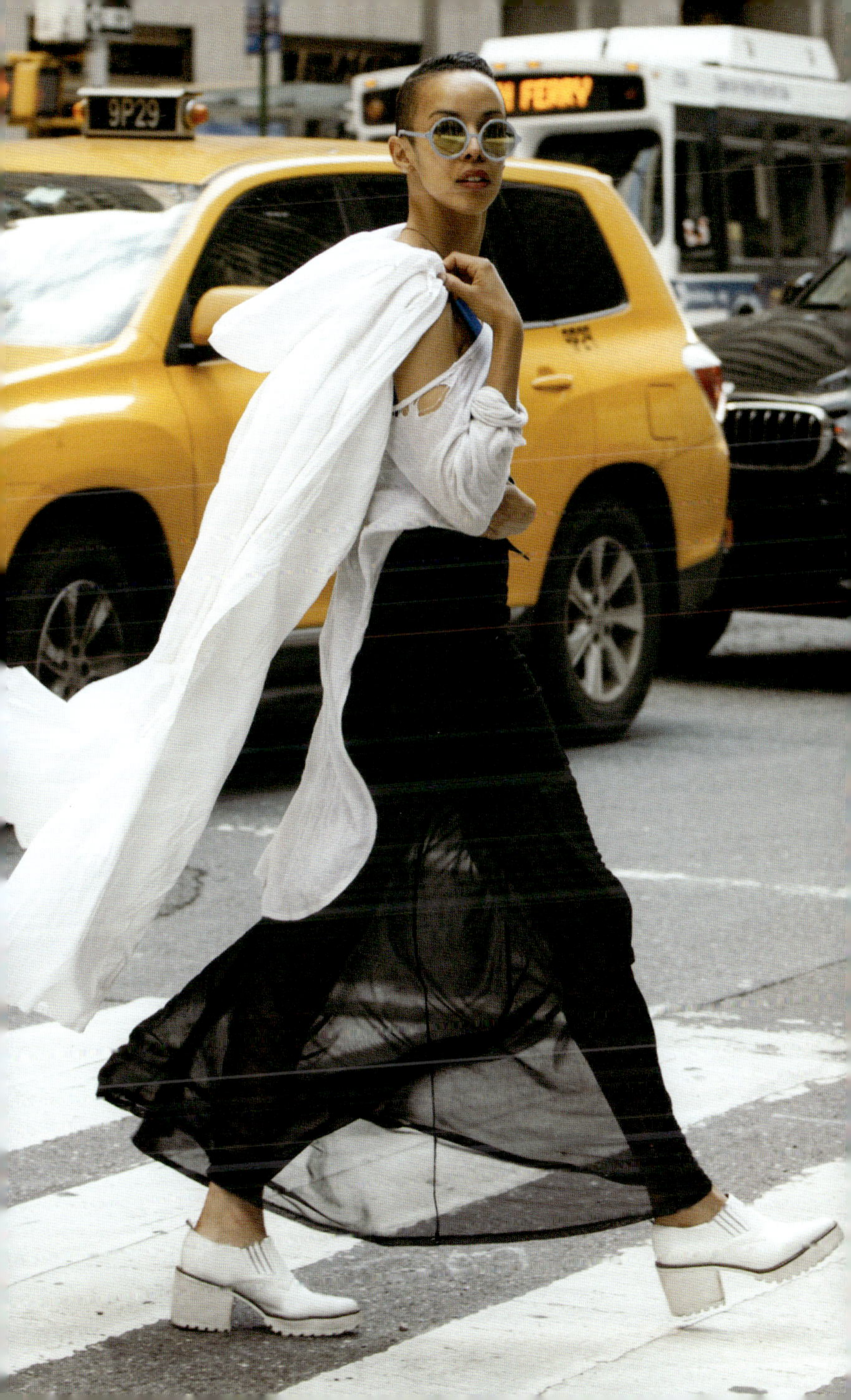
9P29
FERRY

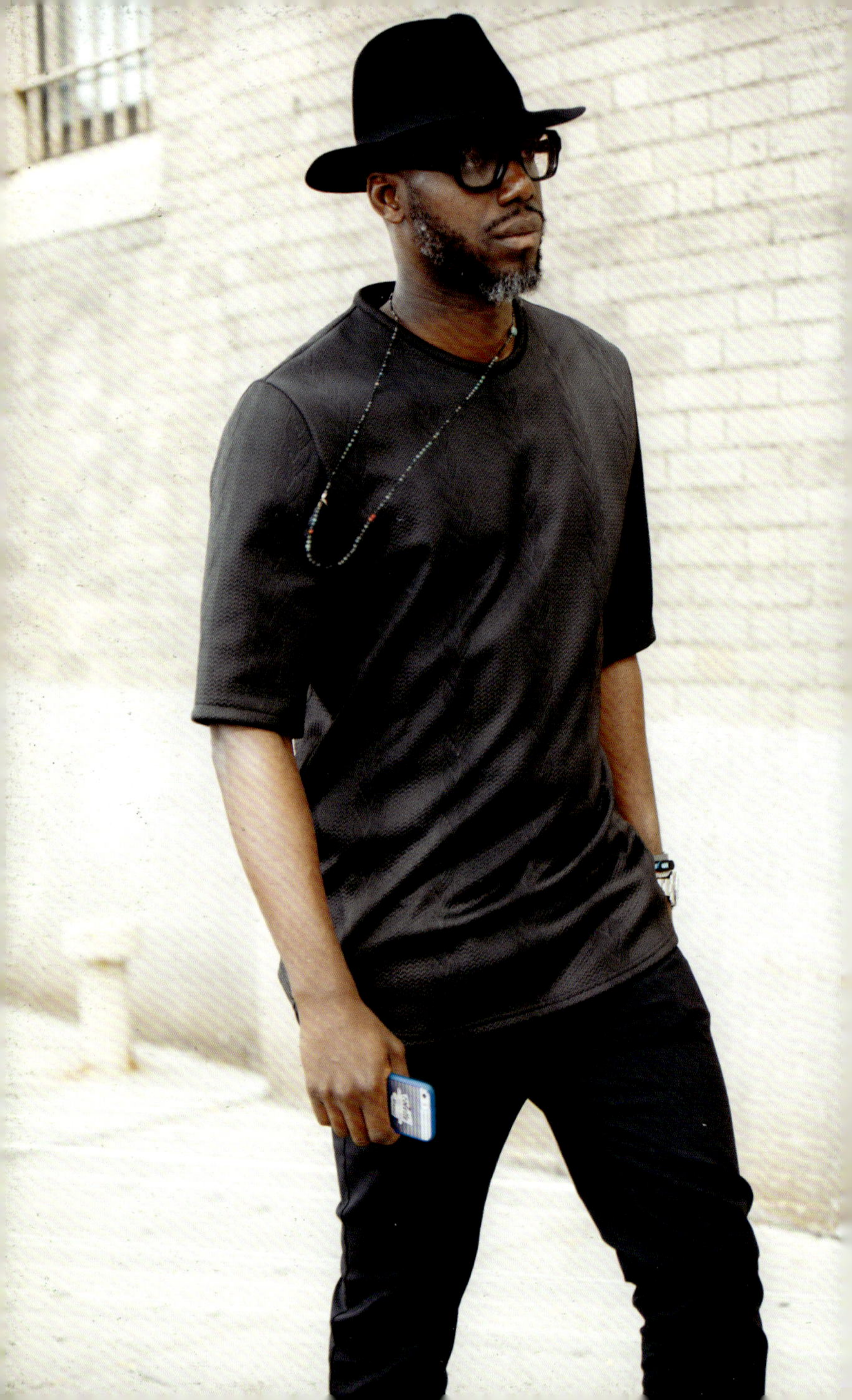

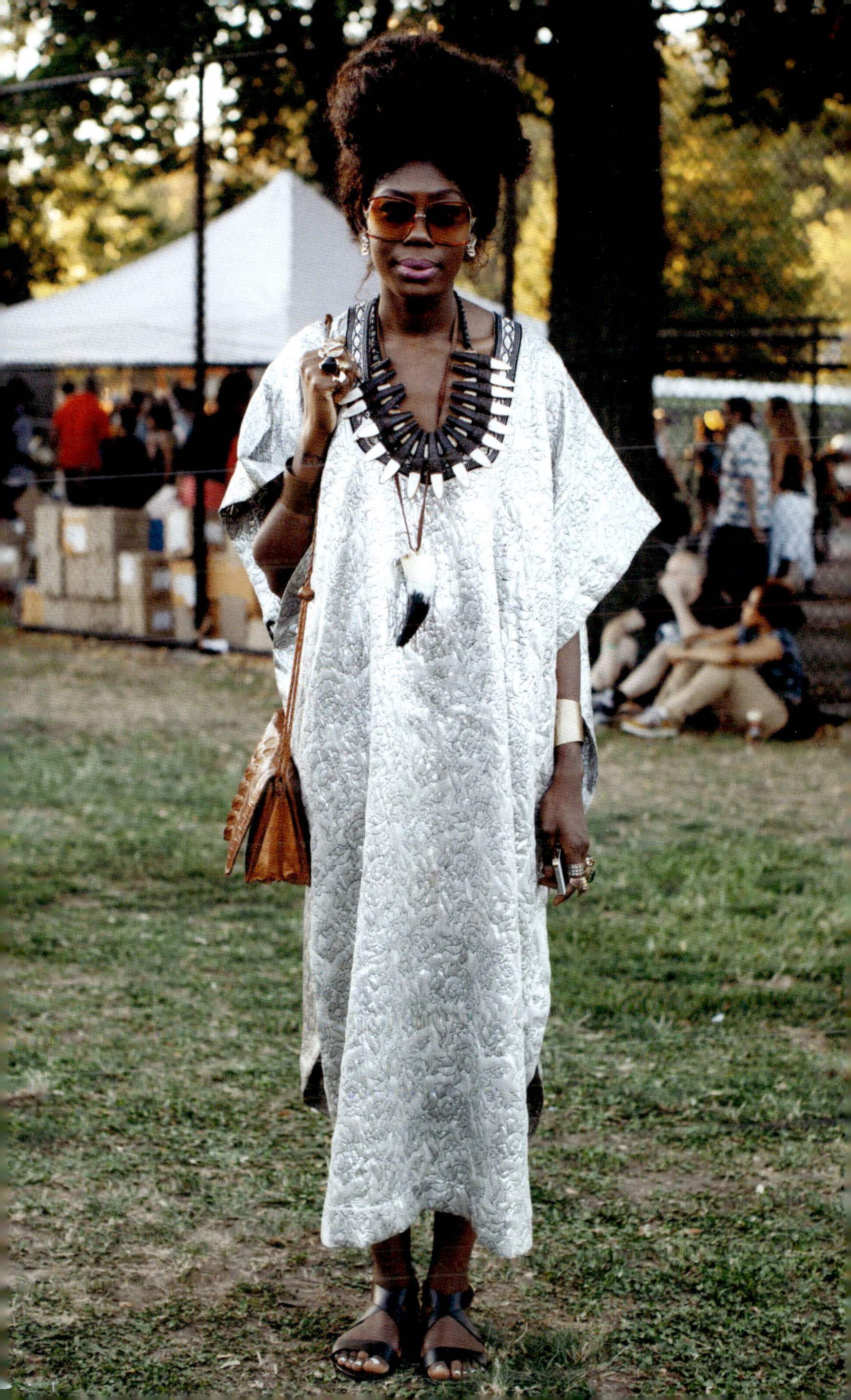

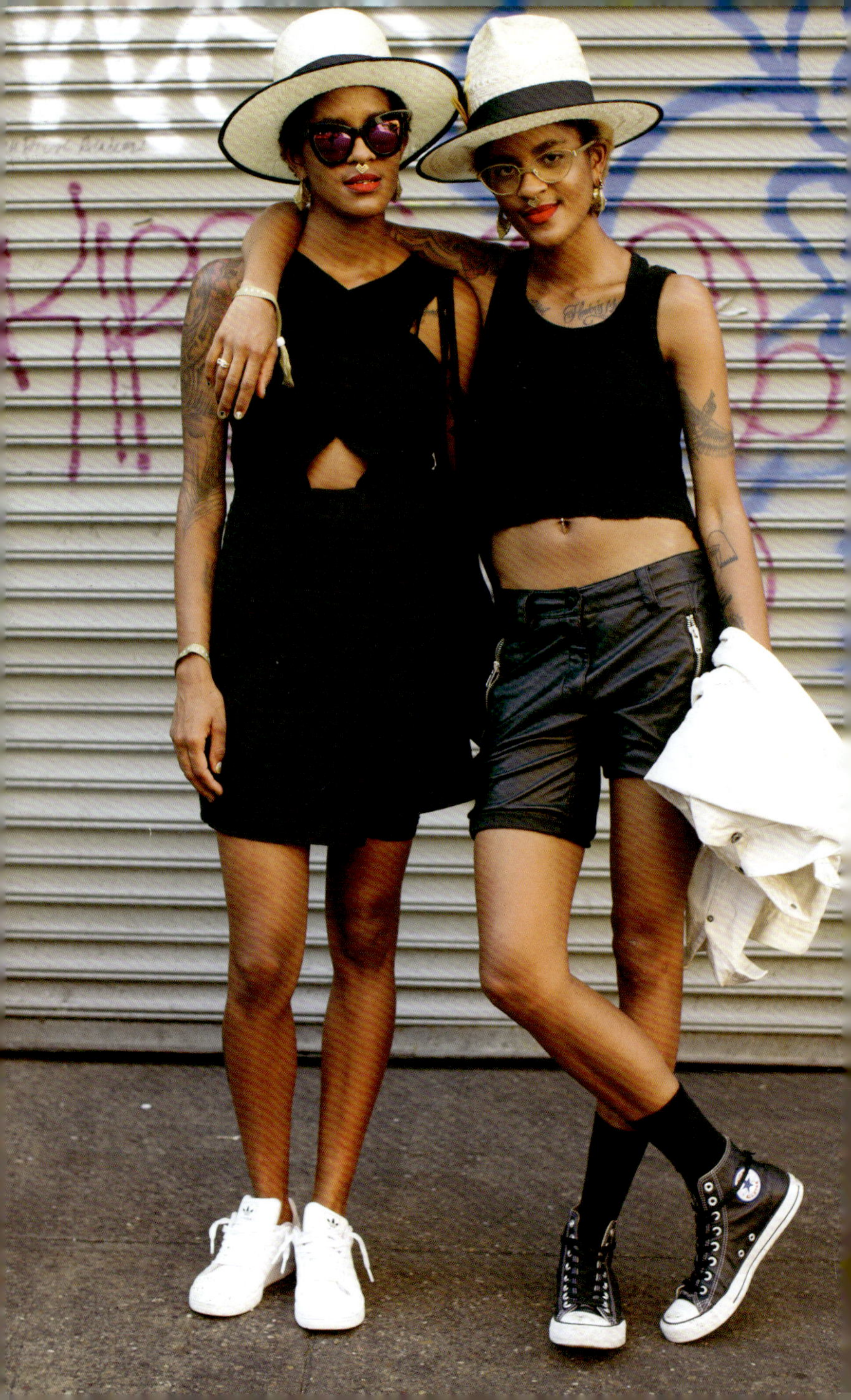

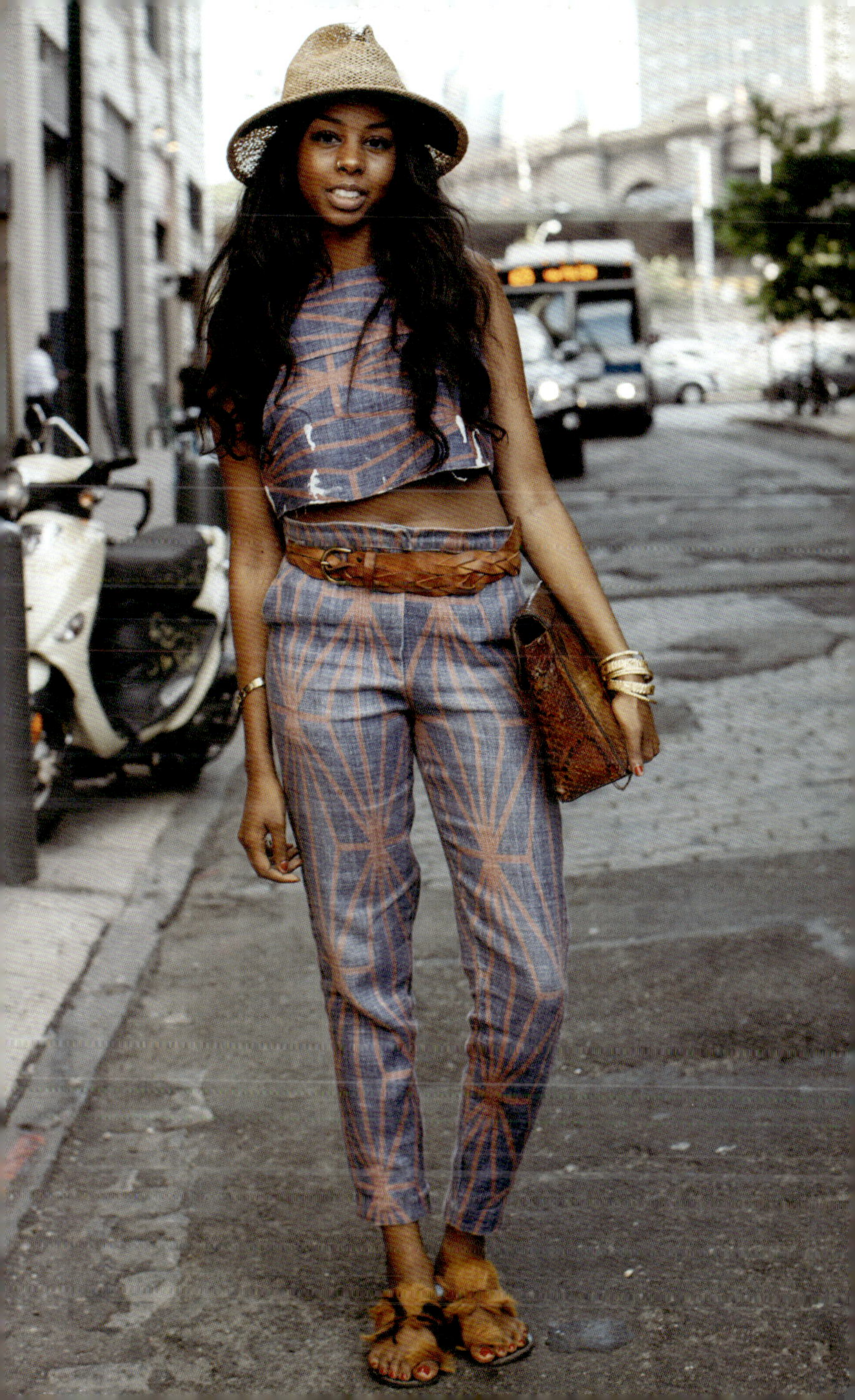

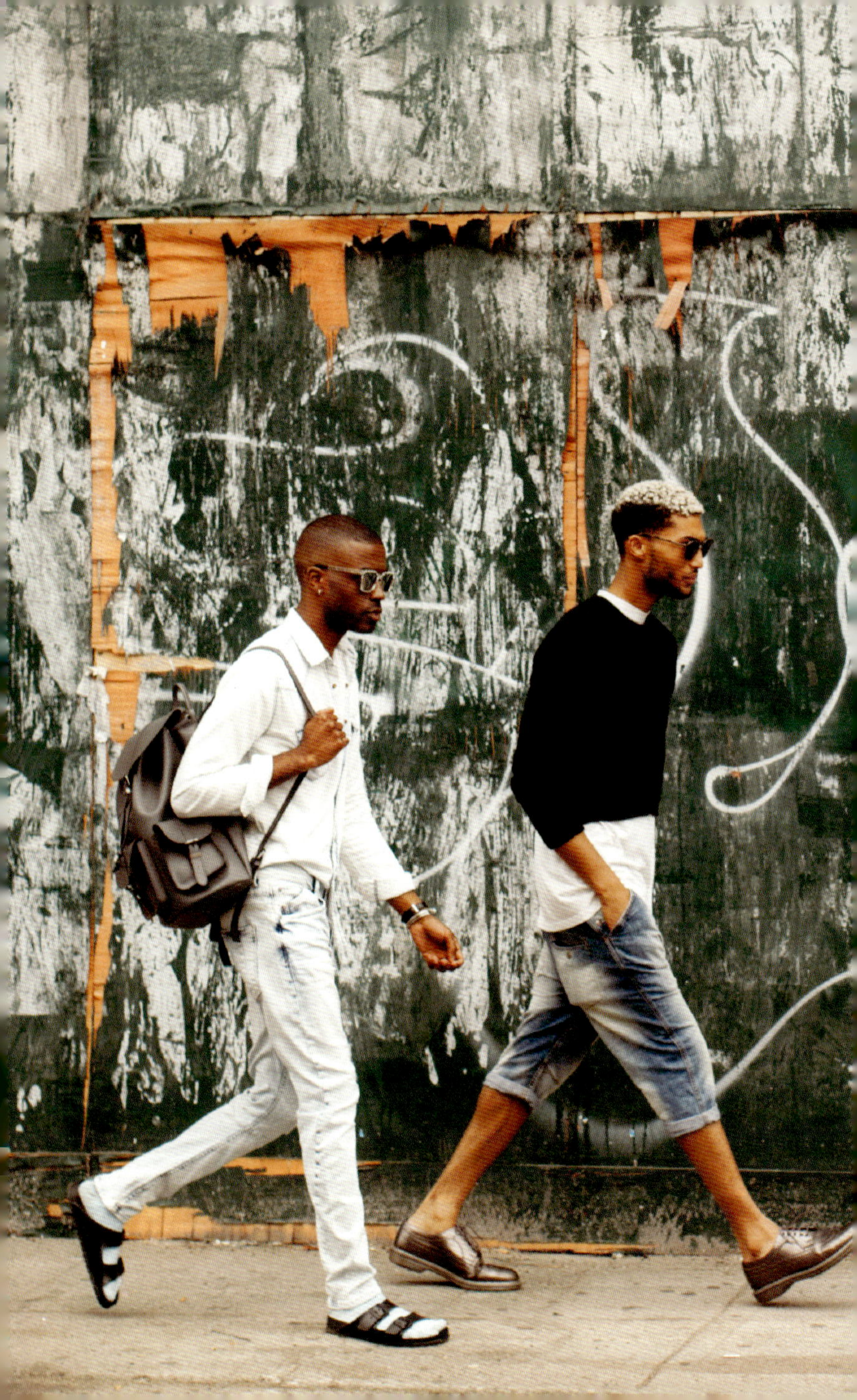

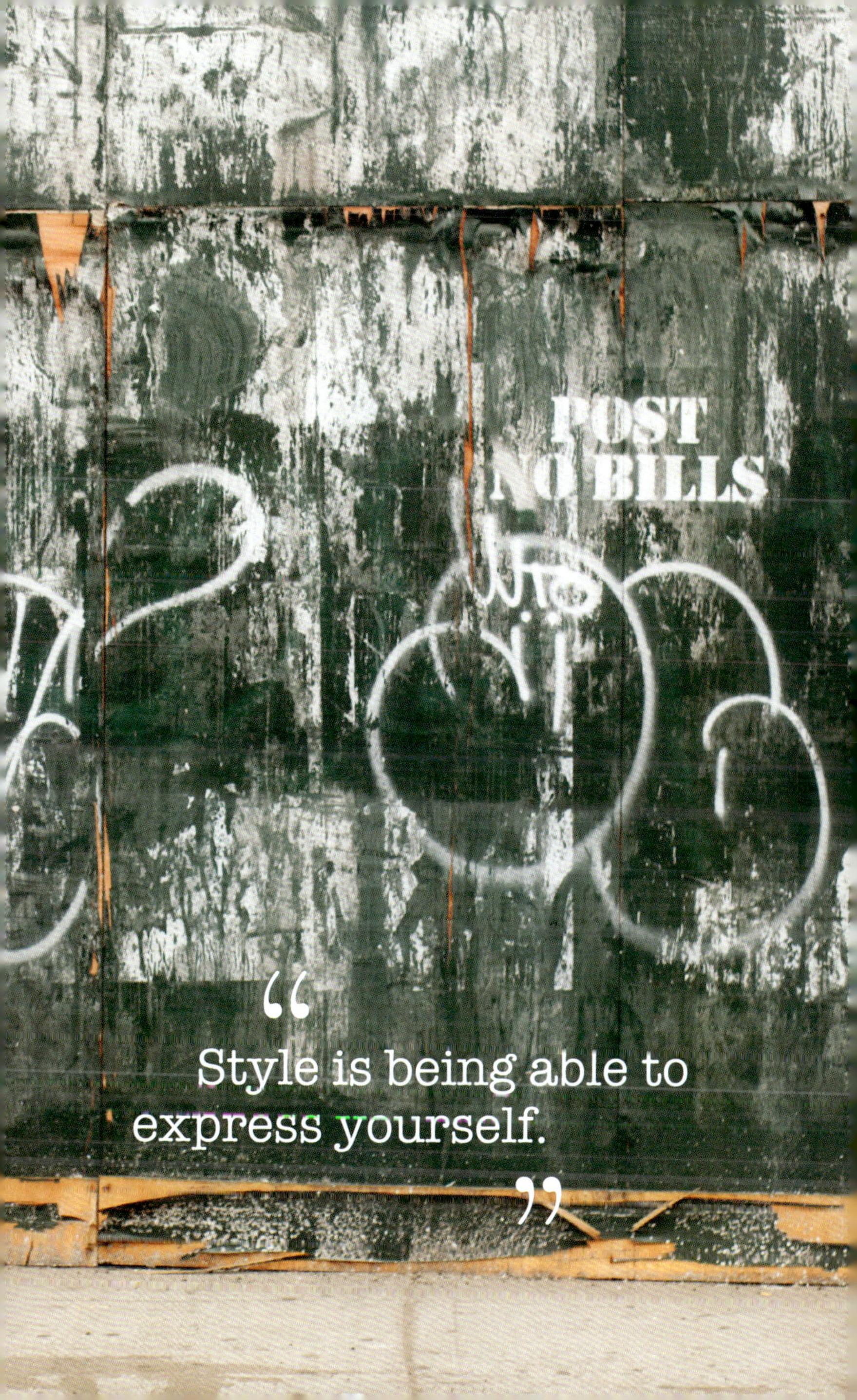

"Style is being able to express yourself."

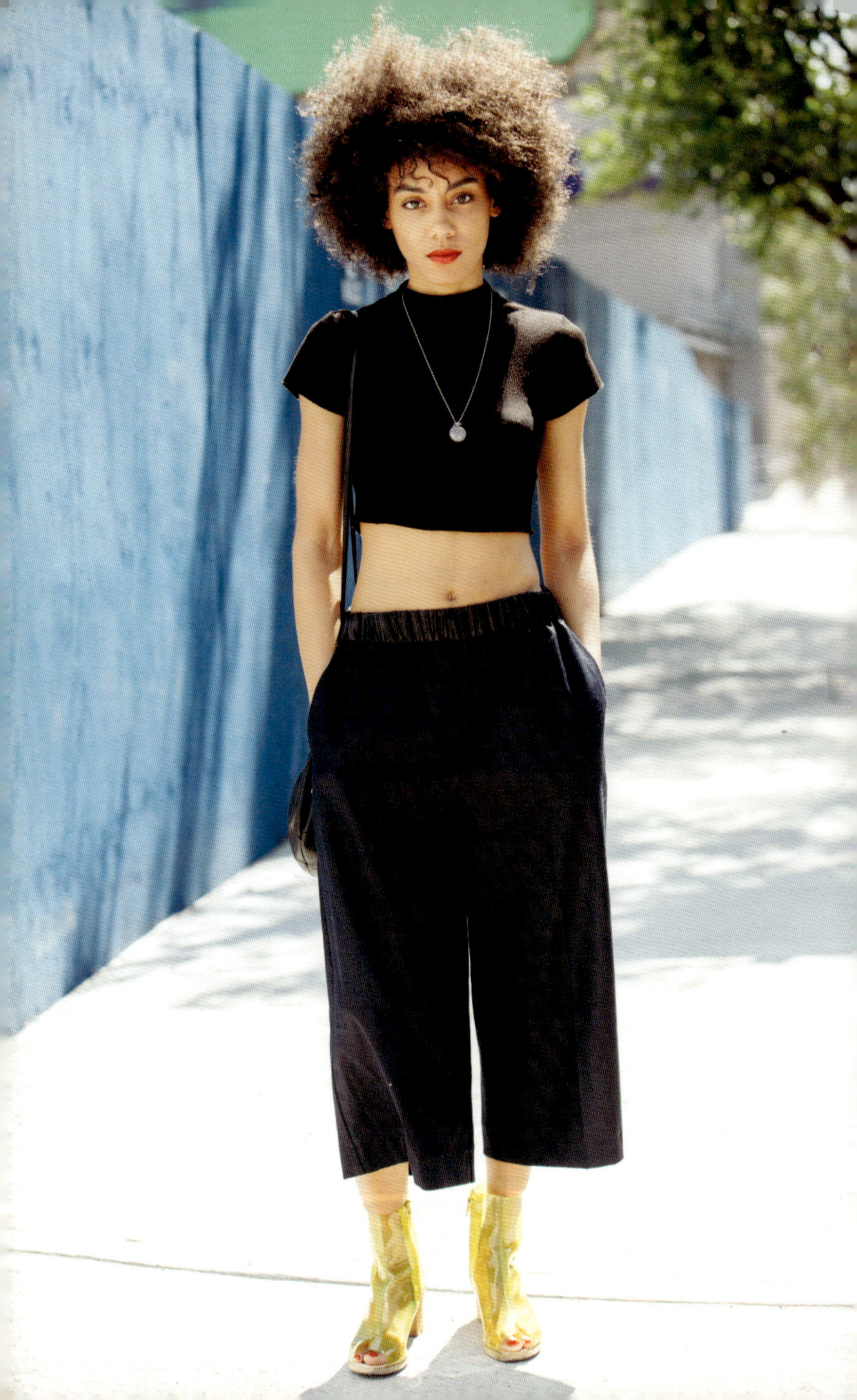

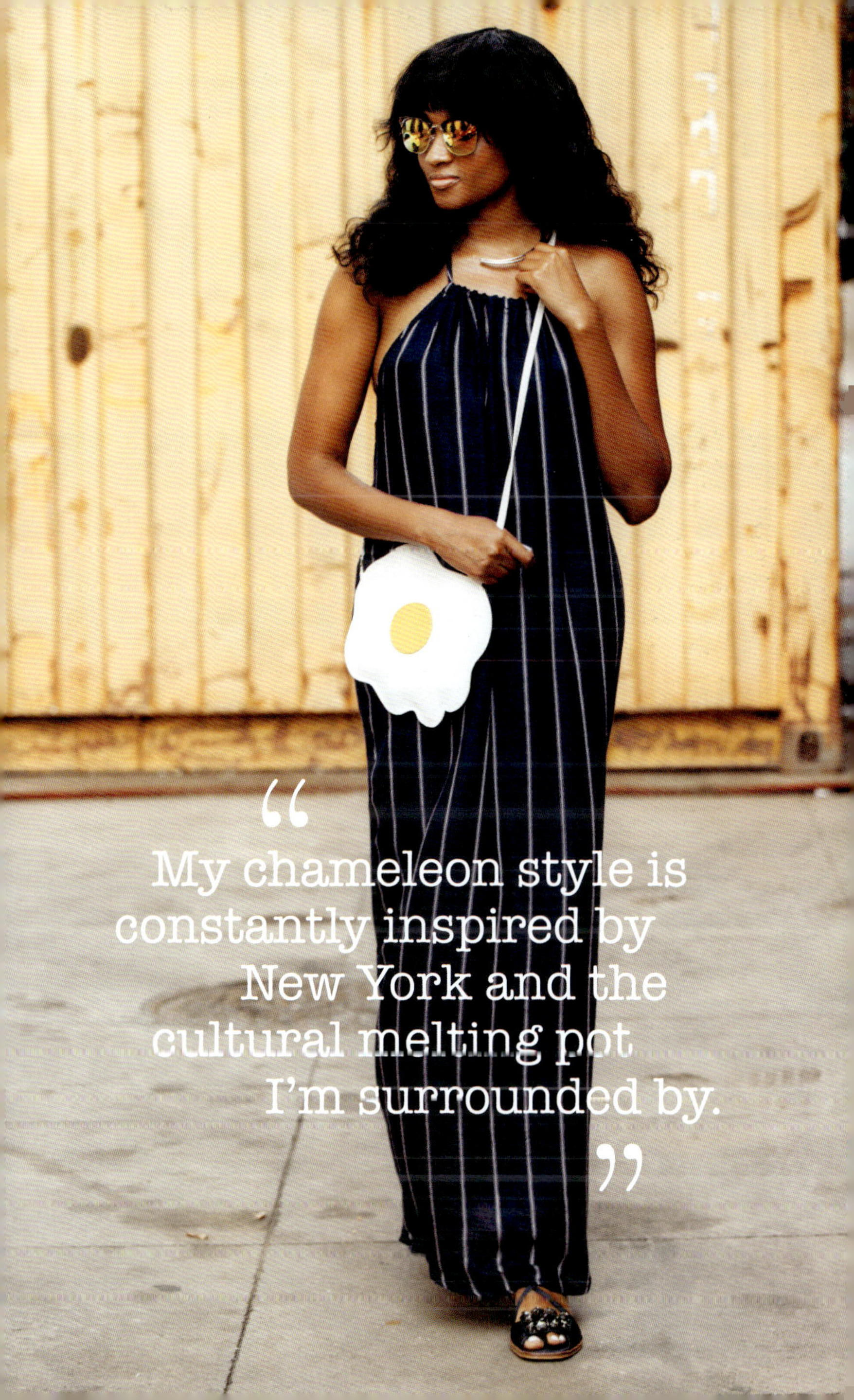
"My chameleon style is constantly inspired by New York and the cultural melting pot I'm surrounded by."

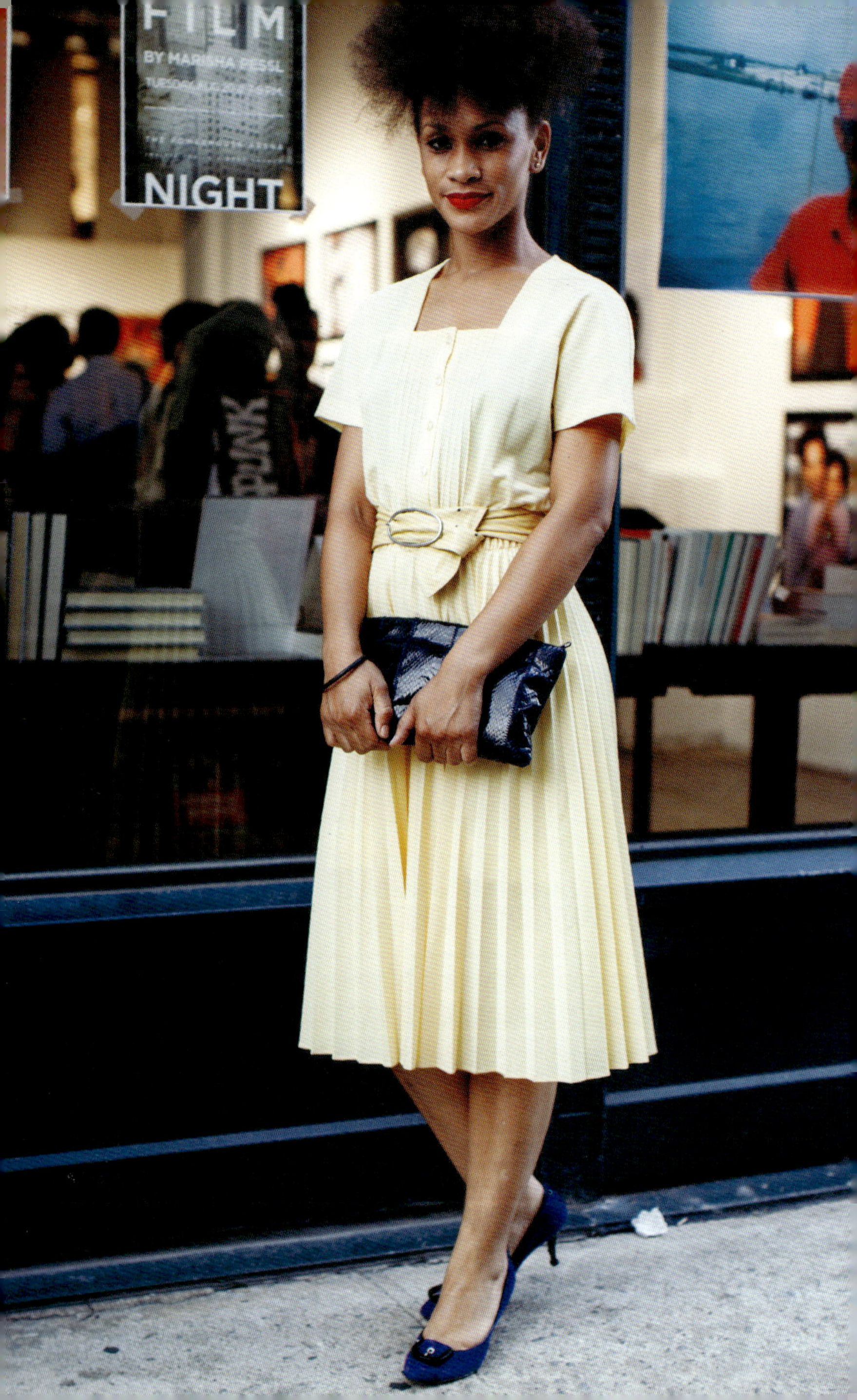
FILM
NIGHT

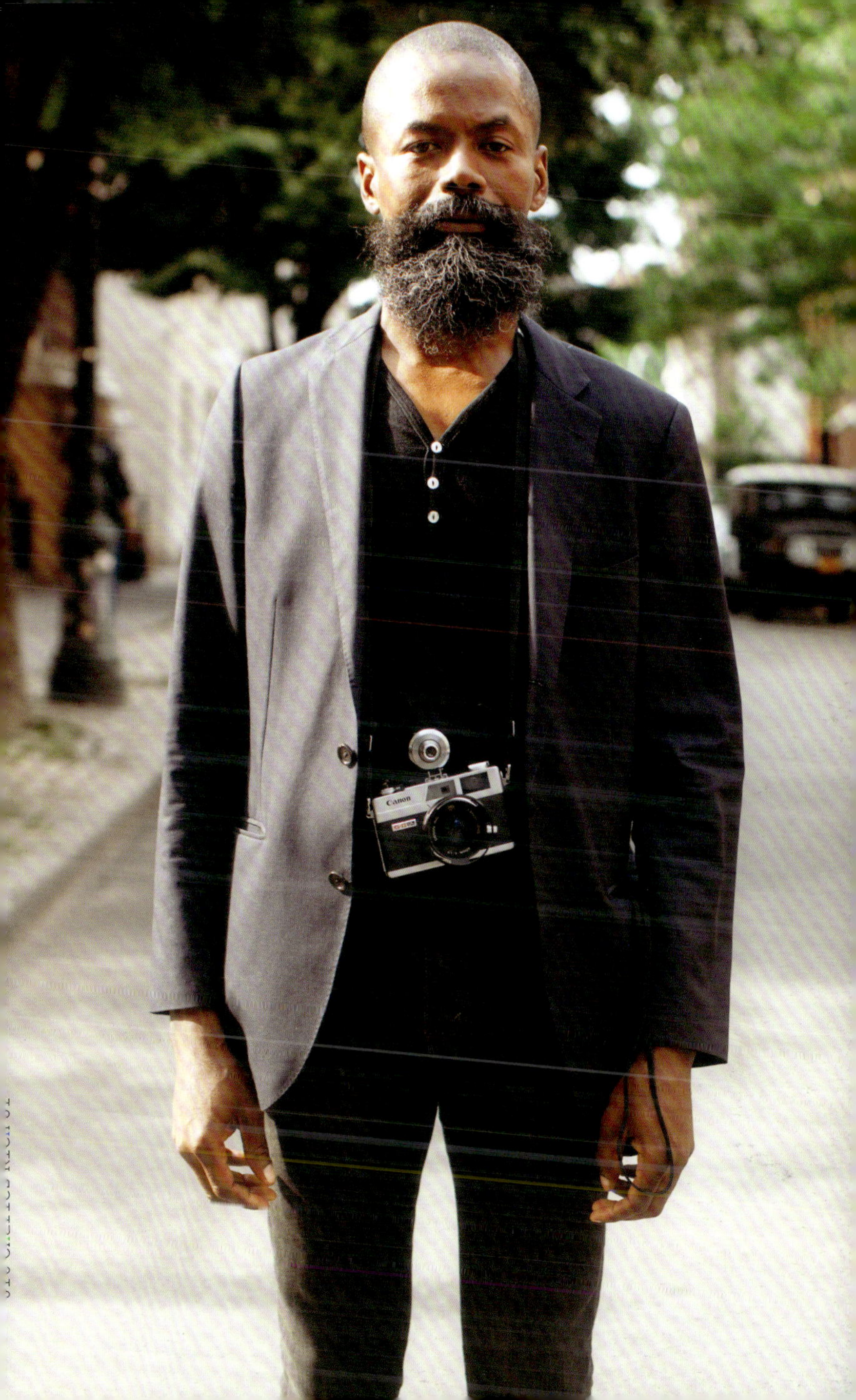

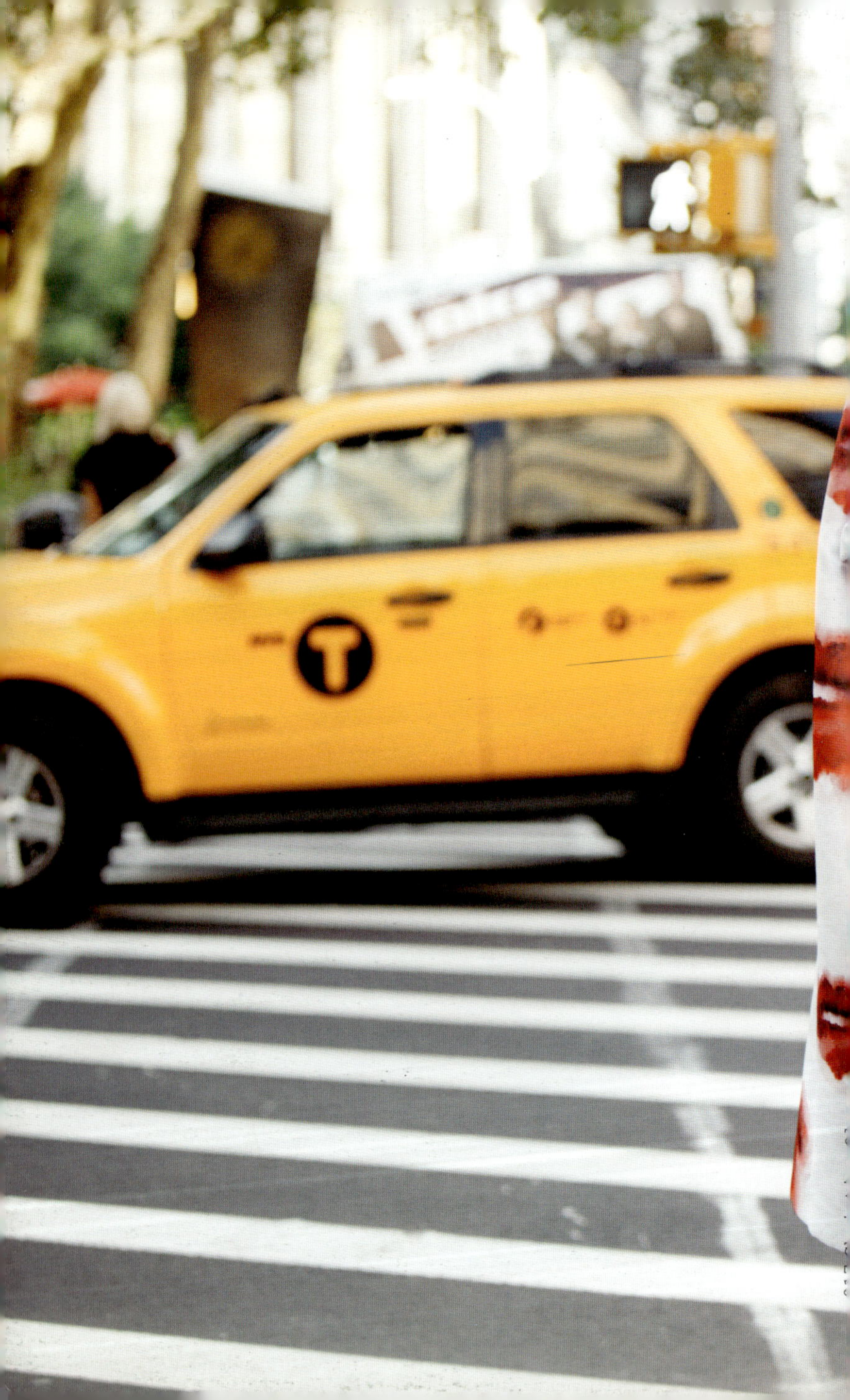

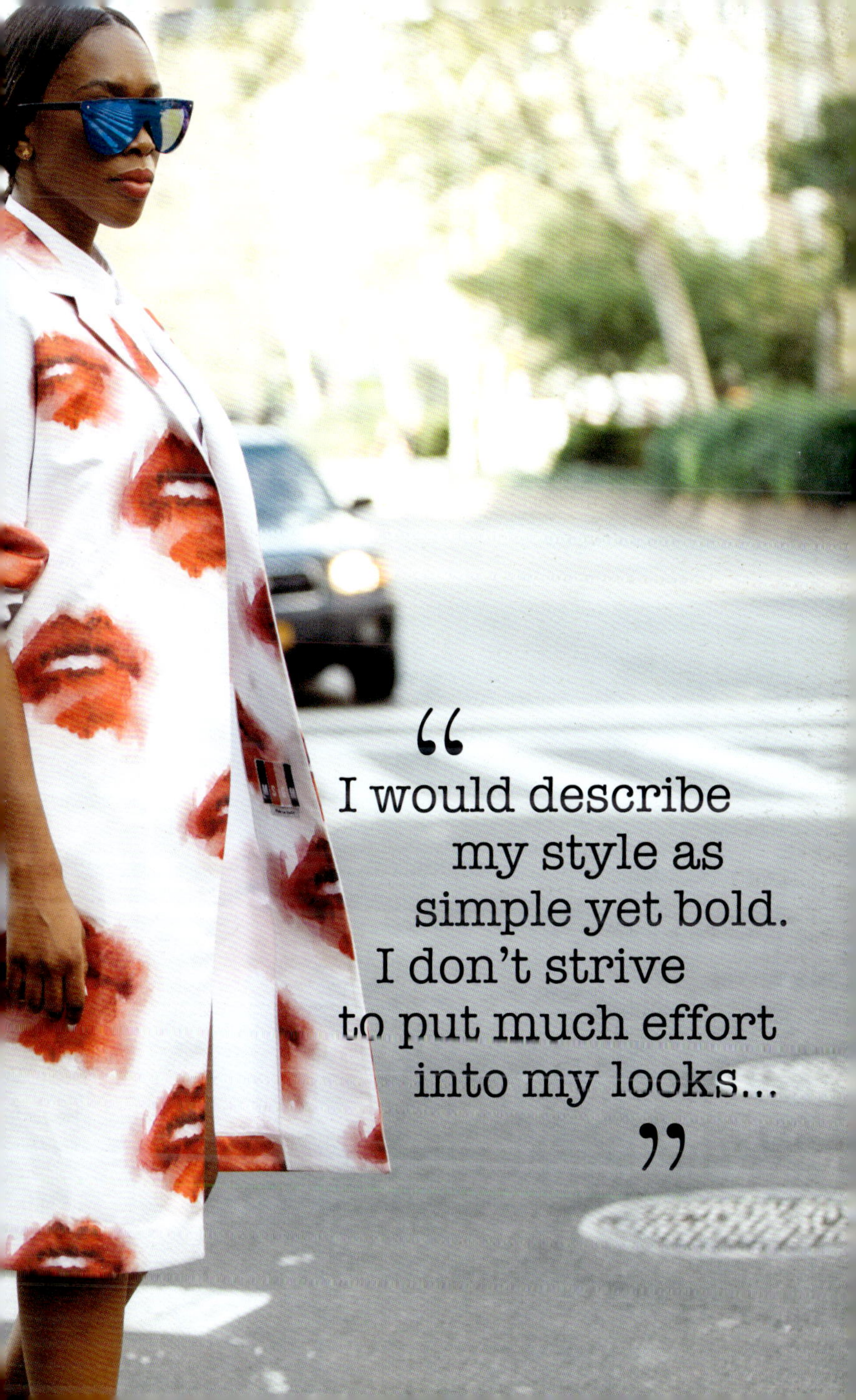
"I would describe my style as simple yet bold. I don't strive to put much effort into my looks..."

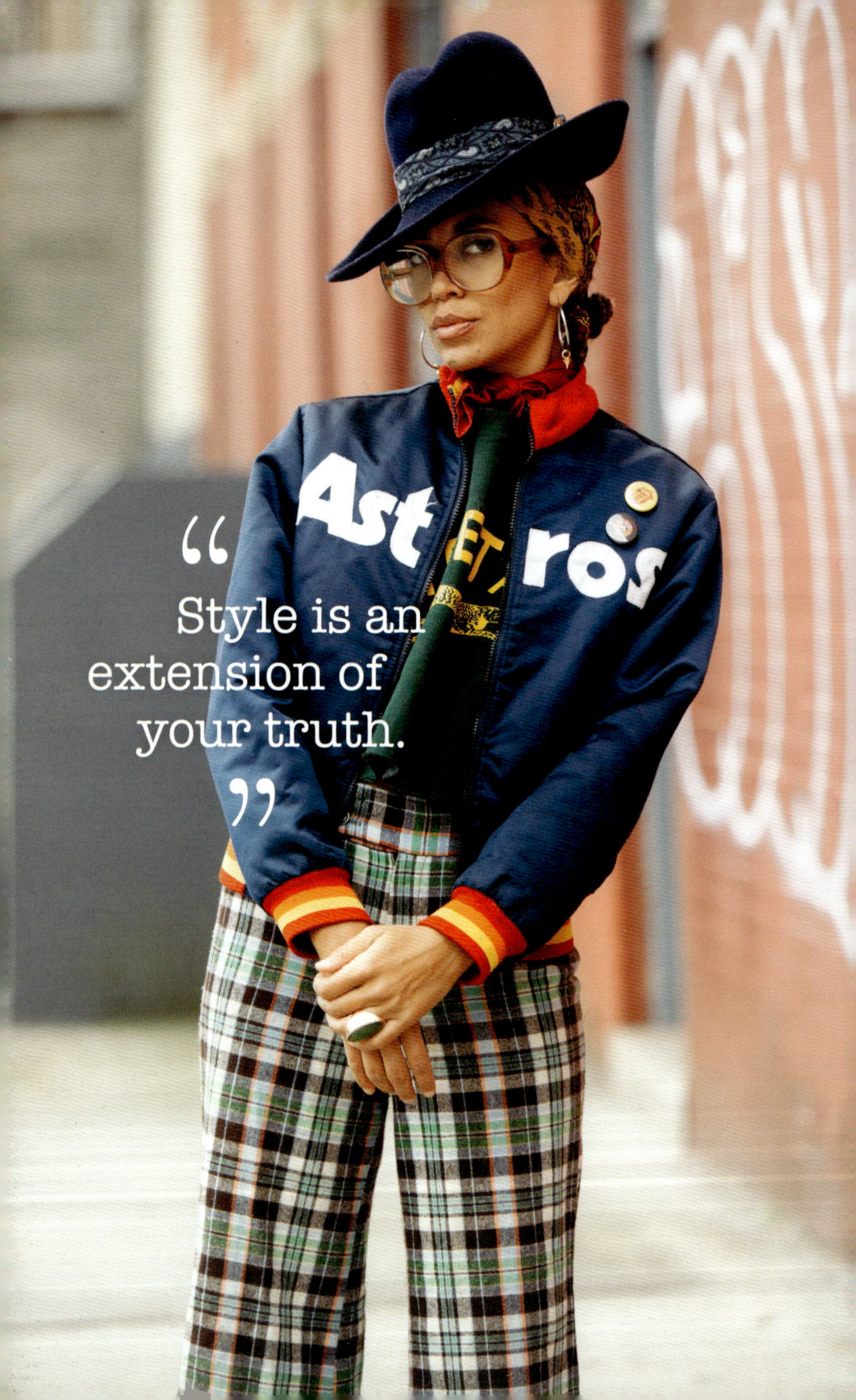

"Style is an extension of your truth."

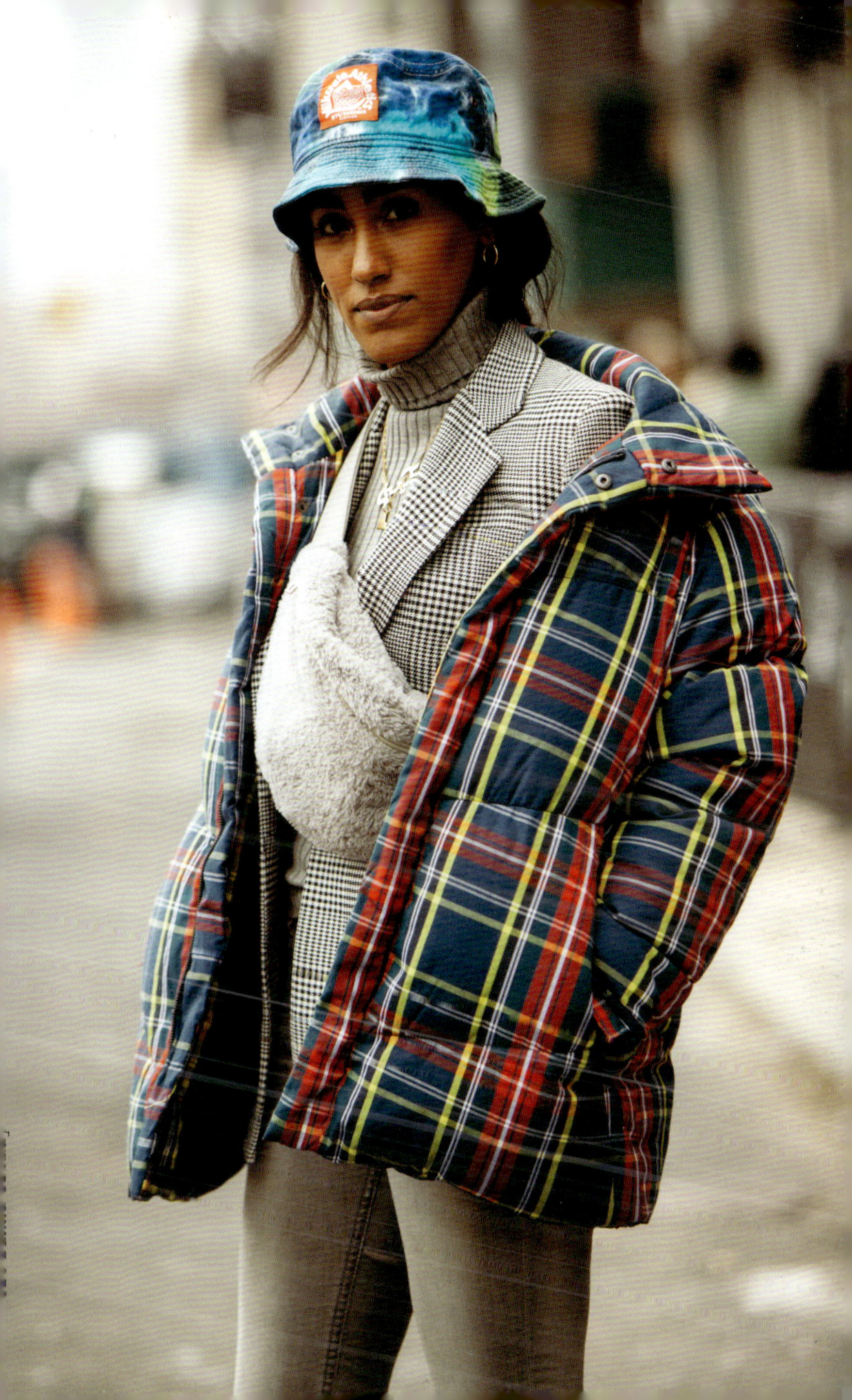

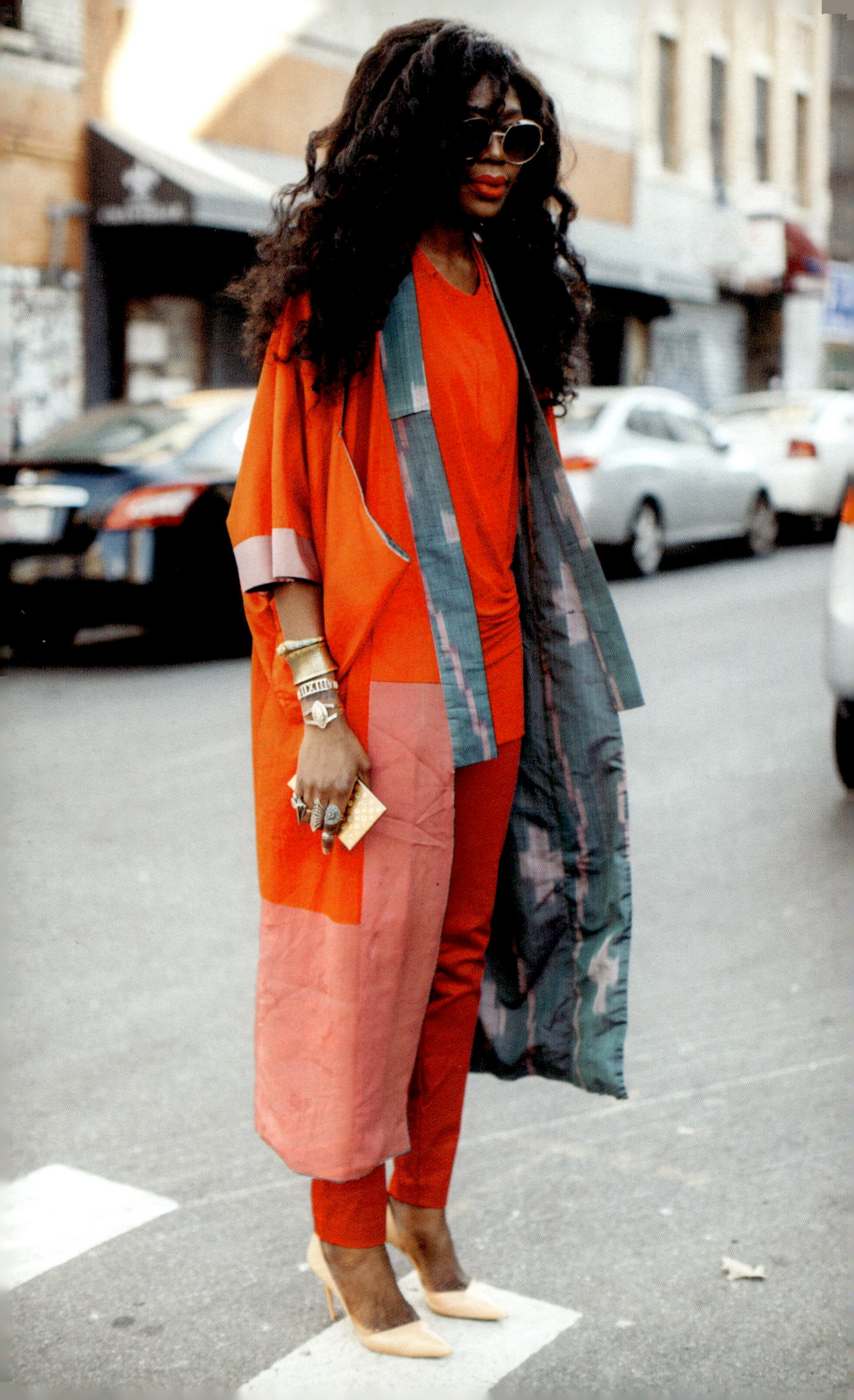

“My fashion aesthetic is greatly influenced by world culture.”

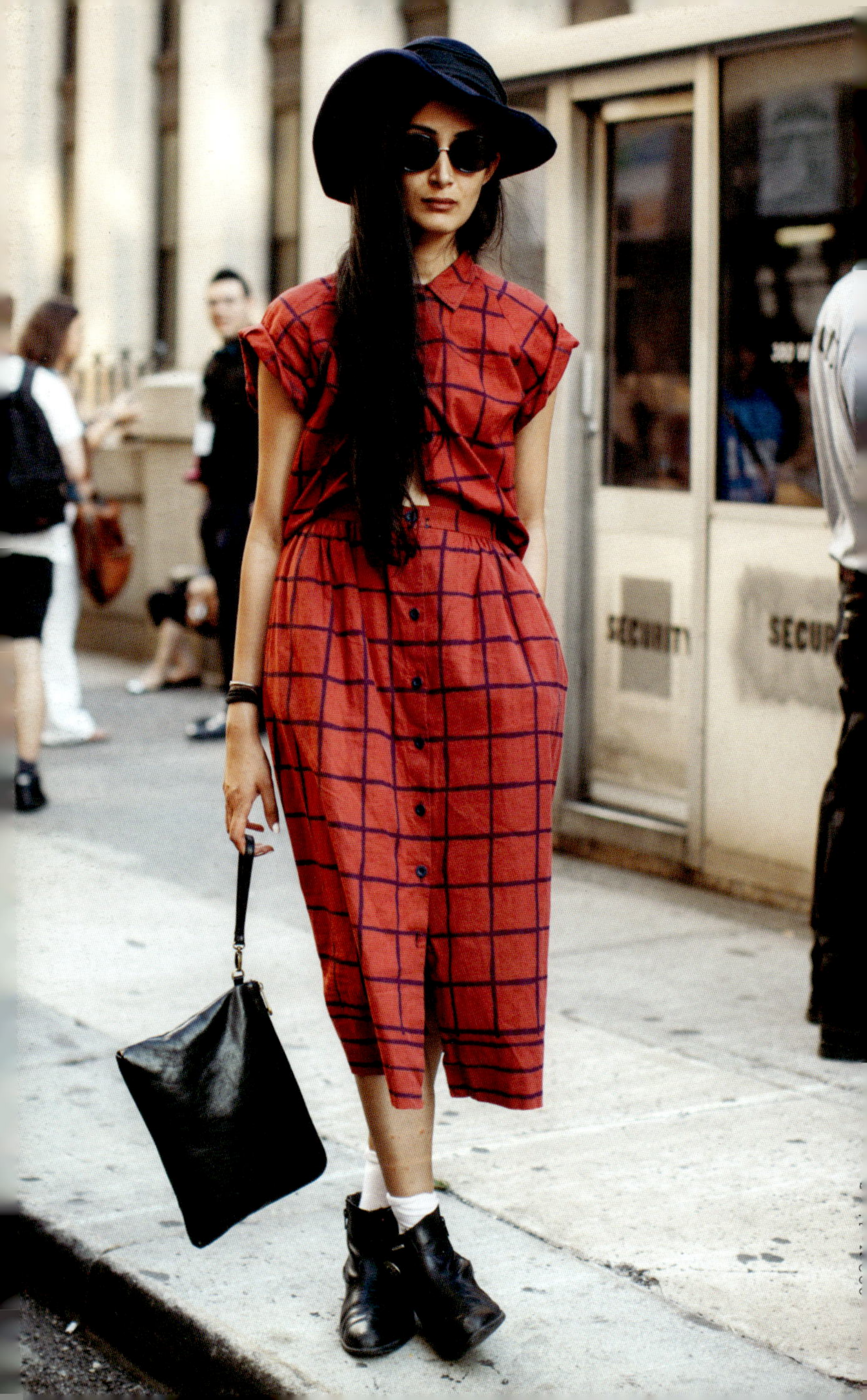
SECURITY

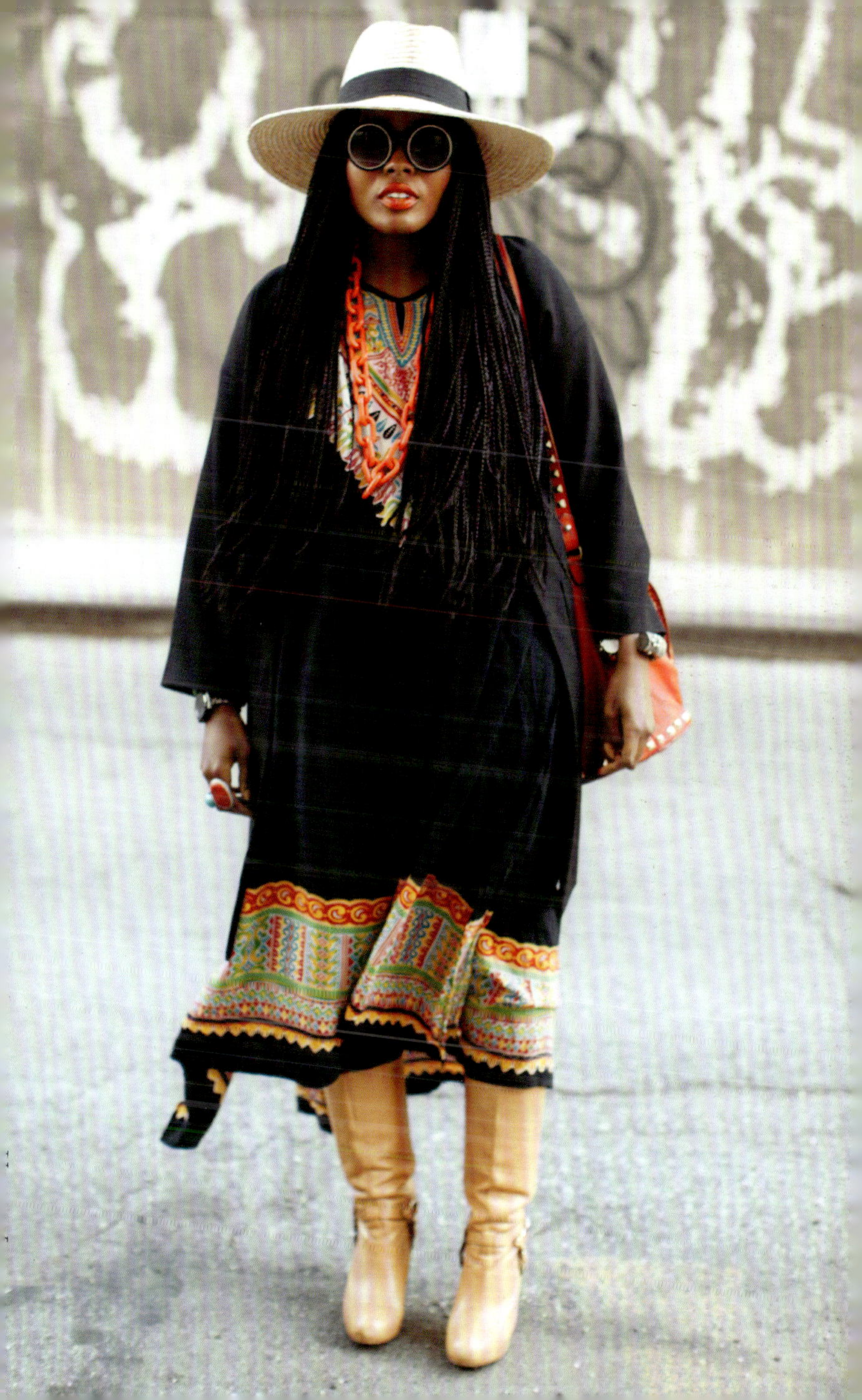

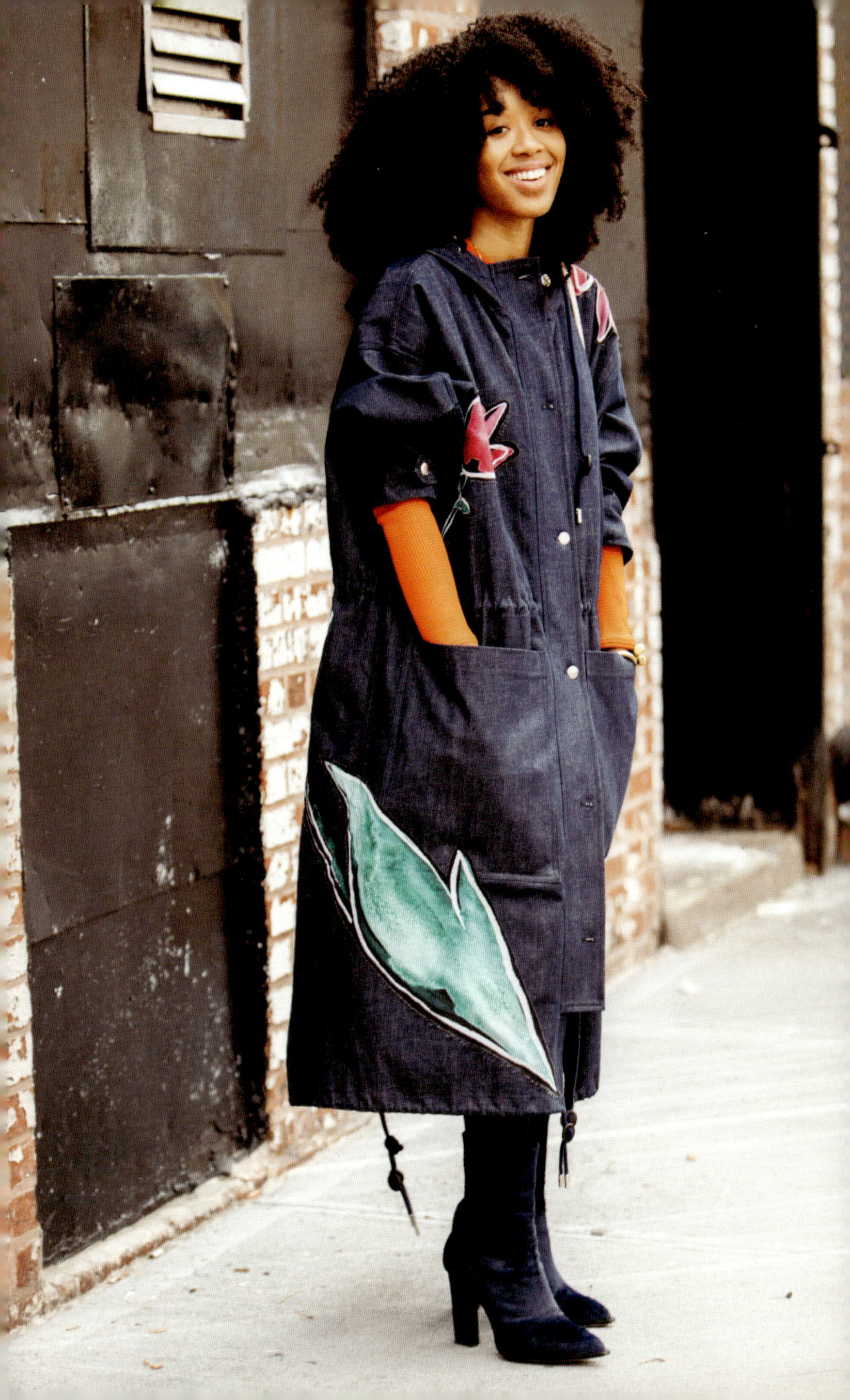

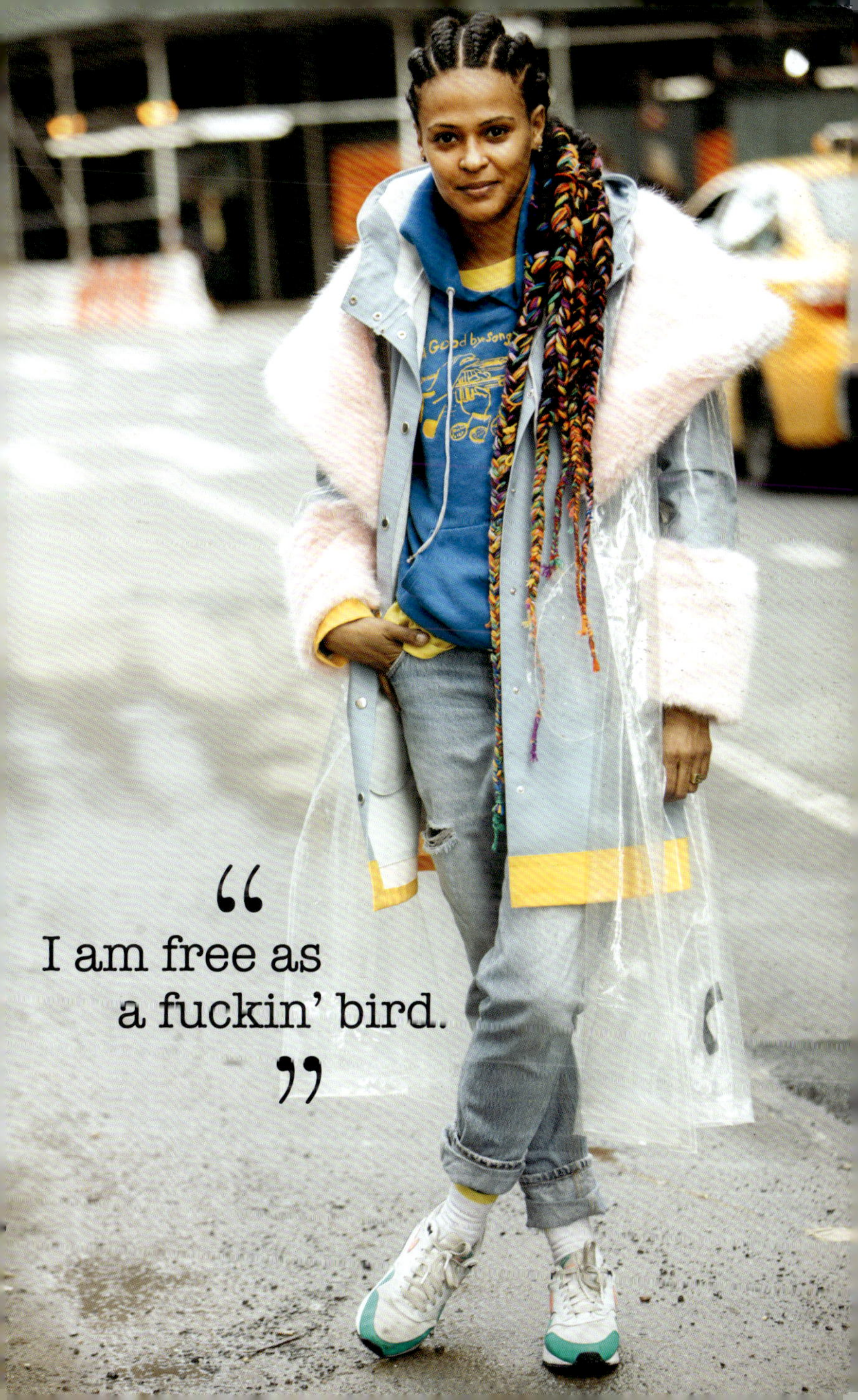
“I am free as
a fuckin’ bird.”

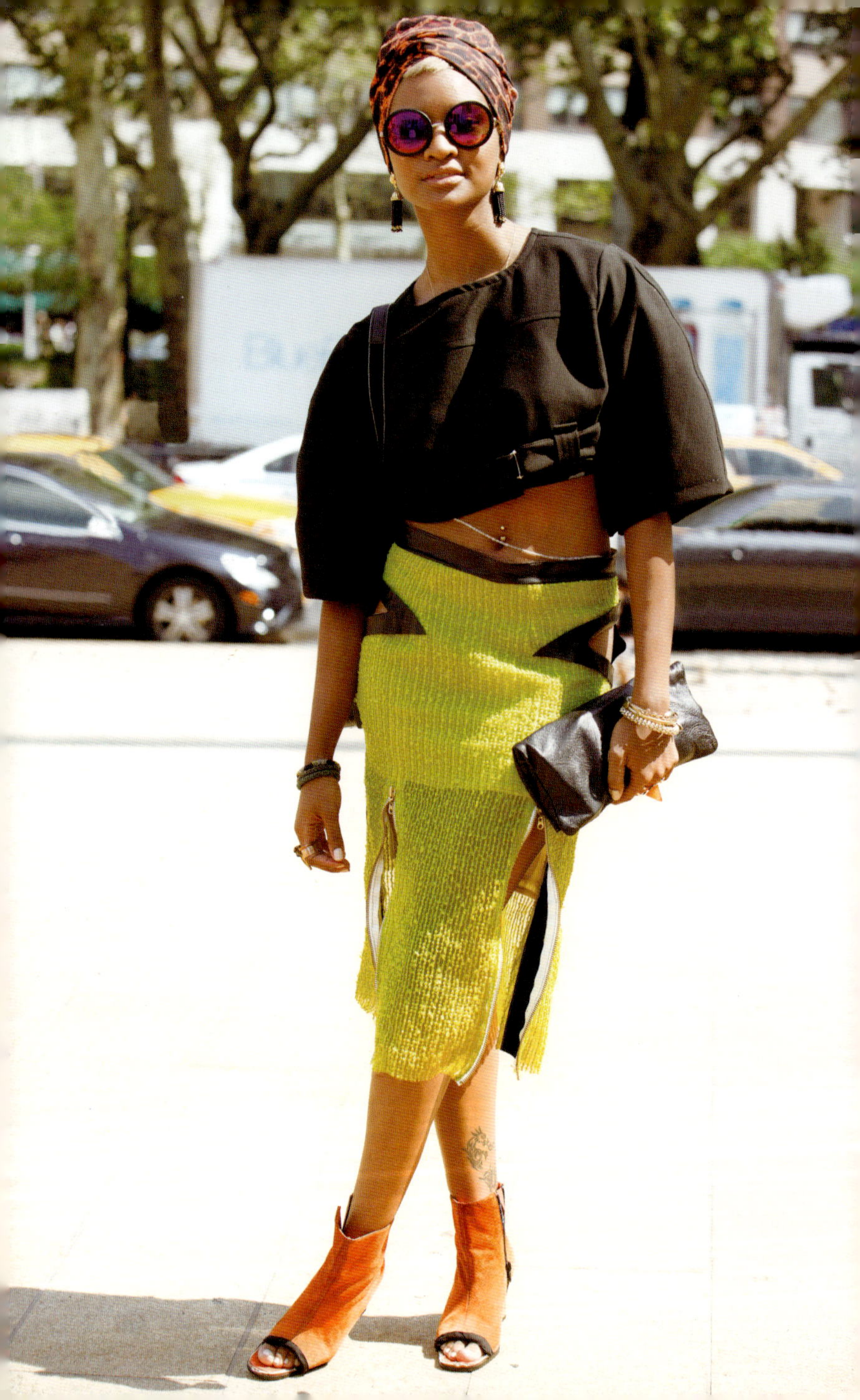

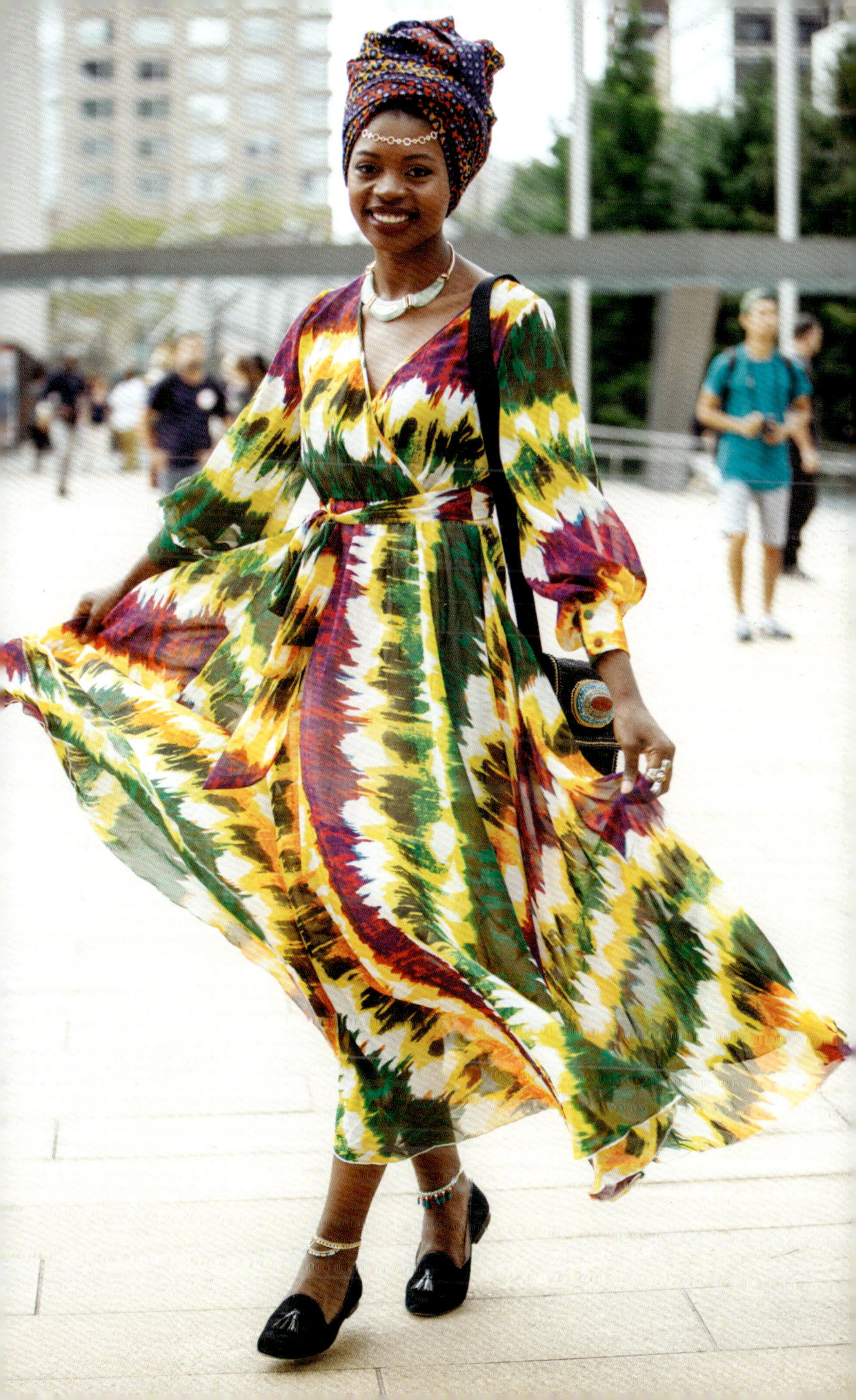

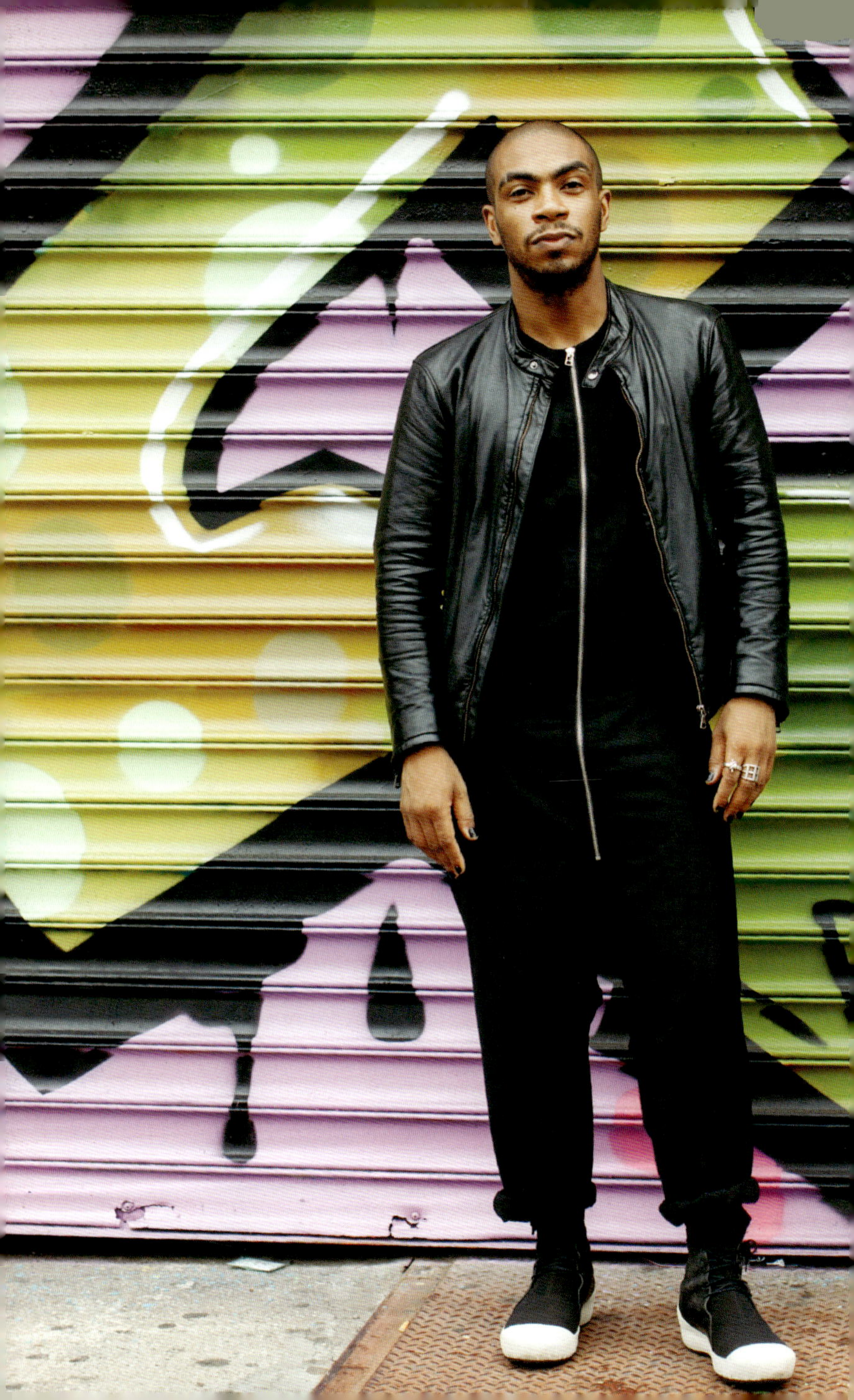

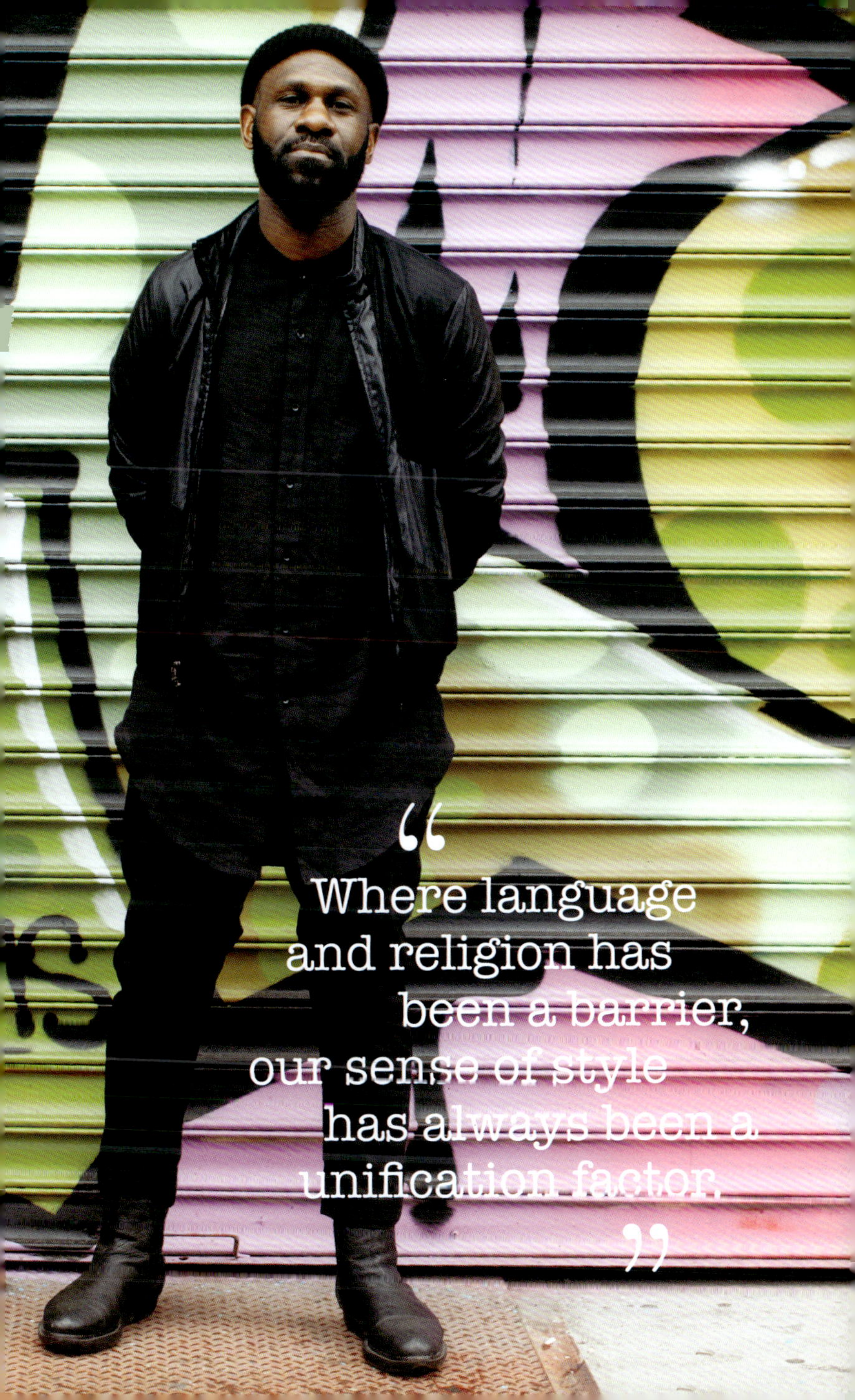
"Where language and religion has been a barrier, our sense of style has always been a unification factor."

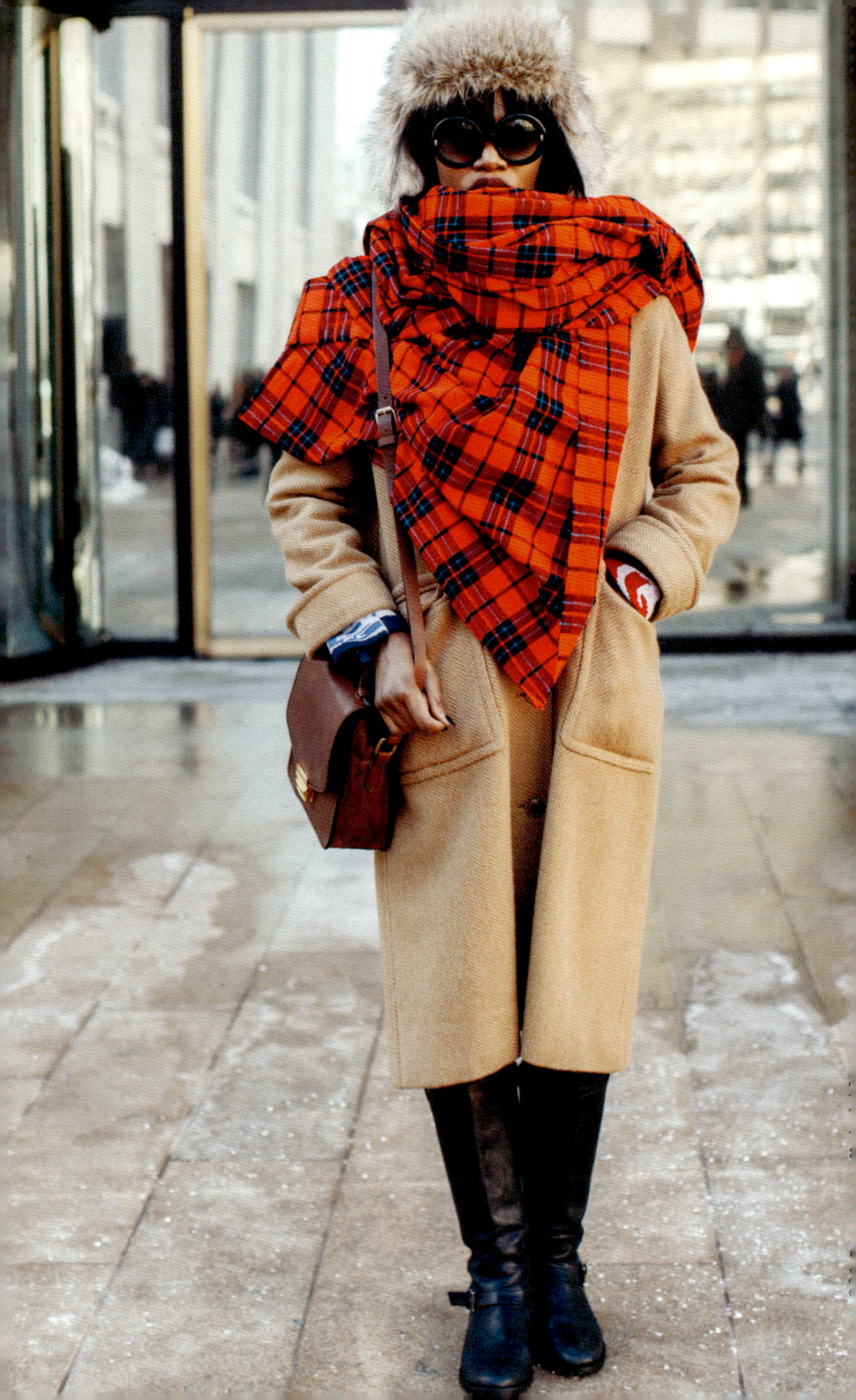

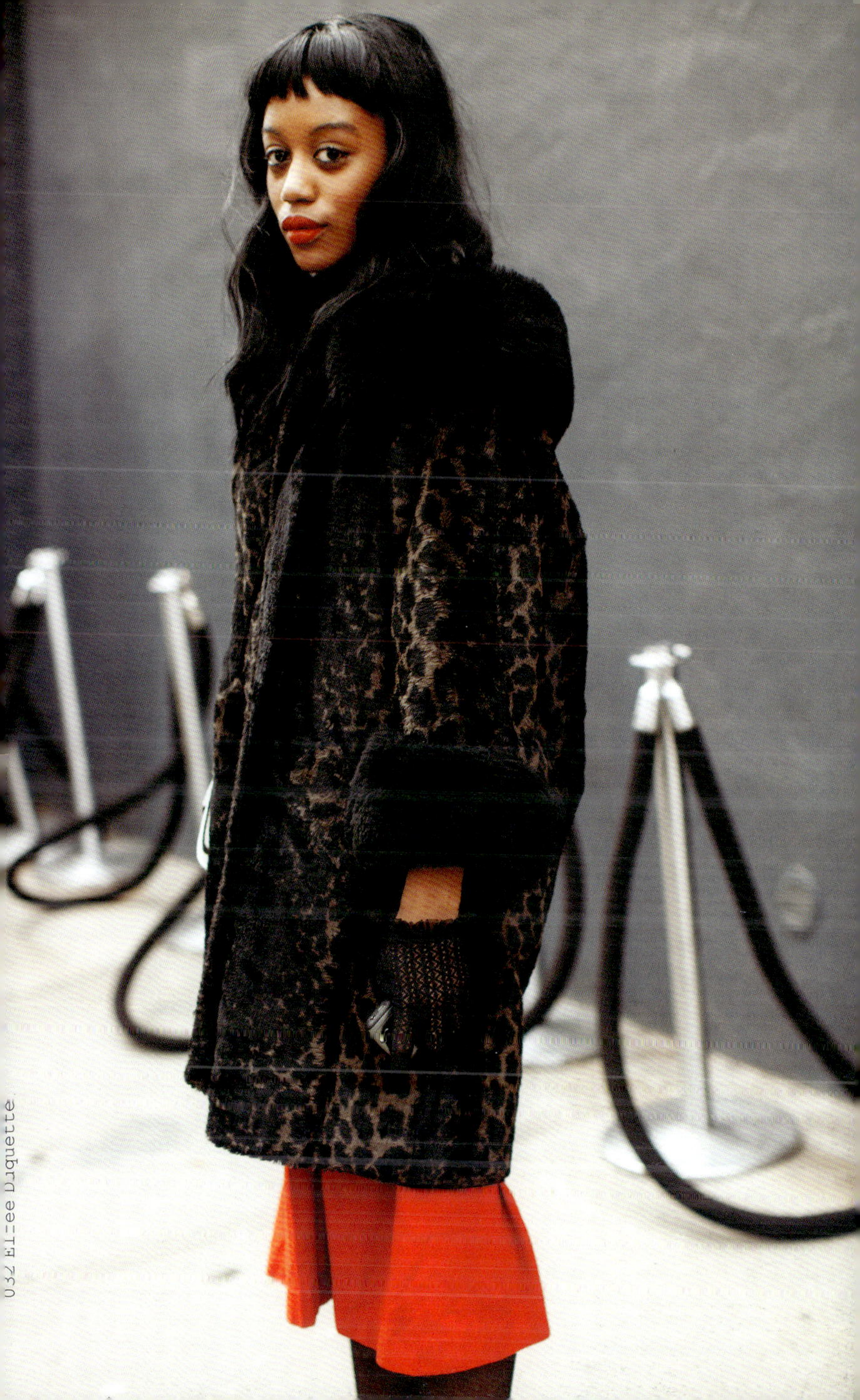

032 Elizee Diquette

“I am forever evolving yet consistently the same.”

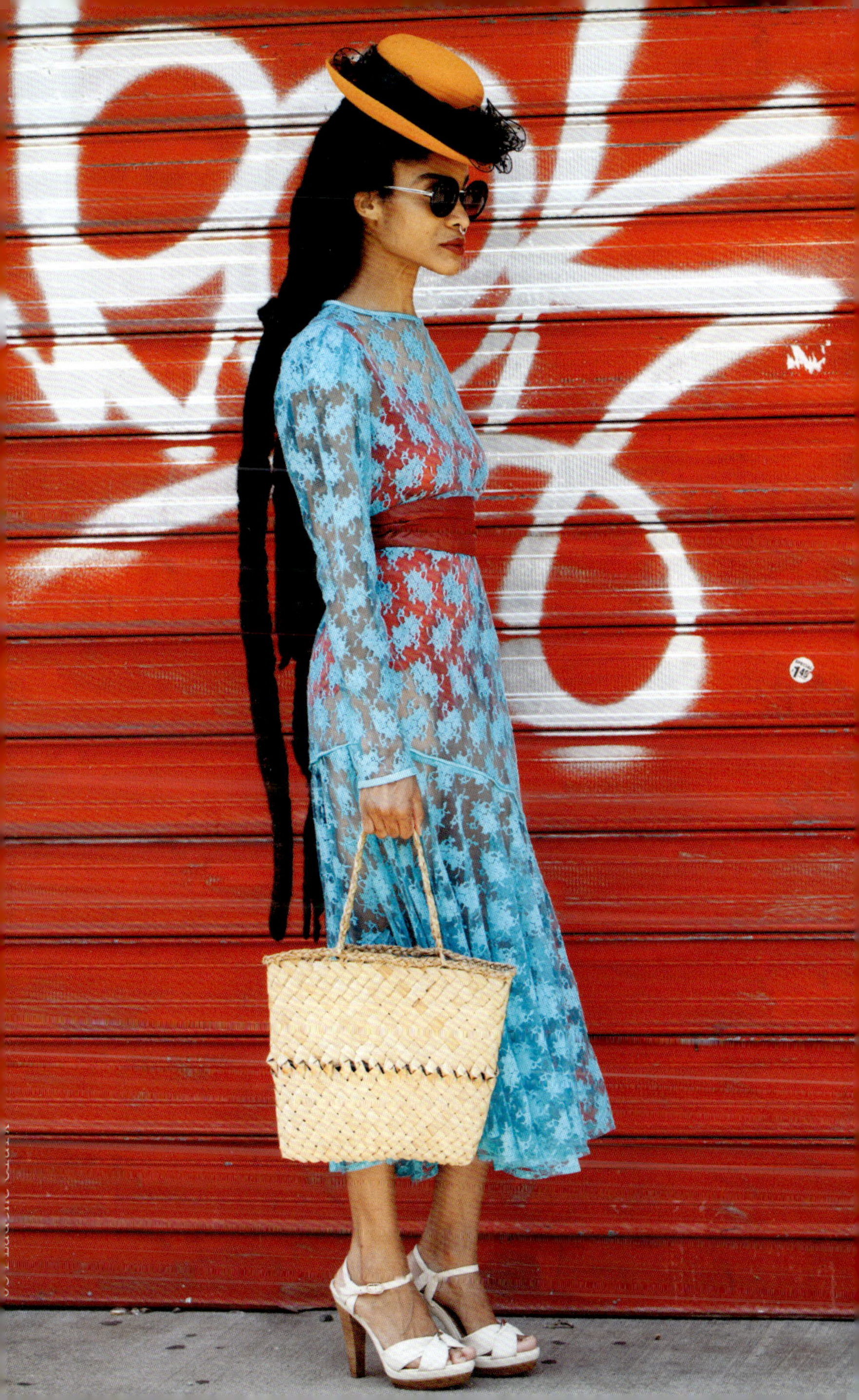

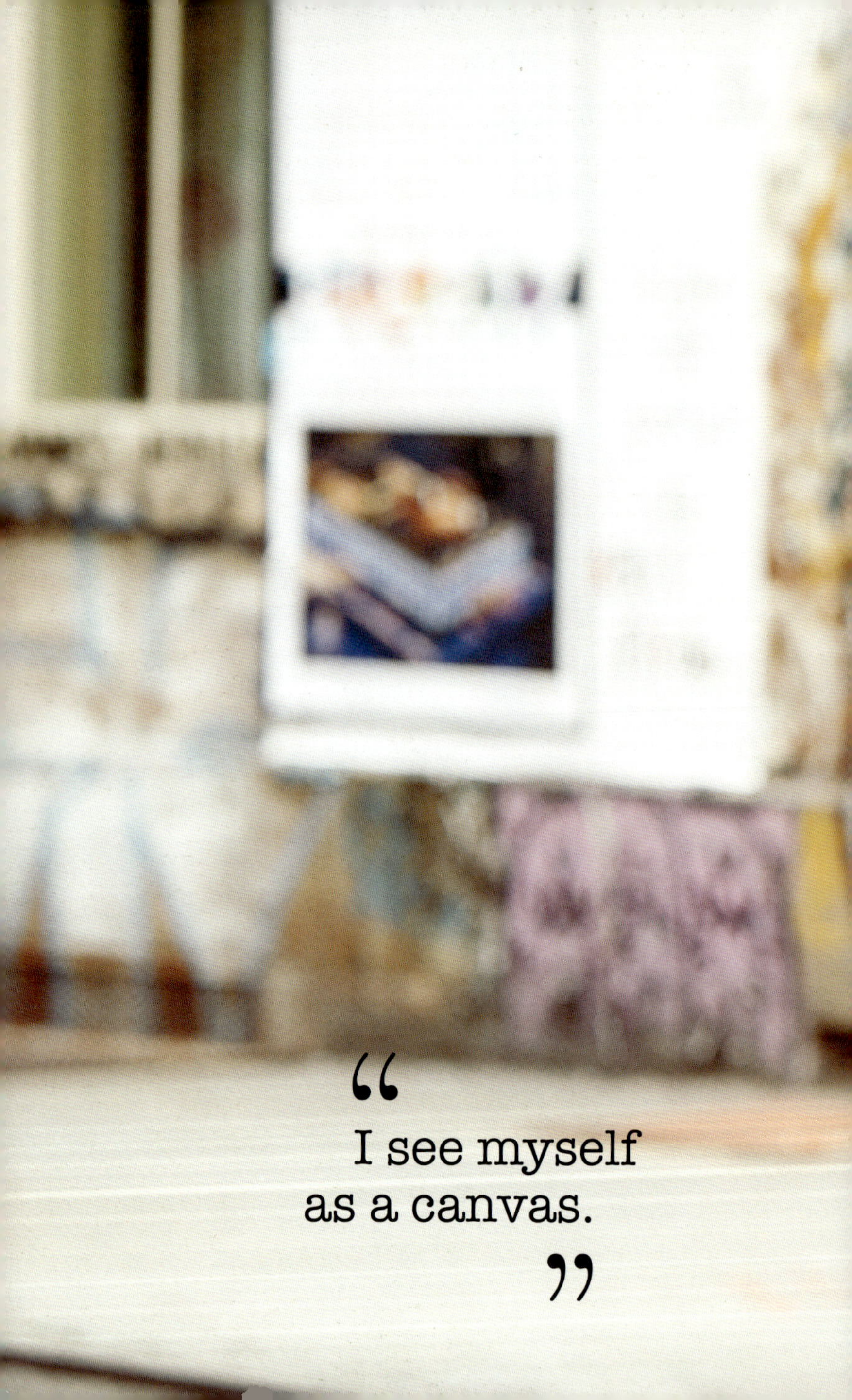
"I see myself
as a canvas."

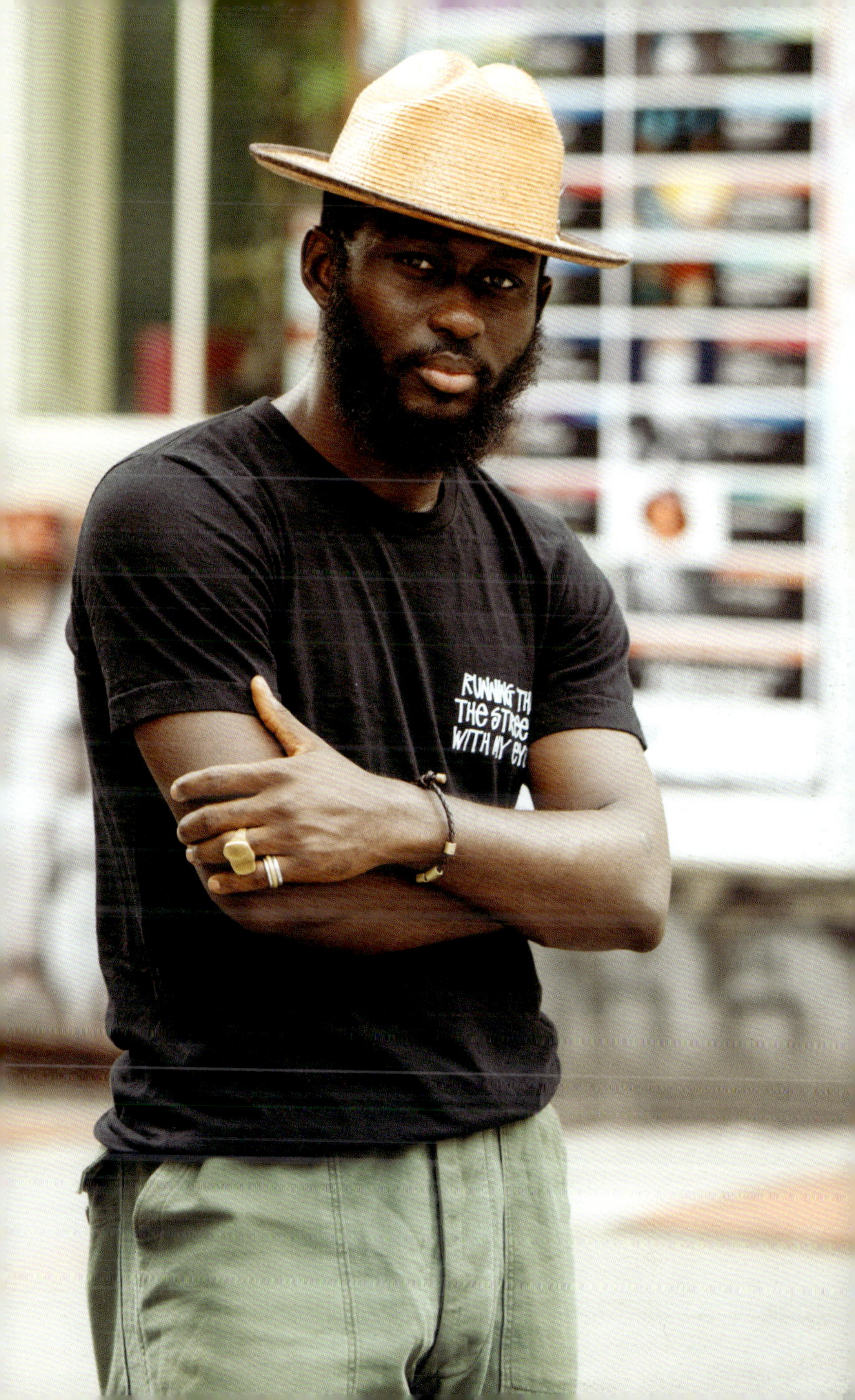
RUNNING TH
THE STREE
WITH MY EY

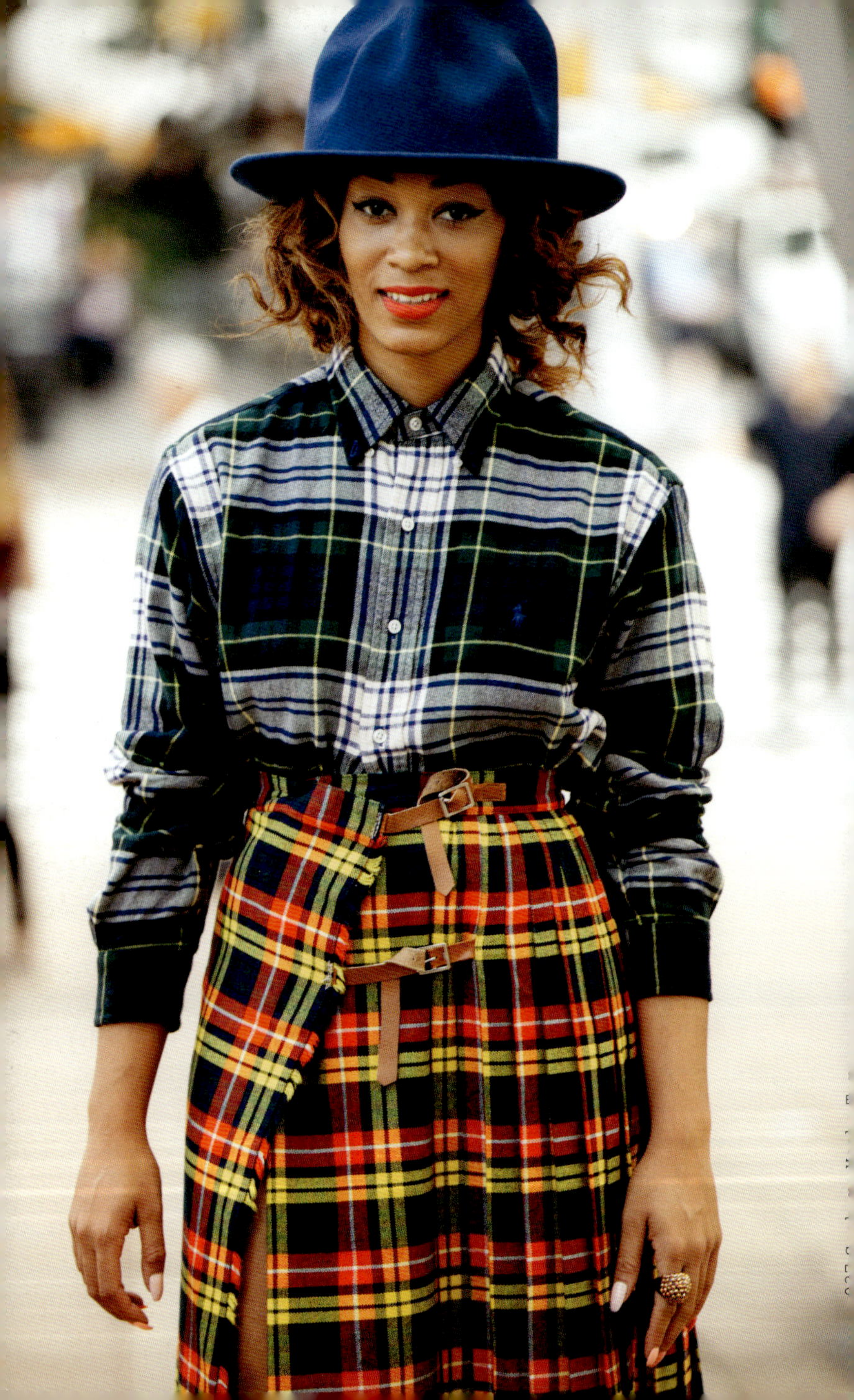

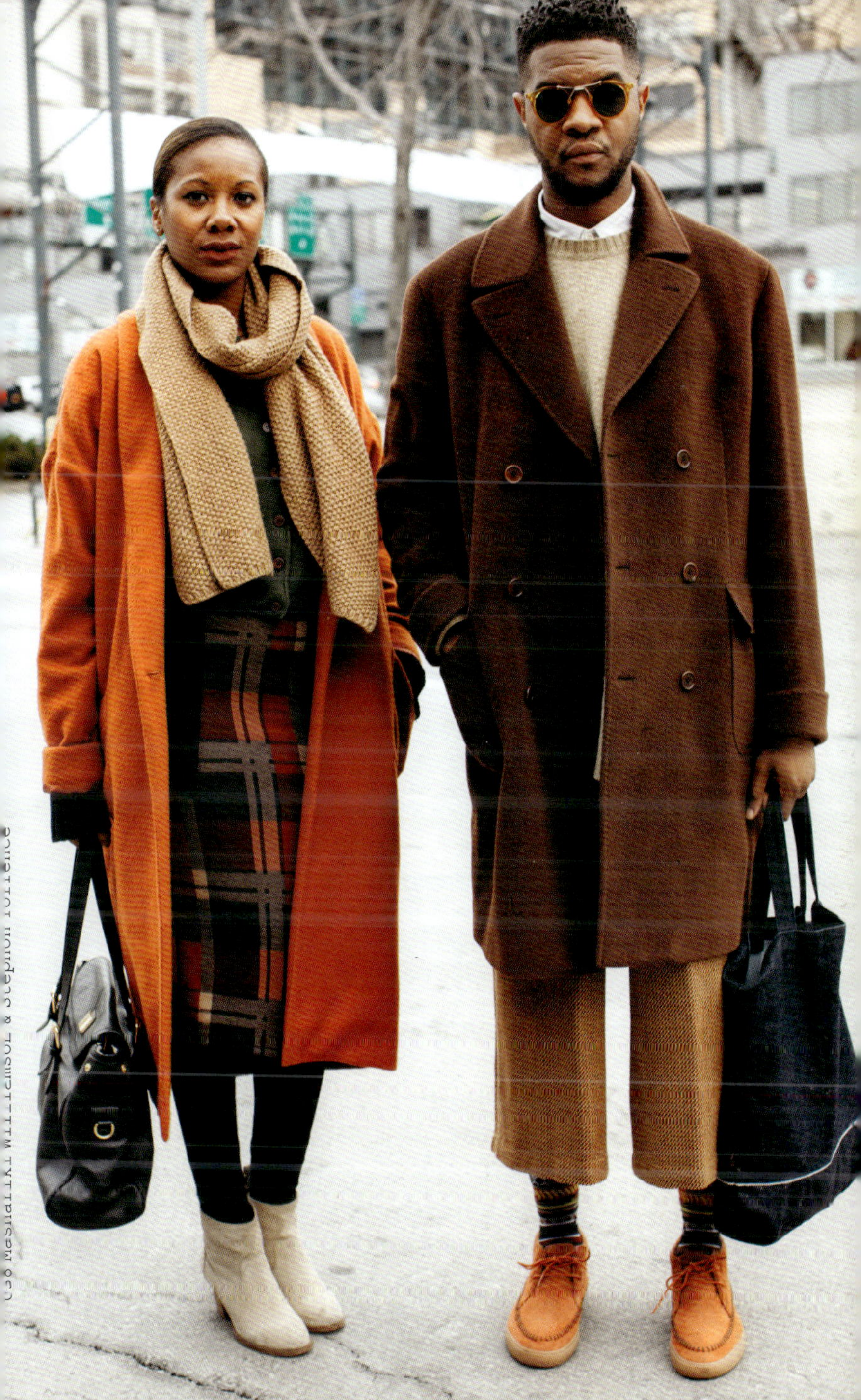

038 Mashariki Williamson & Stephon Torrence

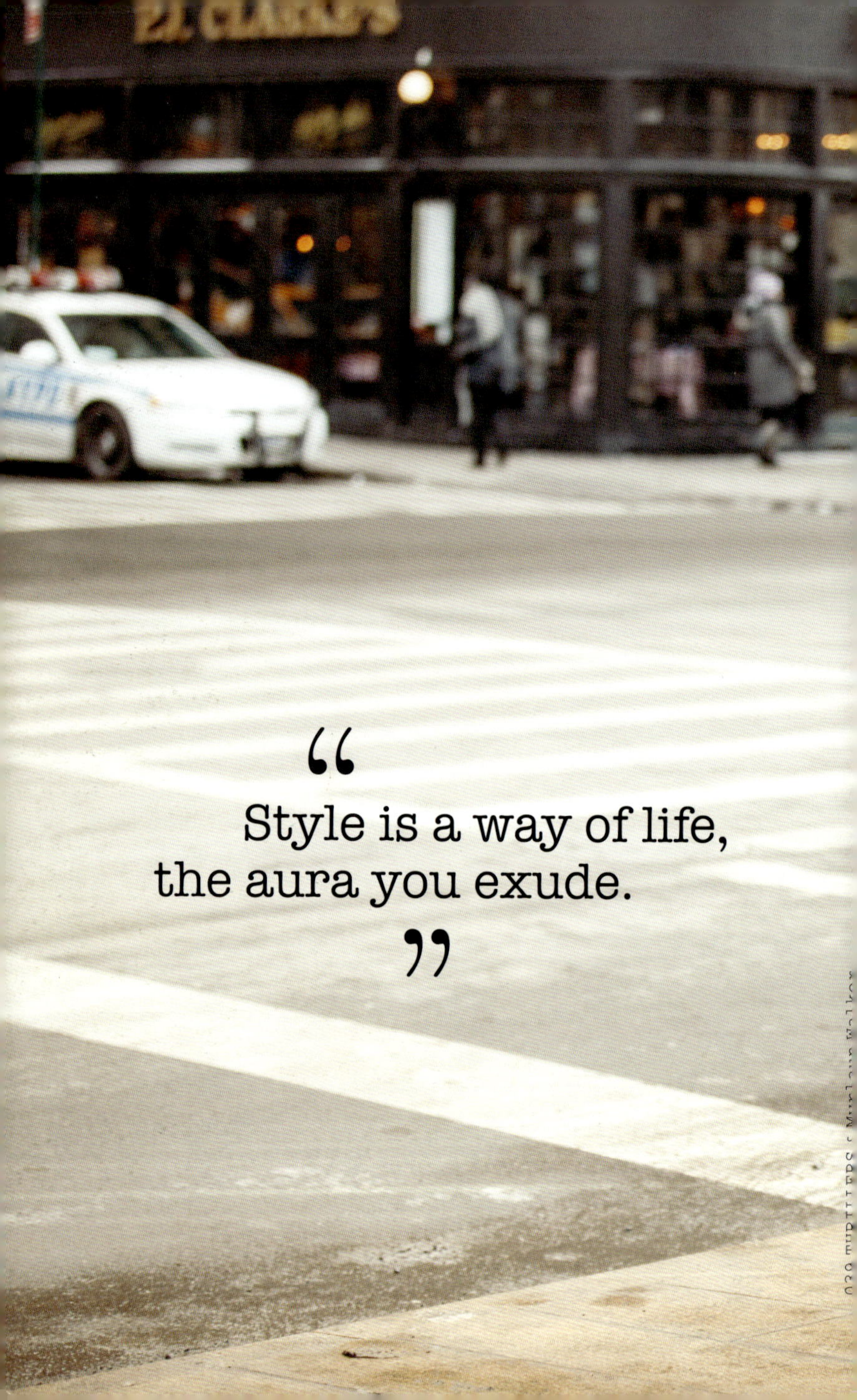
“Style is a way of life,
the aura you exude.”

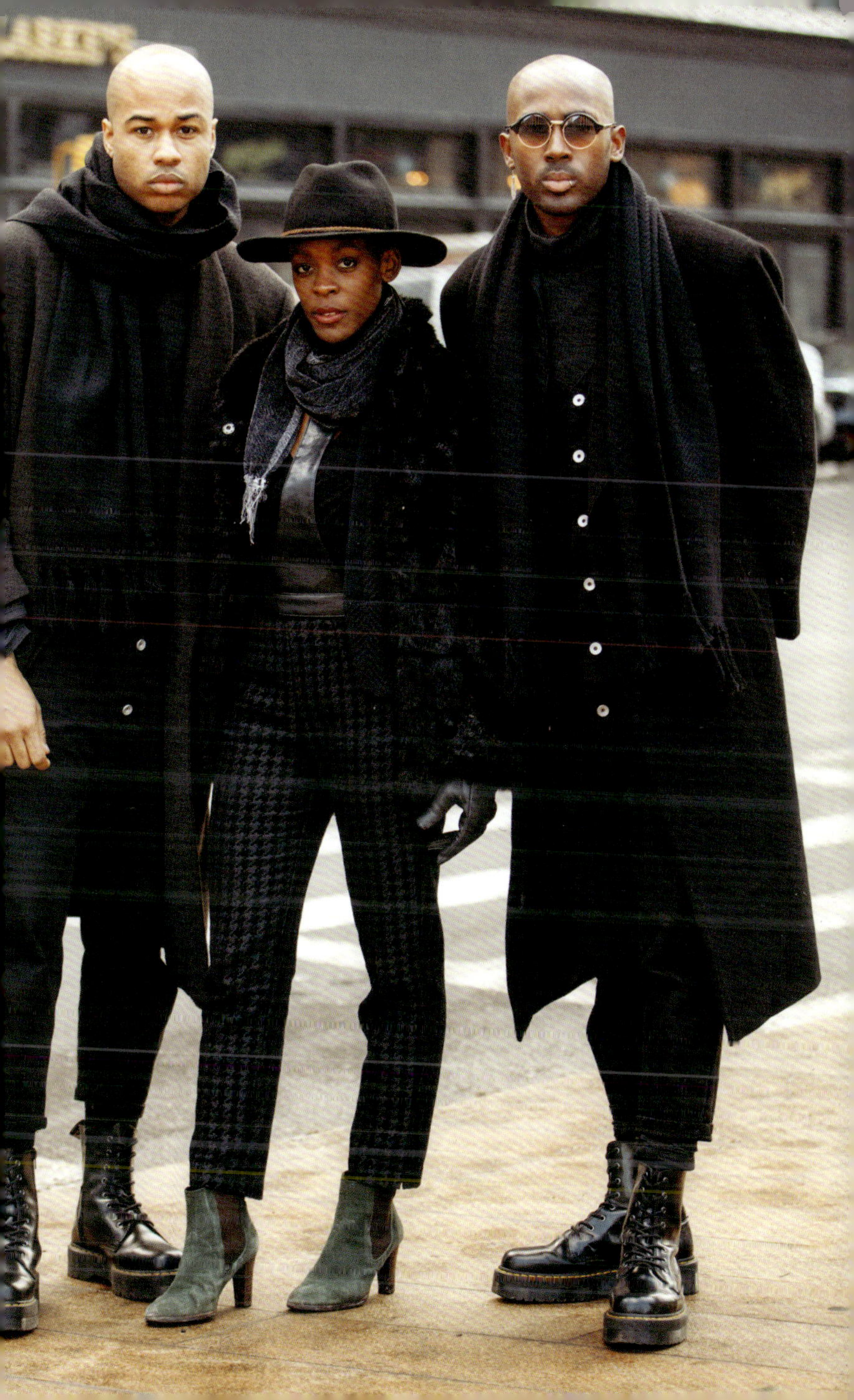

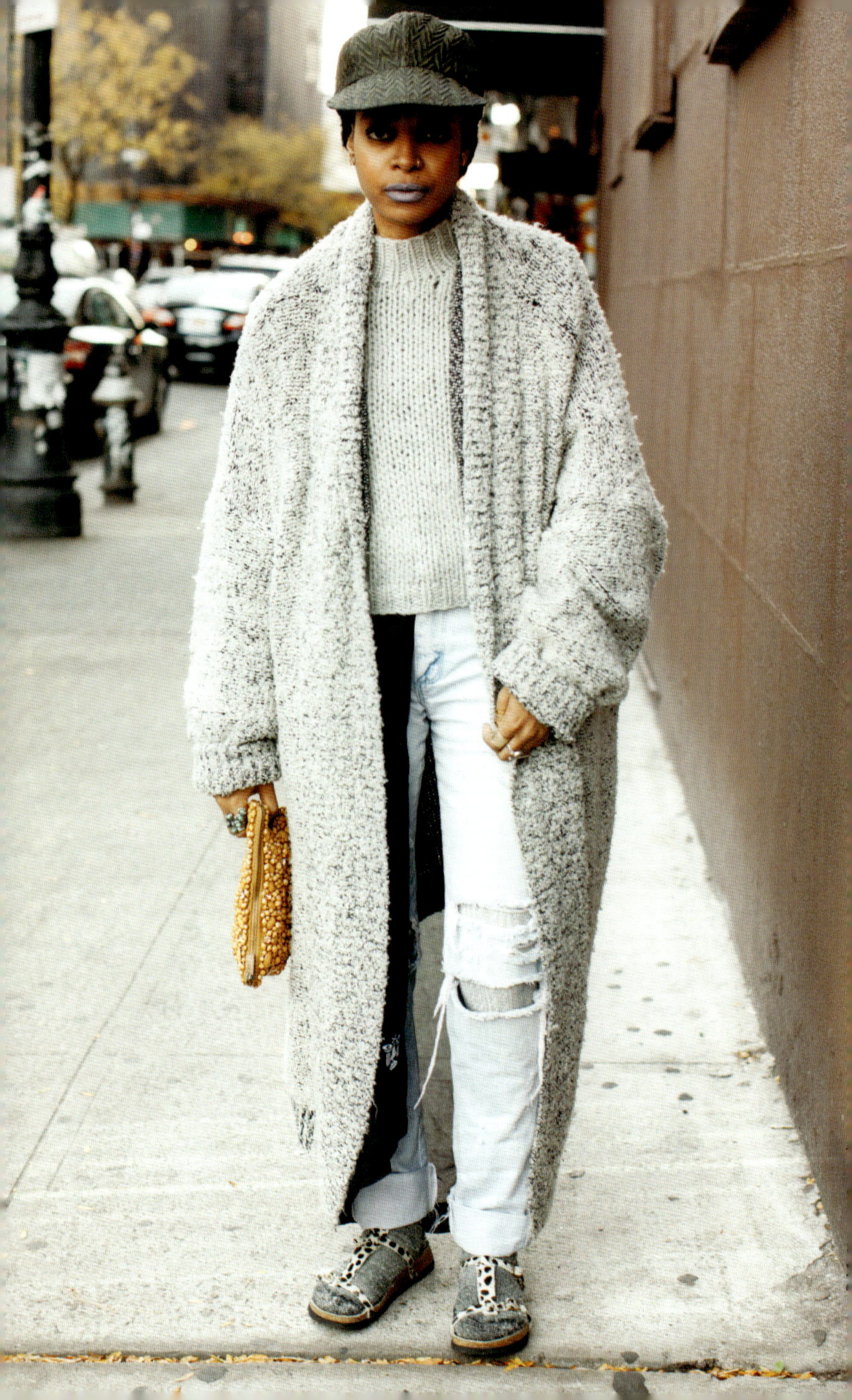

“

I’m inspired by my diaspora and the way in which we have adorned ourselves throughout history.

”

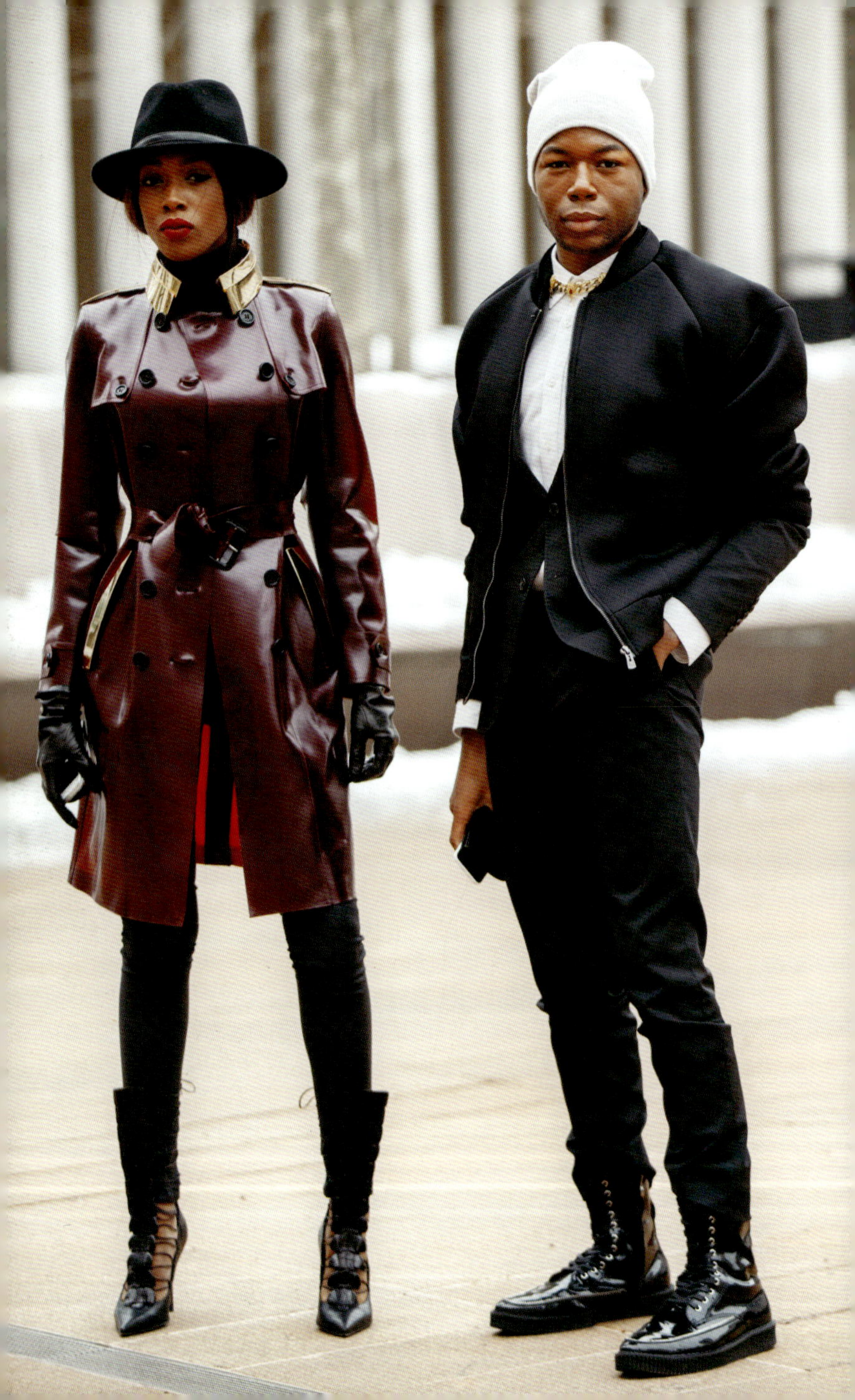

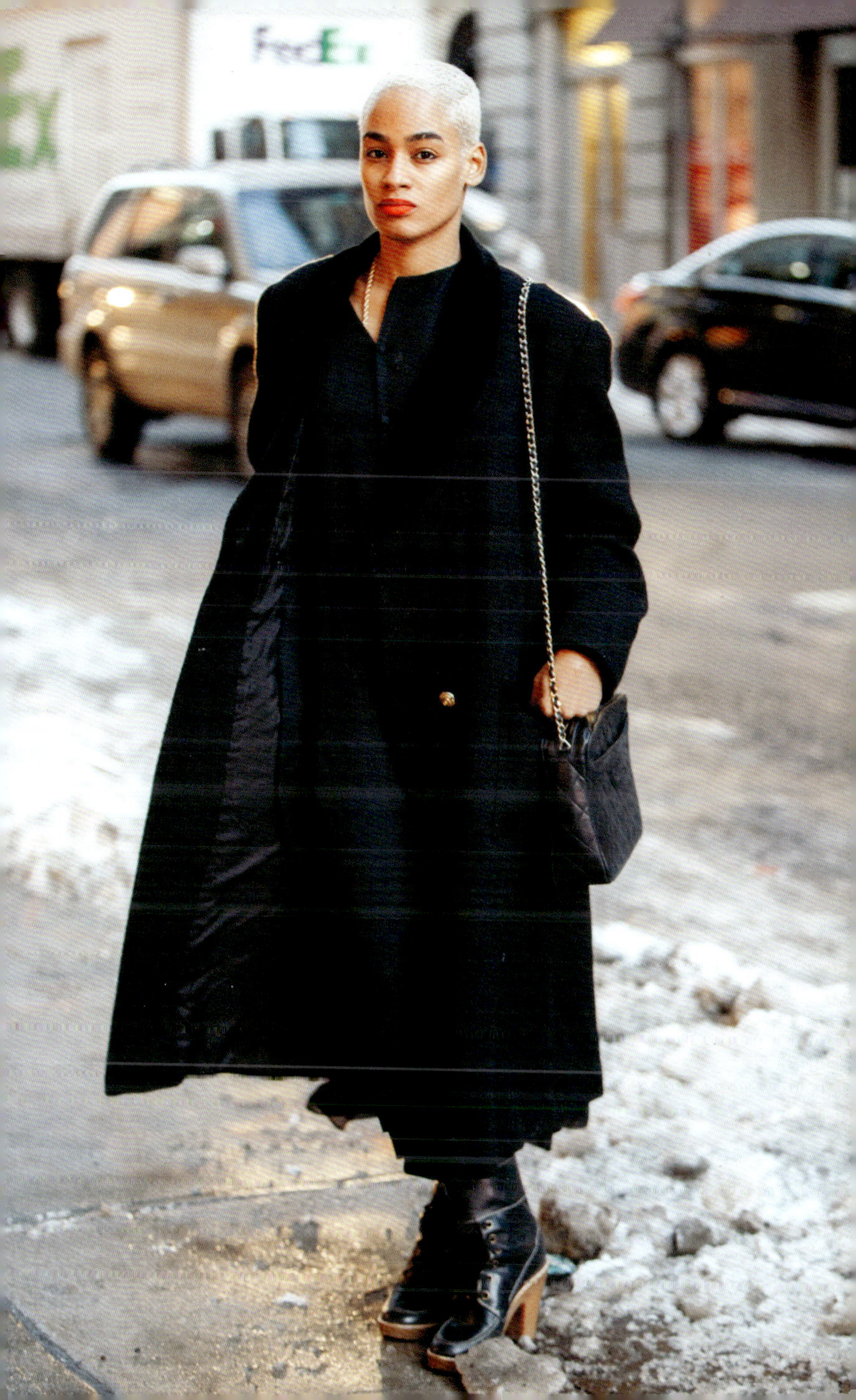
FedEx

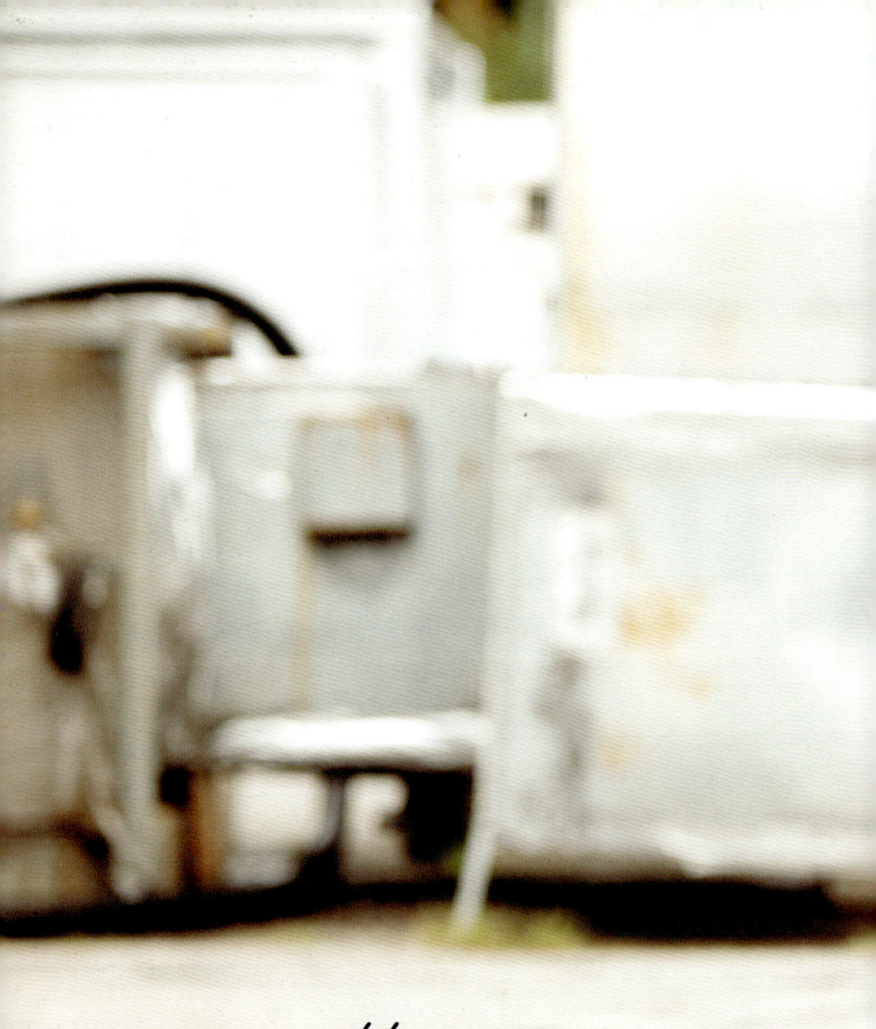

“My style is
an evolution
of who I am.”

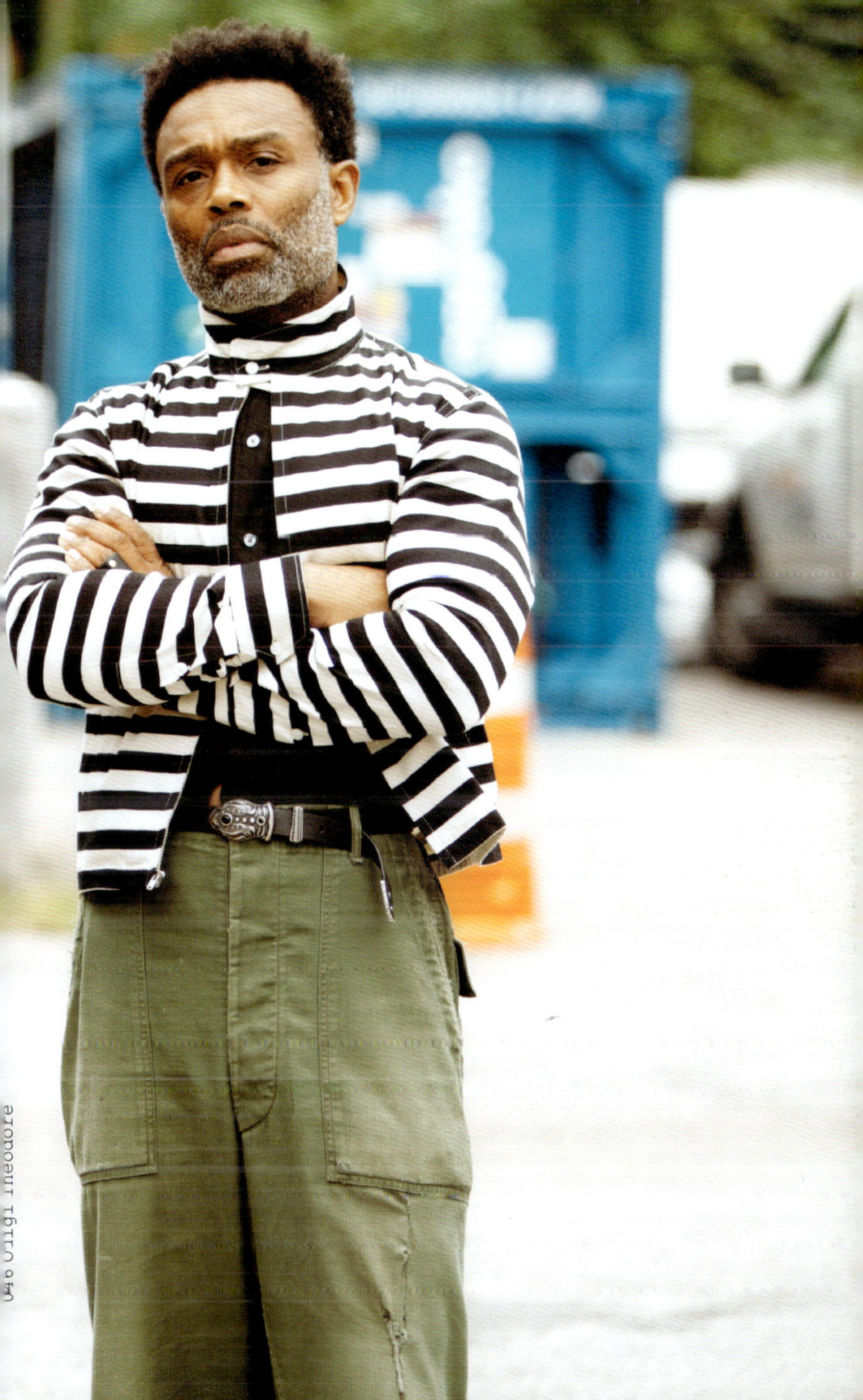

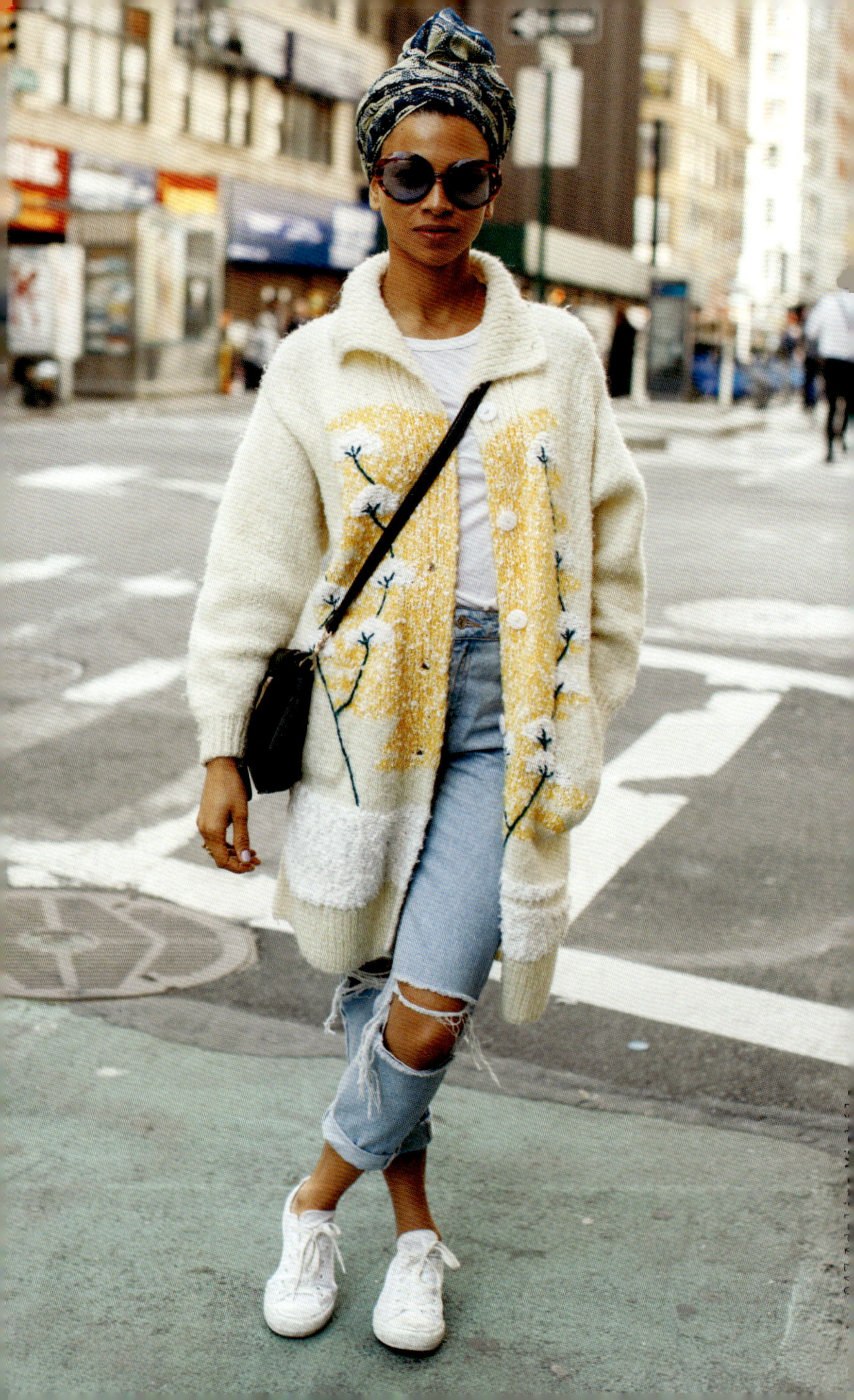

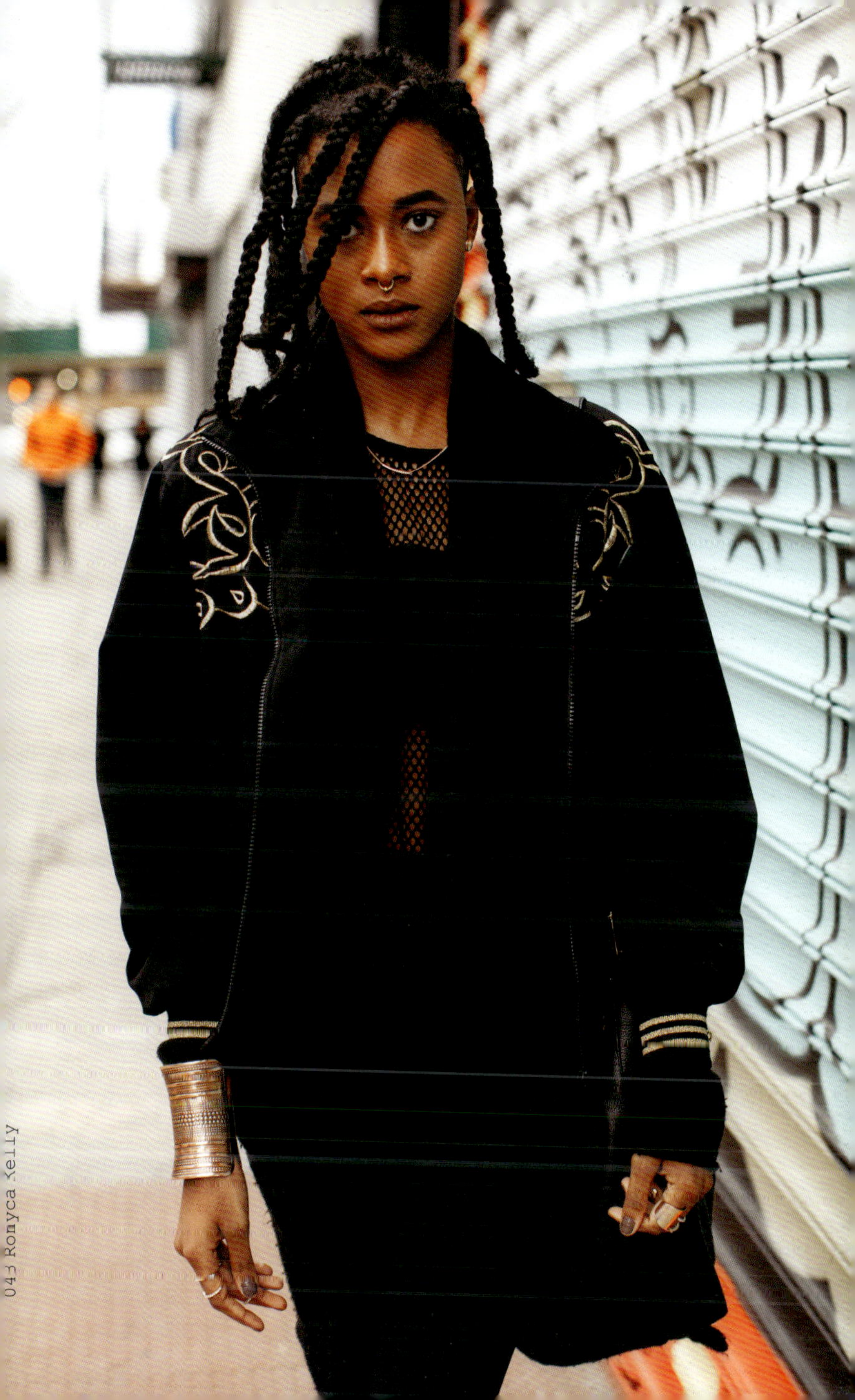

043 Ronyca Kelly

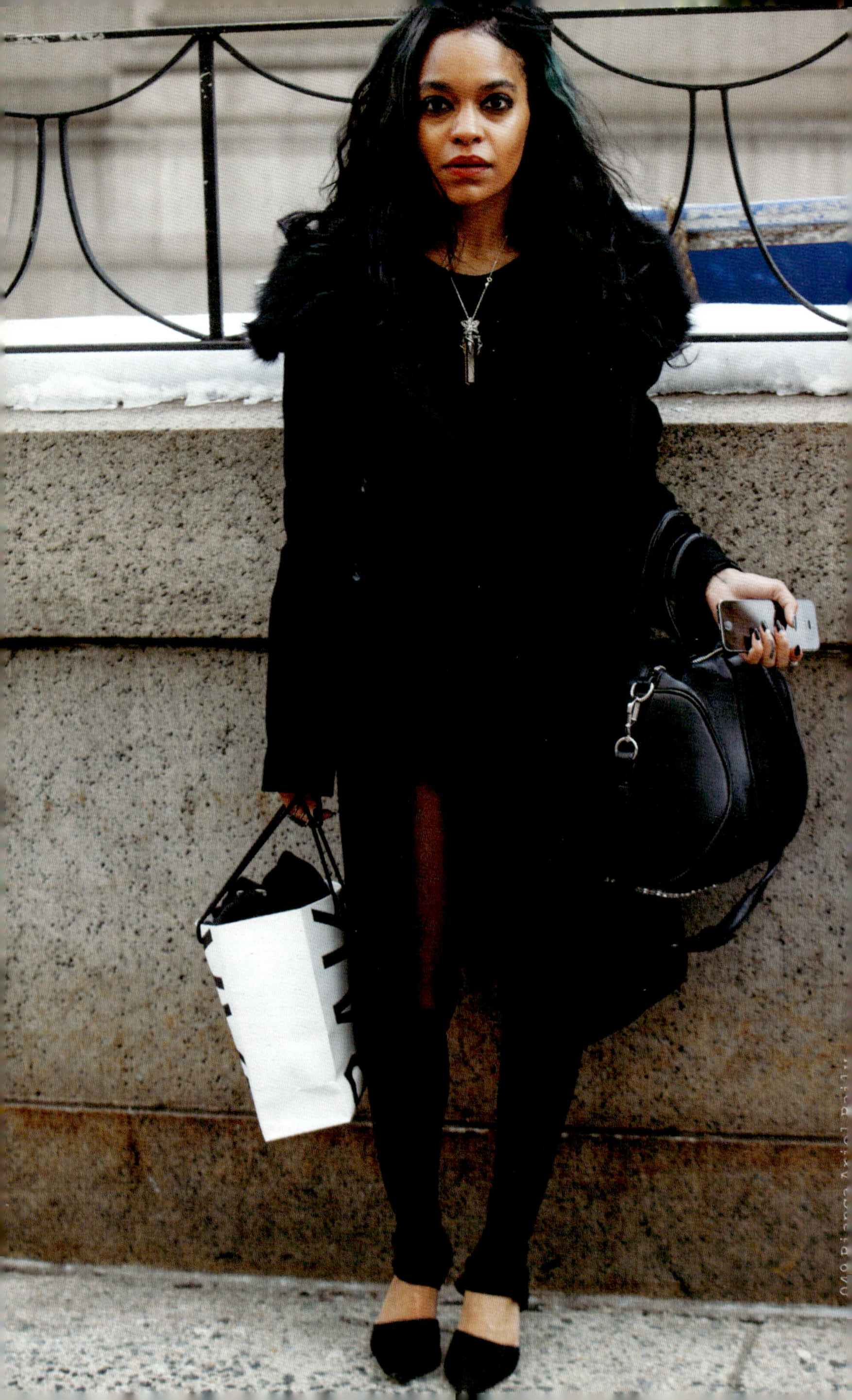

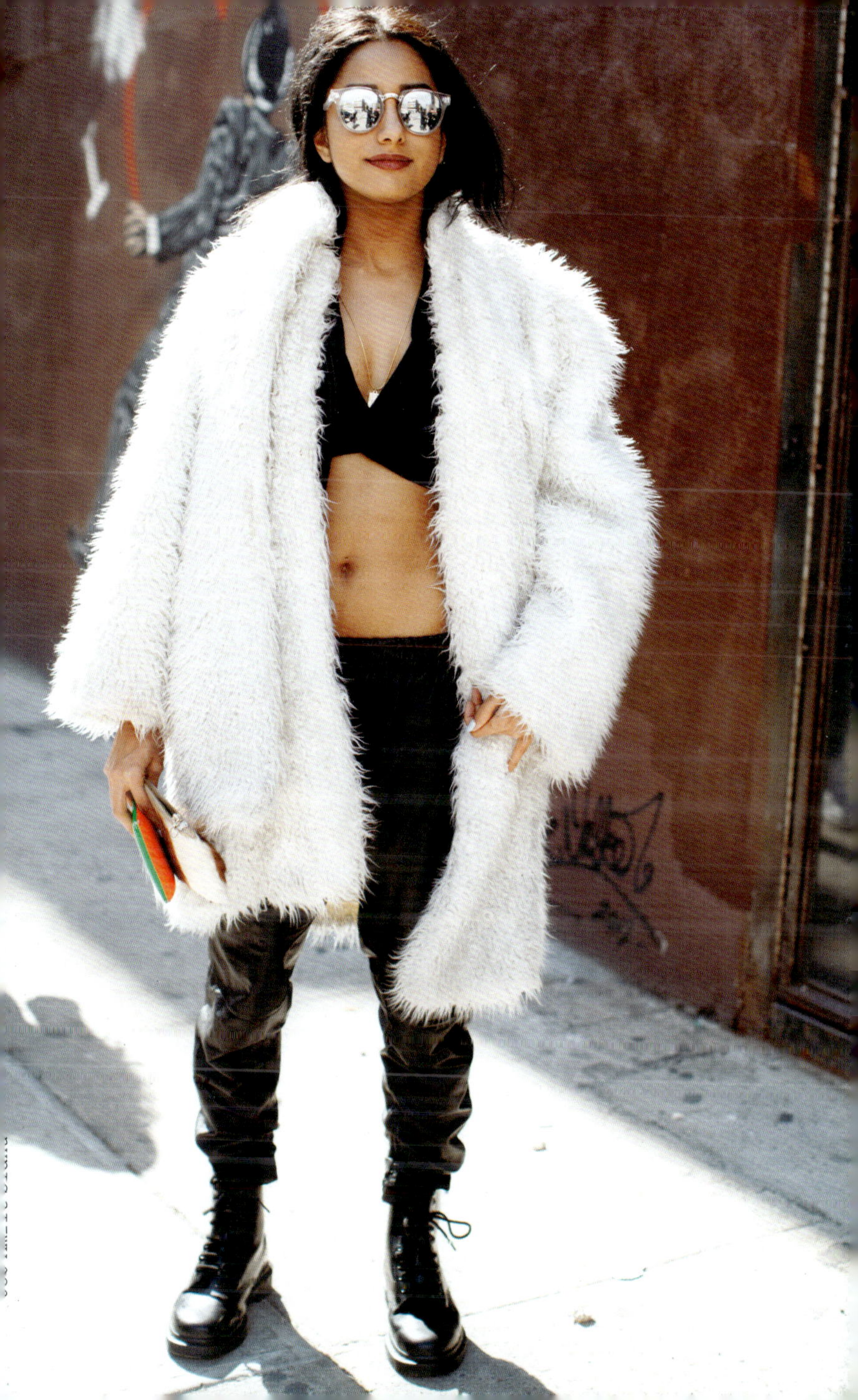

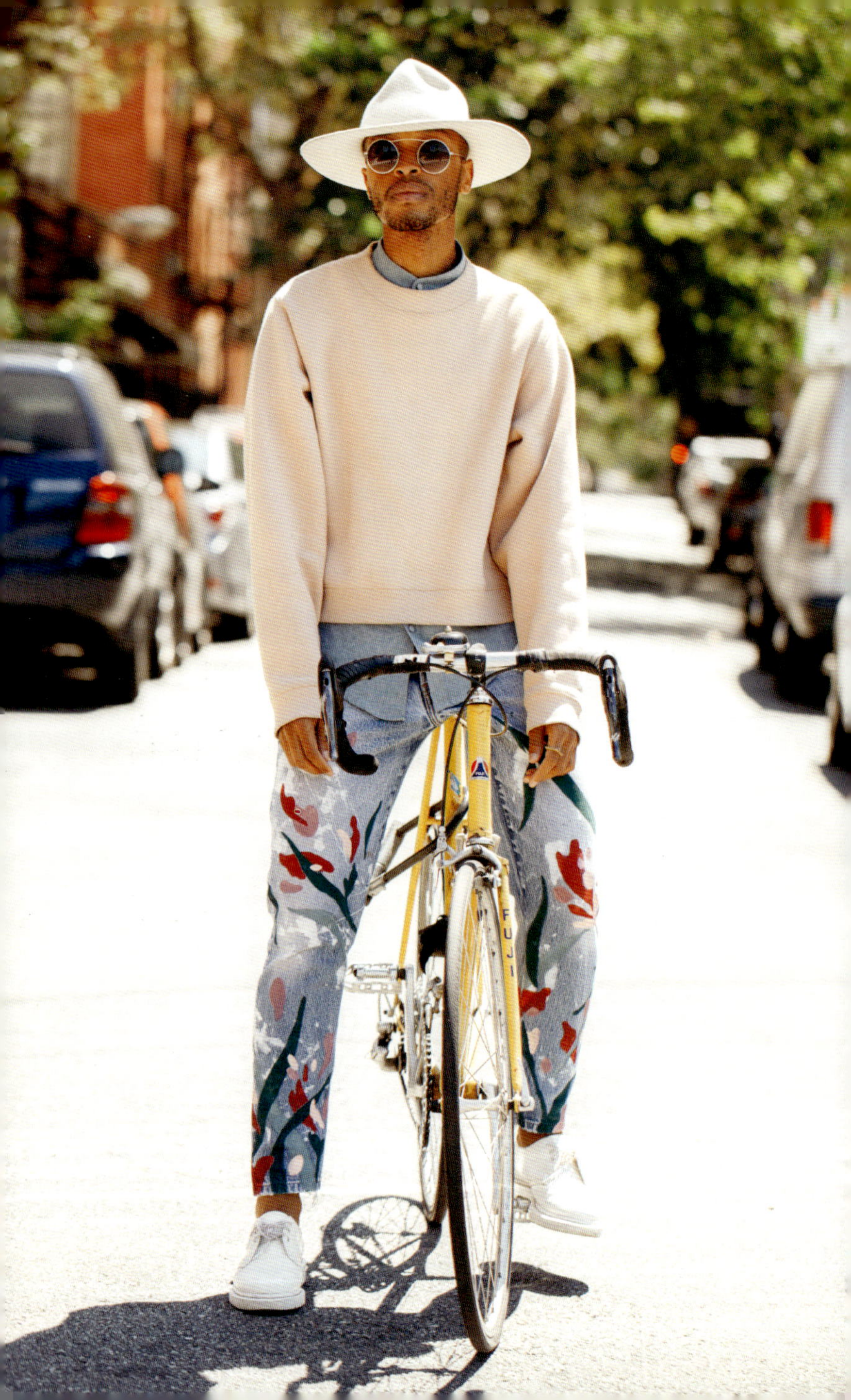
FUJI

"I feel as though my style has matured with me, and though it is still experimental at times, the backbone is a clean aesthetic."

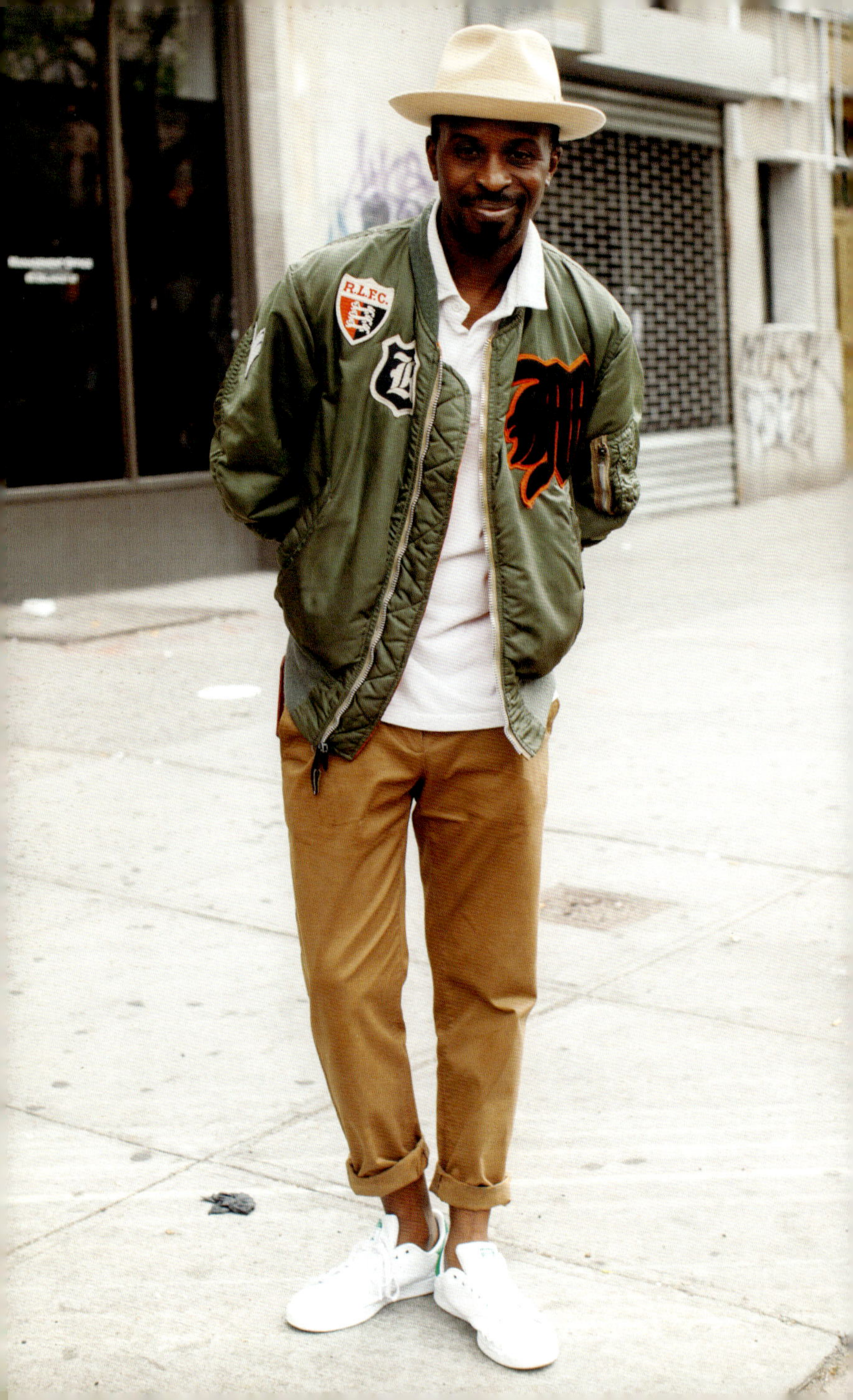
R.L.F.C.

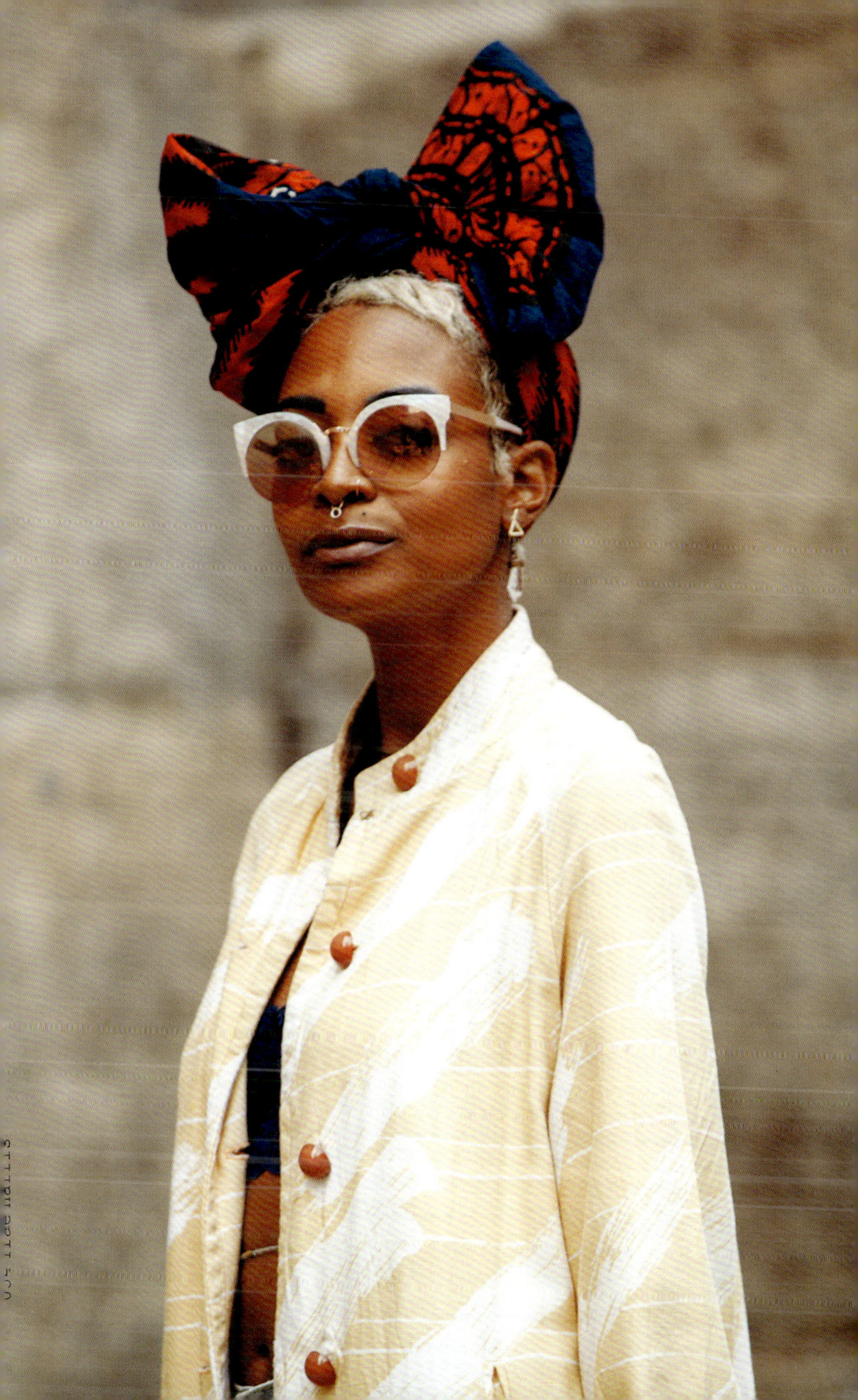

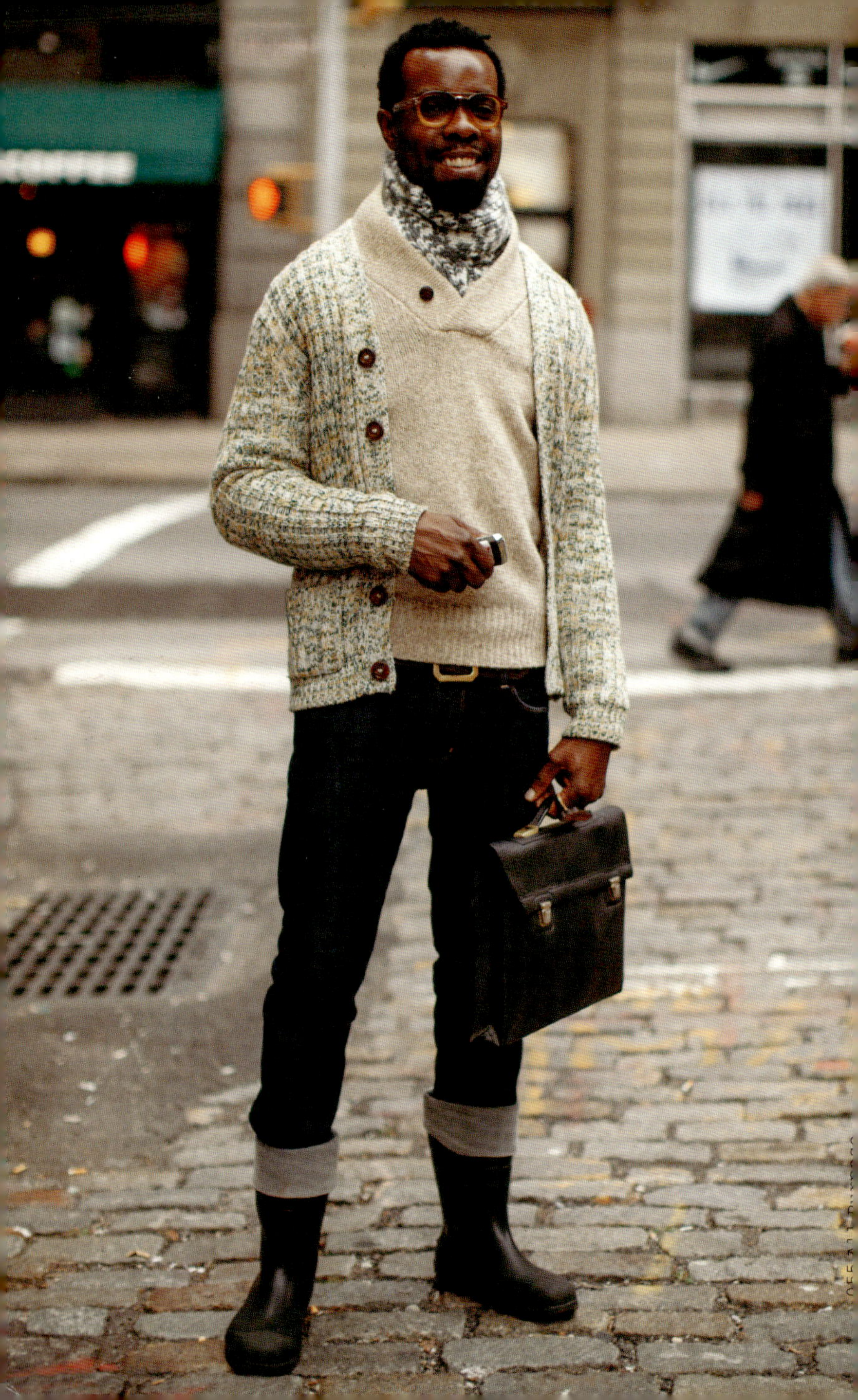

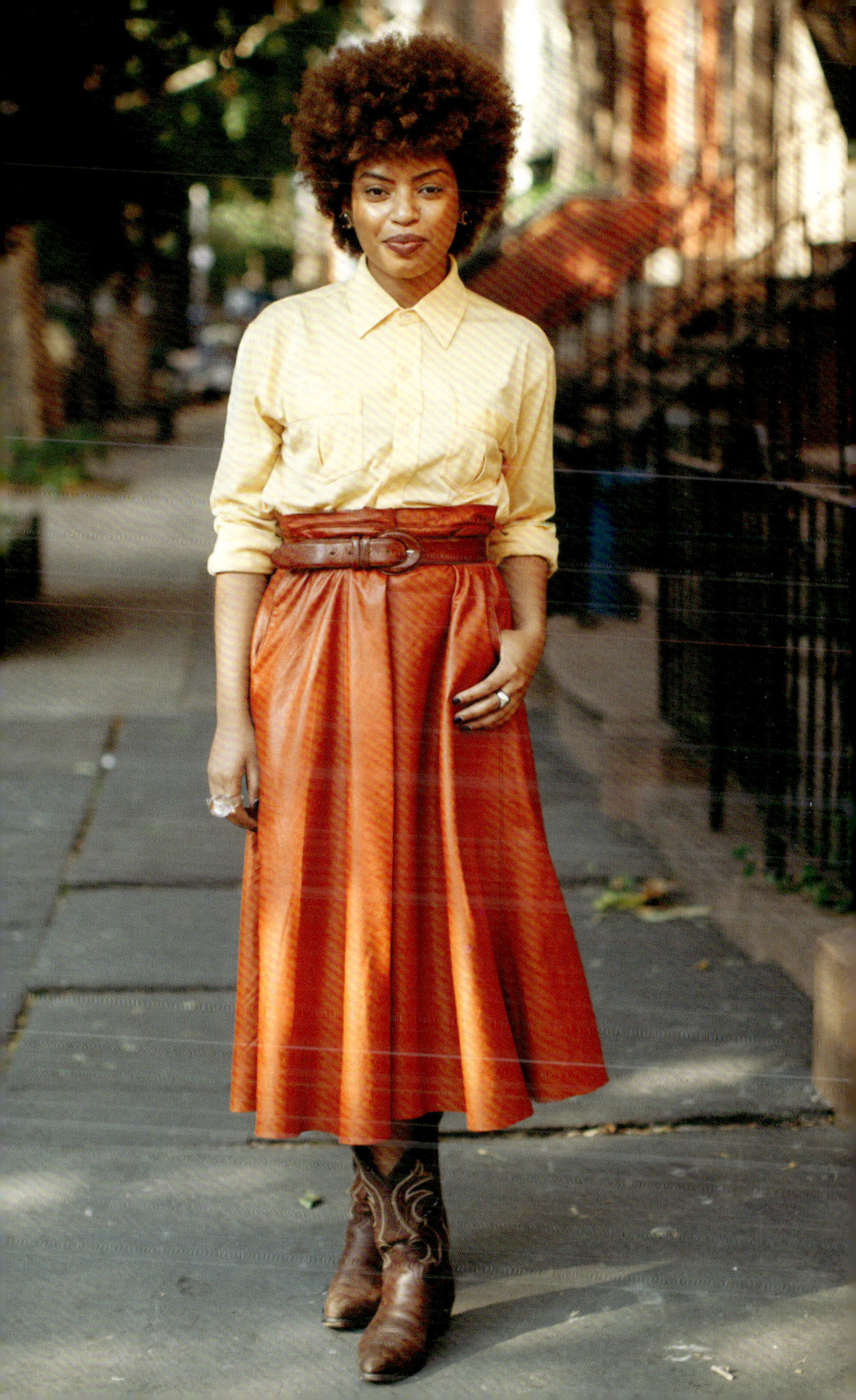

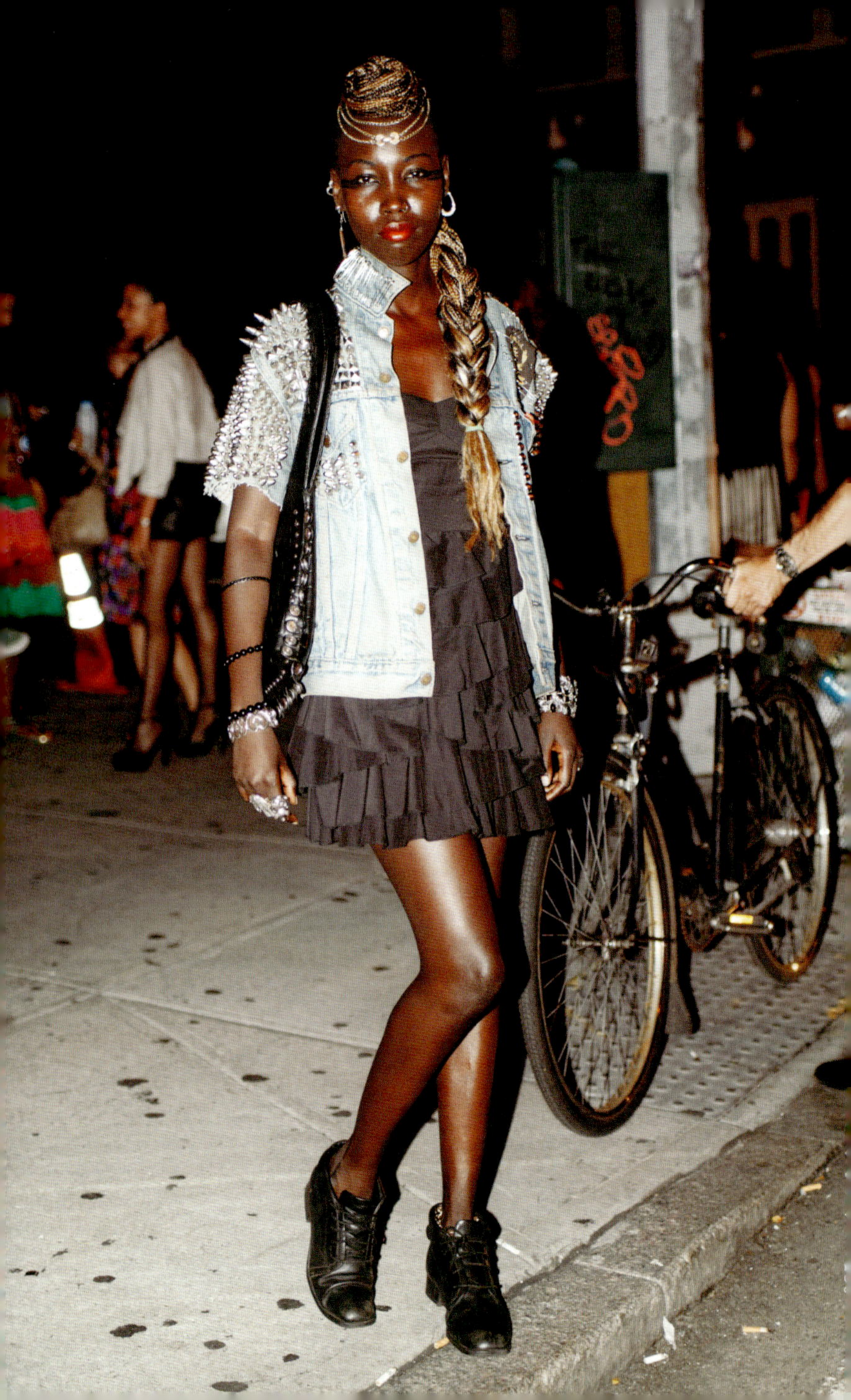

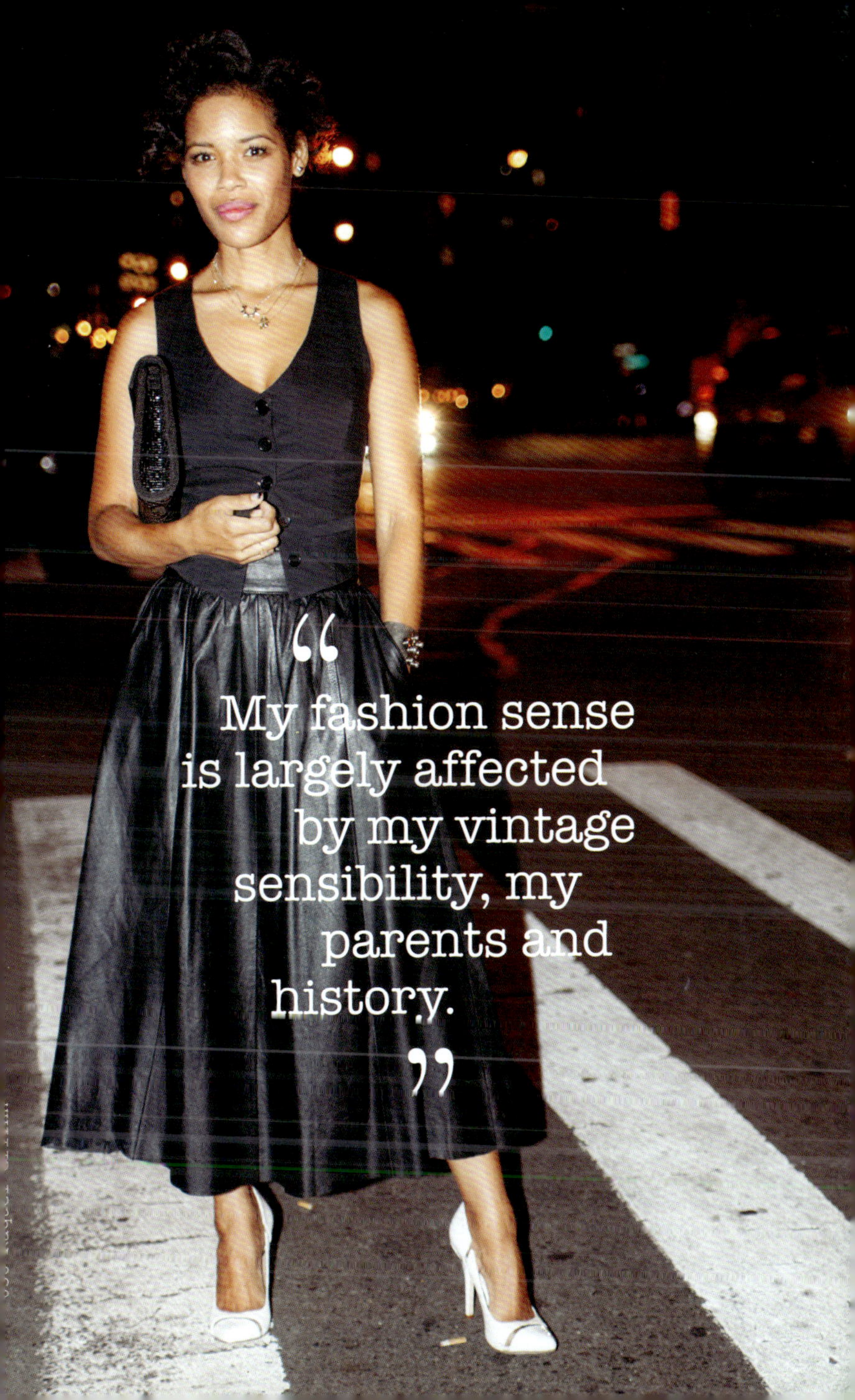
"My fashion sense is largely affected by my vintage sensibility, my parents and history."

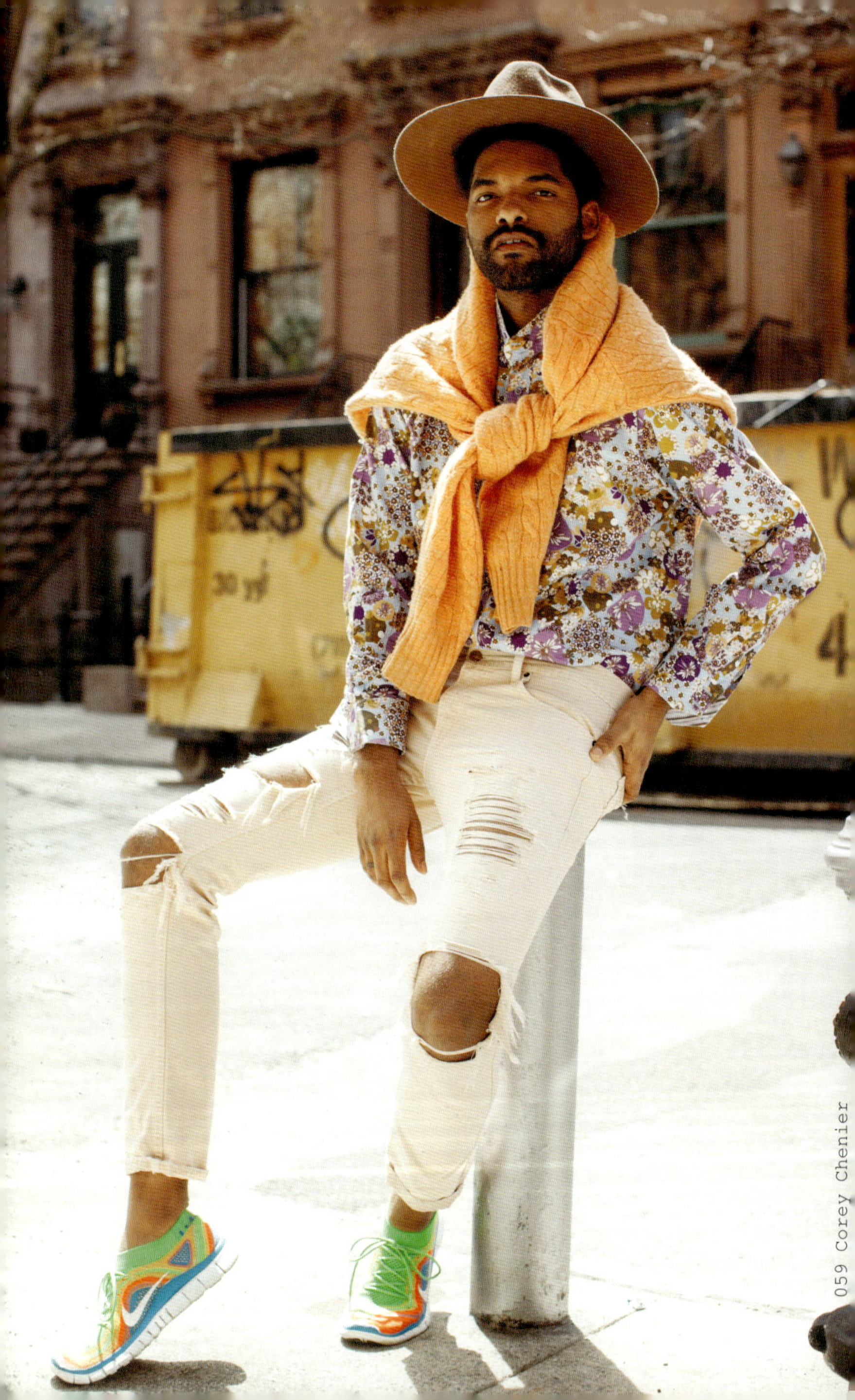

059 Corey Chenier

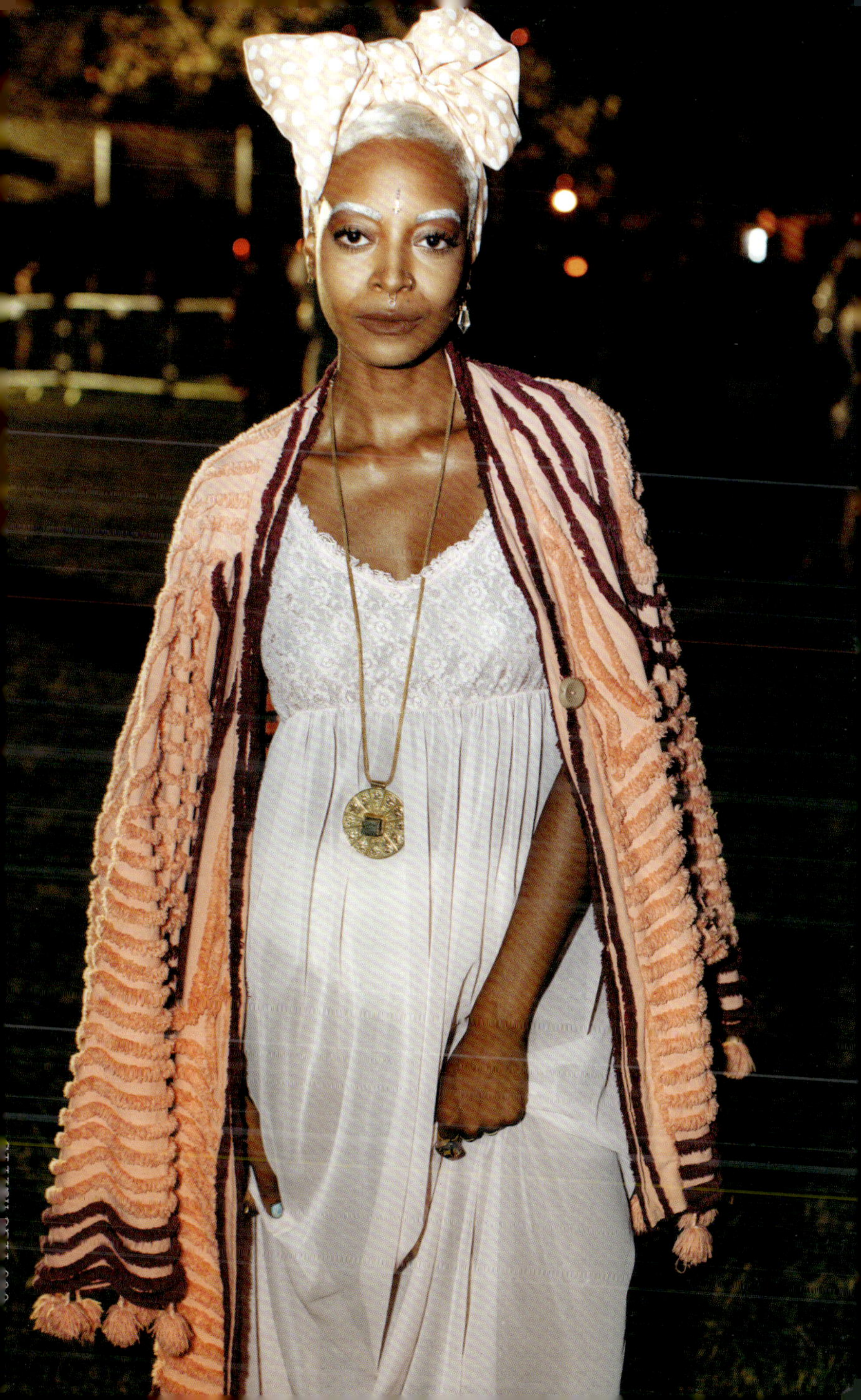

“Style is what you make it. It’s an outward expression of who you are.”

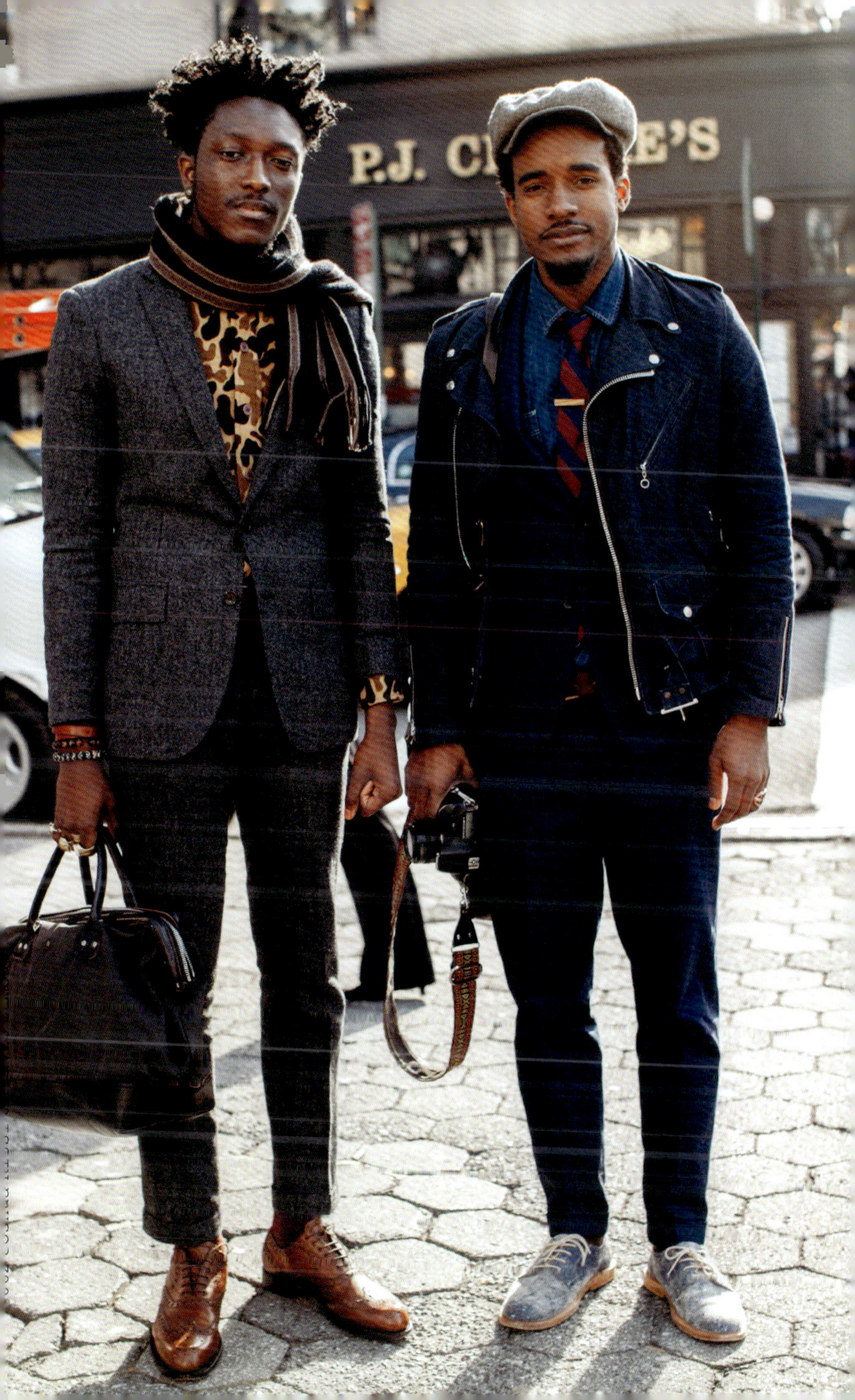
P.J.

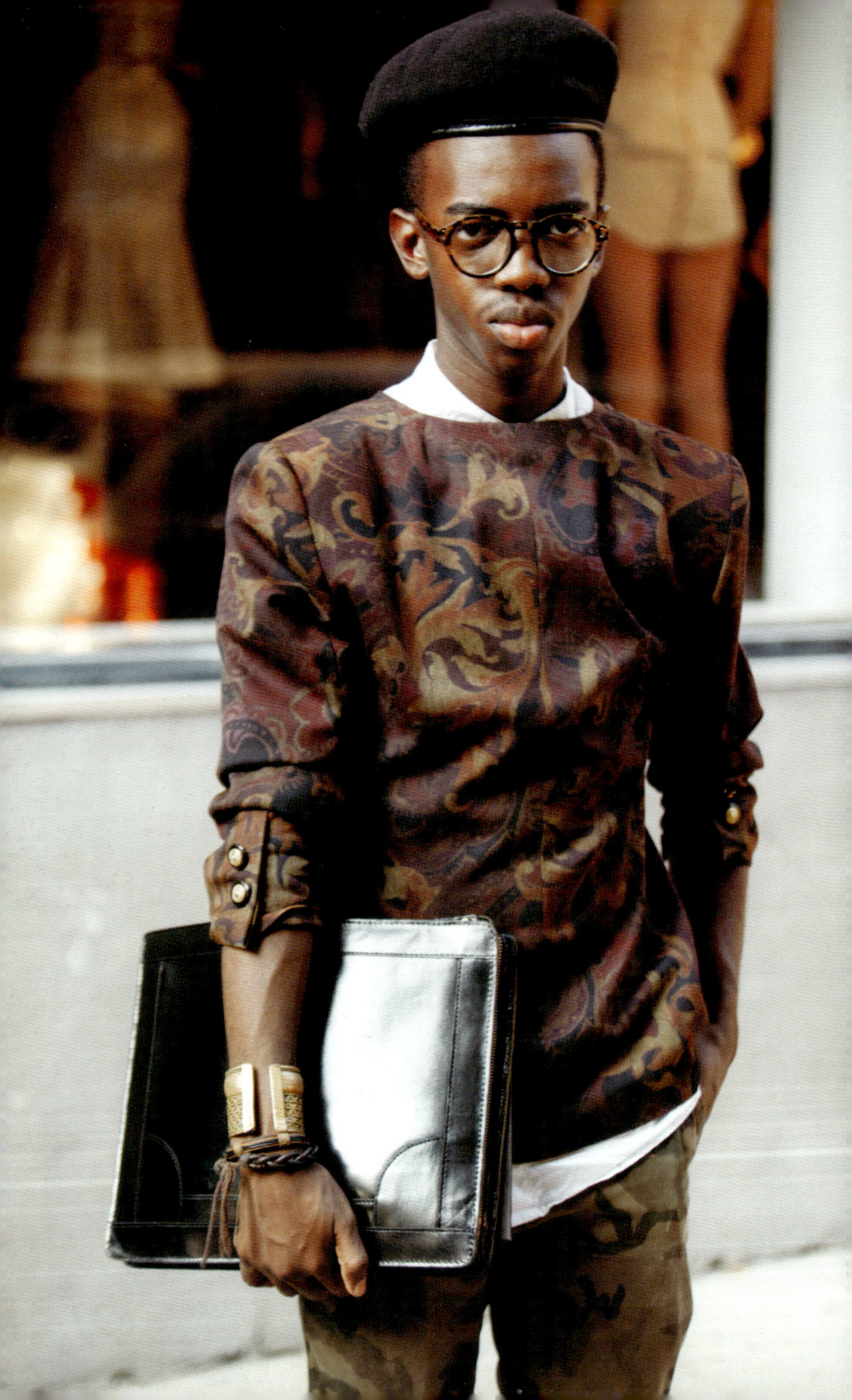

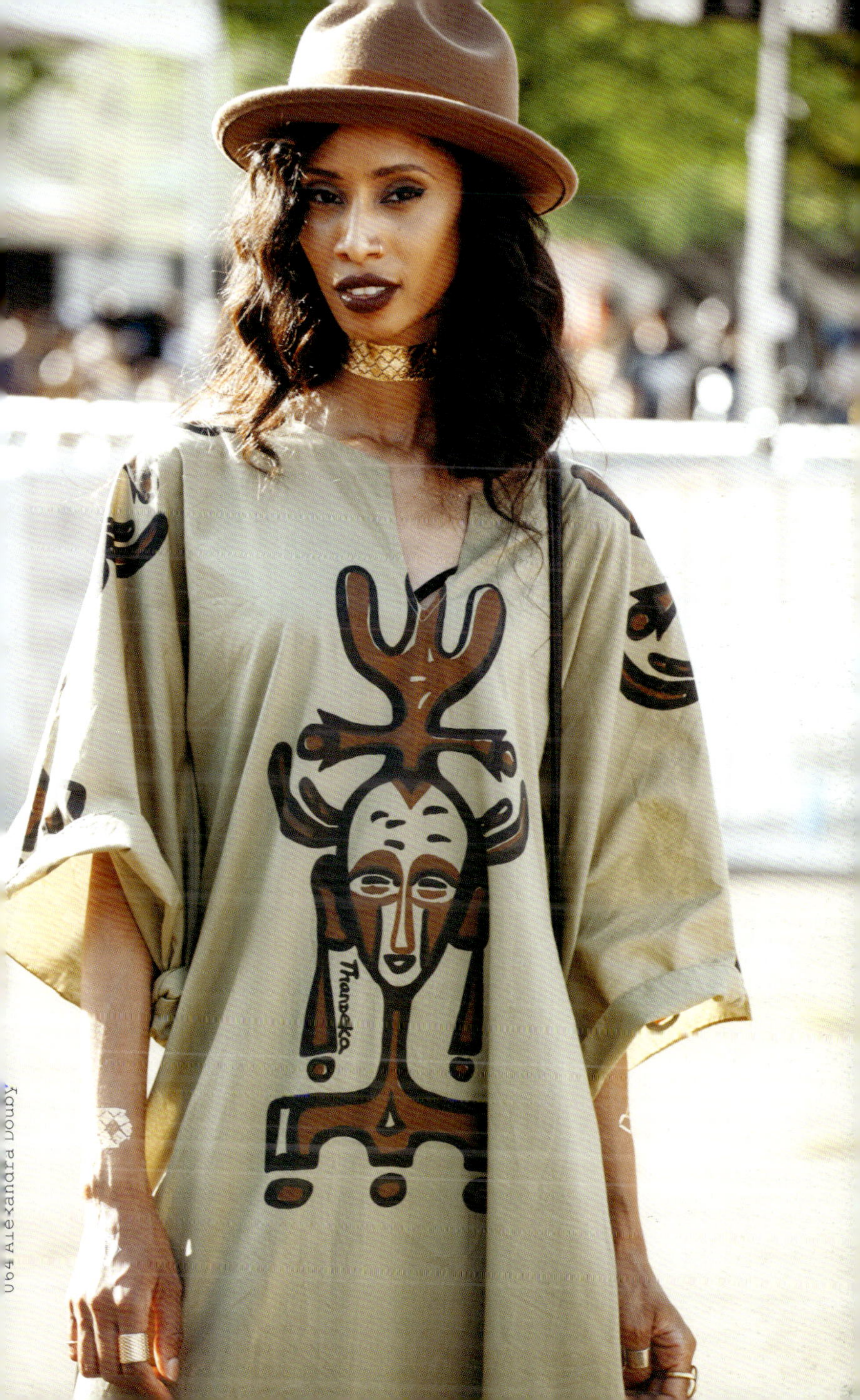

064 Alexandra Dondy

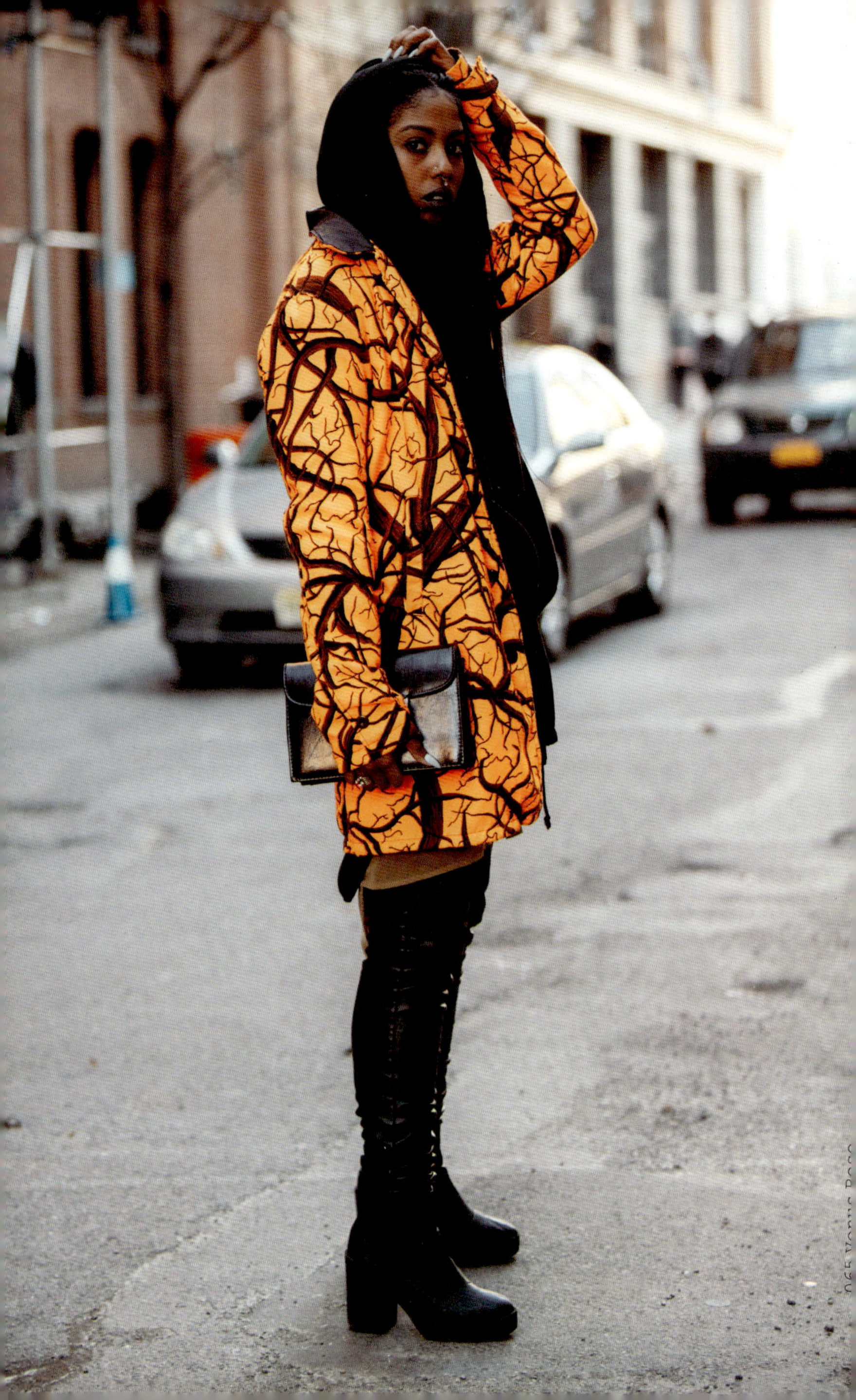

065 Venus Rose

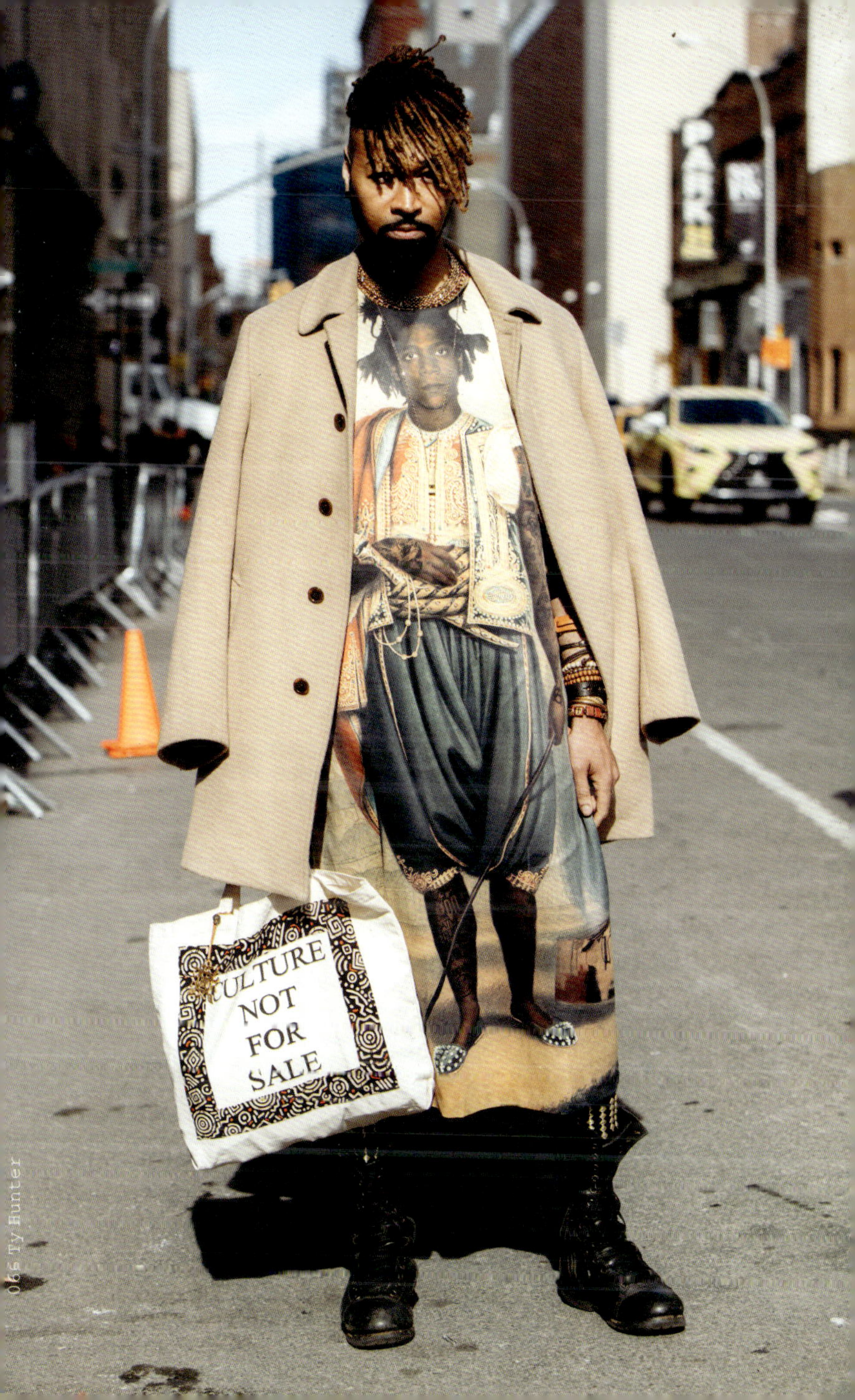

065 Ty Hunter

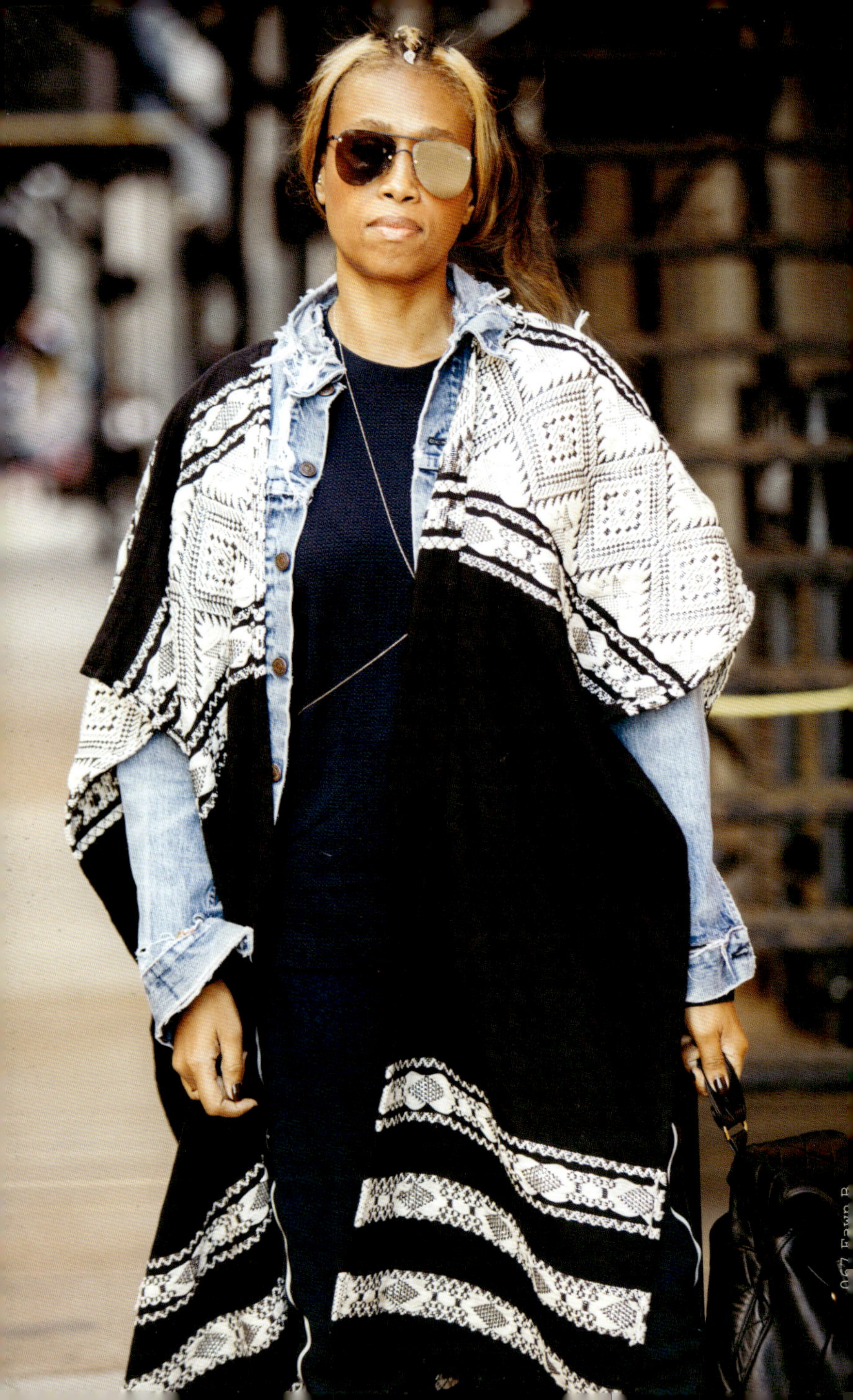

067 Fawn B

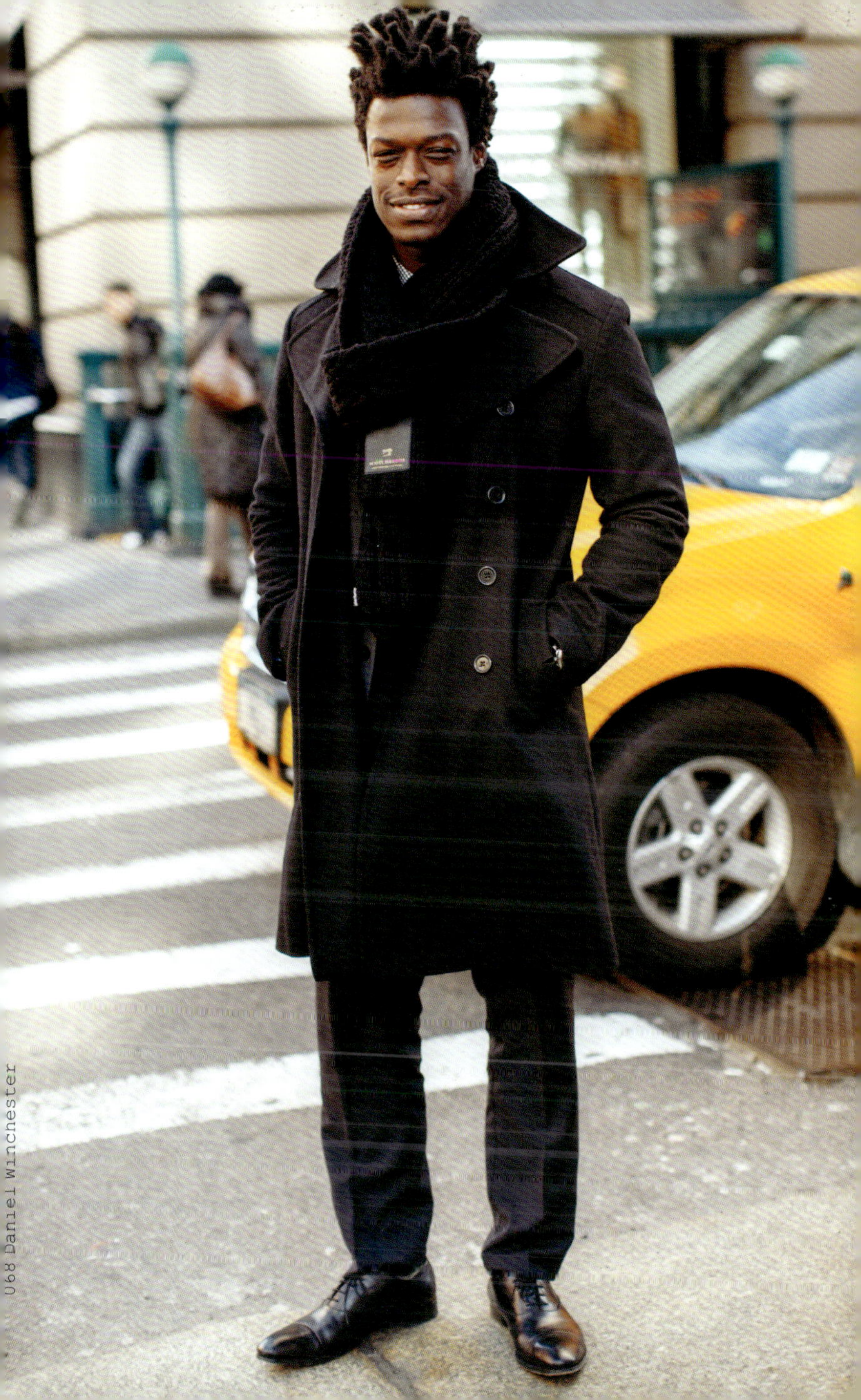

068 Daniel Winchester

“True style cannot be faked. It is in the tilt of a neck, the tie of a scarf, the strut of the heel and in the layers of an outfit.”

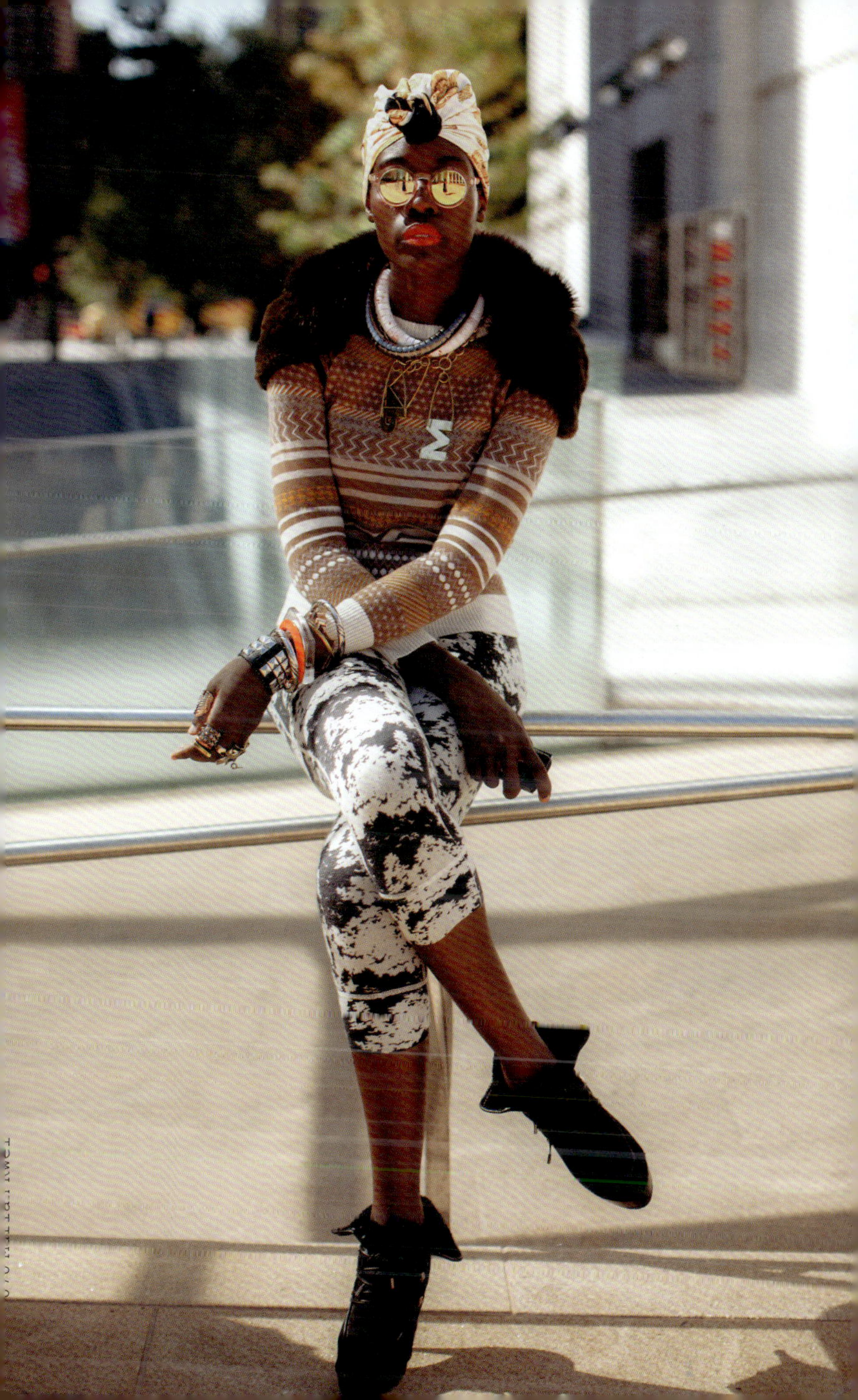

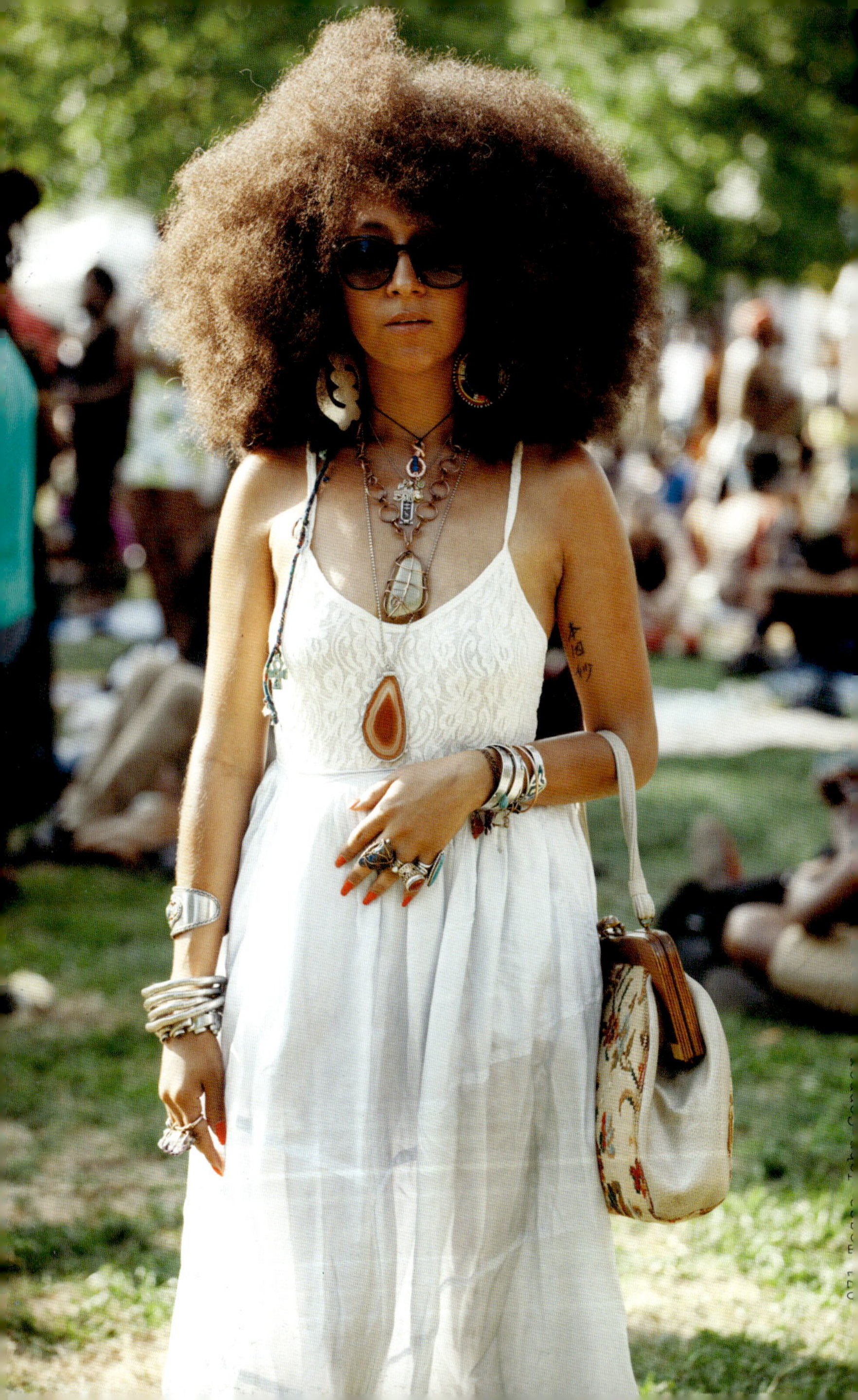

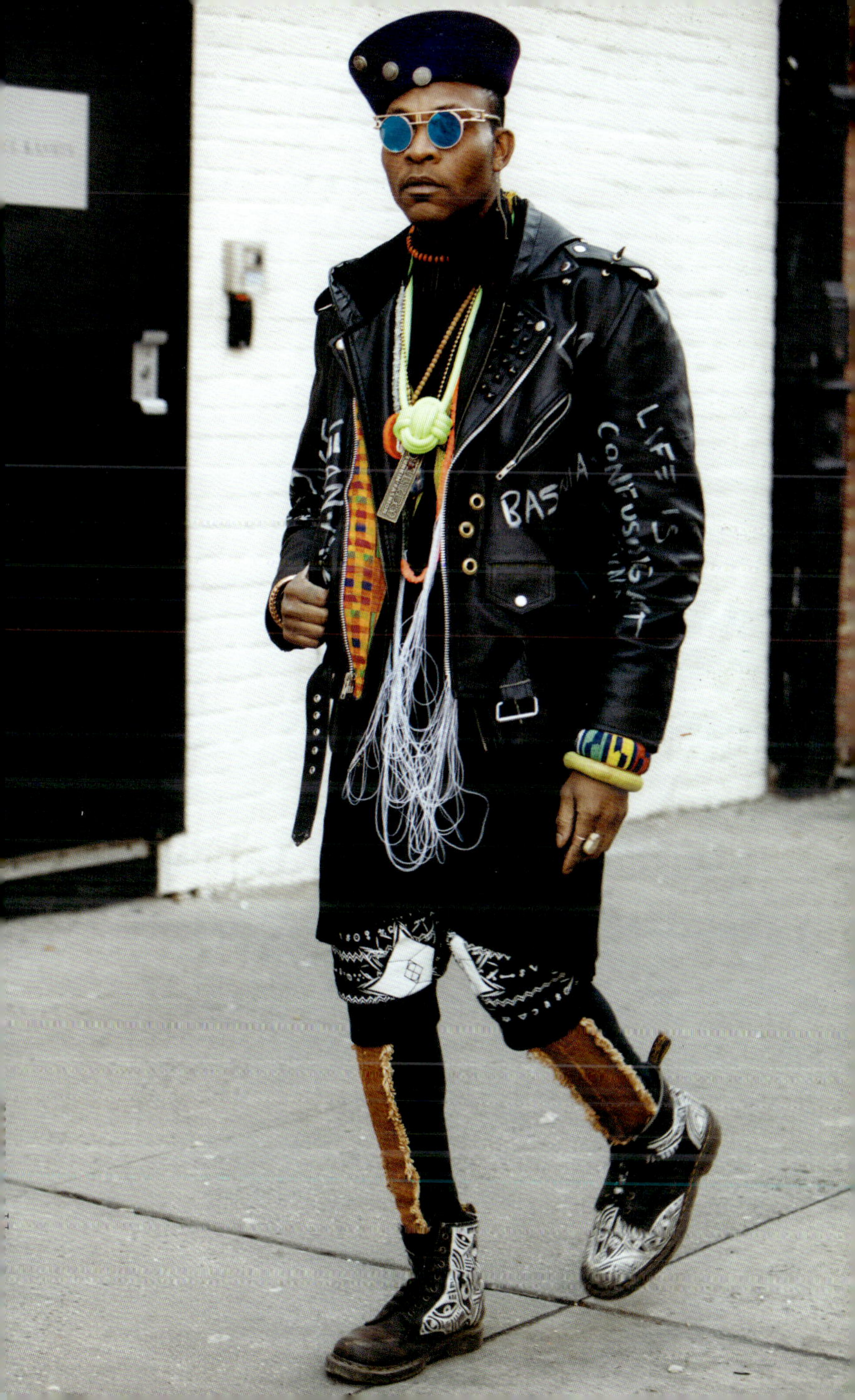

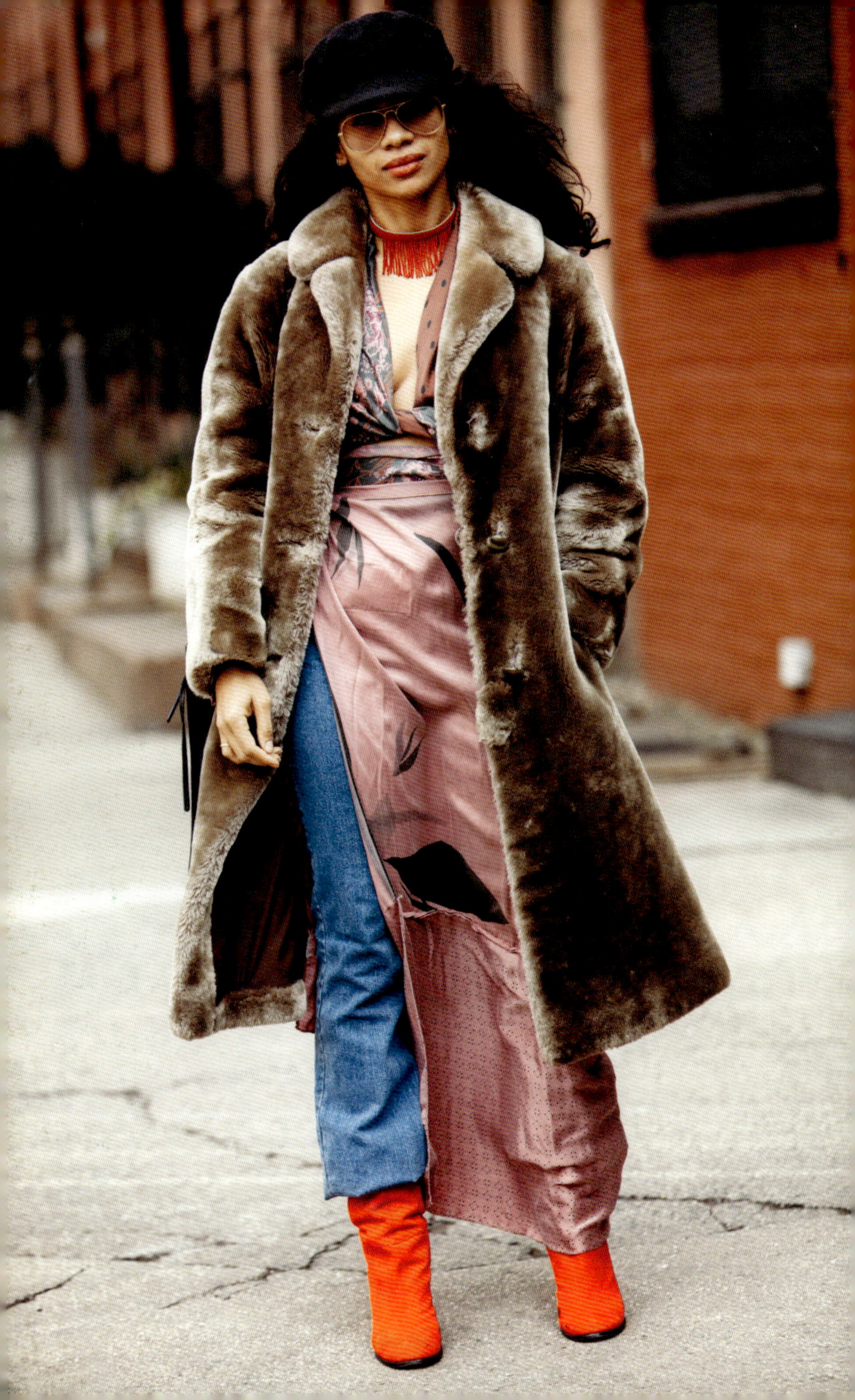

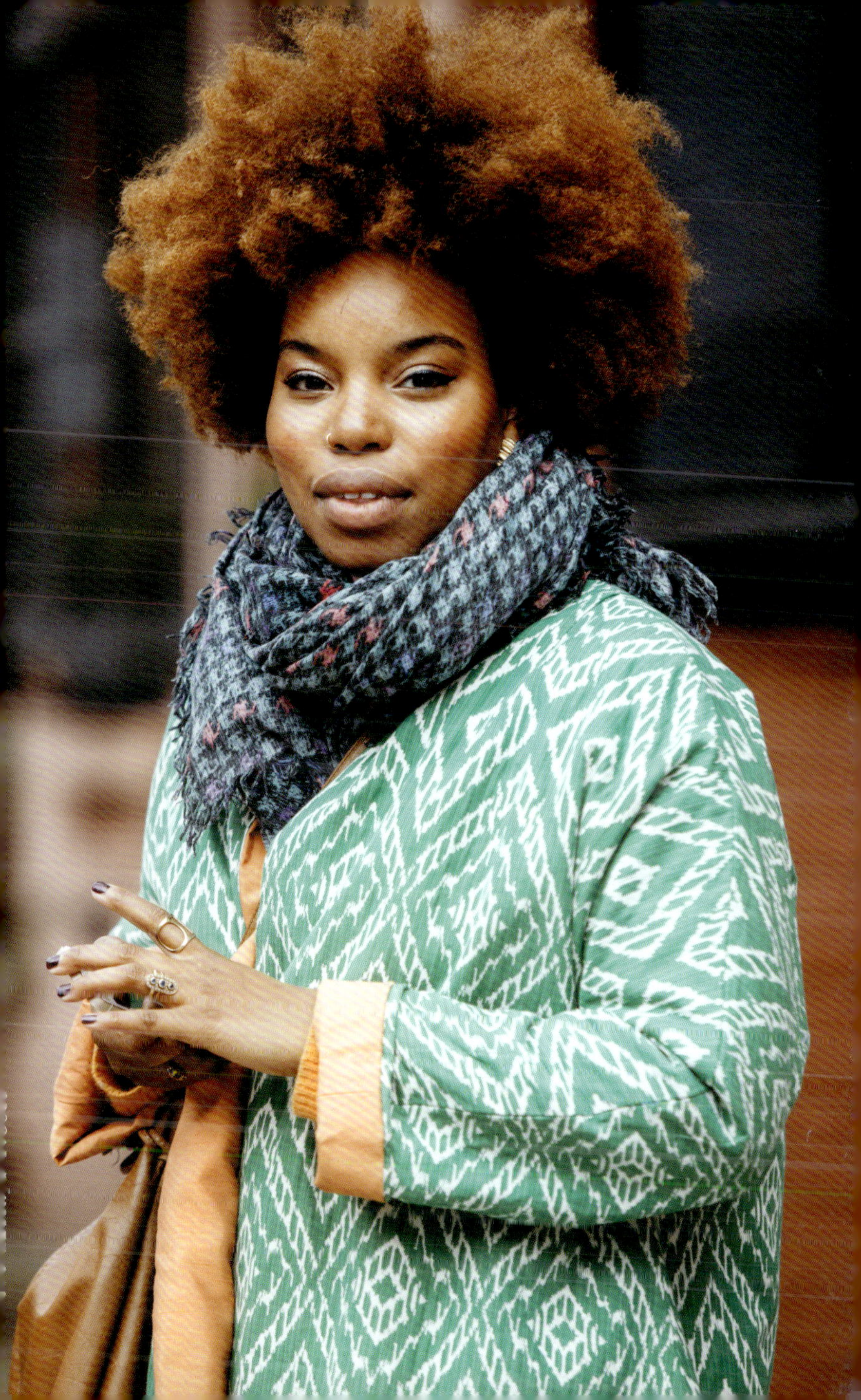

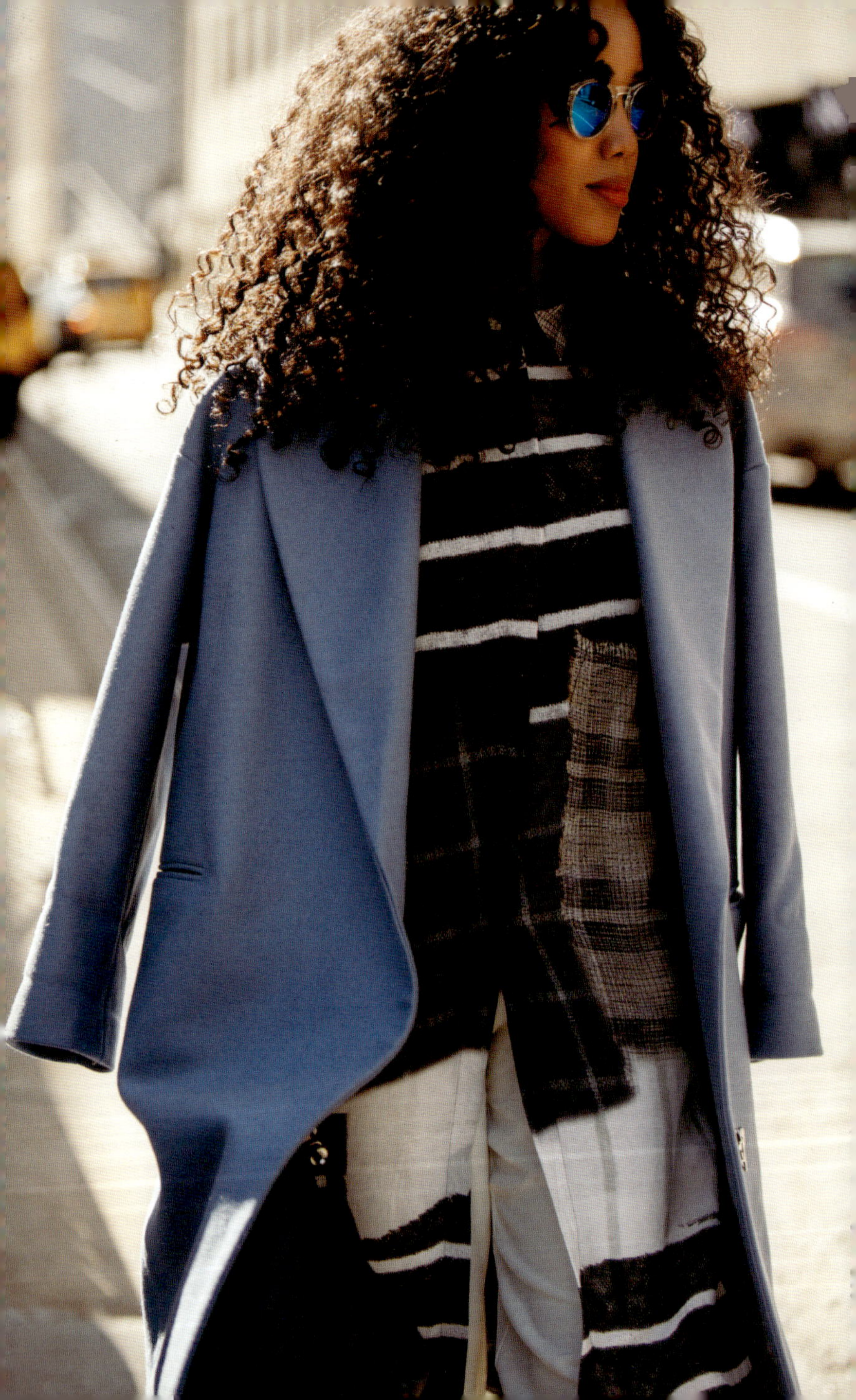

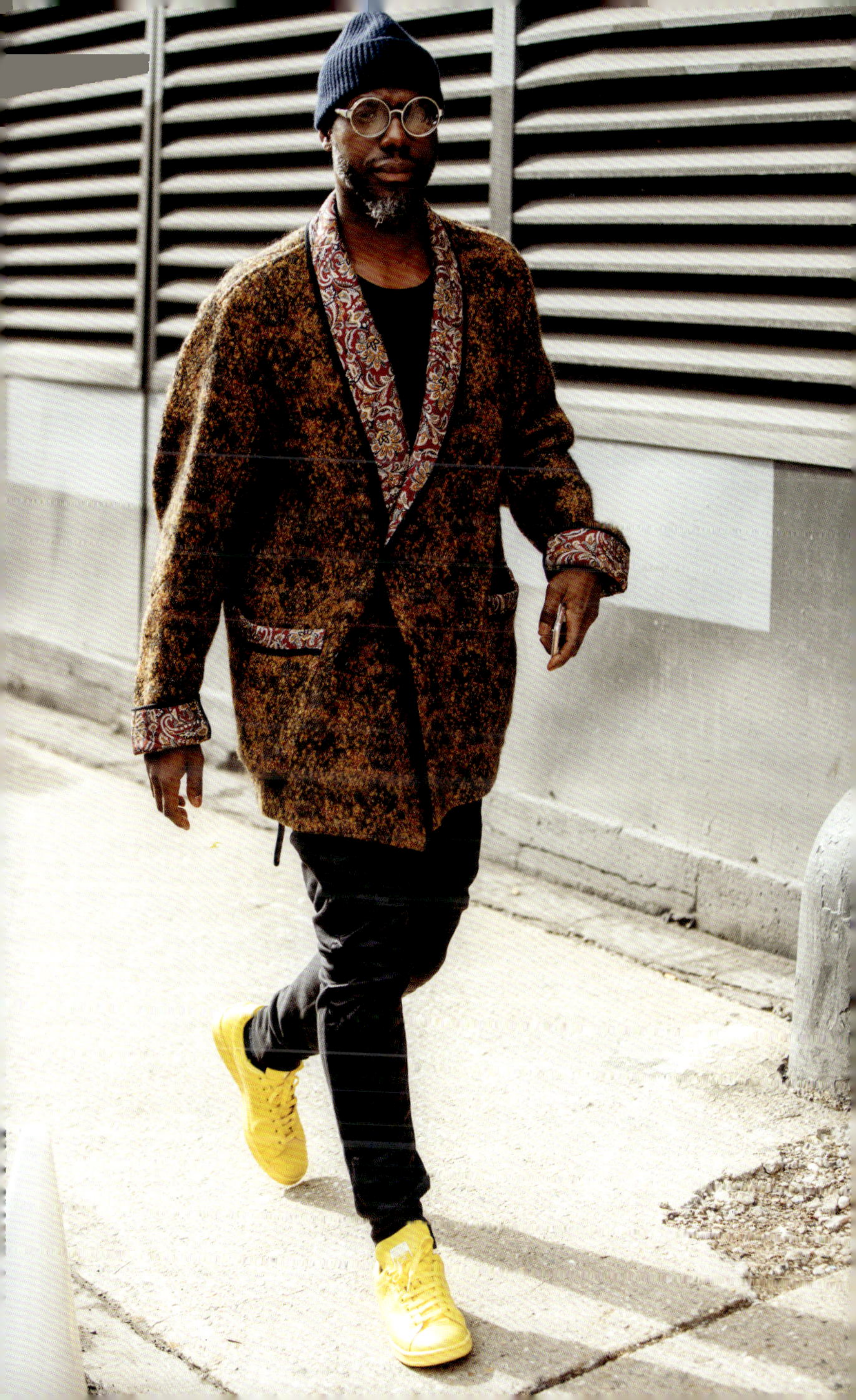

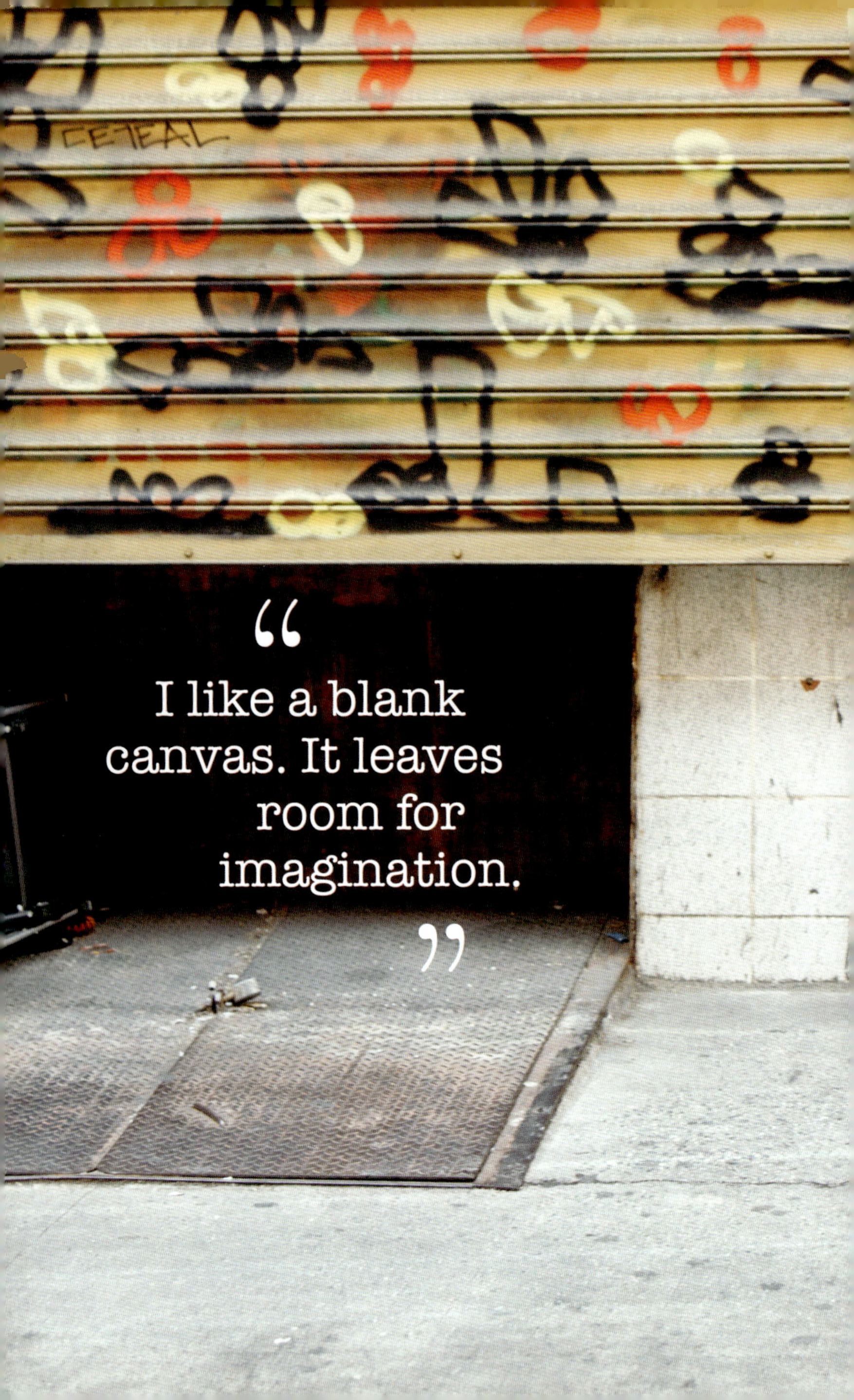
“I like a blank canvas. It leaves room for imagination.”

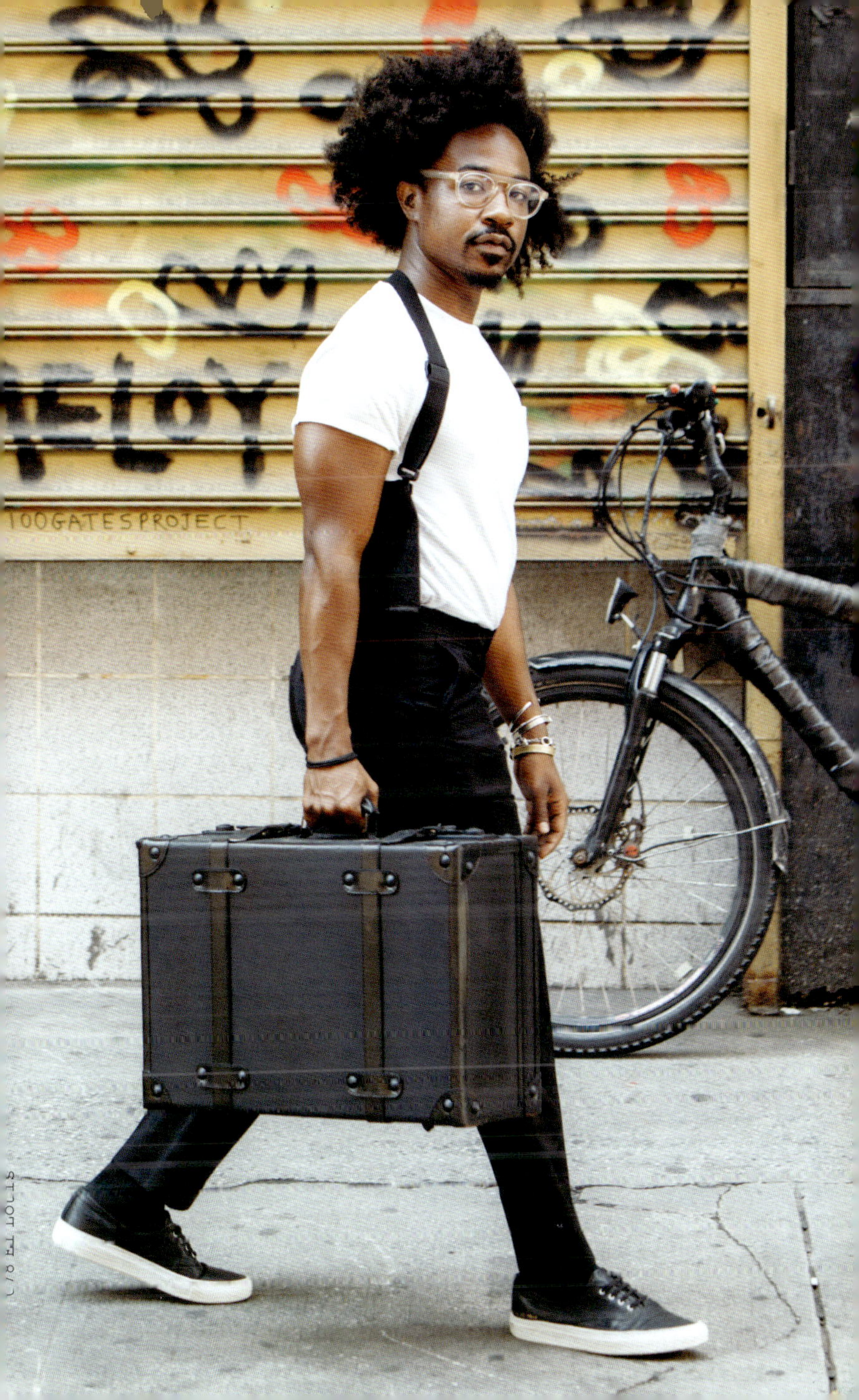
100GATESPROJECT

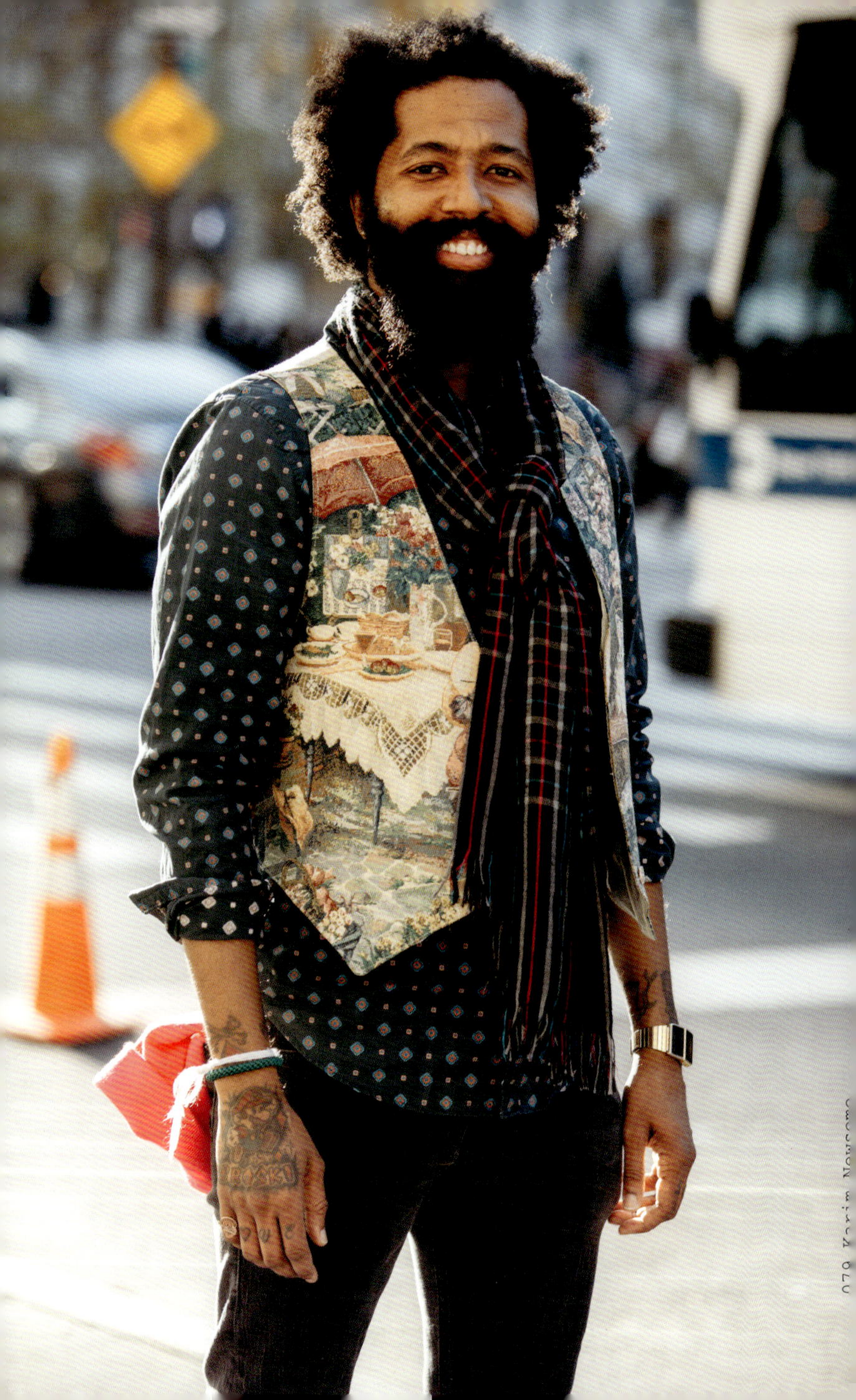

079 Karim Newsome

“

I am a seeker.
Doing my best to
unlearn lies
and learn truths and
dancing as much
as I can in
between.

”

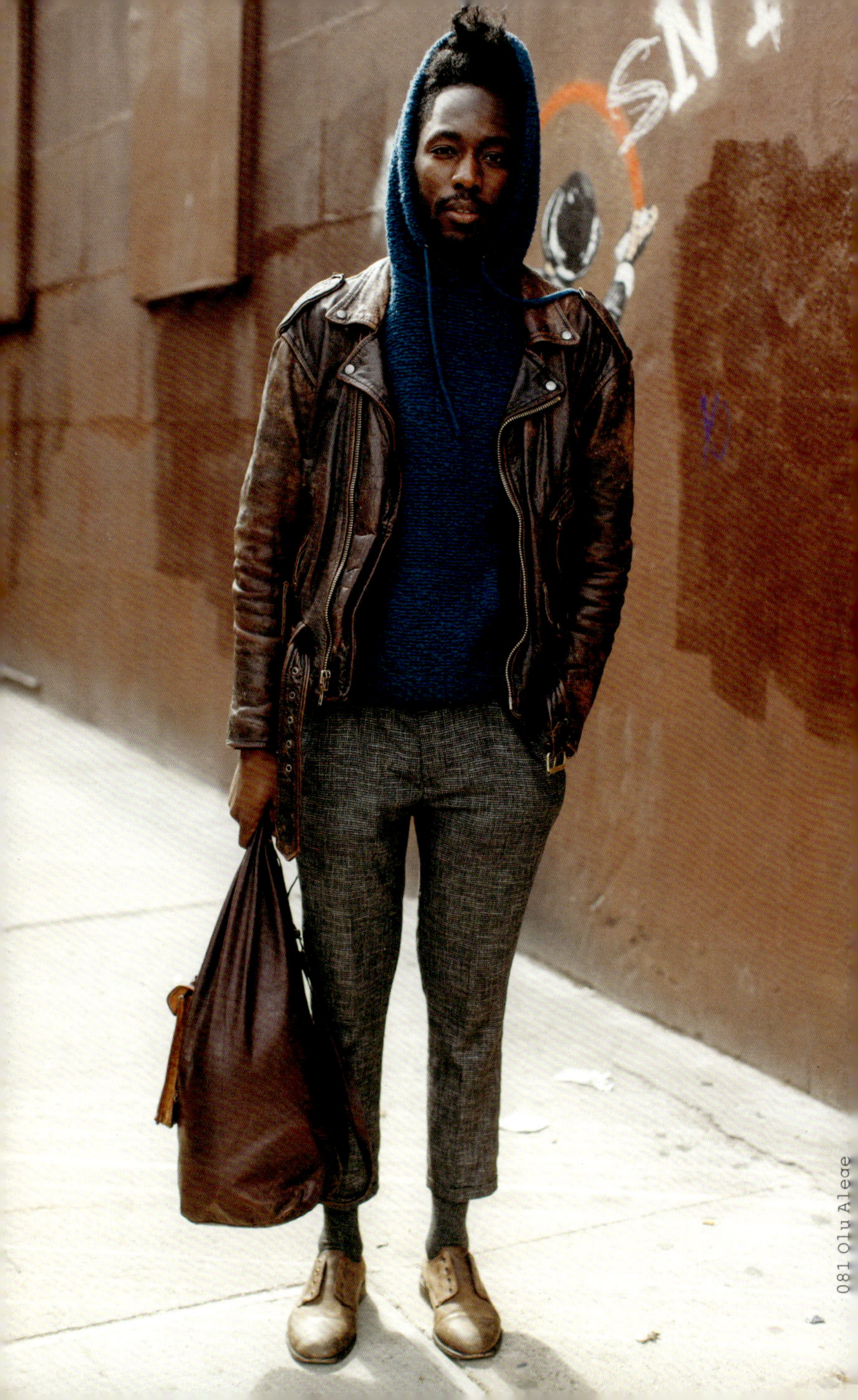

081 Olu Aleae

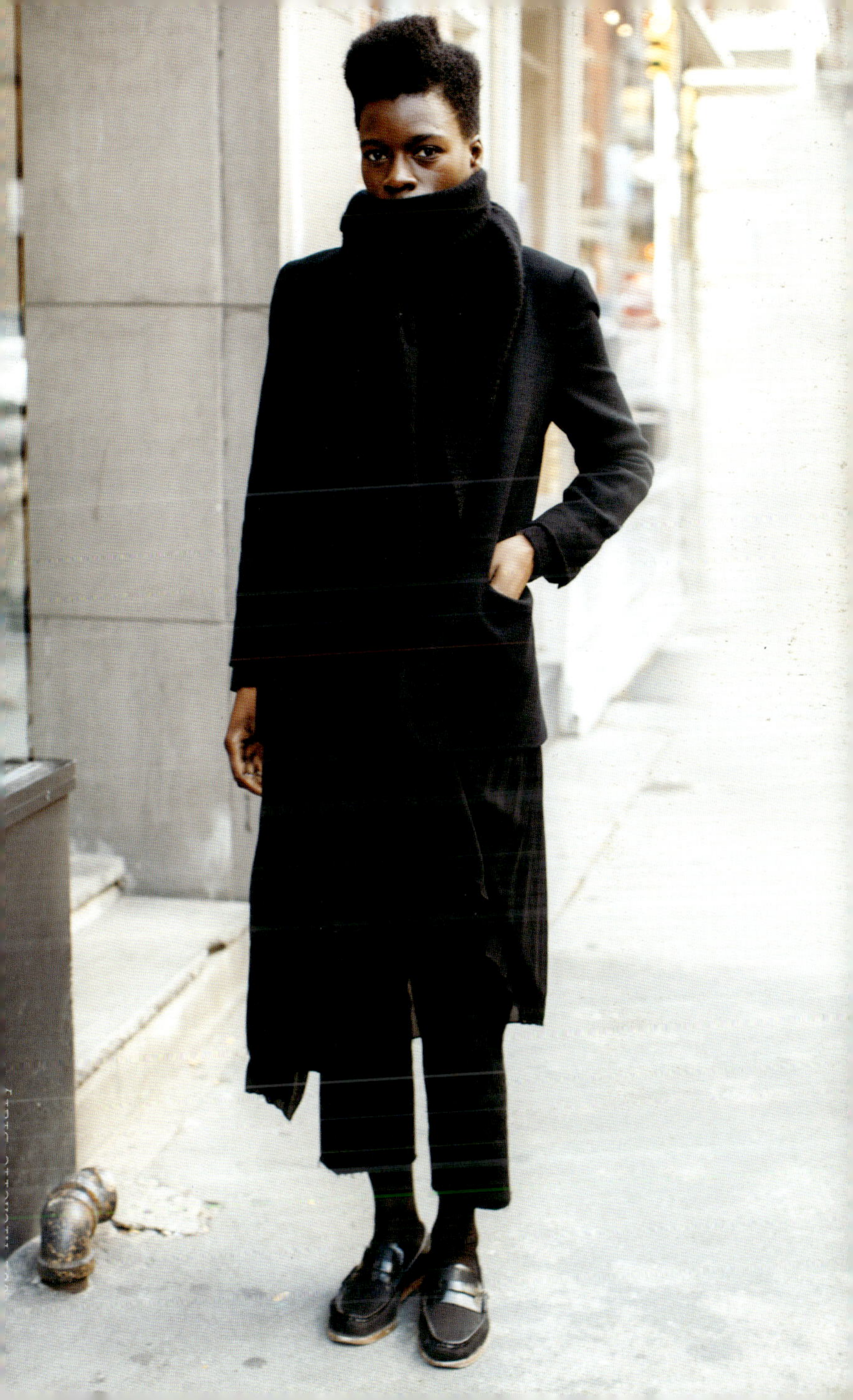

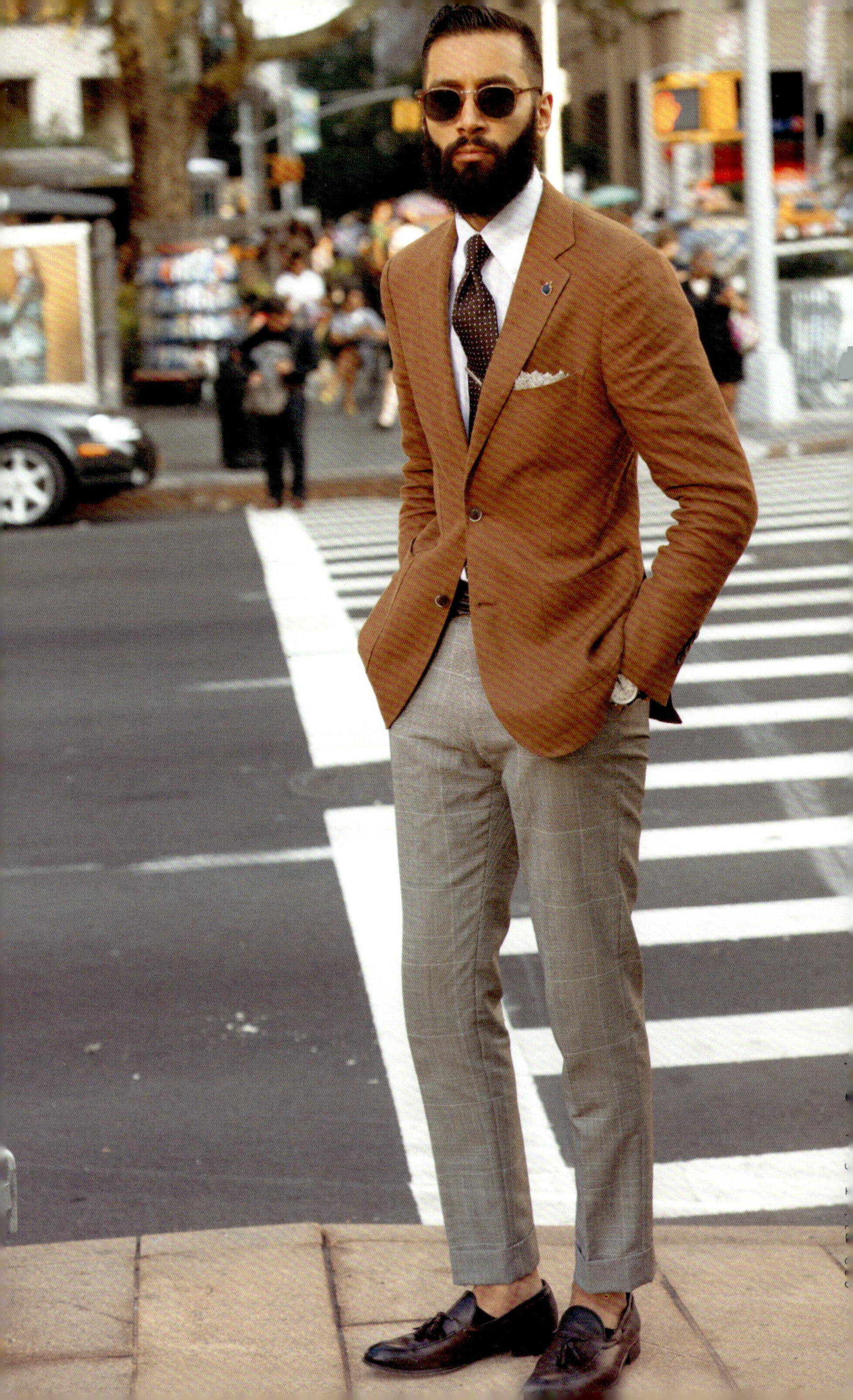

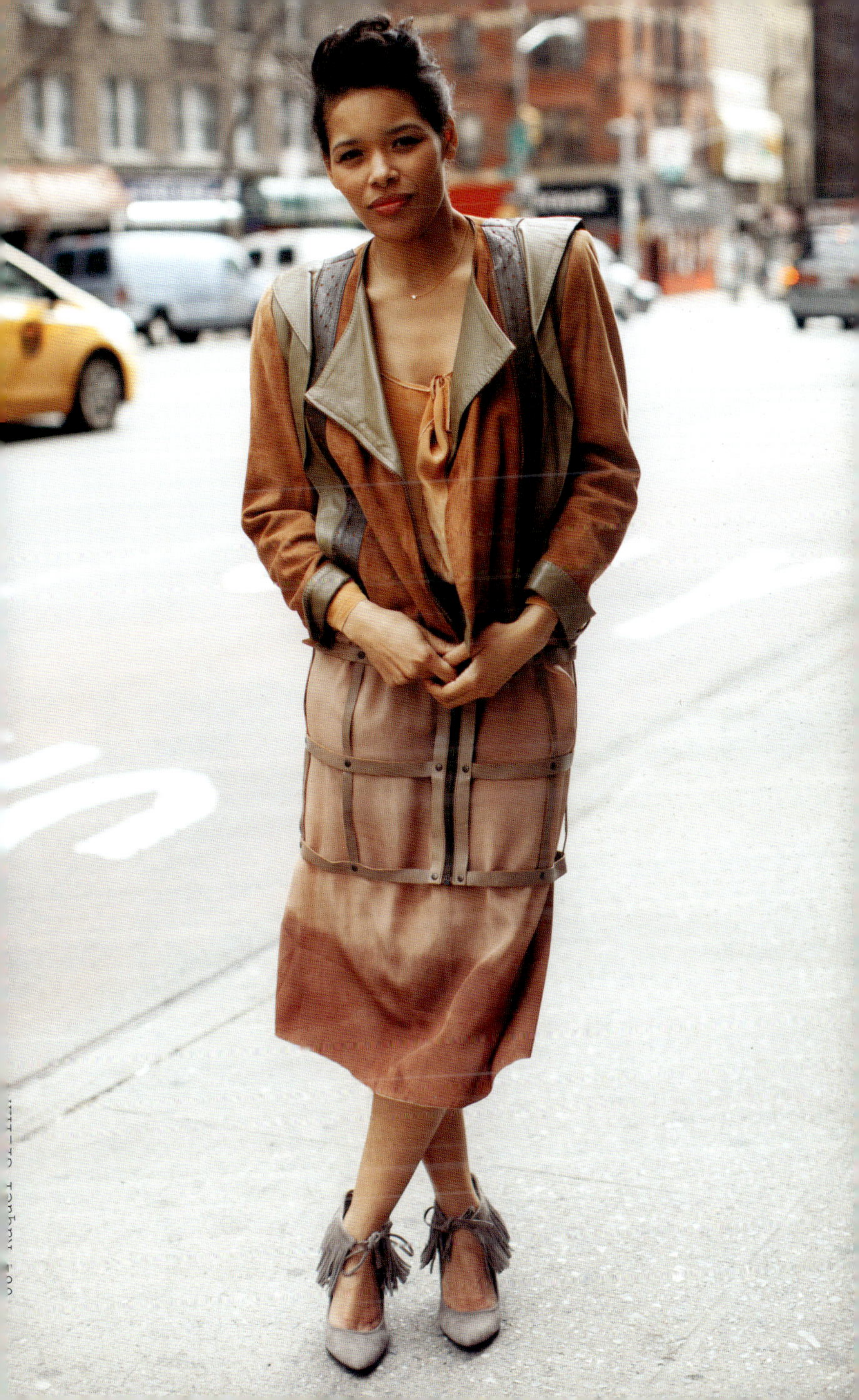

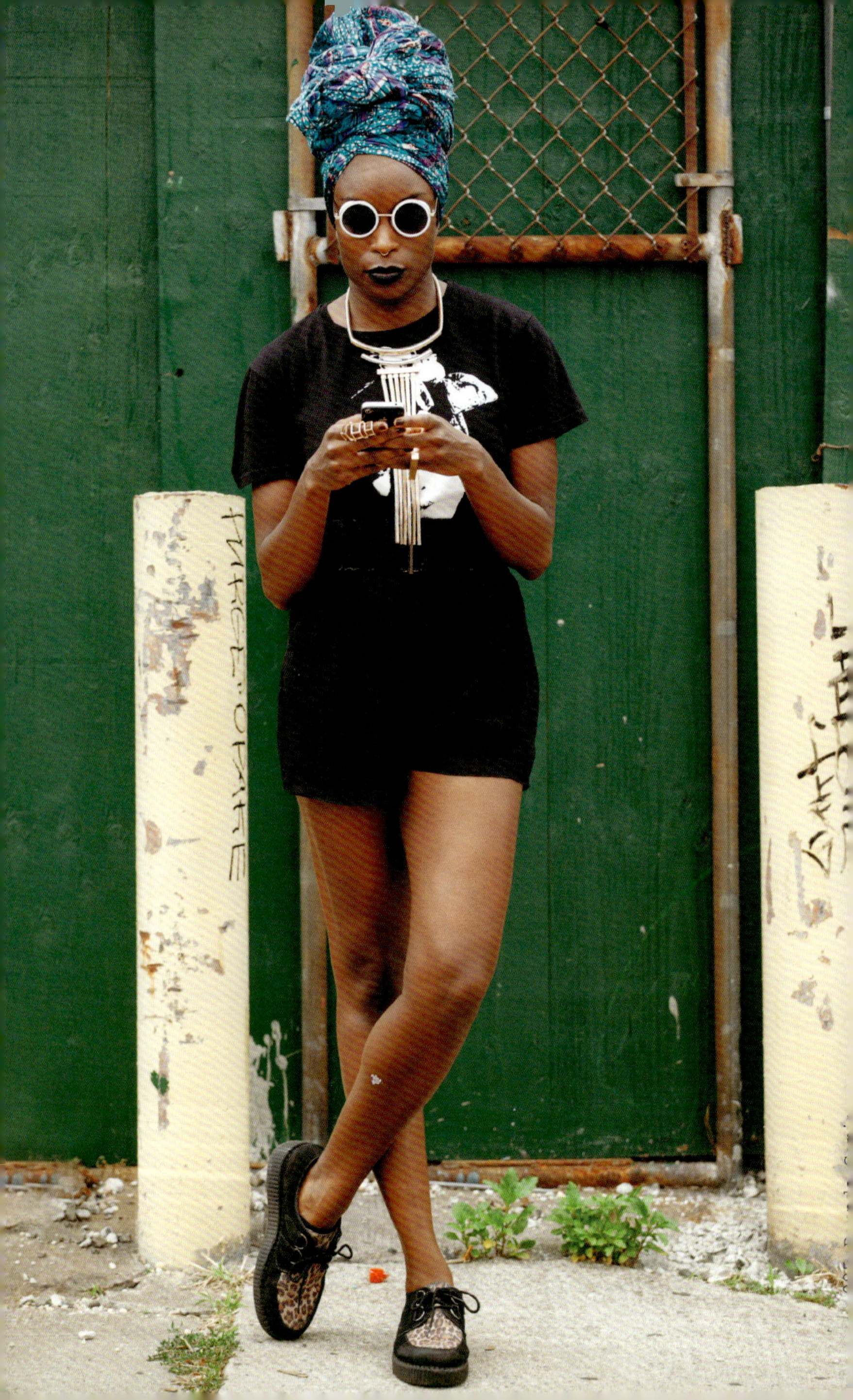

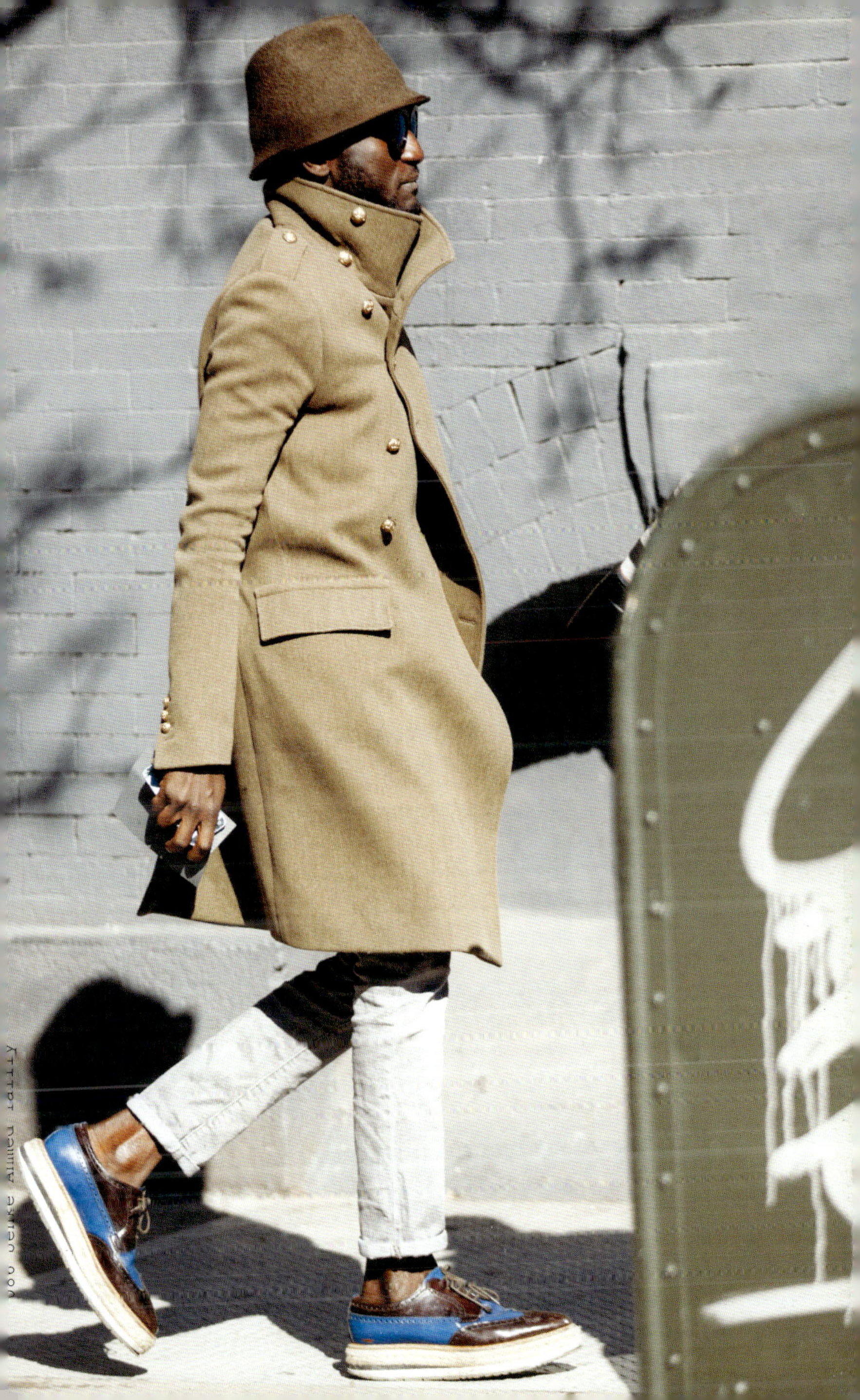

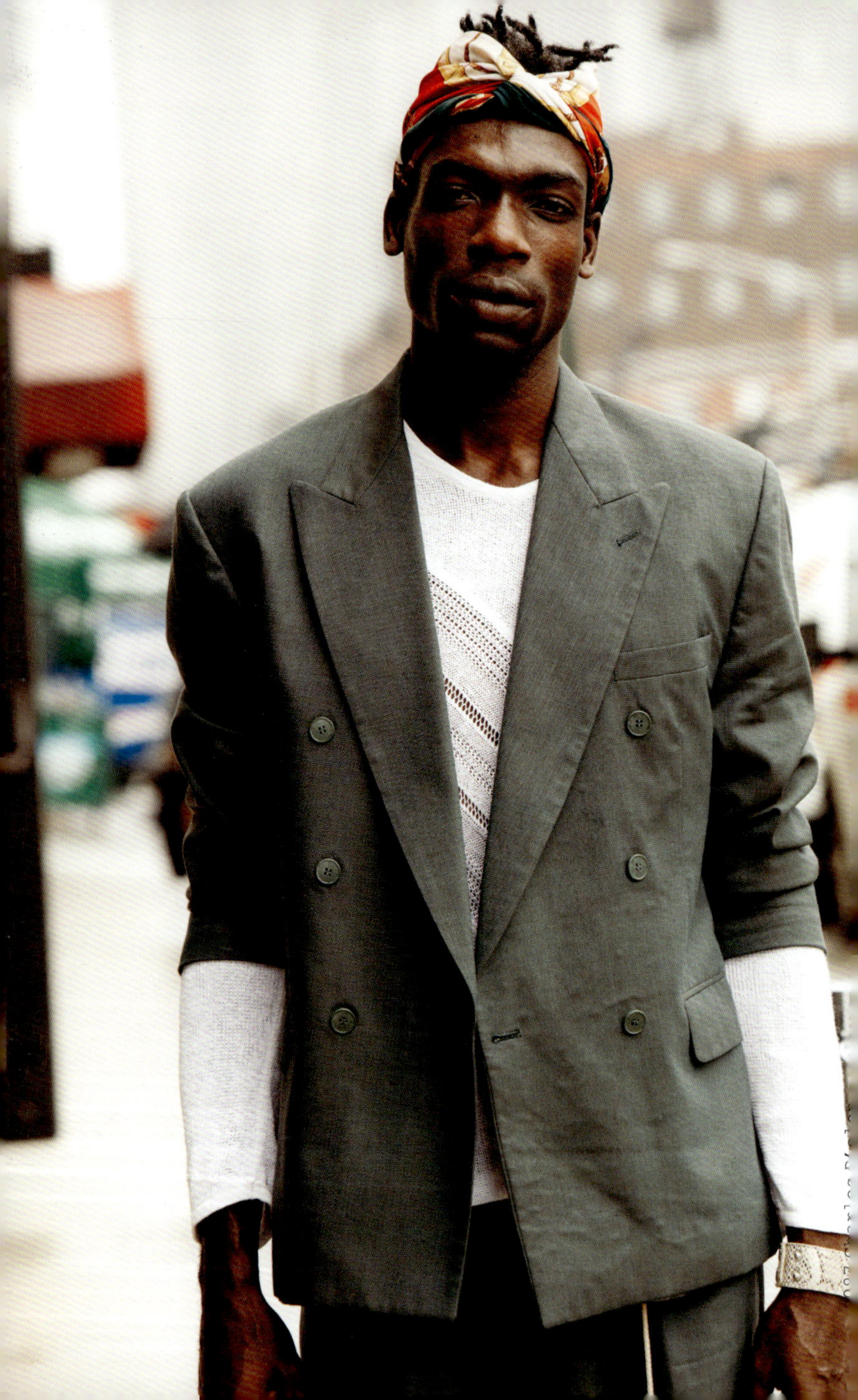

“

I let my clothing
and their colors
inspire me.

”

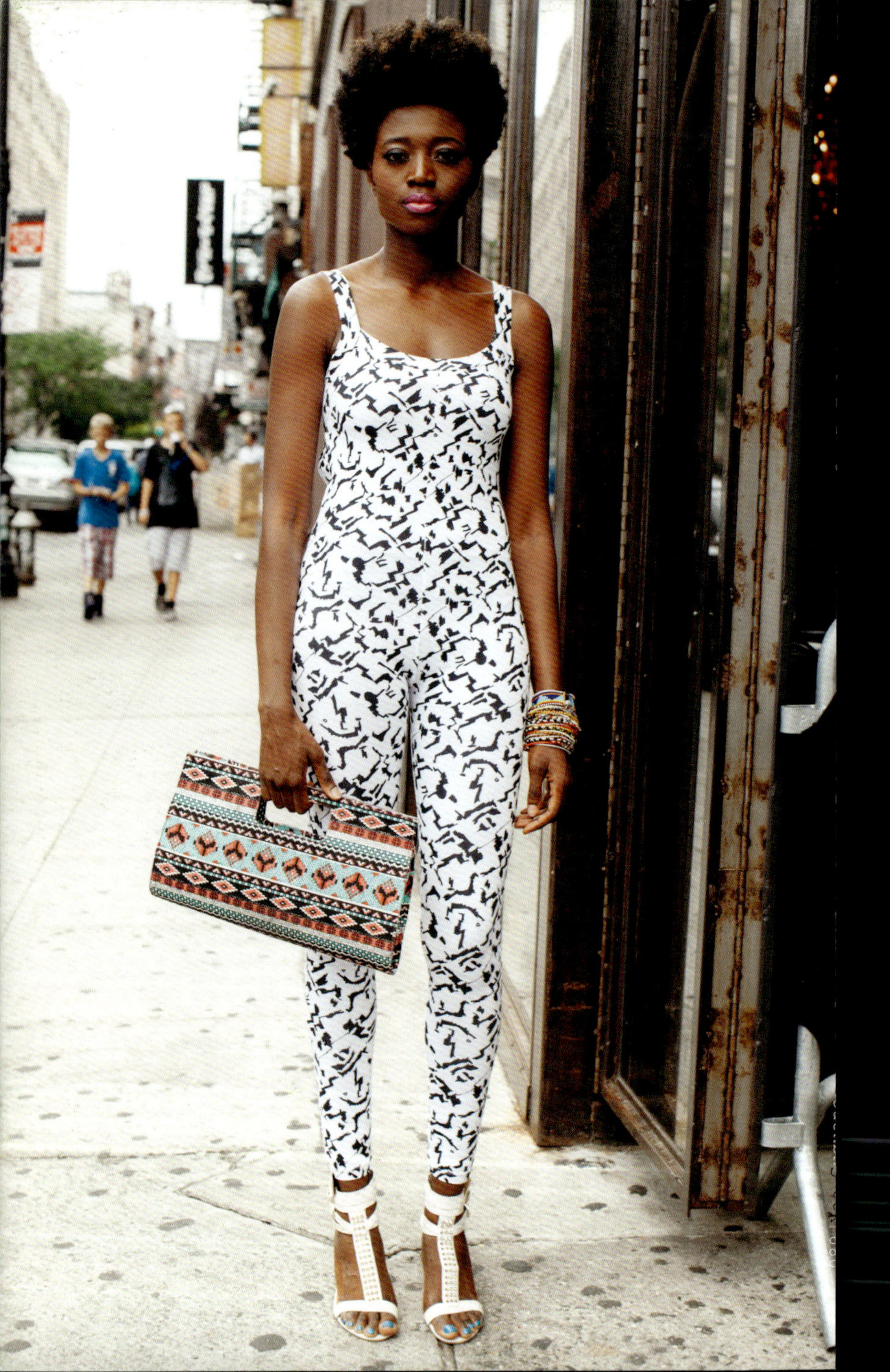

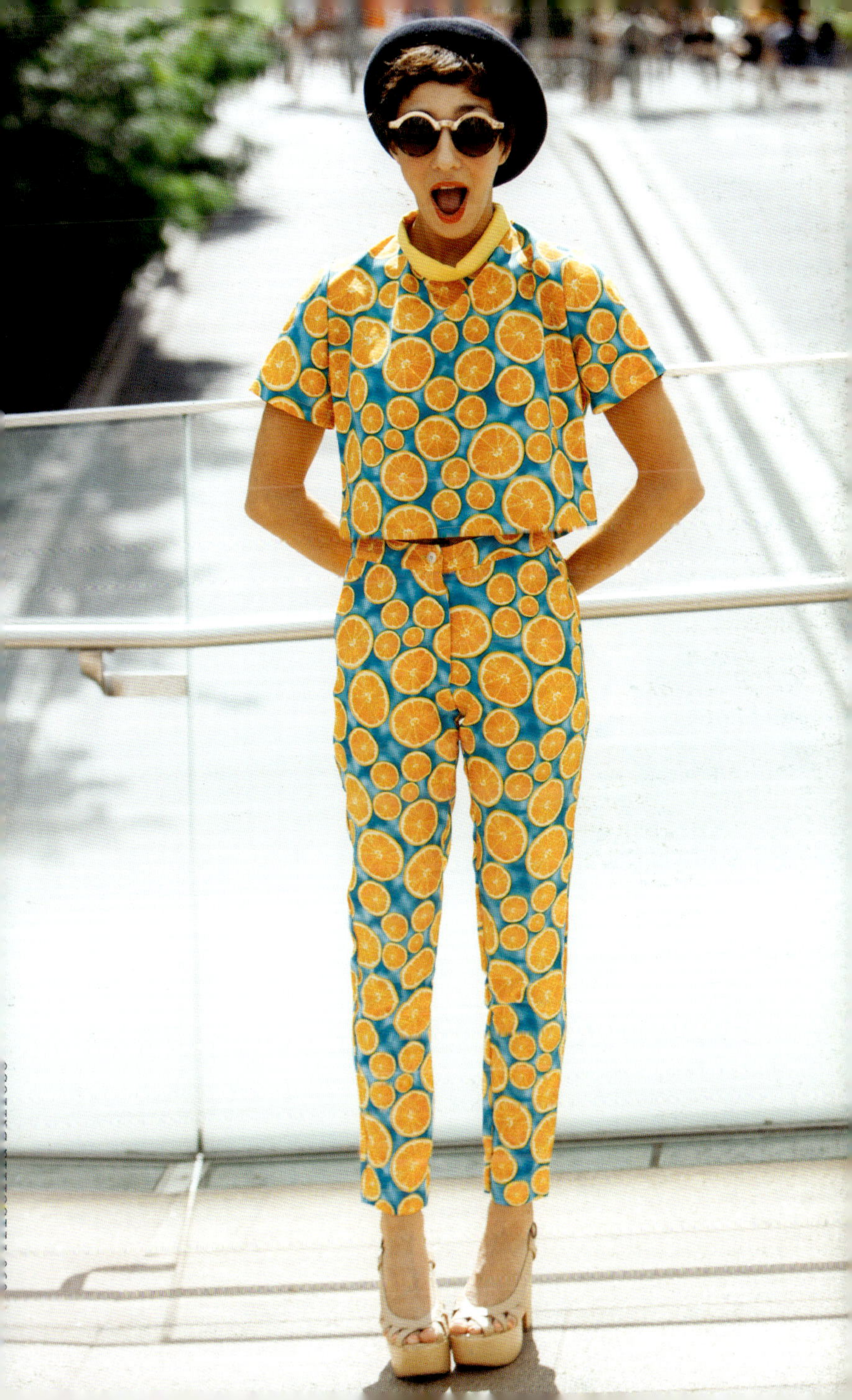

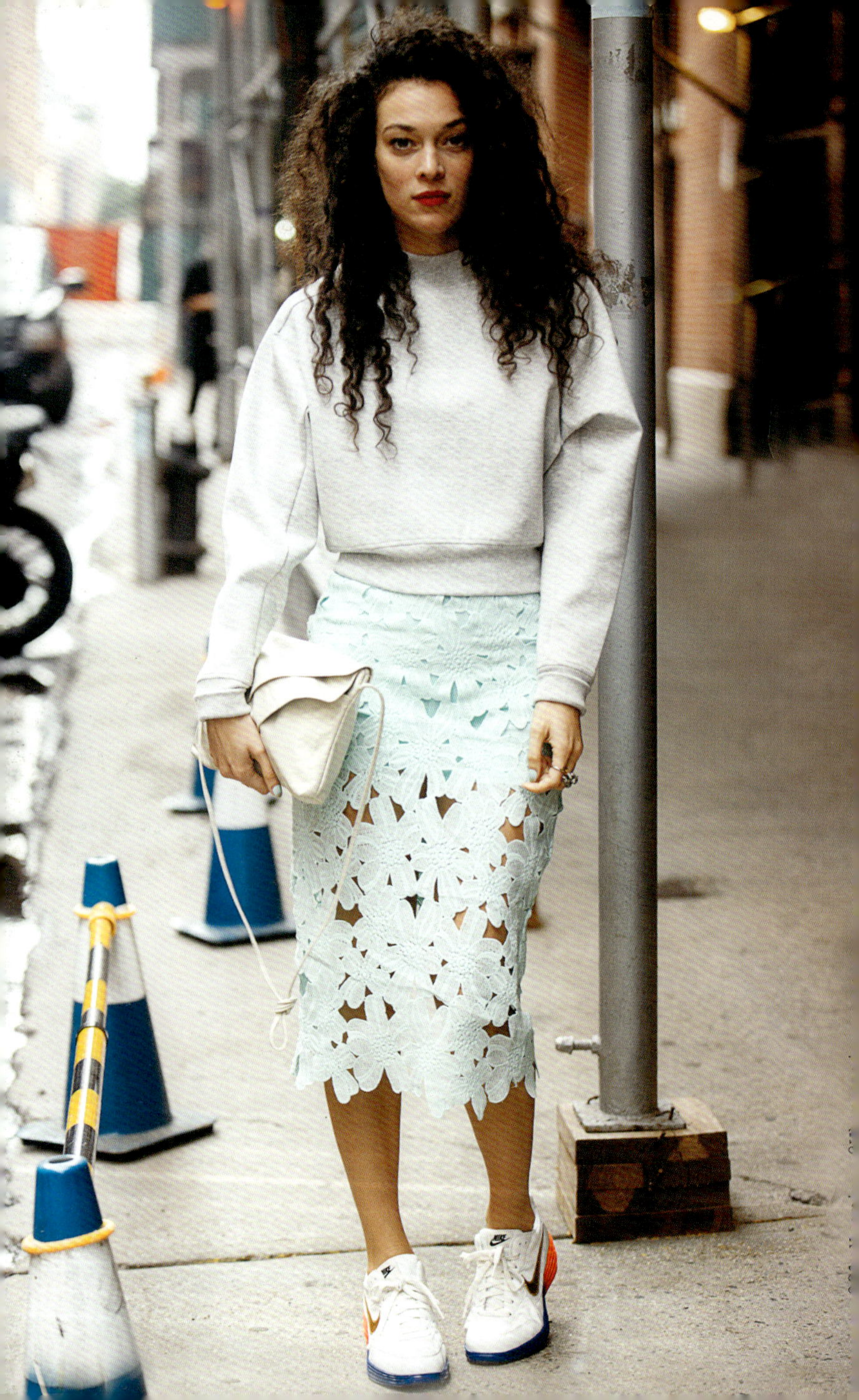

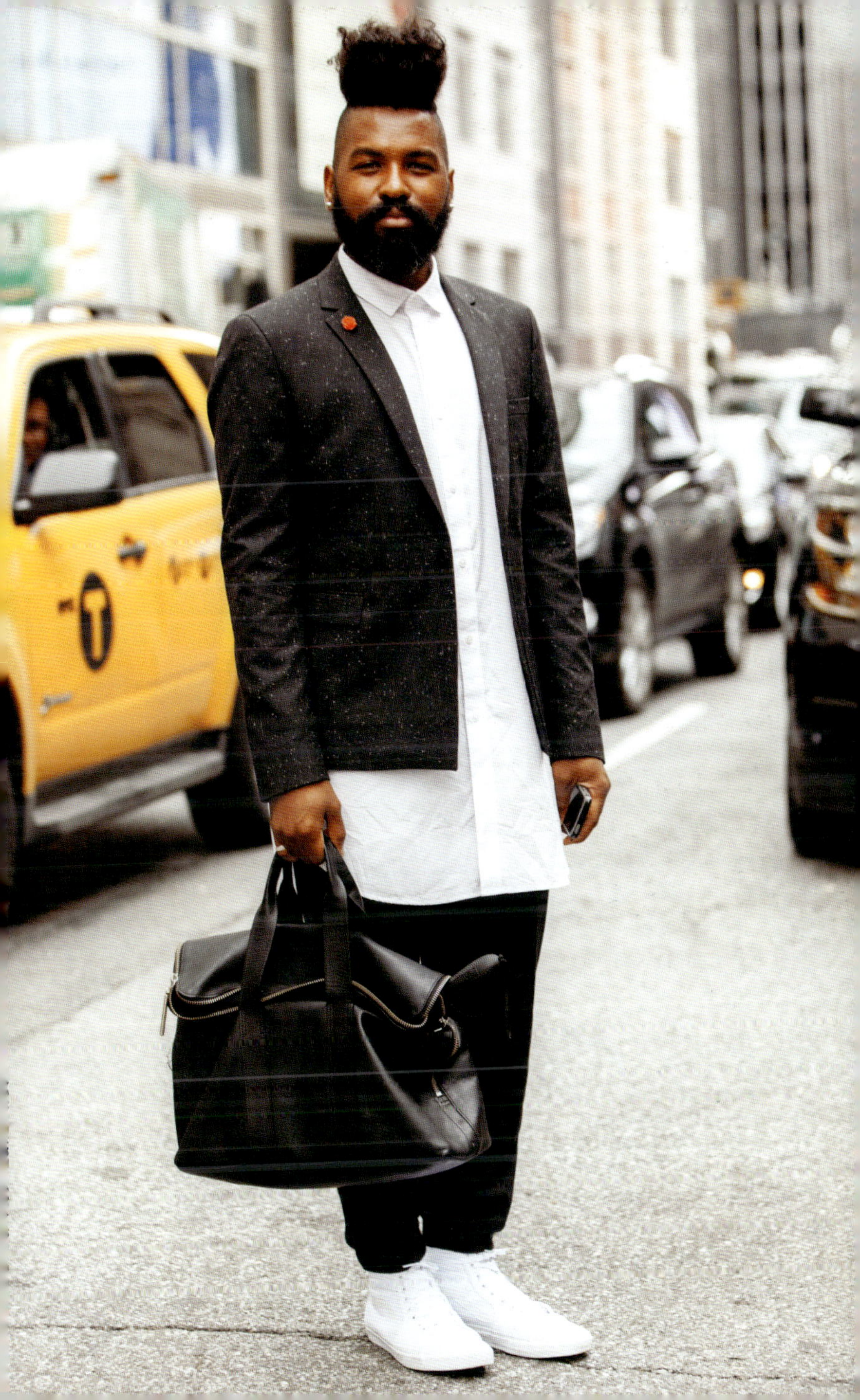

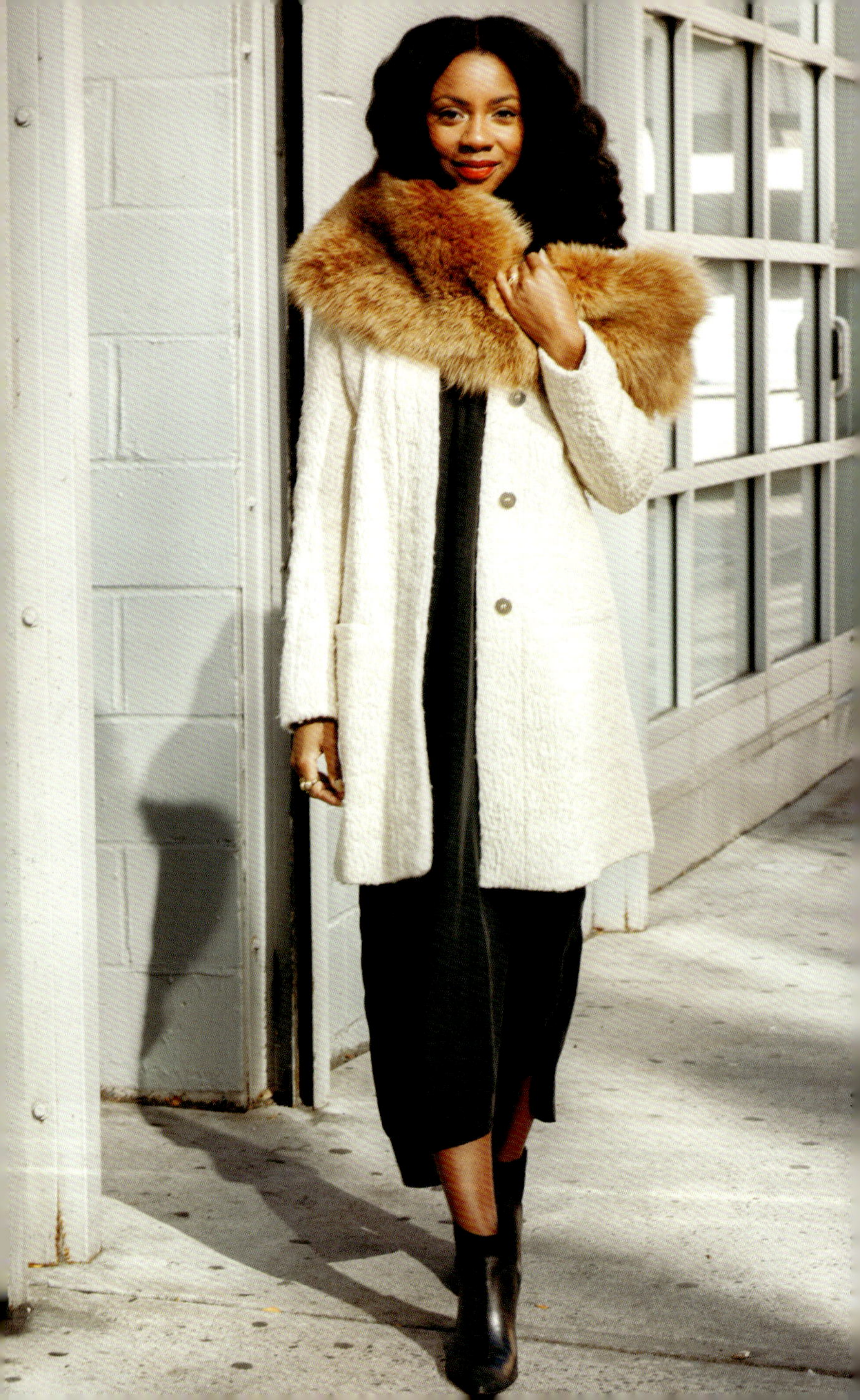

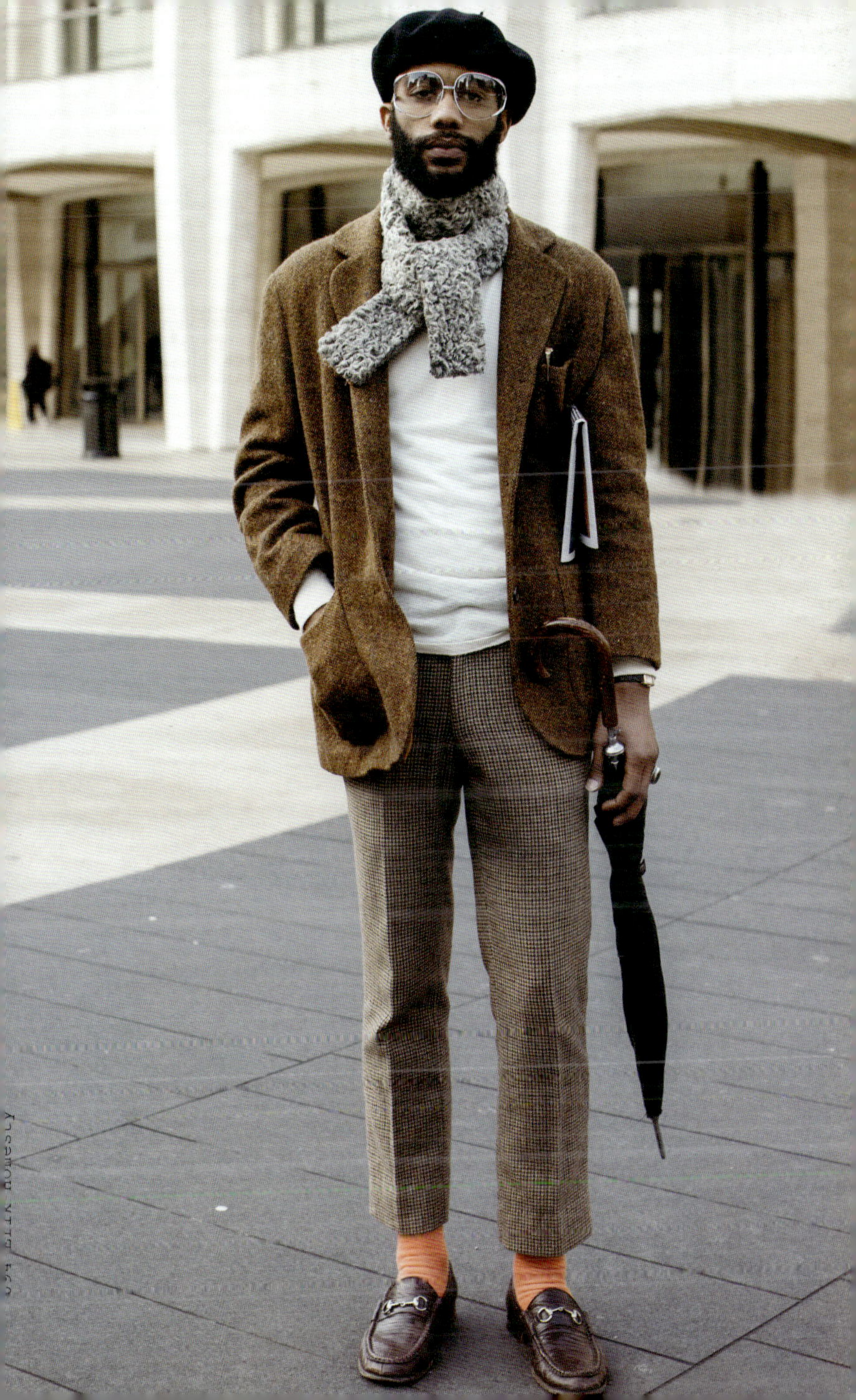

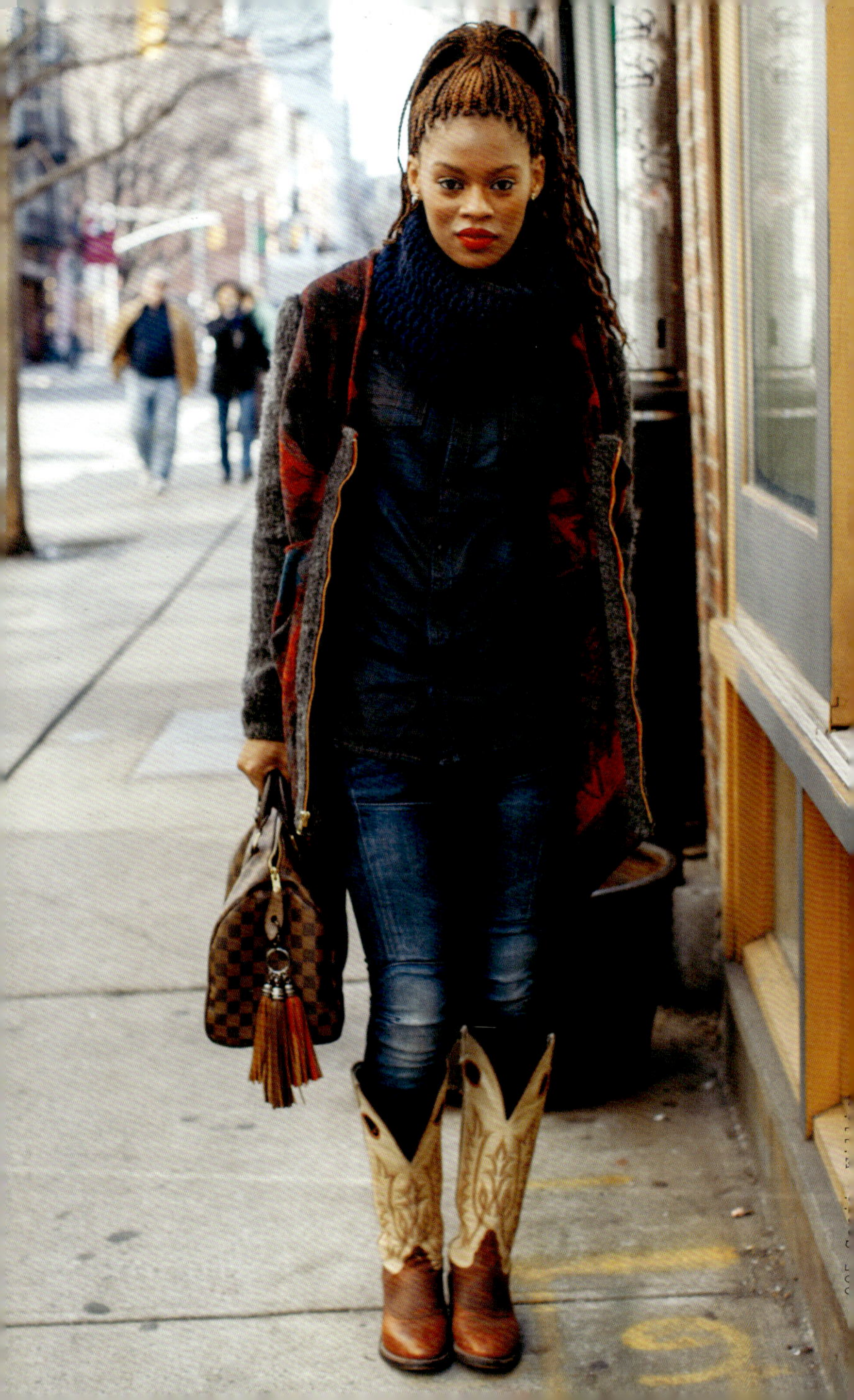

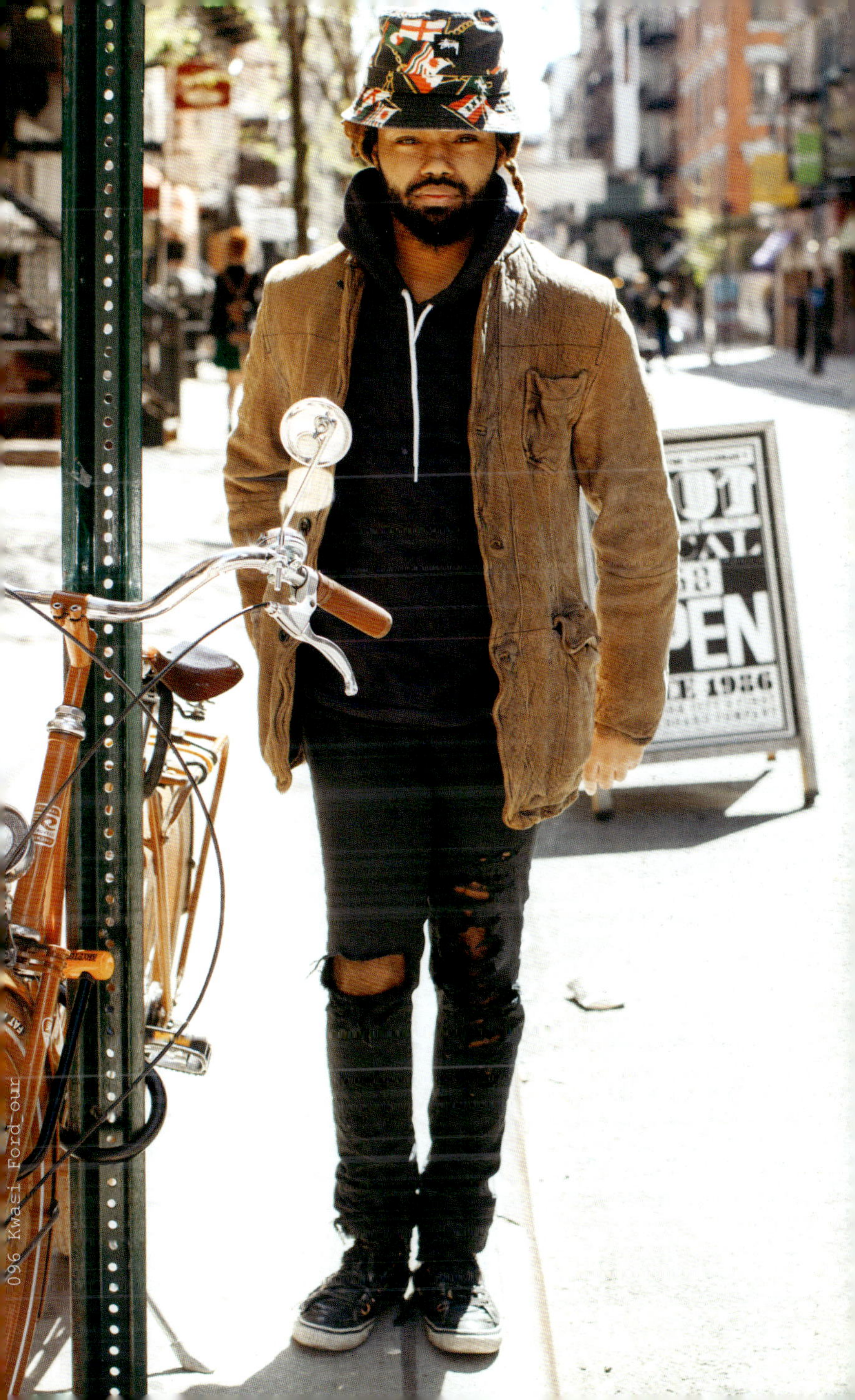

096 Kwasi Ford_our

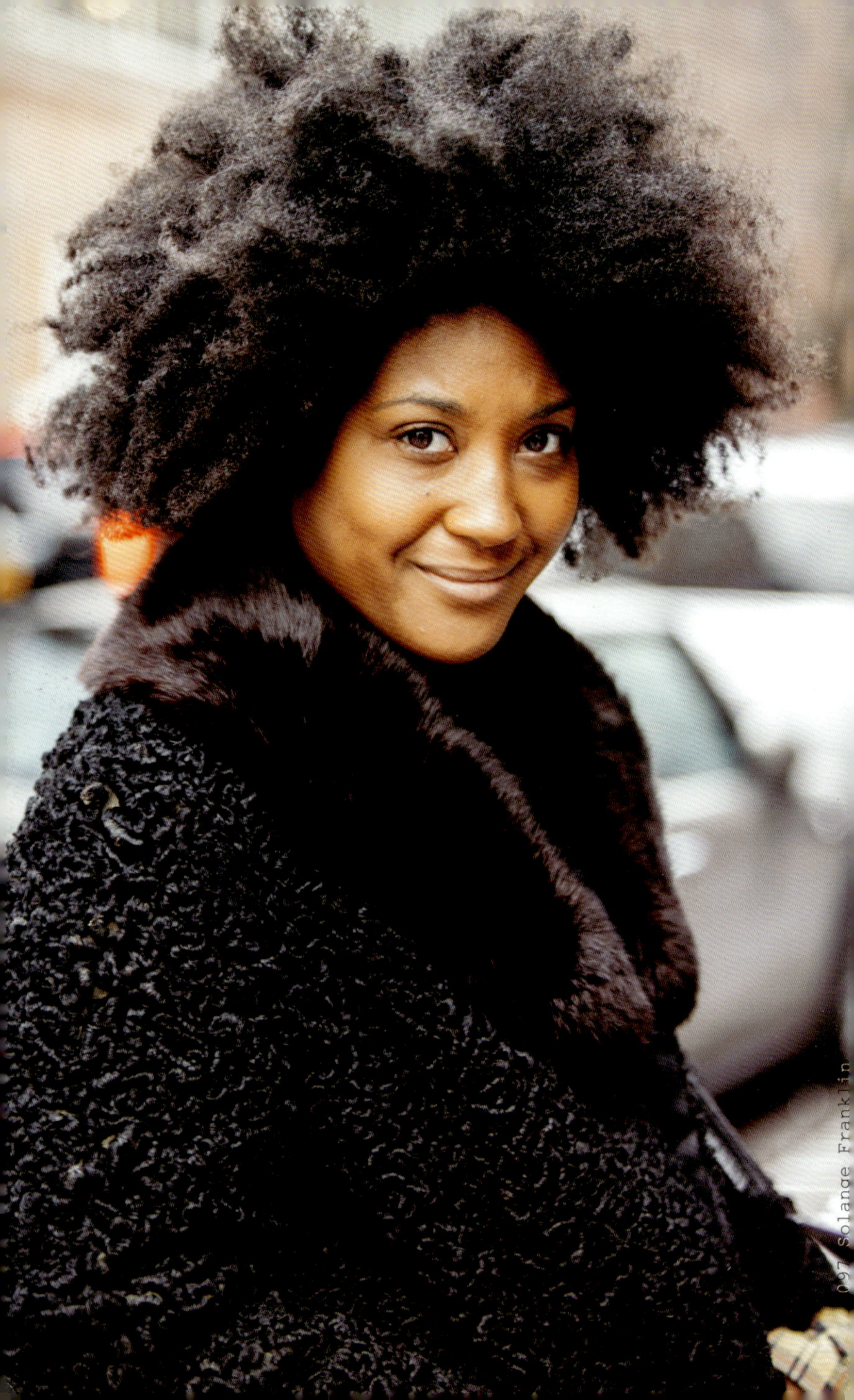

097 Solange Franklin

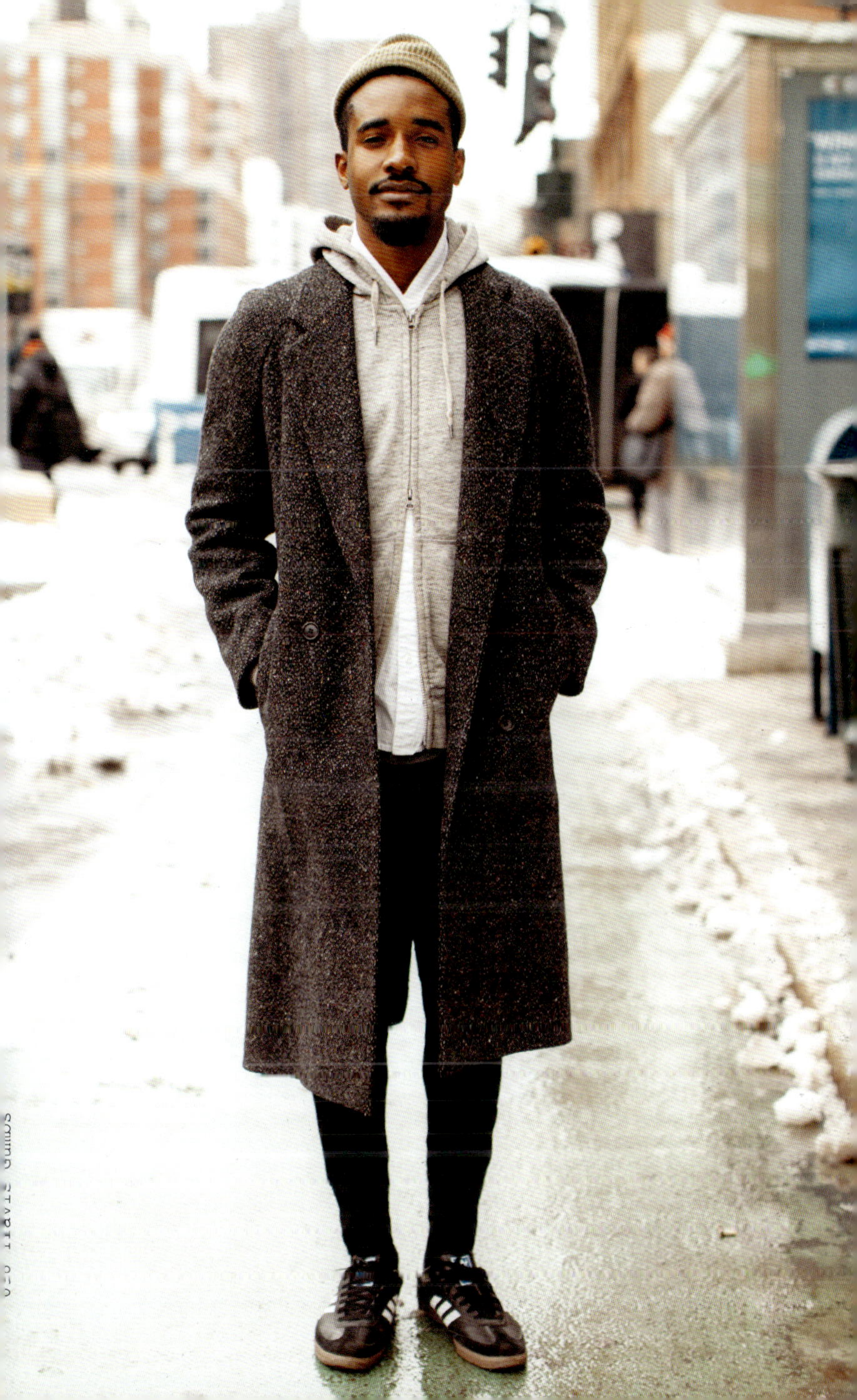

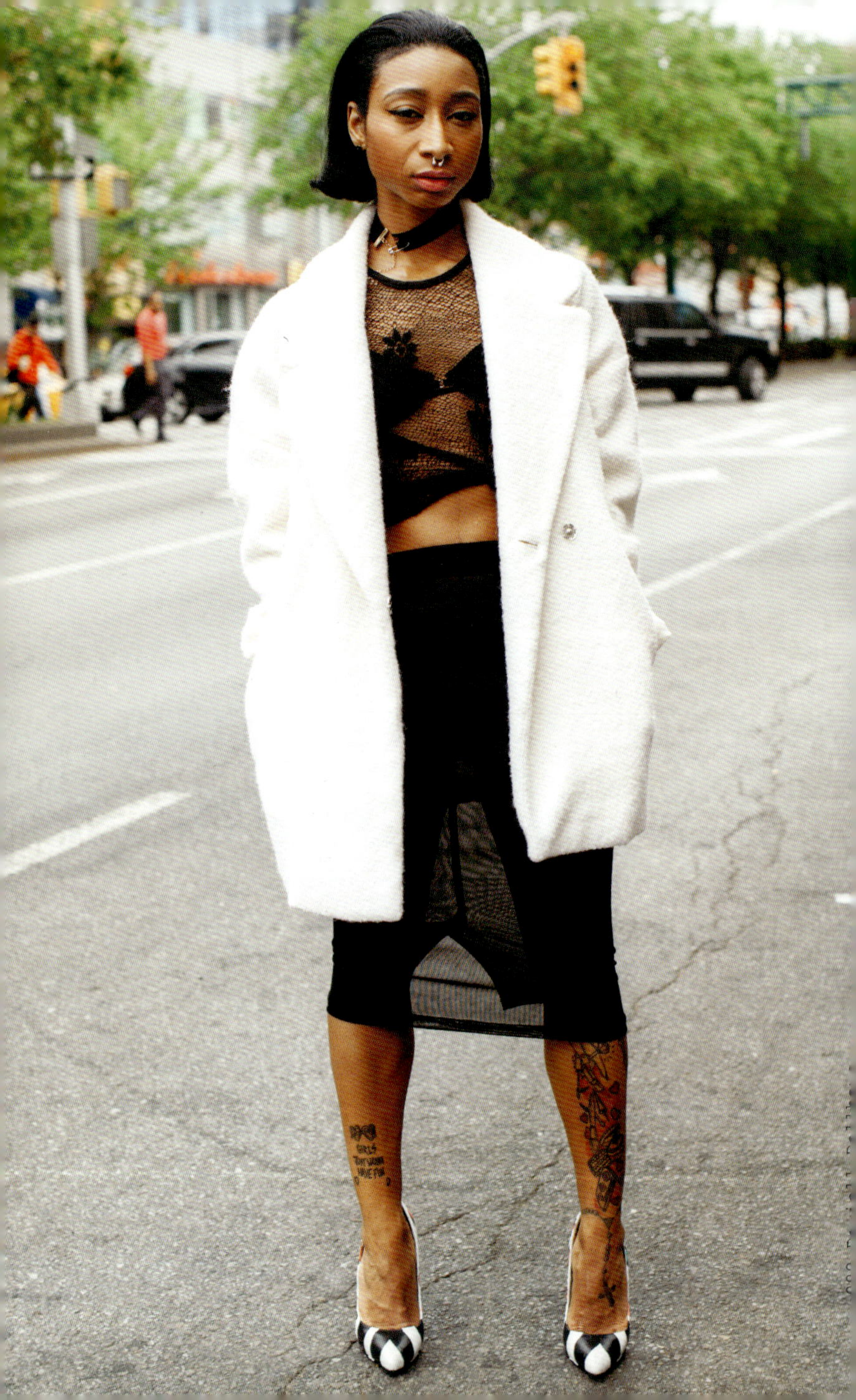

"I have to dress in a way that complements my perception of myself."

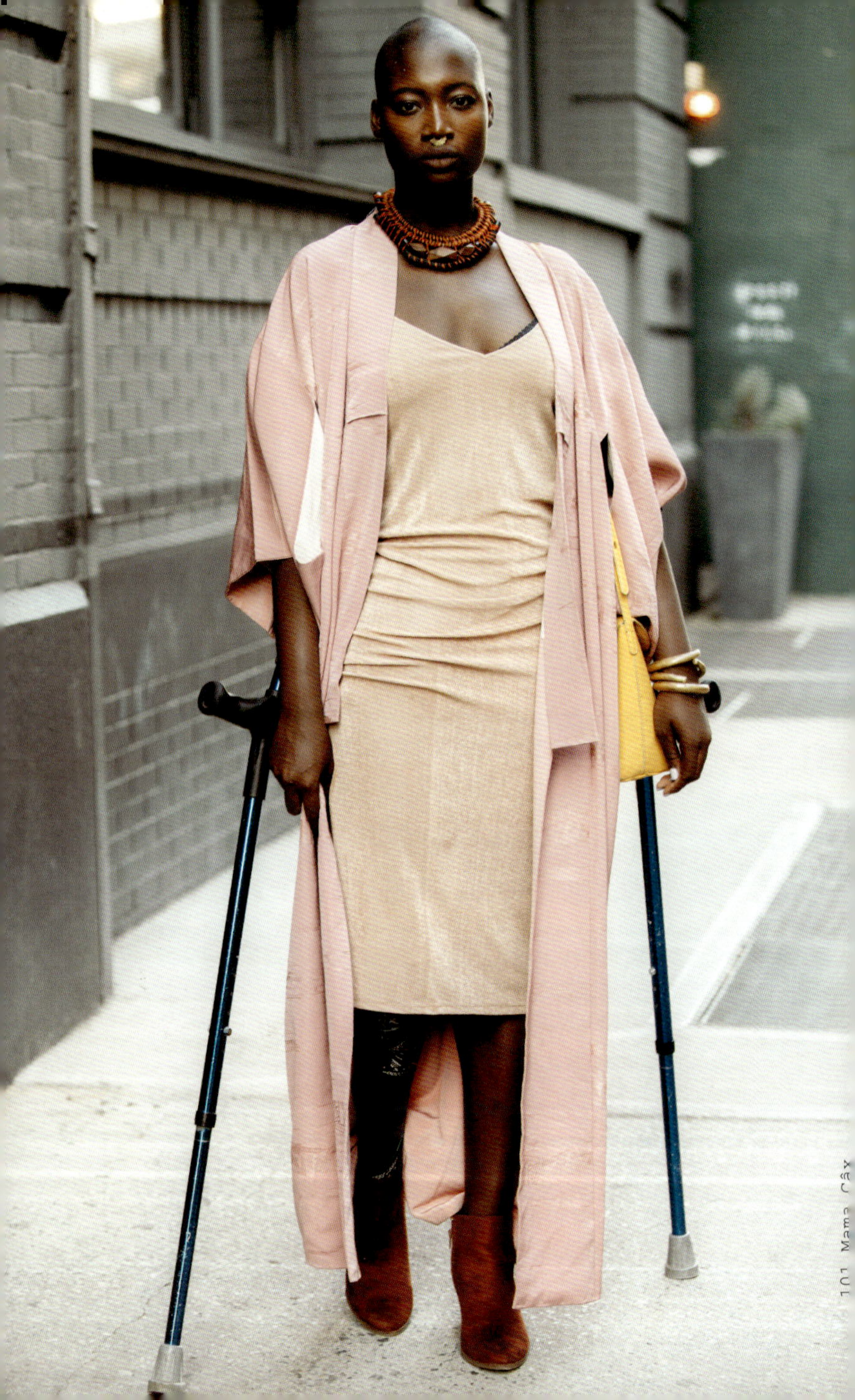

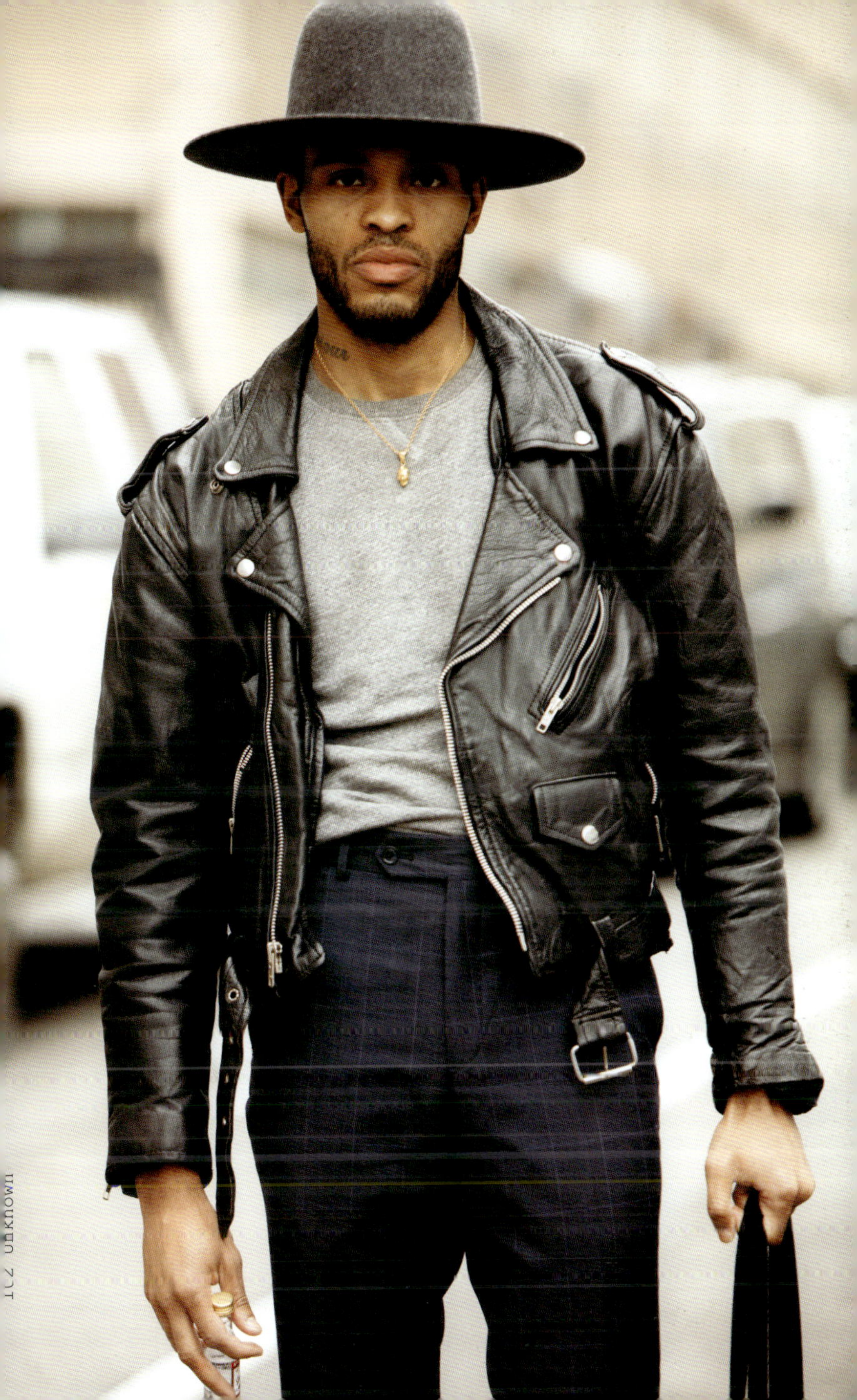

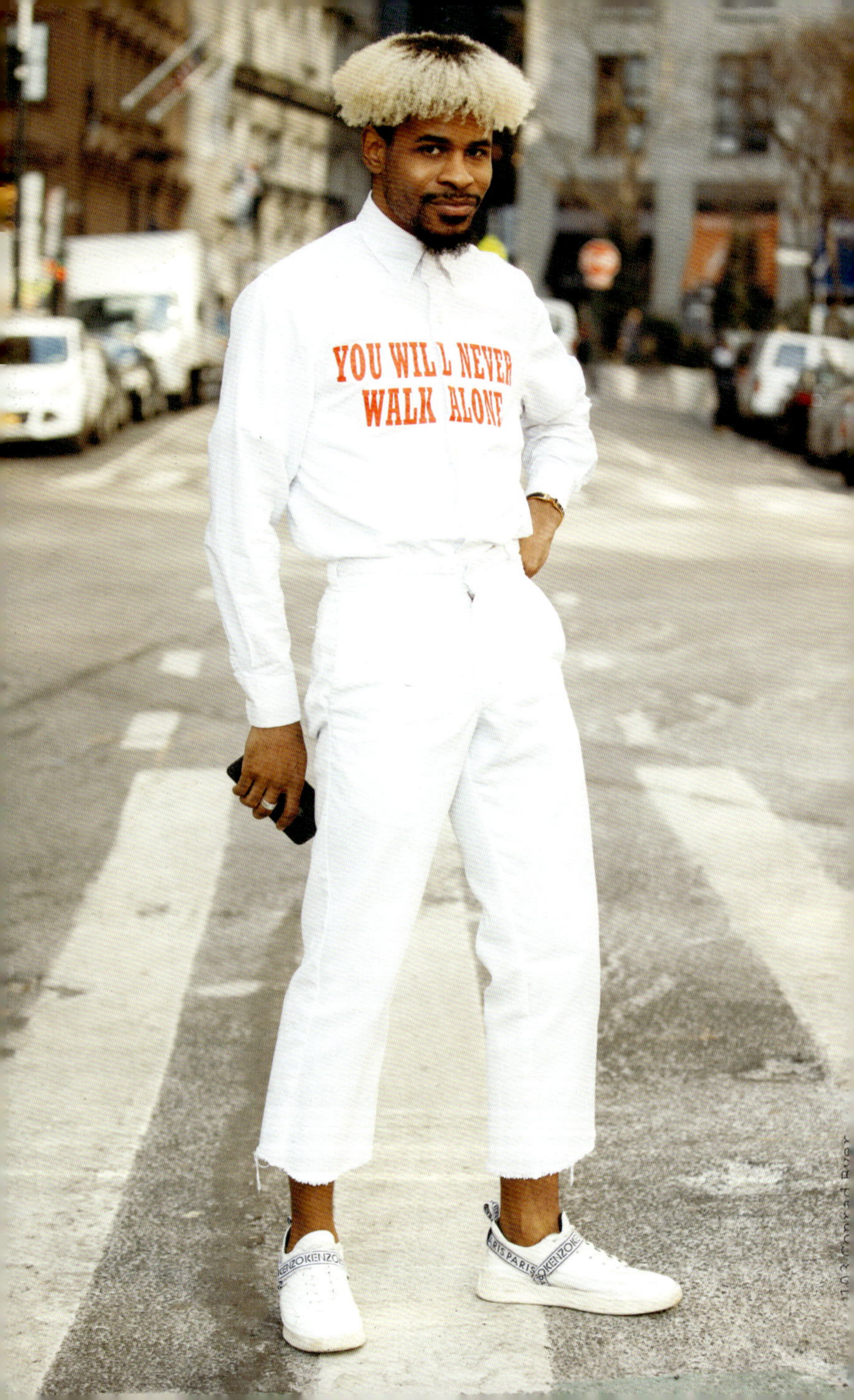

© Conrad Ryer

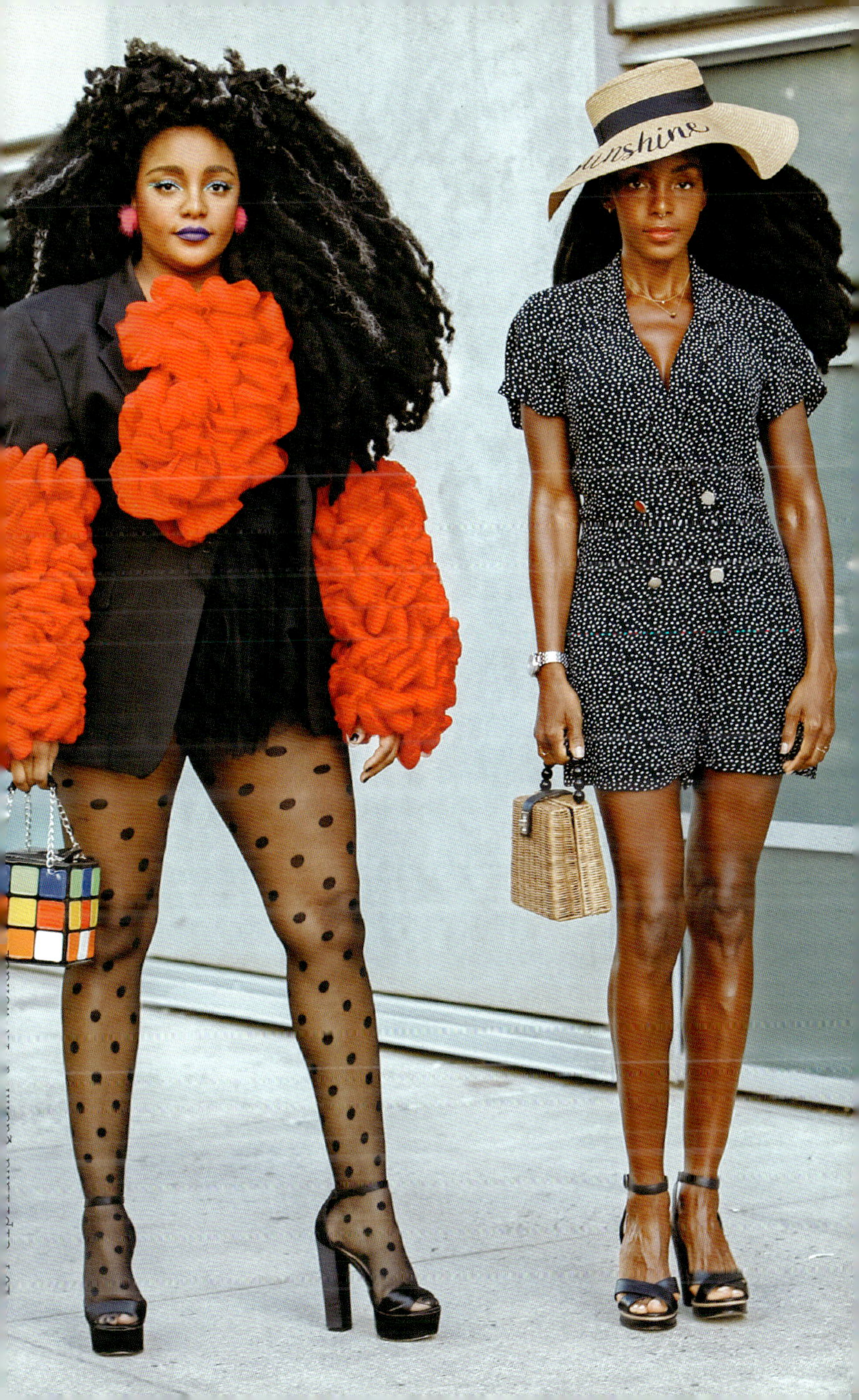
unshine

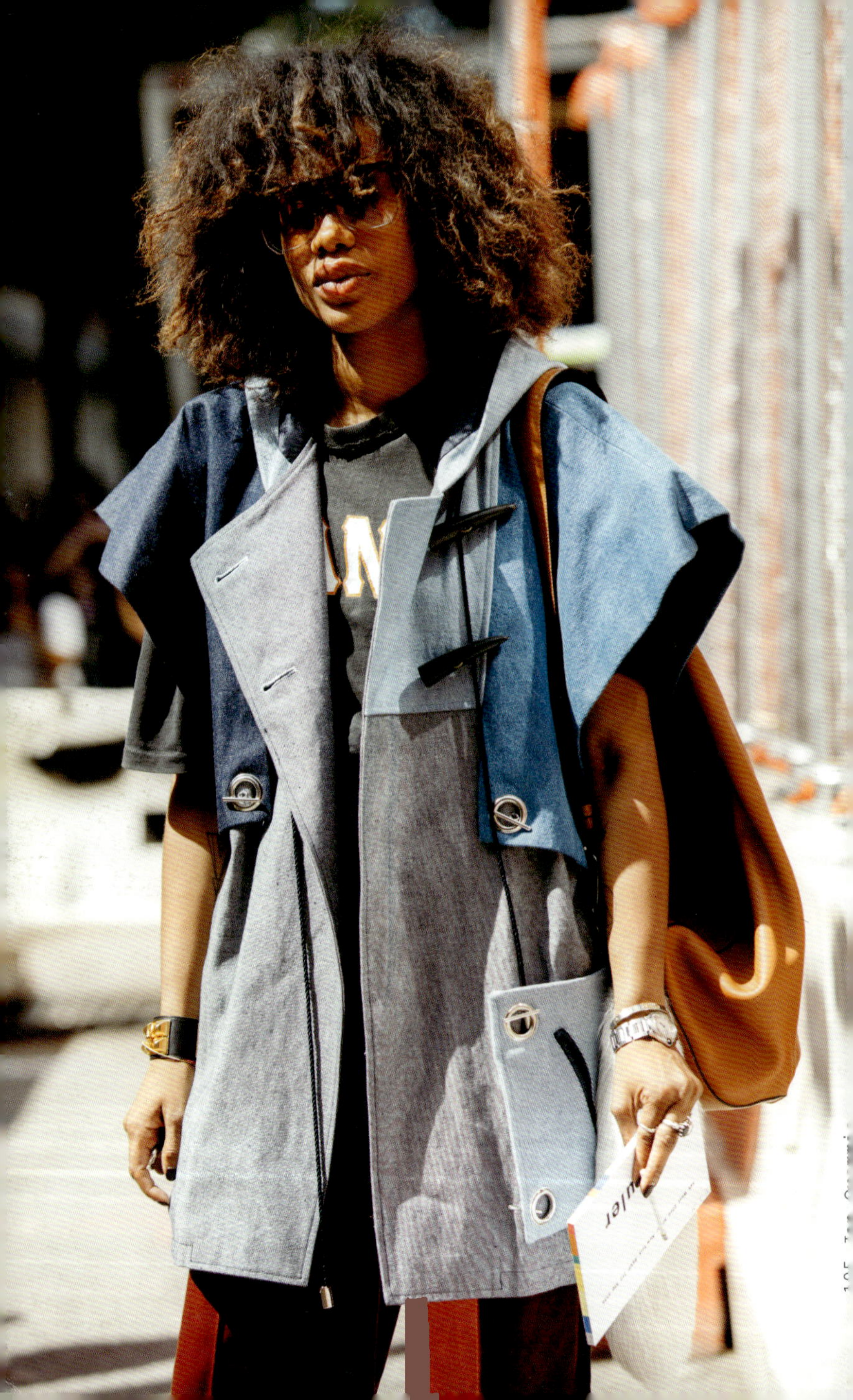

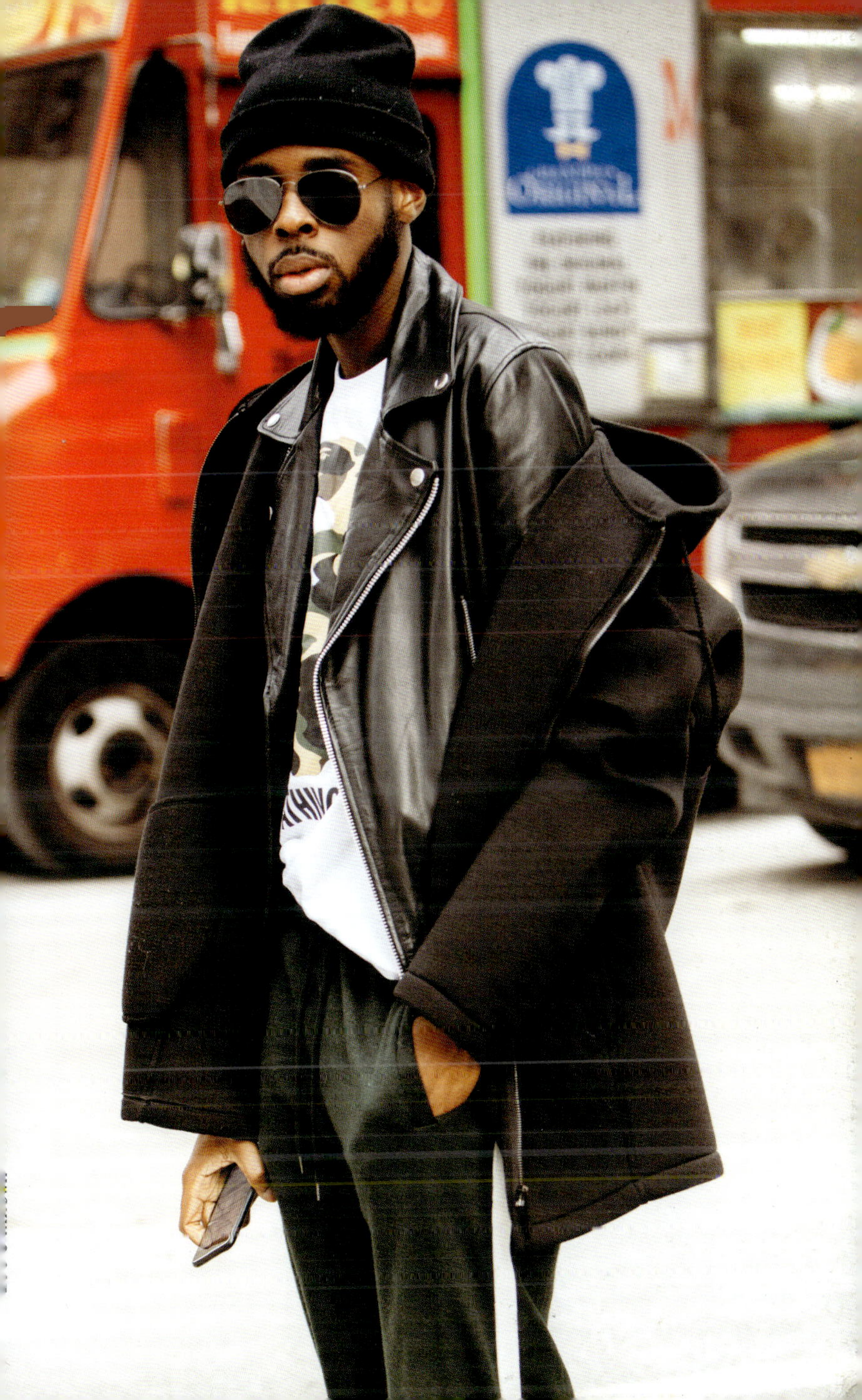

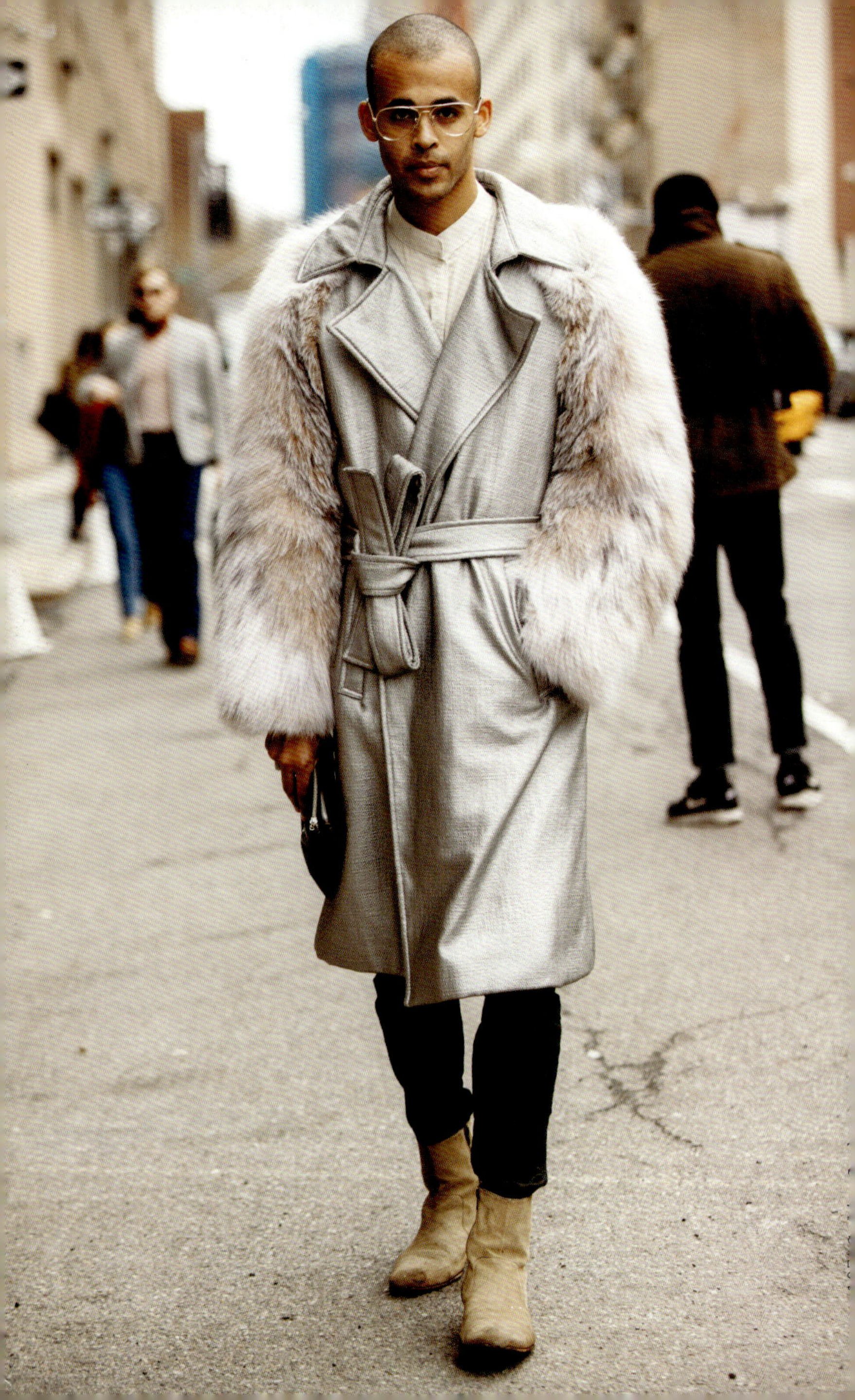

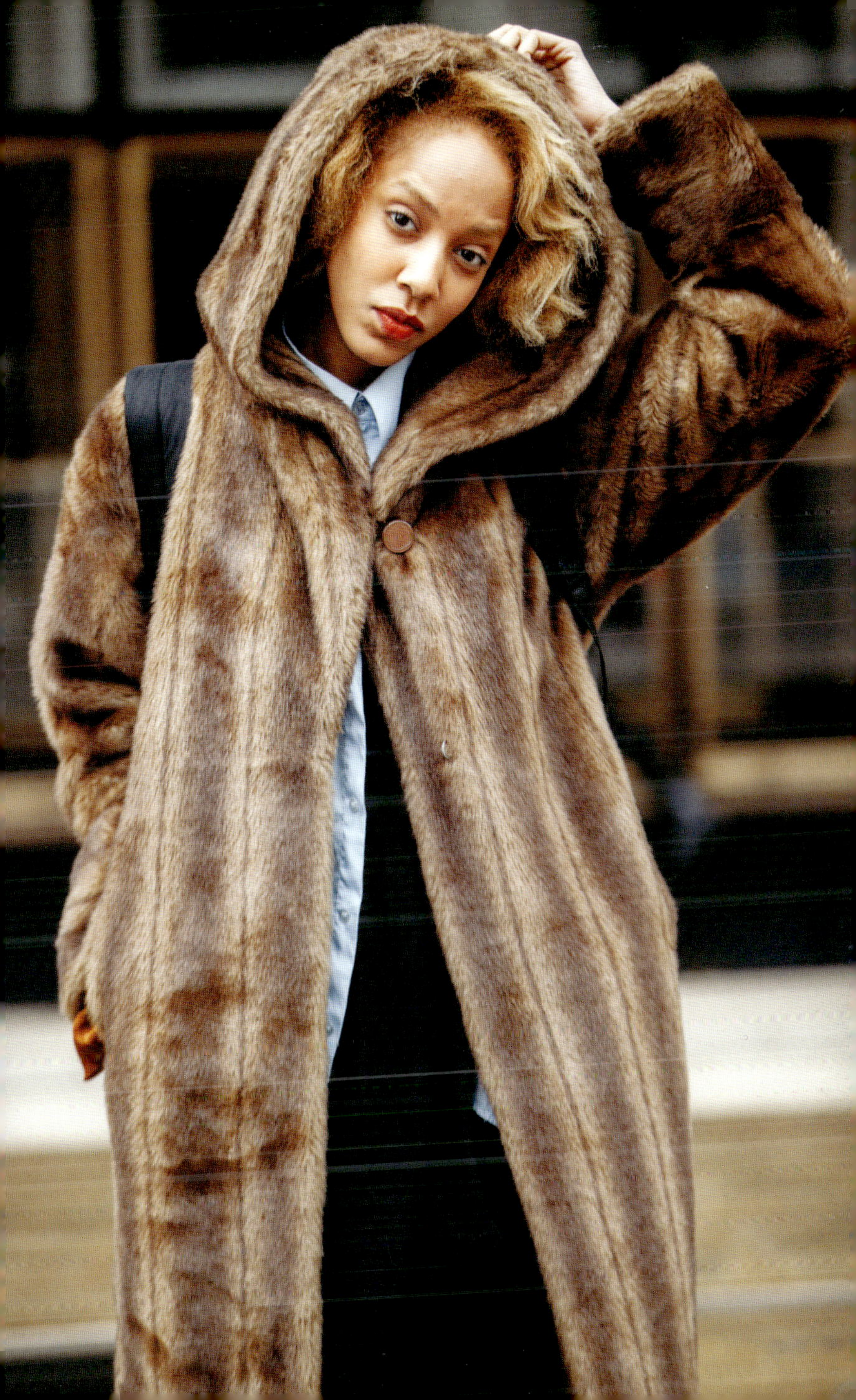

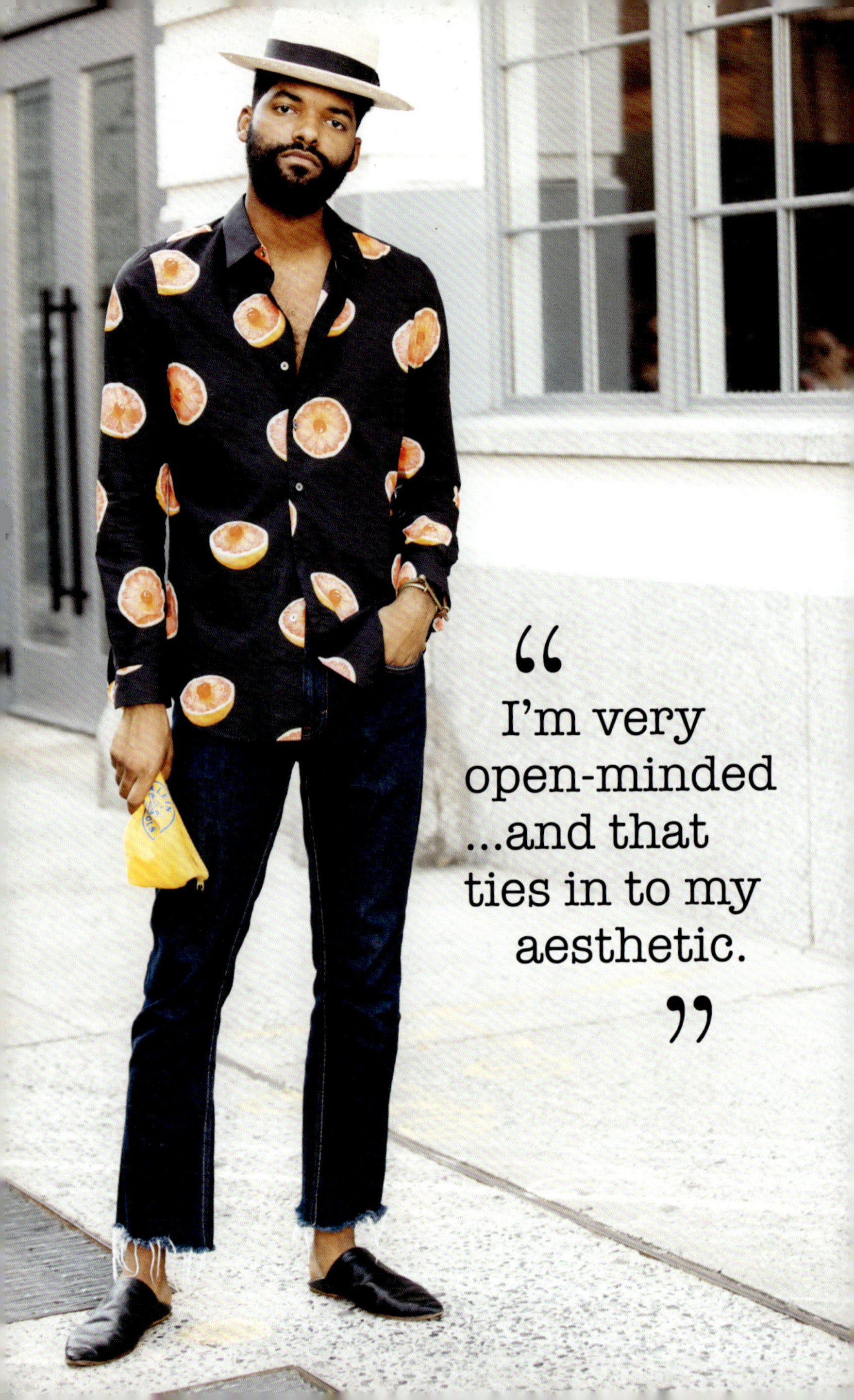
“I’m very open-minded ...and that ties in to my aesthetic.”

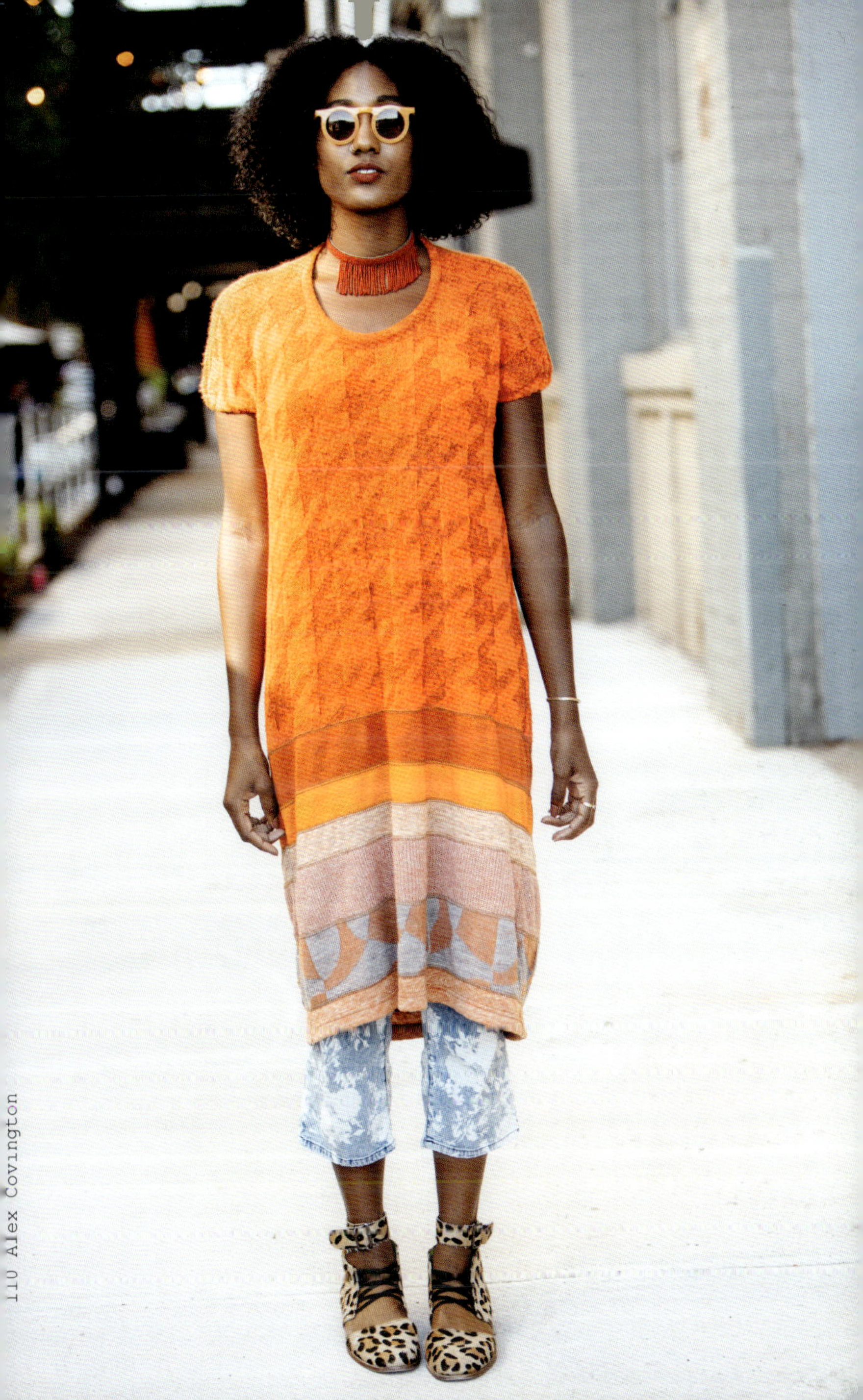

“The most stylish people I know aren’t at all trendy. They possess timeless and classic style.”

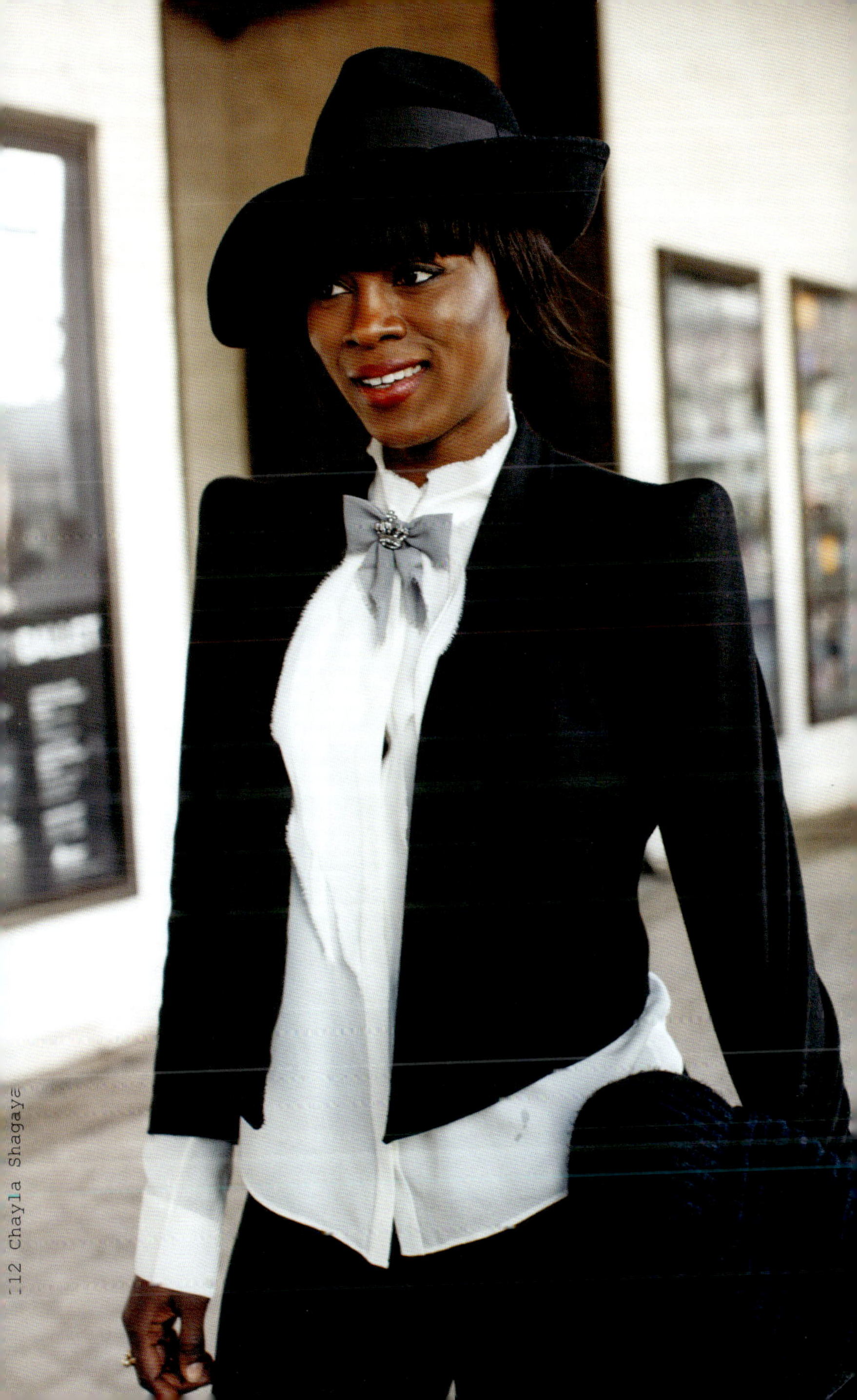

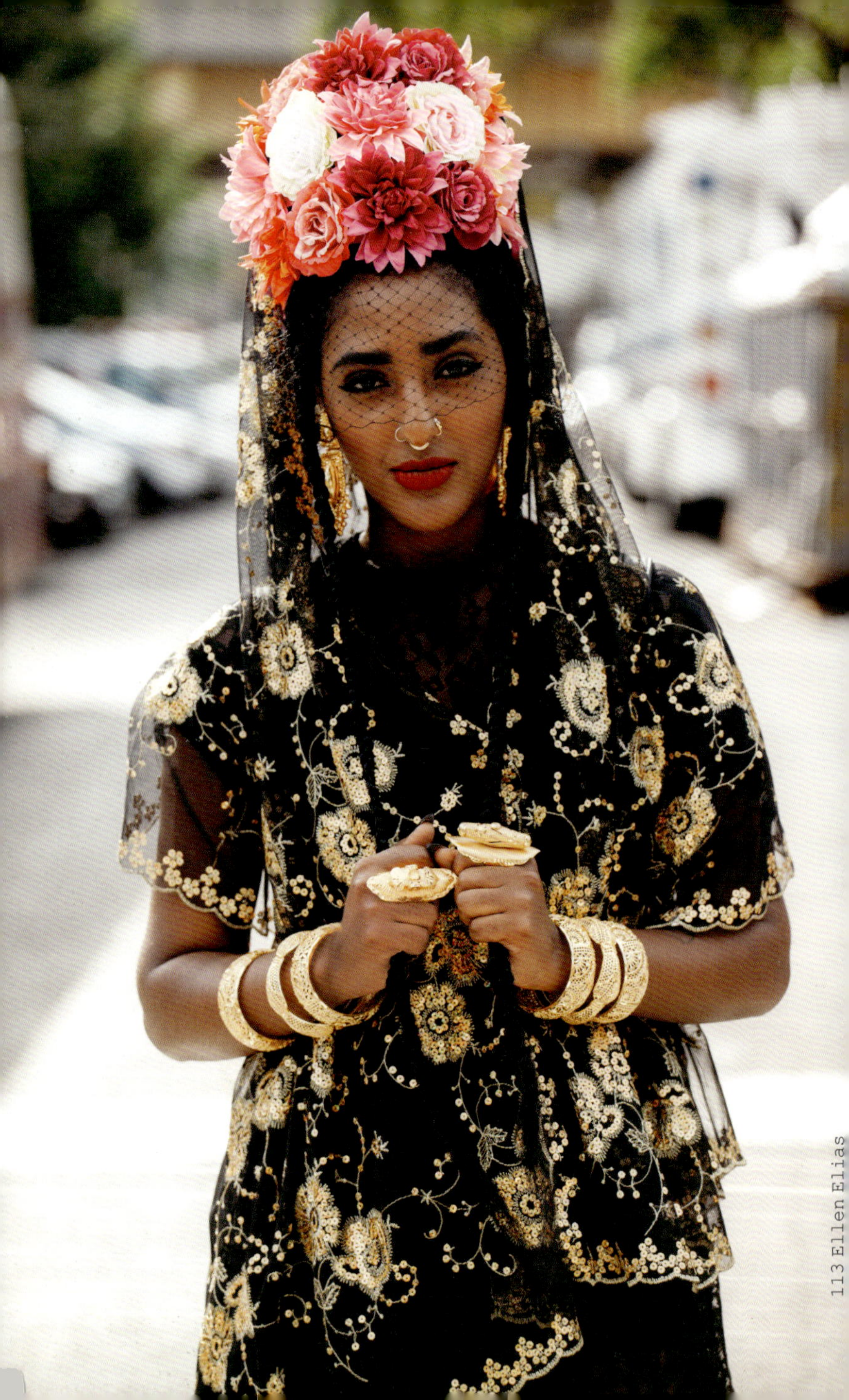

113 Ellen Elias

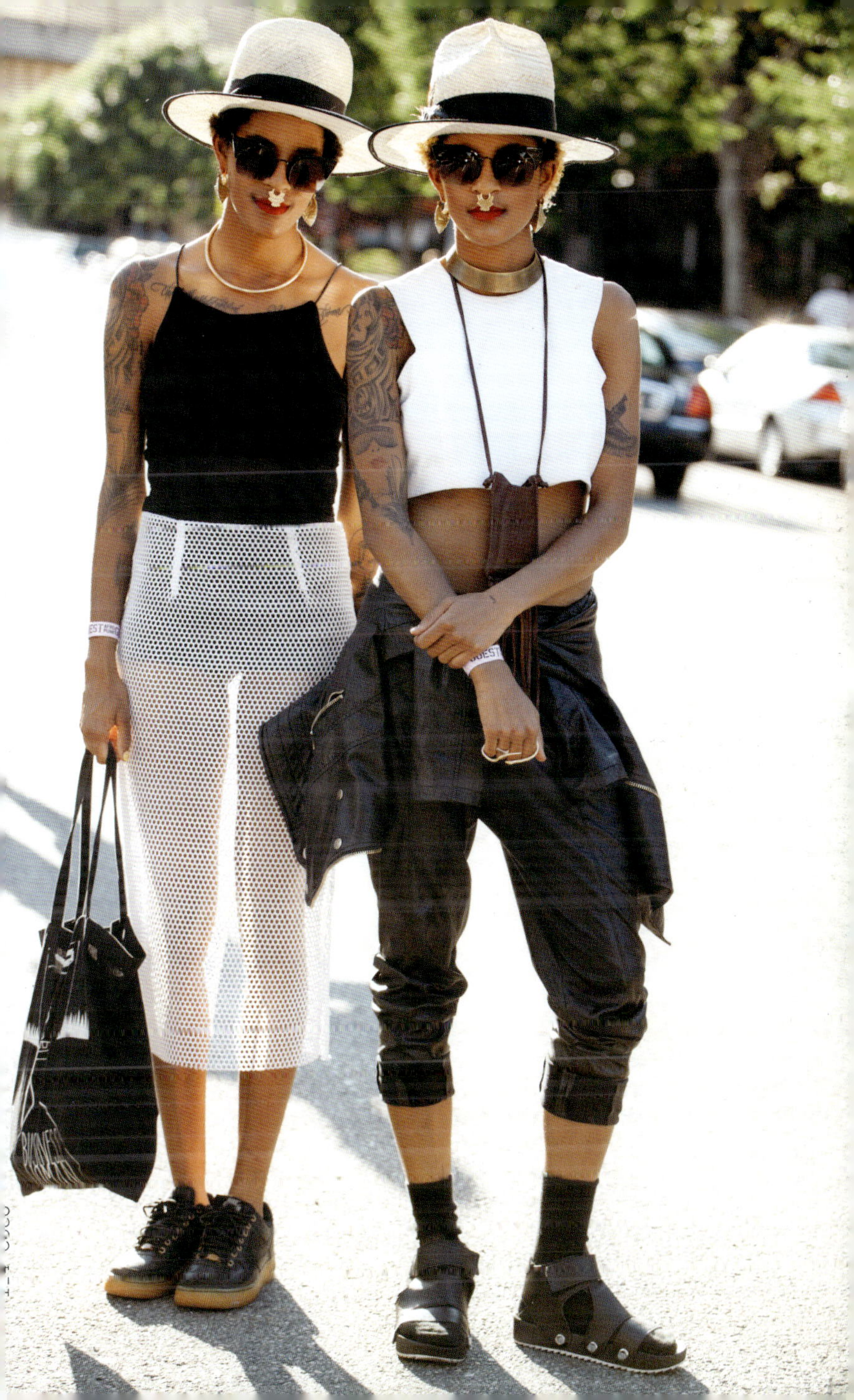

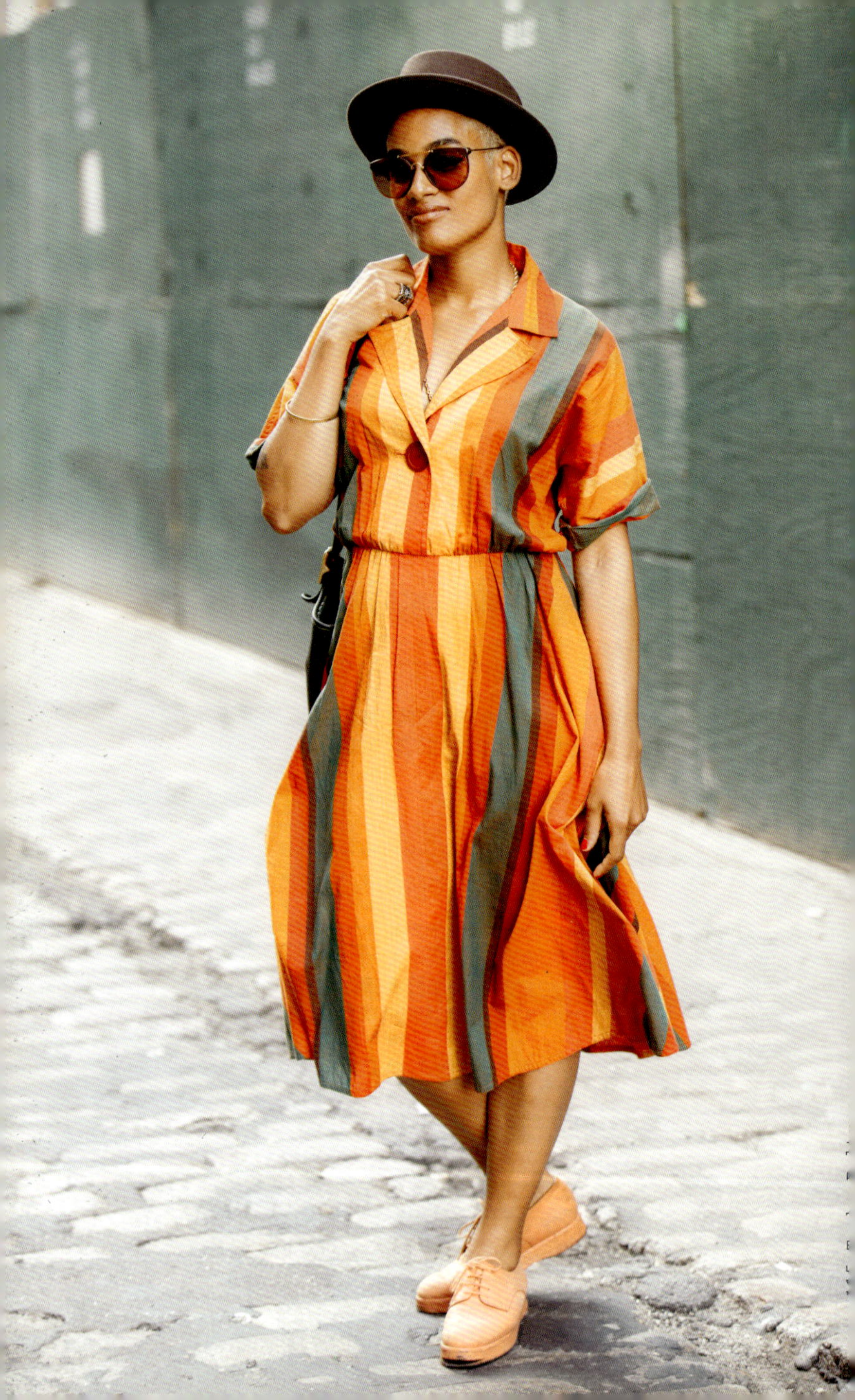

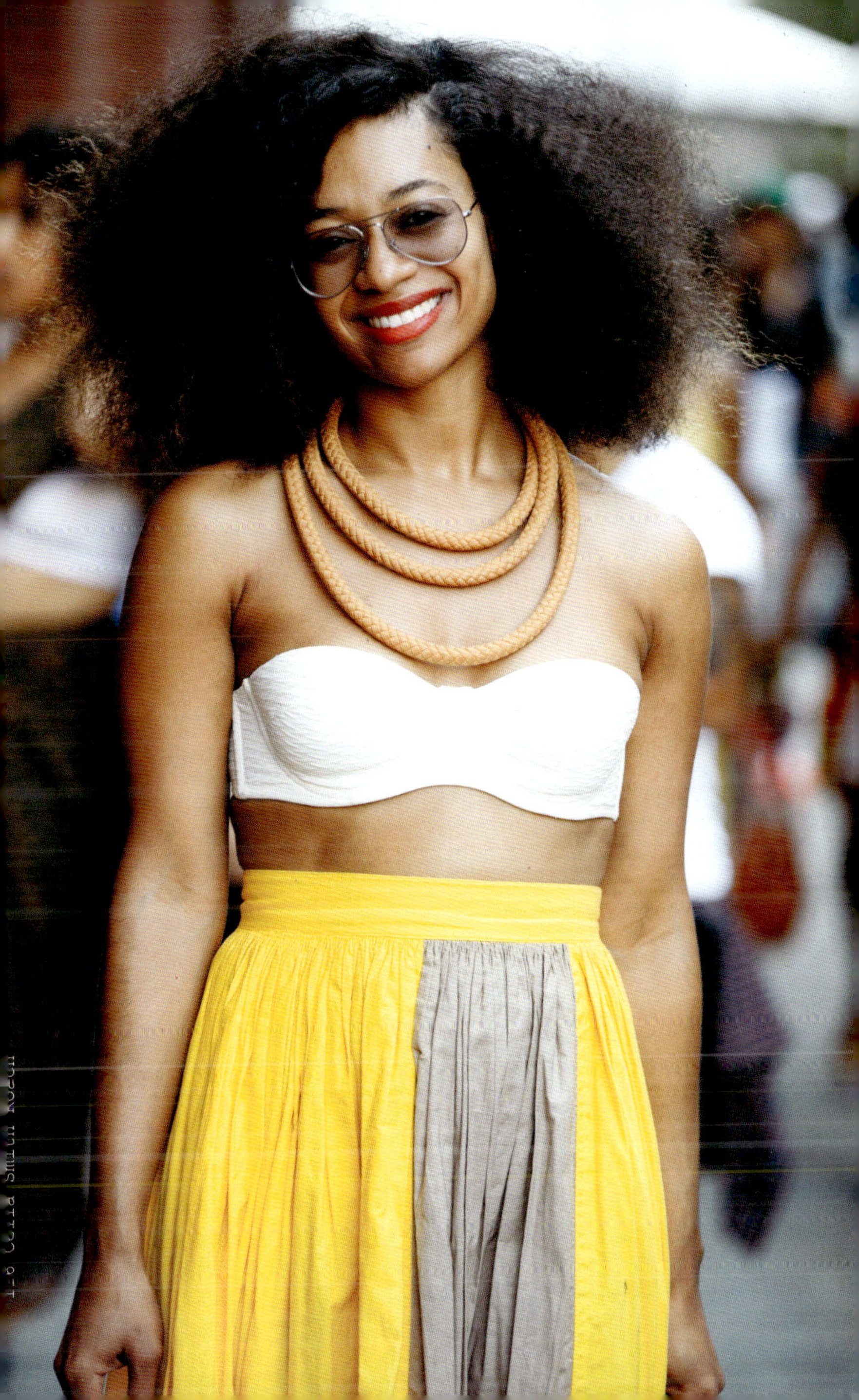

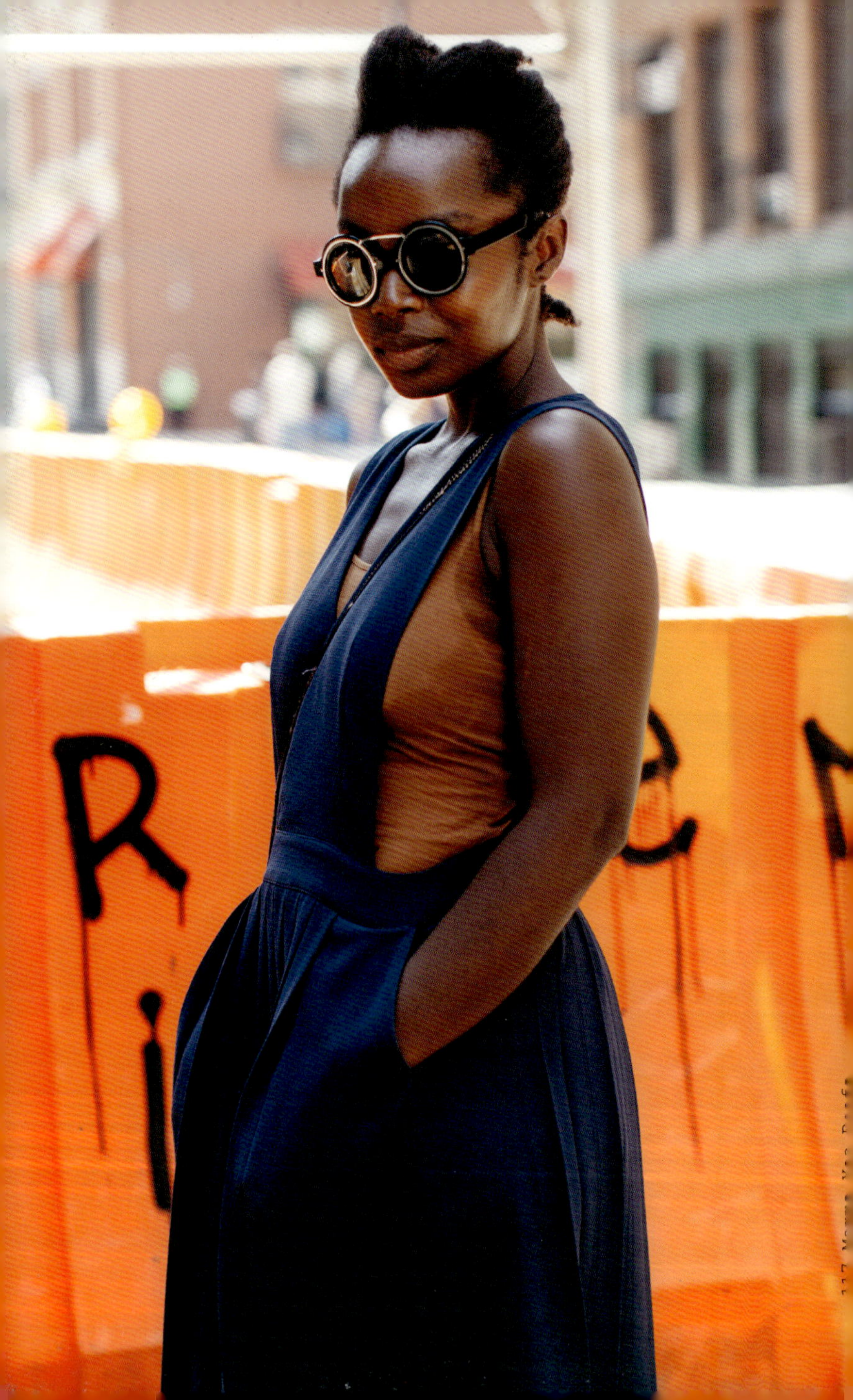

117 Mame Yaa Boafo

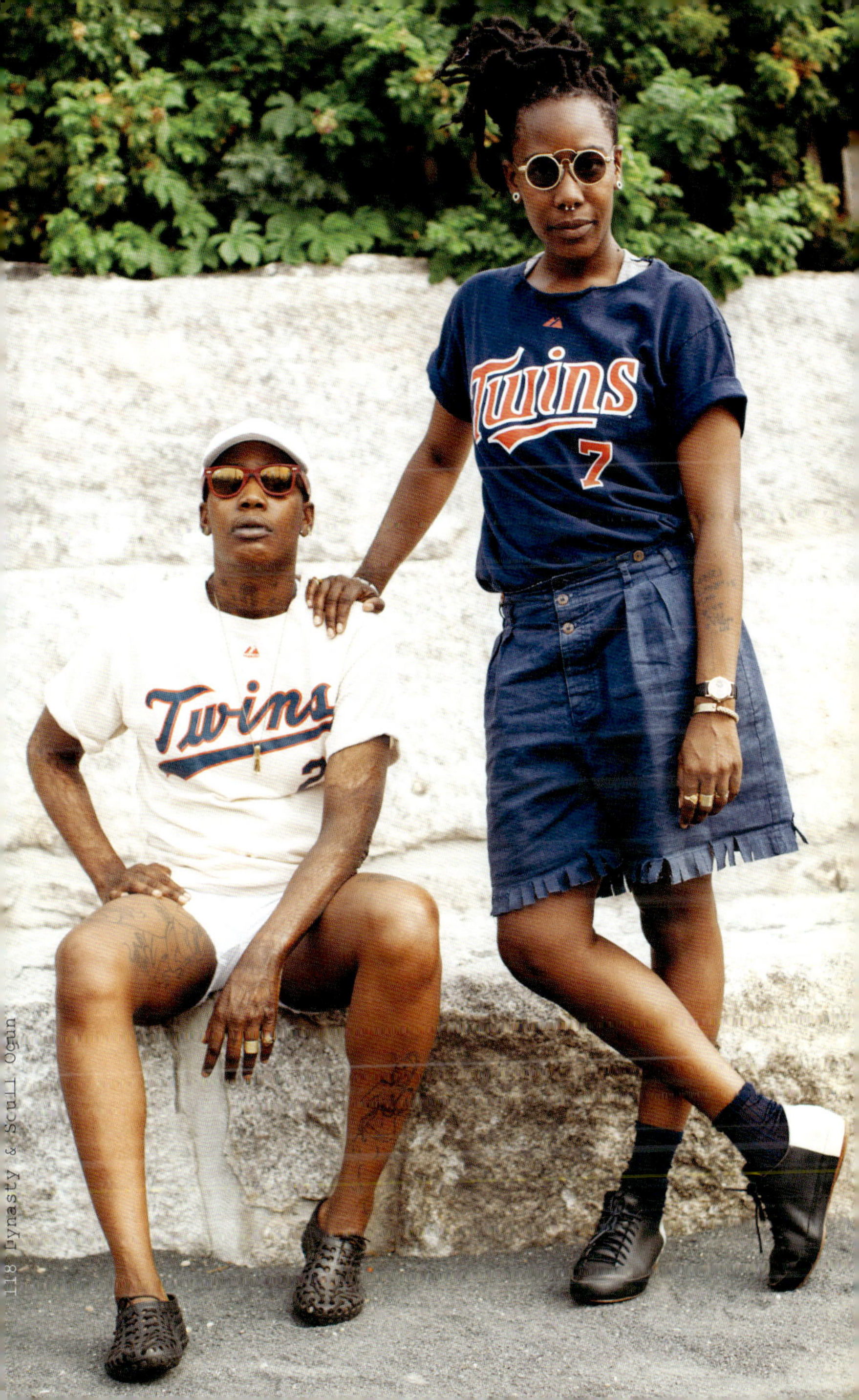

 Dynasty & Scull Ogun

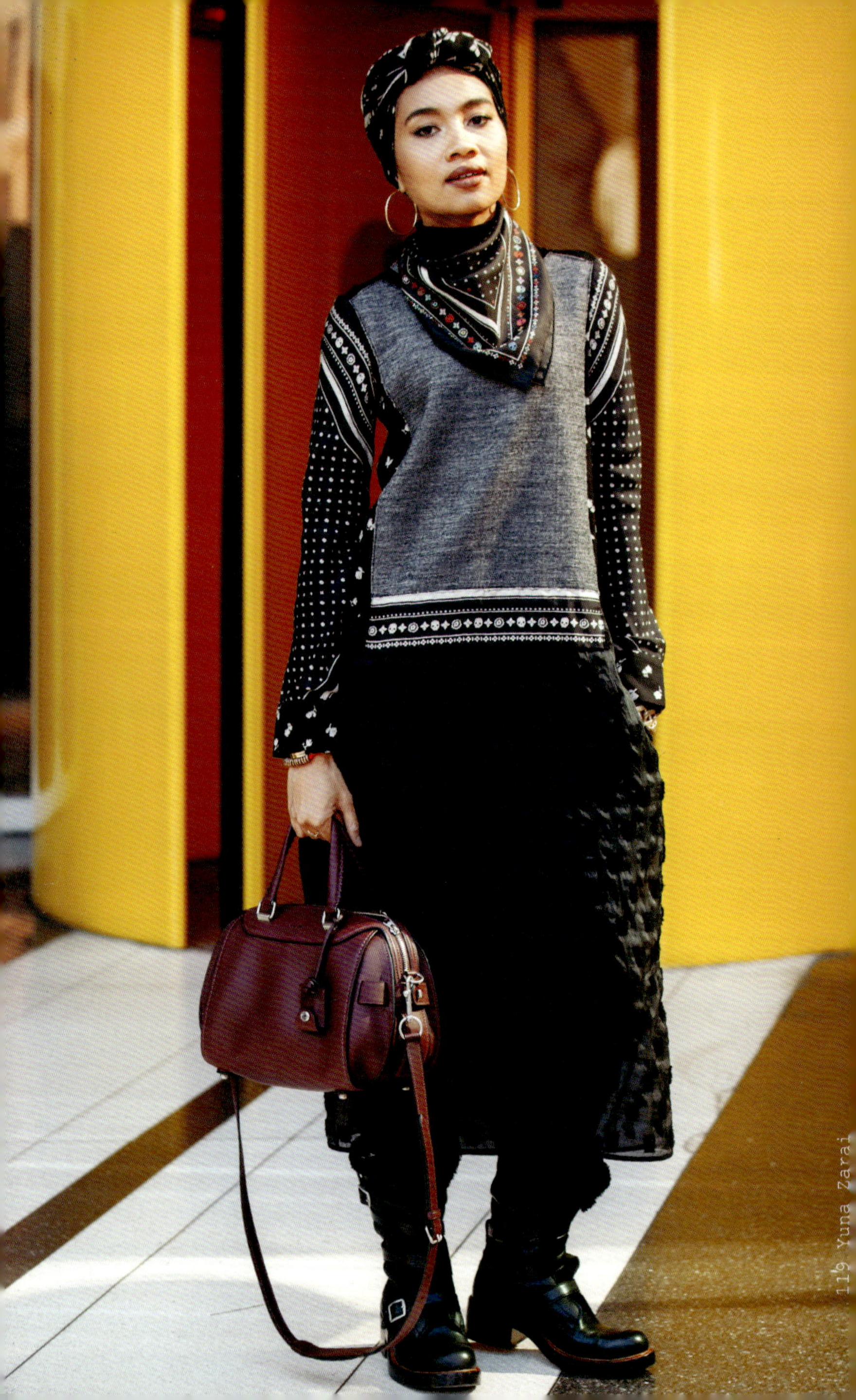

119 Yuna Zarai

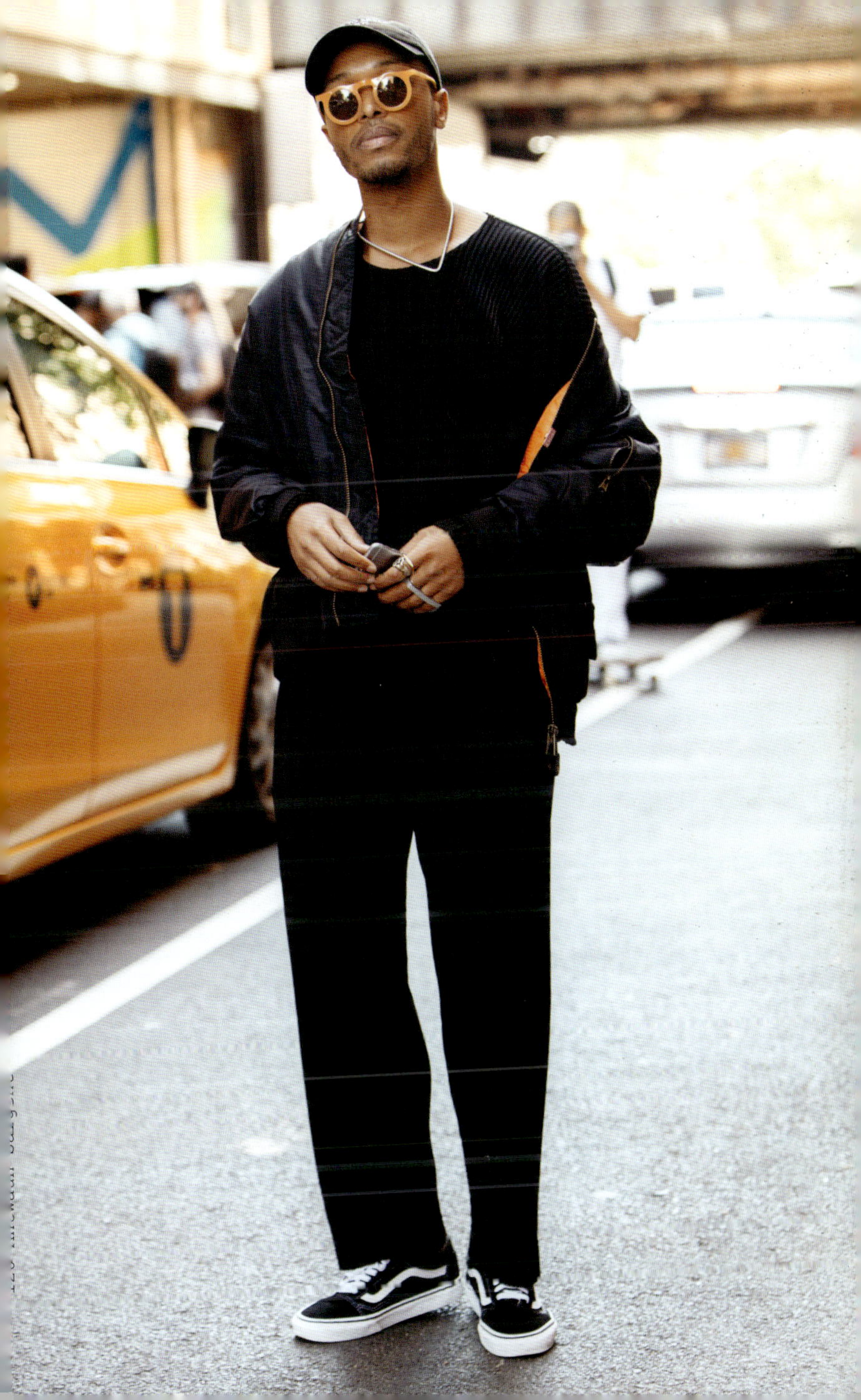

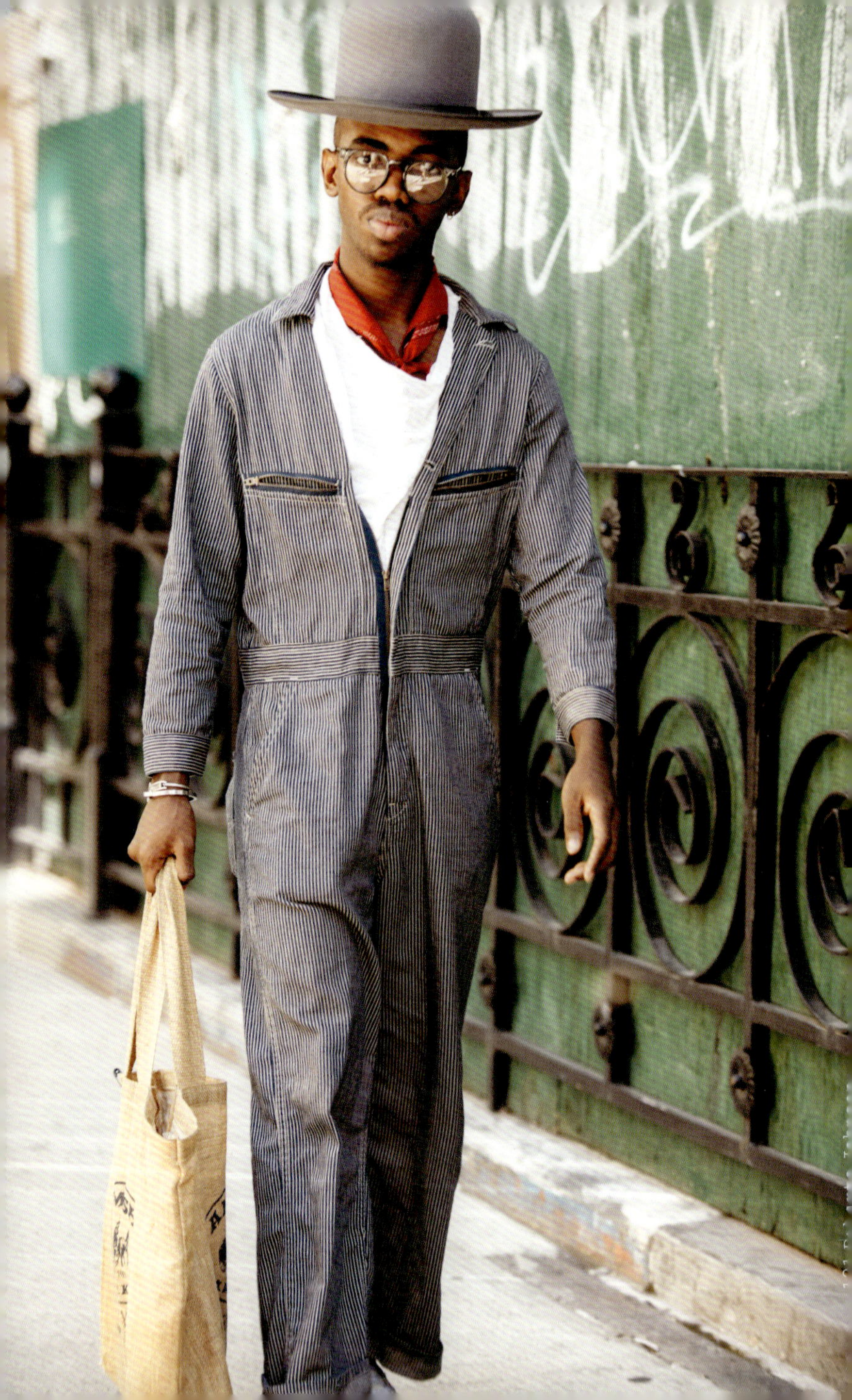

“I think of movies and eras of time, ’20s, ’40s, and ’60s; that is what shapes my lifestyle.”

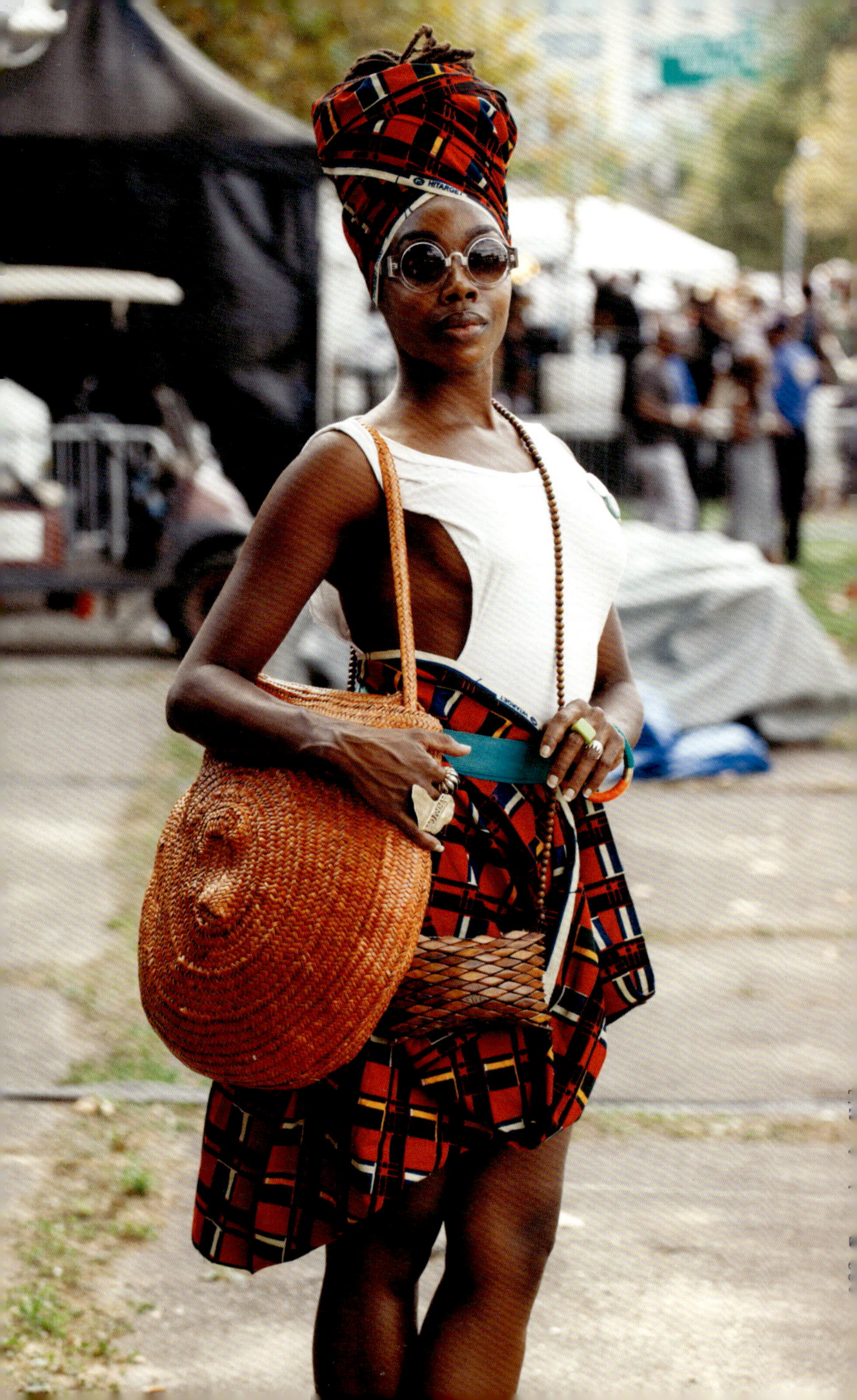

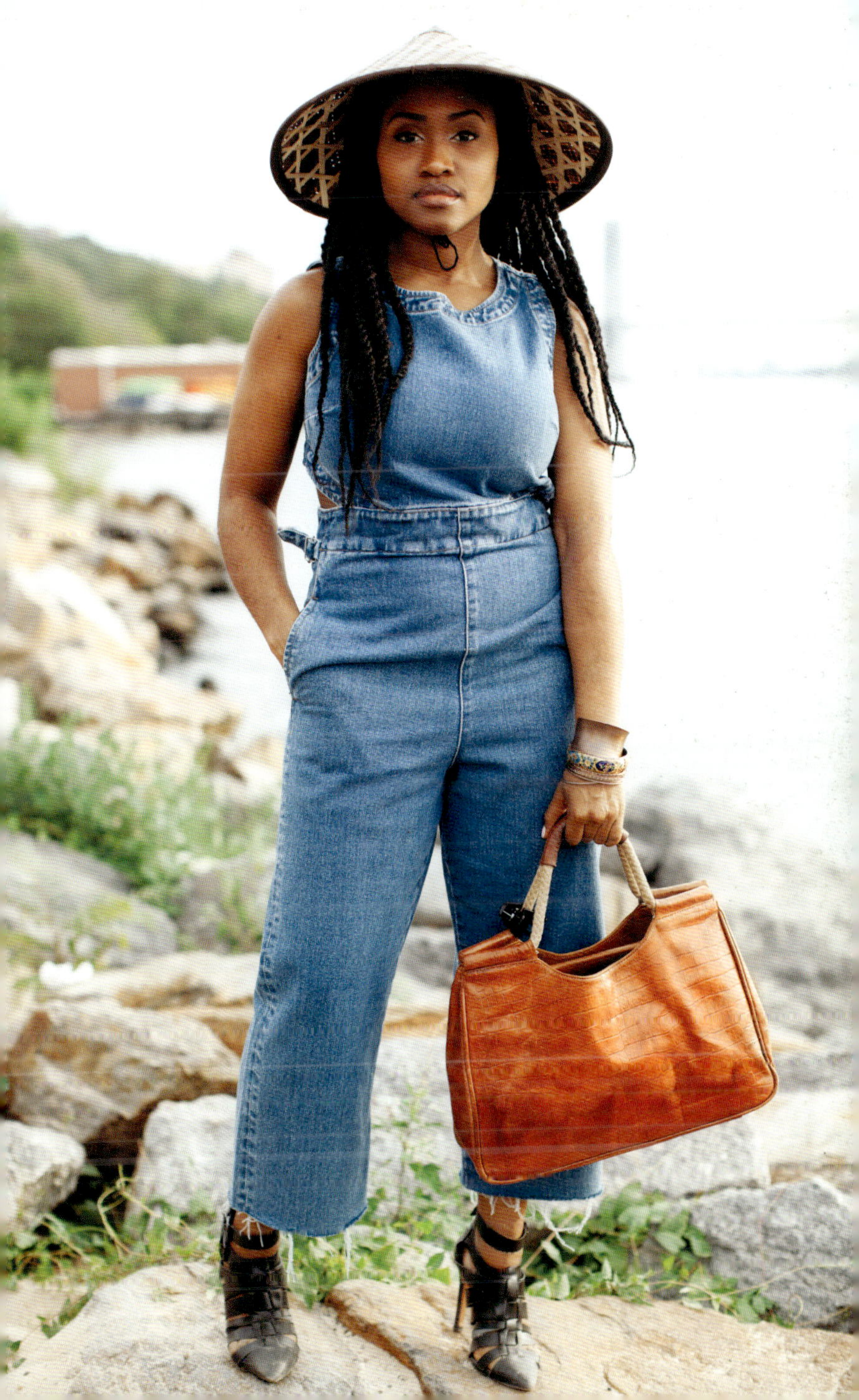

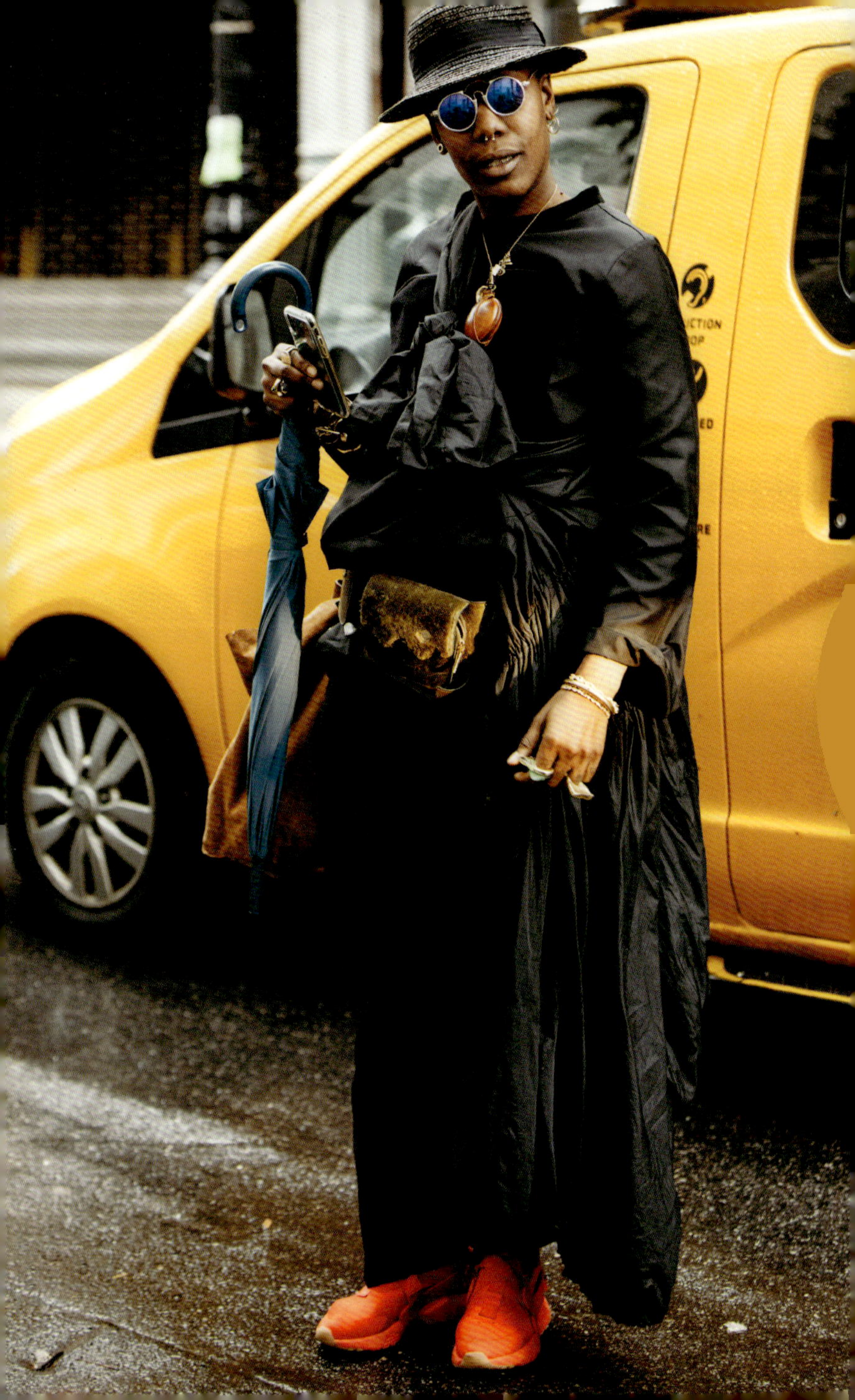

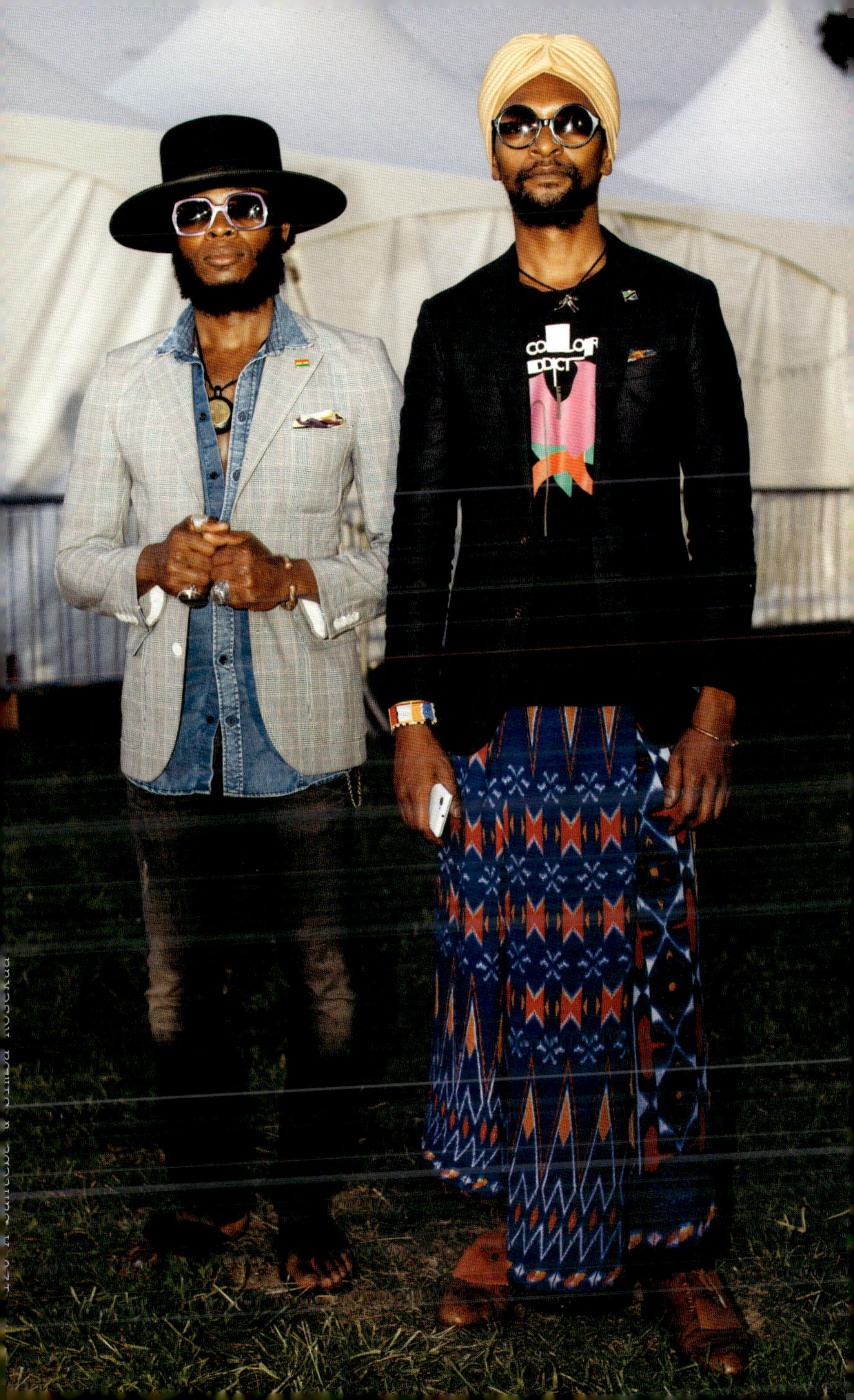

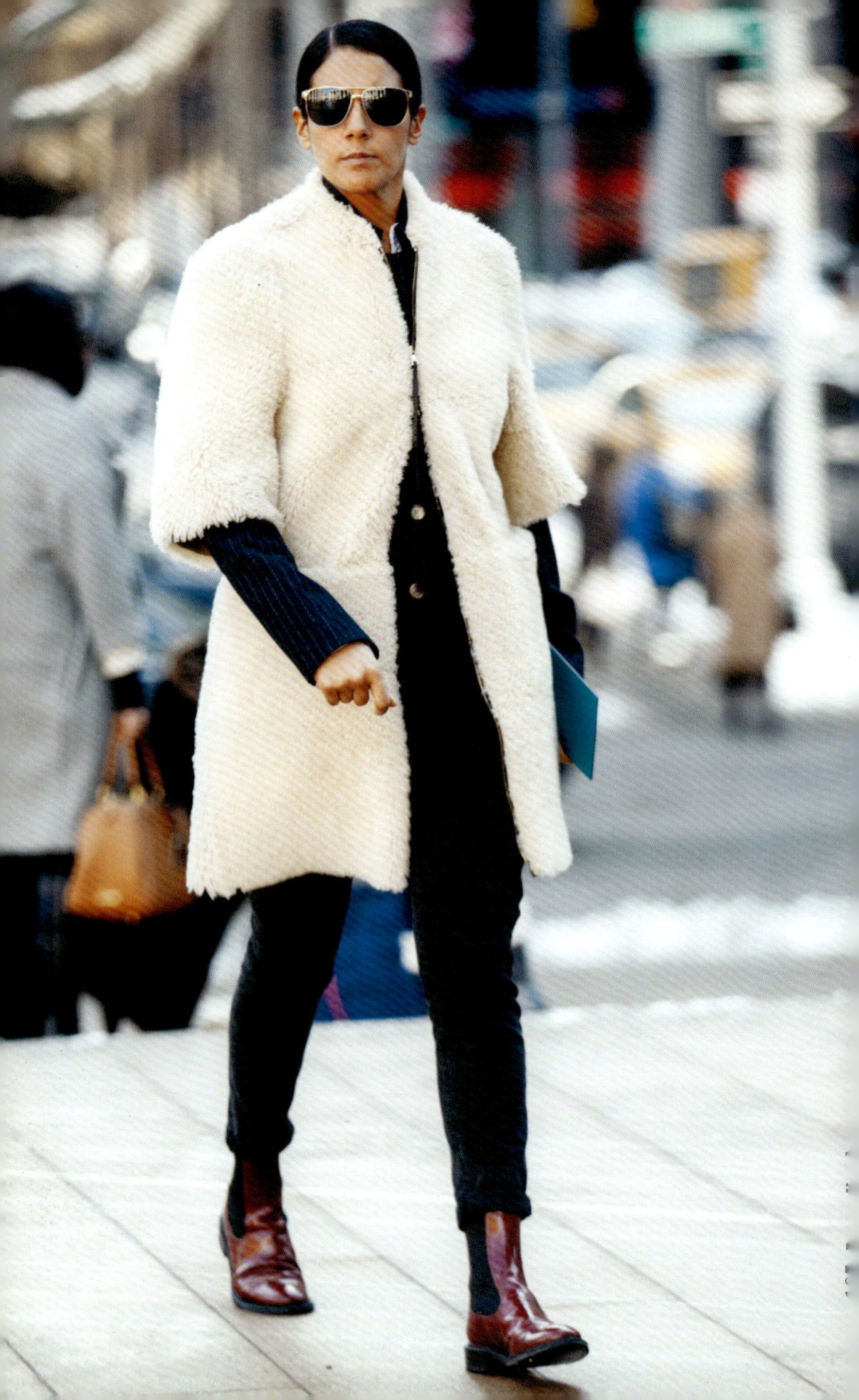

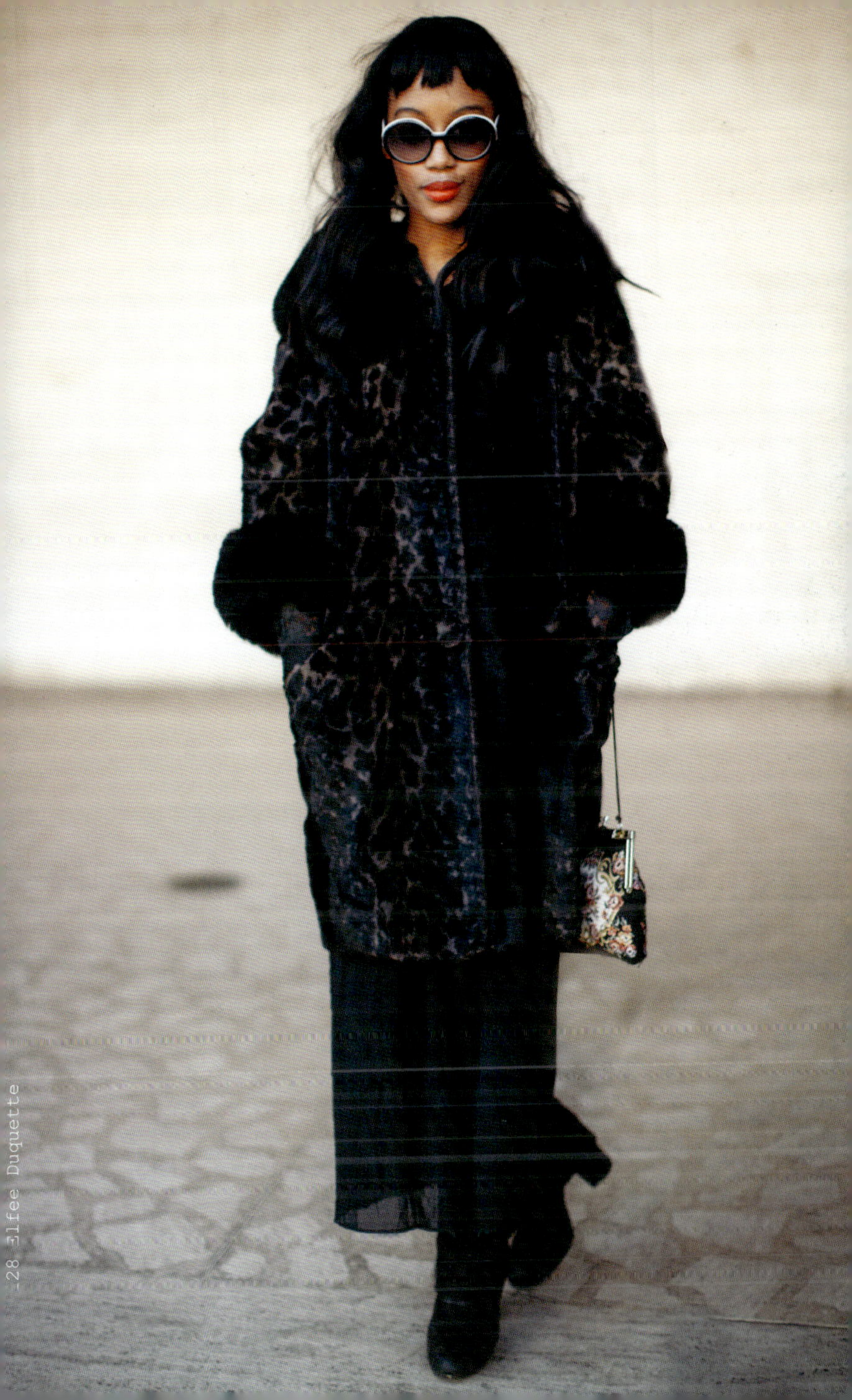

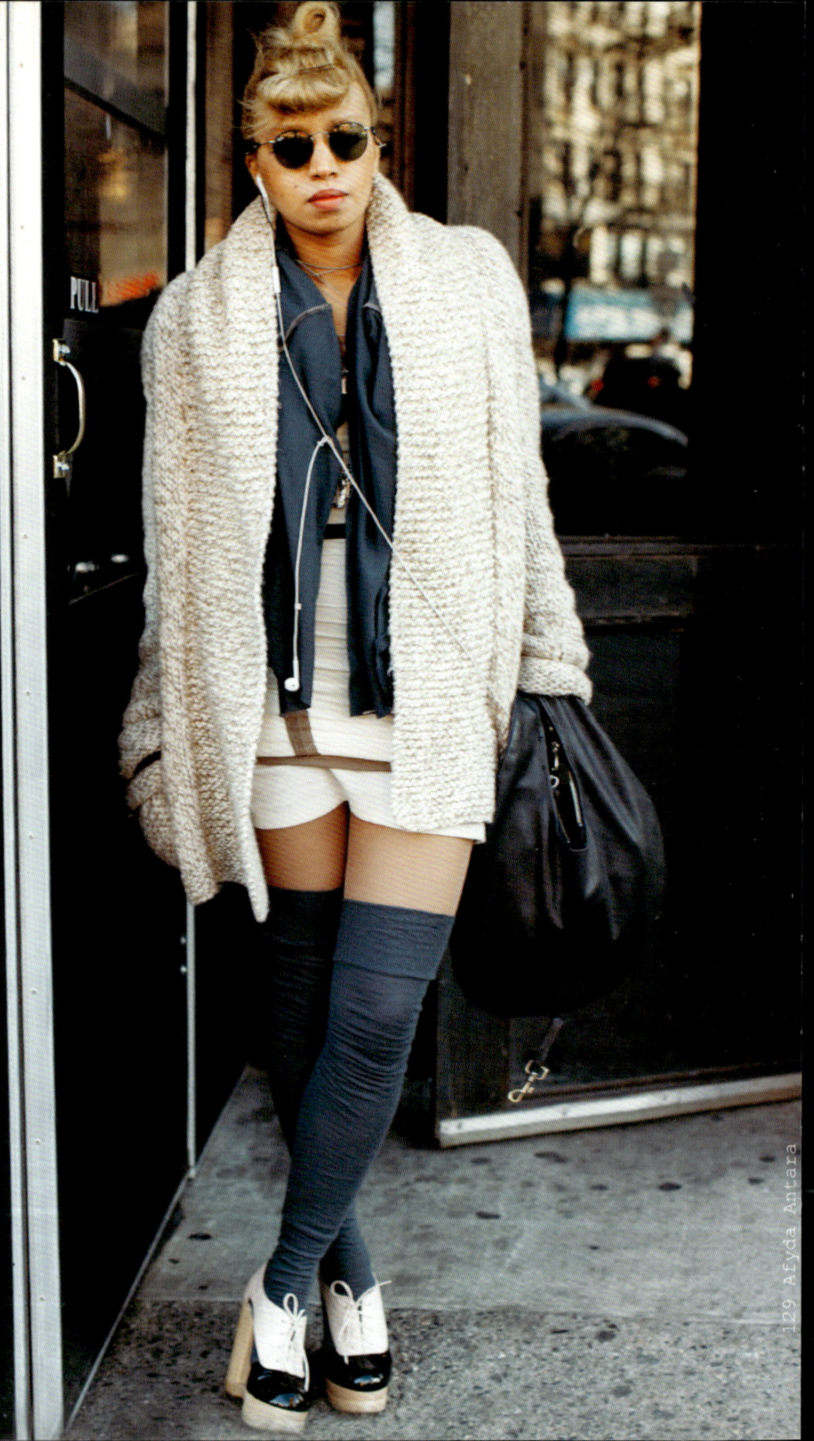

129 Afyda Antara

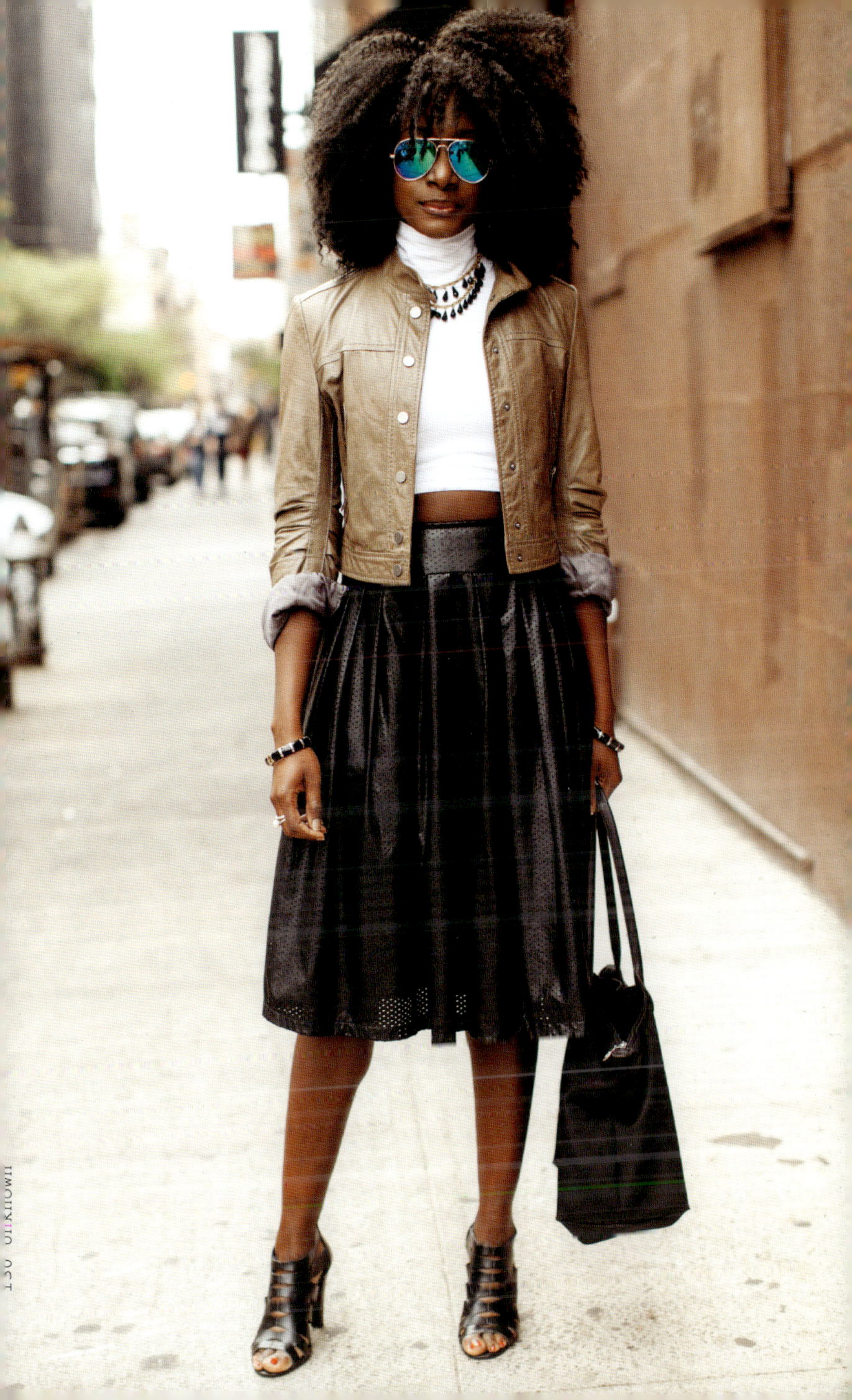

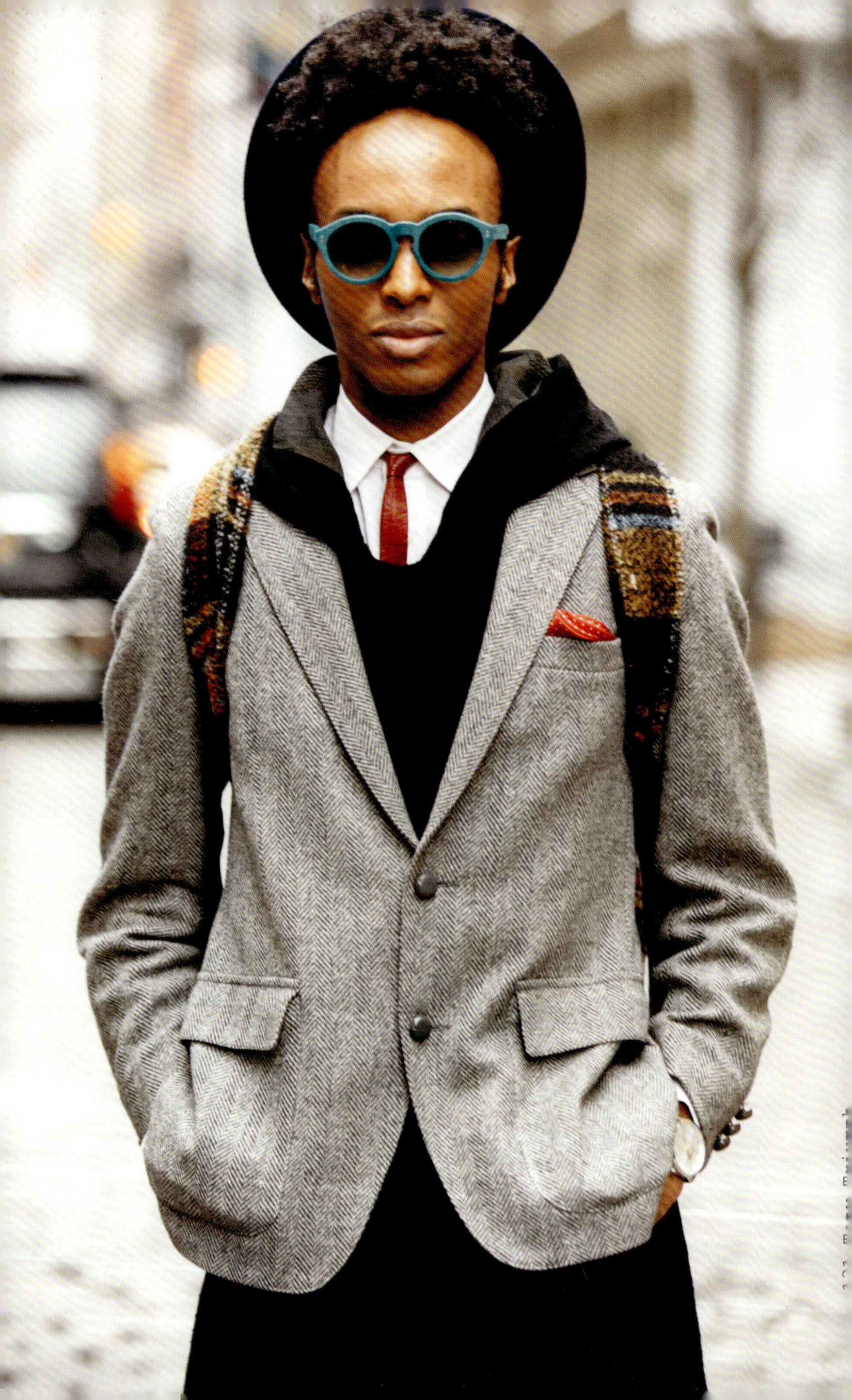

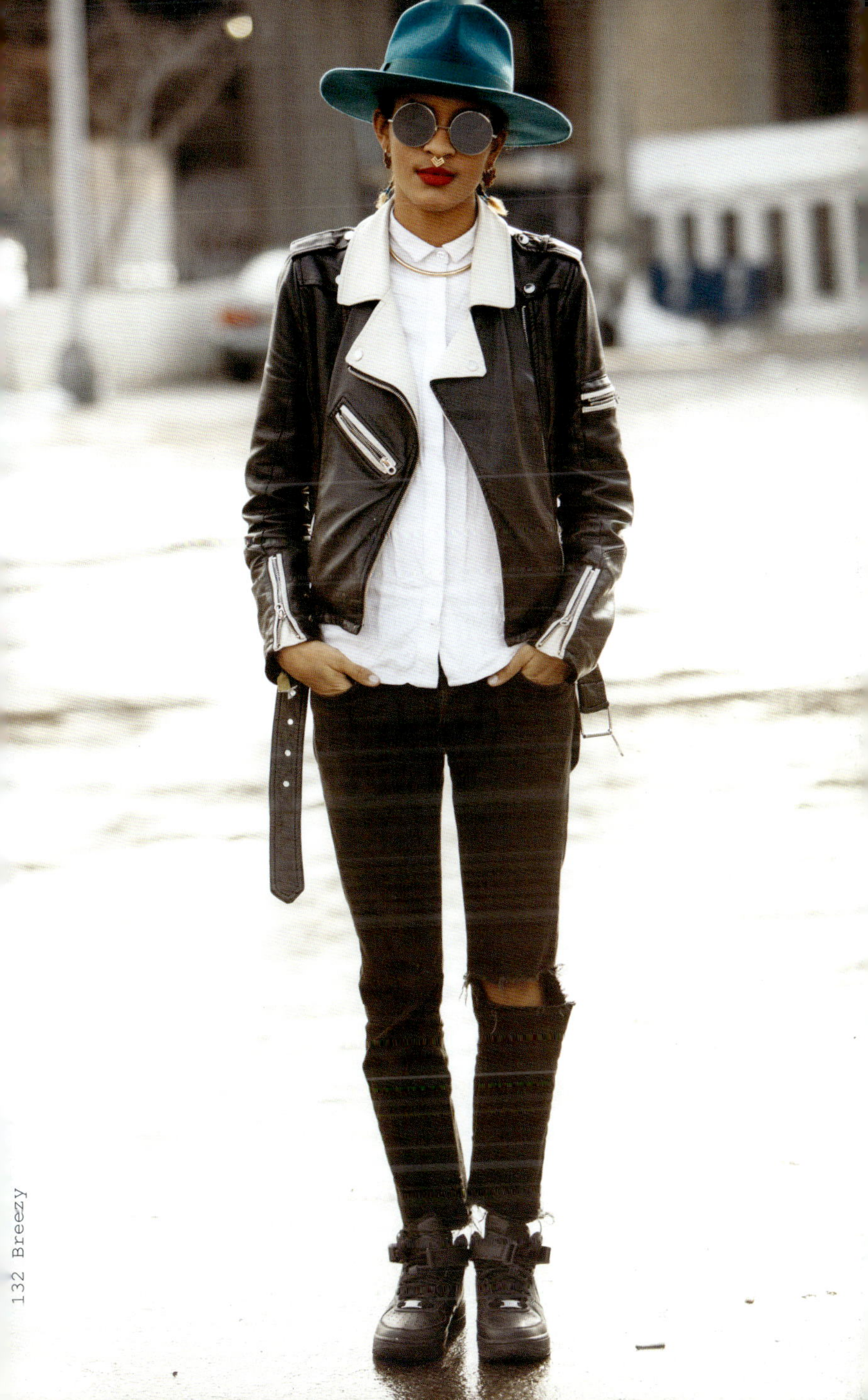

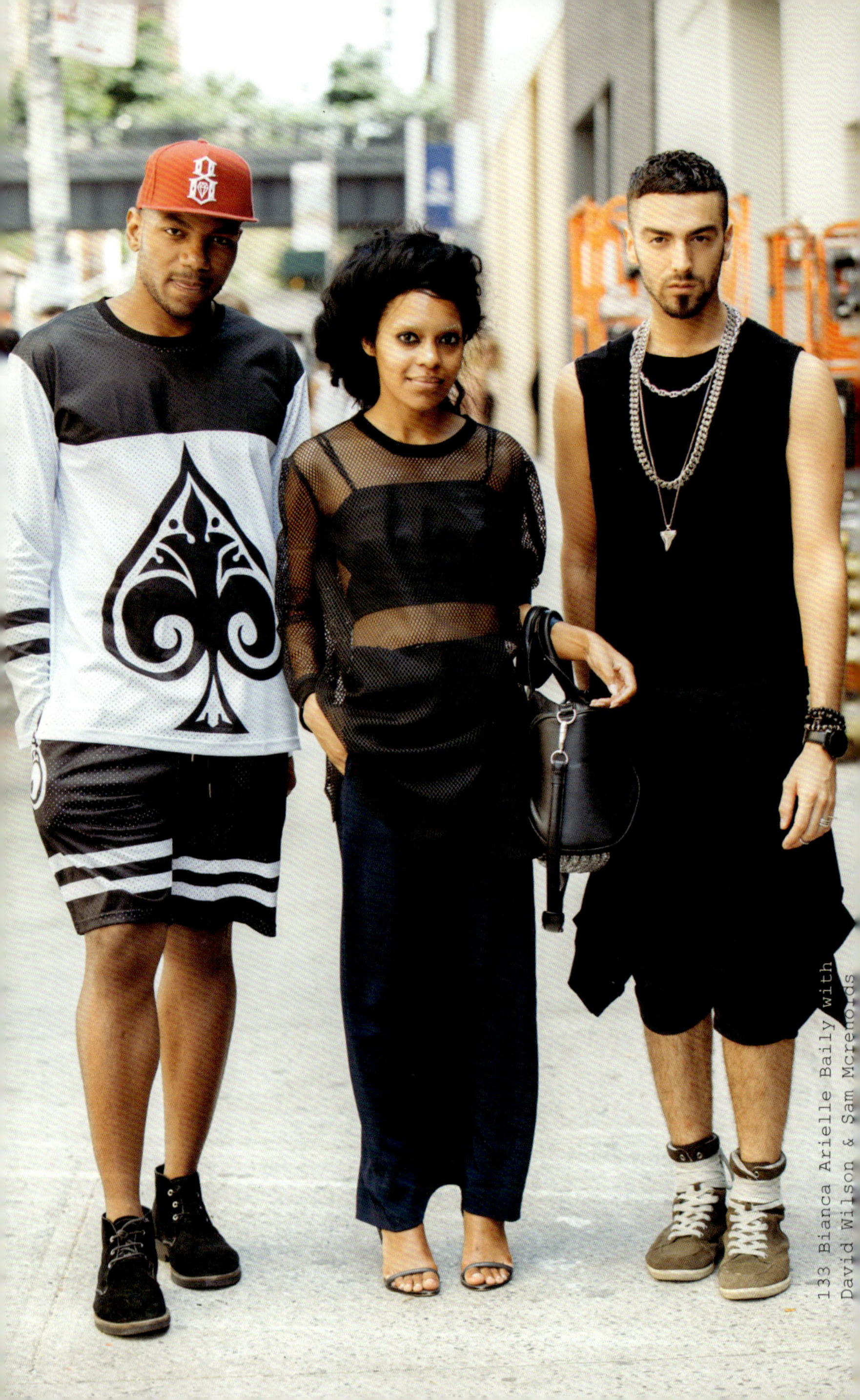

133 Bianca Arielle Baily with
David Wilson & Sam Mcrenolds

"Everything I do is a reflection of who I am. That is my inspiration."

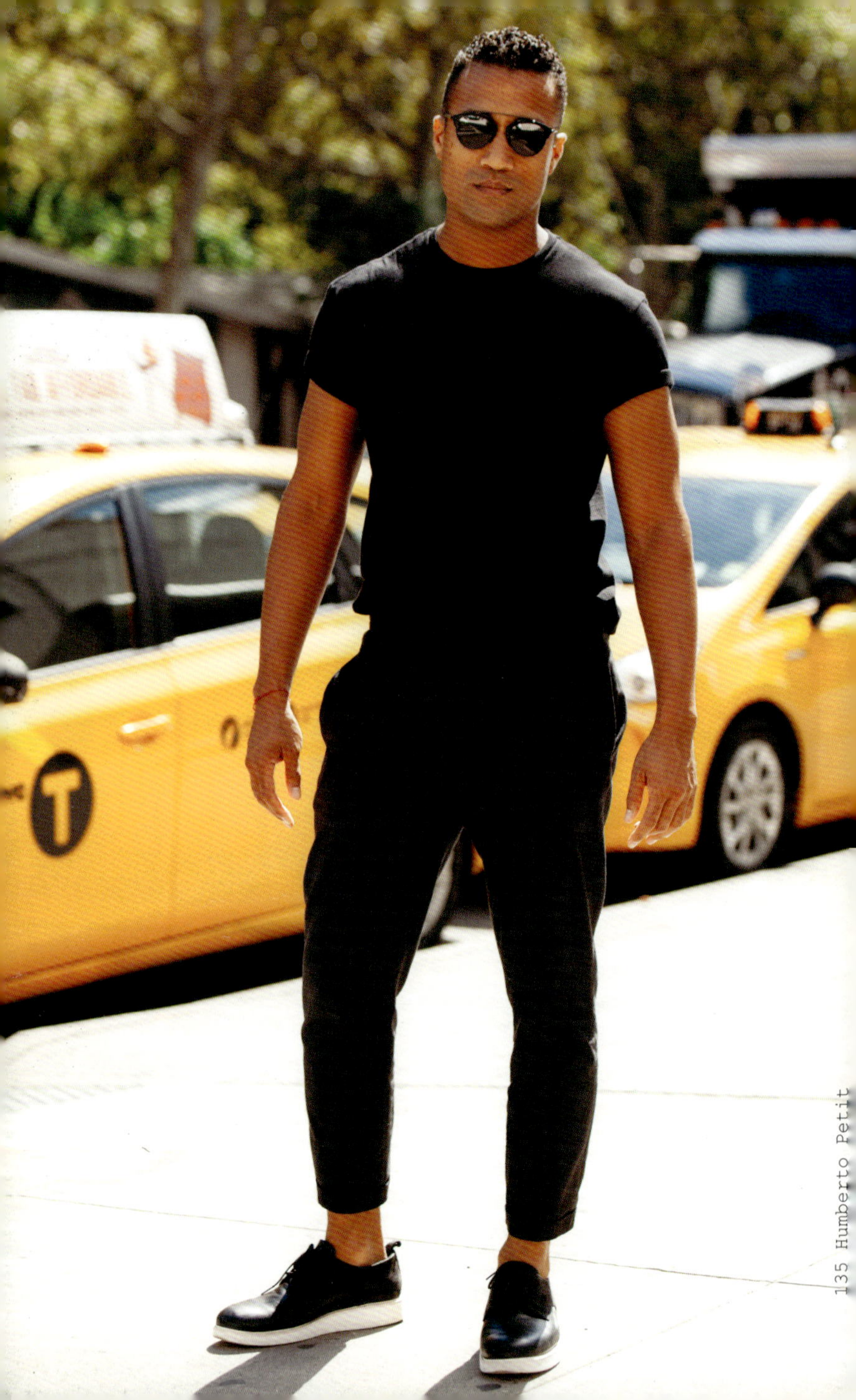

135 Humberto Petit

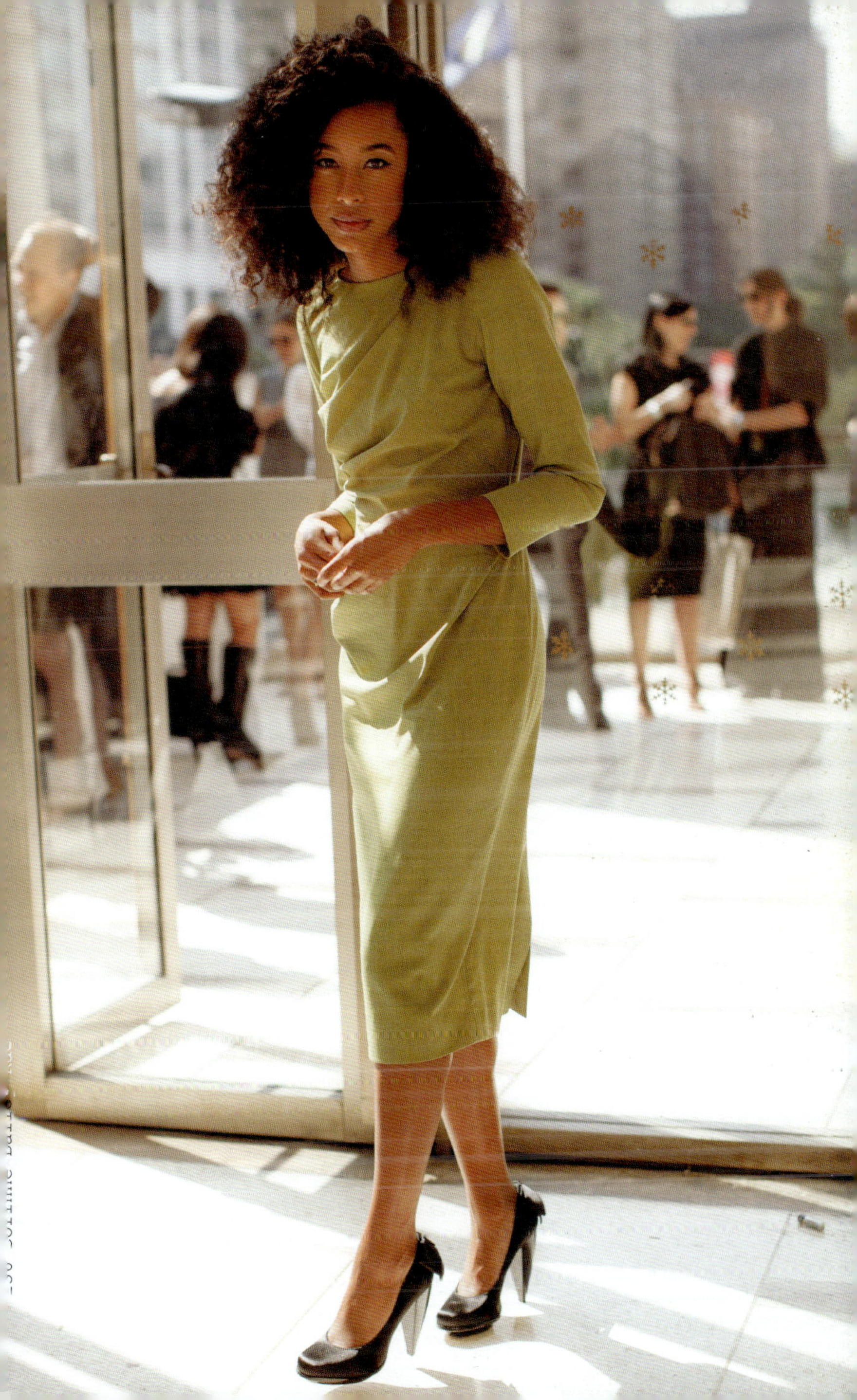

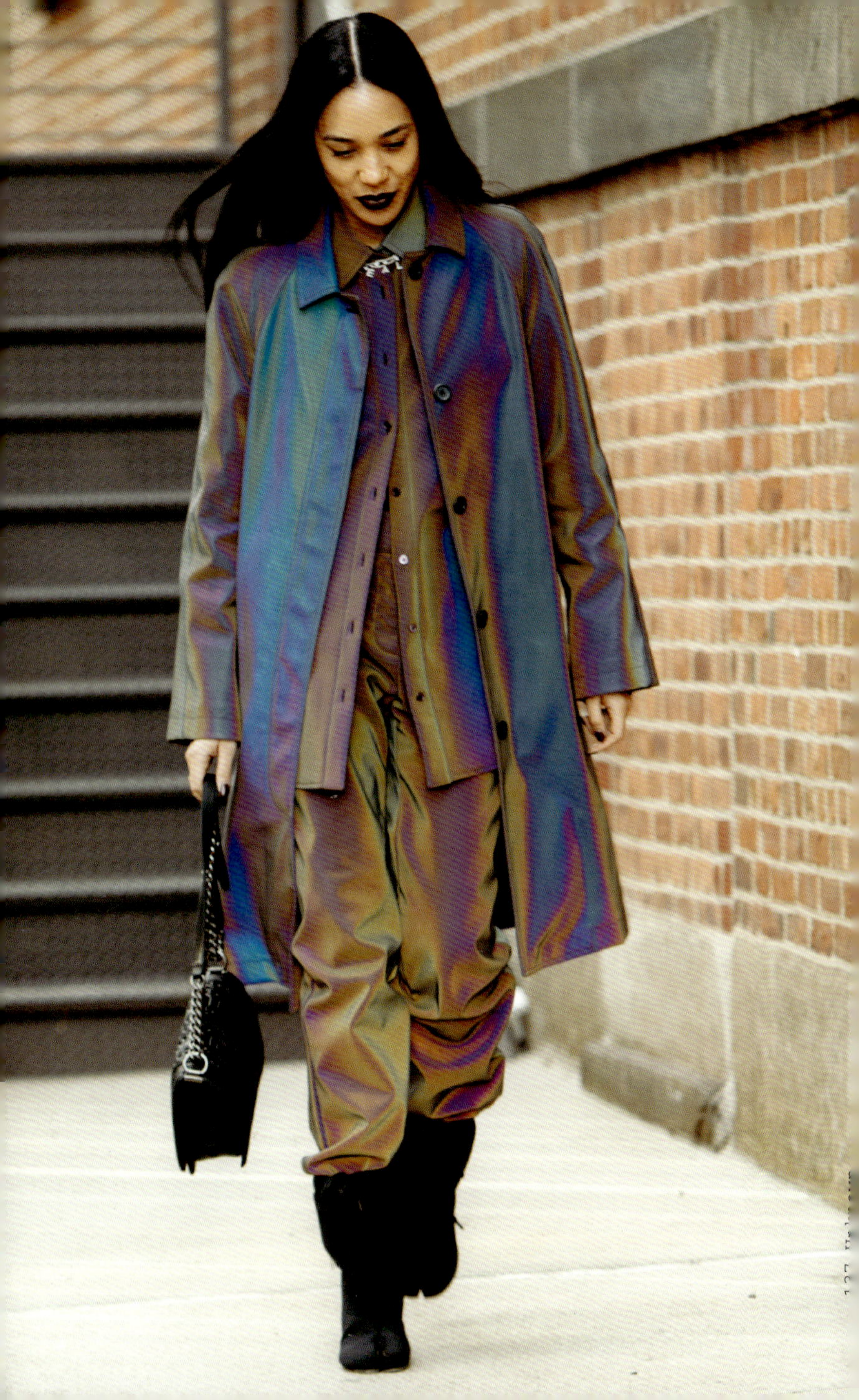

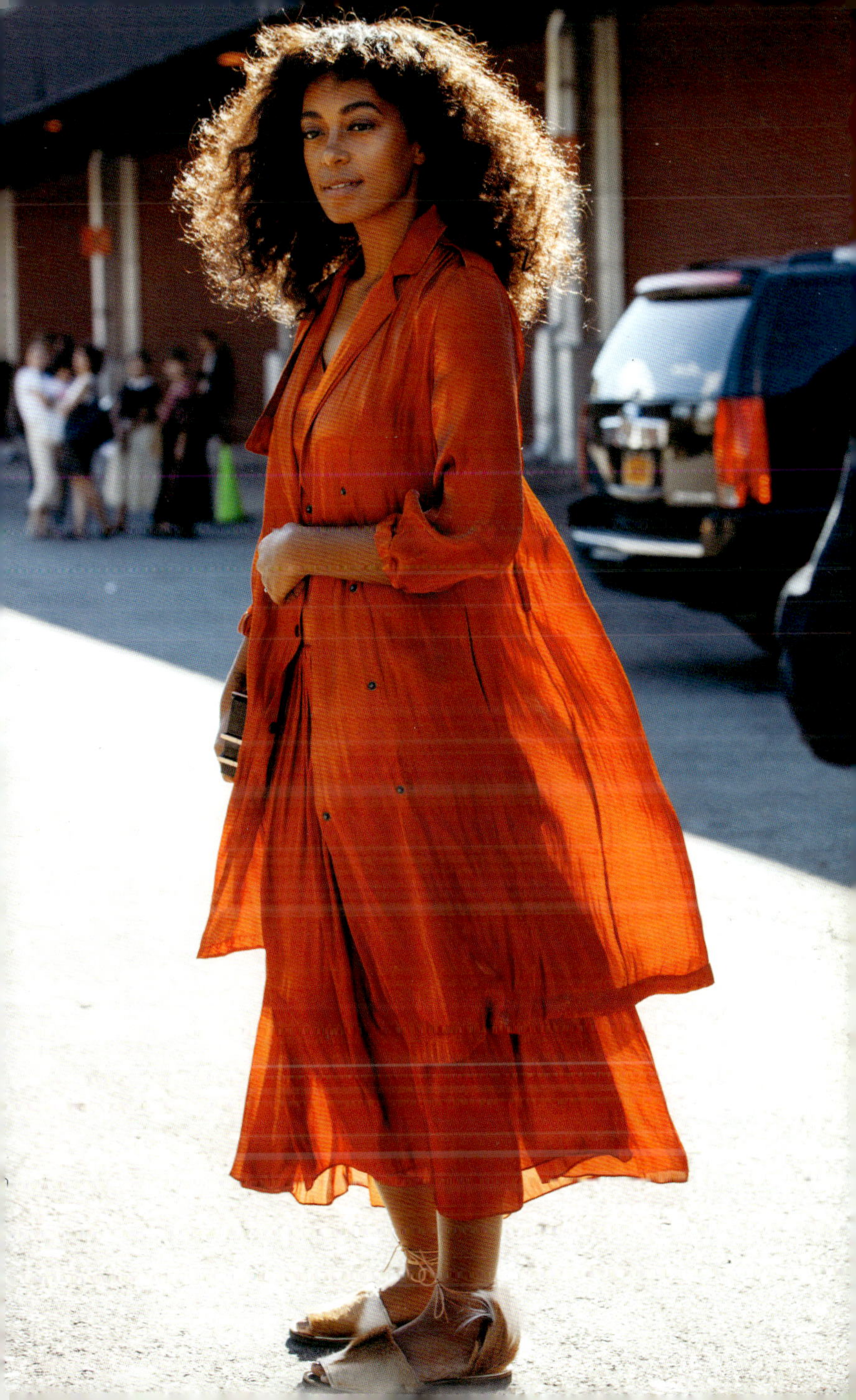

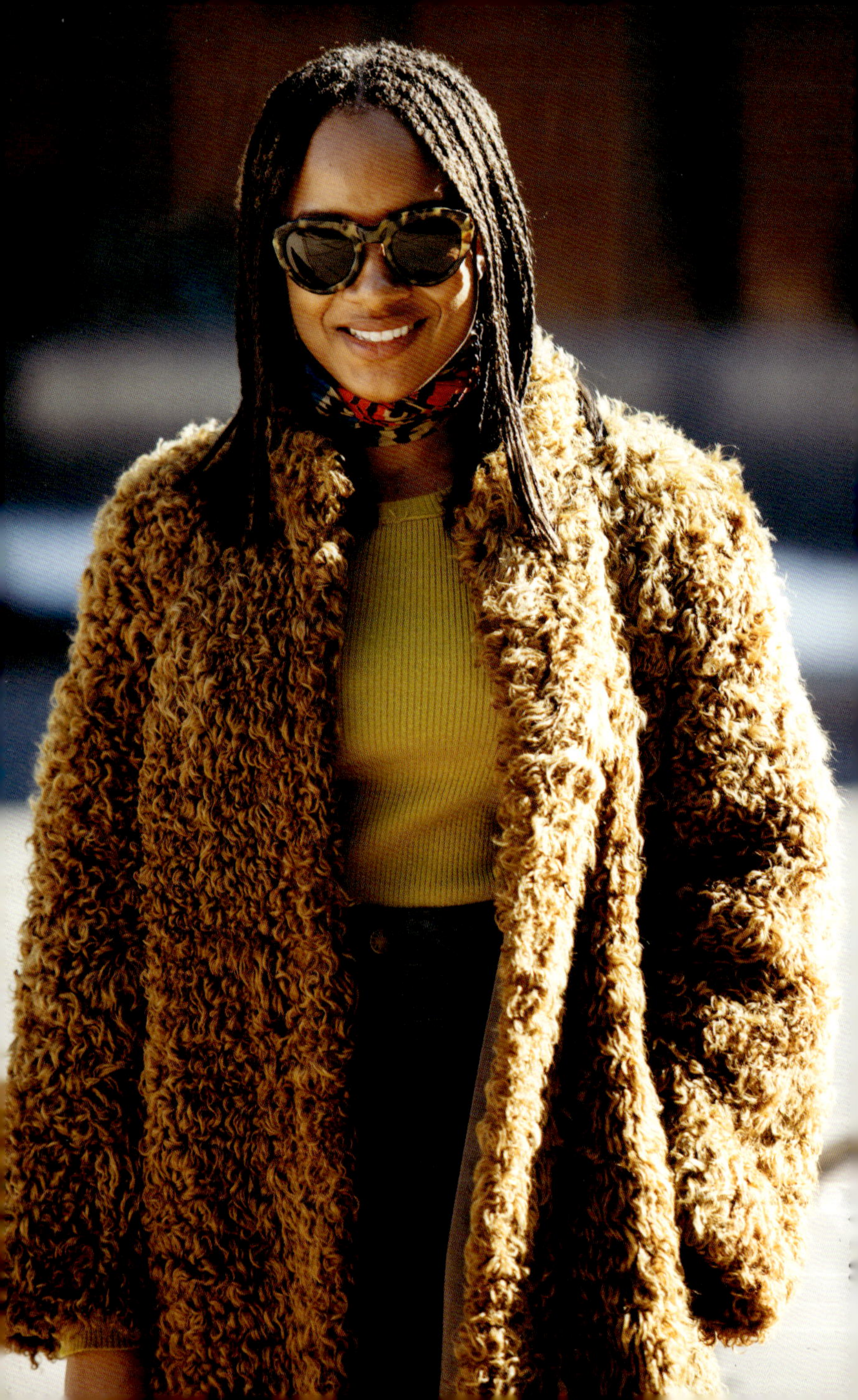

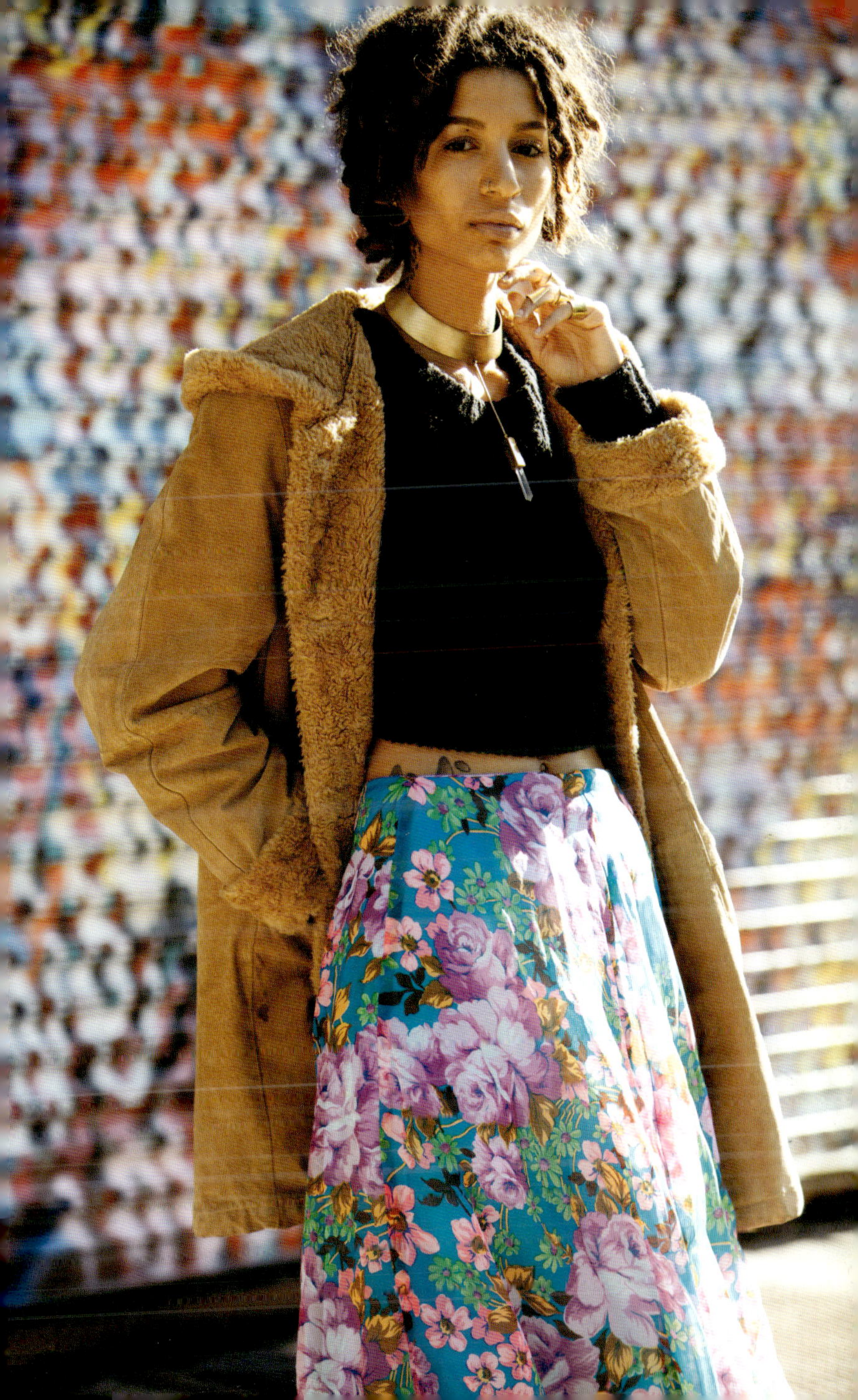

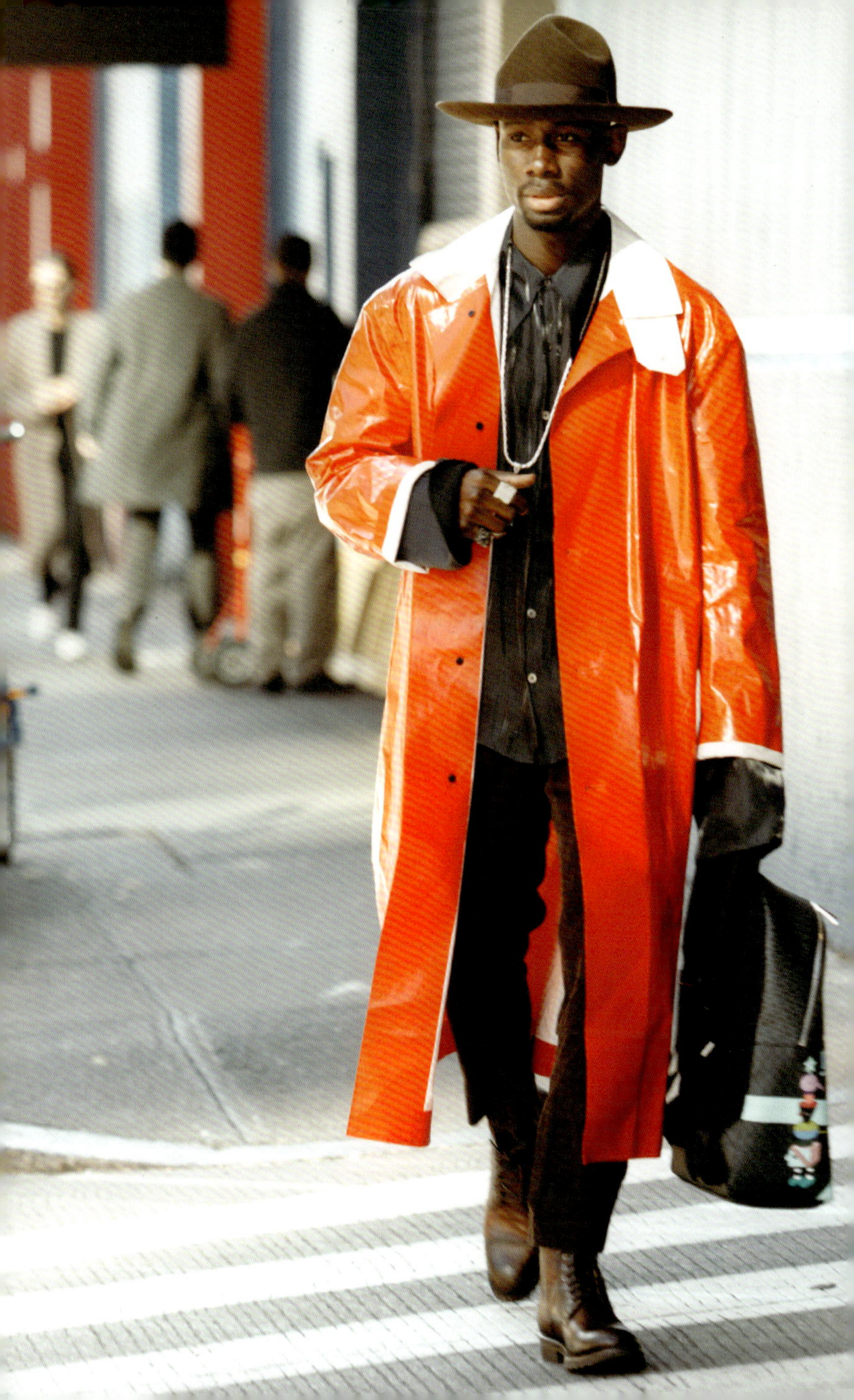

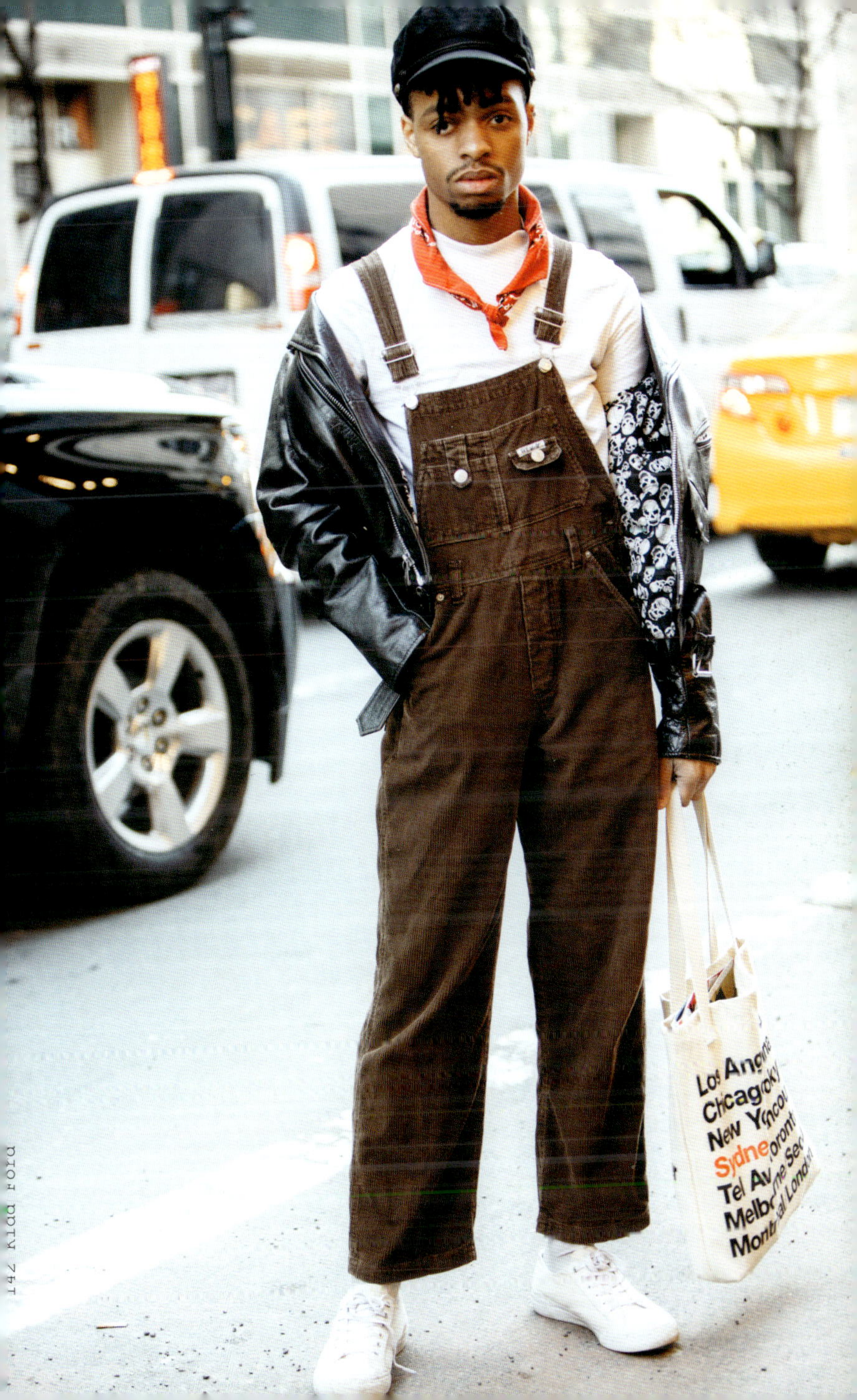

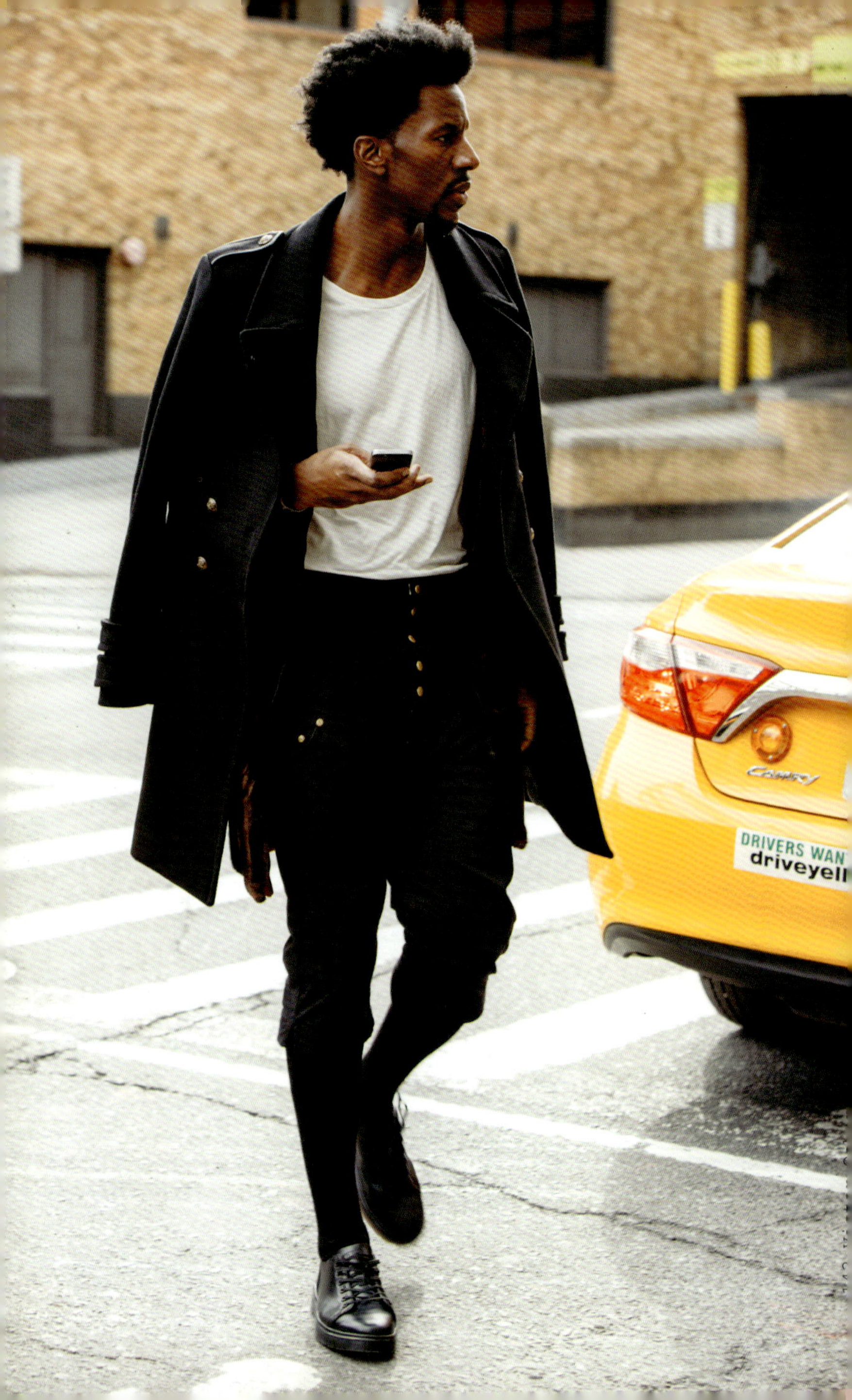
CAMRY
DRIVERS WAN
driveyell

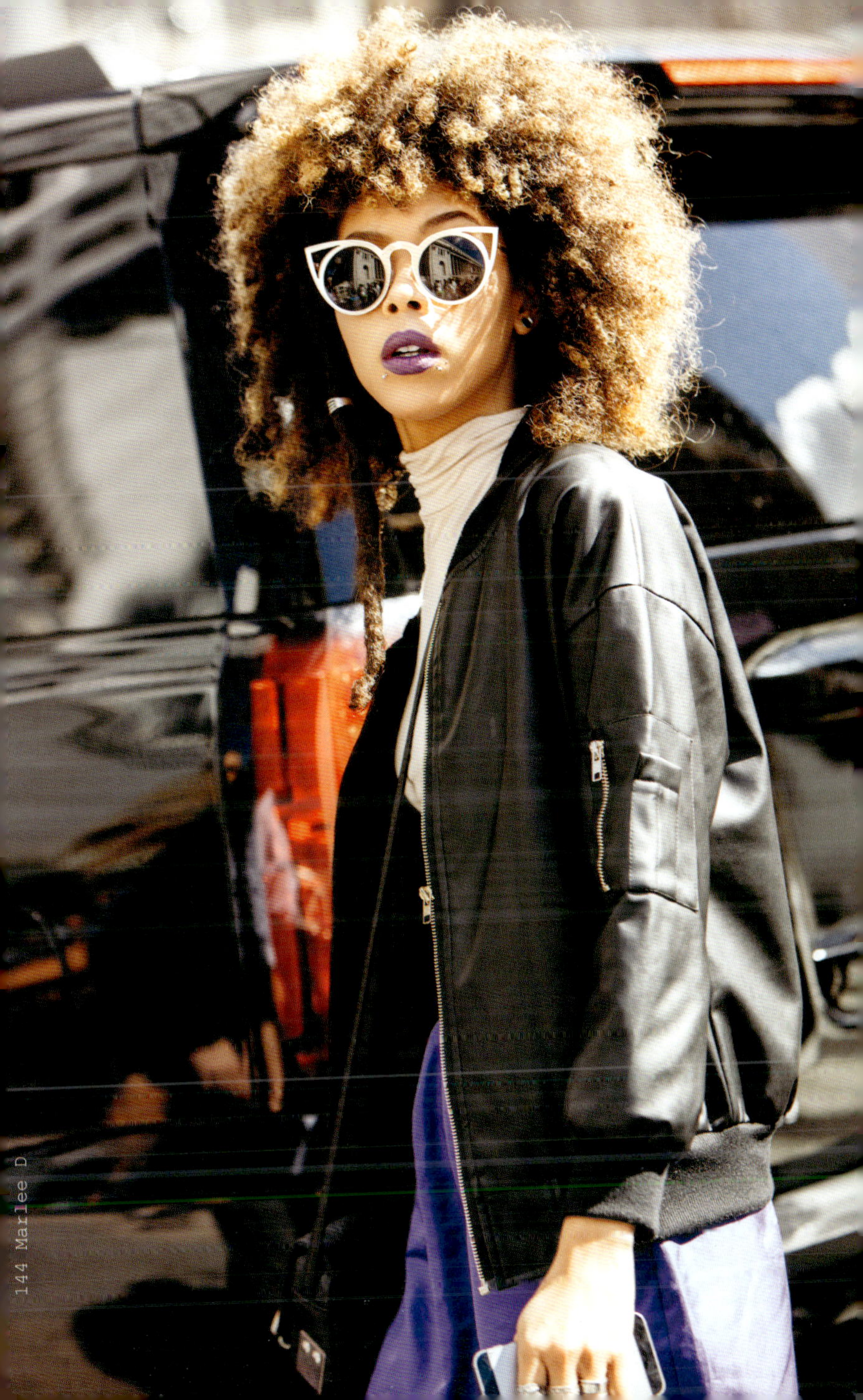

 Marlee D

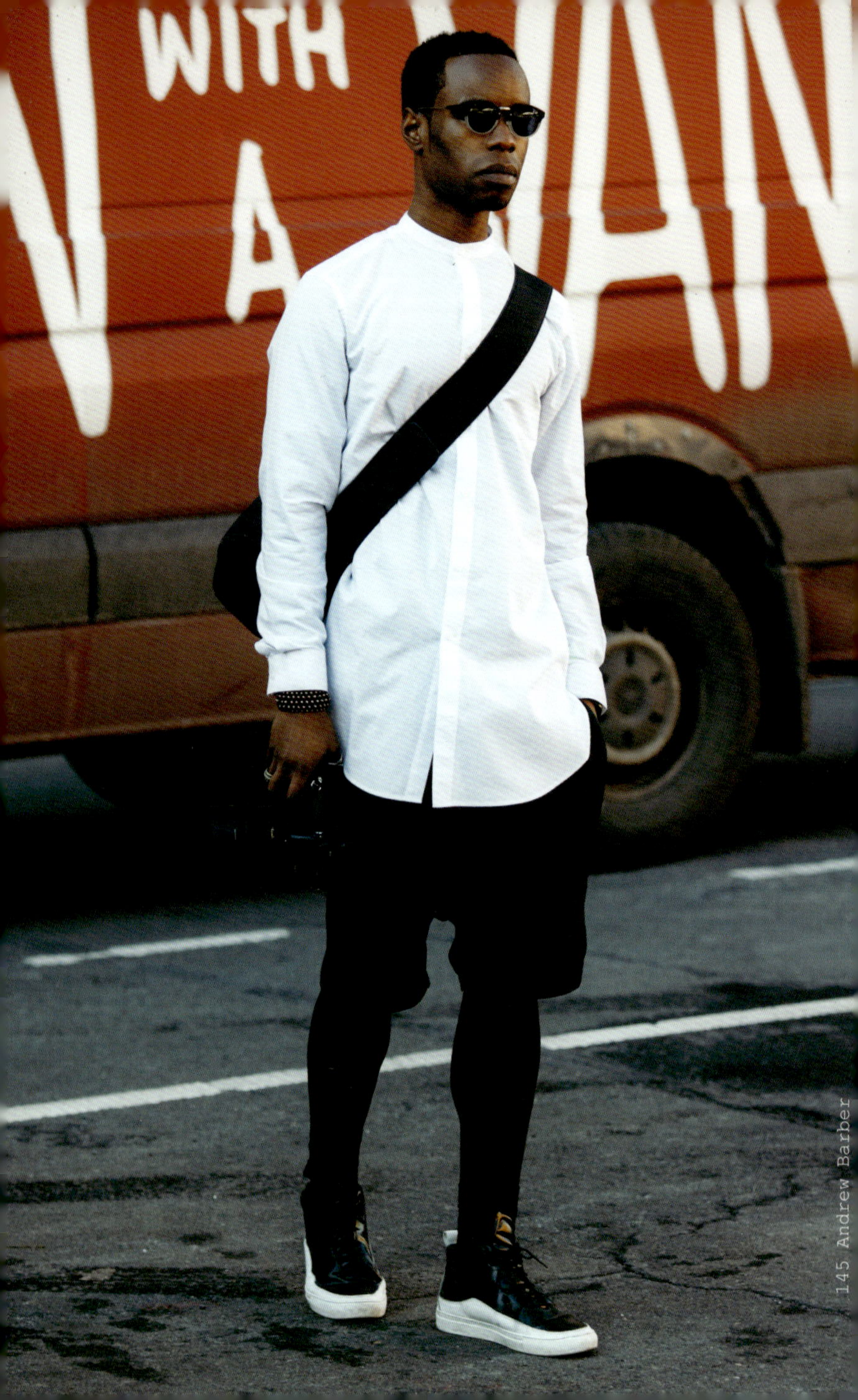

145 Andrew Barber

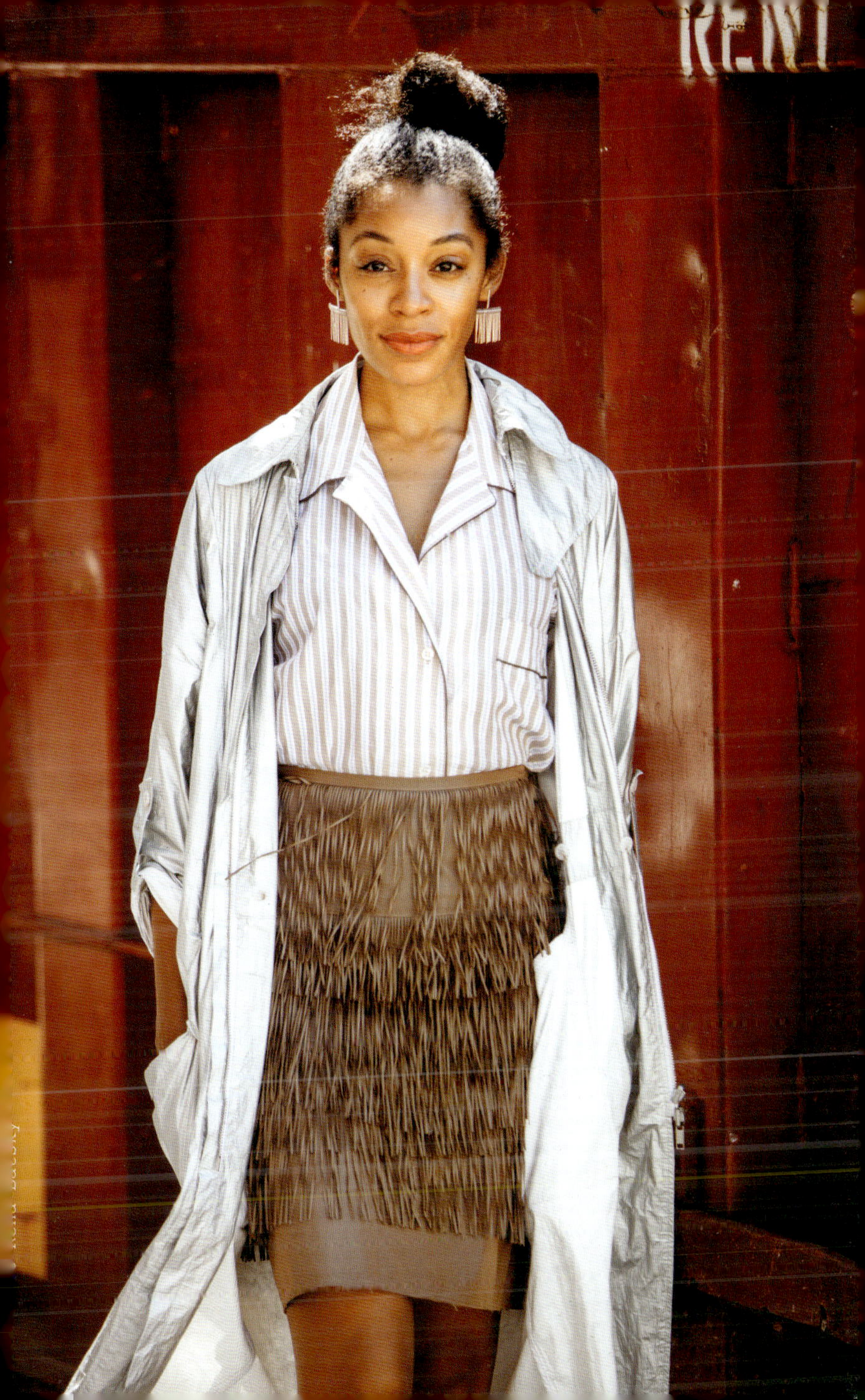
RENT

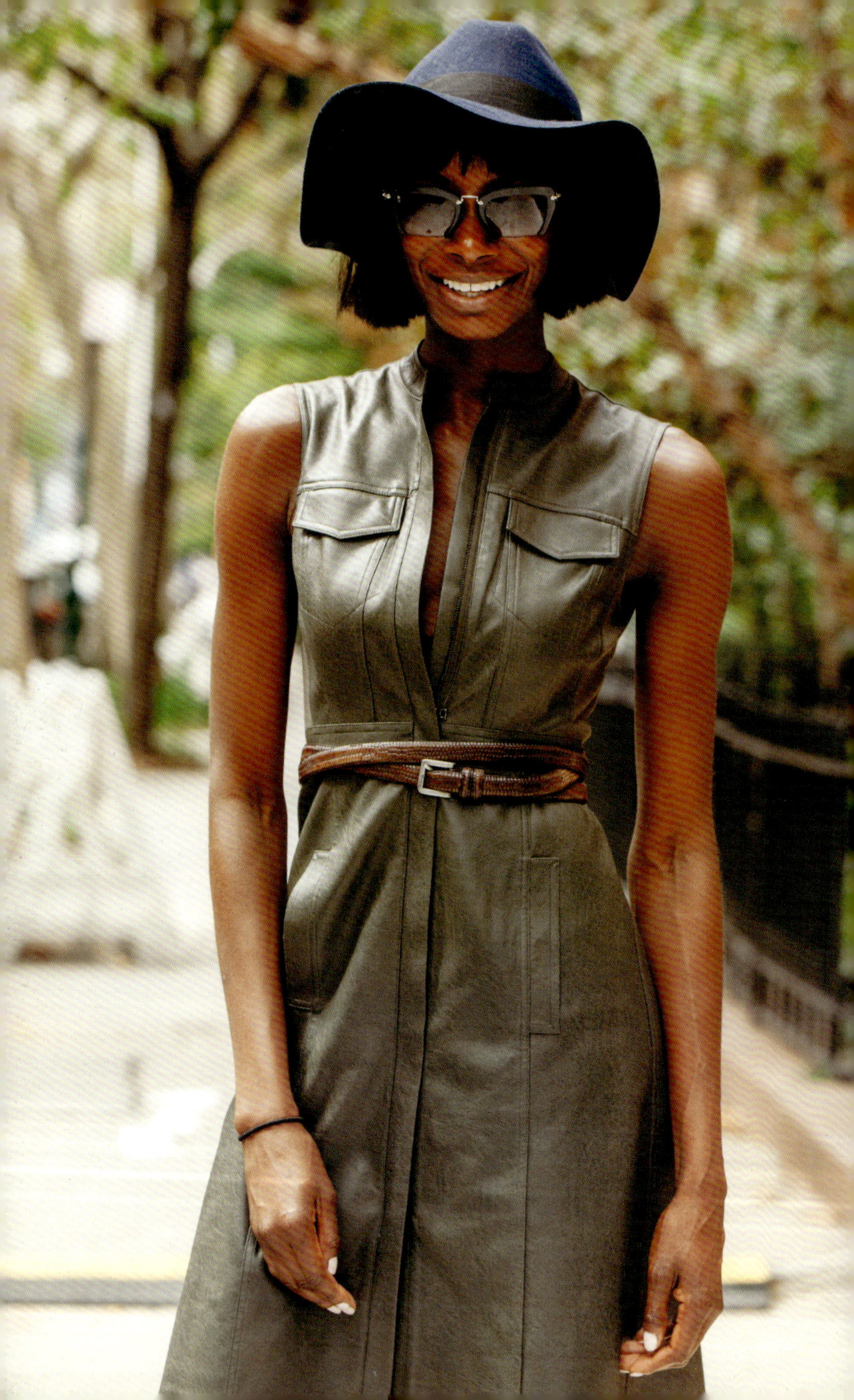

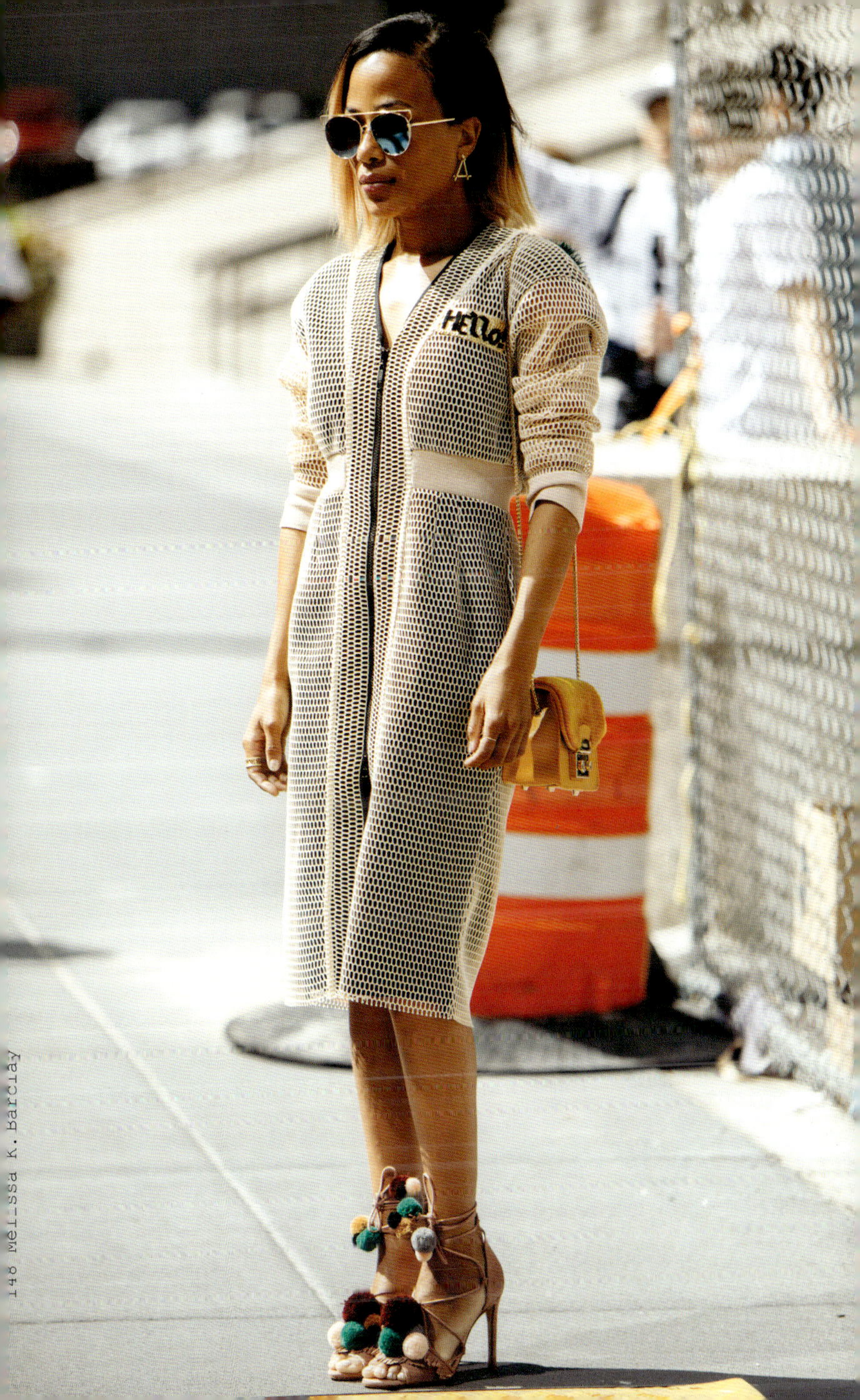
HEllo!

“Indigenous southern bohemian gal, from the east side of Saturn.”

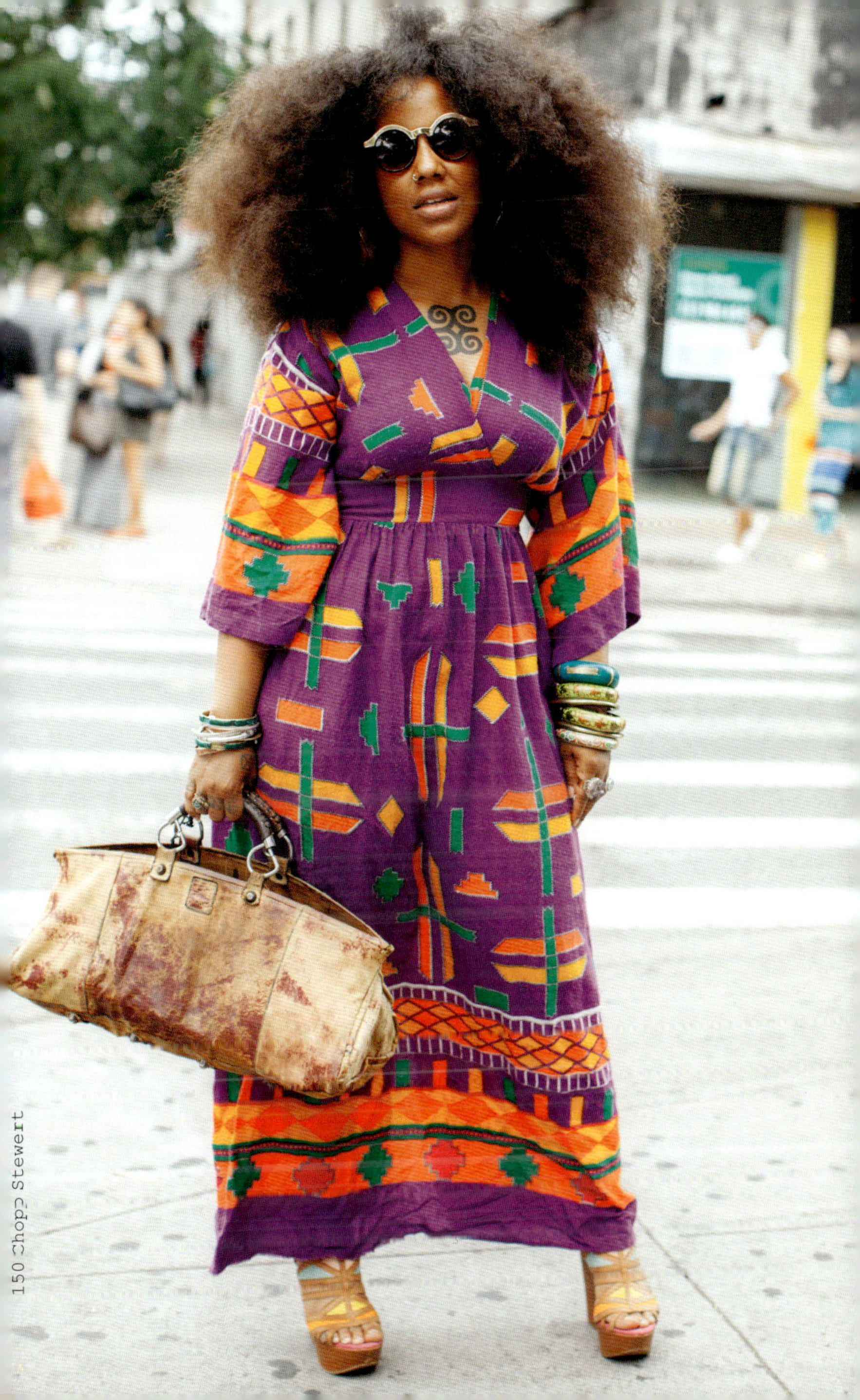

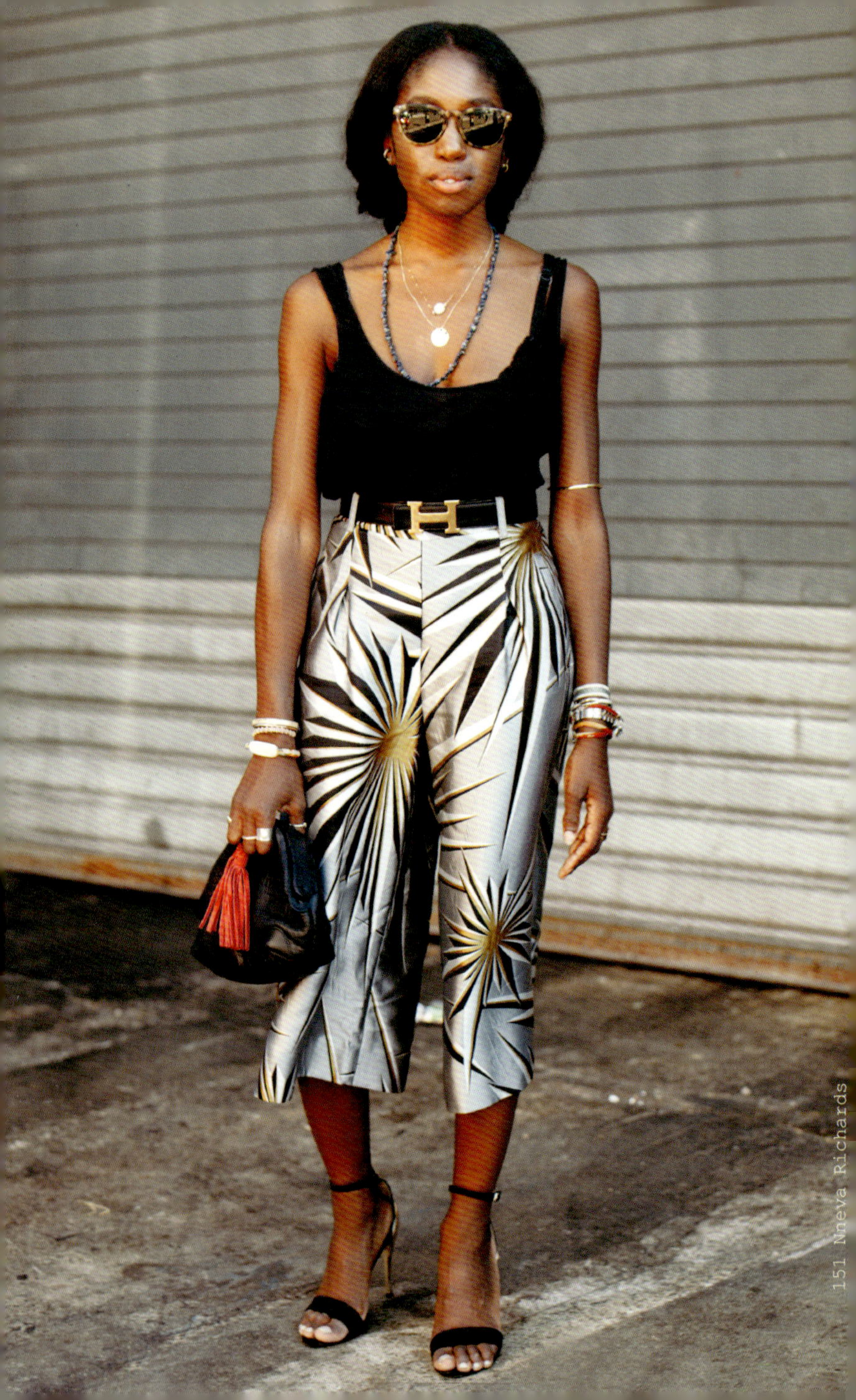

151 Nneva Richards

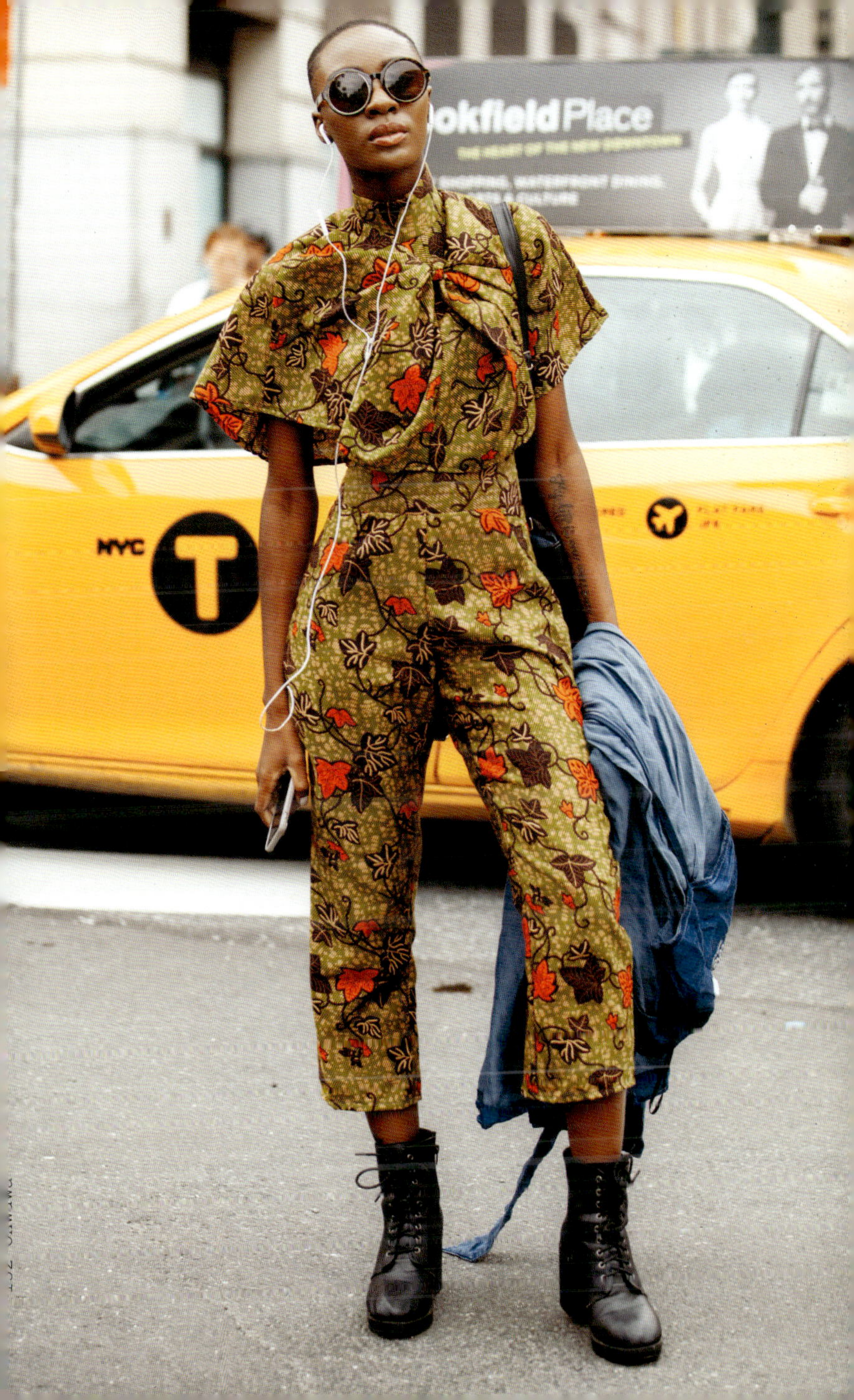
okfield Place
NYC
T

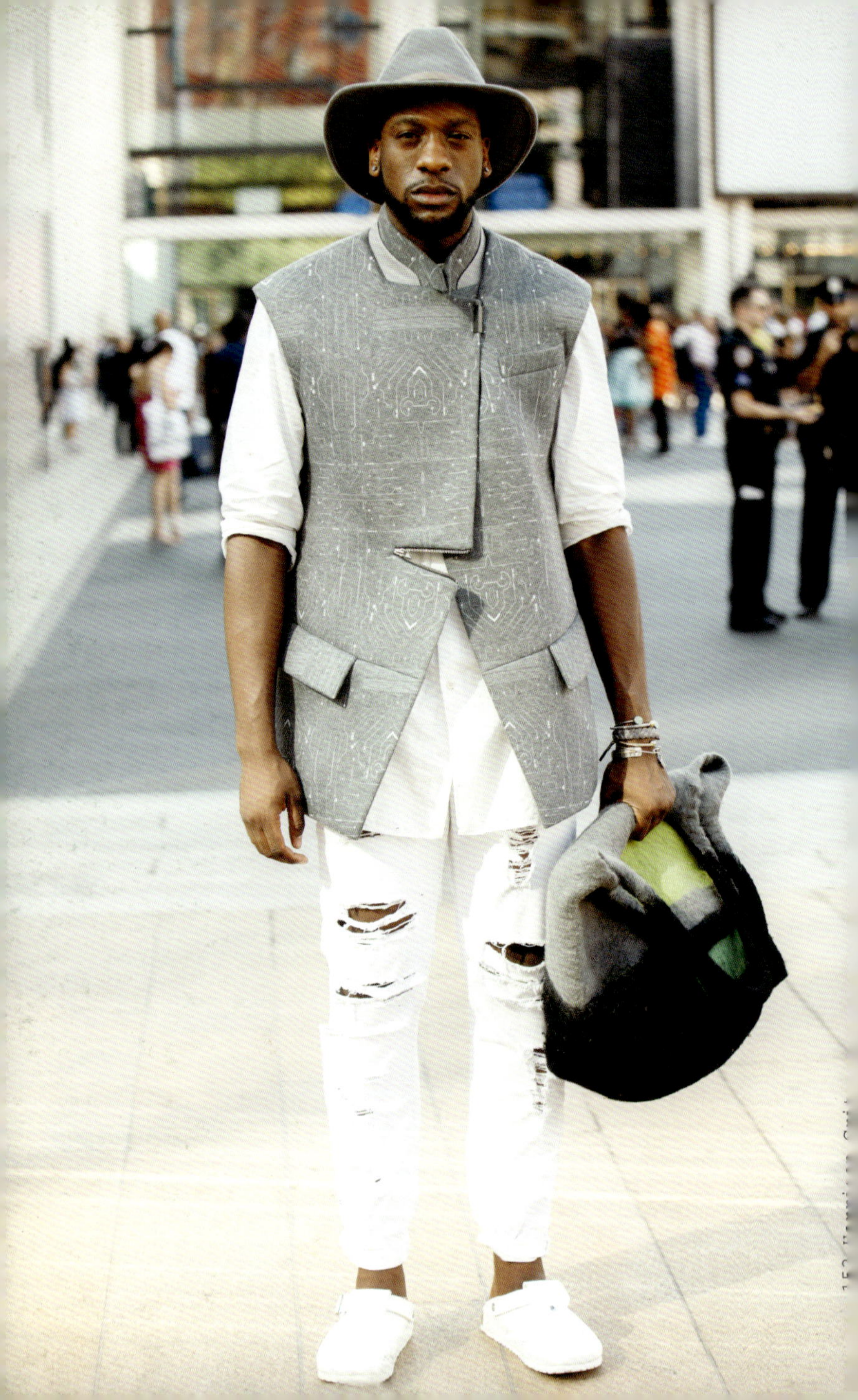

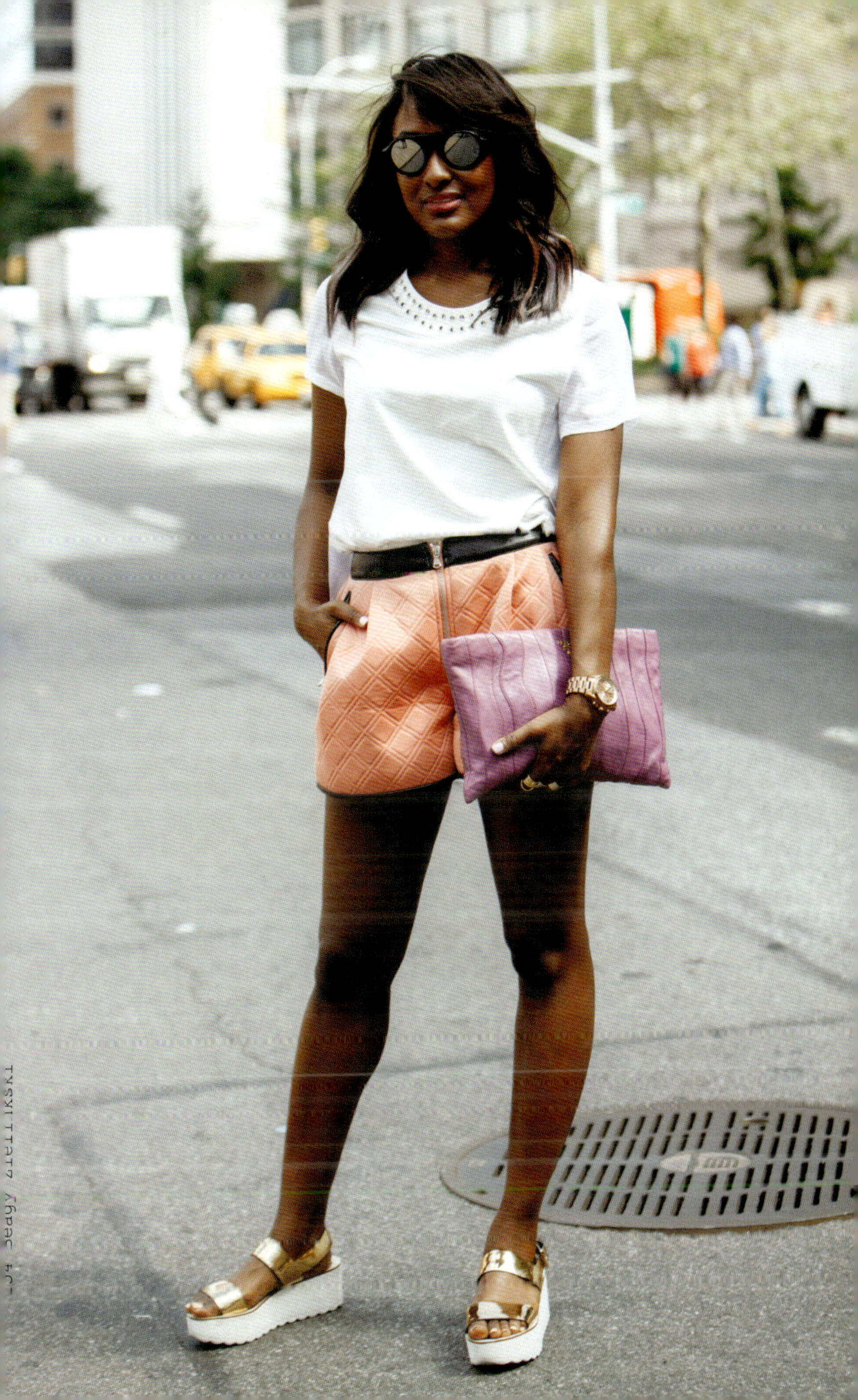

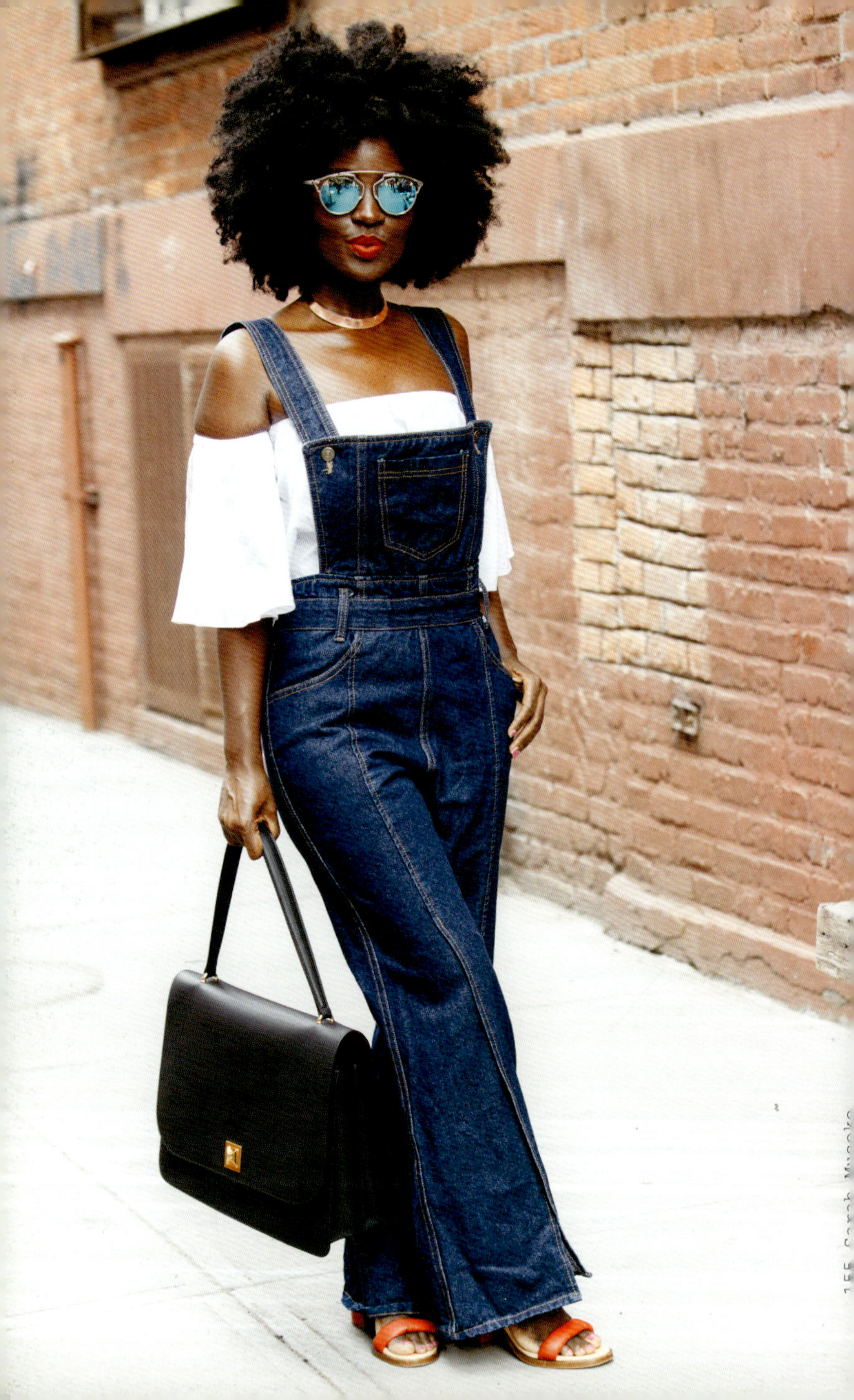

155 Sarah

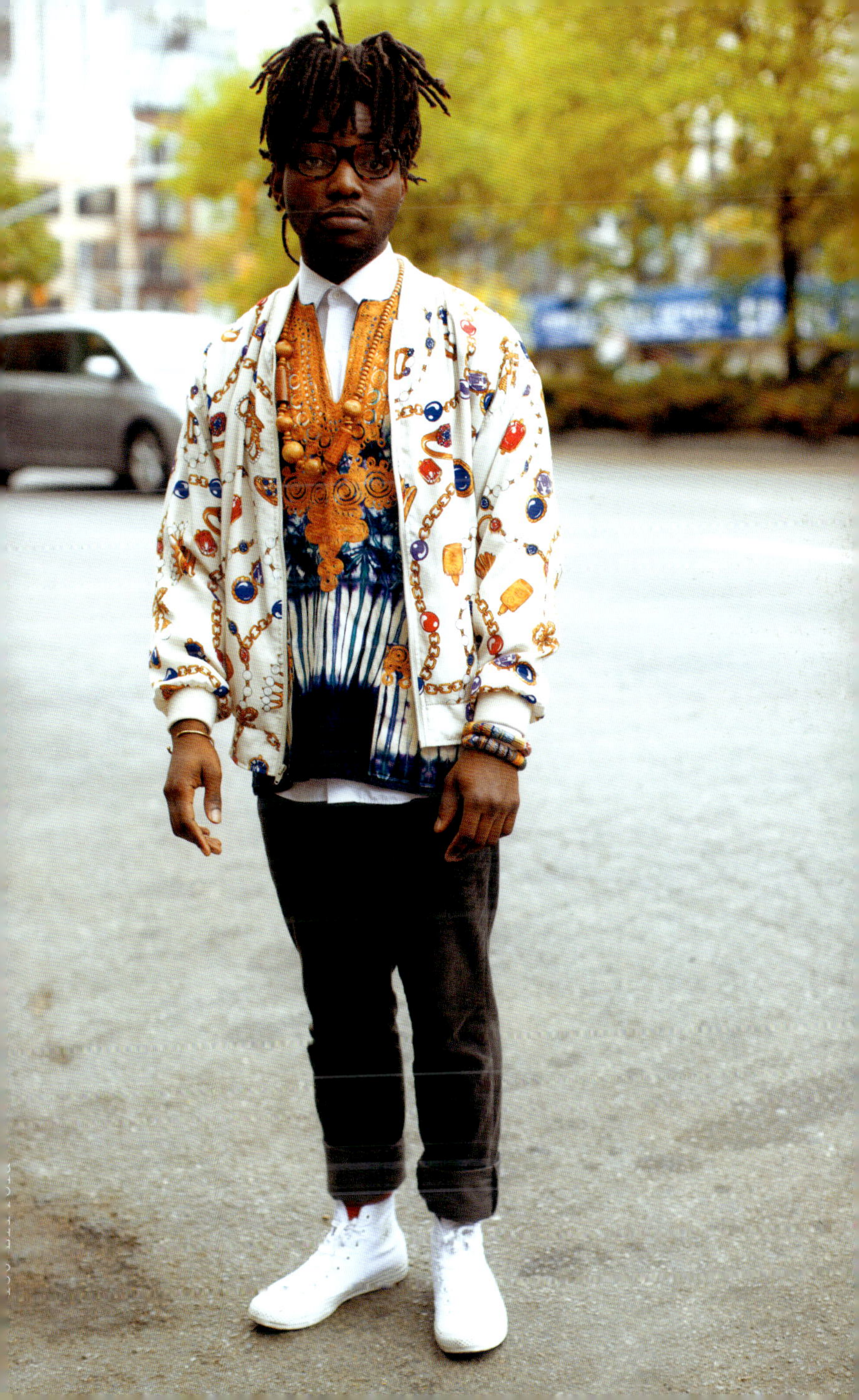

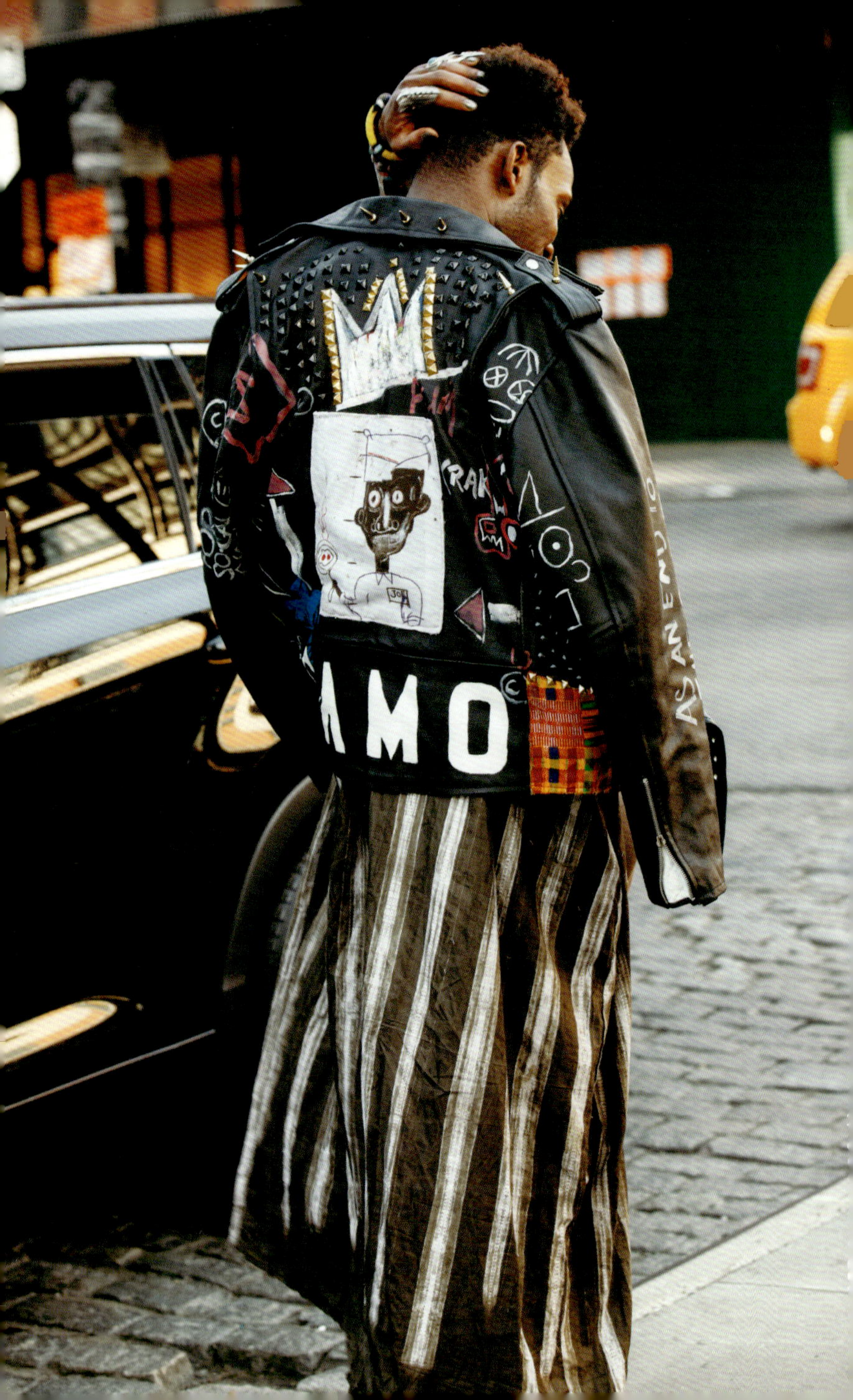
AMO
AS AN END TO

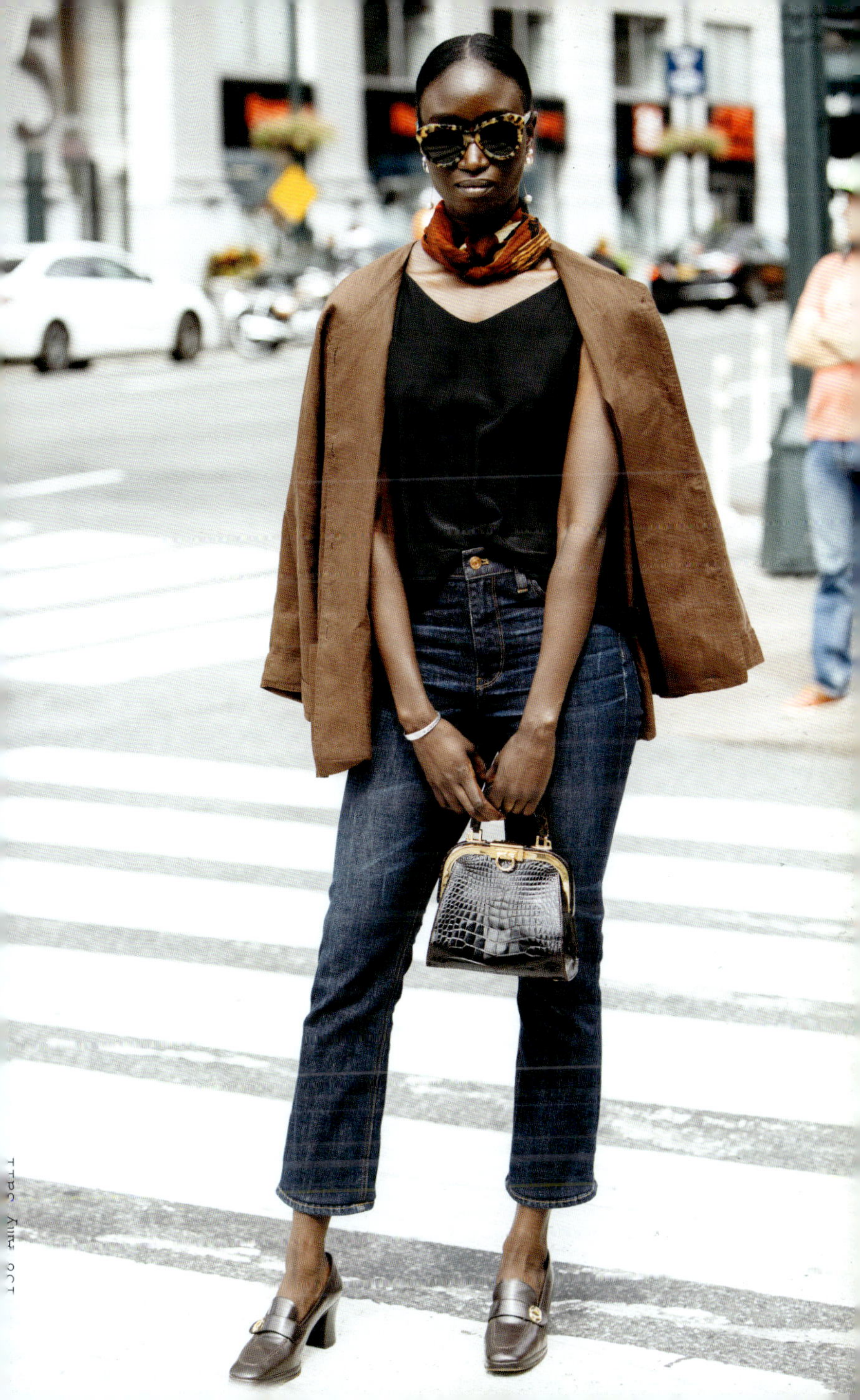

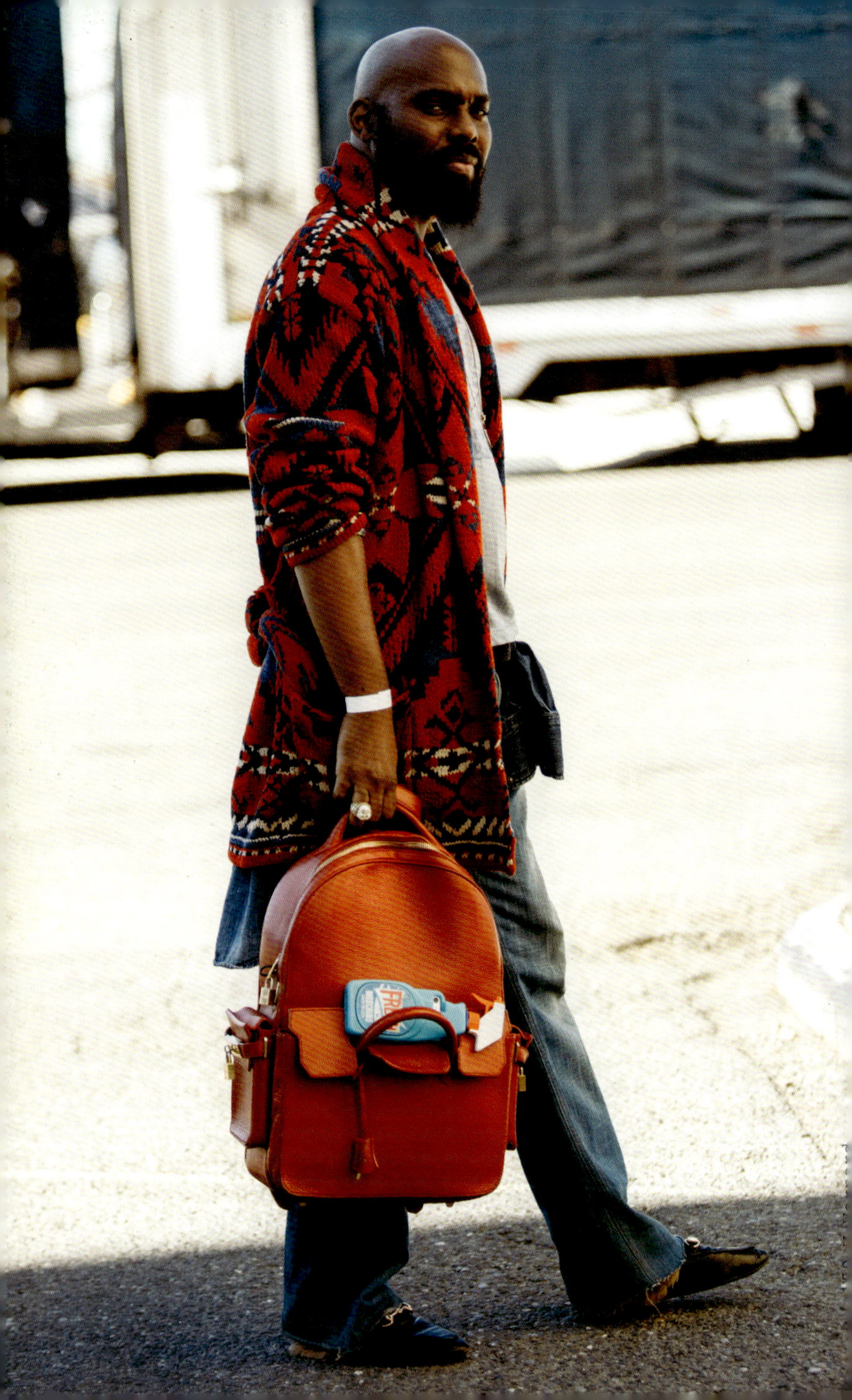

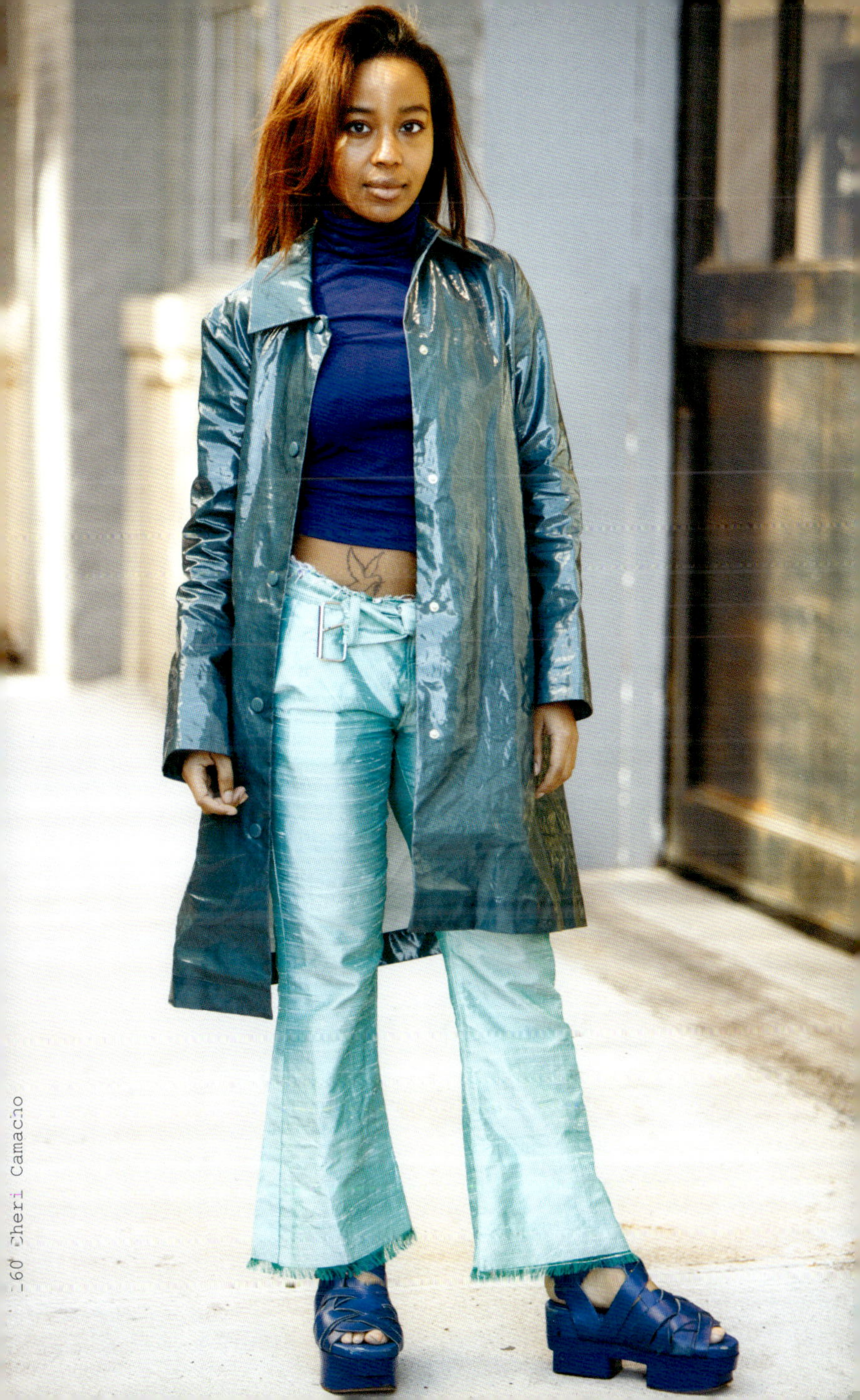

160 Cheri Camacho

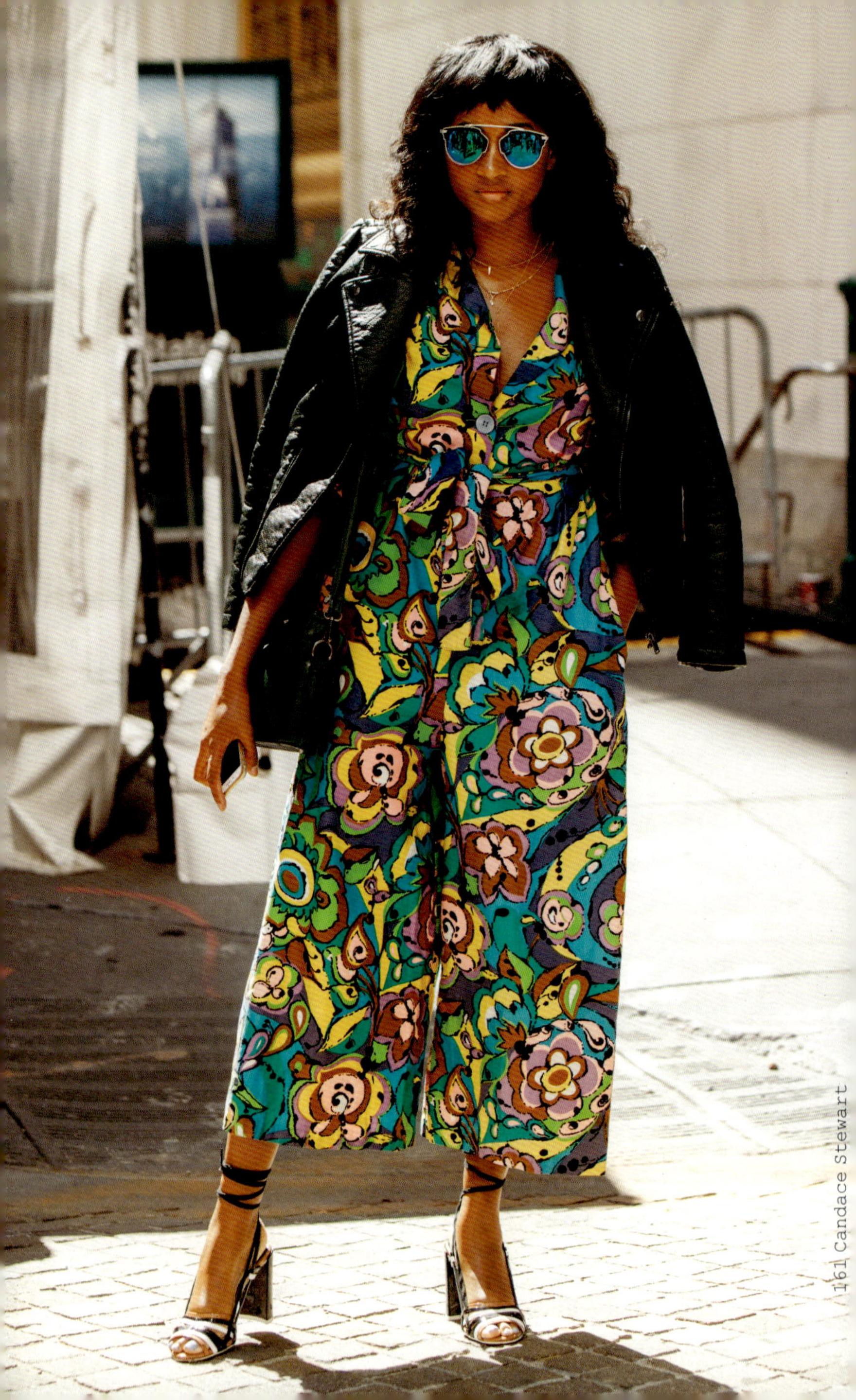

161 Candace Stewart

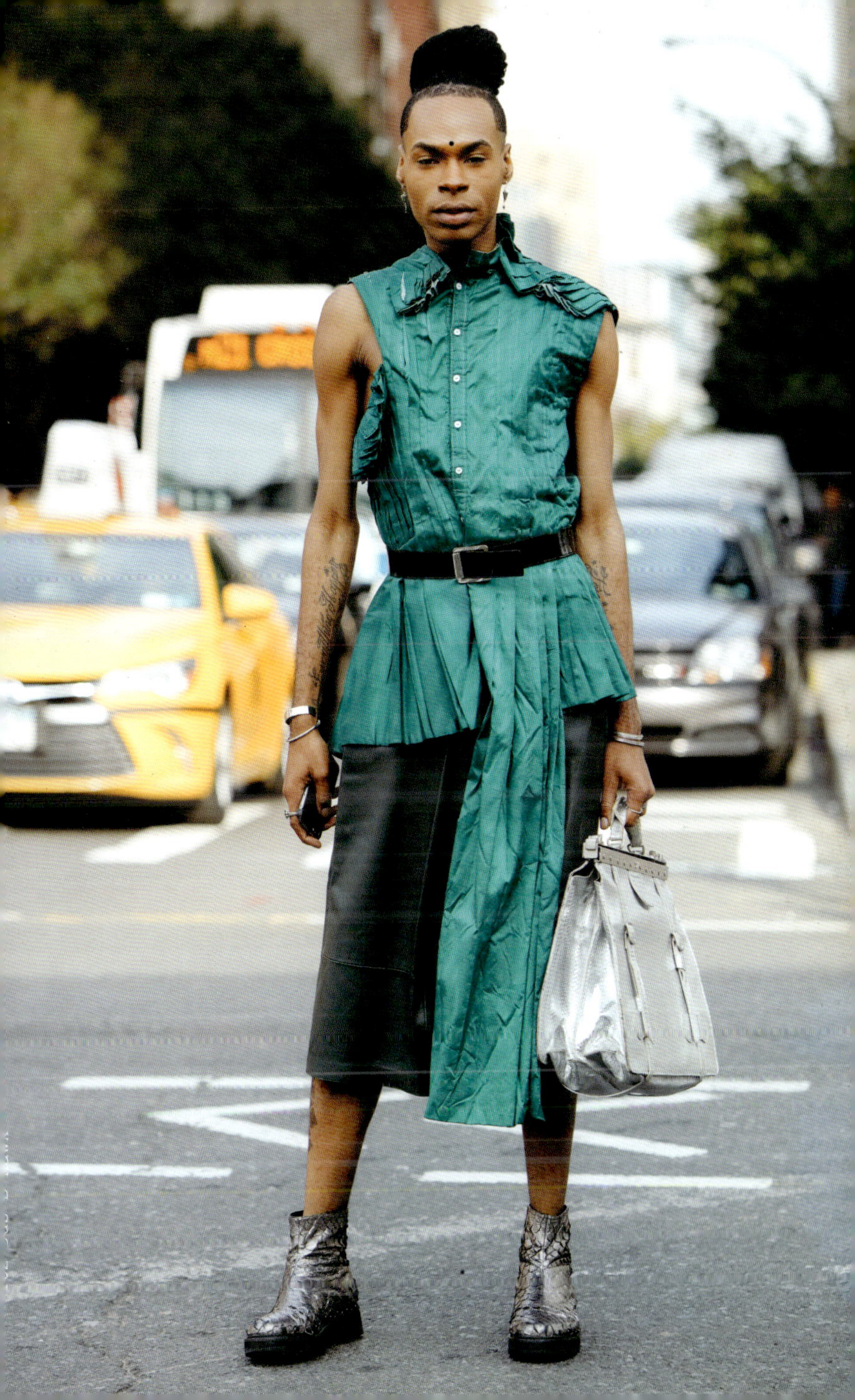

"My style is always evolving with whatever is going on in my life."

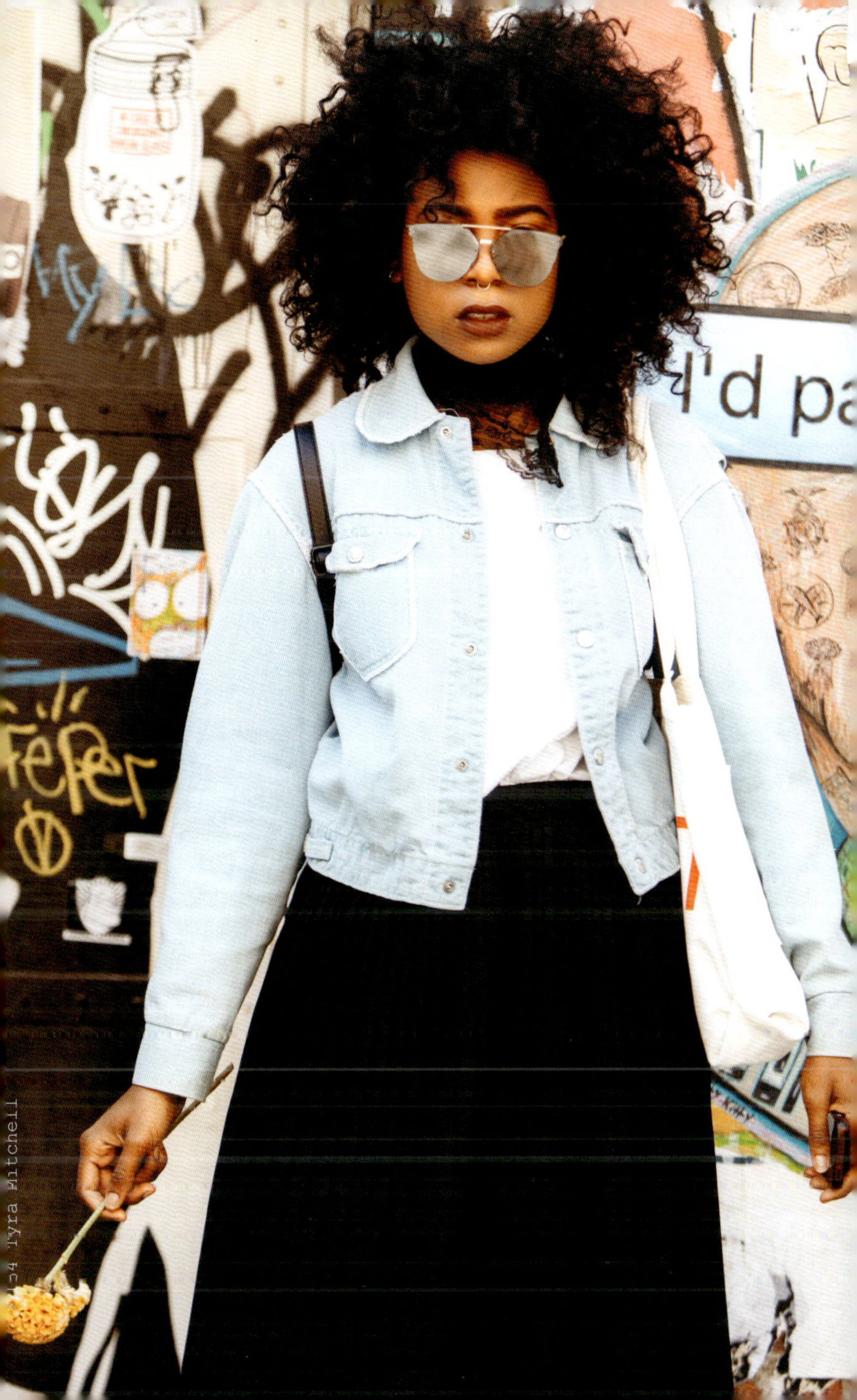
I'd pa

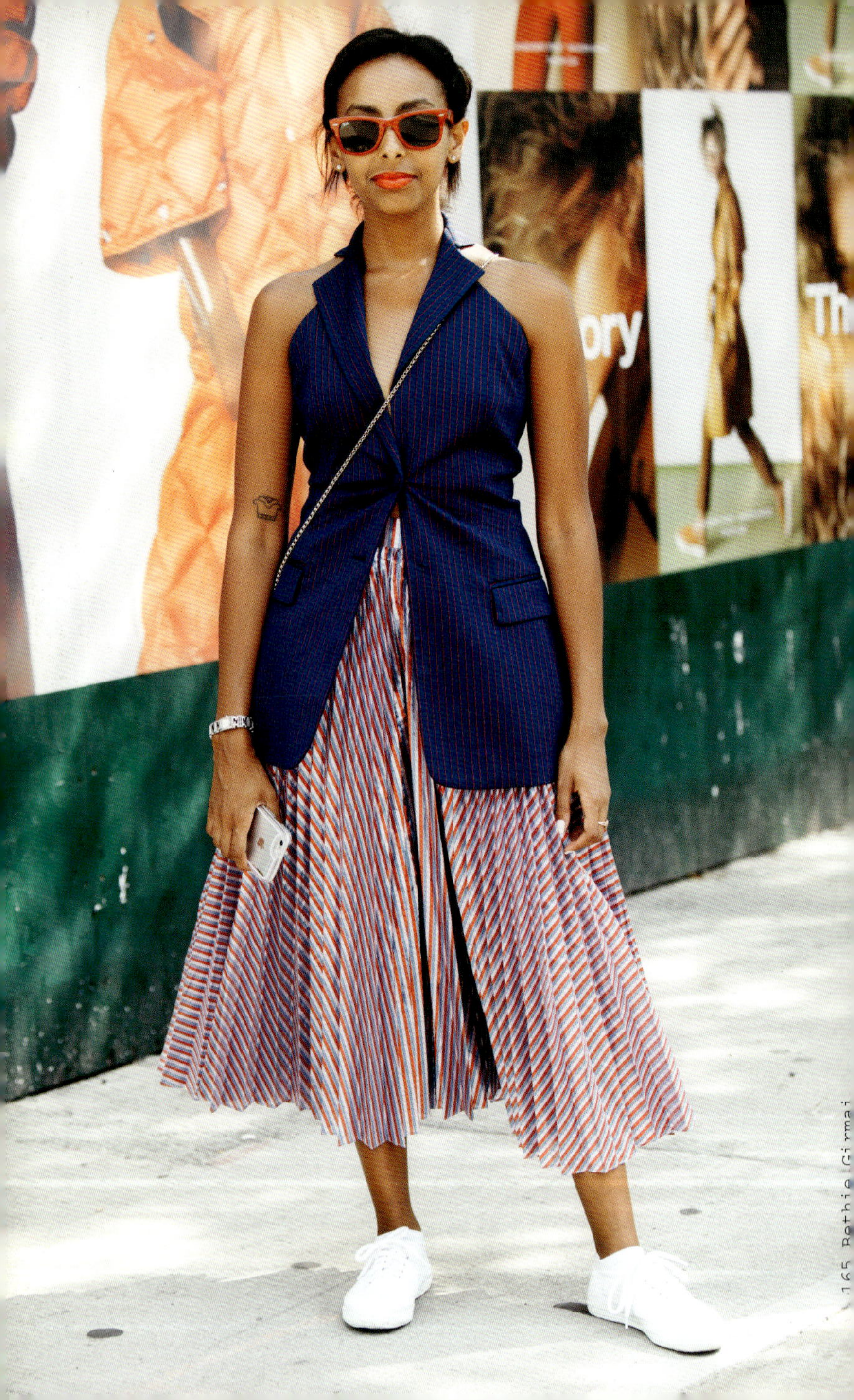

165 Bethie Girmai

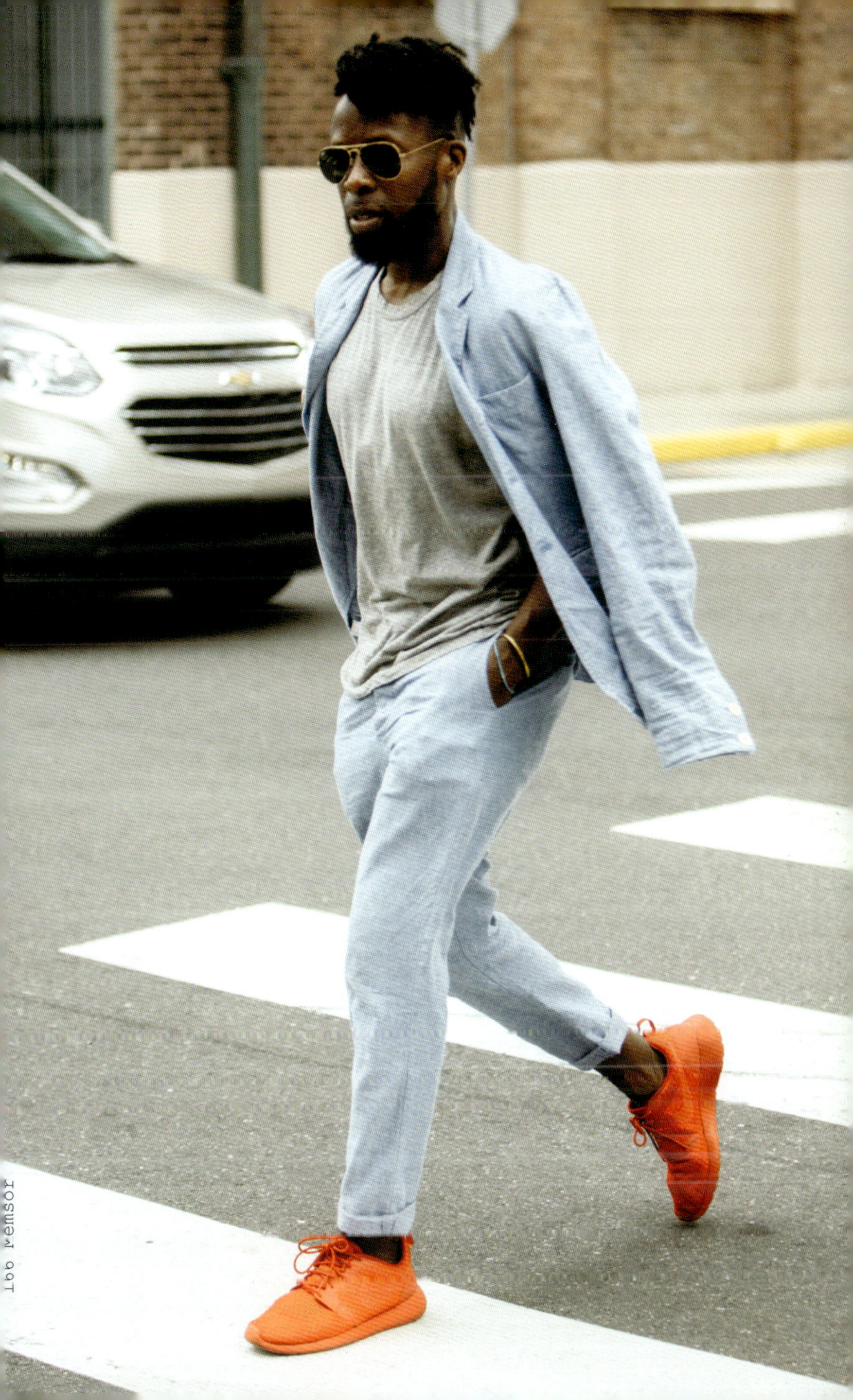

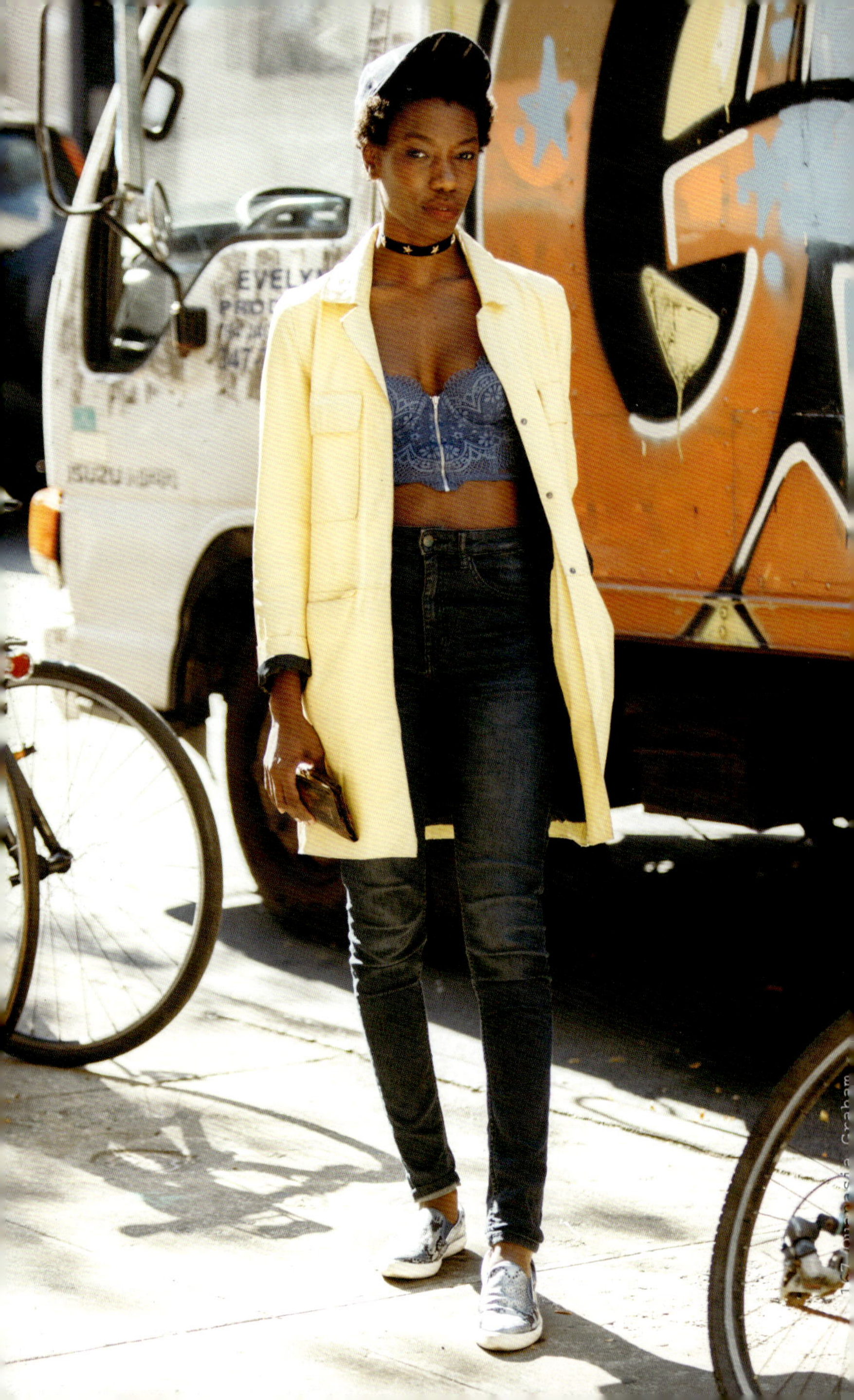

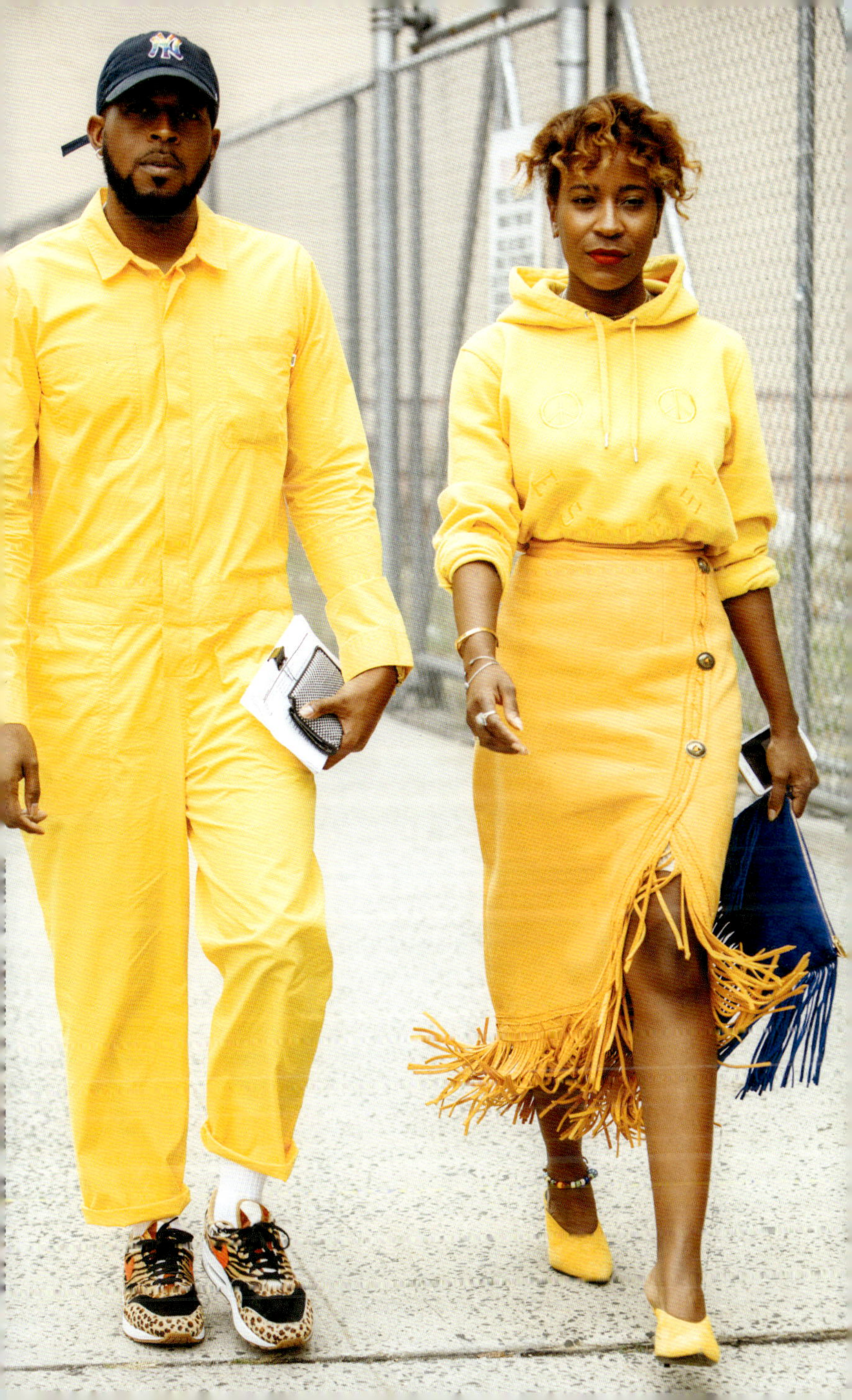

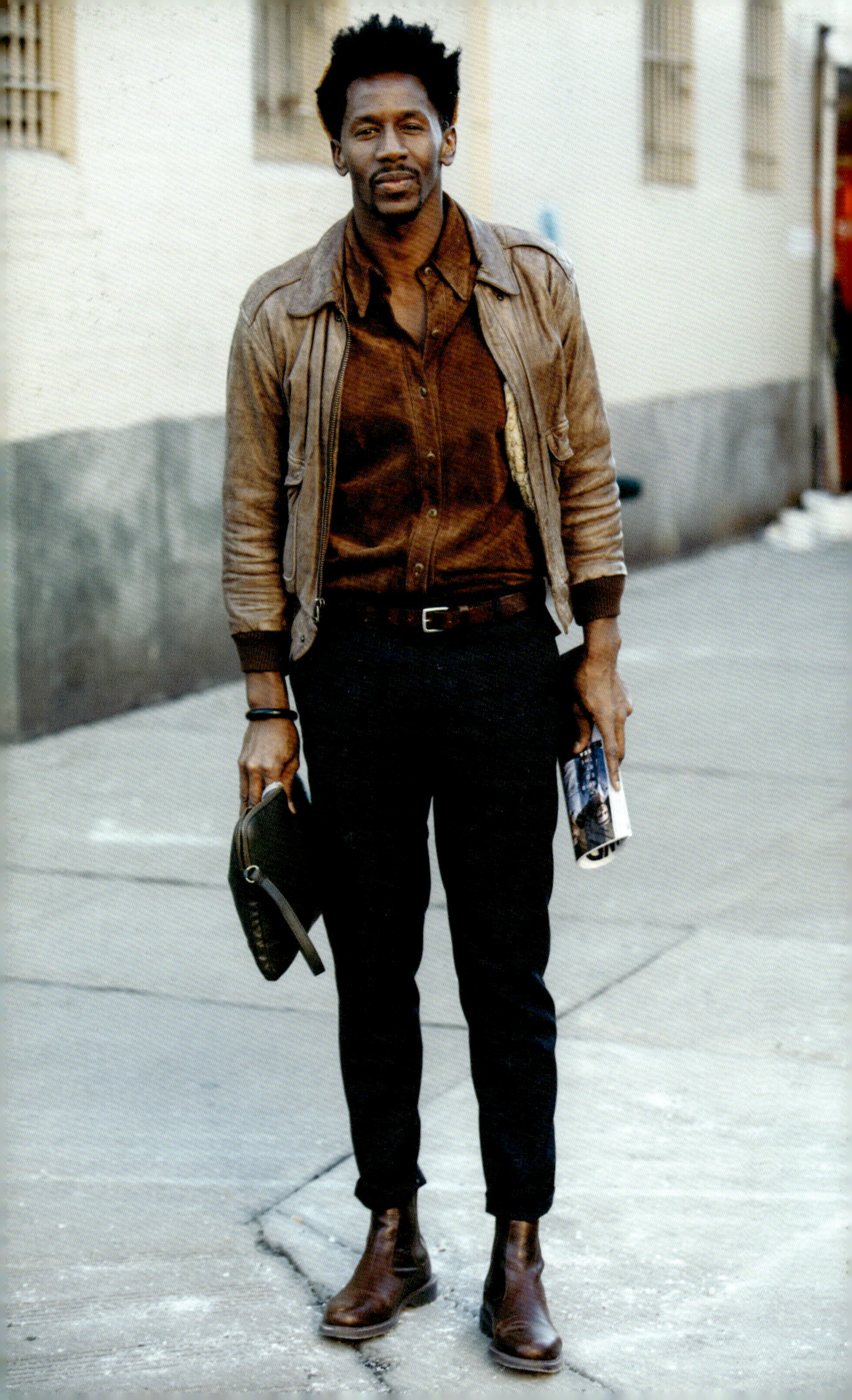

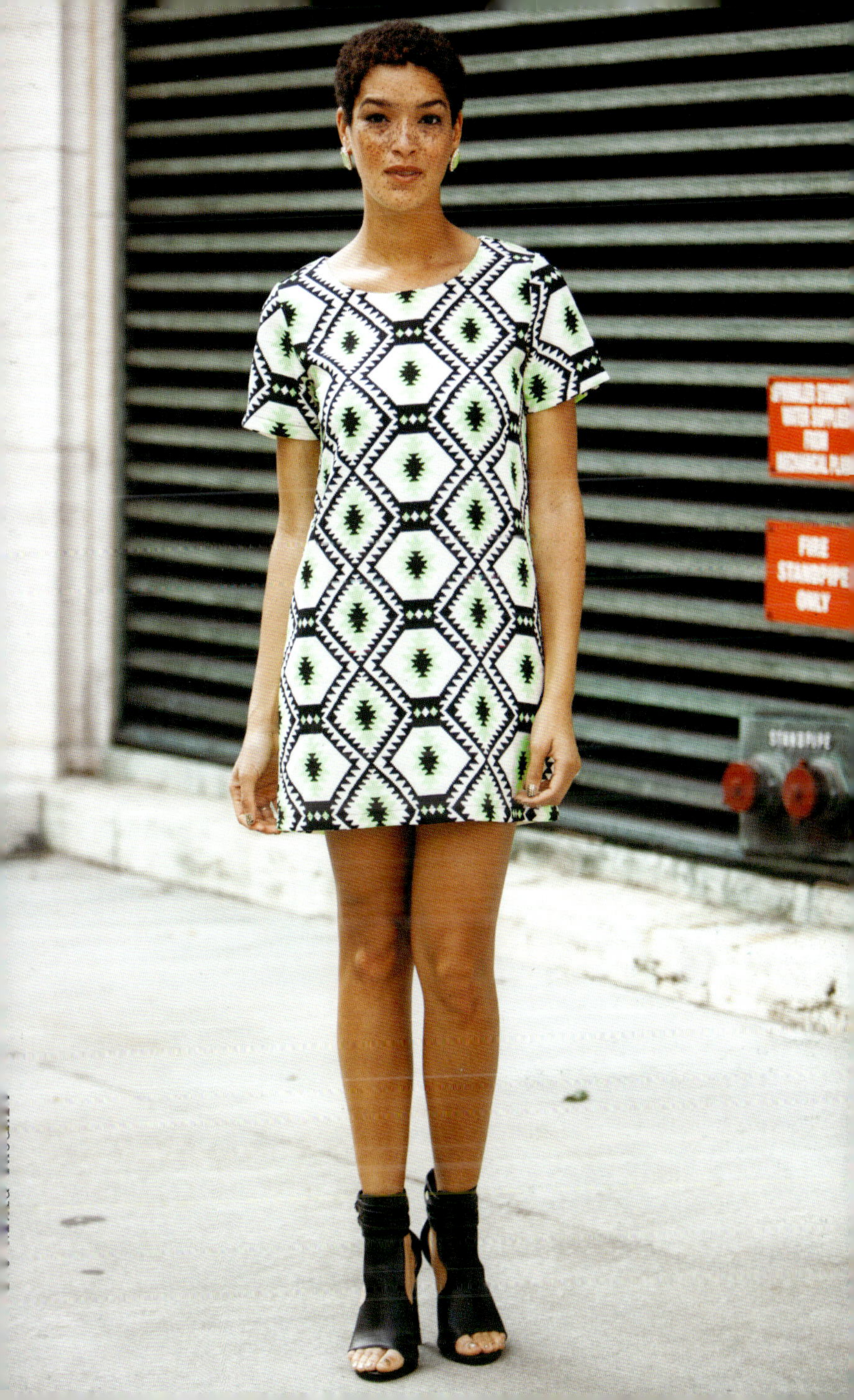
FIRE
STANDPIPE
ONLY
STANDPIPE

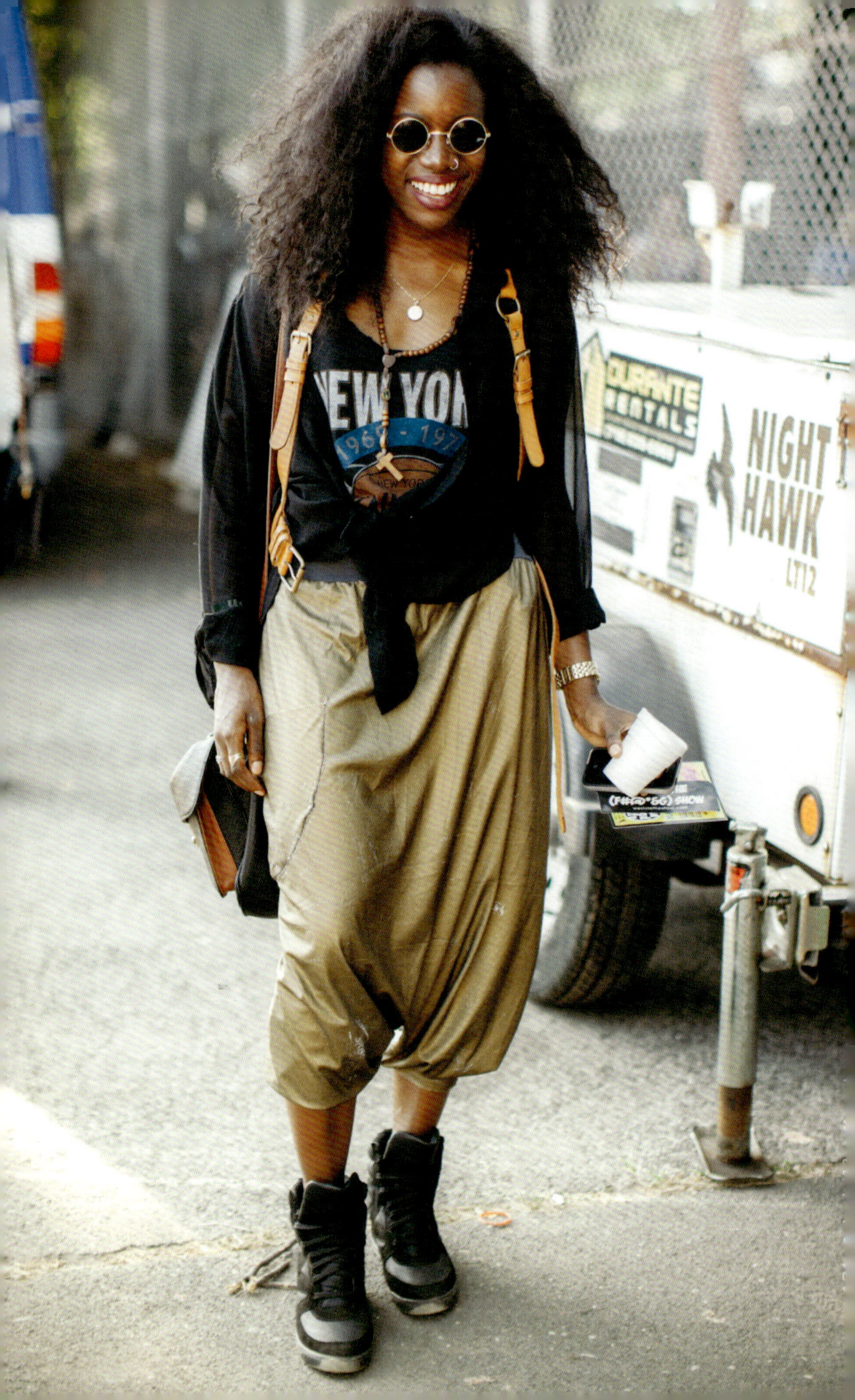
NIGHT
HAWK
LT12

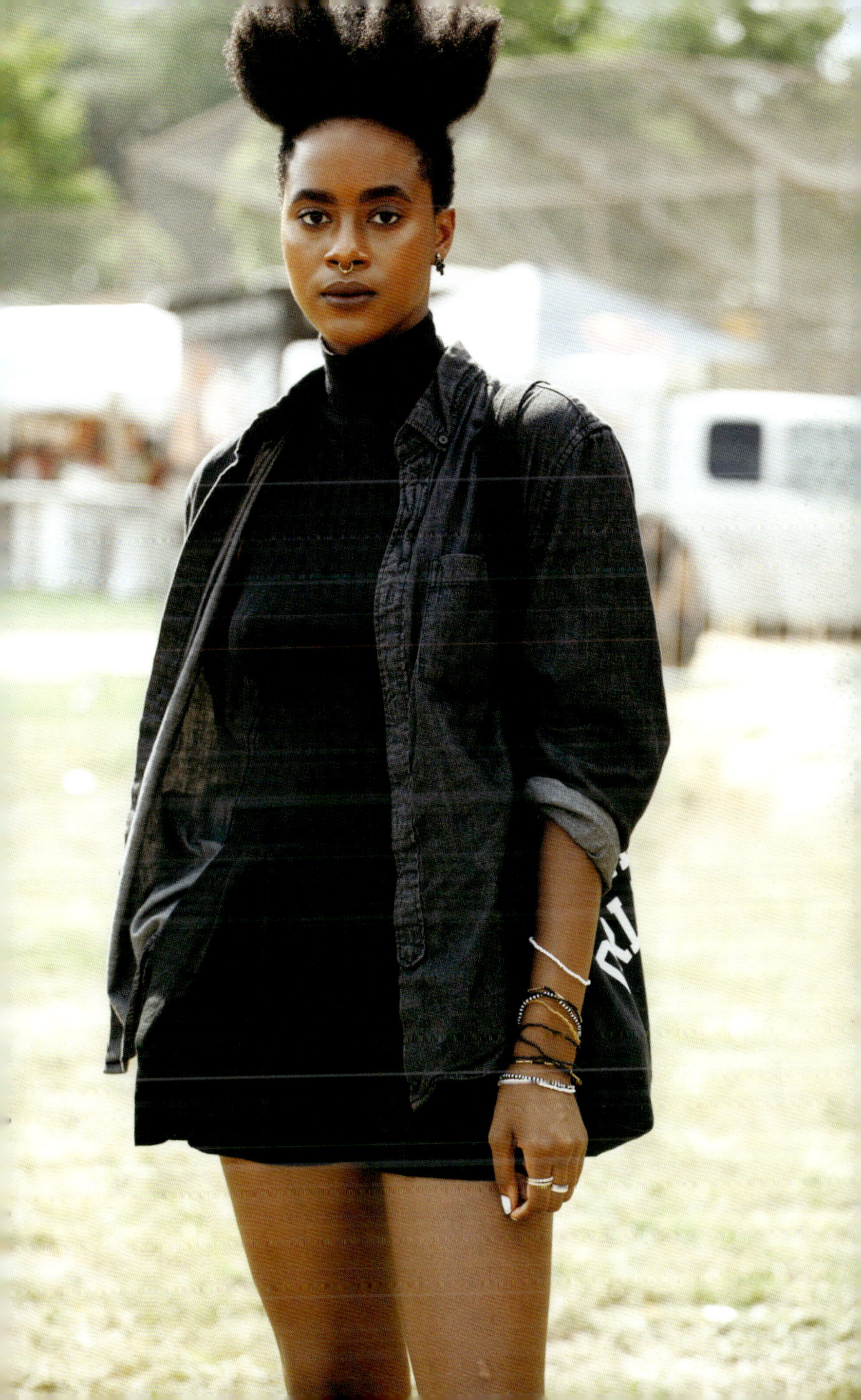

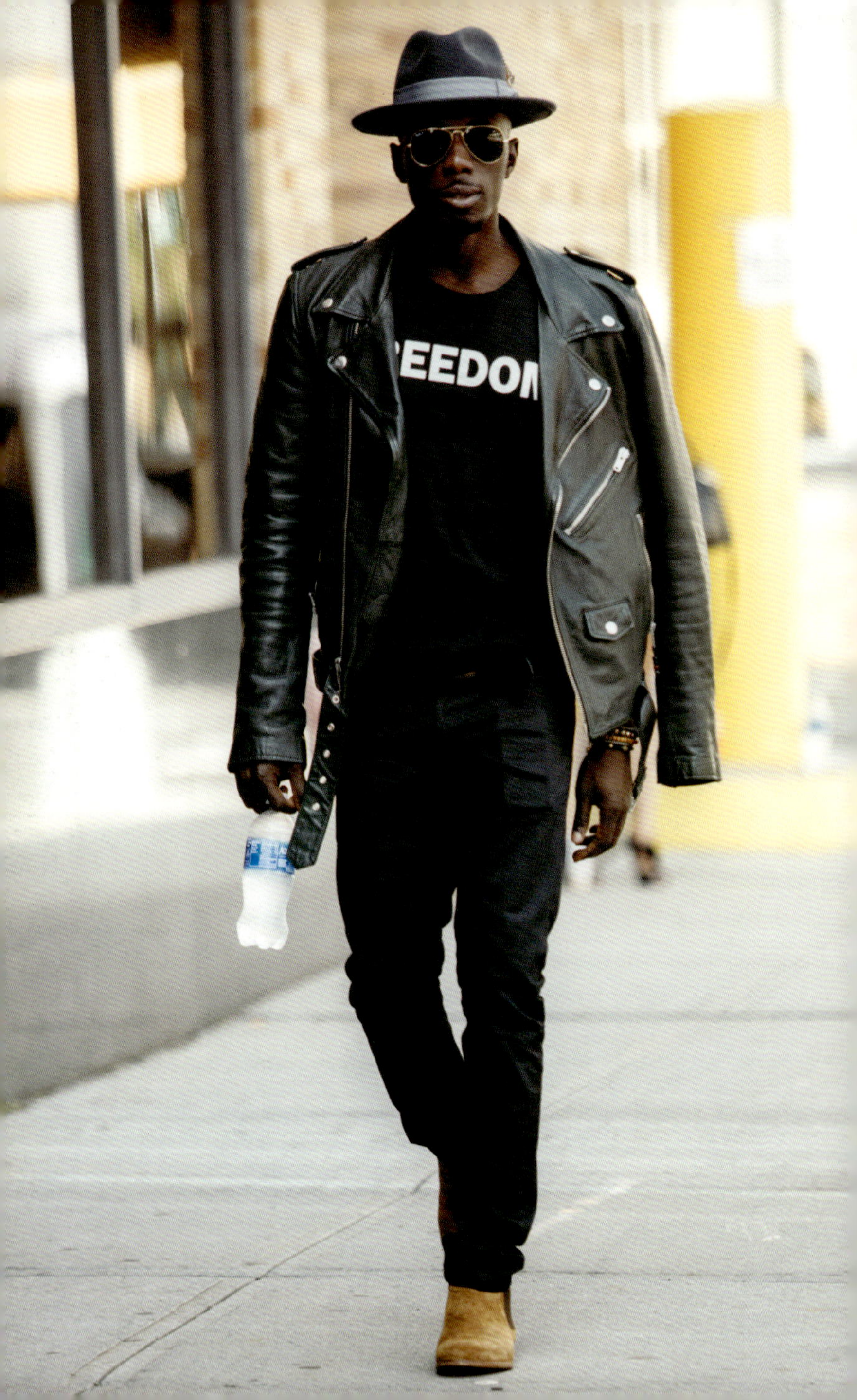
EEDOM

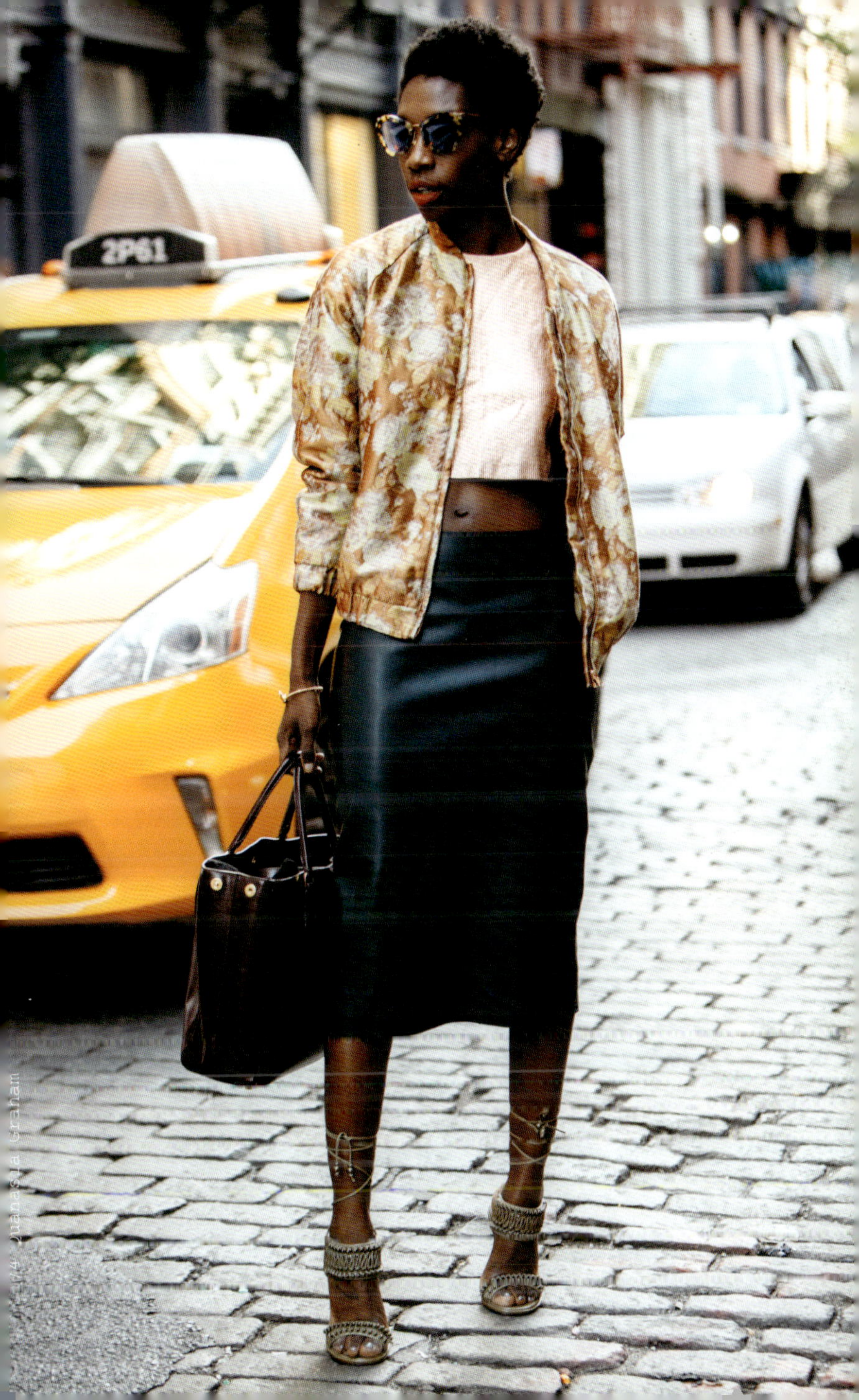
2P61

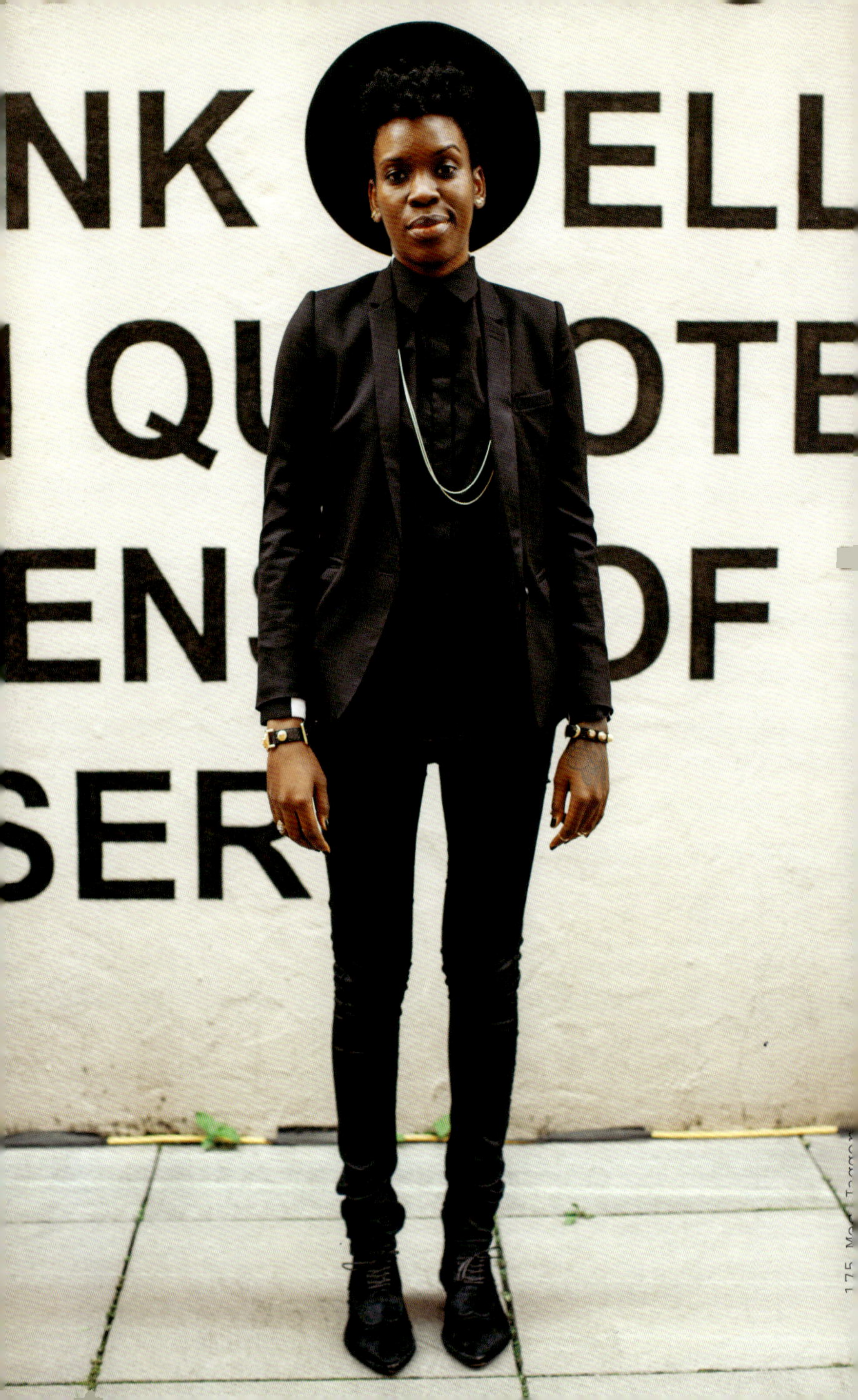

175

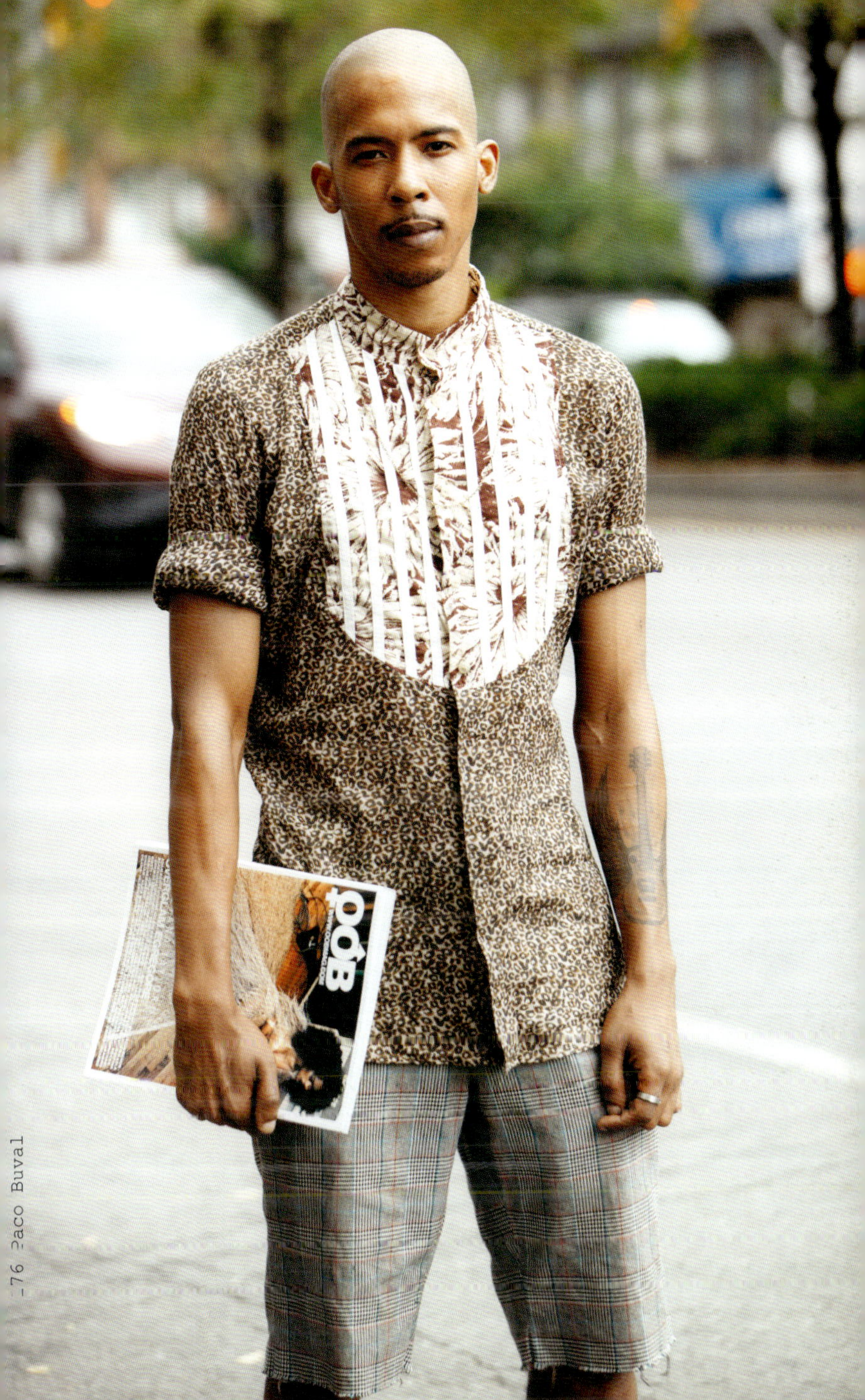

 Paco Buval

“My style and accessories are inspired by every goddess, princess, queen, past, present, and future.”

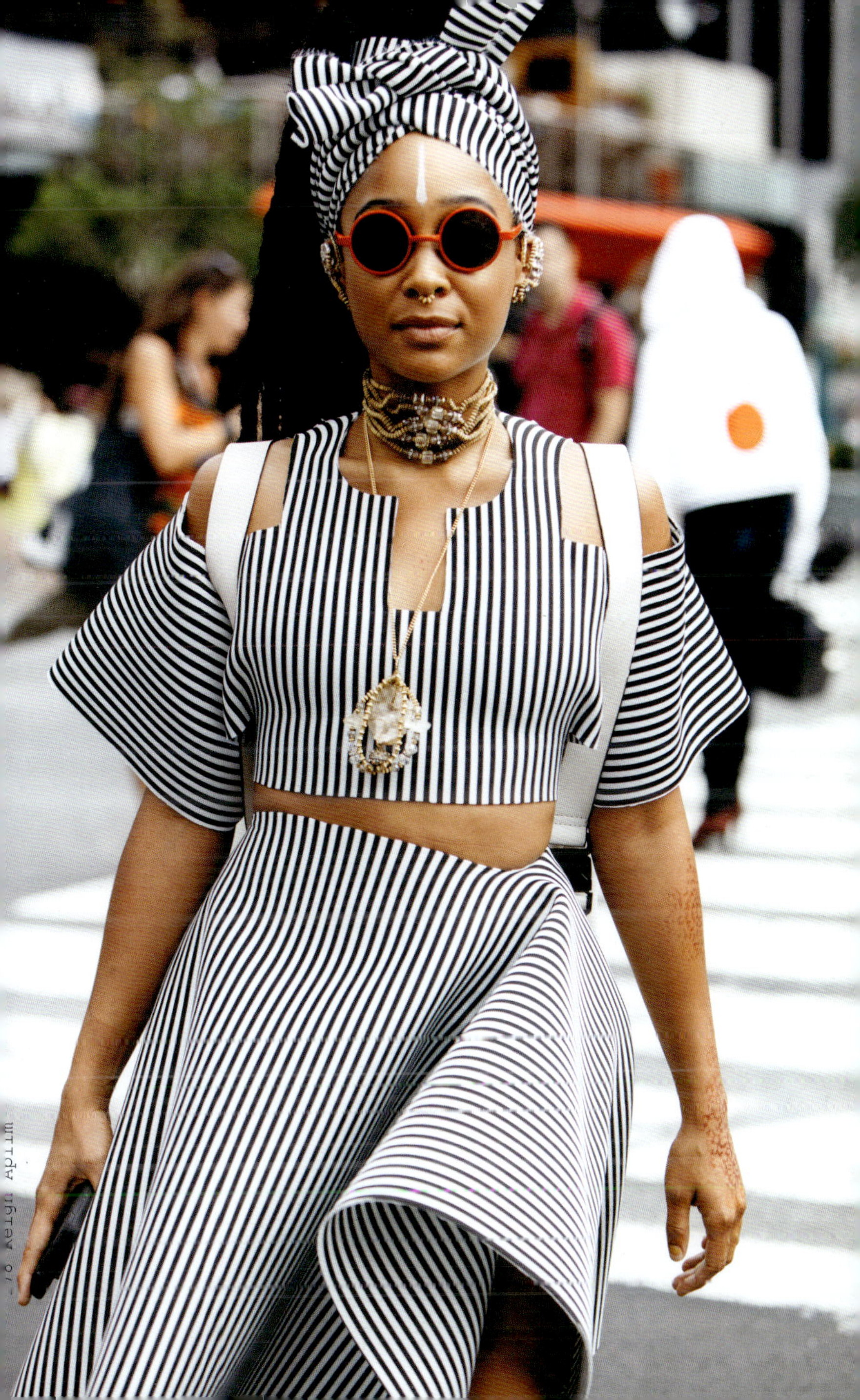

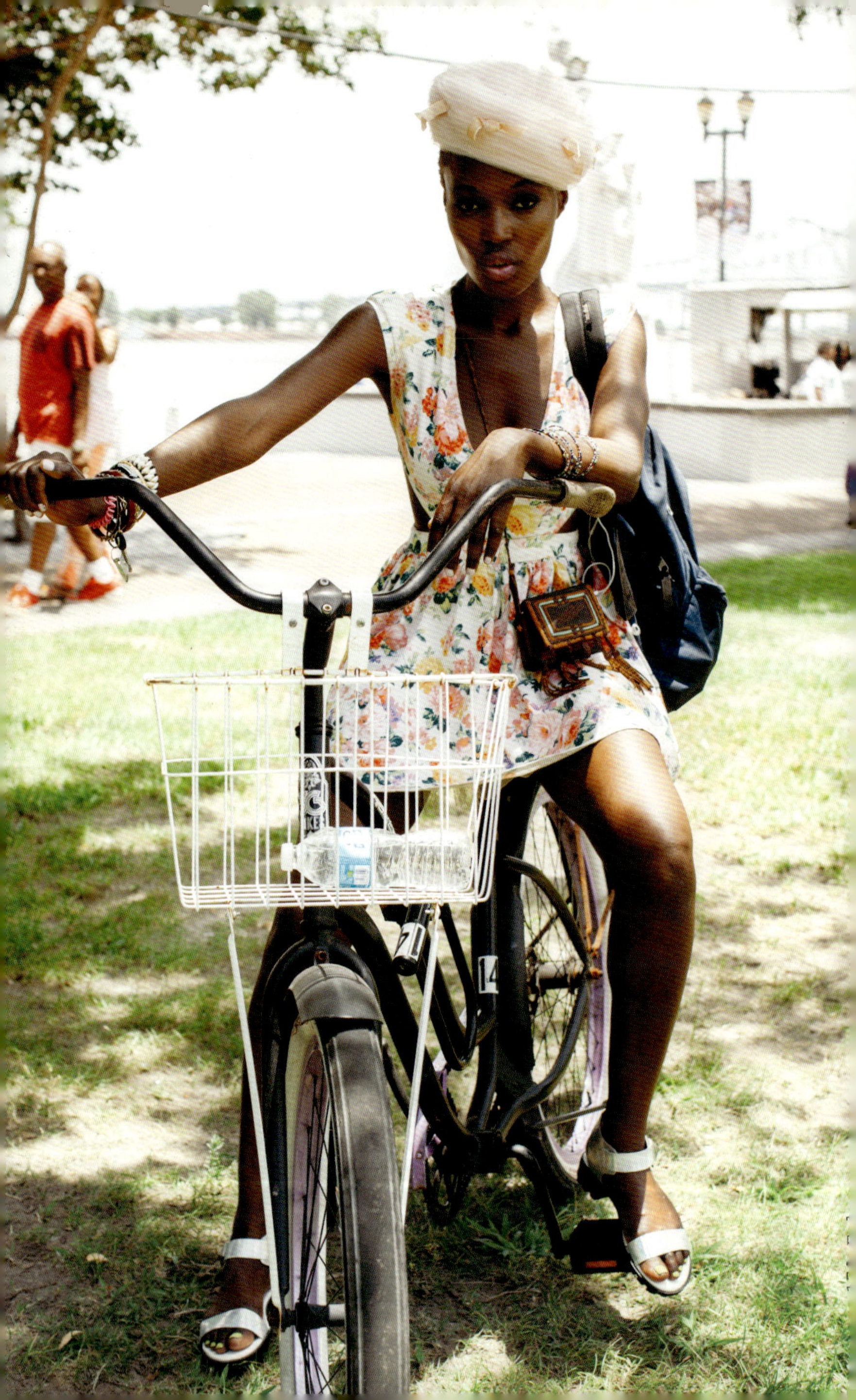

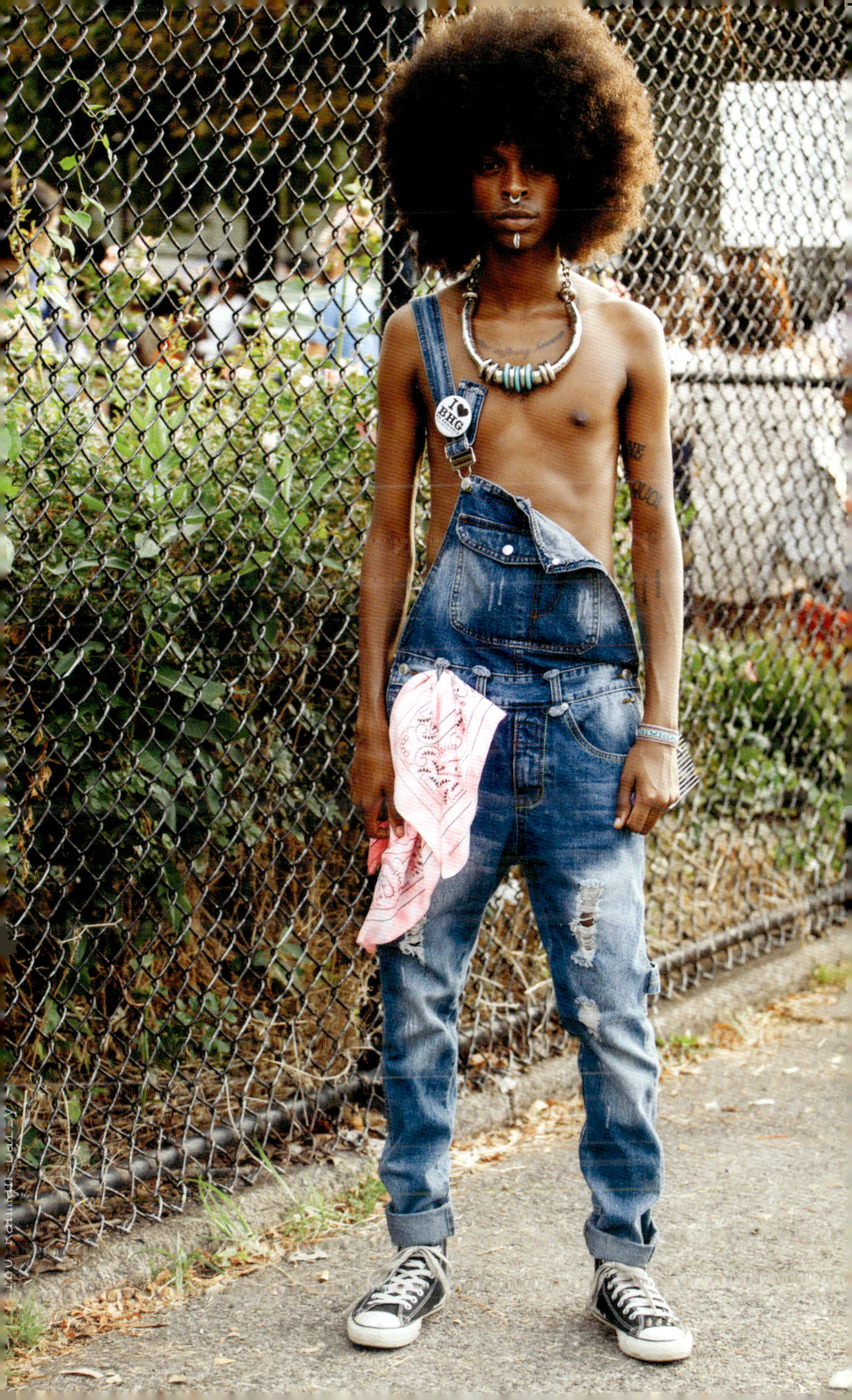
I ♥ BHG

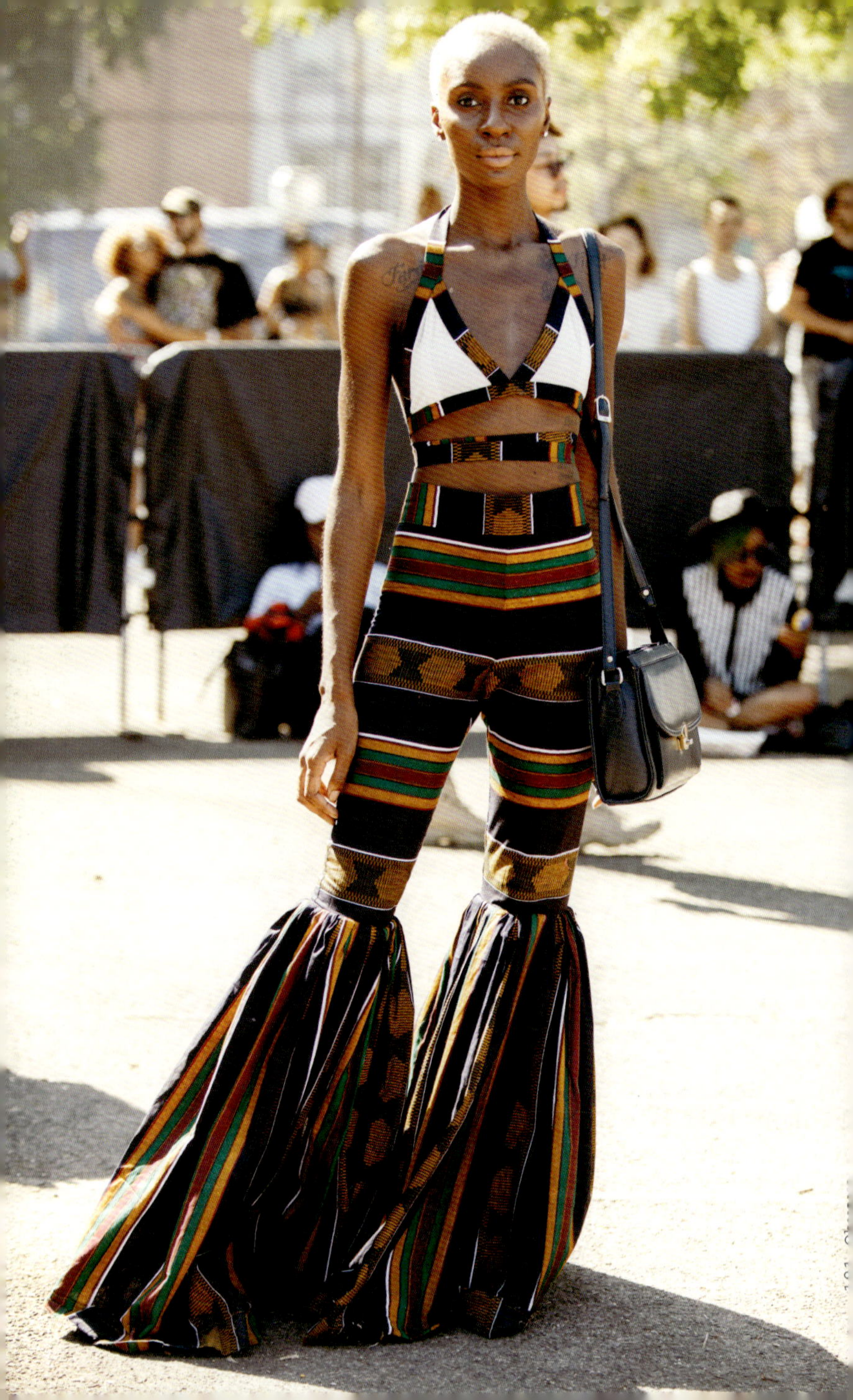

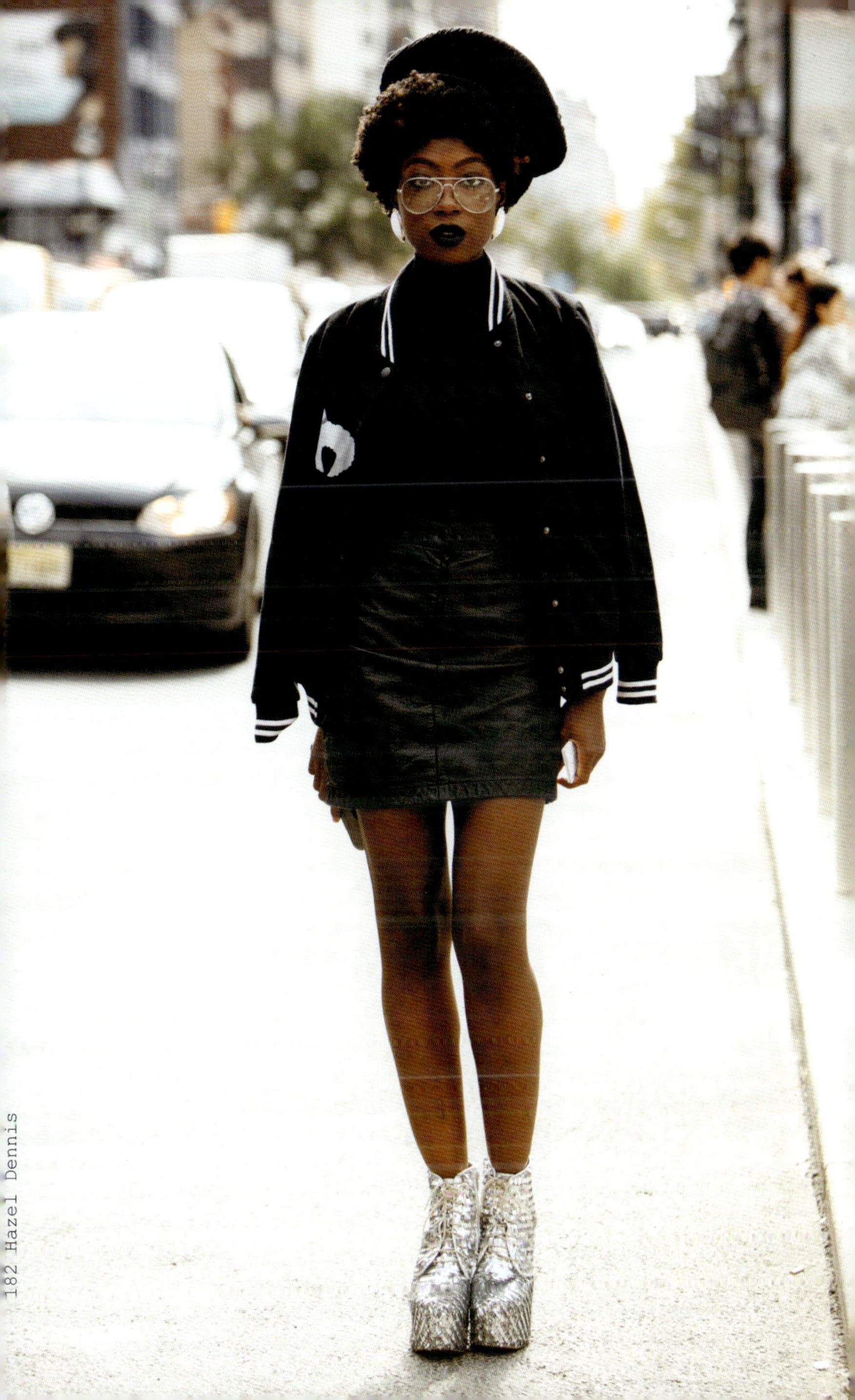

182 Hazel Dennis

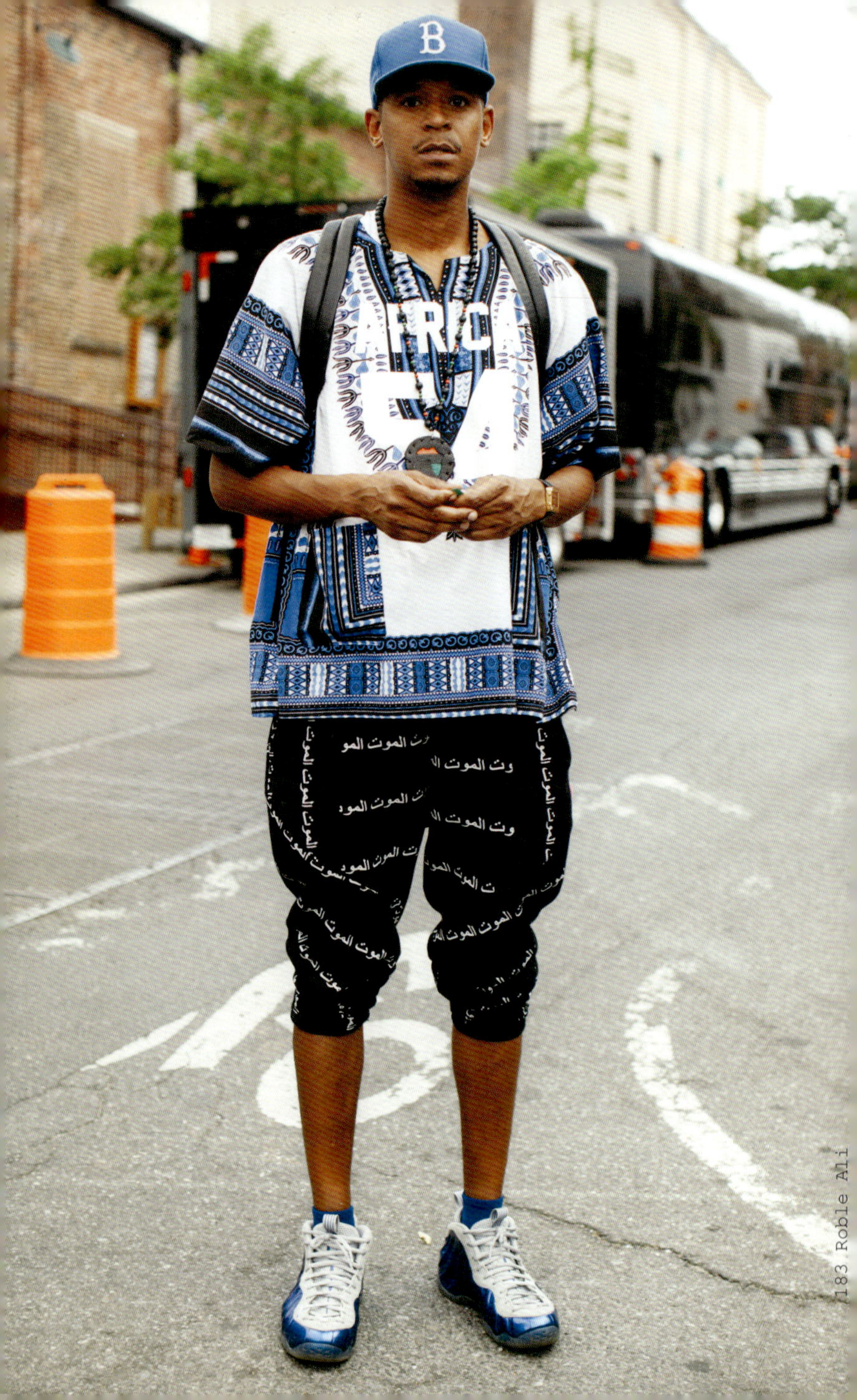

183 Roble Ali

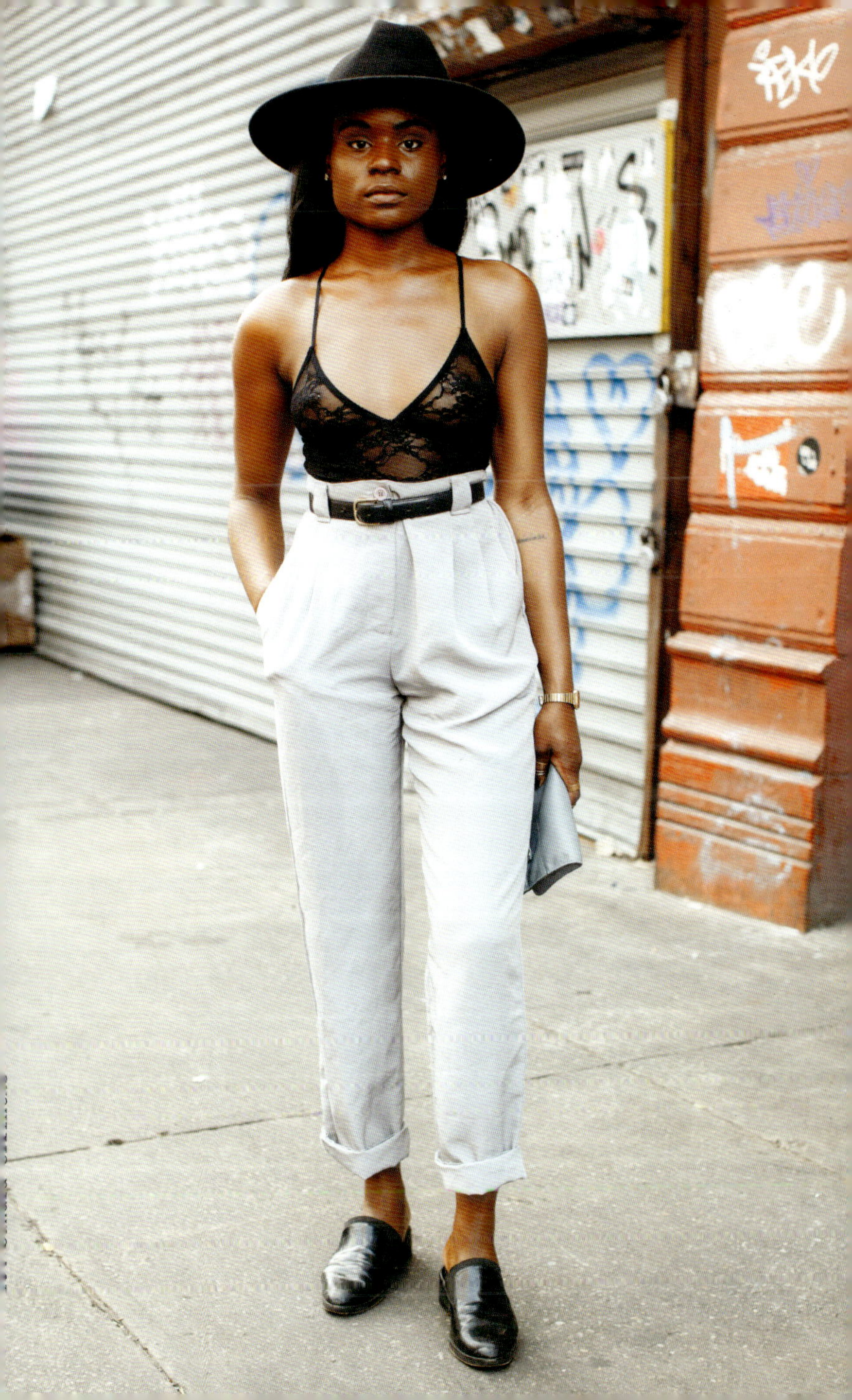

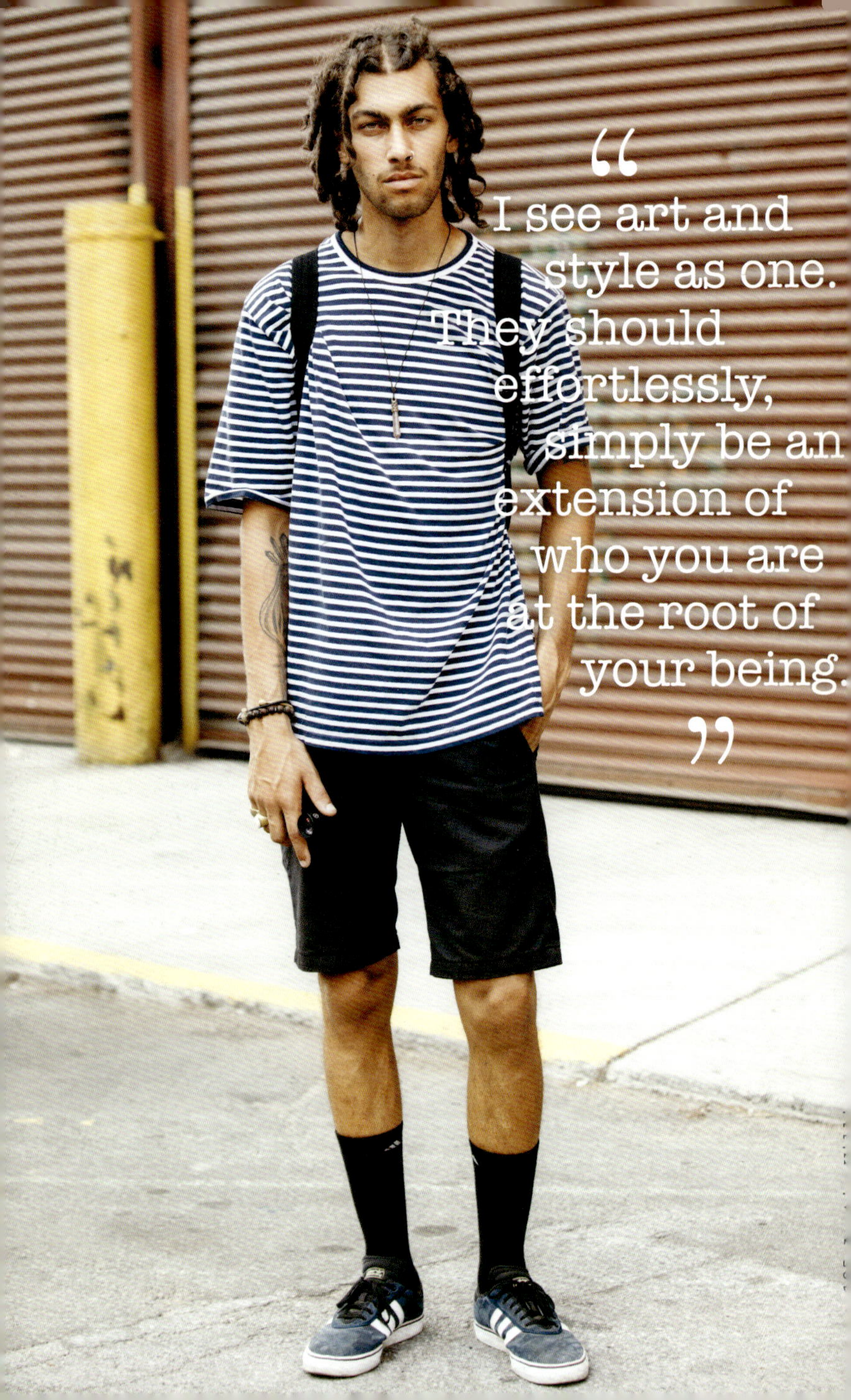
“
I see art and
style as one.
They should
effortlessly,
simply be an
extension of
who you are
at the root of
your being.
”

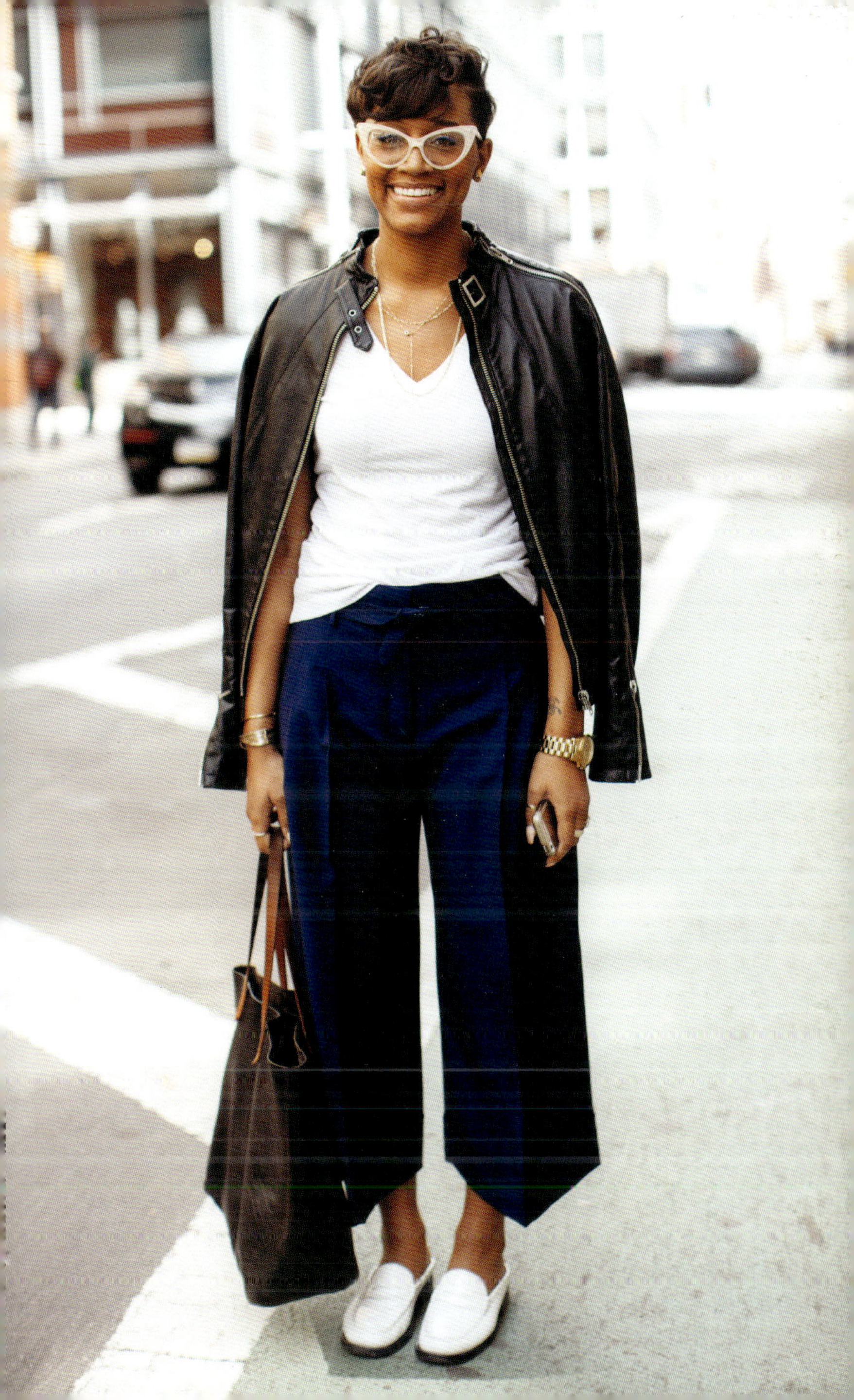

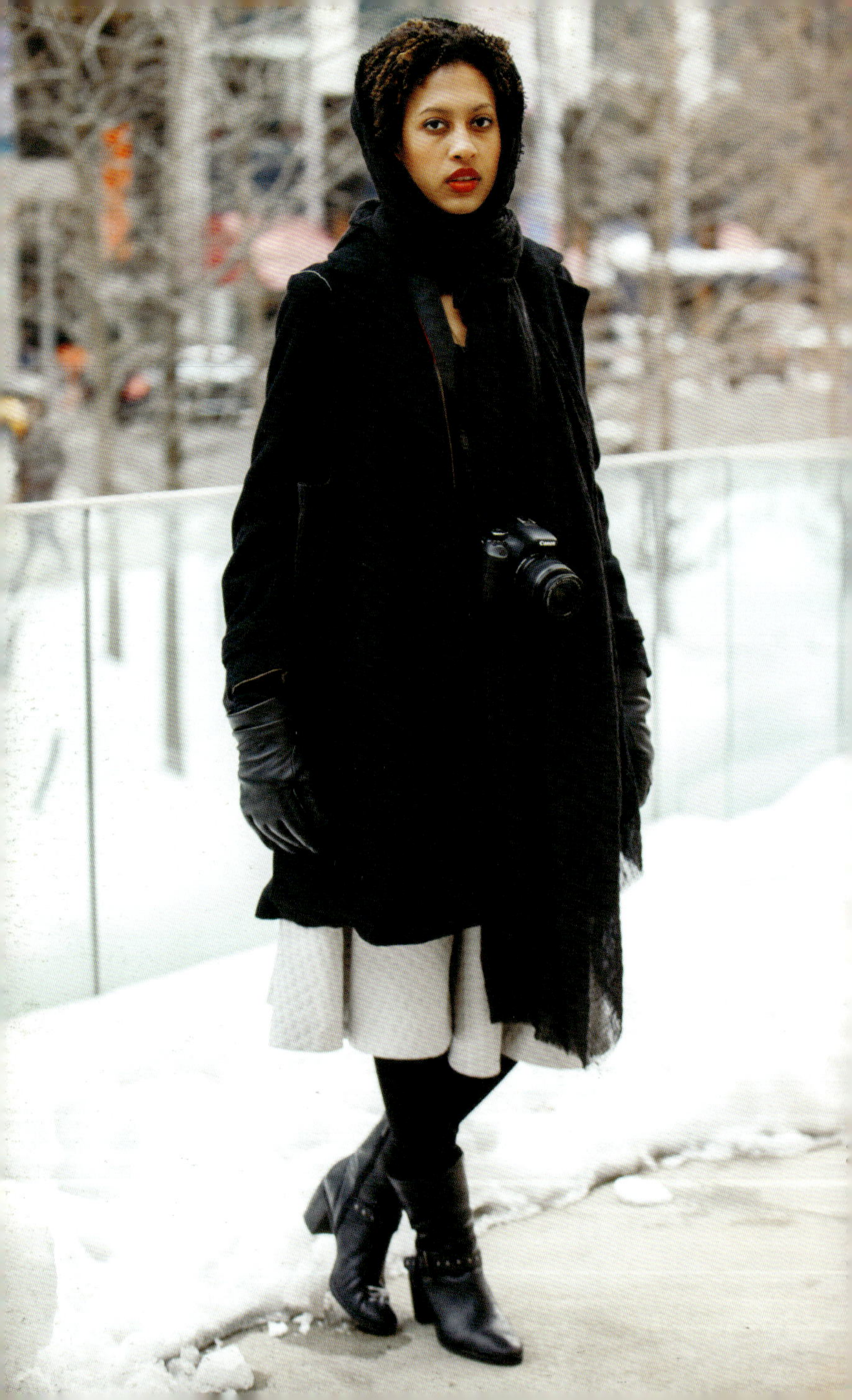

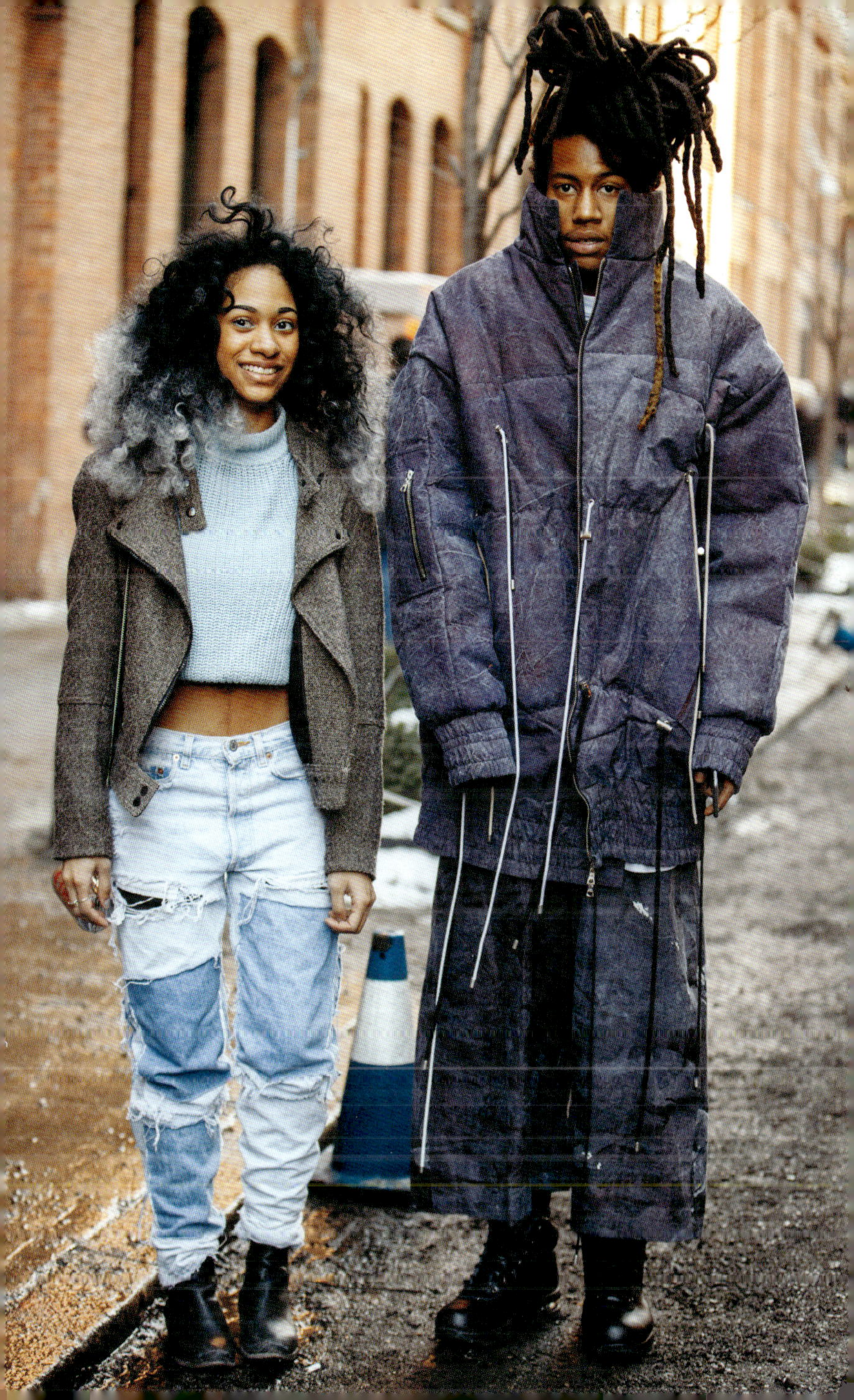

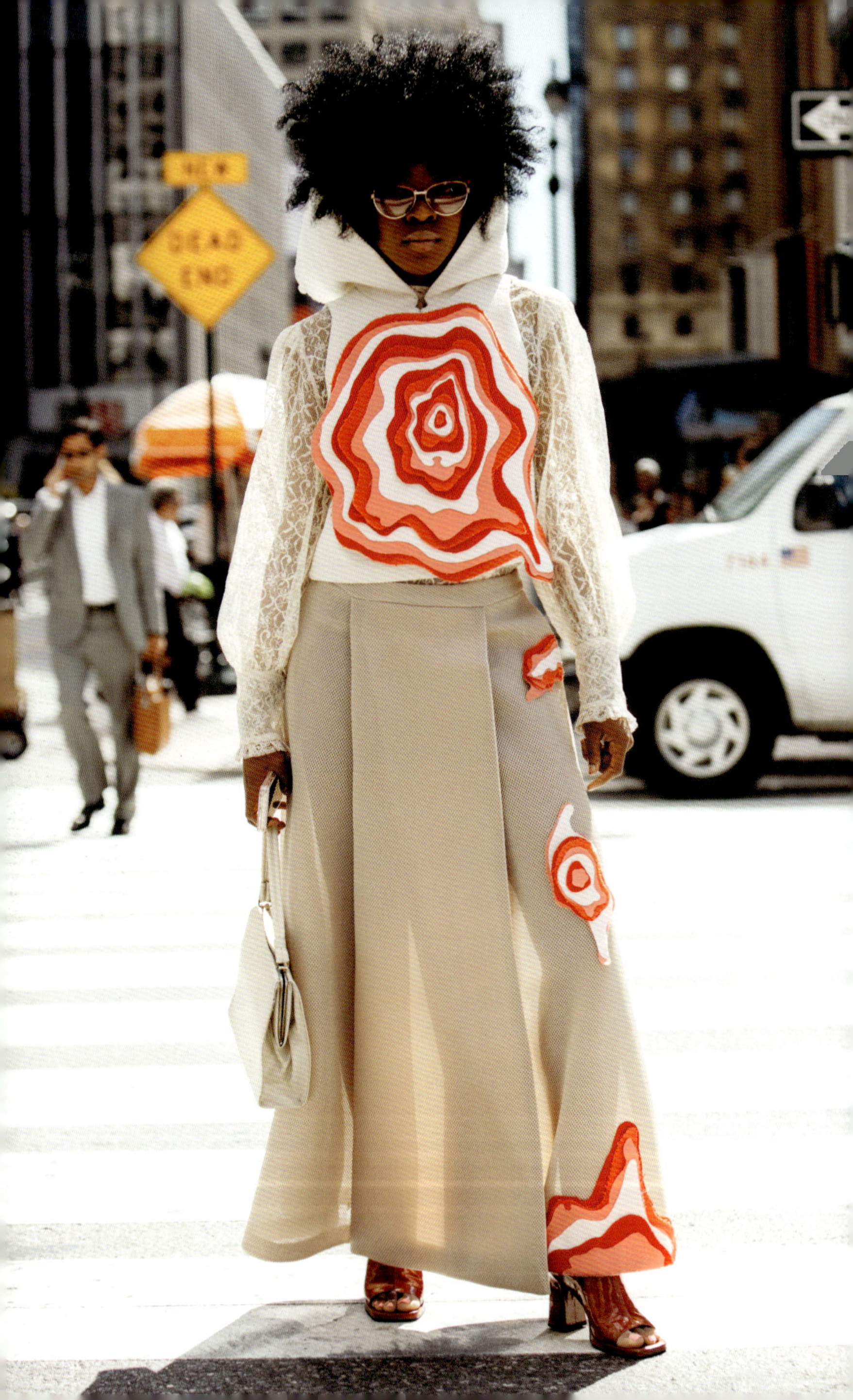
NEW
DEAD END

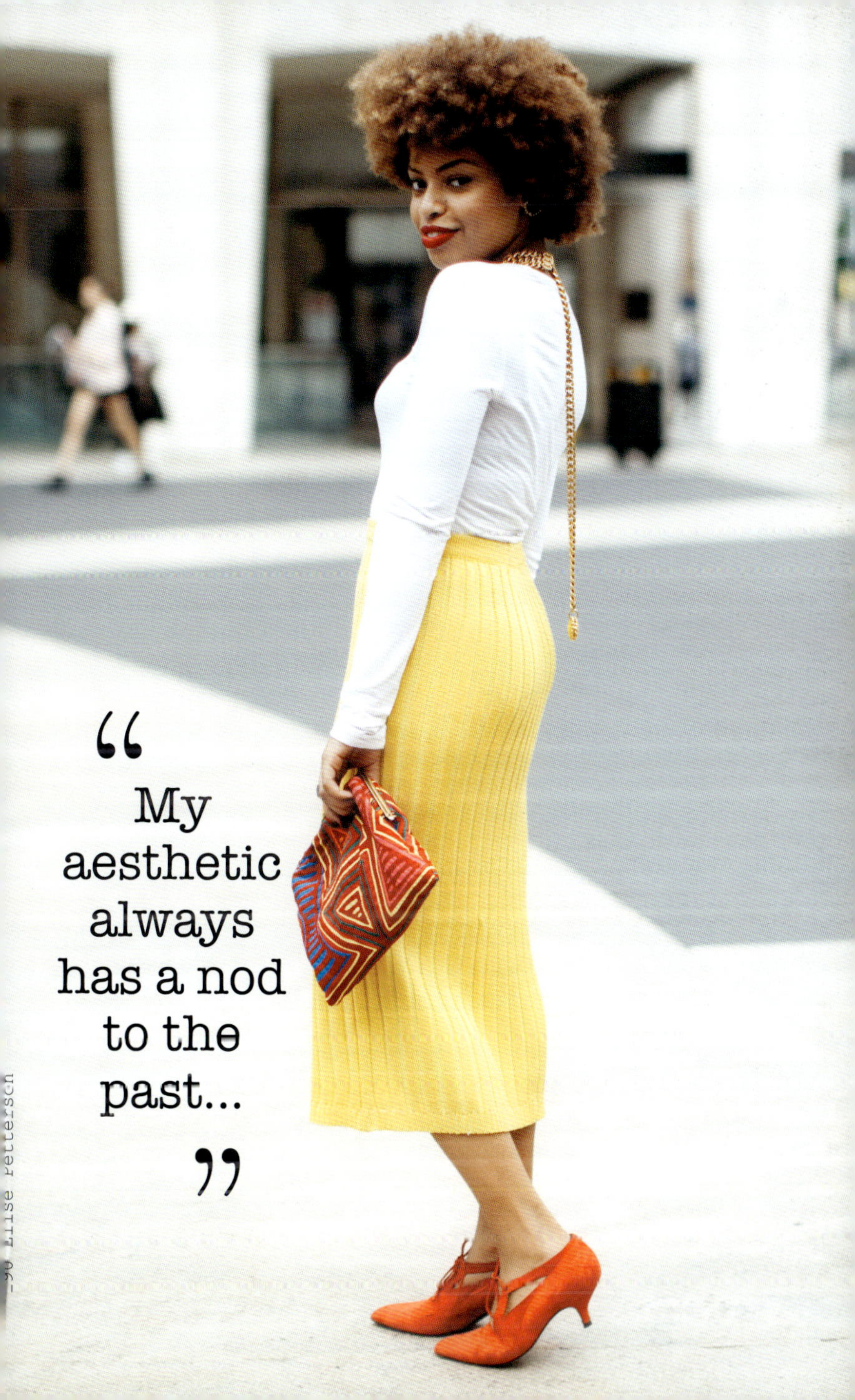
"My aesthetic always has a nod to the past..."

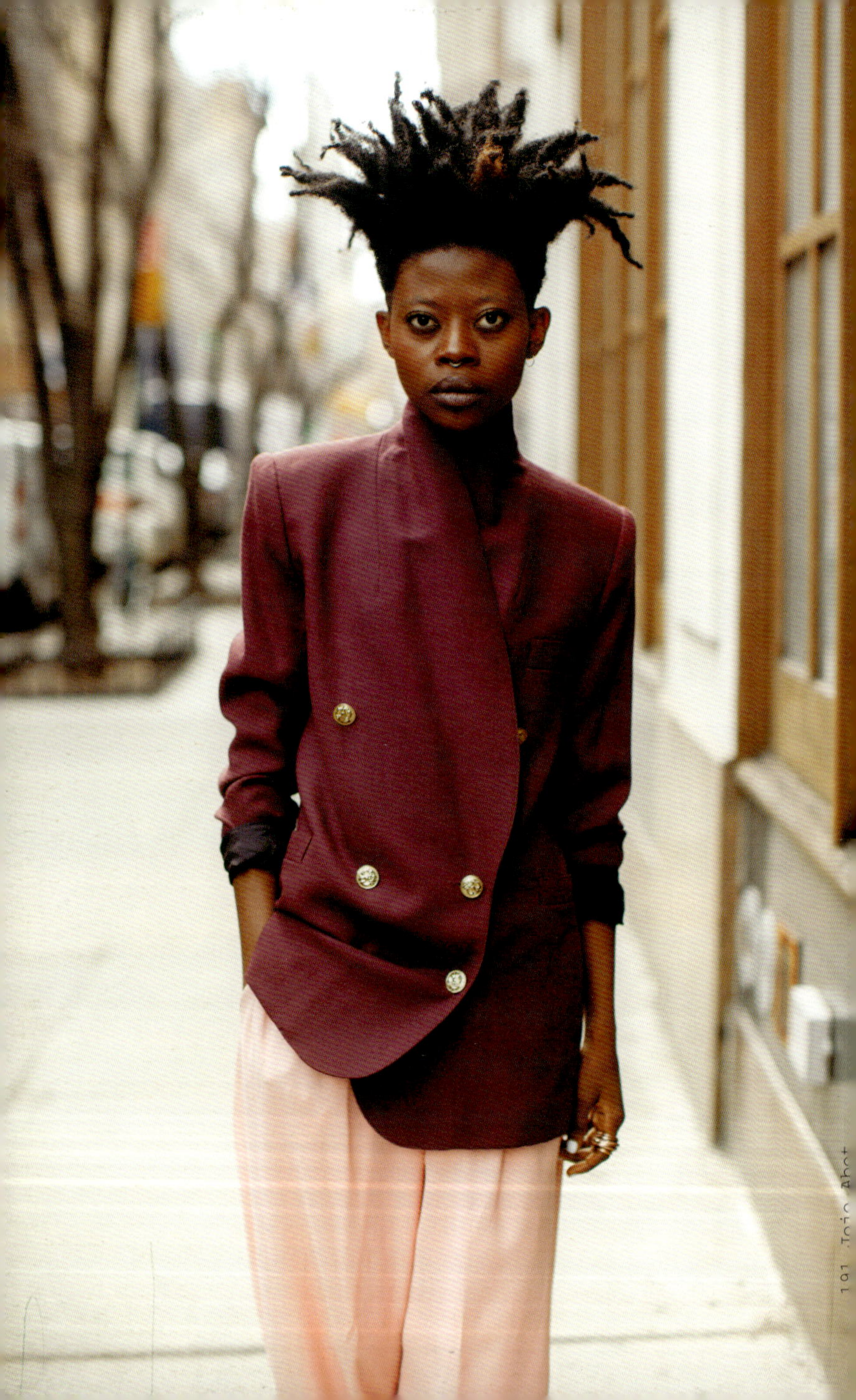

191 Tojo Abot

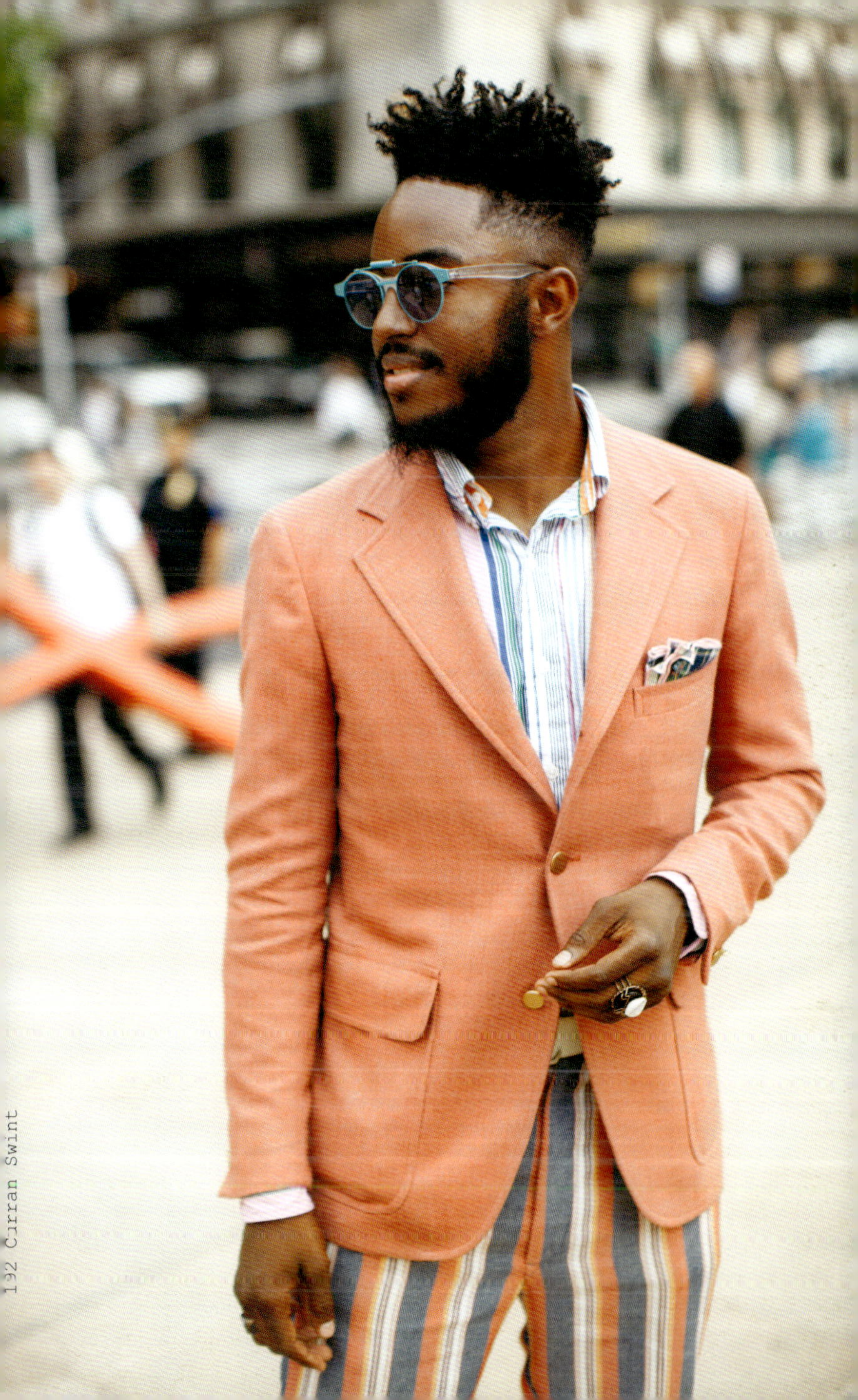

 Cirran Swint

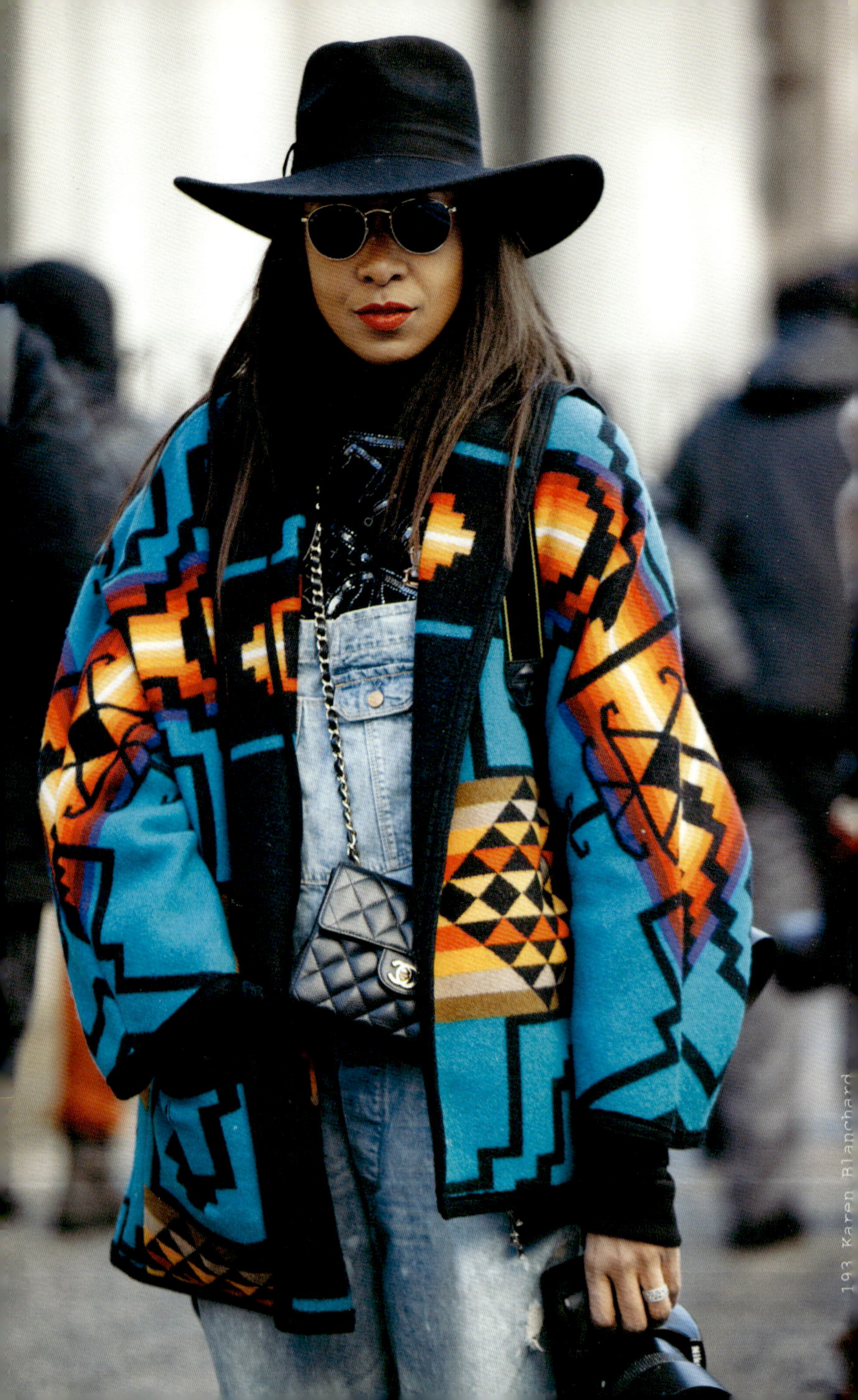

193 Karen Blanchard

“Cobalt blue is my favorite. It’s rich and seems to glow at the same time. It looks beautiful in any form and I love it against my skin.”

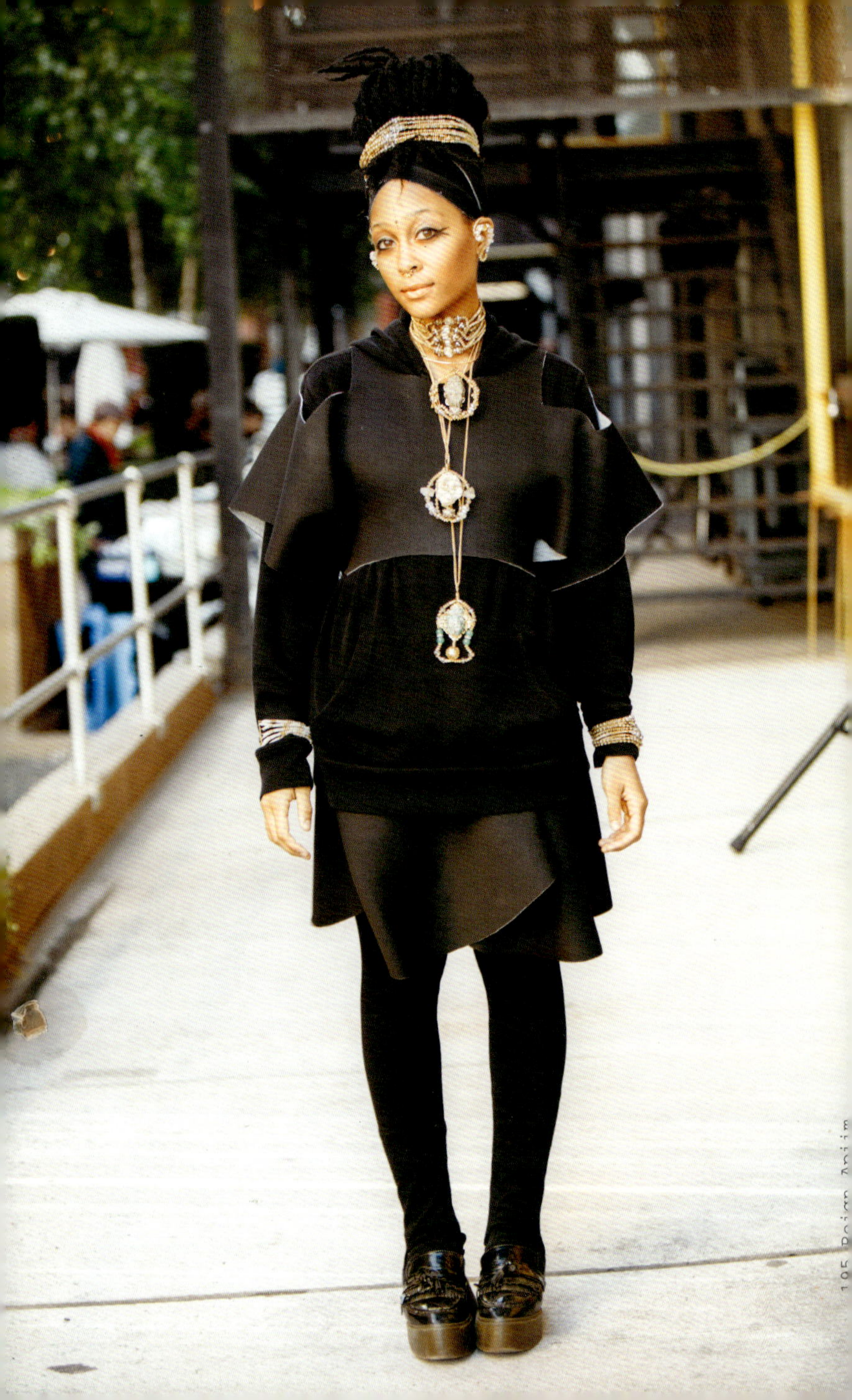

105

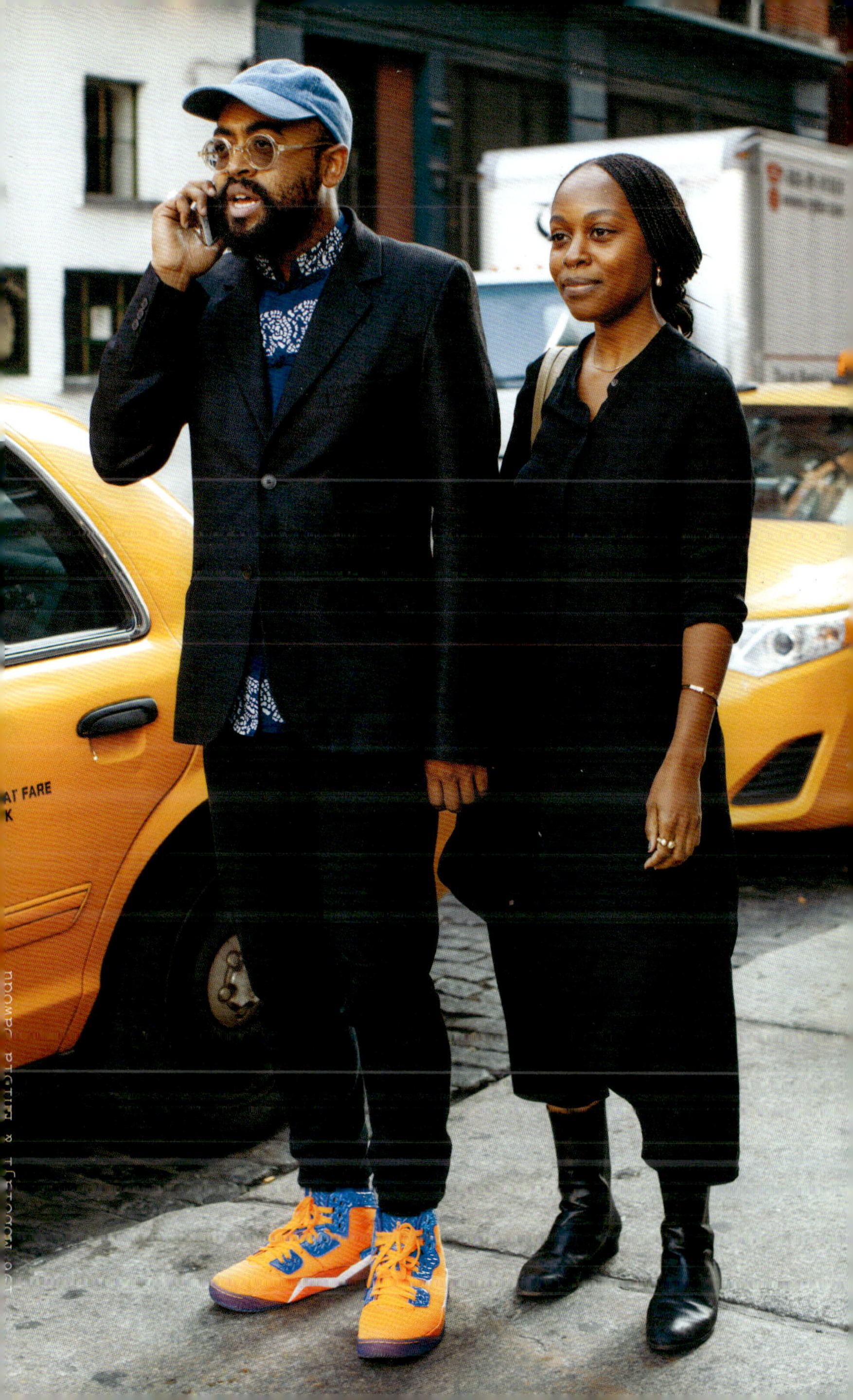

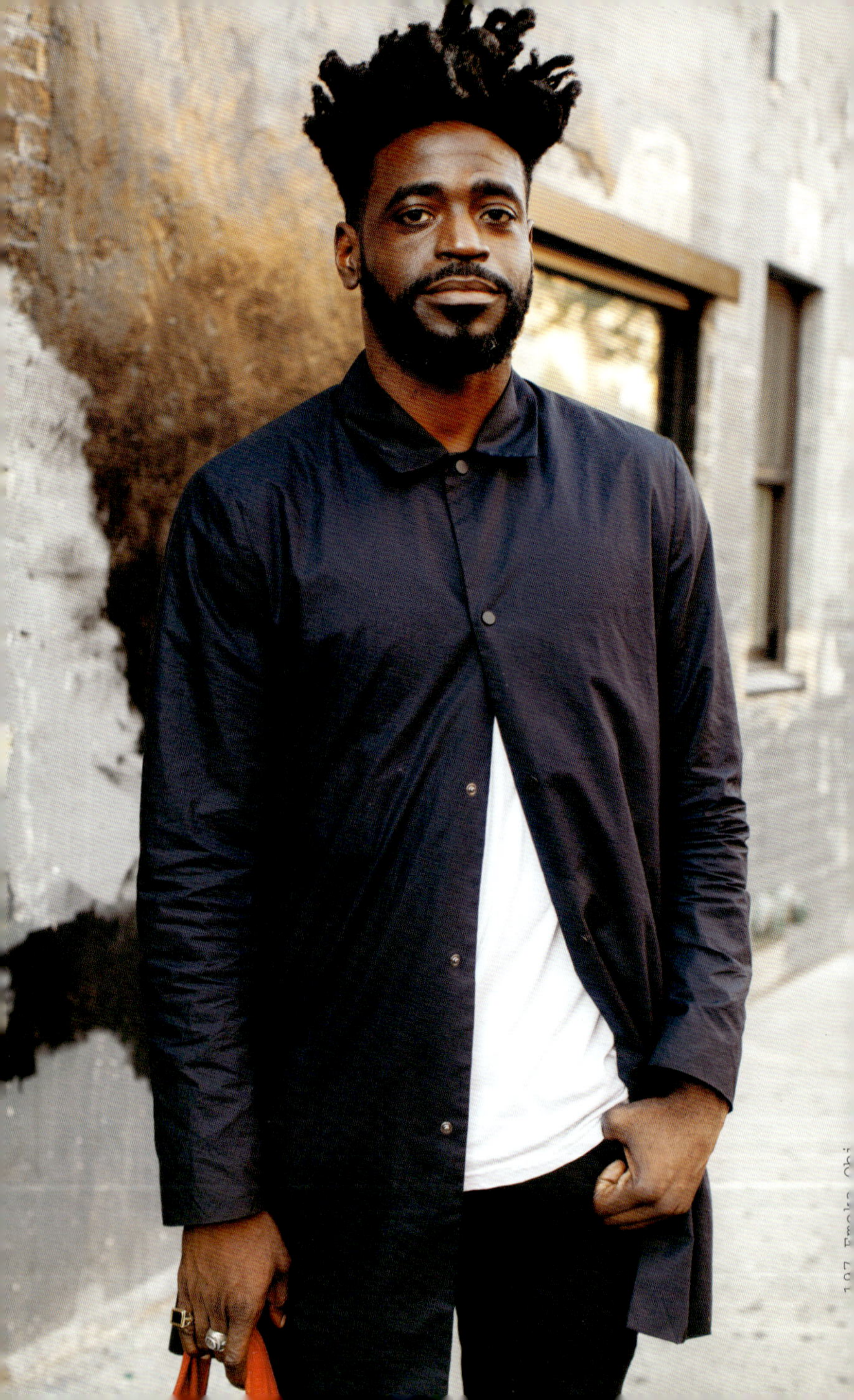

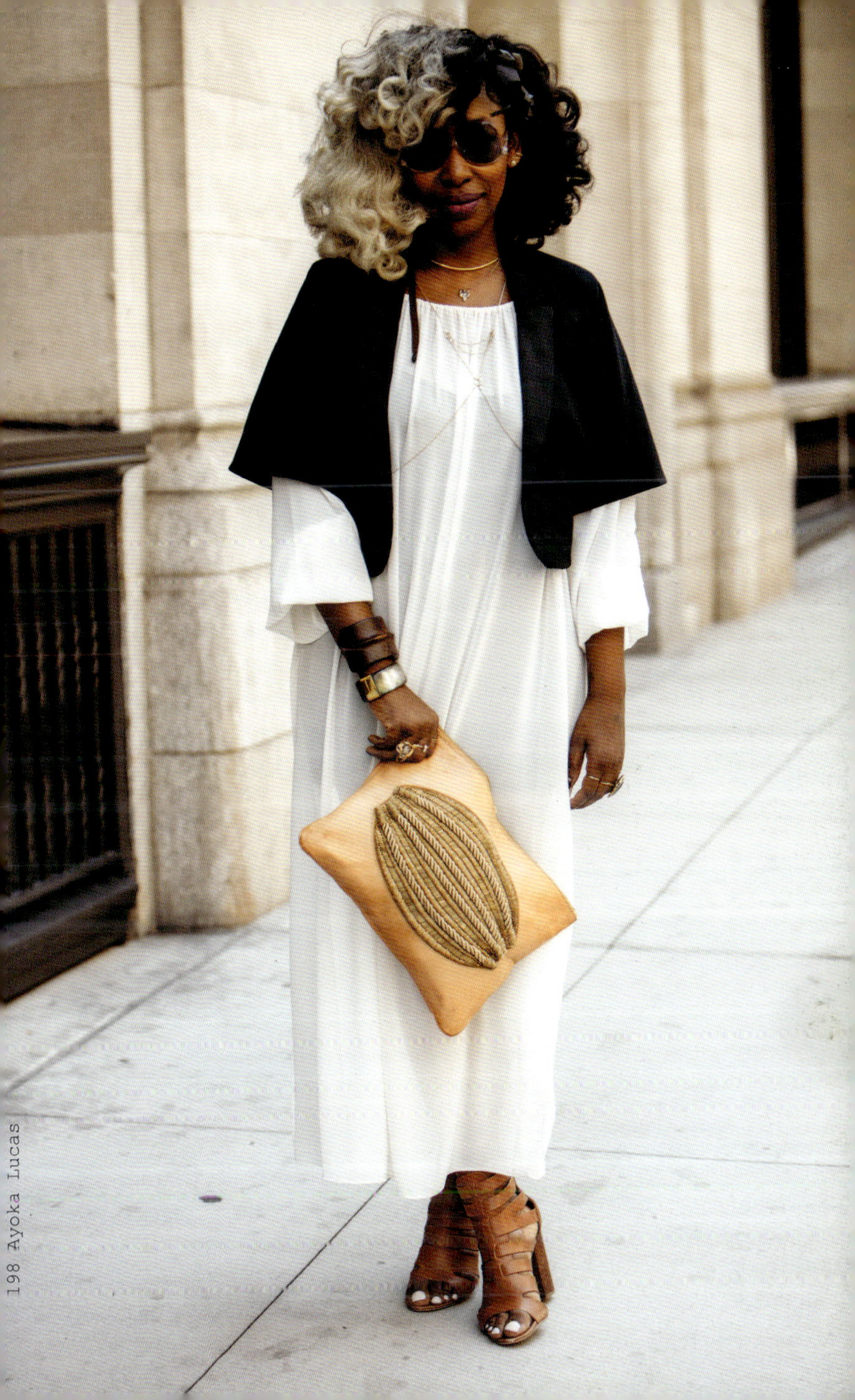

Ayoka Lucas

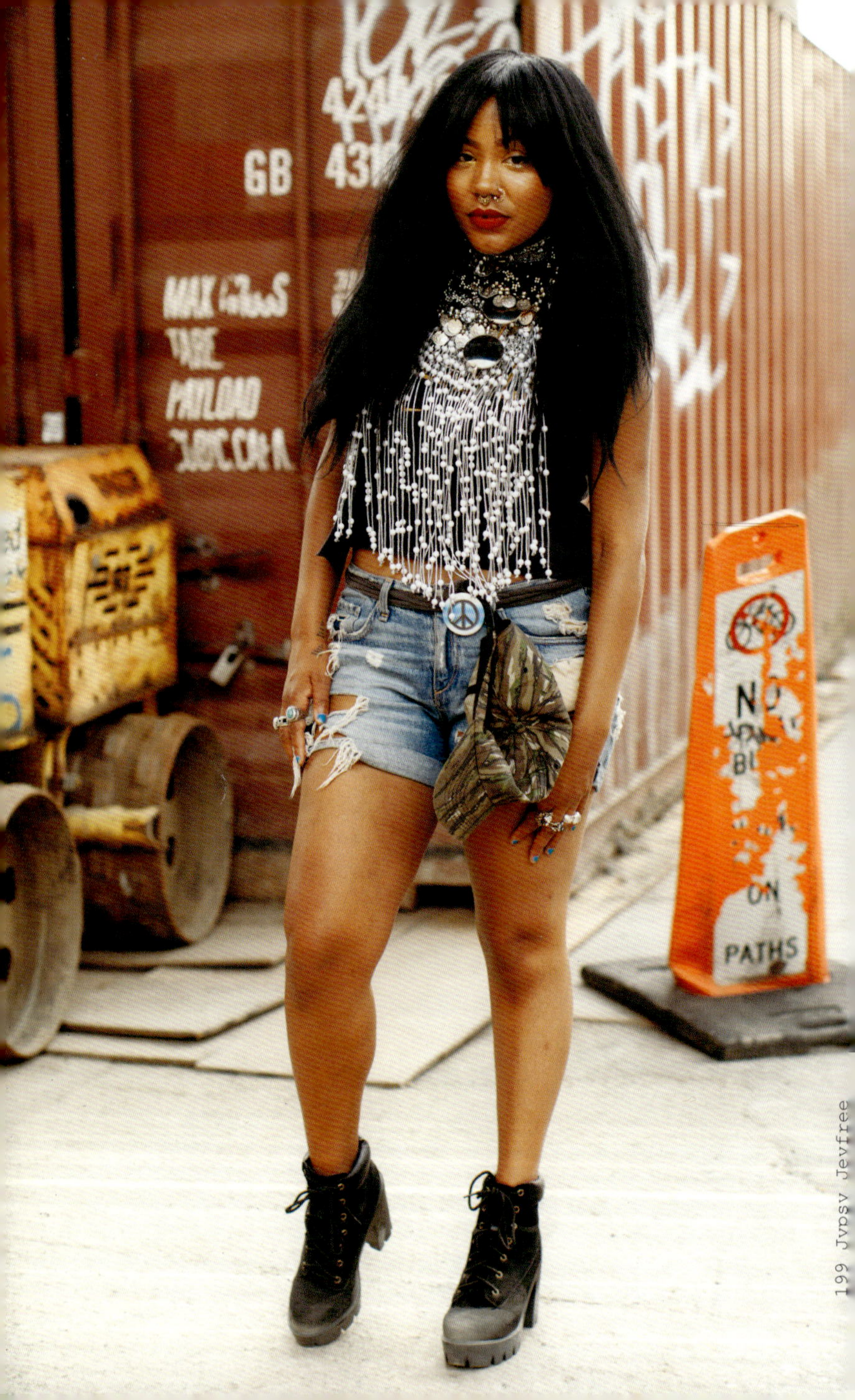

199 Jvpsv Jevfree

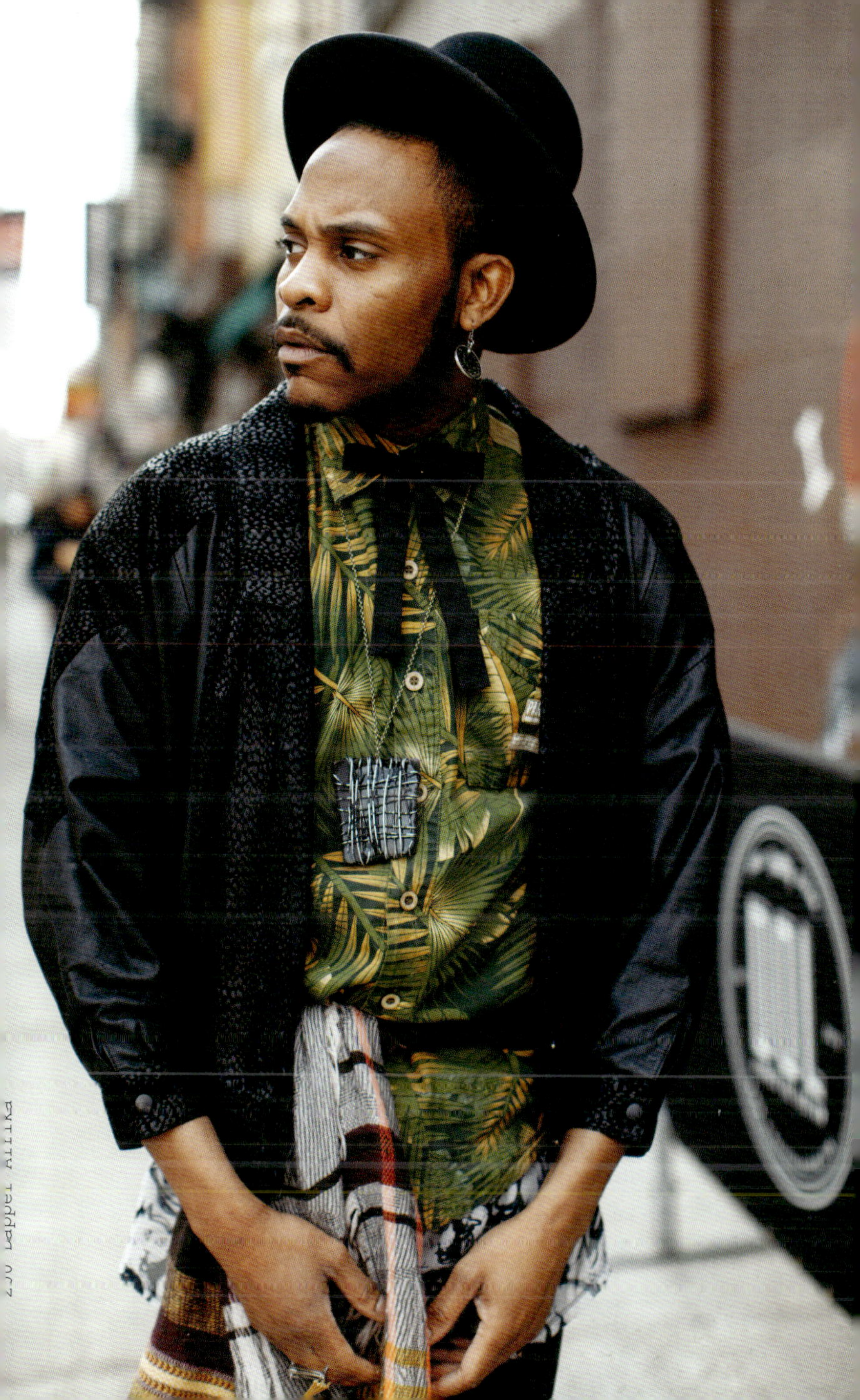

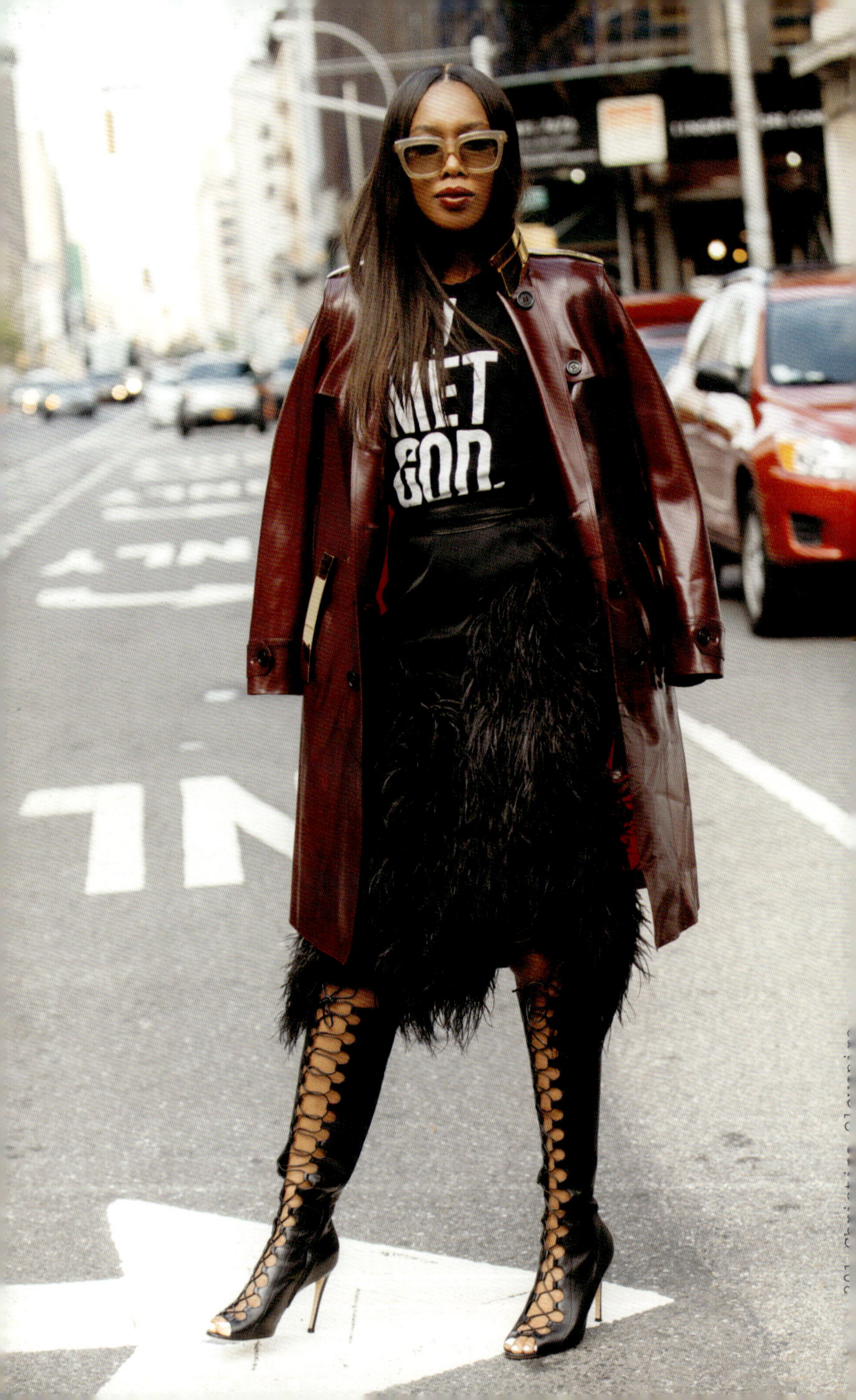
MET
GOD.

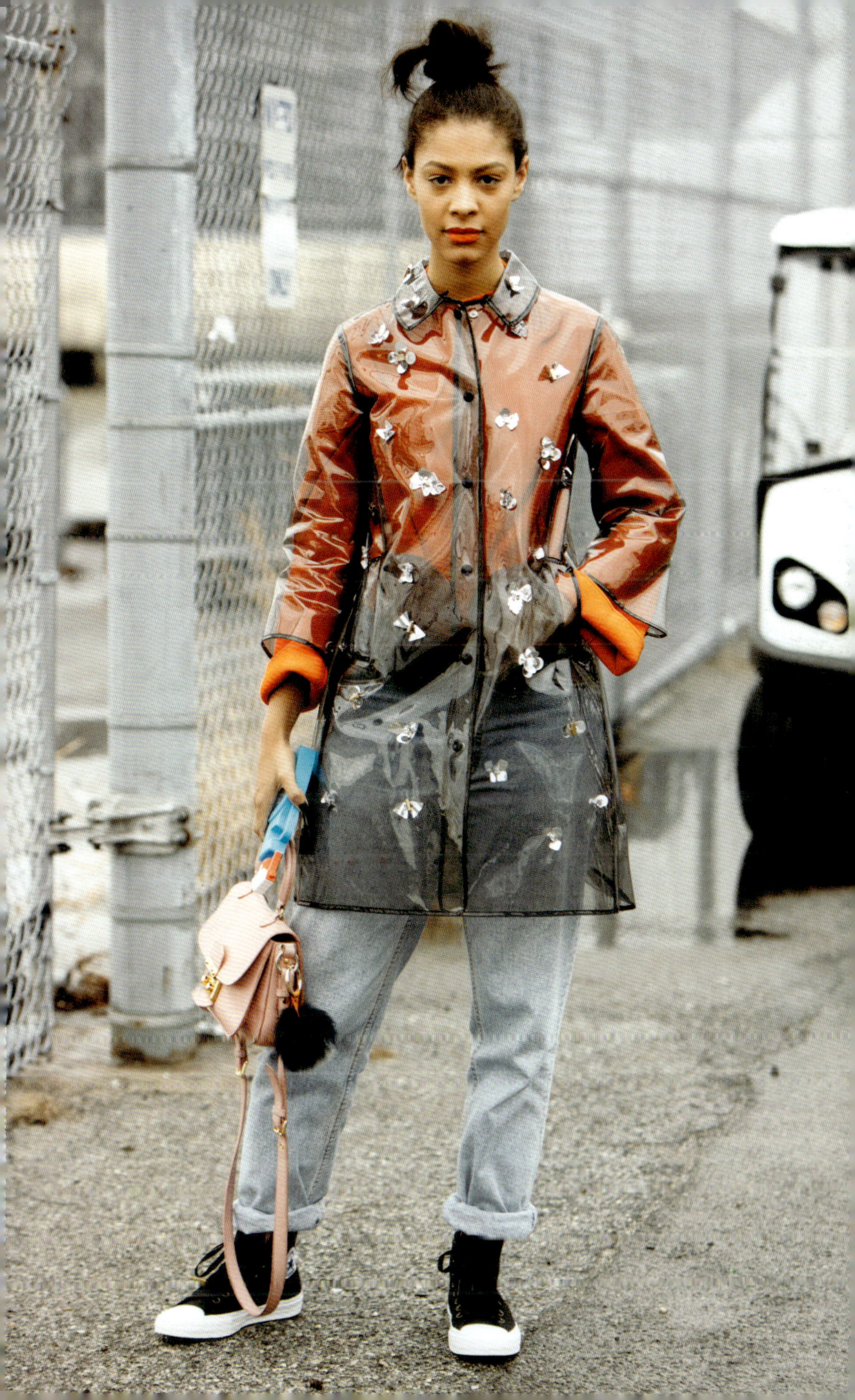

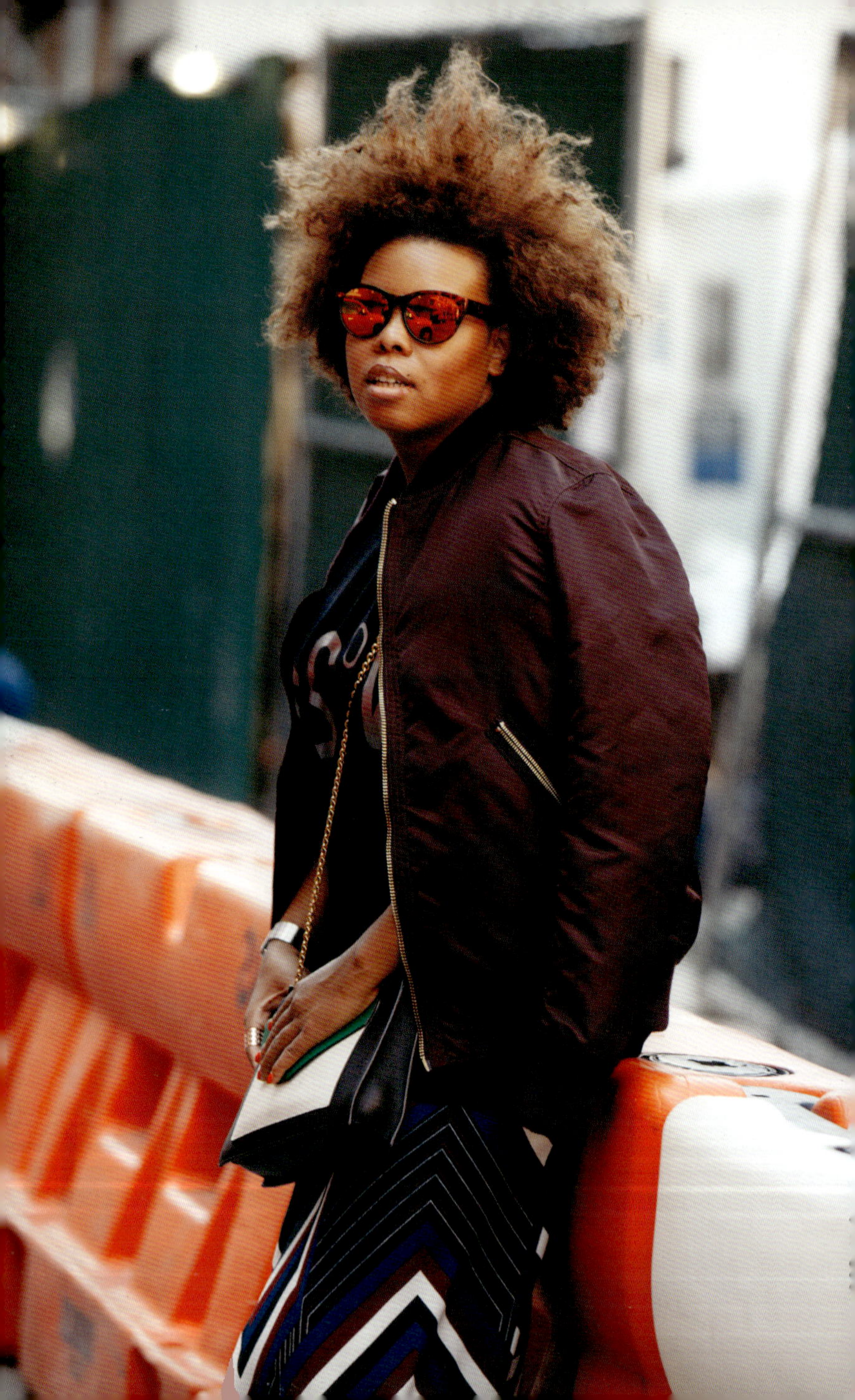

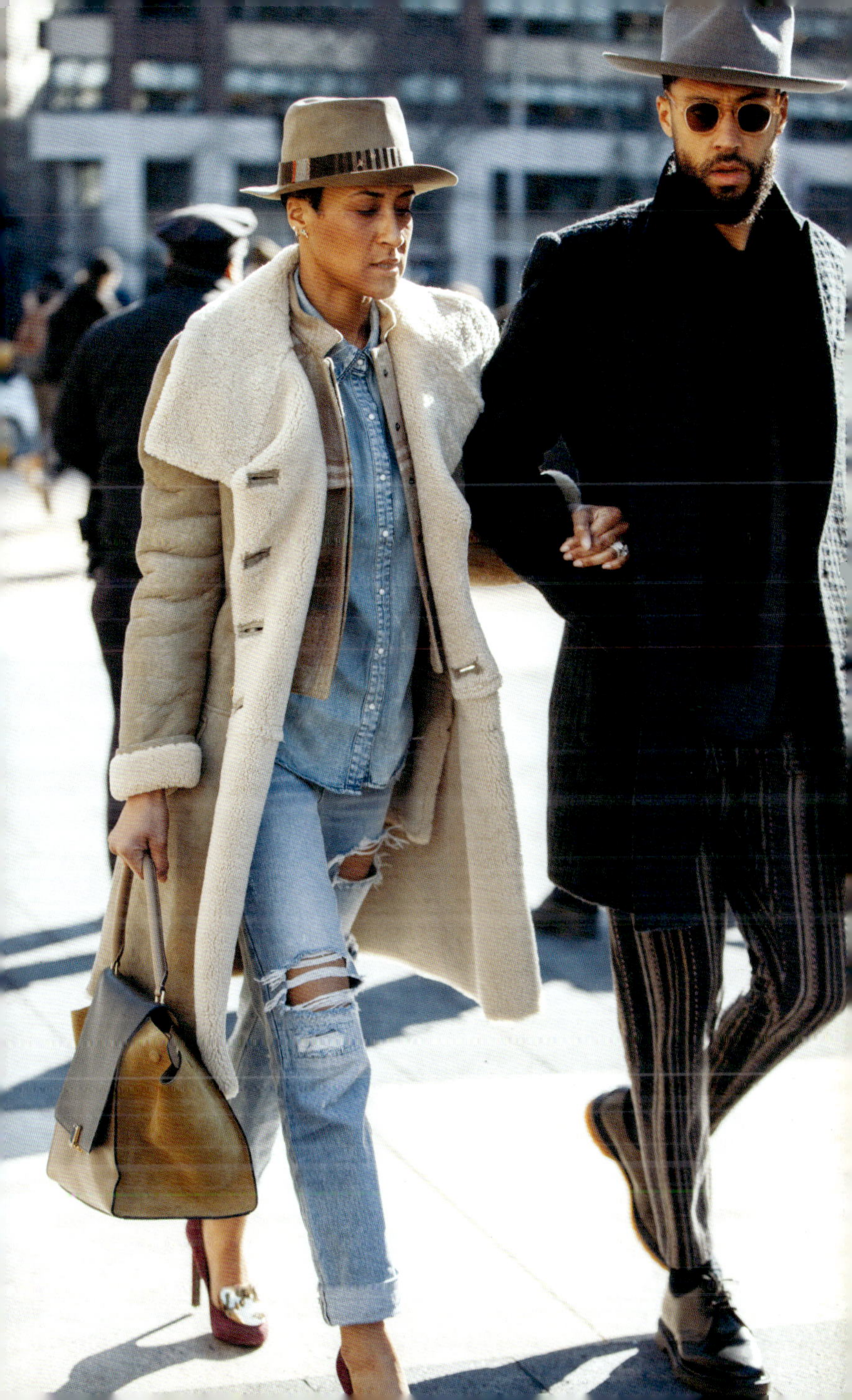

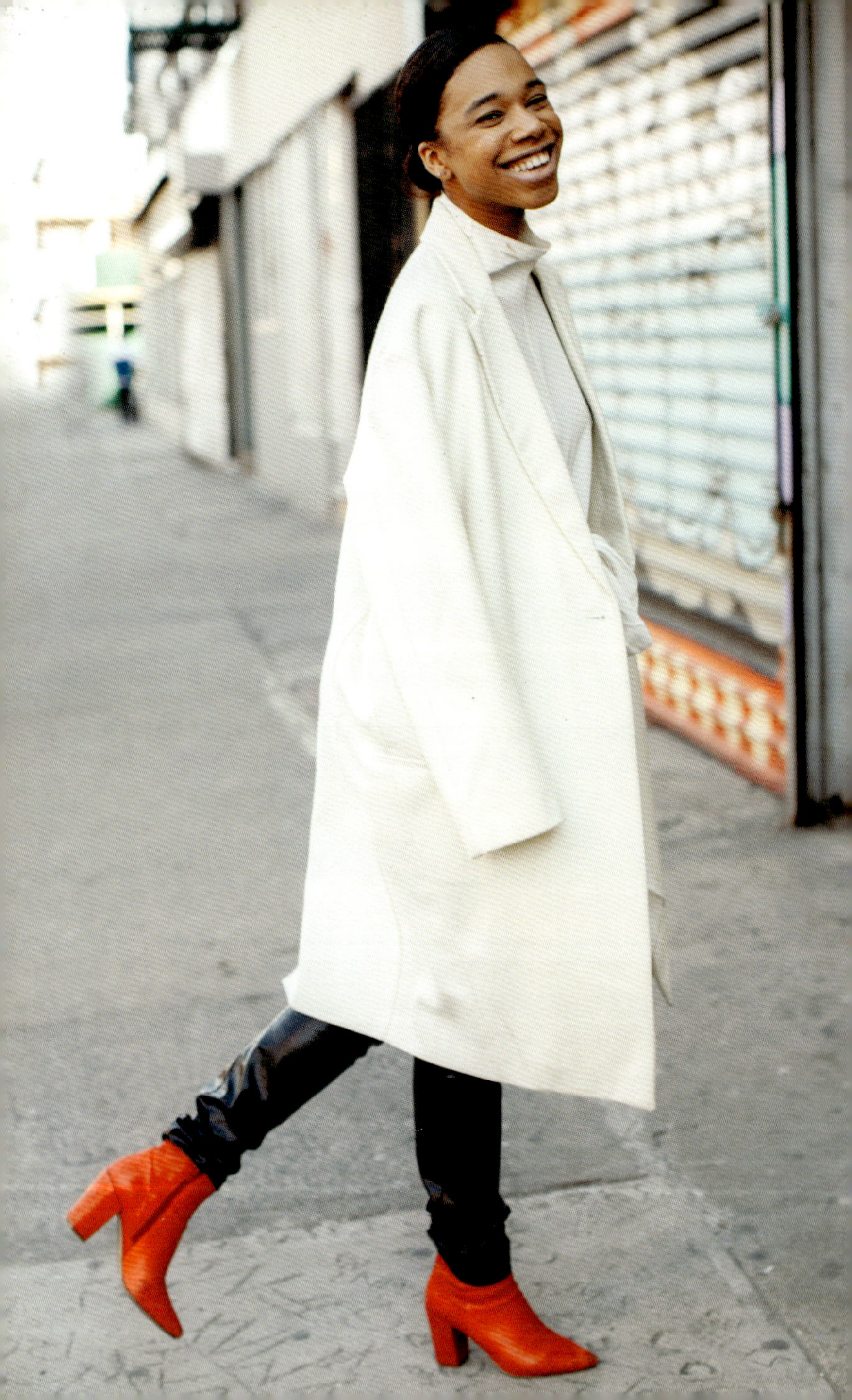

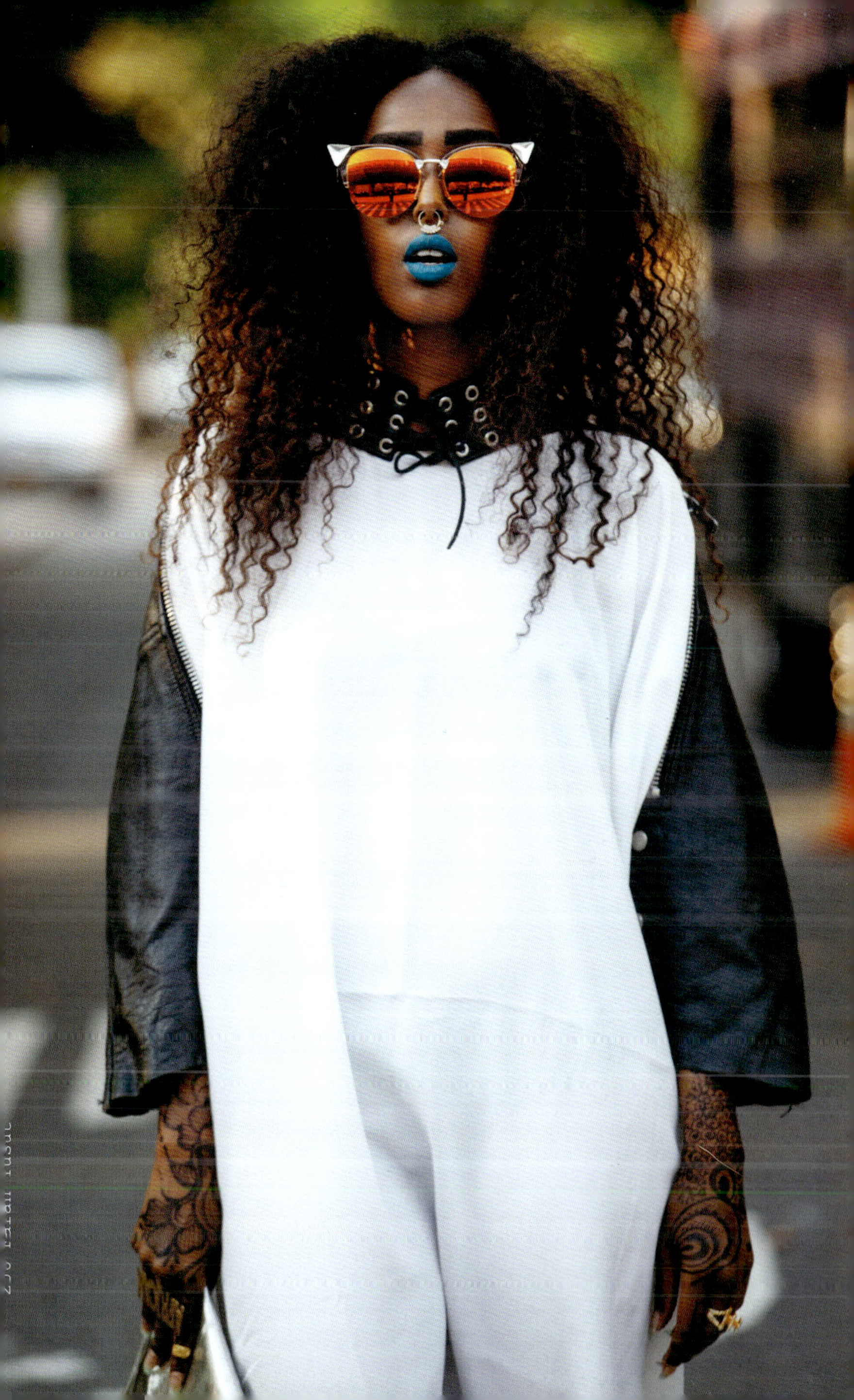

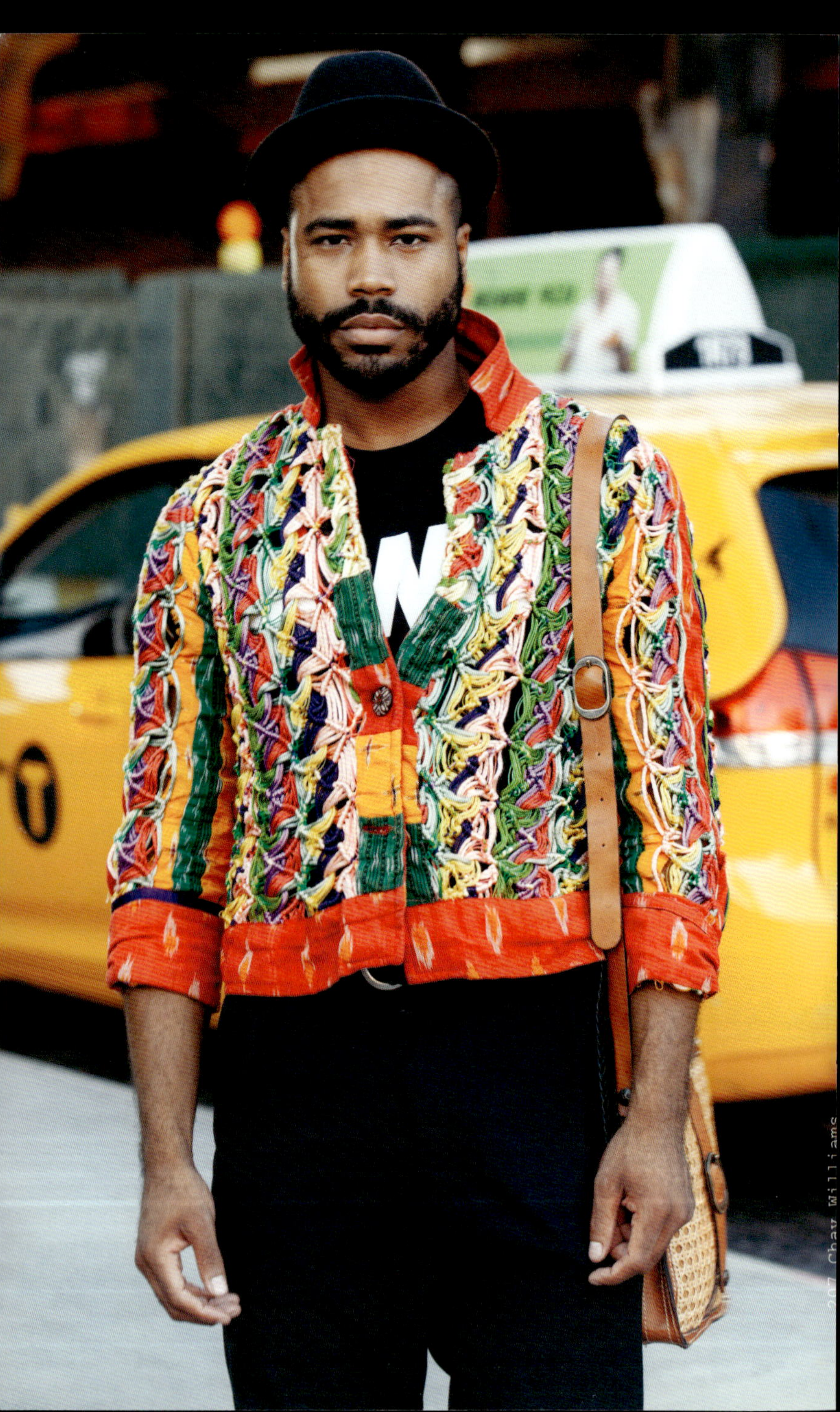

 Chav Williams

“Fashion is both the projection of your fantasy and a conversation with your ancestors.”

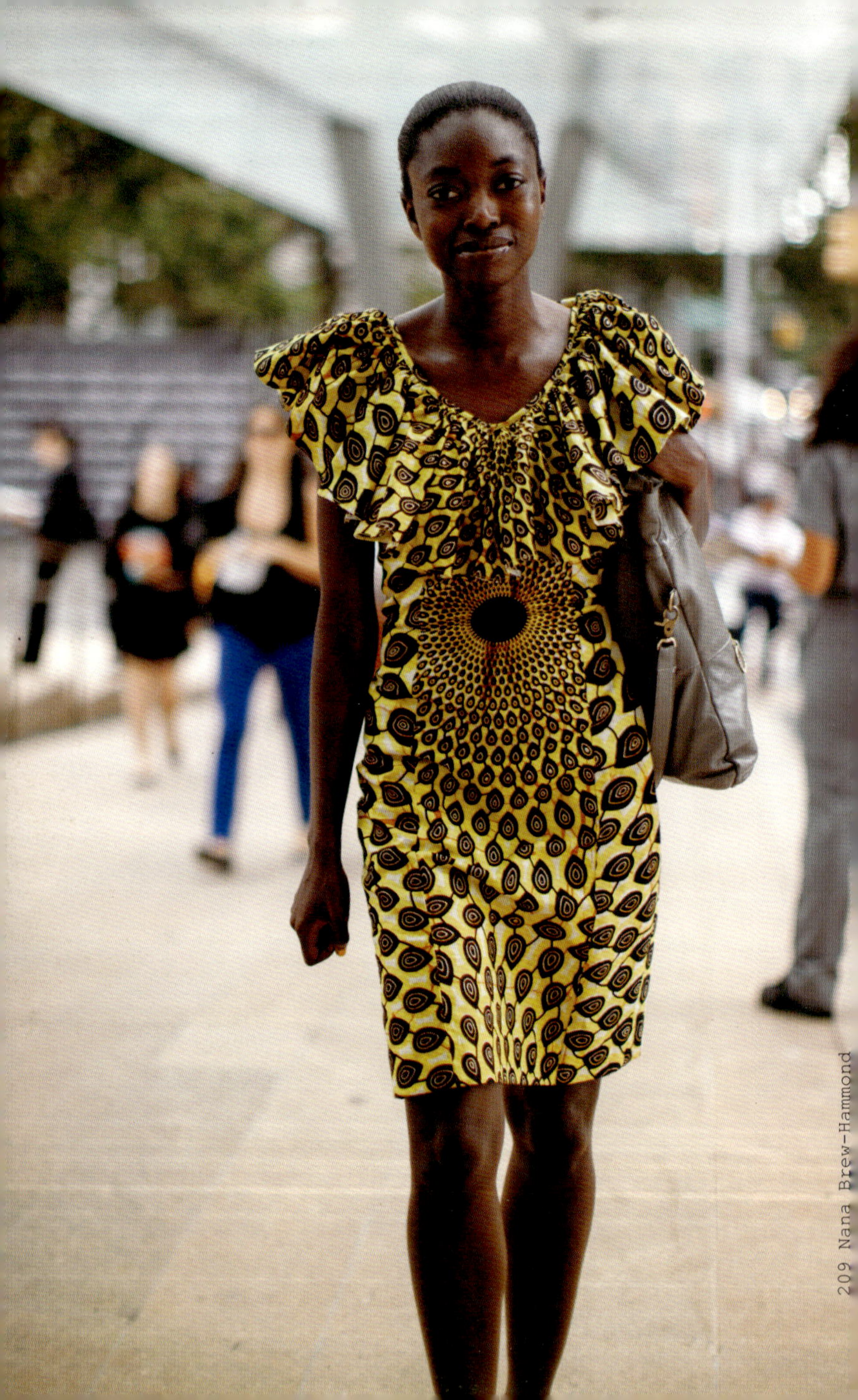

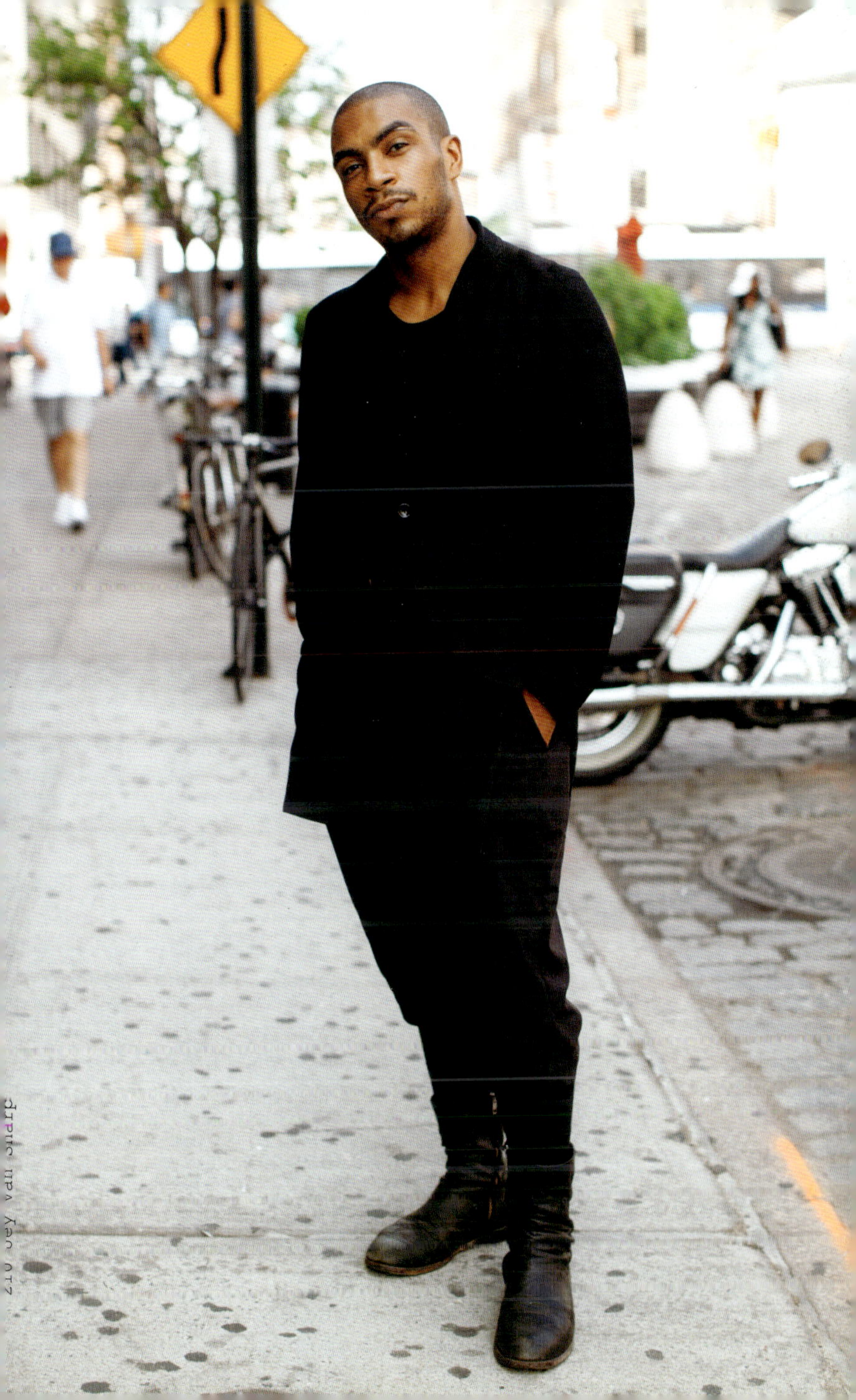

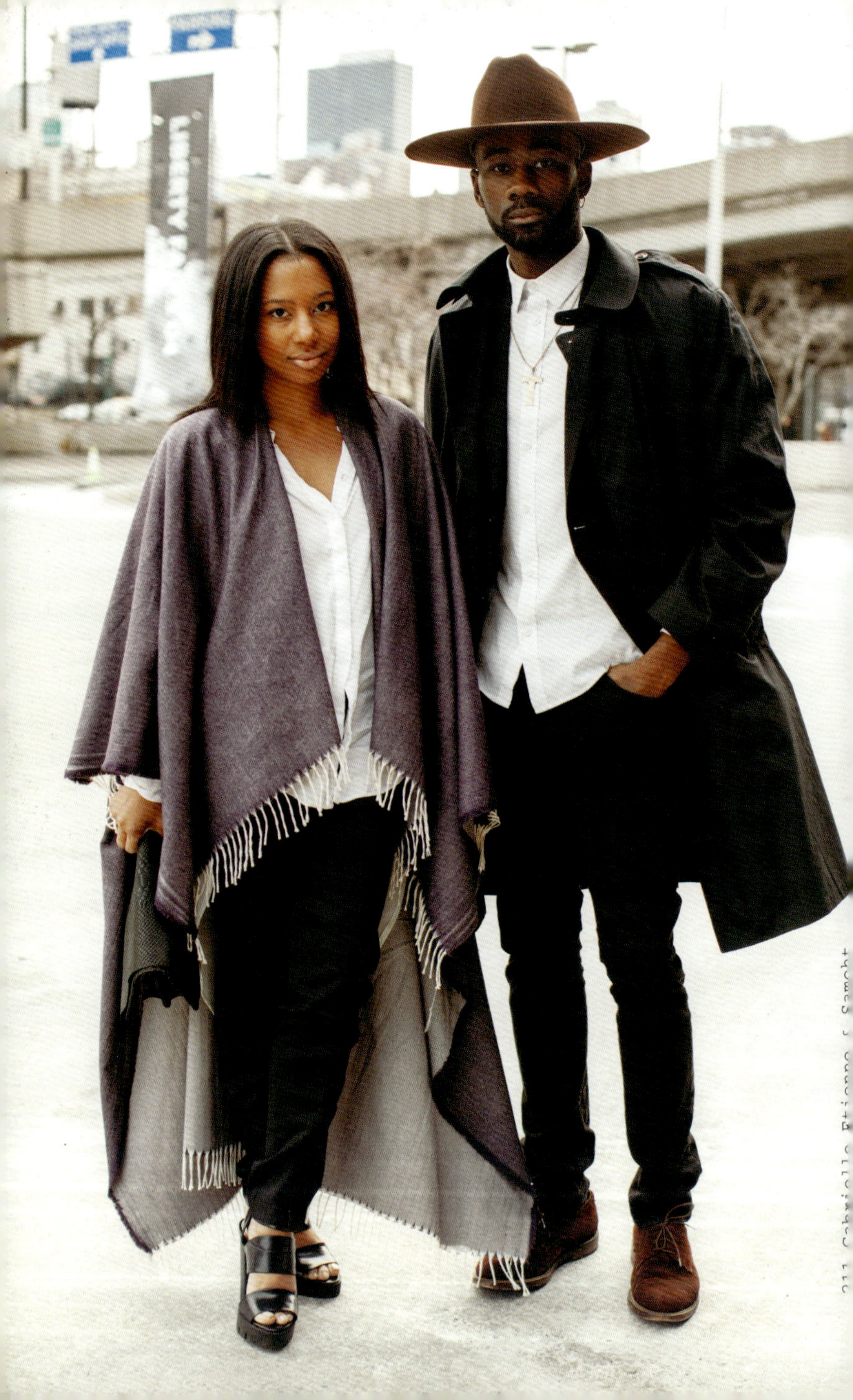

211 Gabrielle Etienne & Samcht

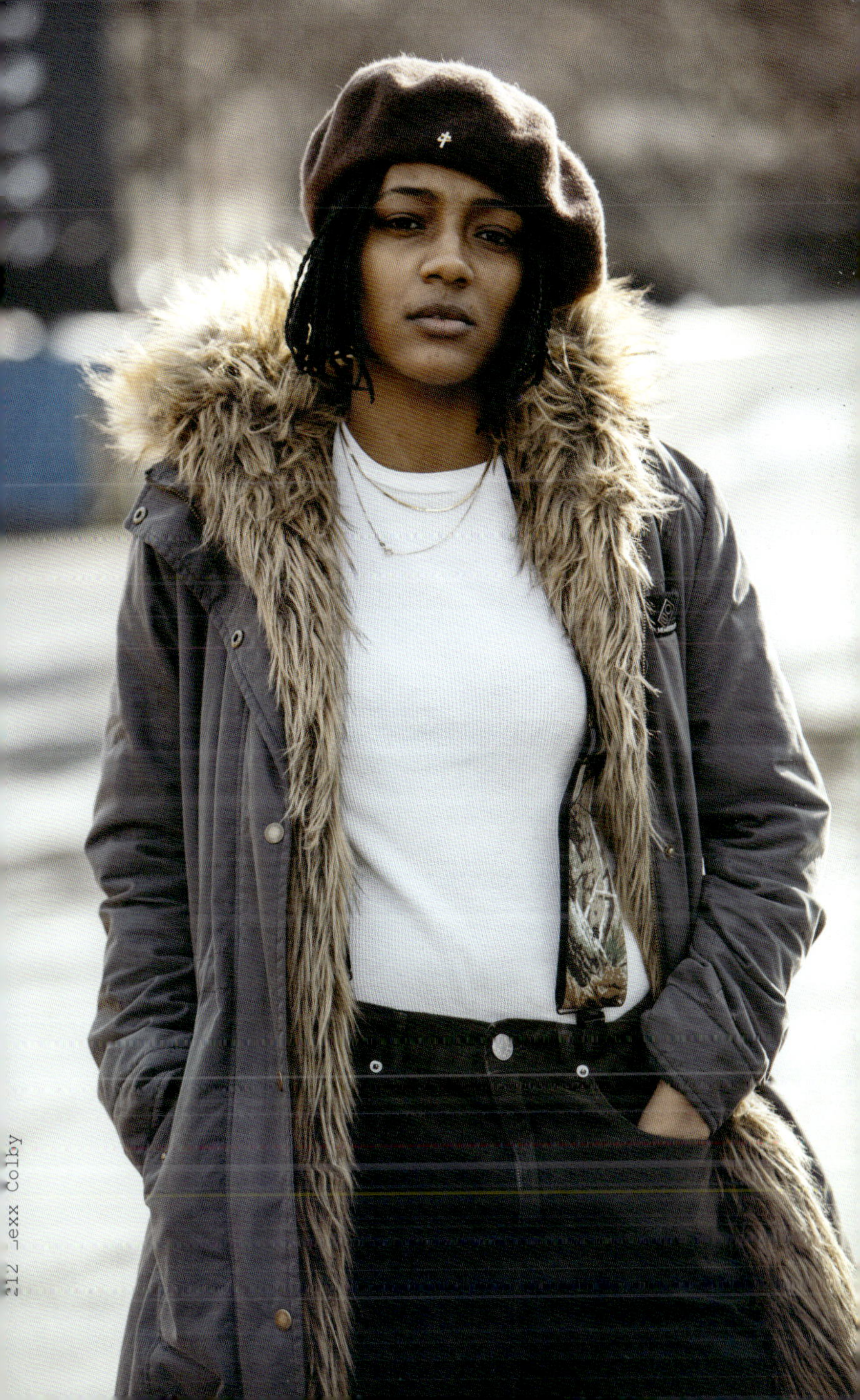

 Jexx Colby

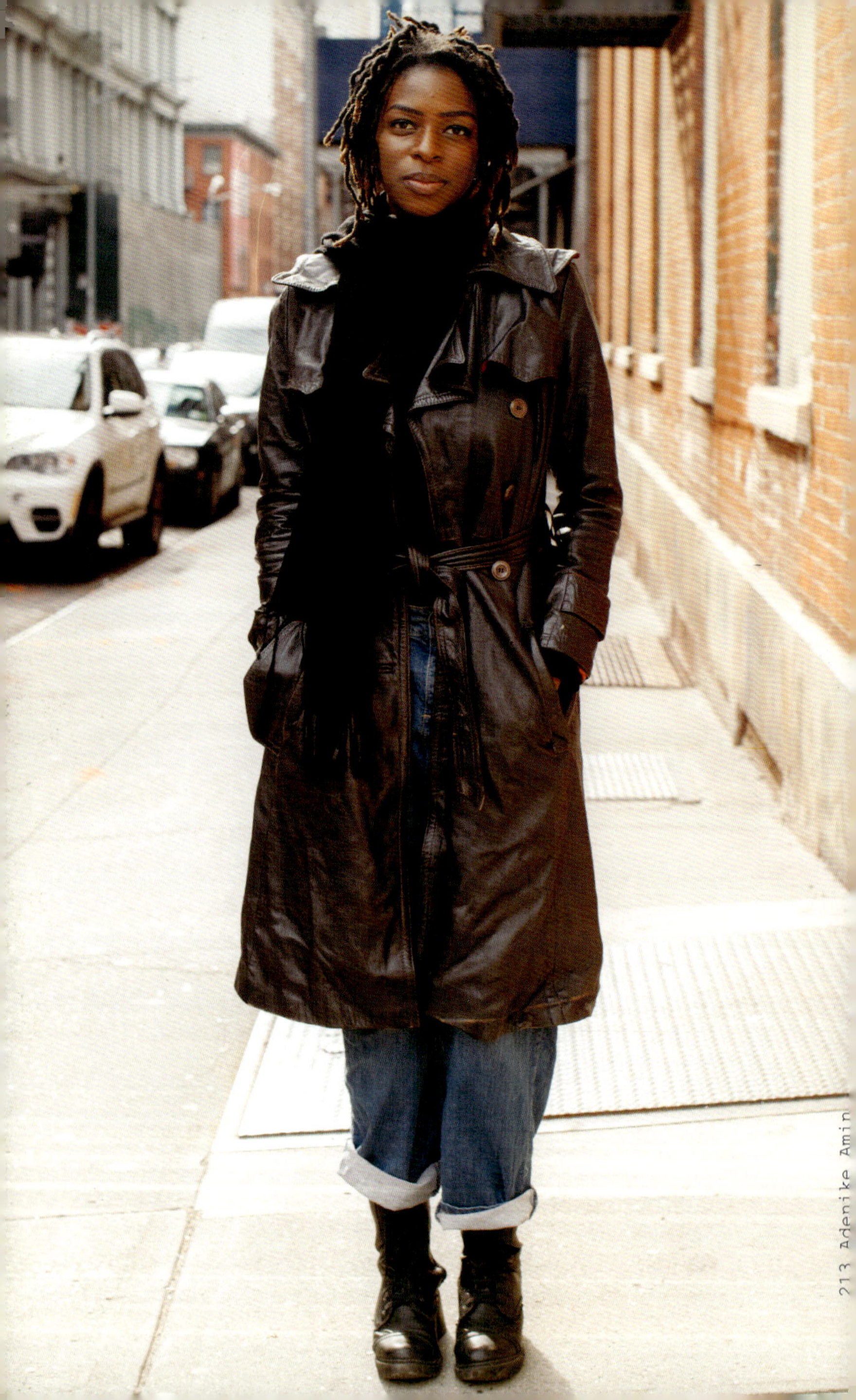

 Adenike Amin

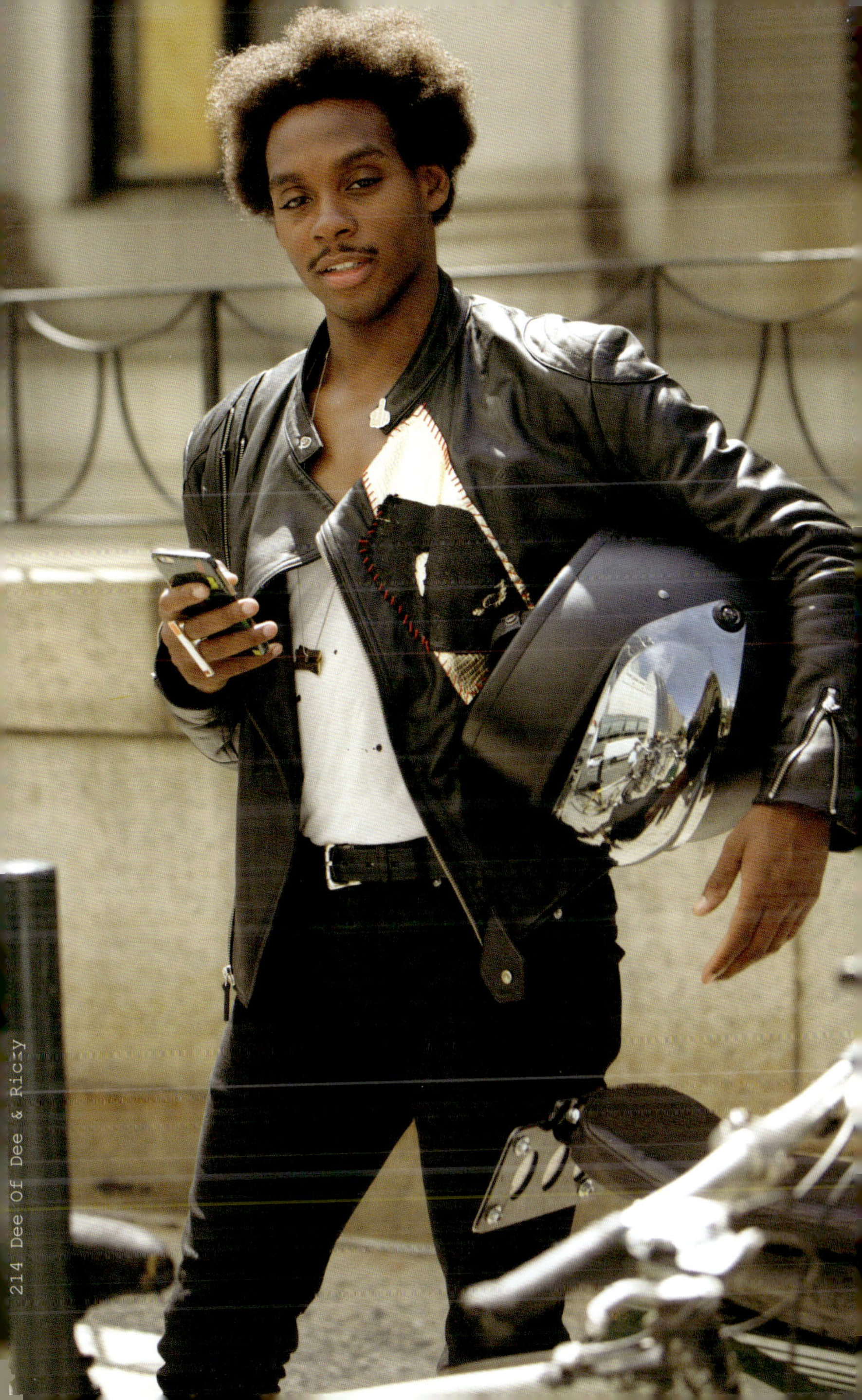

 Dee Of Dee & Ricky

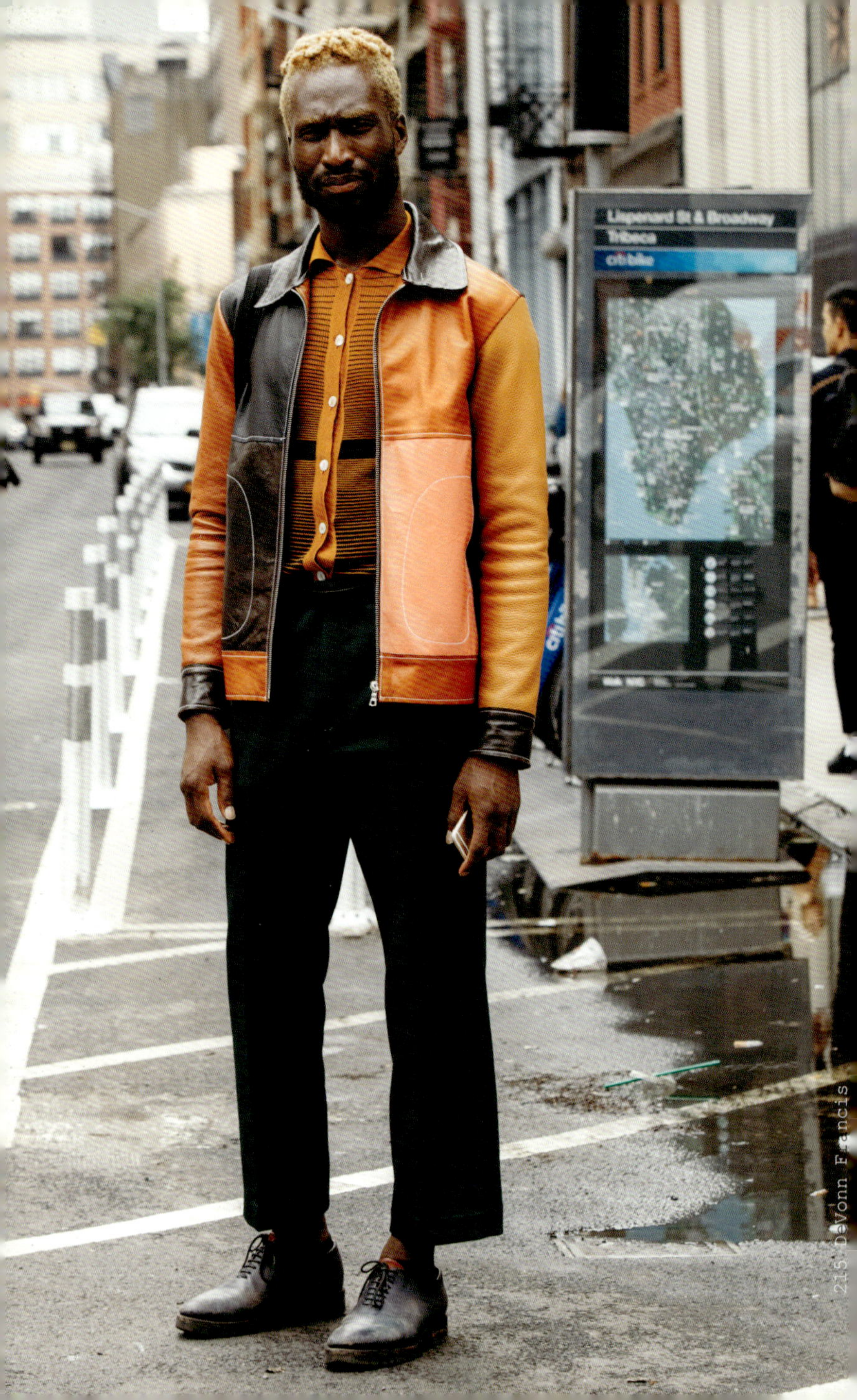

215 DeVonn Francis

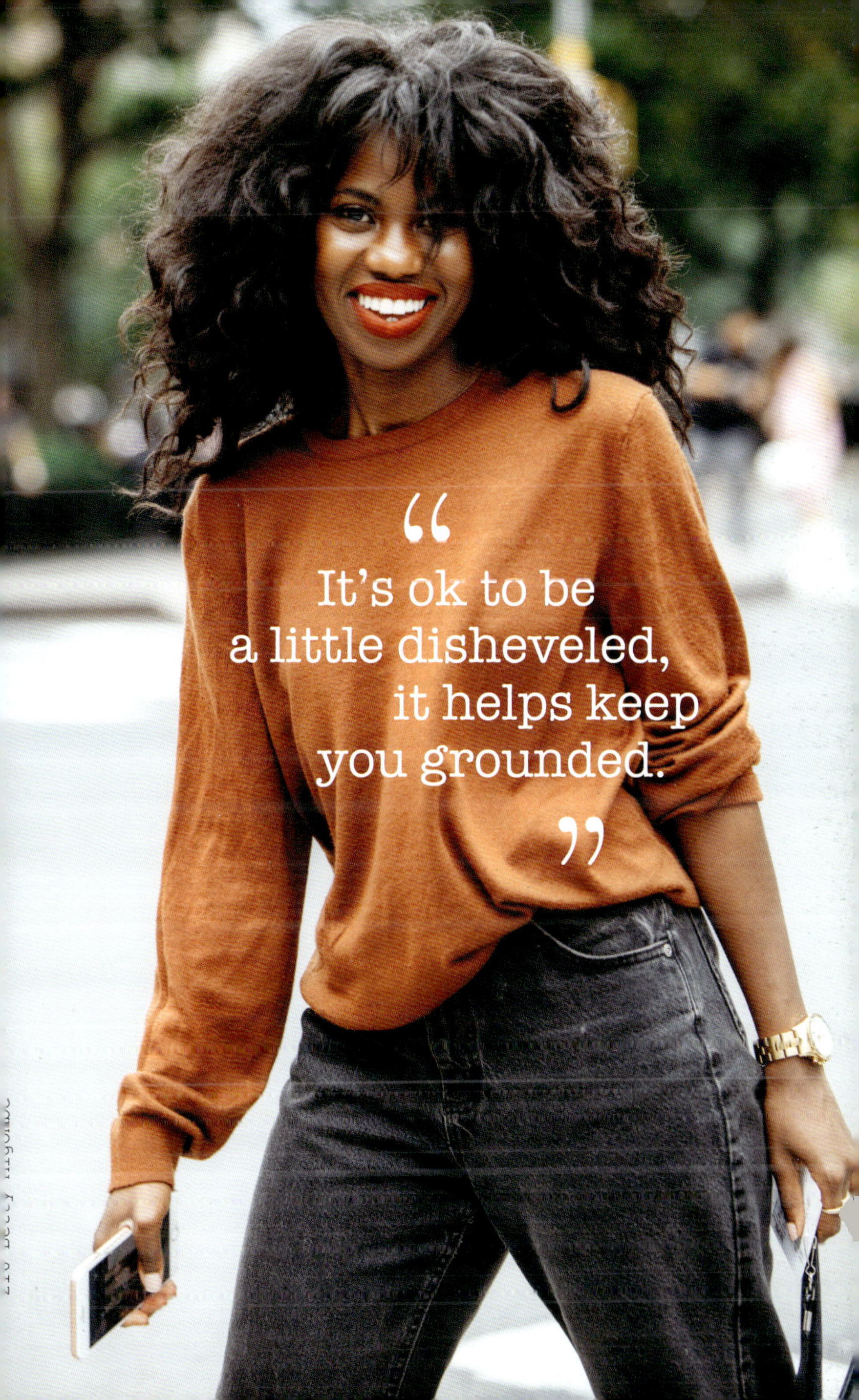
"It's ok to be
a little disheveled,
it helps keep
you grounded."

“Accessories are key to my personal style, it’s what differentiates that item that I and a million other ladies all over the world may own.”

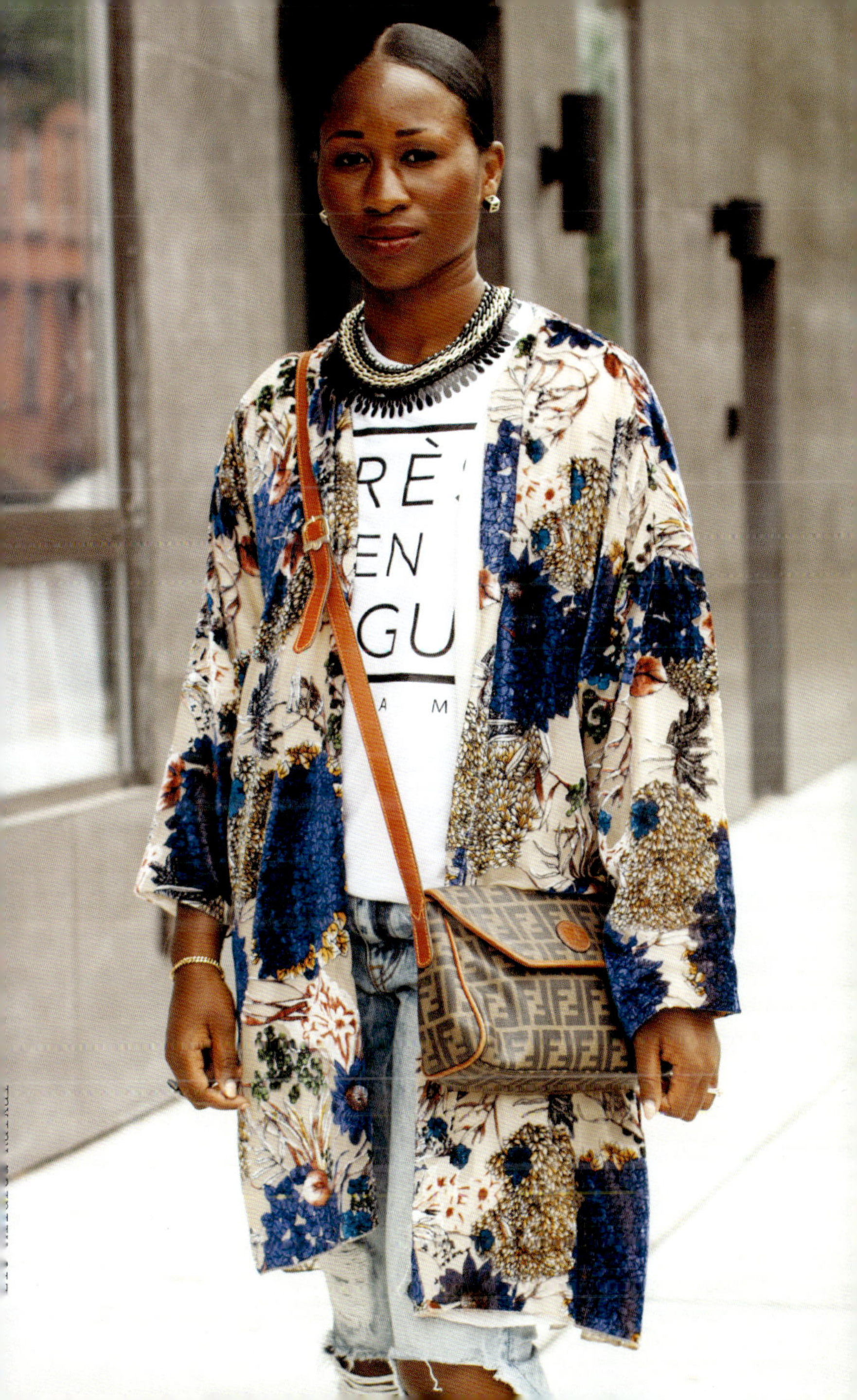
RÈ
EN
GU

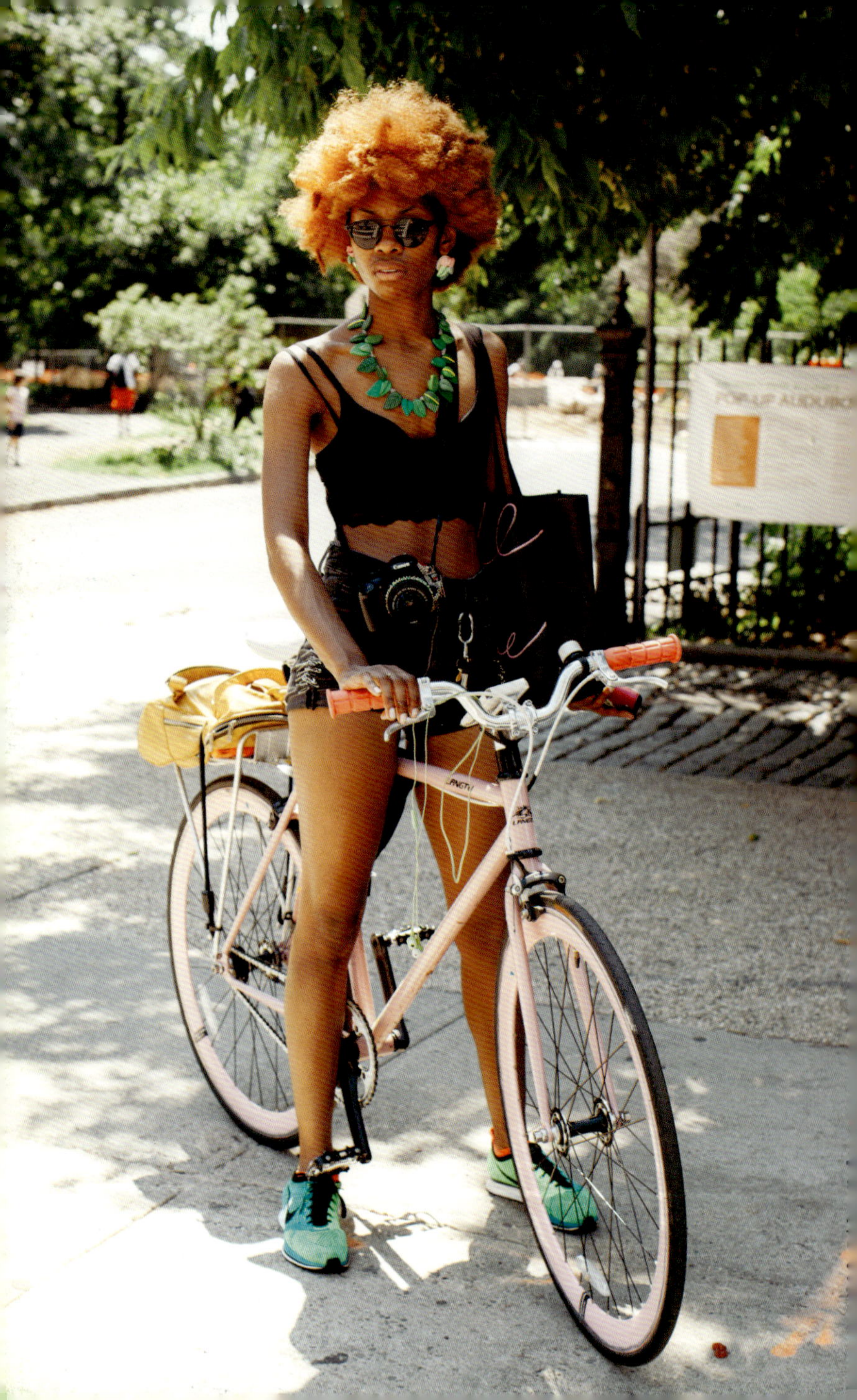

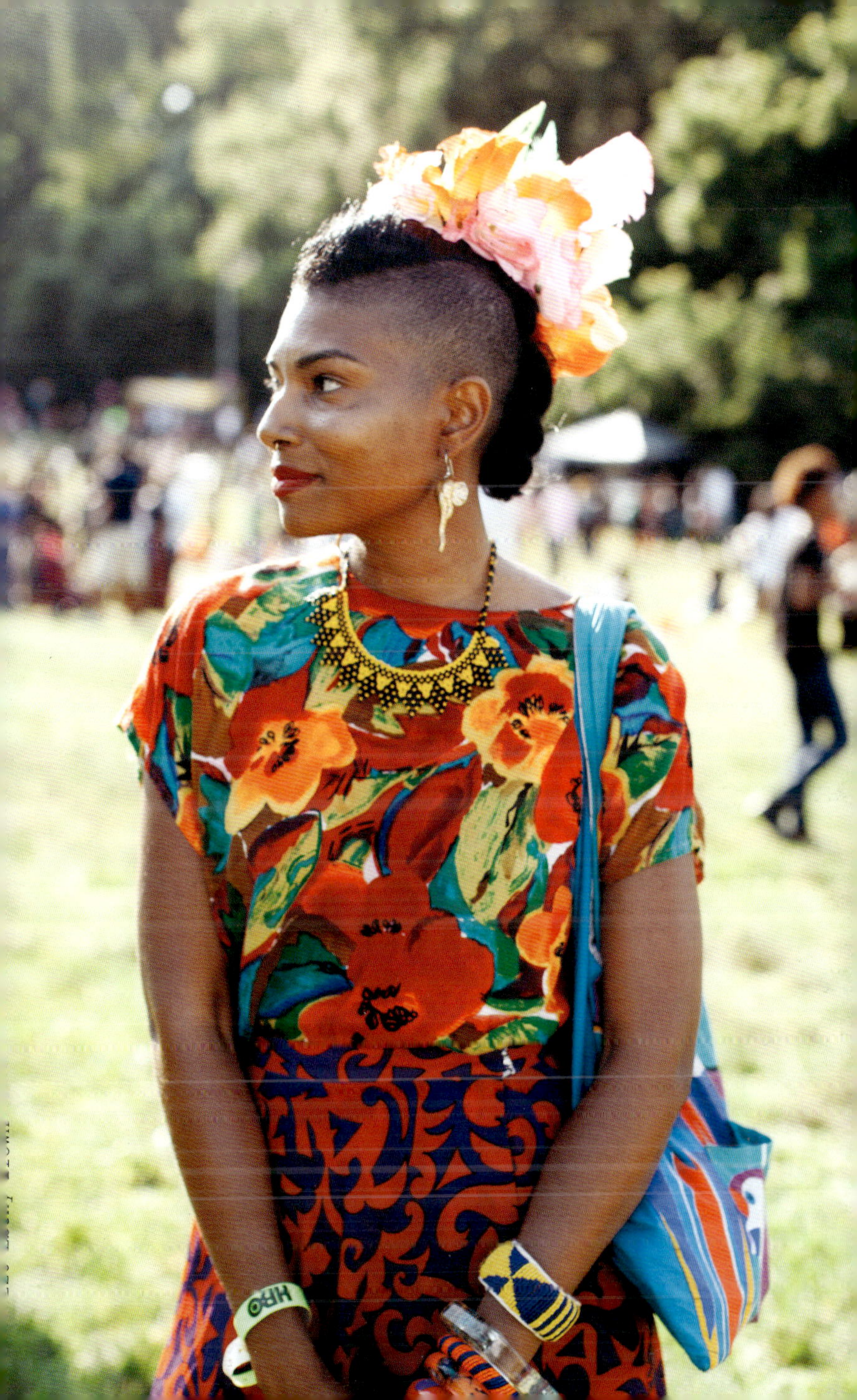

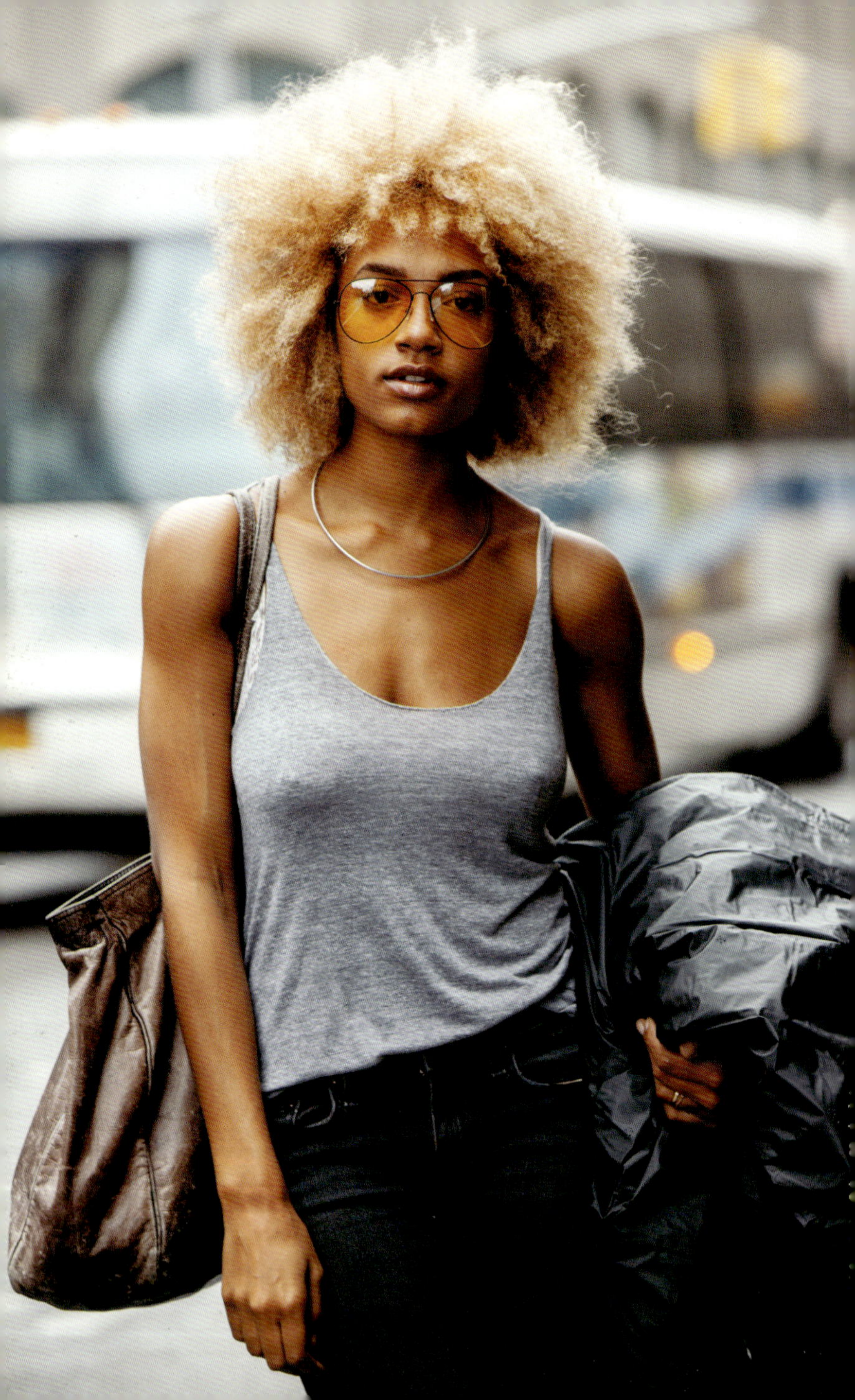

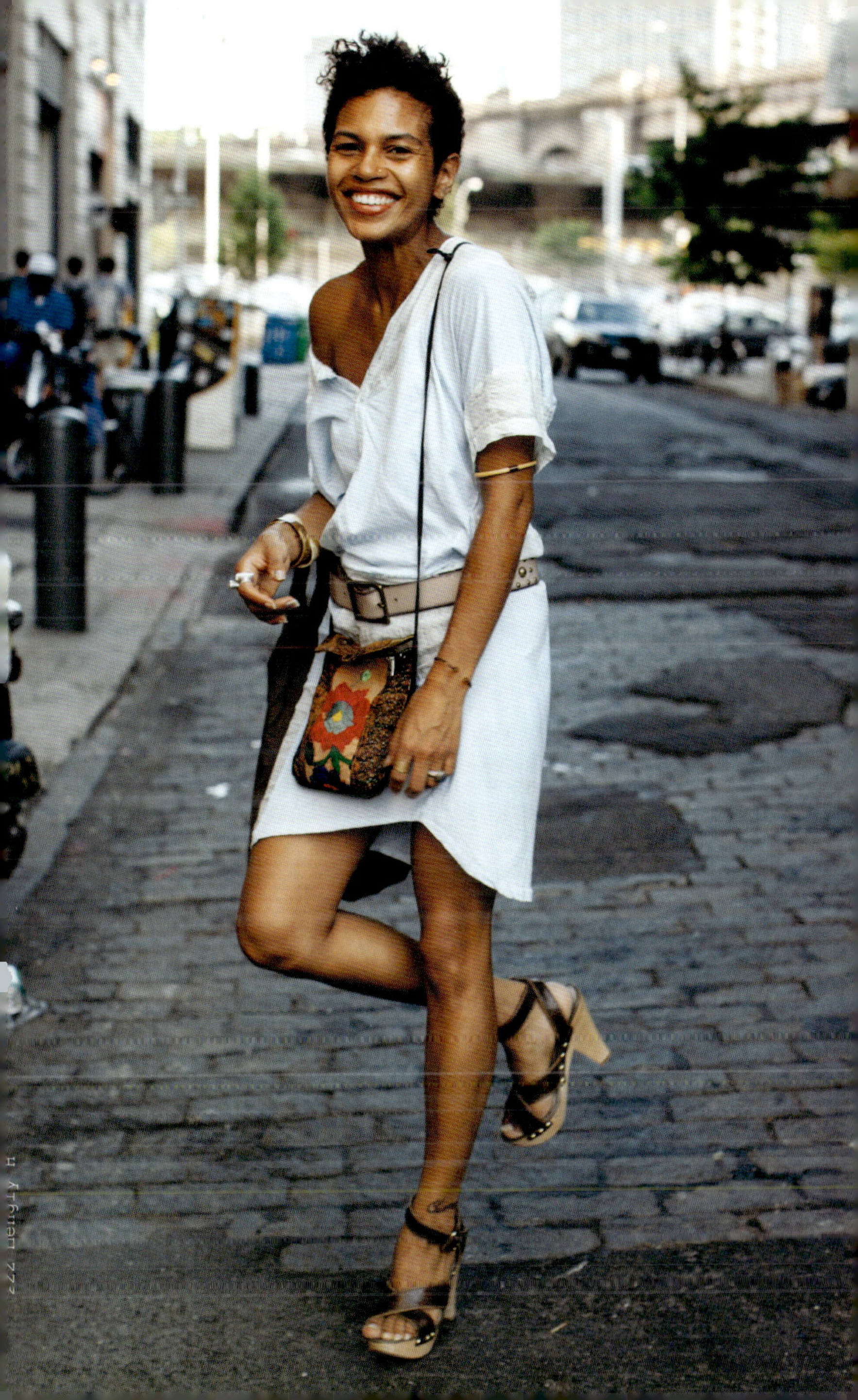

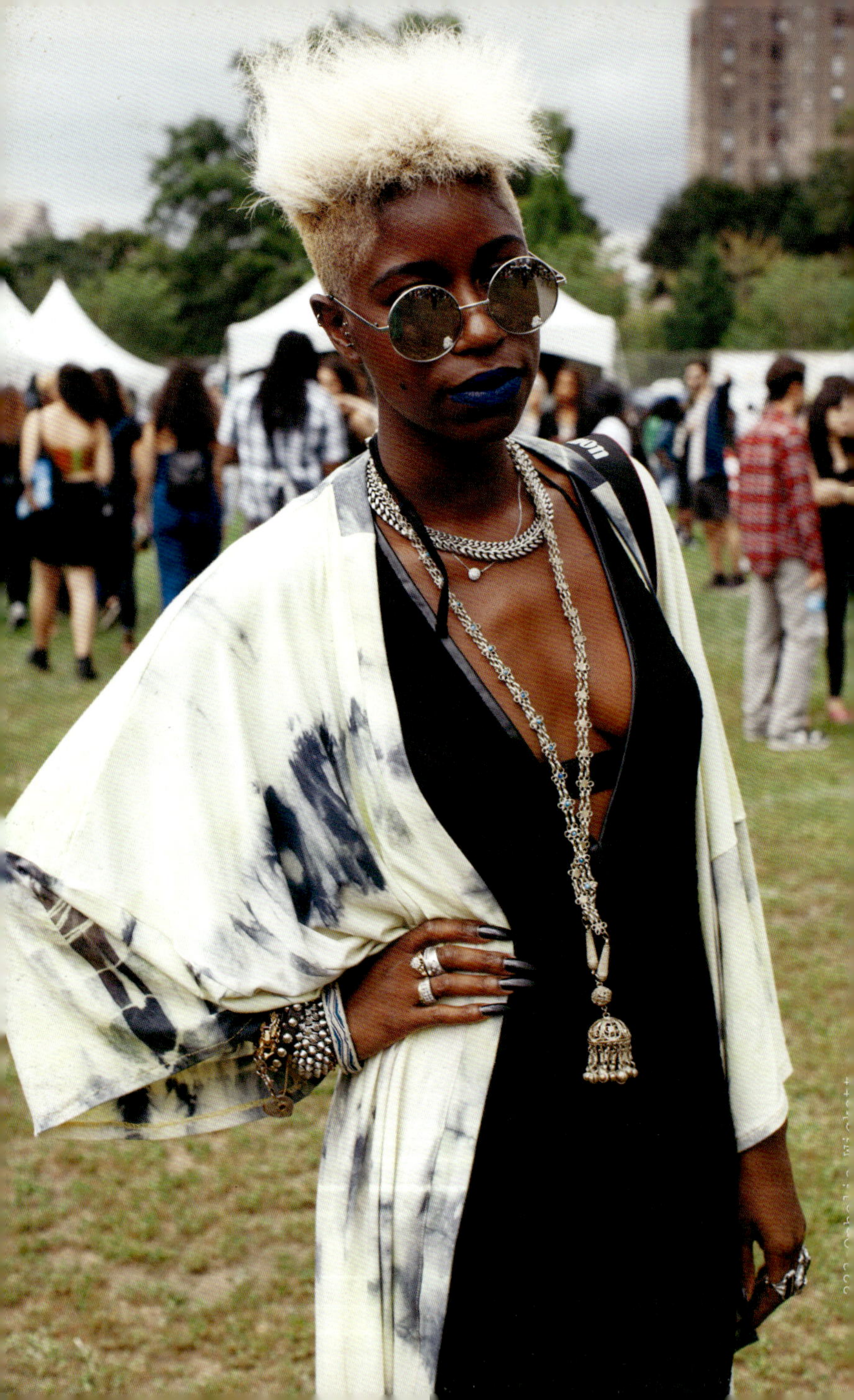

Ophelia Wickett

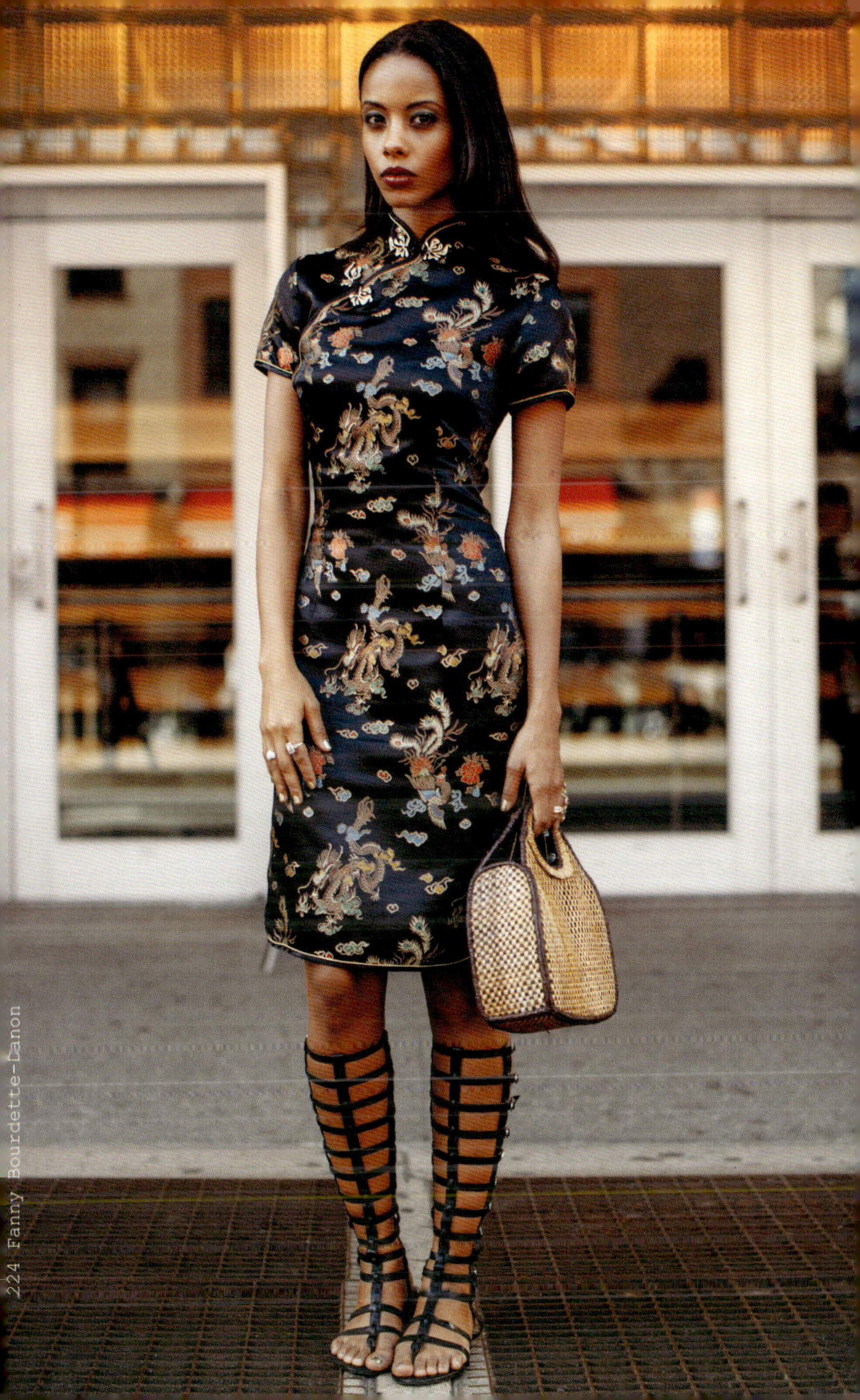

 Fanny Bourdette-Lanon

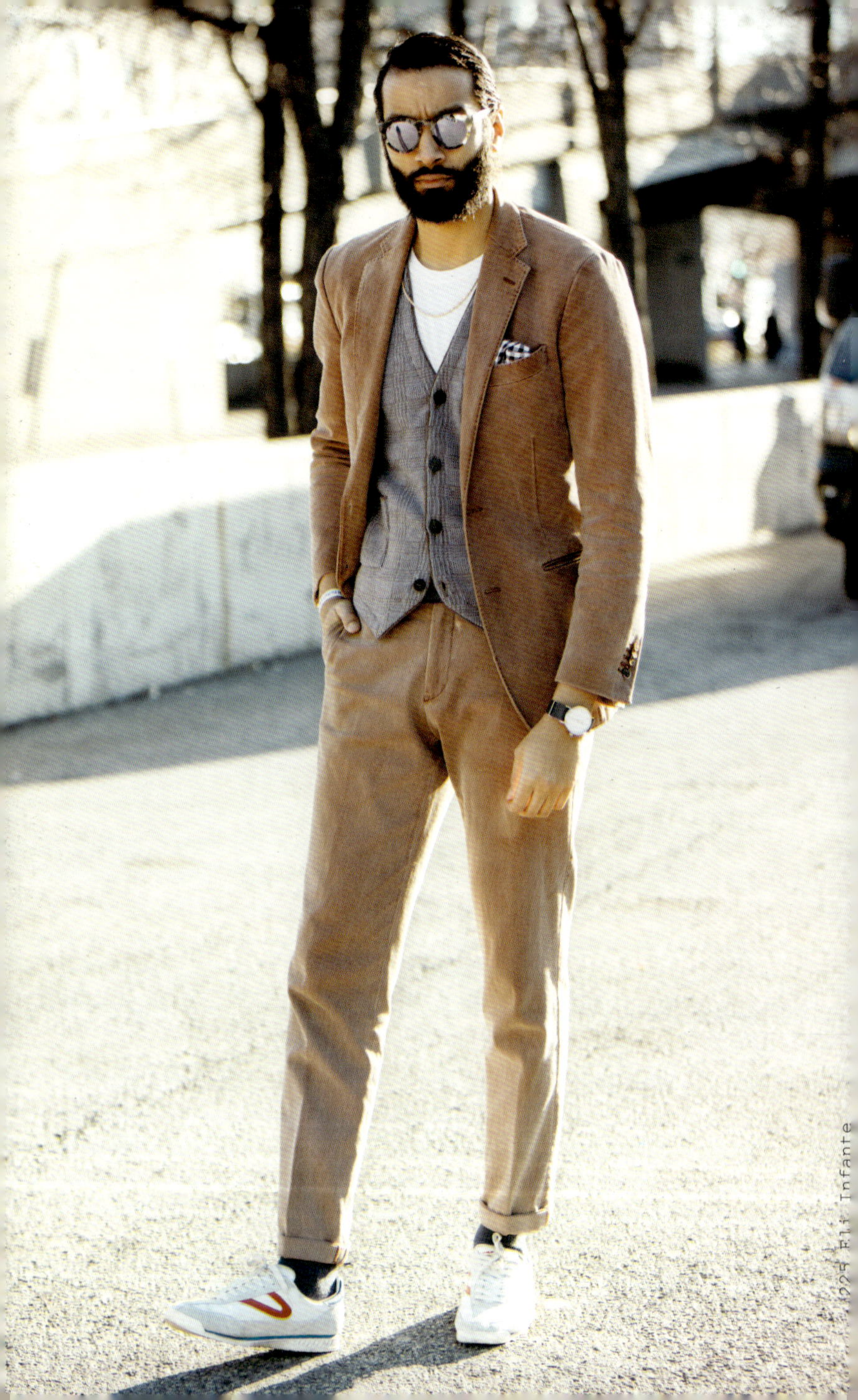

225 Eli Infante

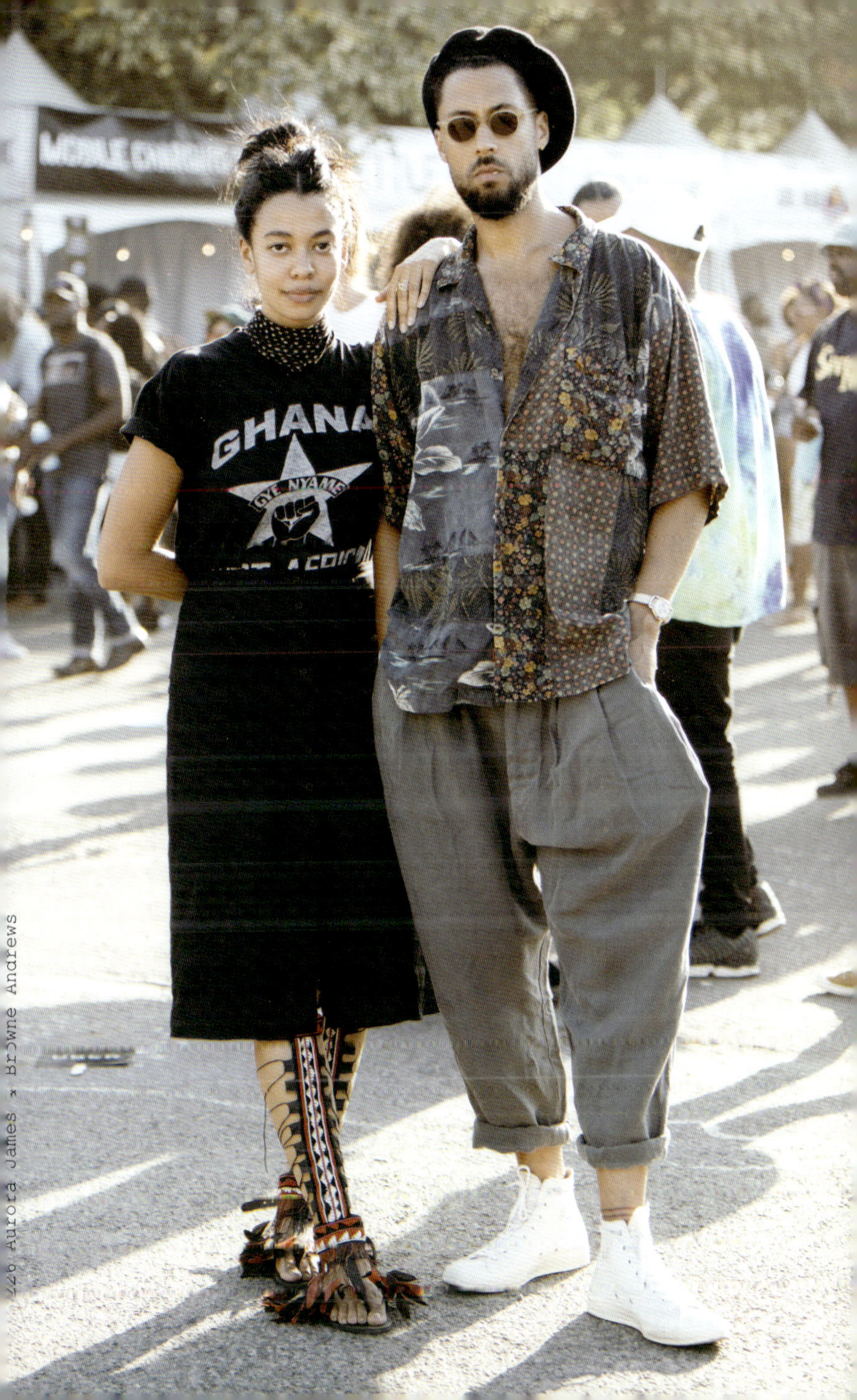

 Aurora James x Browne Andrews

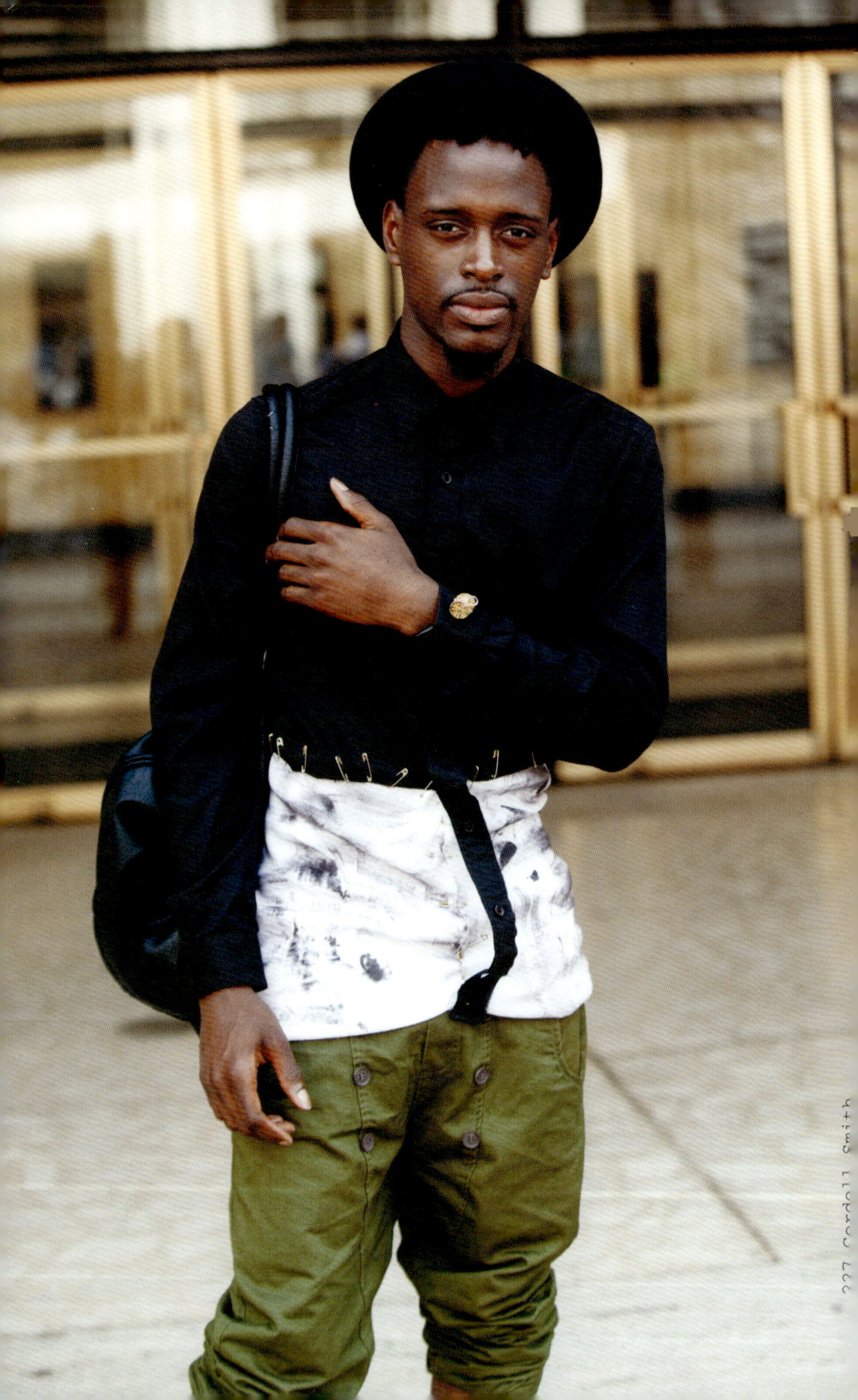

227 Cordell Smith

“

I have always customized my clothes. It’s a reflection of my individual style.

”

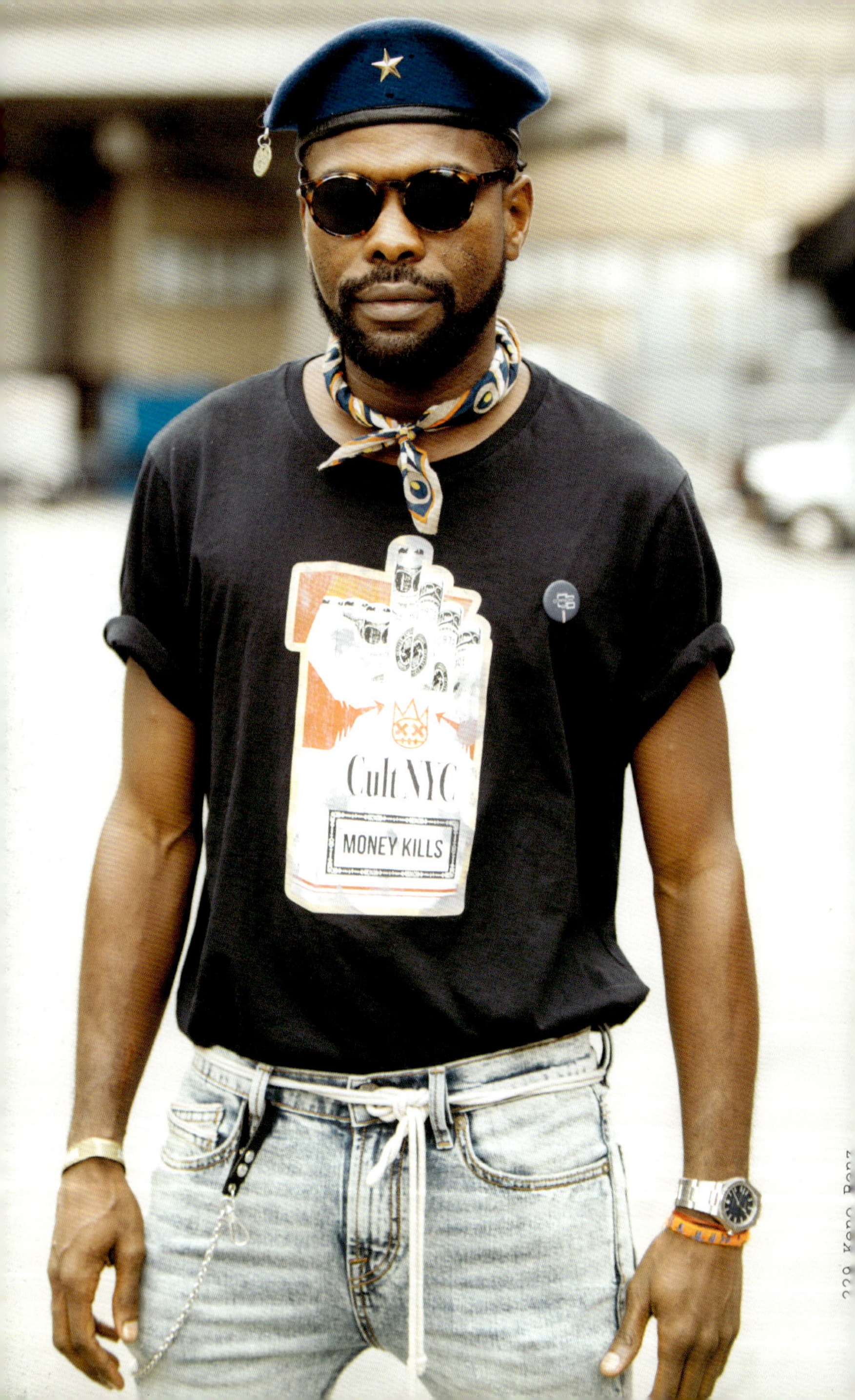
CultNYC
MONEY KILLS

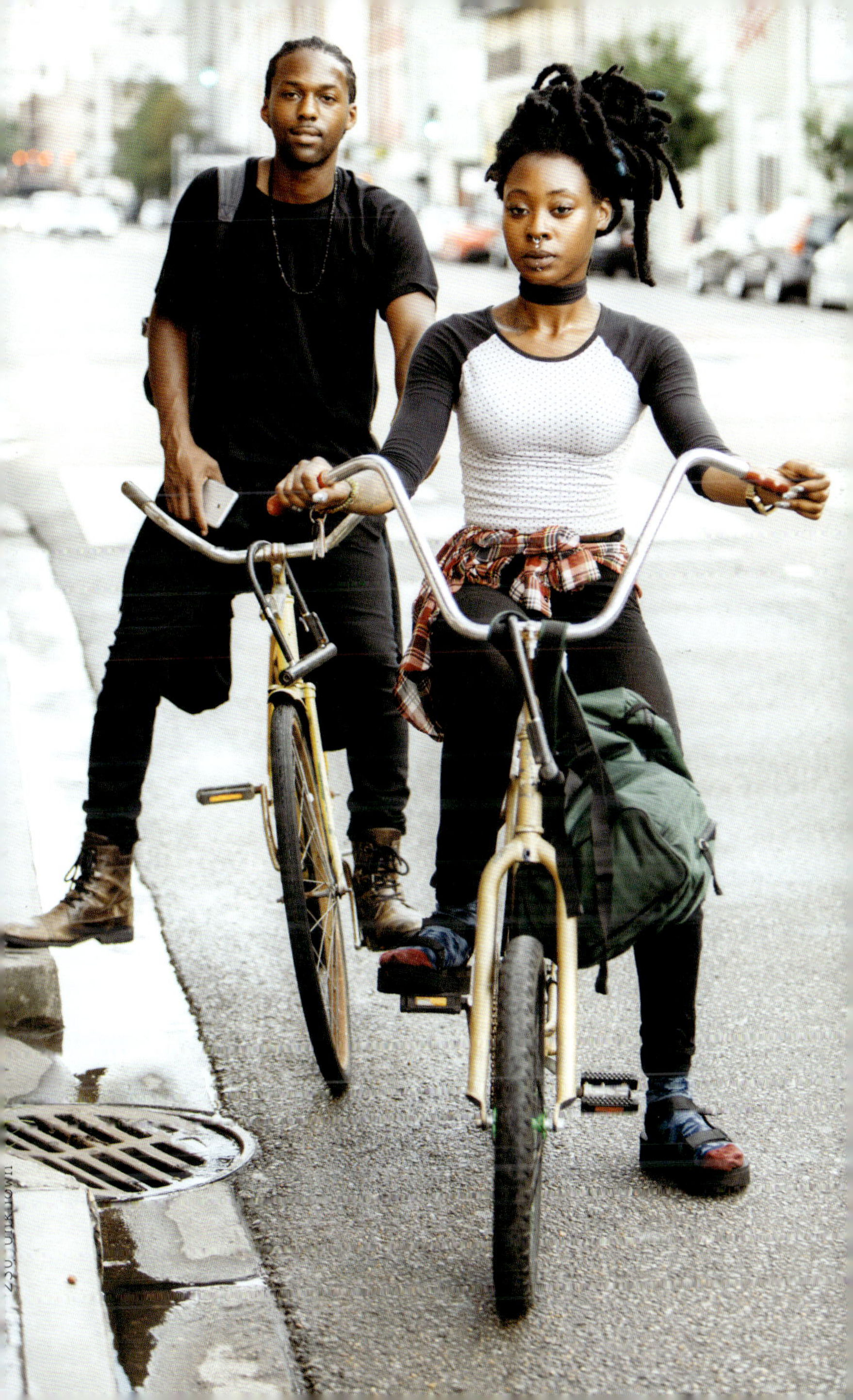

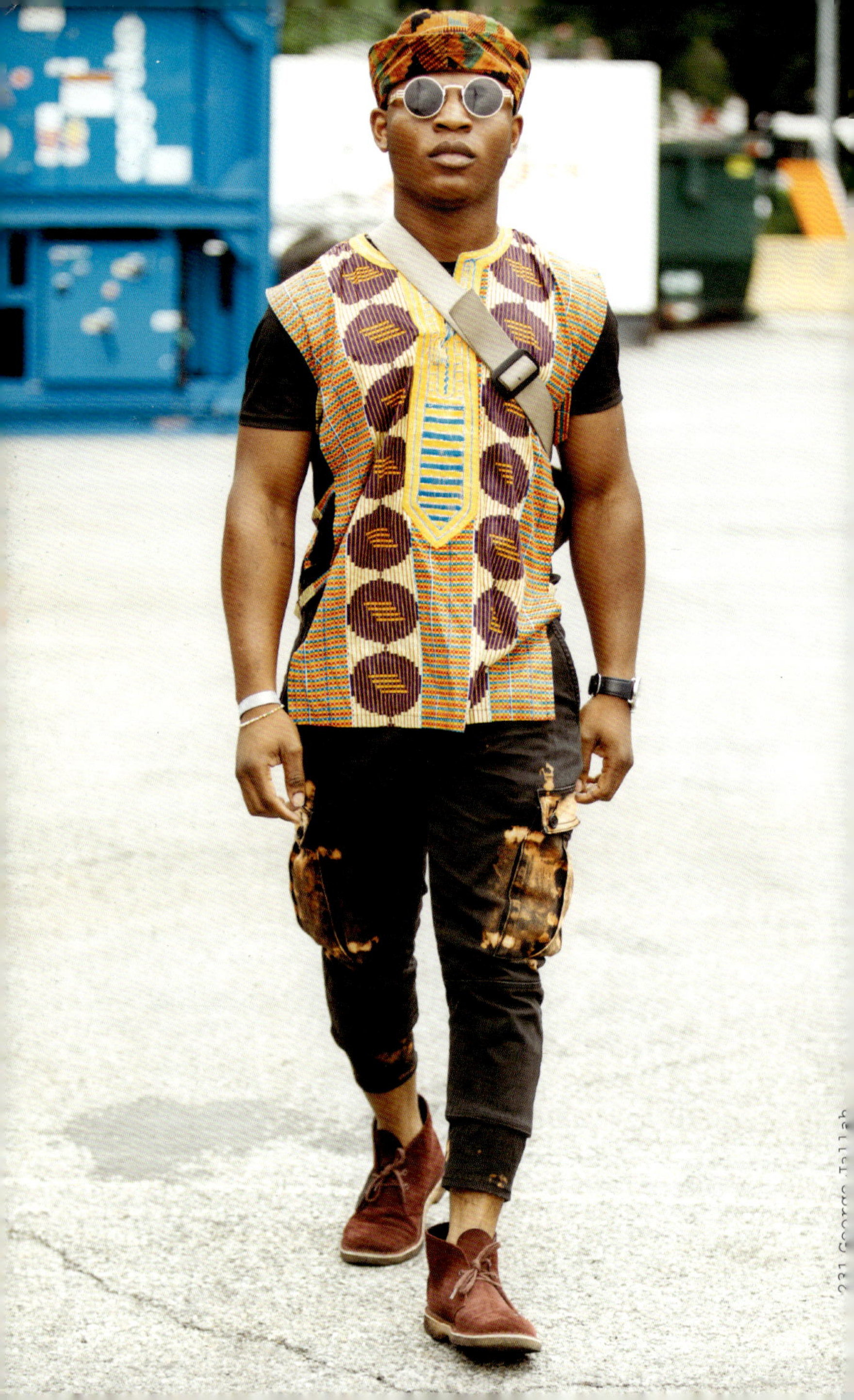

231 George Tallah

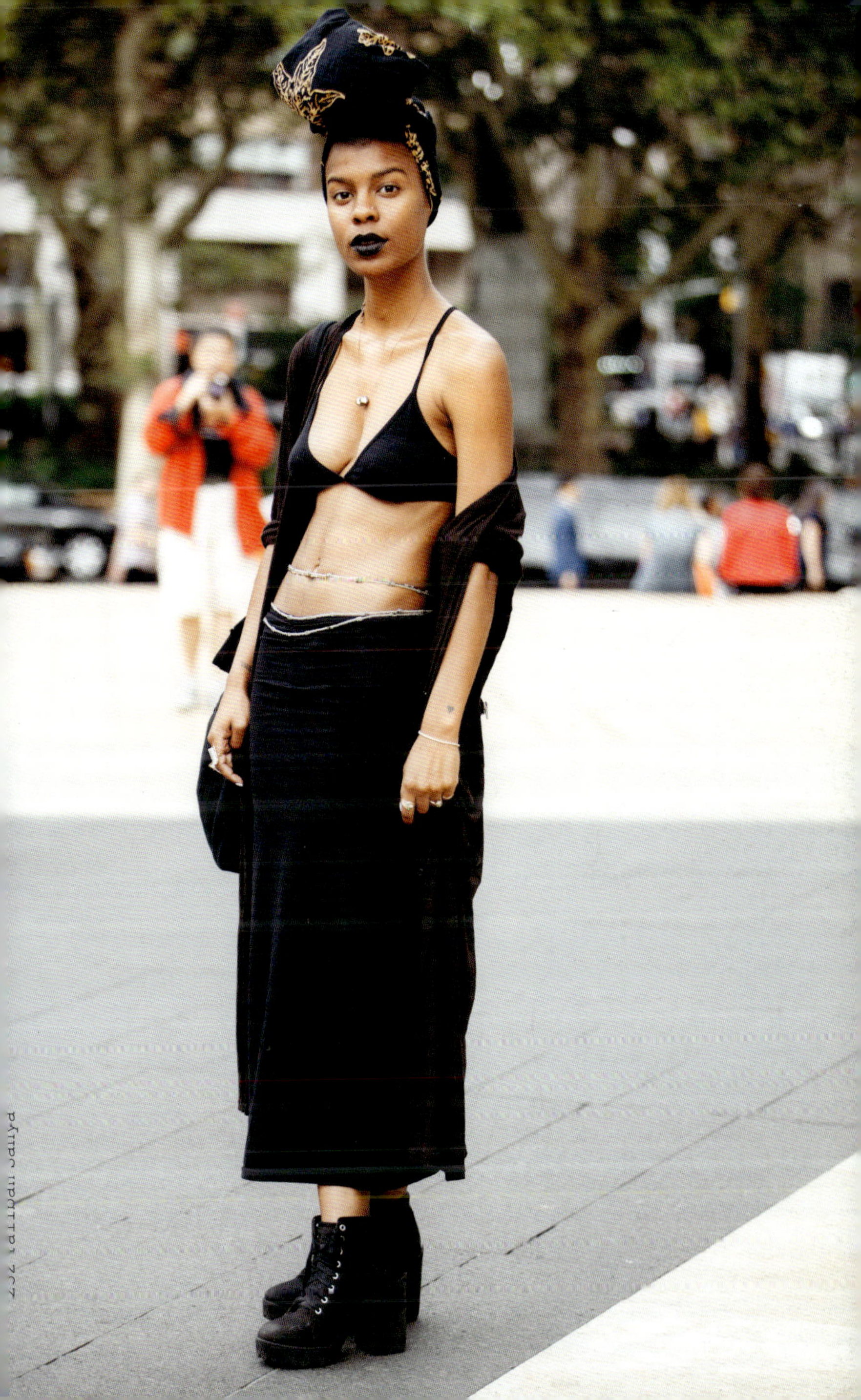

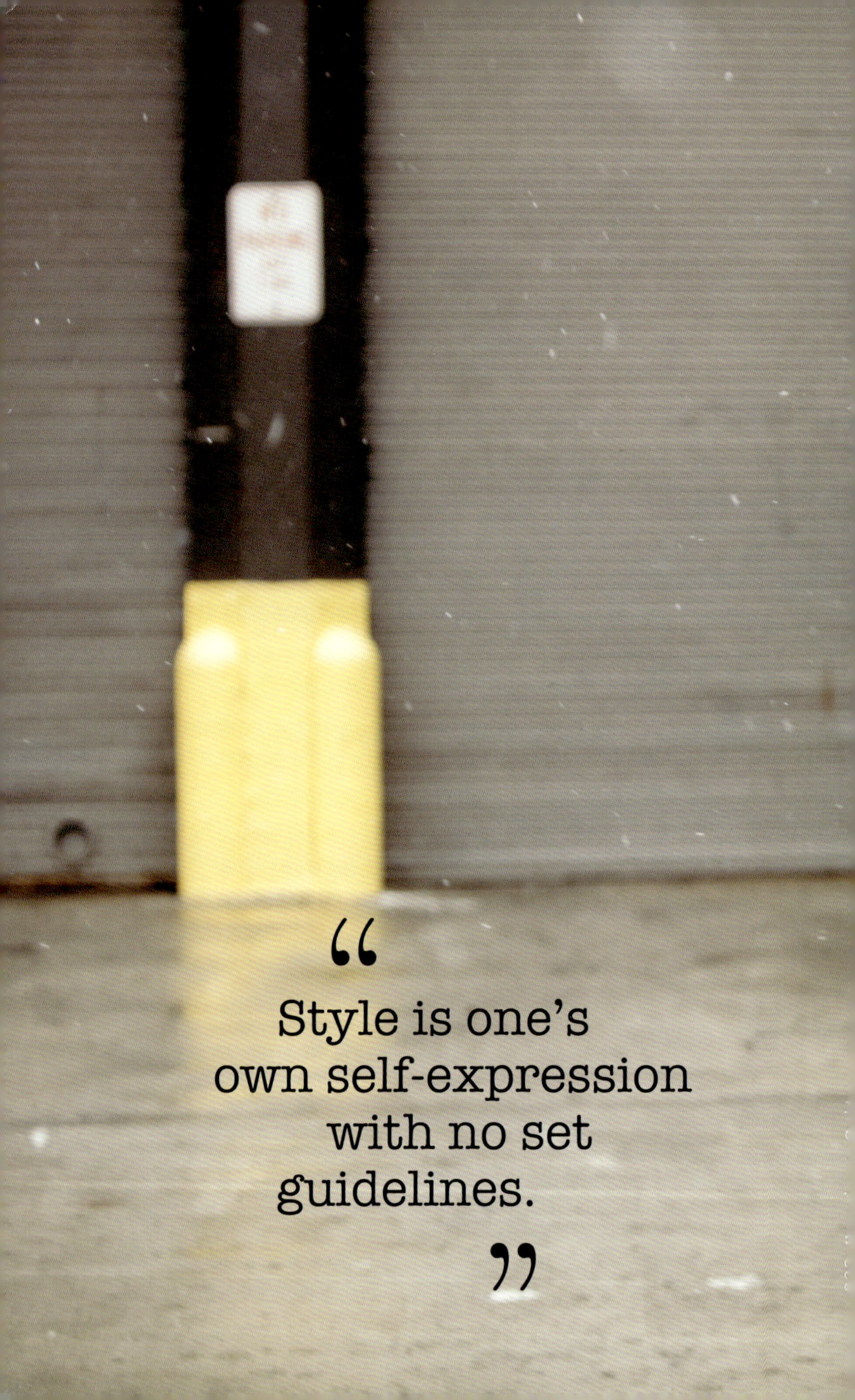

“Style is one’s own self-expression with no set guidelines.”

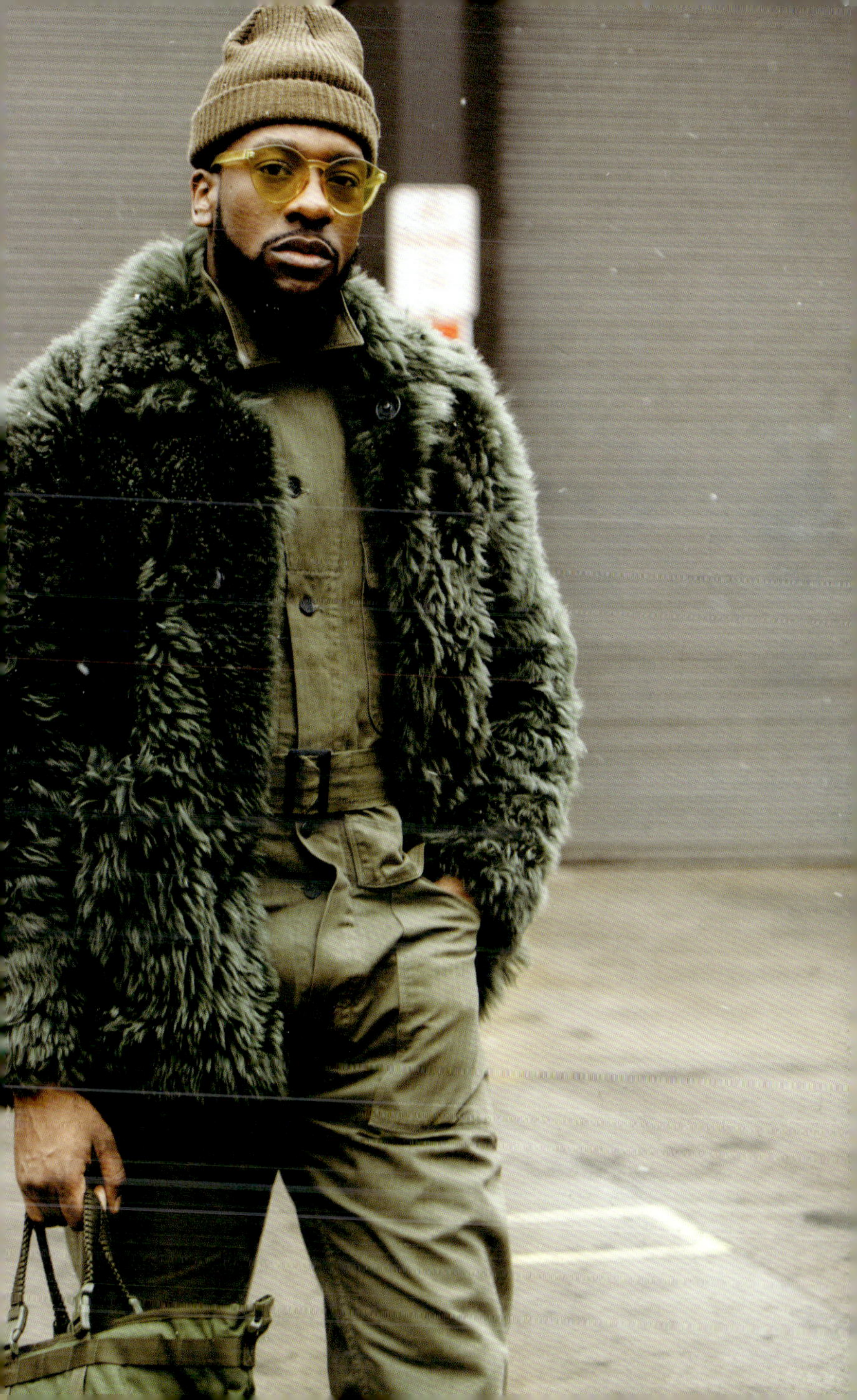

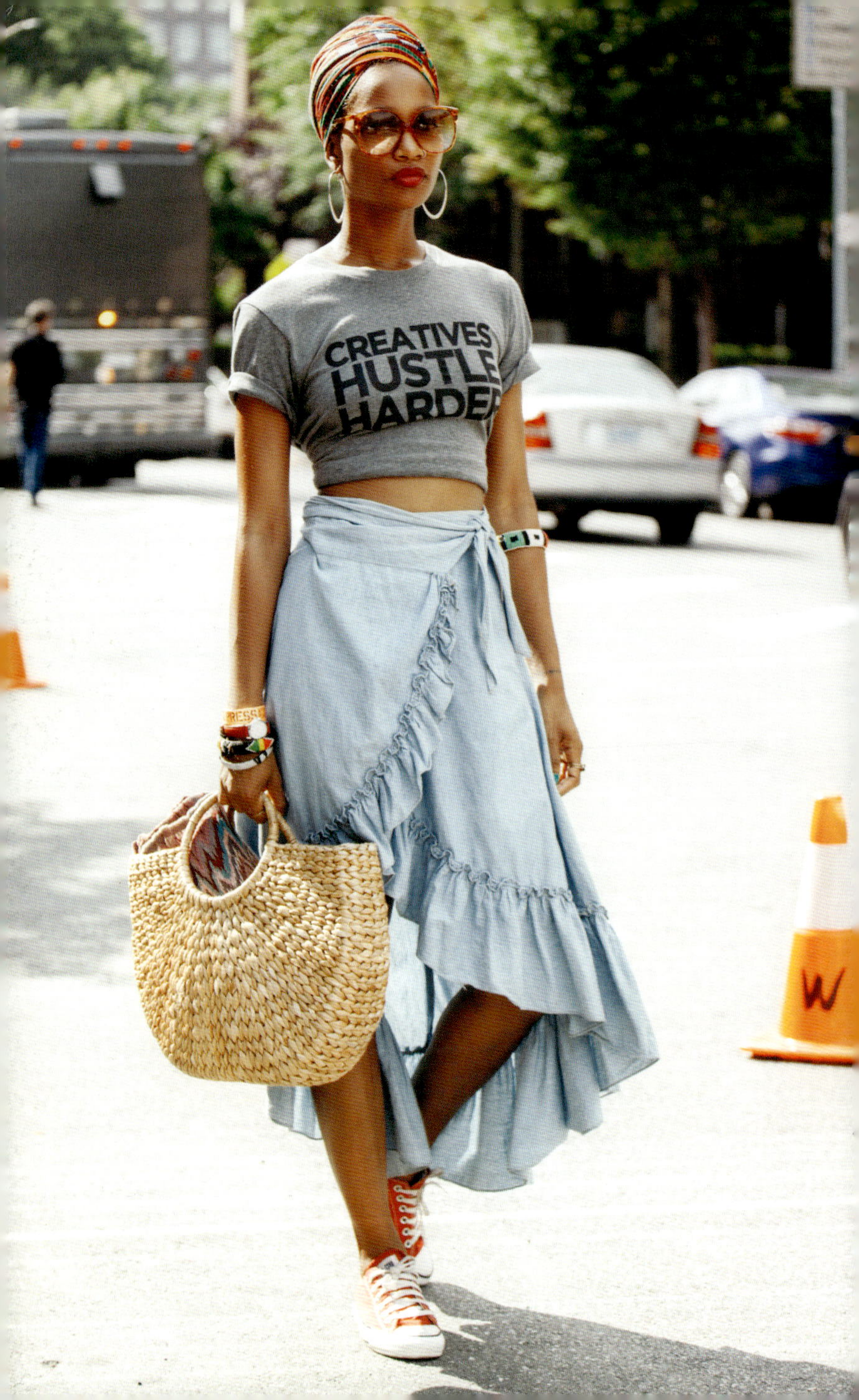
CREATIVES
HUSTLE
HARDER

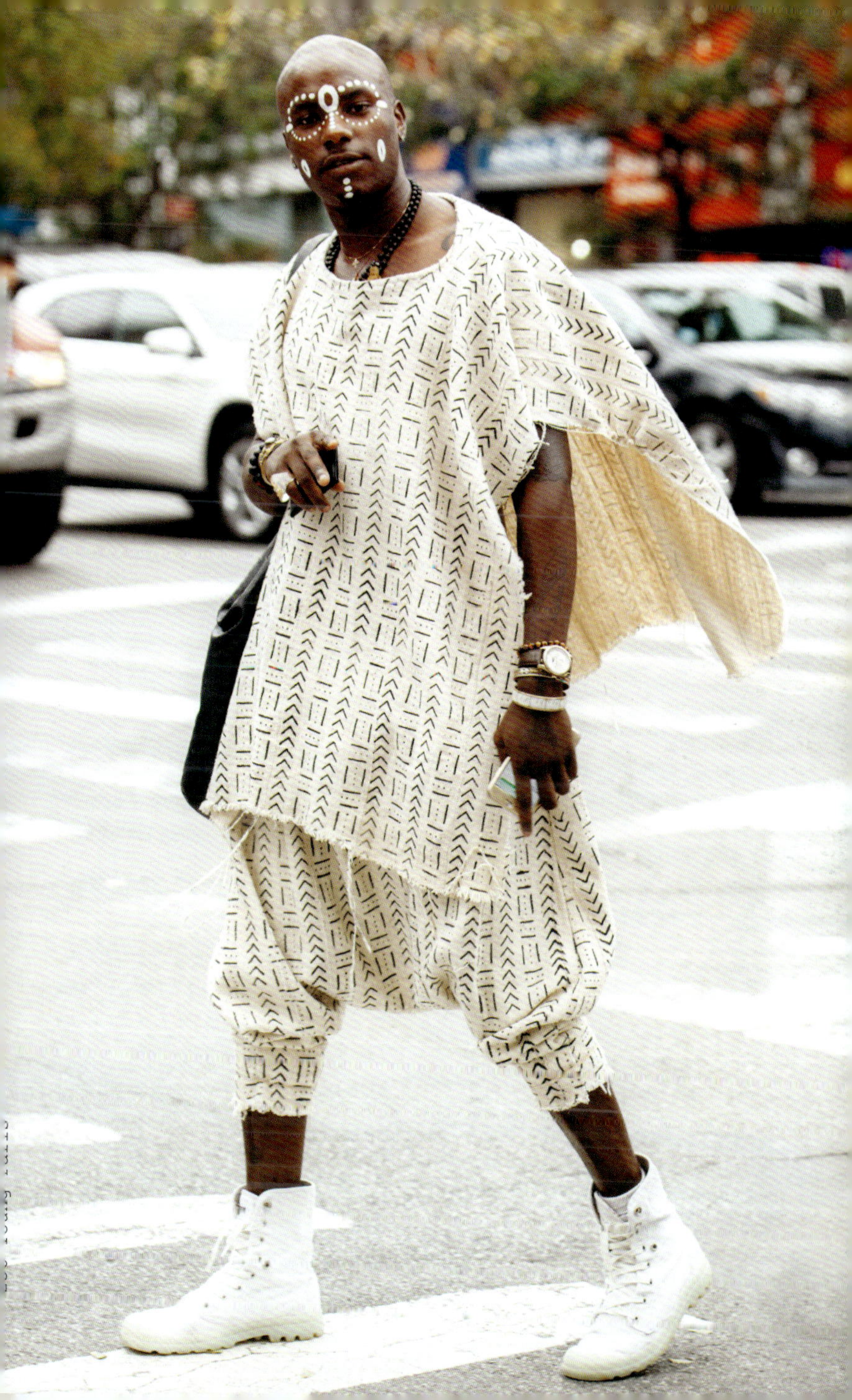

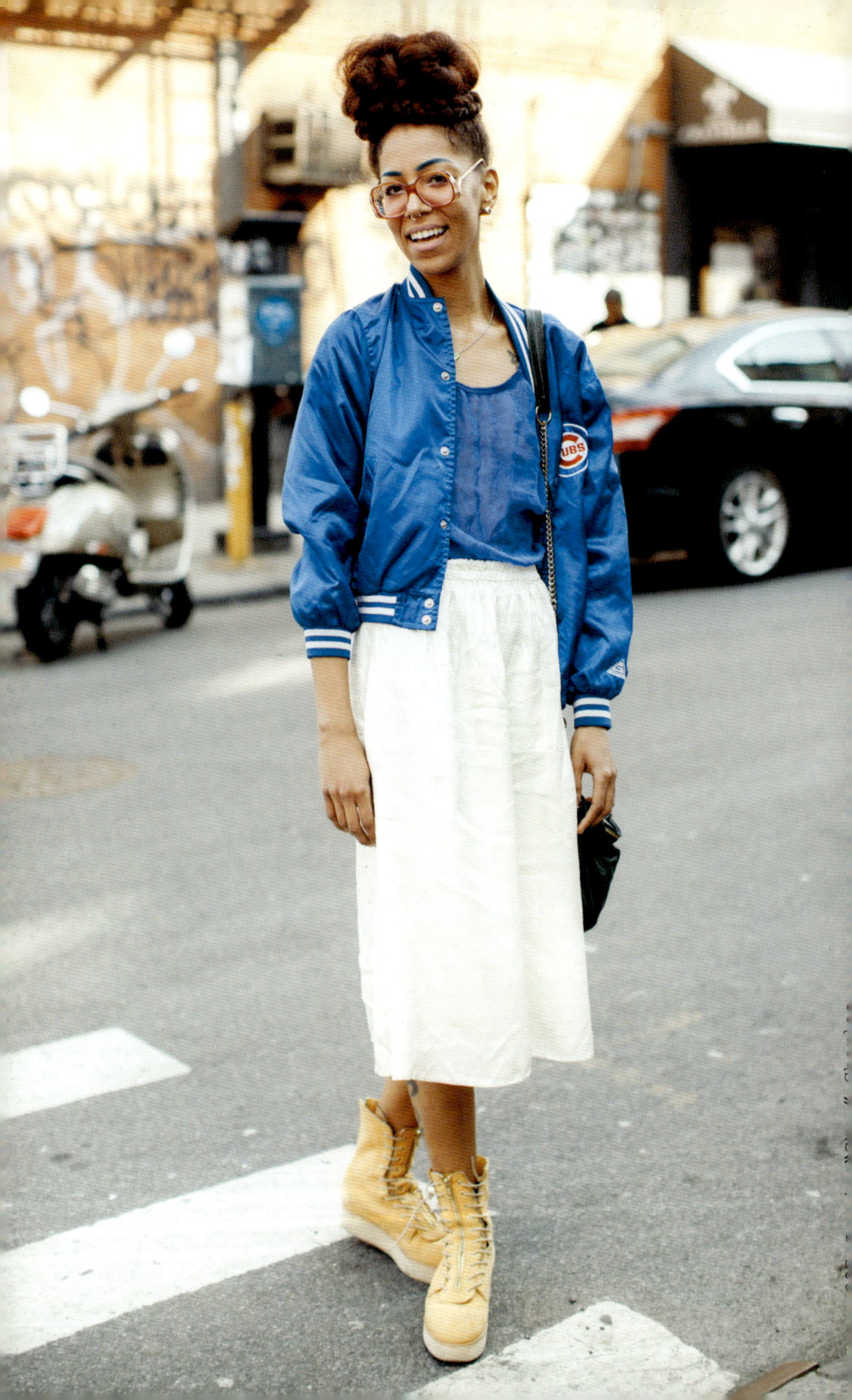
CUBS

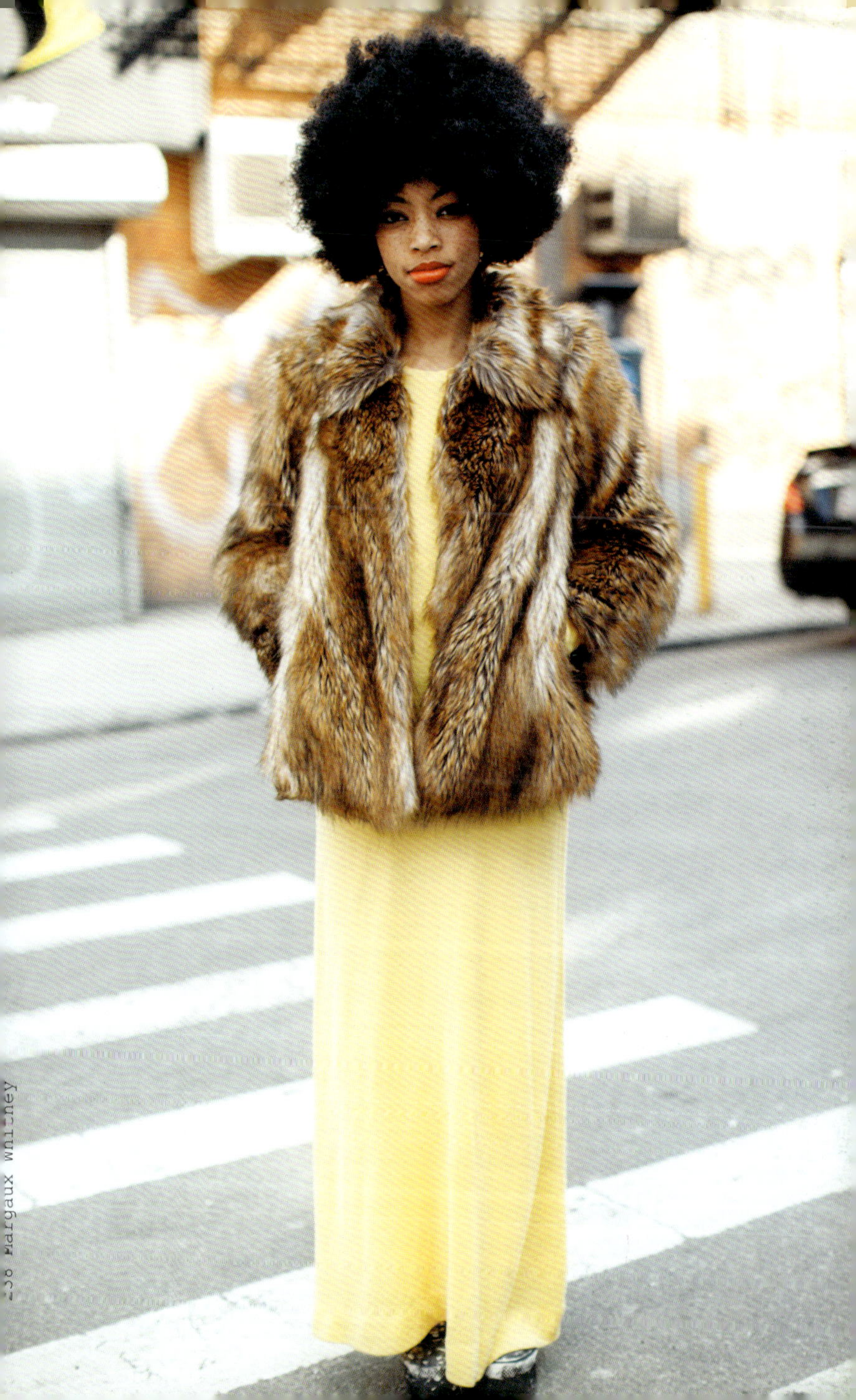

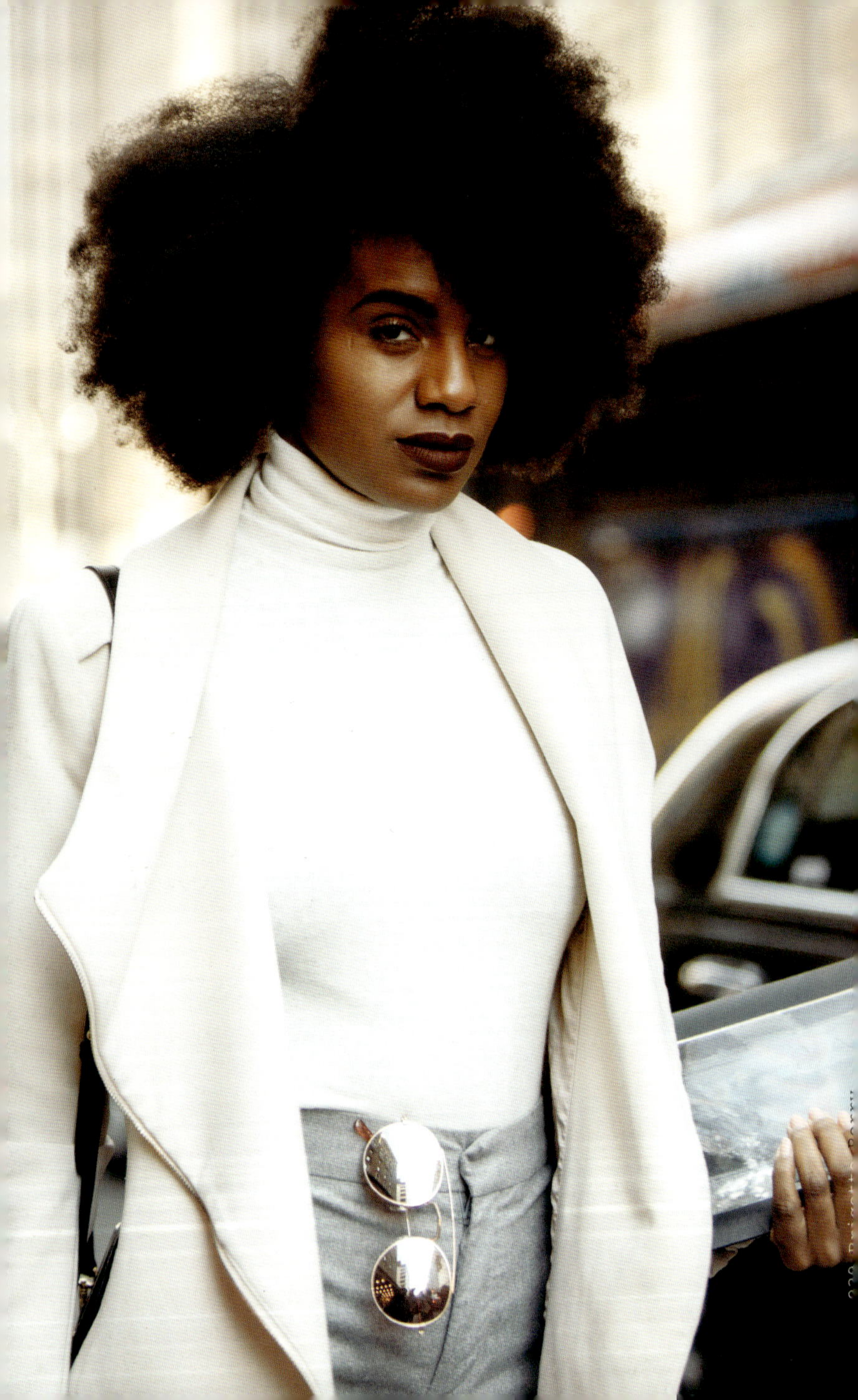

"You have the power to control your own destiny. That includes your happiness."

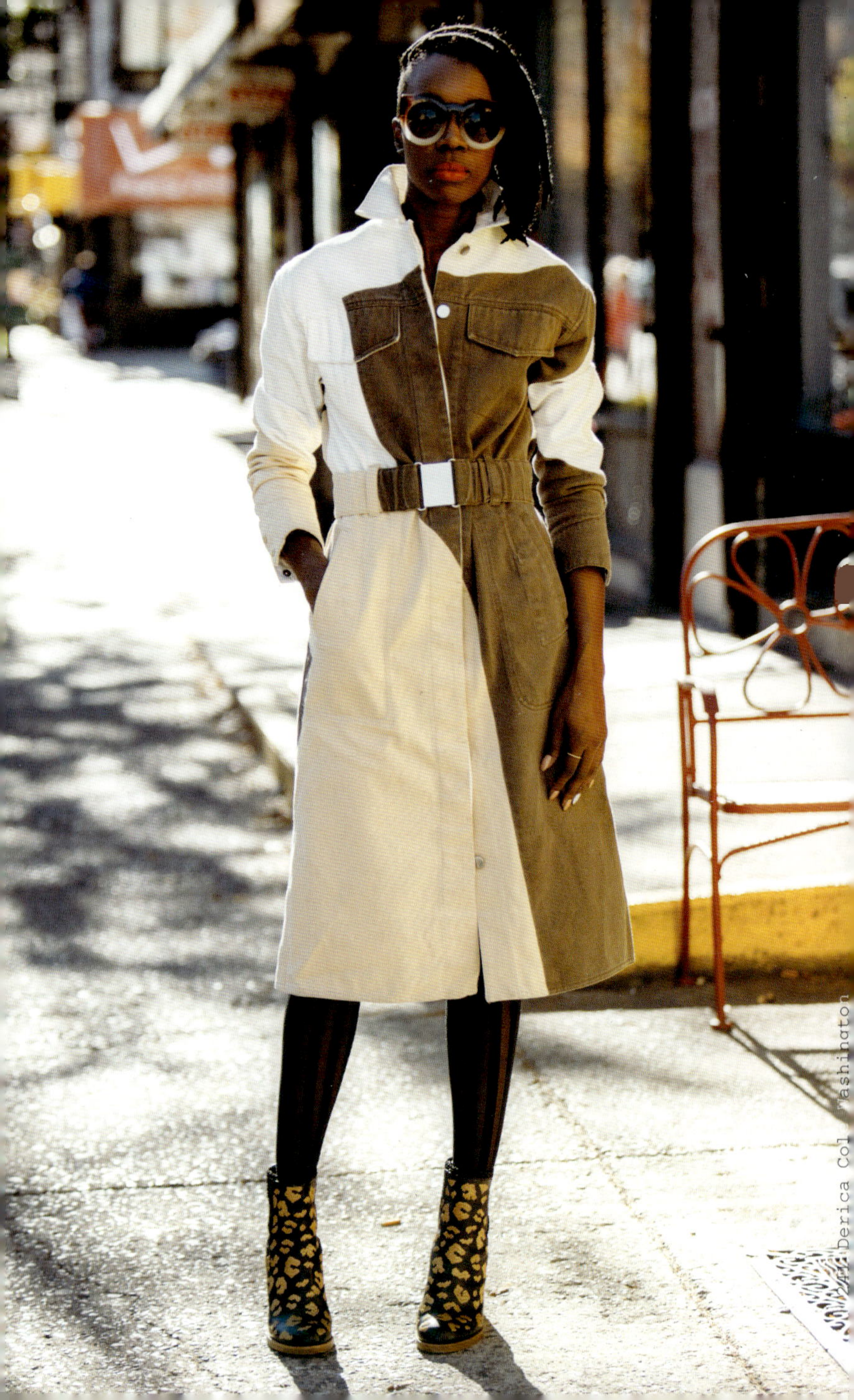

Ari Derica Col Washington

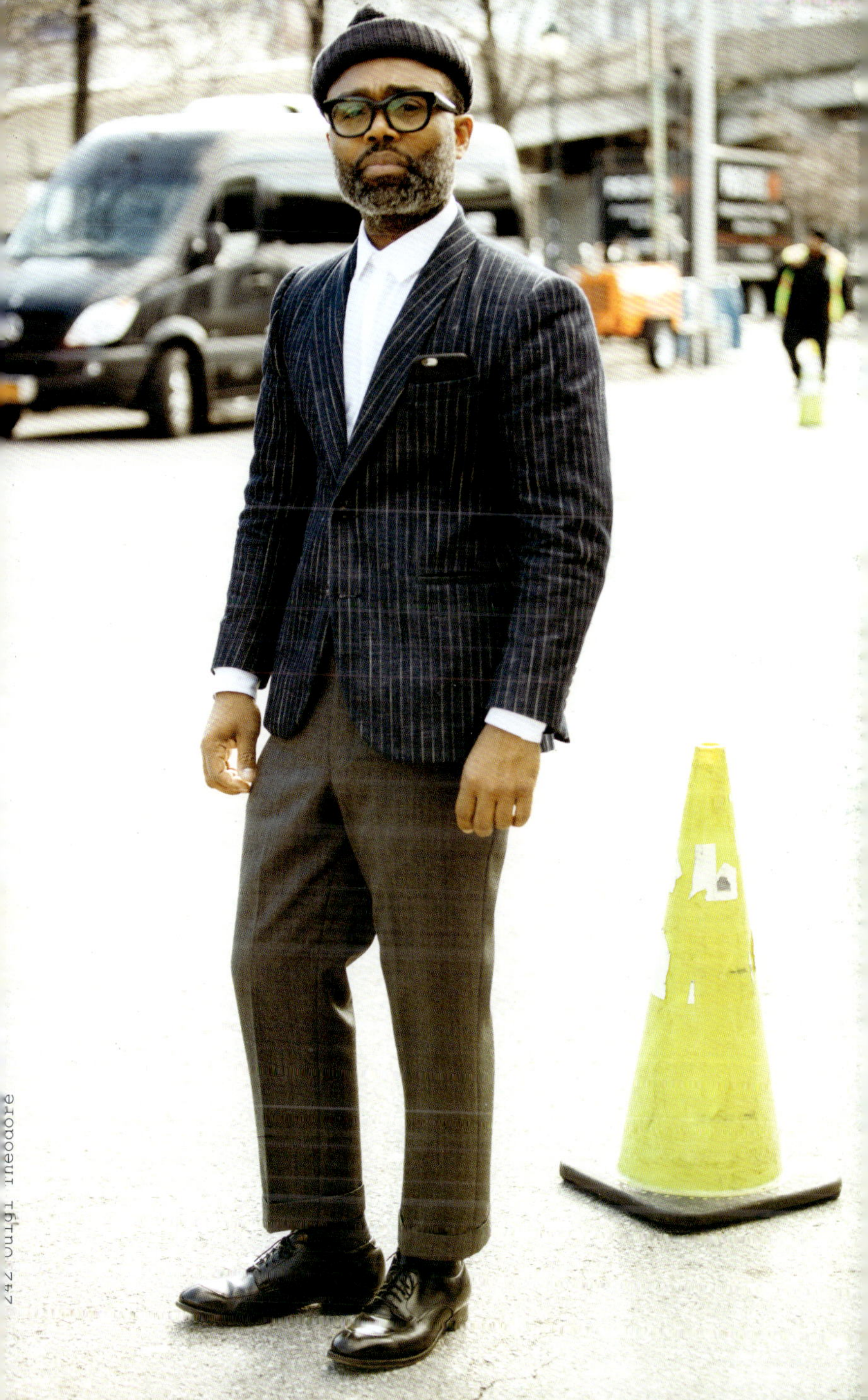

242 Ouigi Theodore

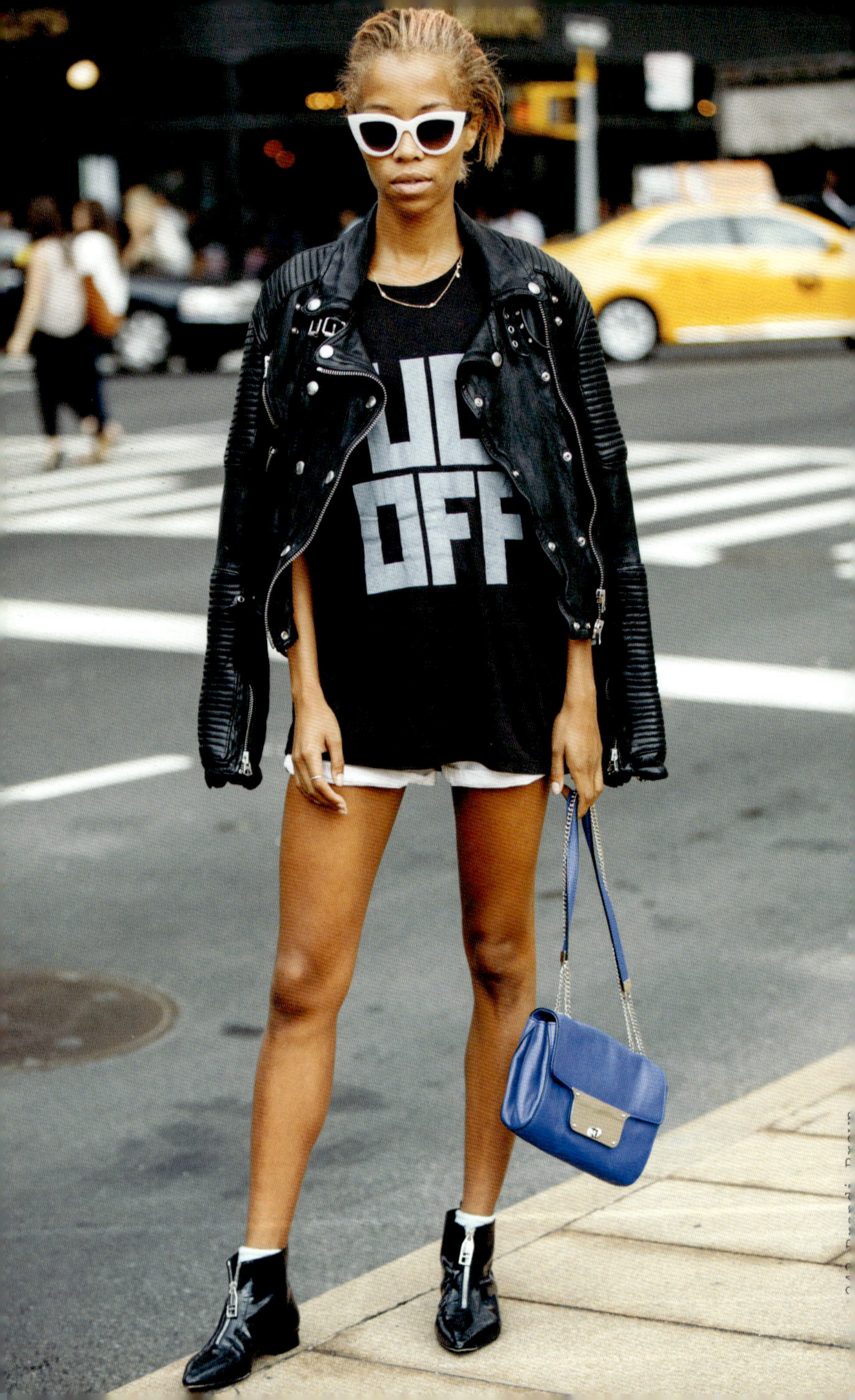
OFF

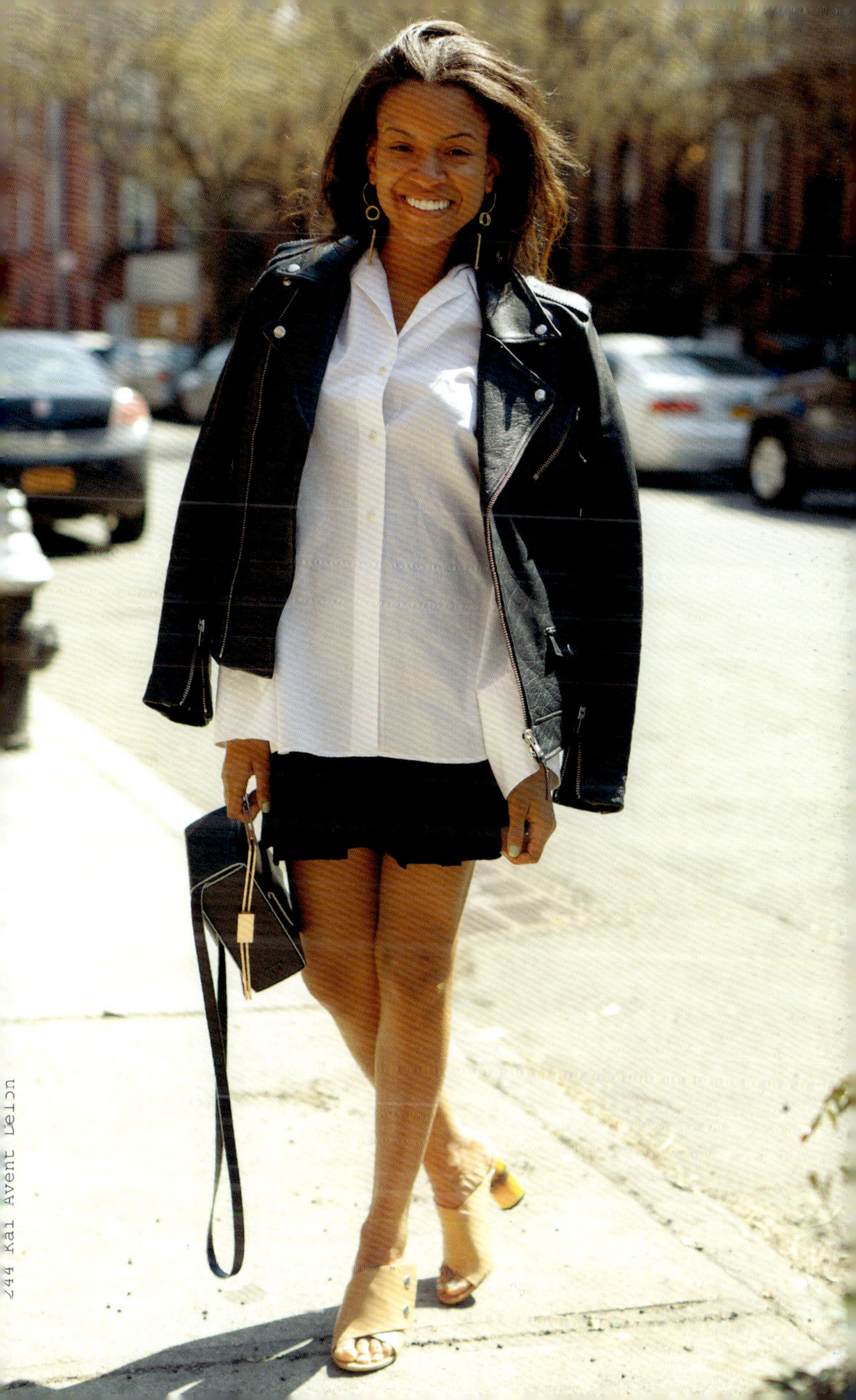

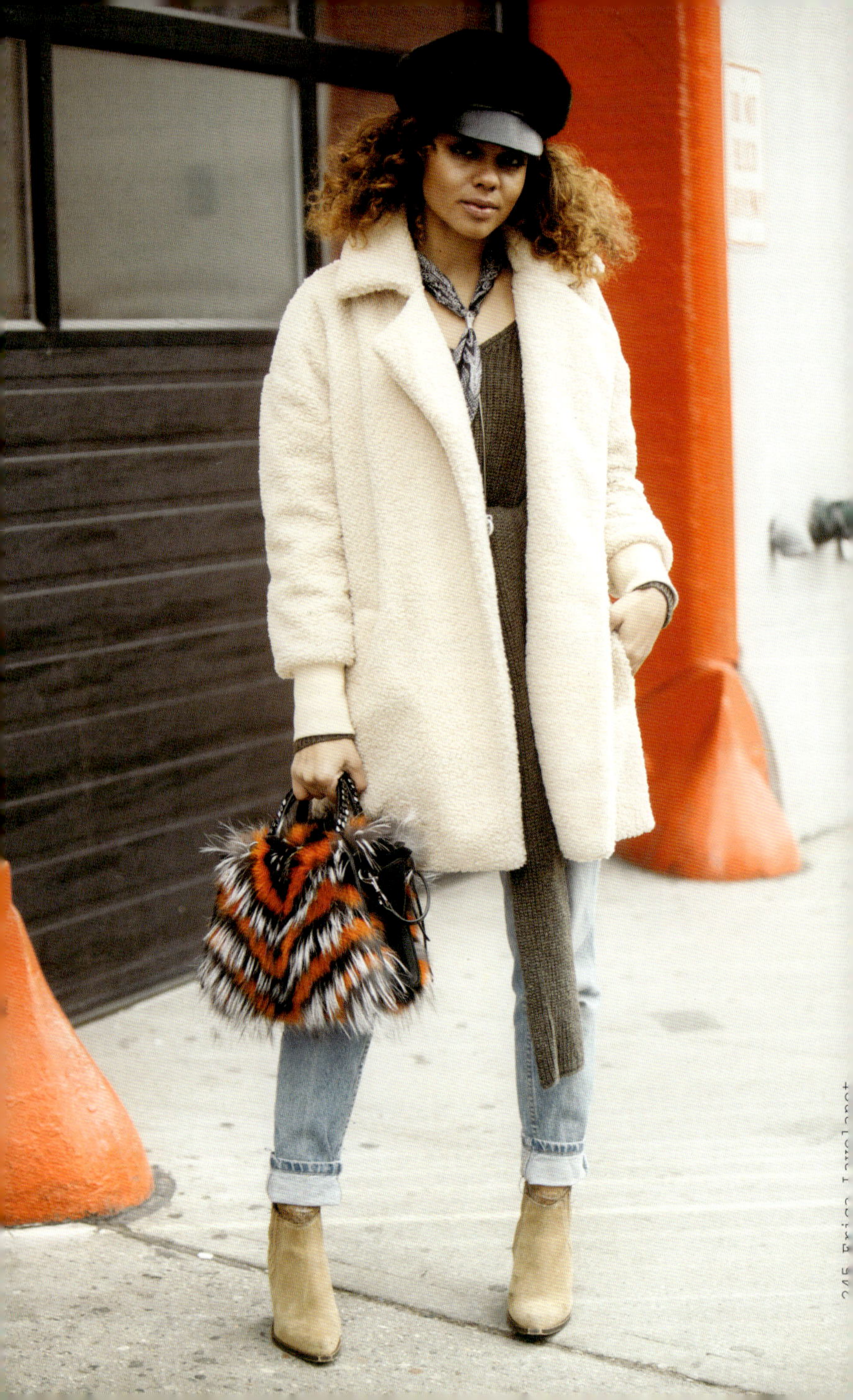

245 Erica Lavelanet

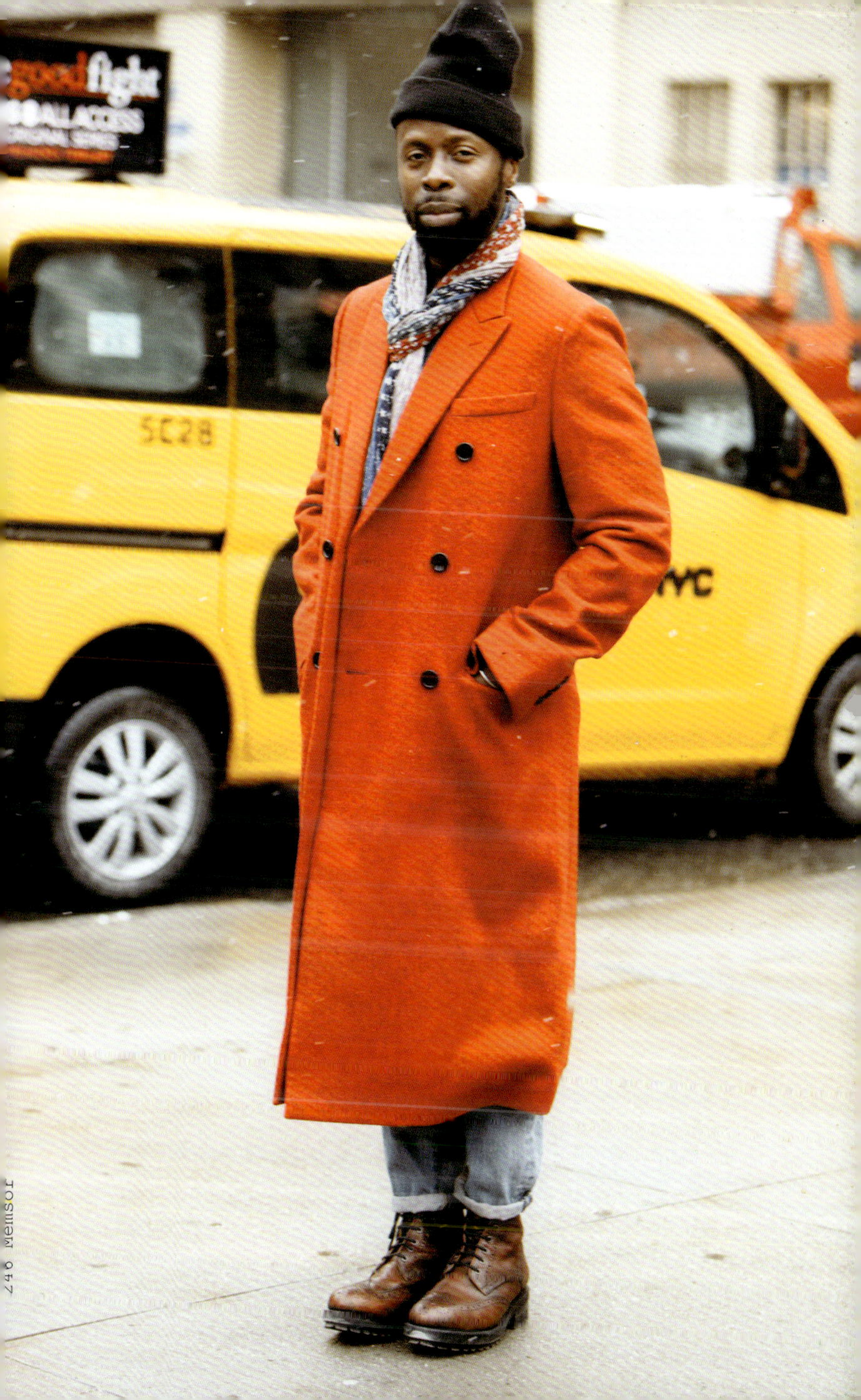
goodfight
ALL ACCESS
ORIGINAL SERIES
5C28
NYC

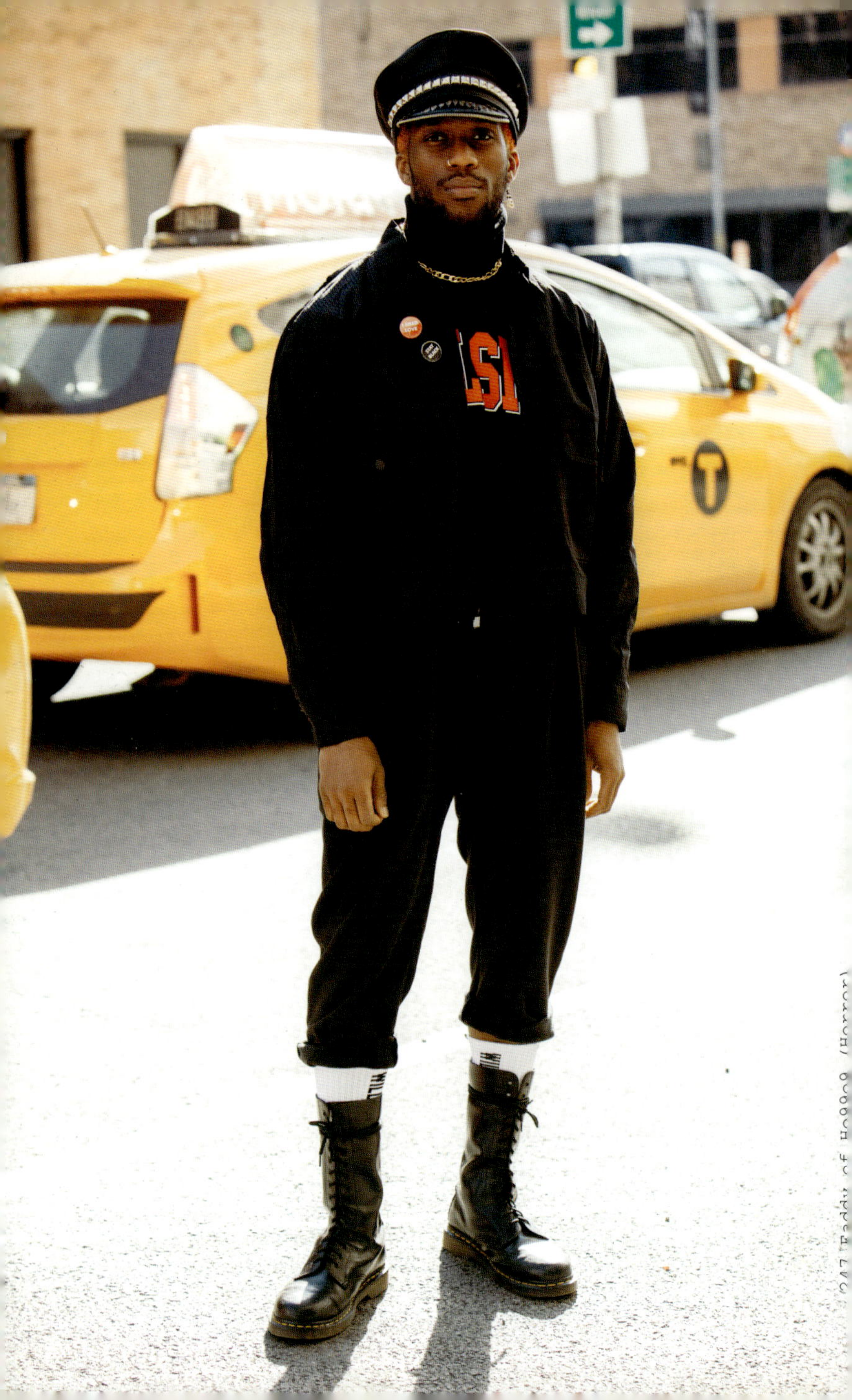

247 Eaddy of Ho99o9 (Horror)

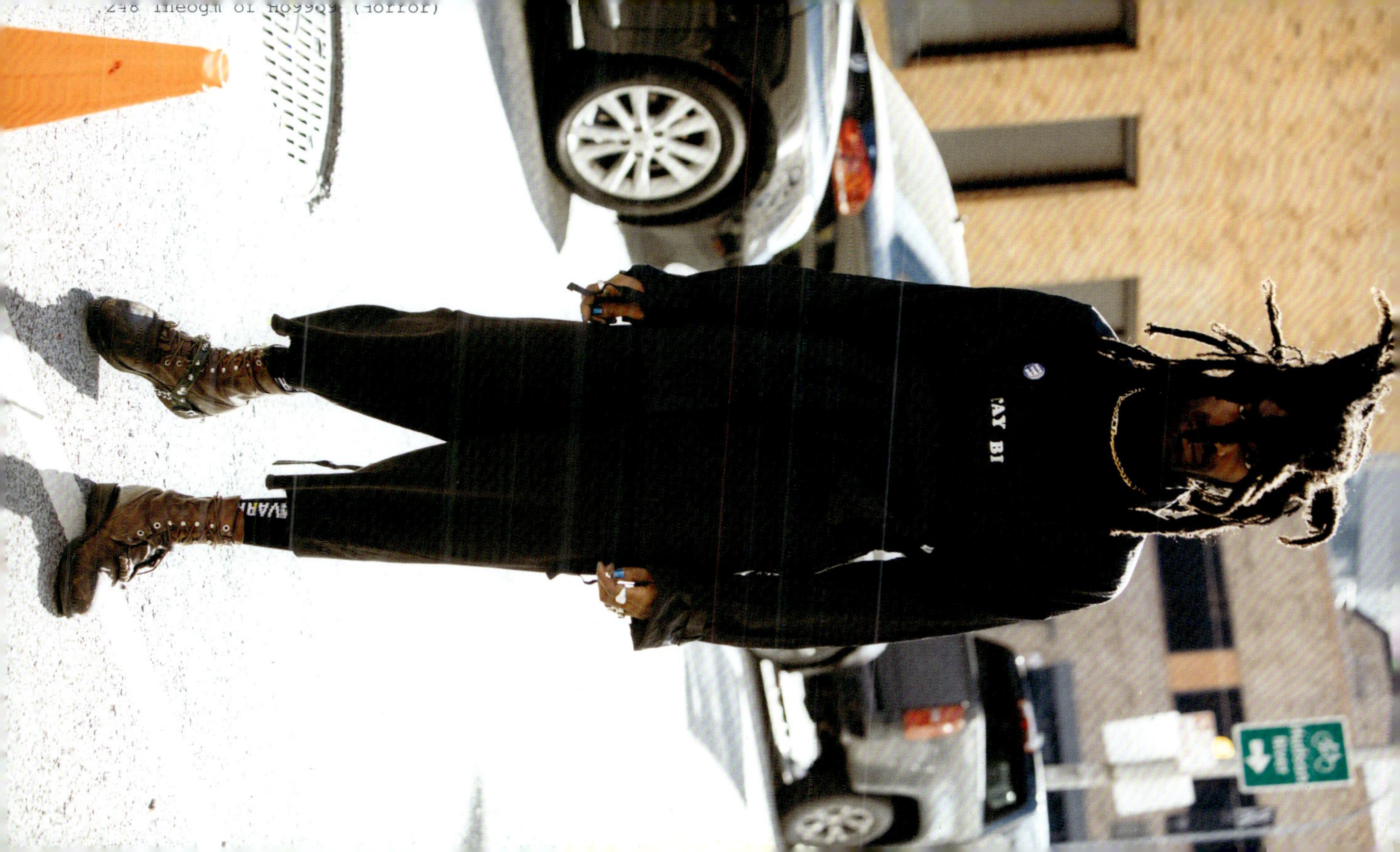

"I think my favorite thing is seeing how my thrifted pieces and my new pieces complement one another."

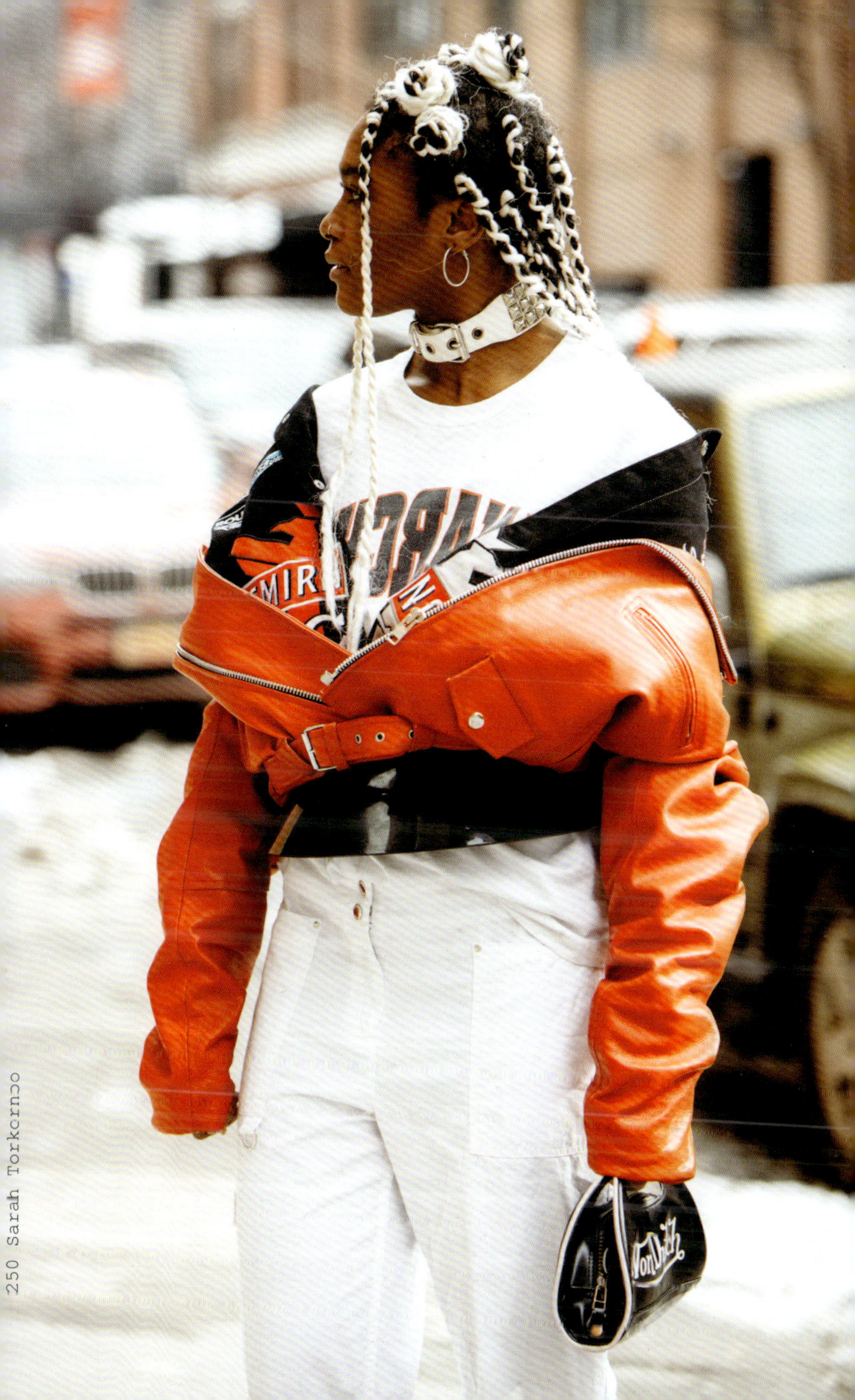

250 Sarah Torkornoo

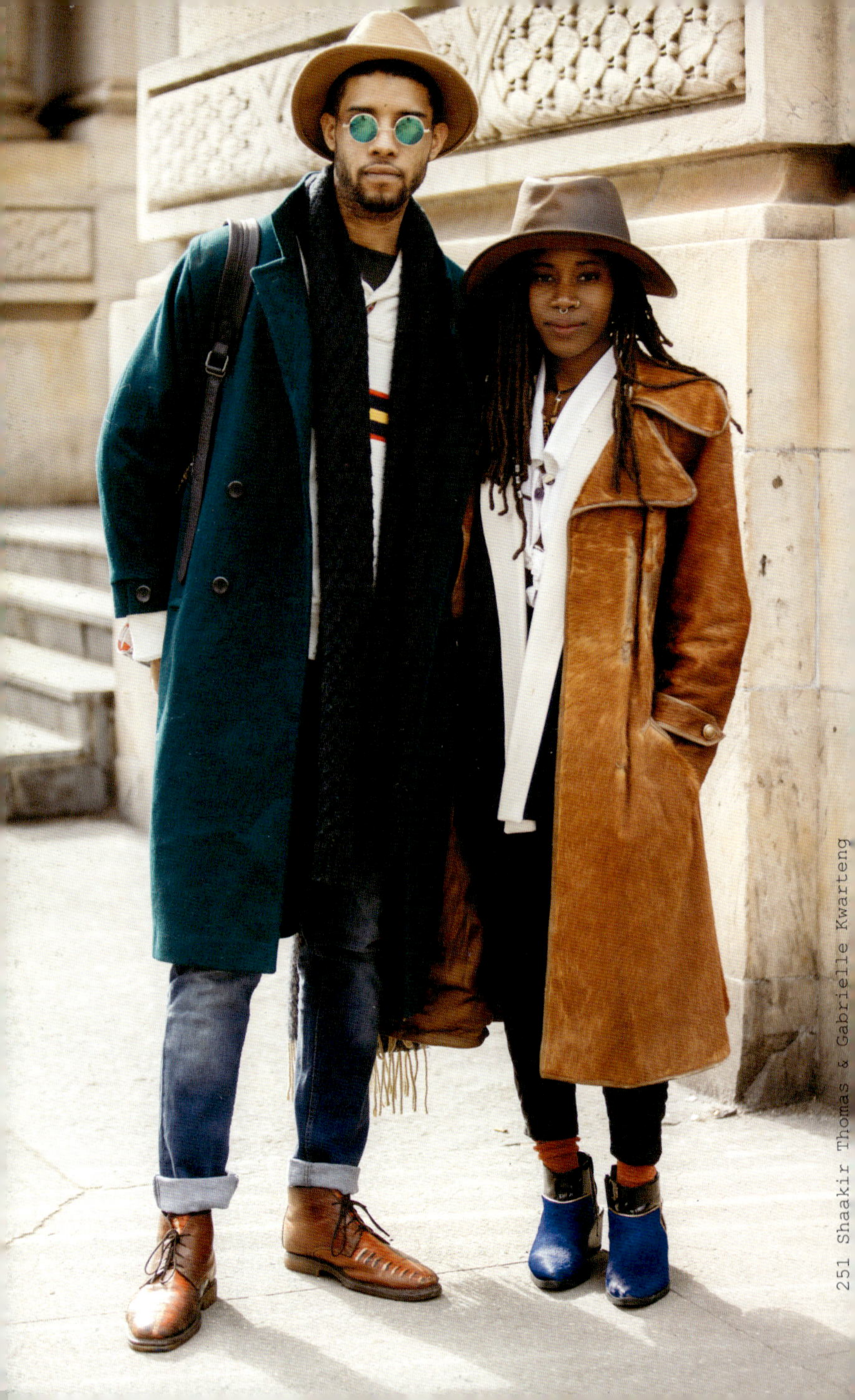

251 Shaakir Thomas & Gabrielle Kwarteng

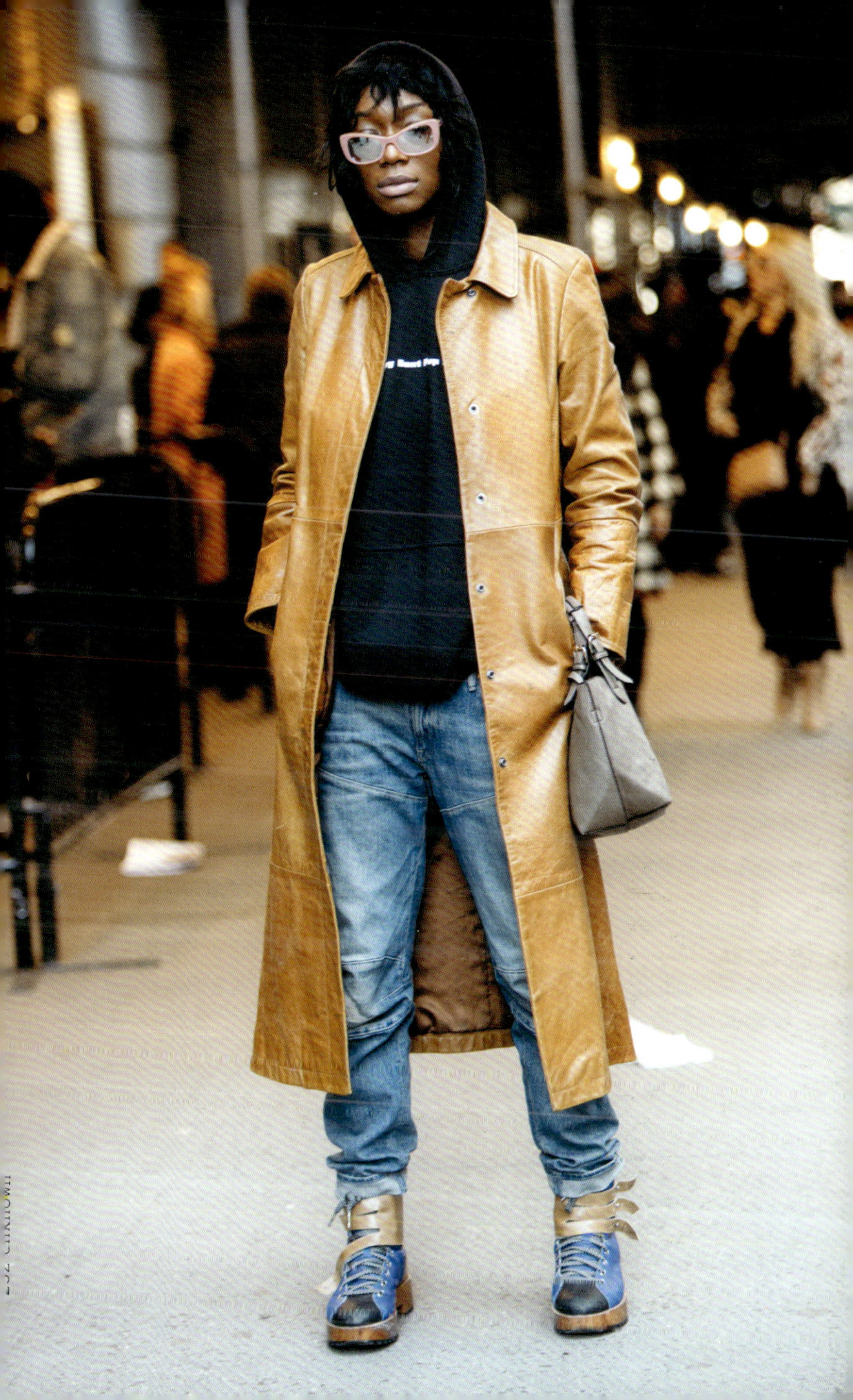

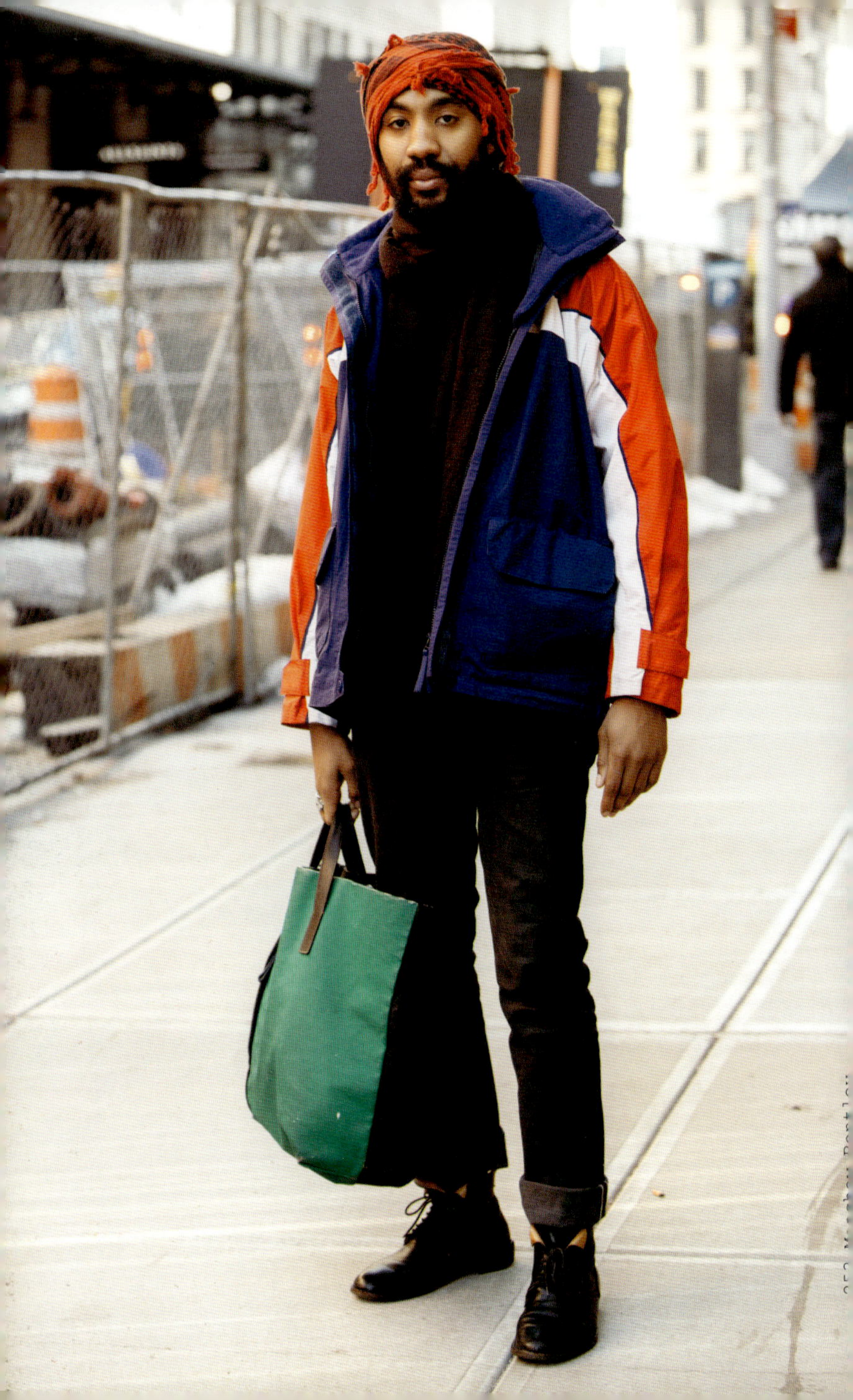

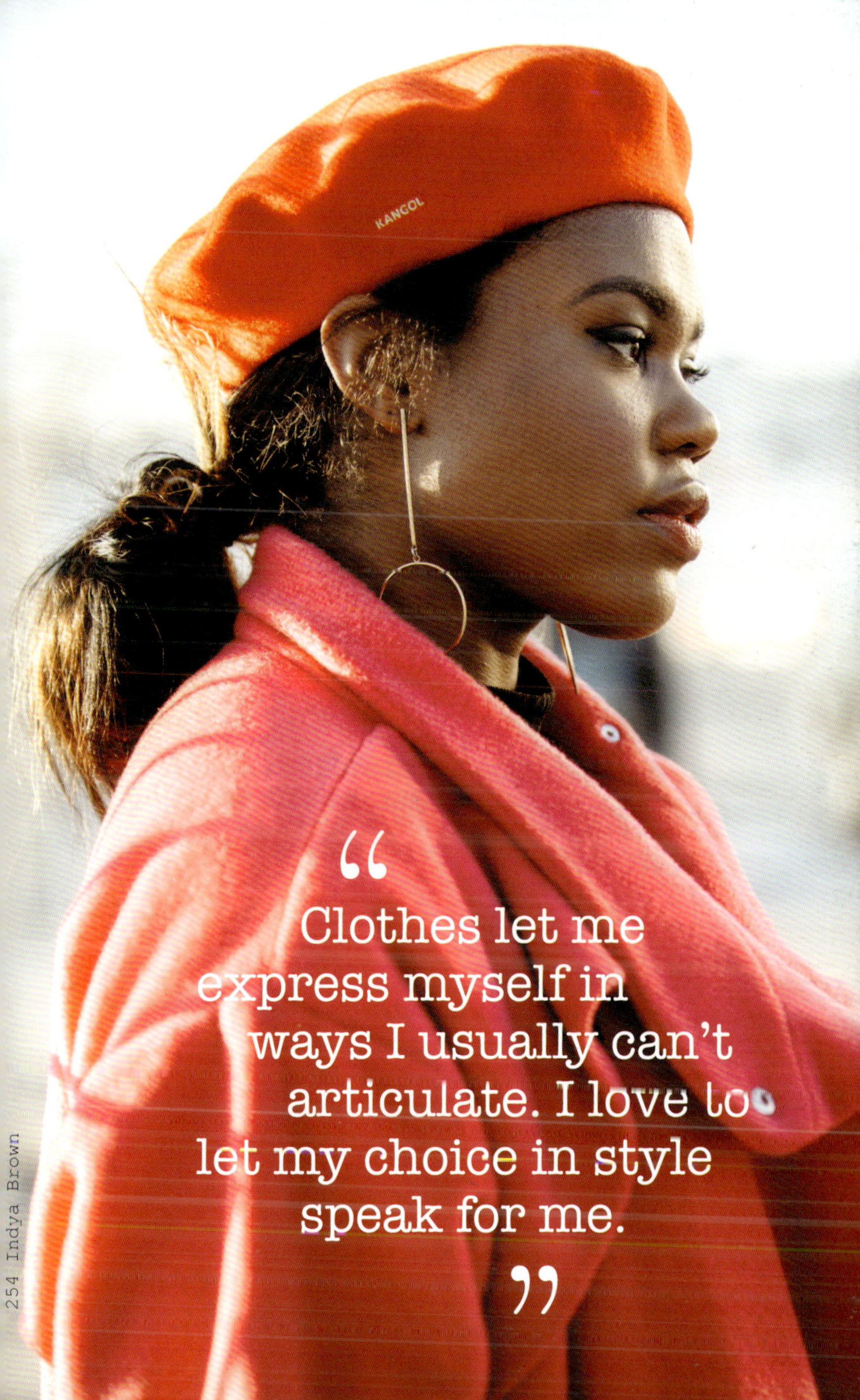
KANGOL
"Clothes let me express myself in ways I usually can't articulate. I love to let my choice in style speak for me."

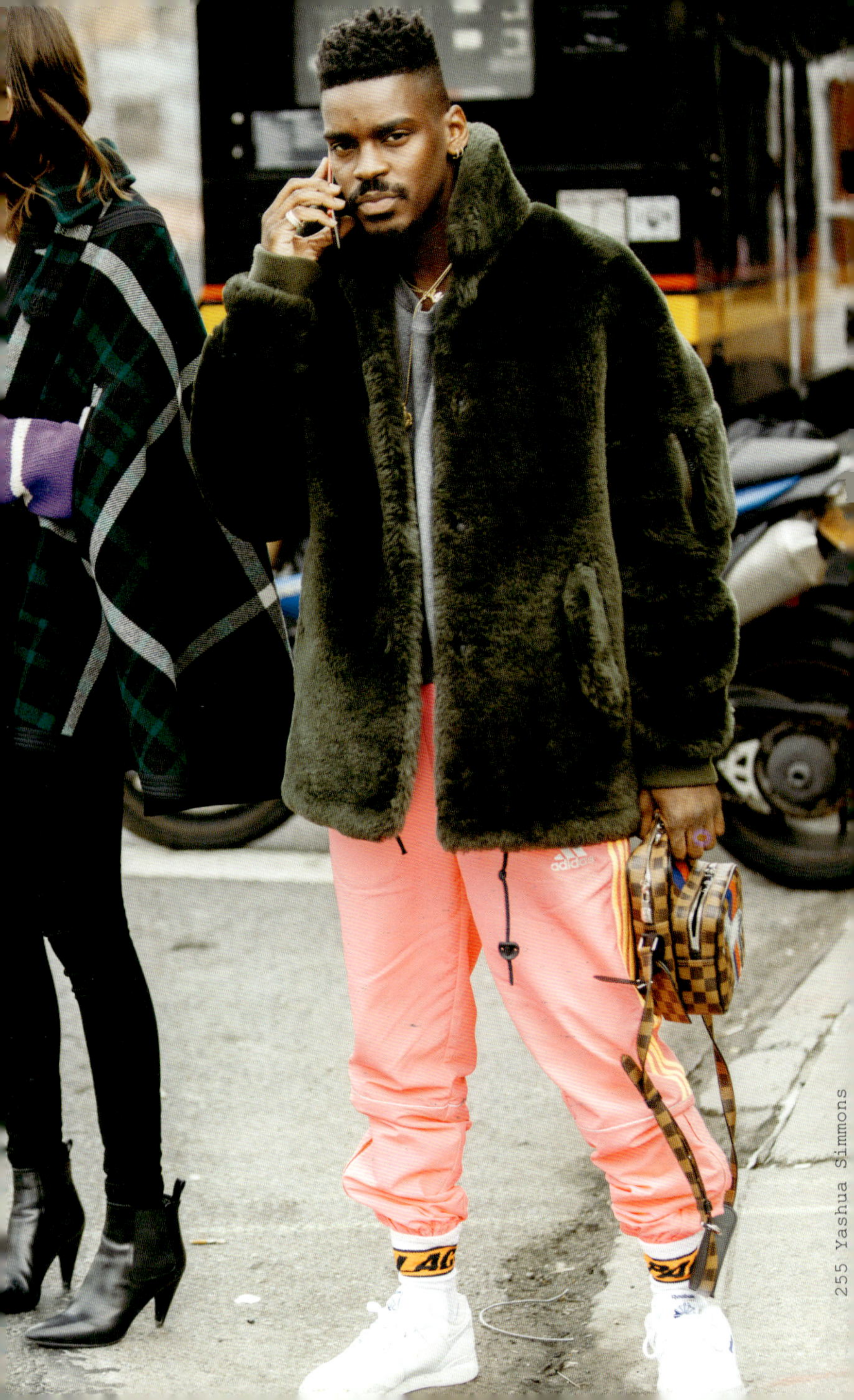

255 Yashua Simmons

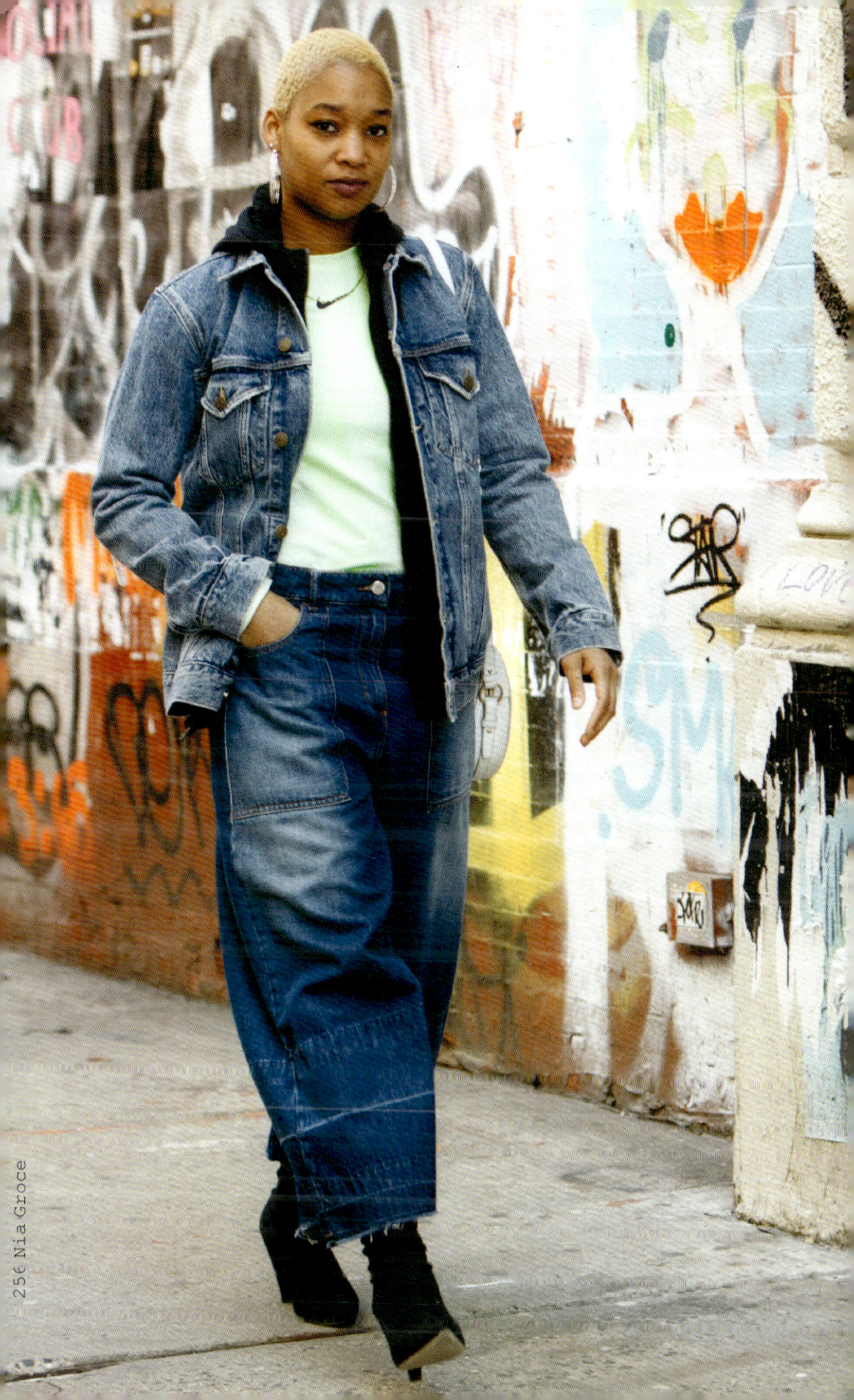

 Nia Groce

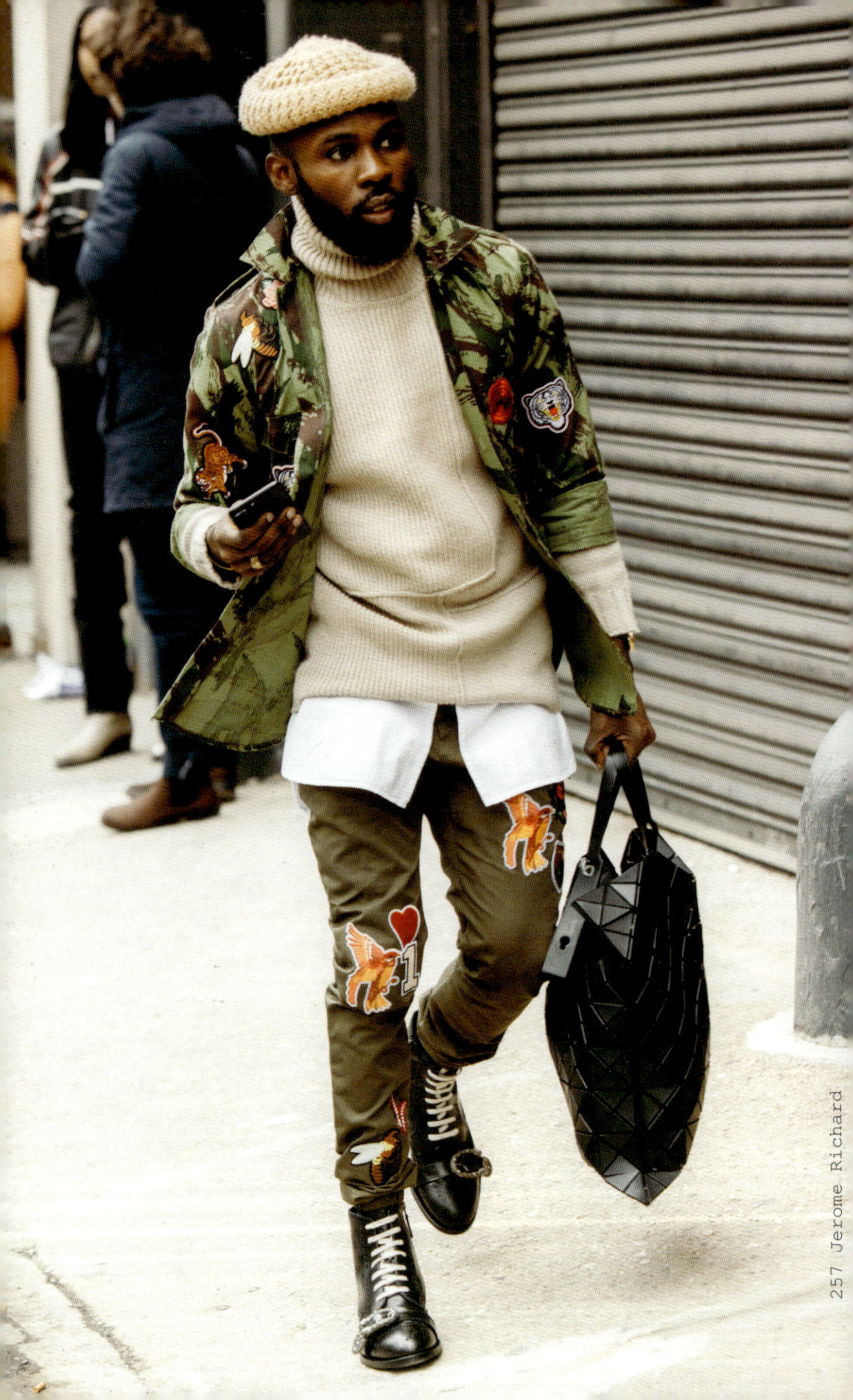

257 Jerome Richard

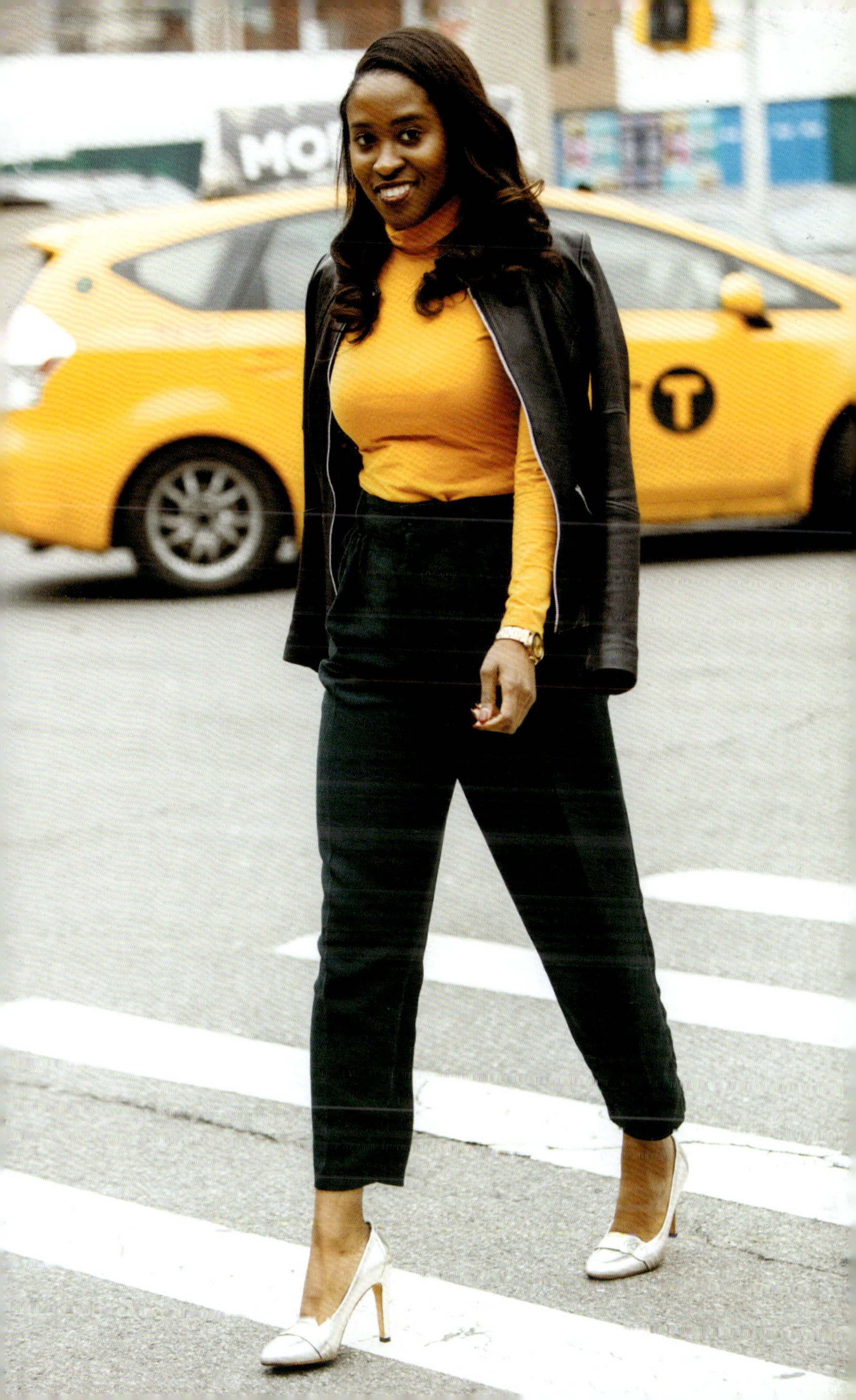

“

‘Tribeca Dad’—
easy clothes, great
fabrics, and living
with the ease of an
eternal Sunday
morning.

”

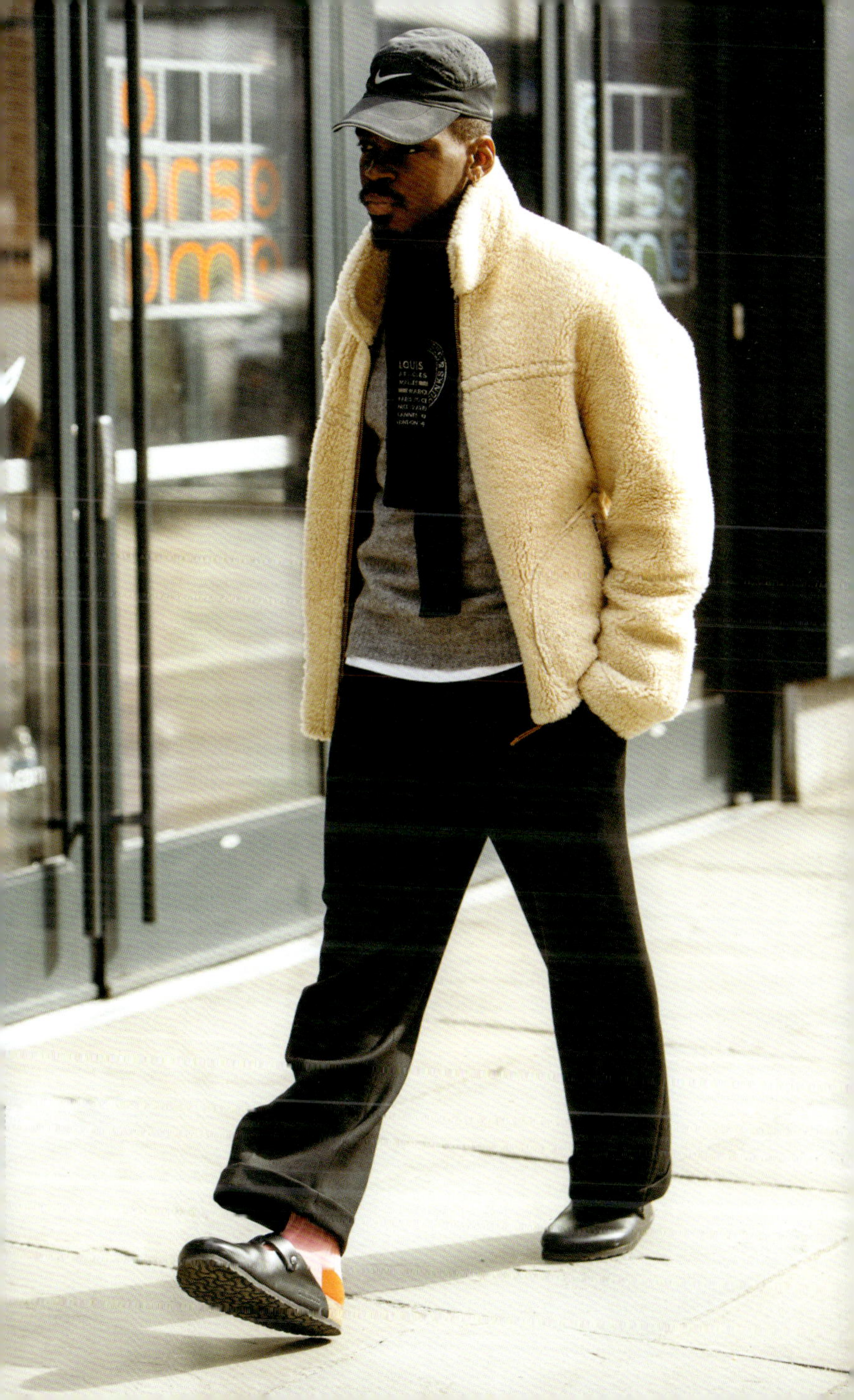
LOUIS

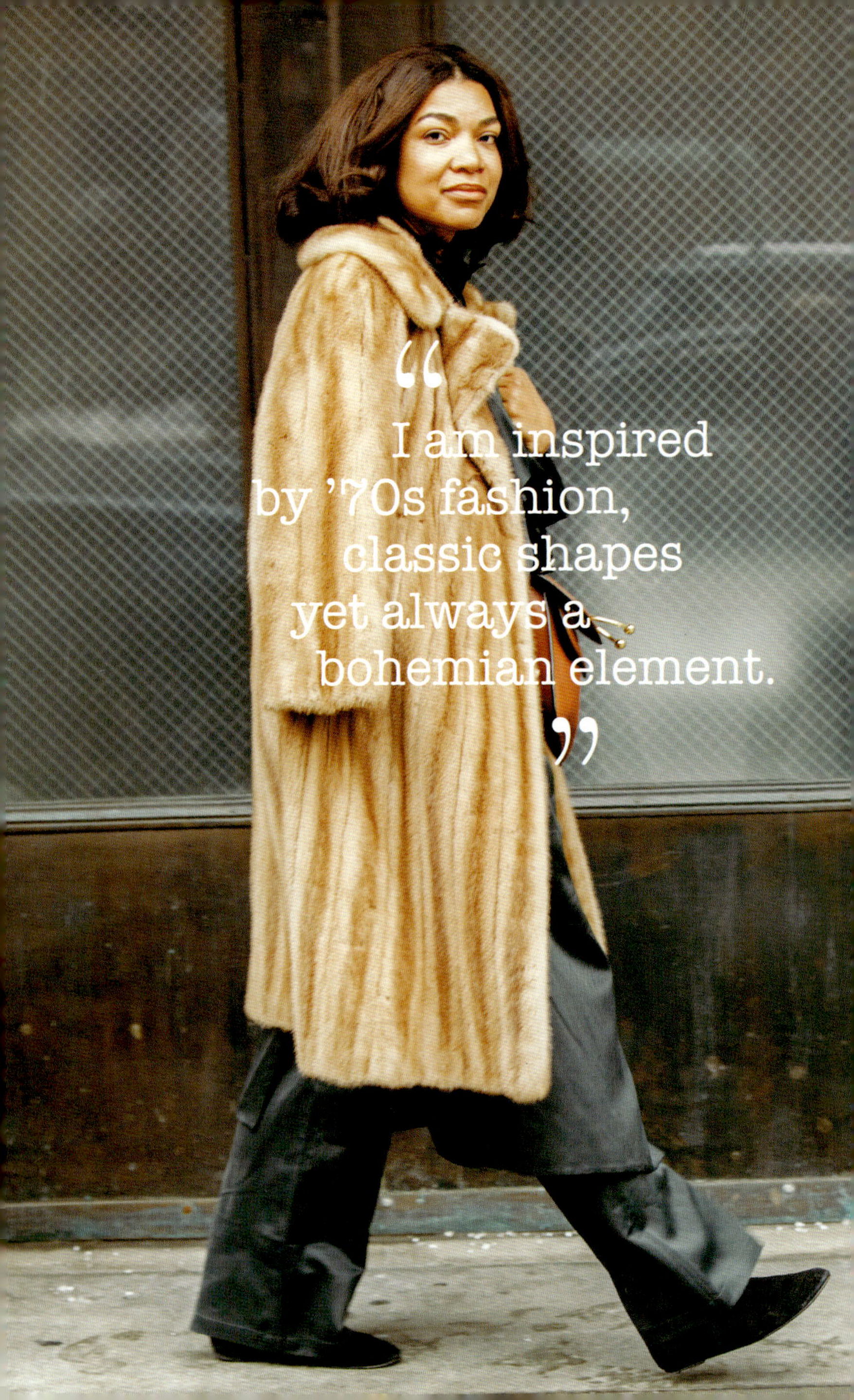
“
I am inspired
by ’70s fashion,
classic shapes
yet always a
bohemian element.
”

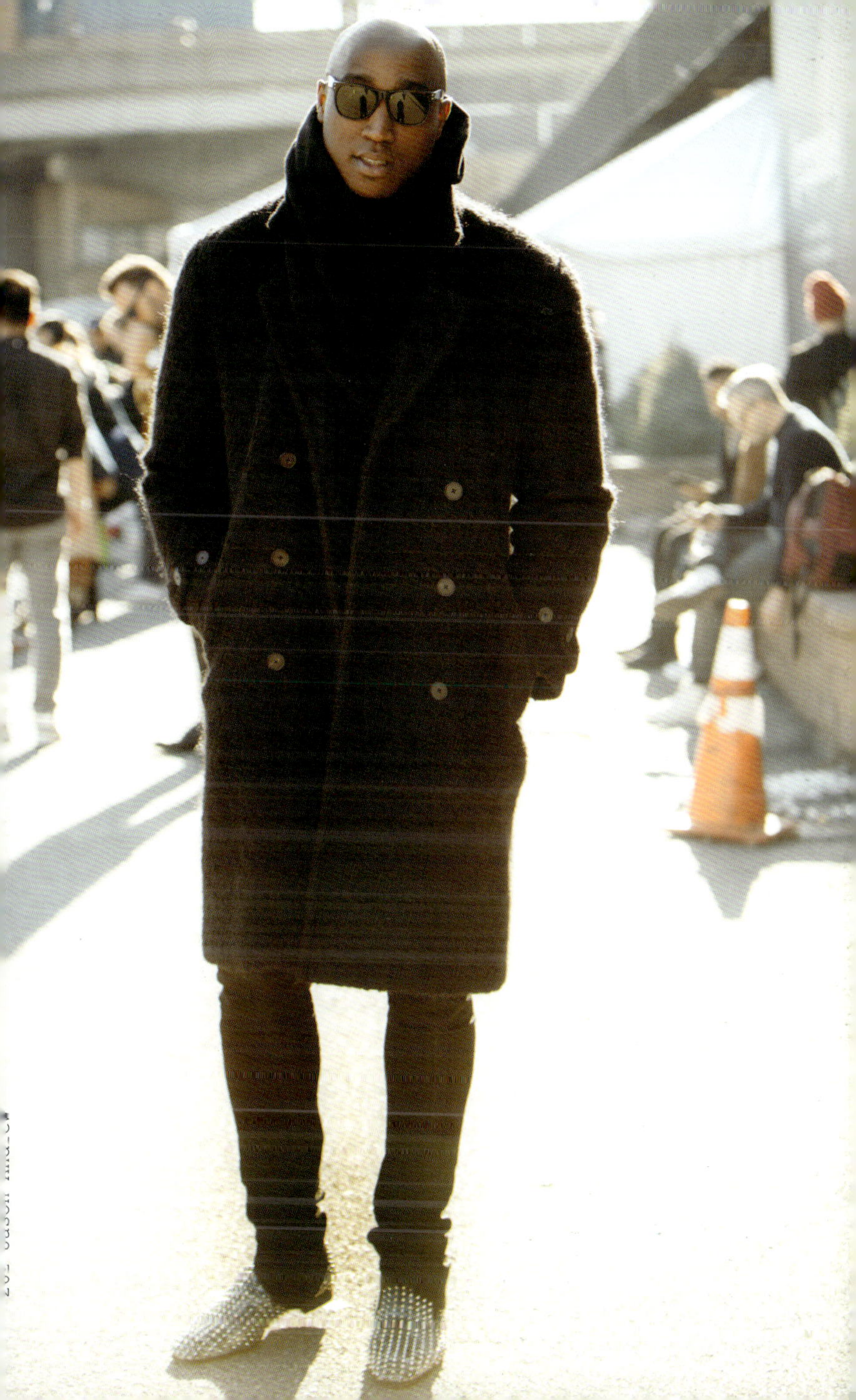

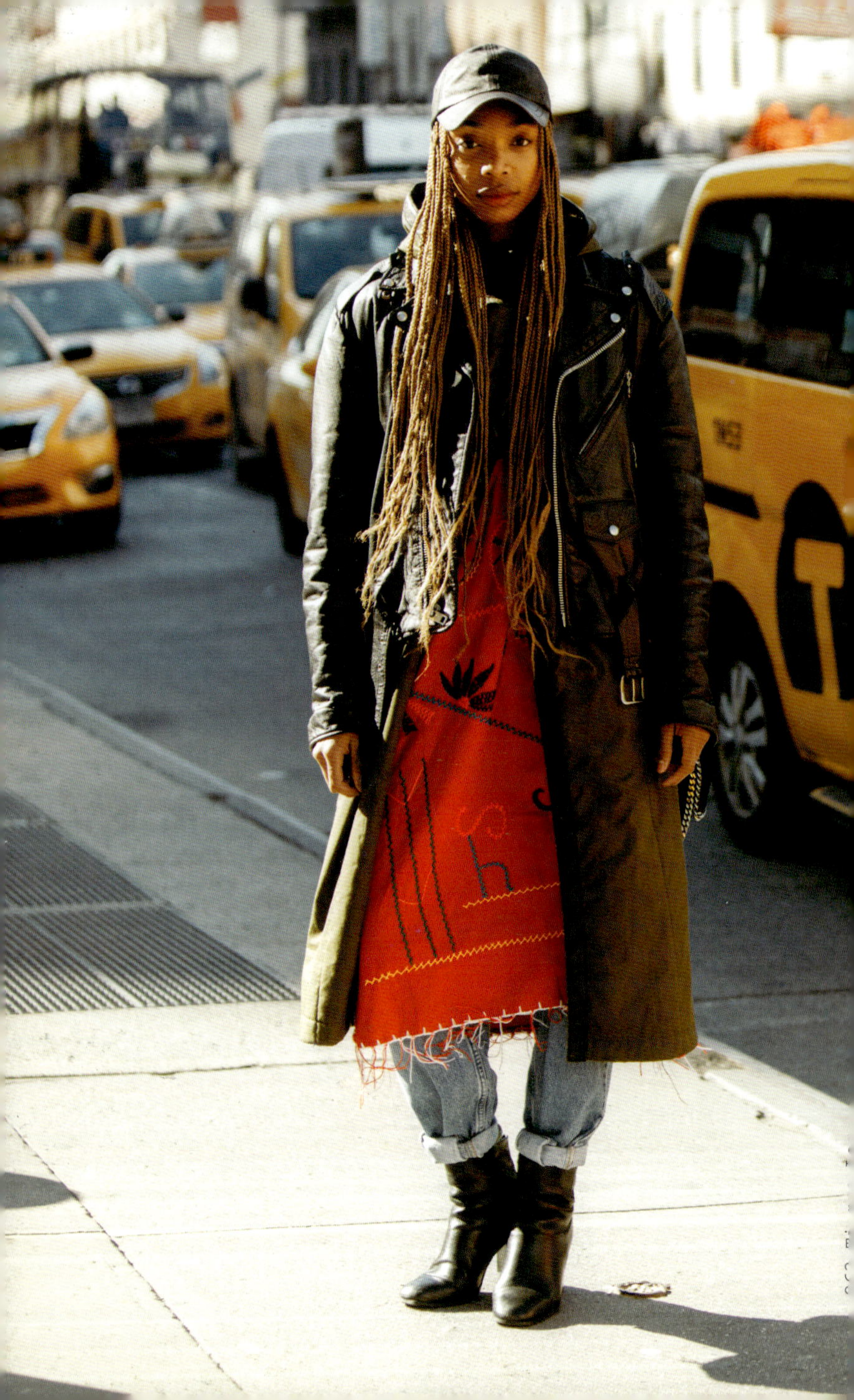

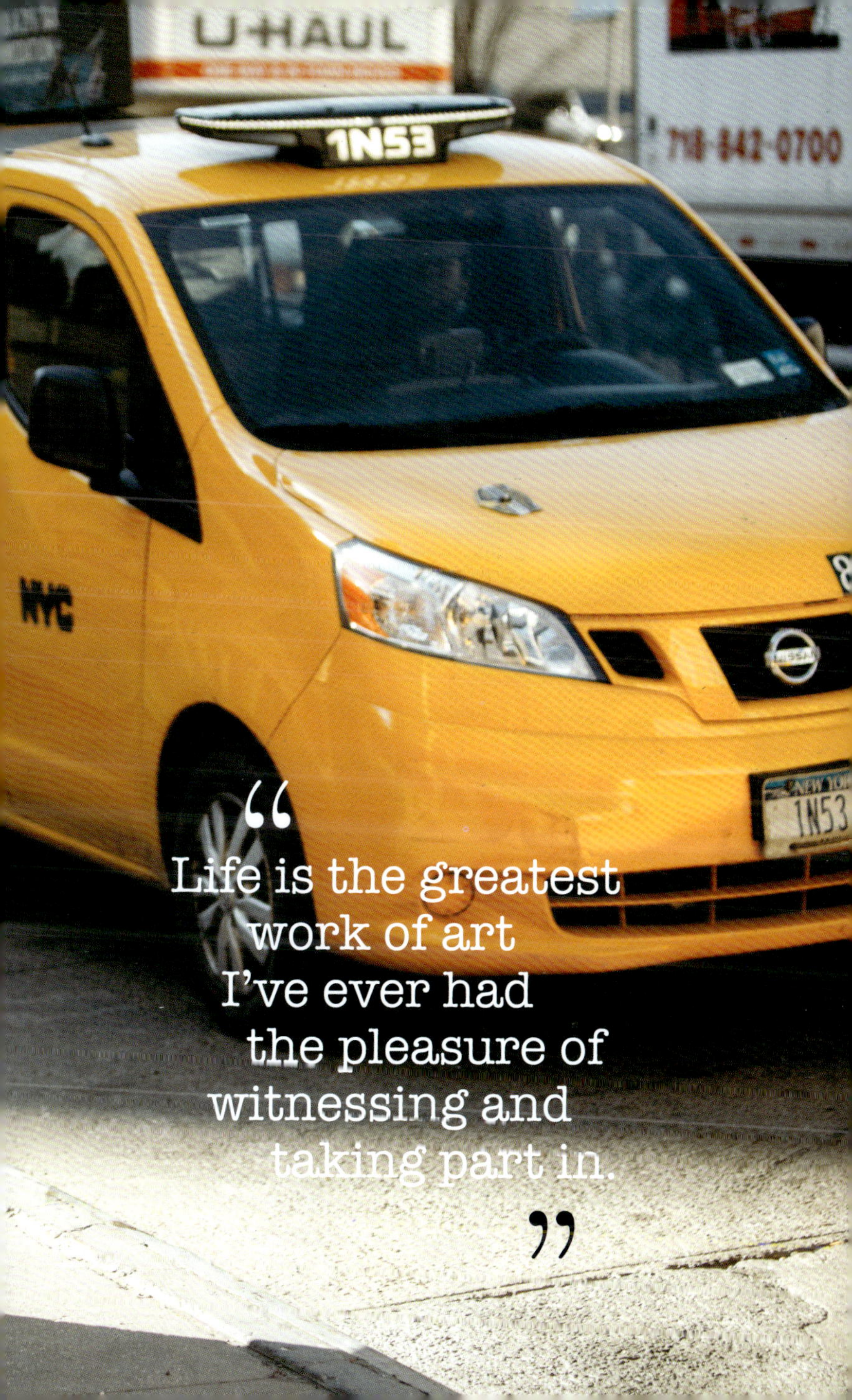

"Life is the greatest work of art I've ever had the pleasure of witnessing and taking part in."

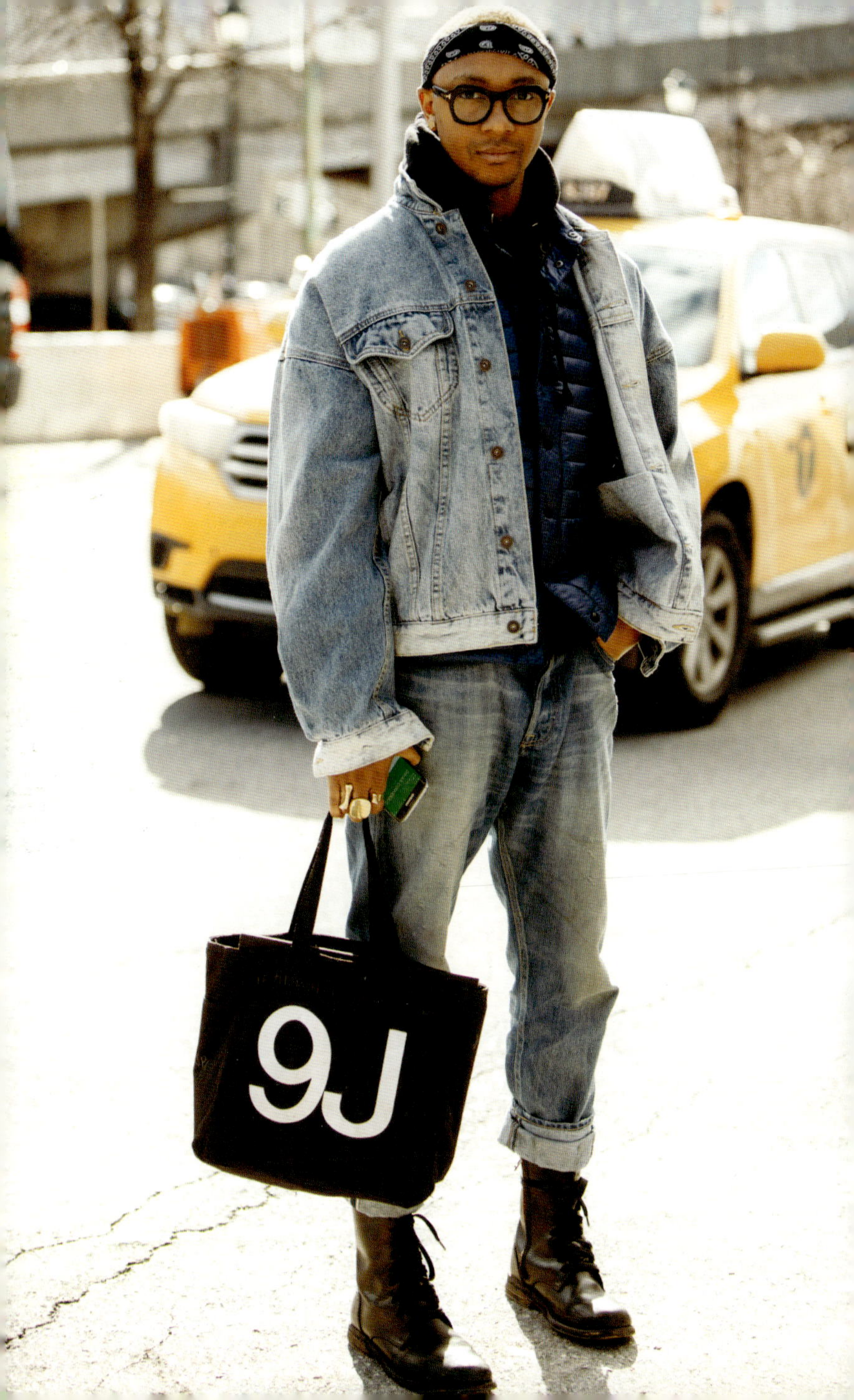
9J

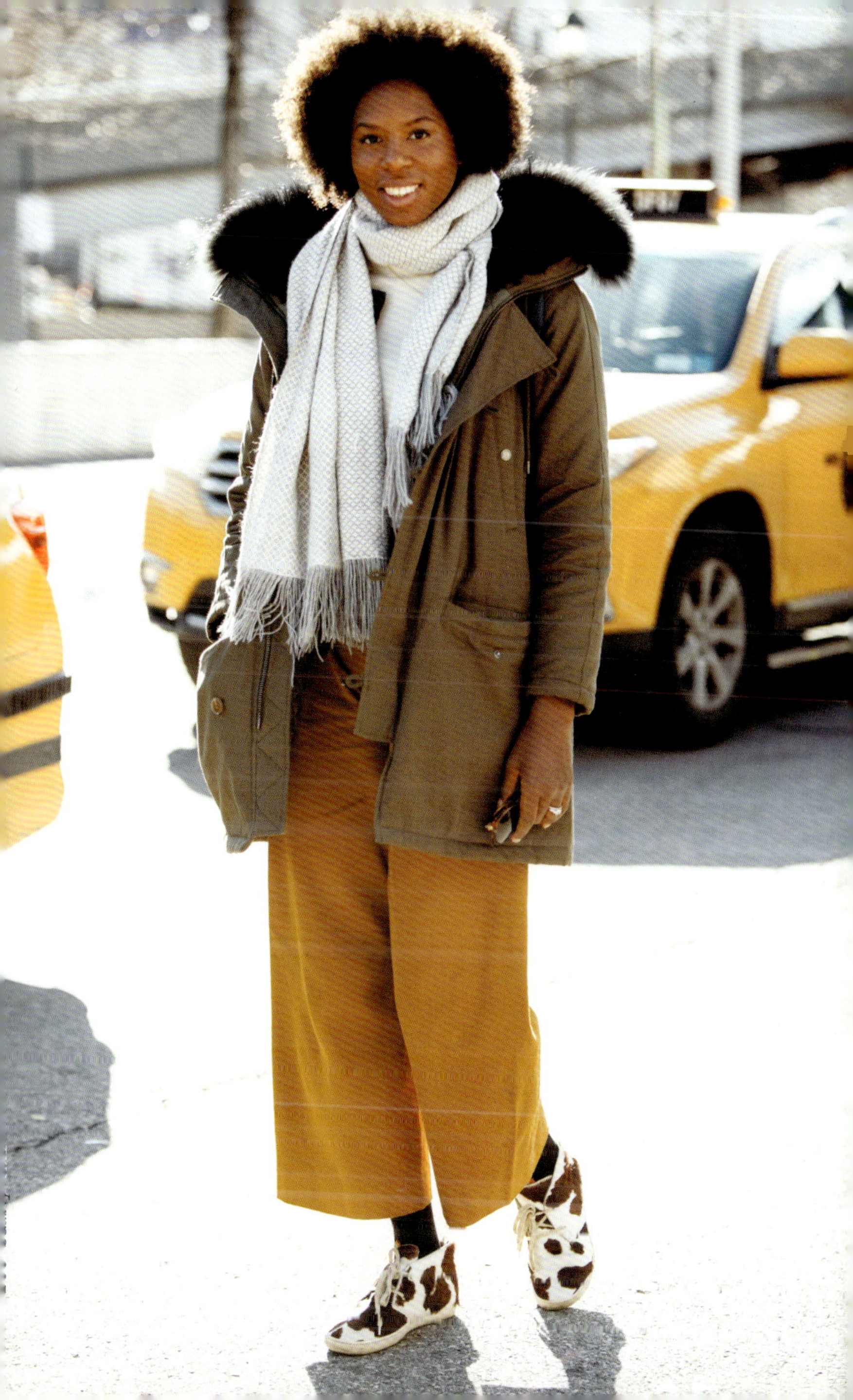

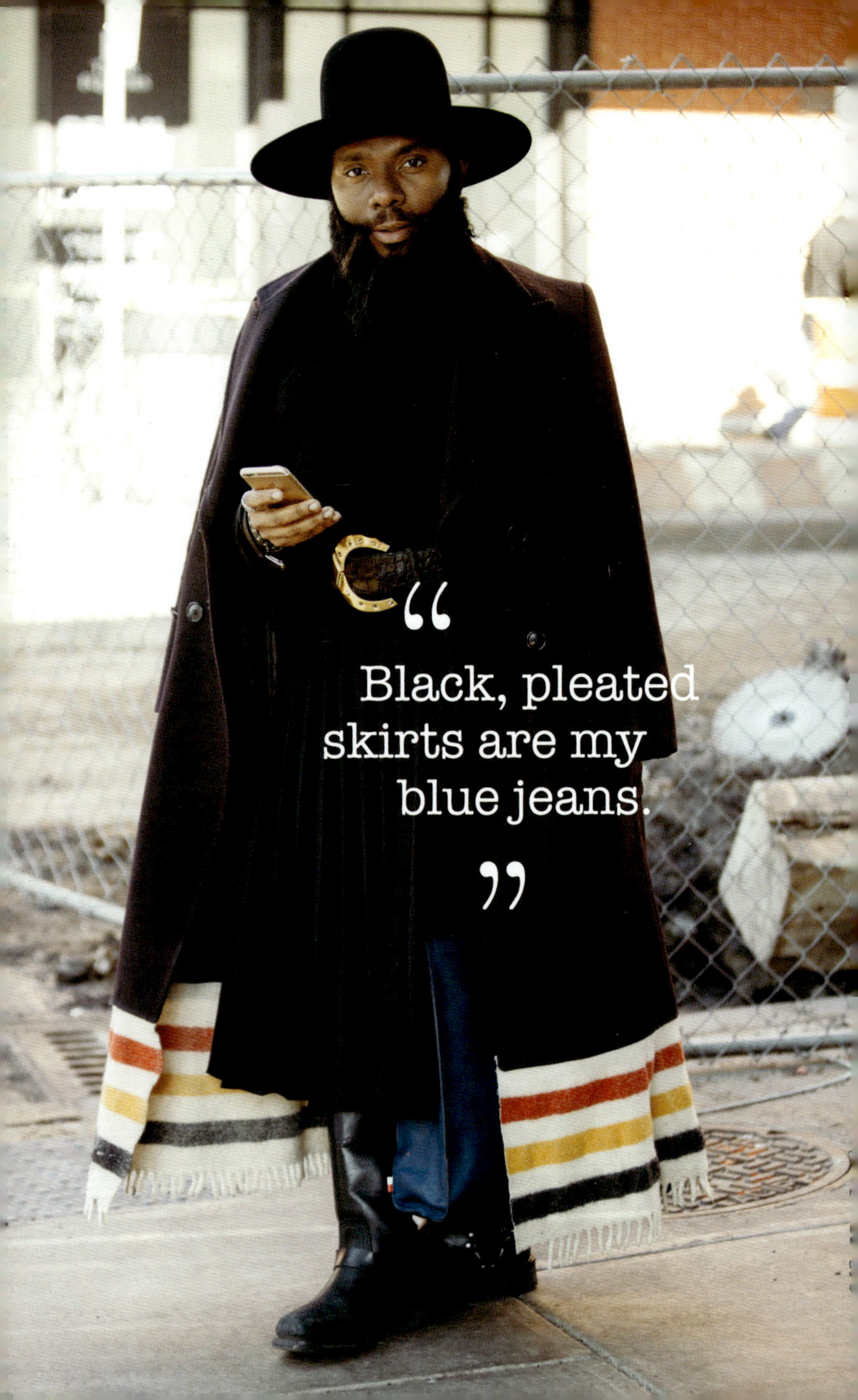
"Black, pleated skirts are my blue jeans."

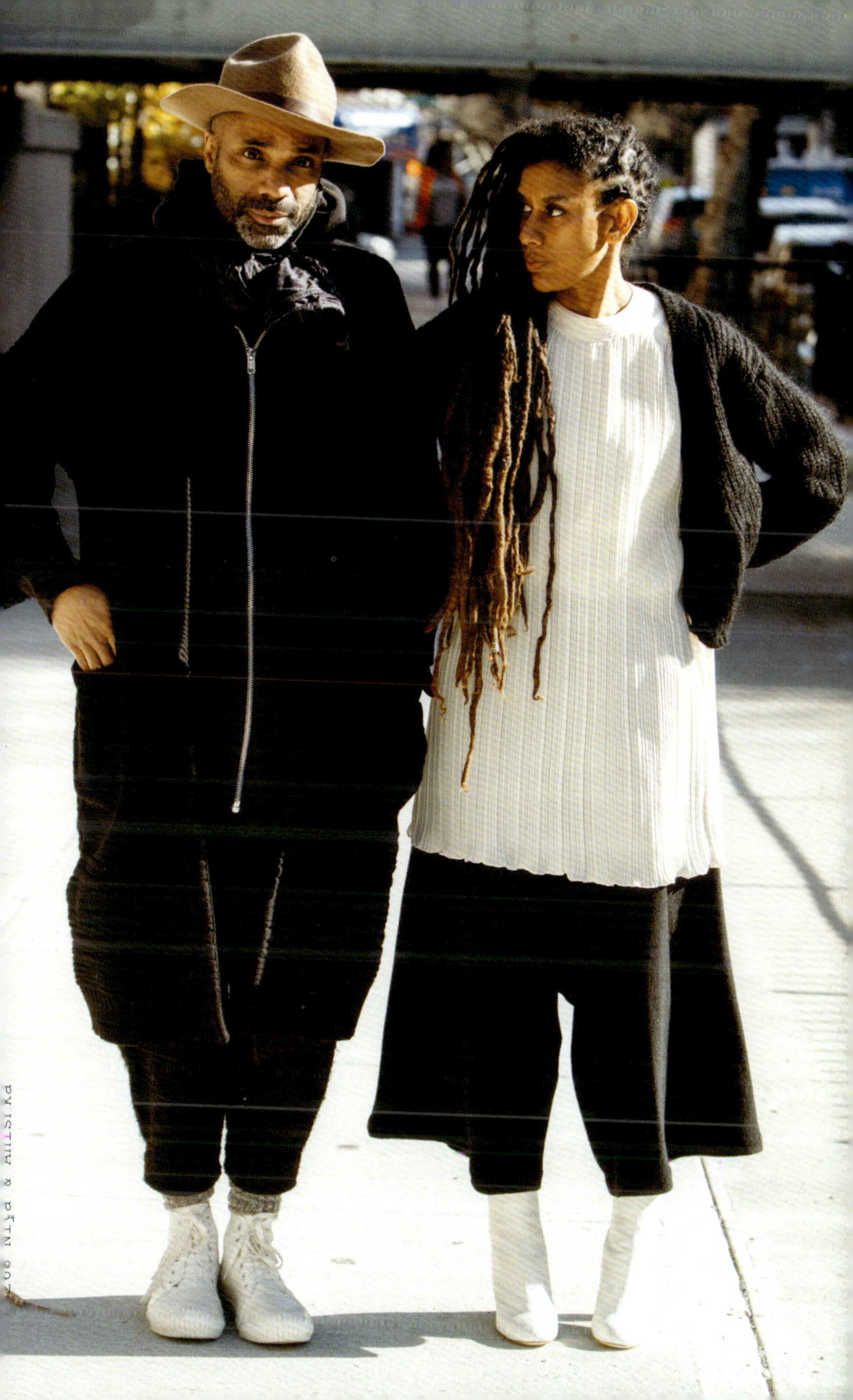

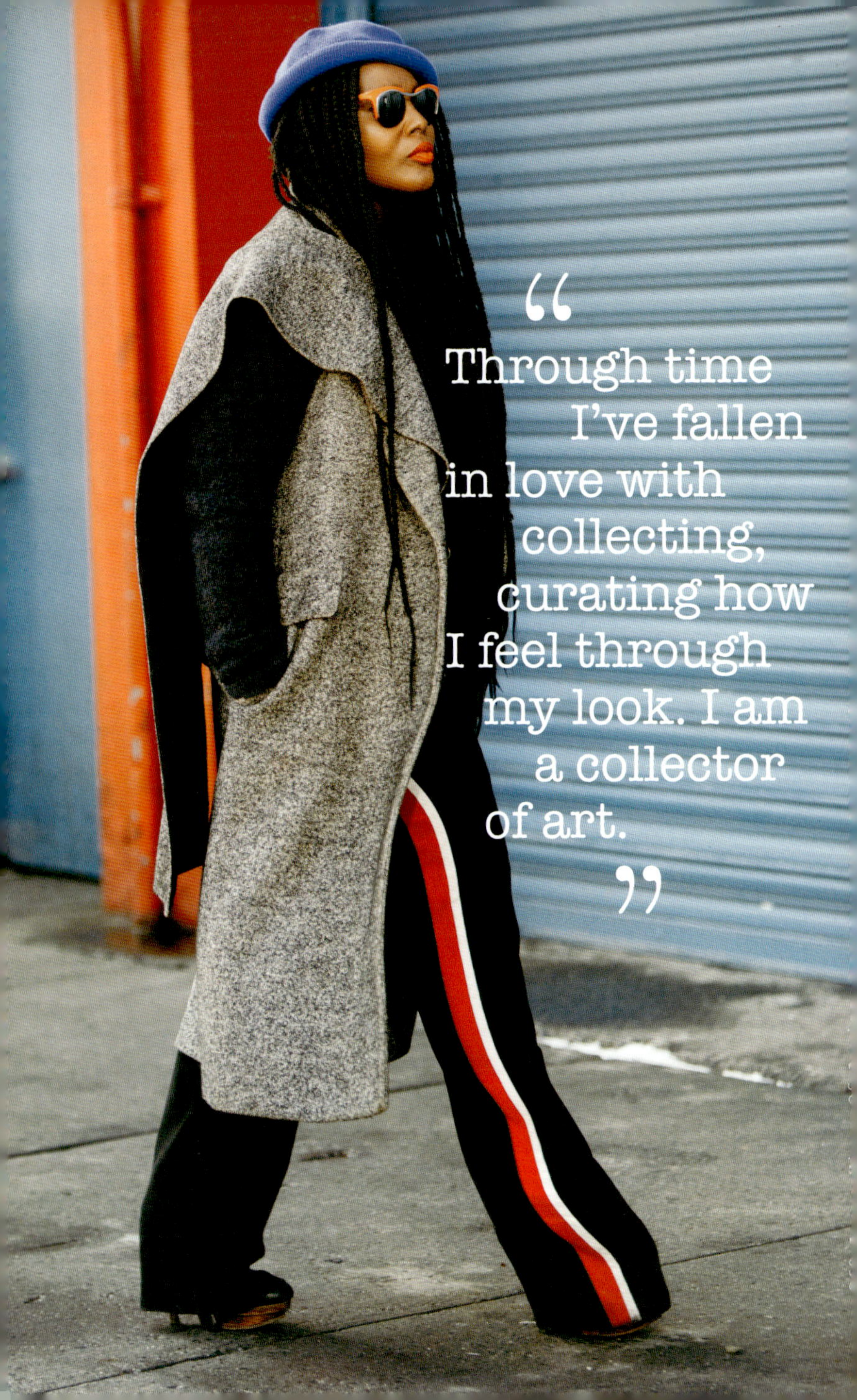
"Through time I've fallen in love with collecting, curating how I feel through my look. I am a collector of art."

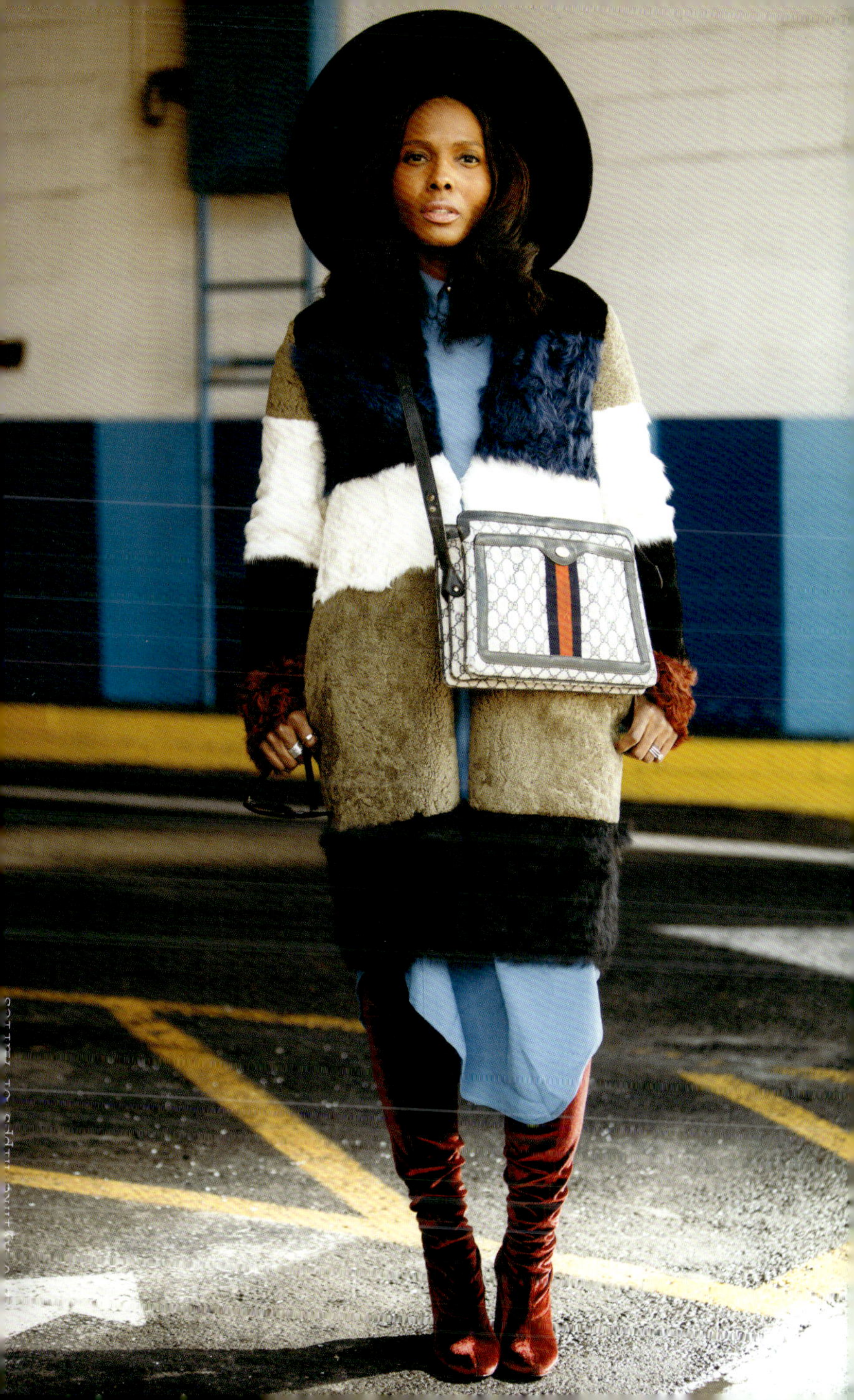

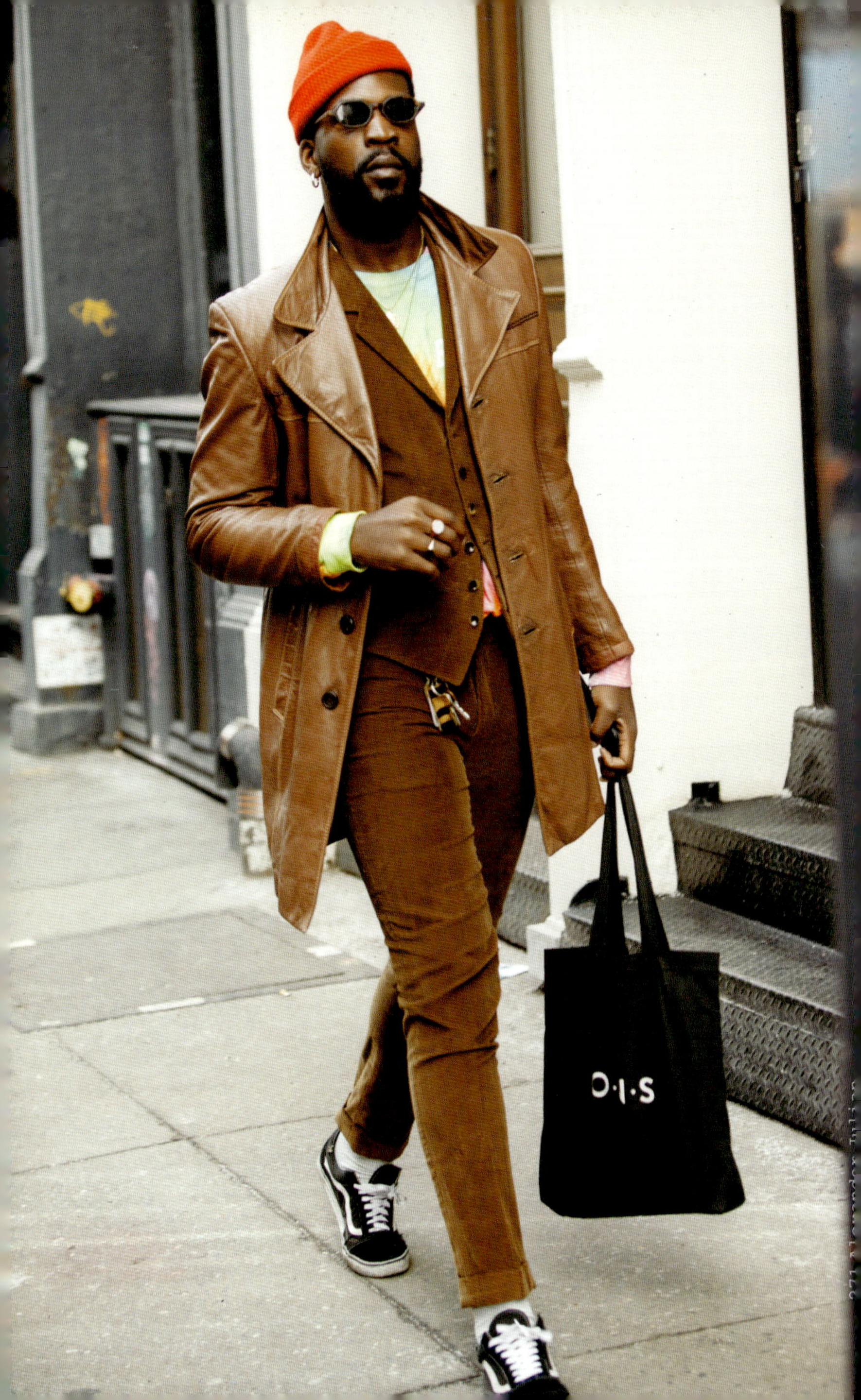

271 Alexander Julian

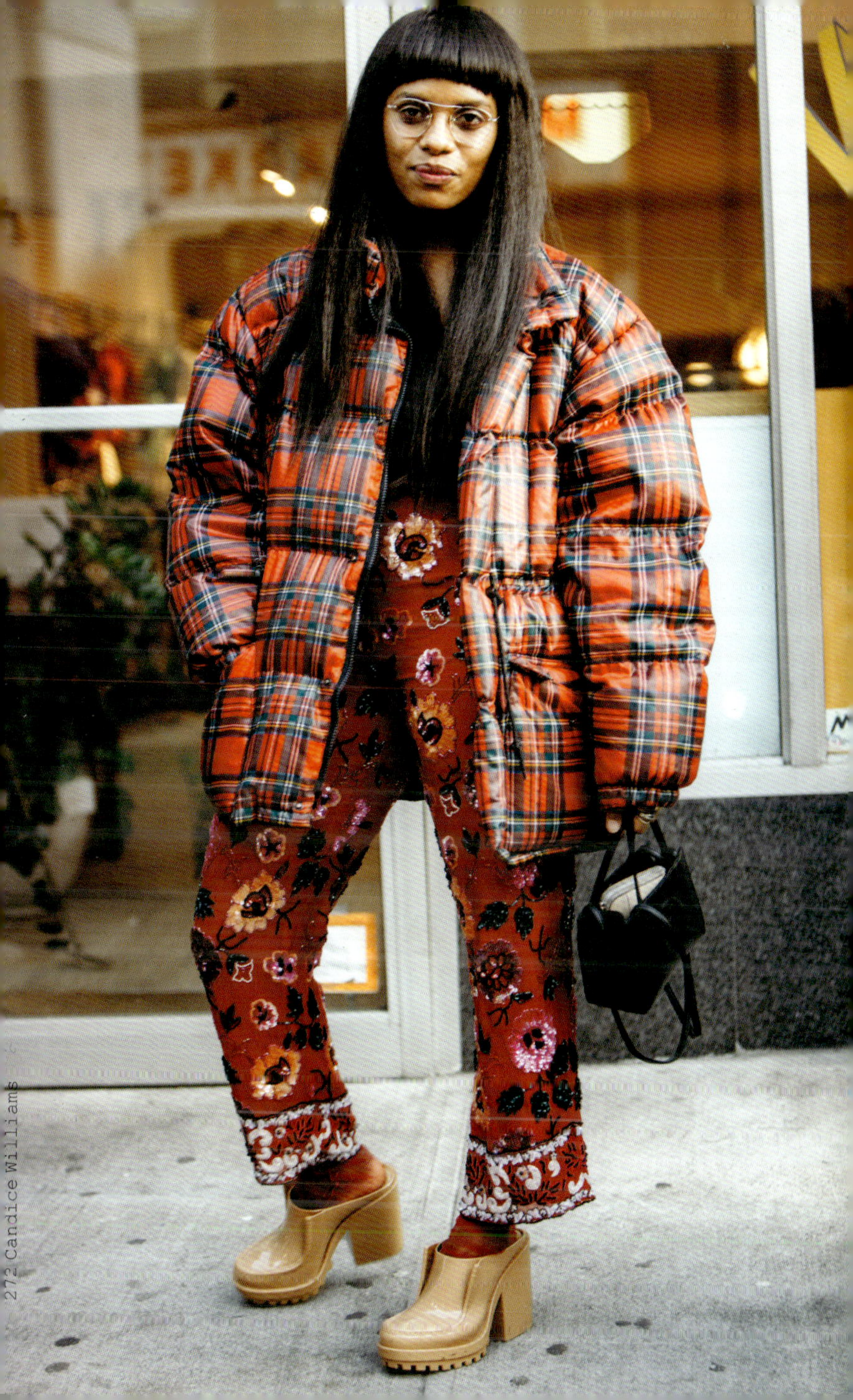

272 Candice Williams

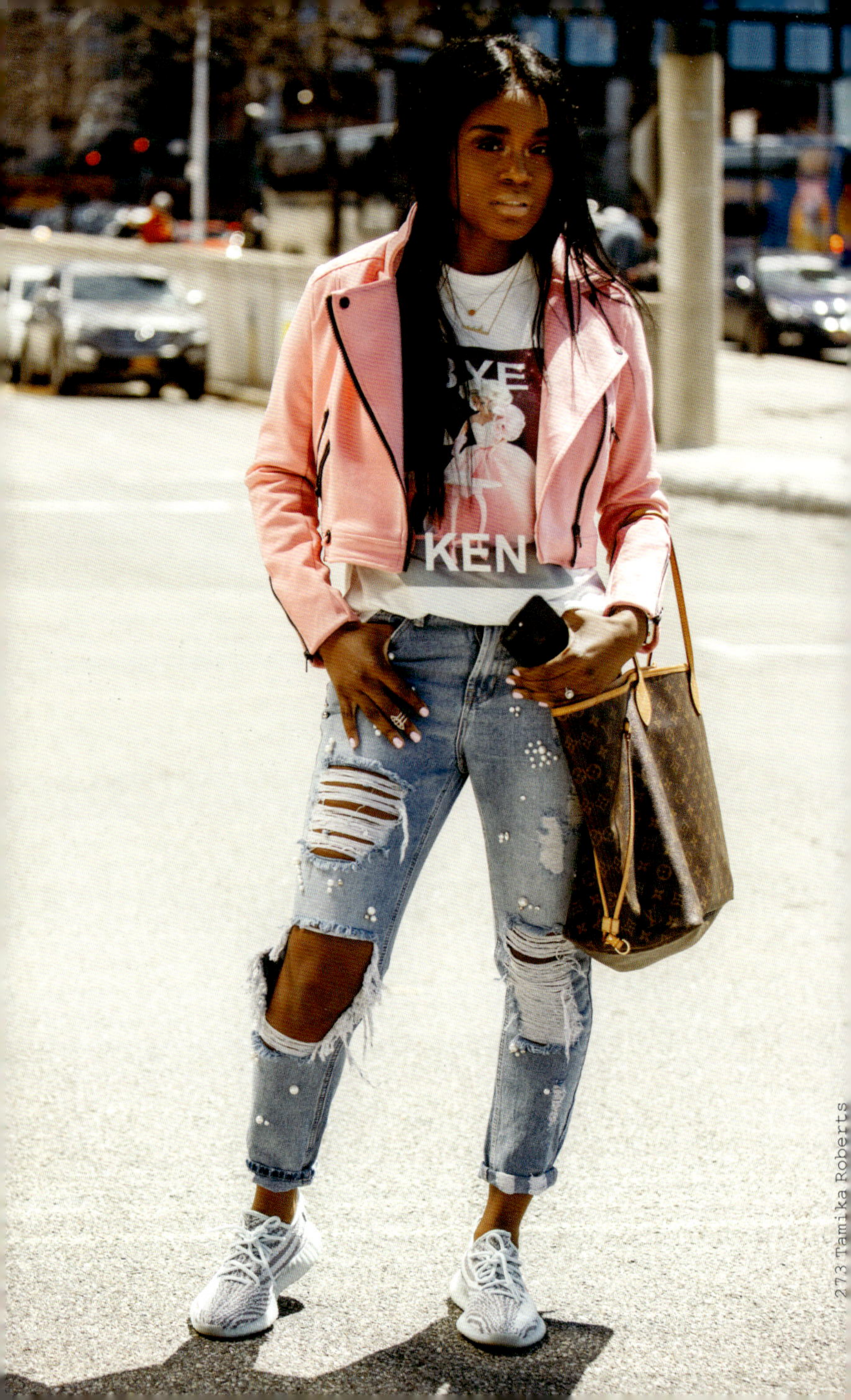

273 Tamika Roberts

“

Fashion is an
escape from hardship
that life sometimes
throws at us.

”

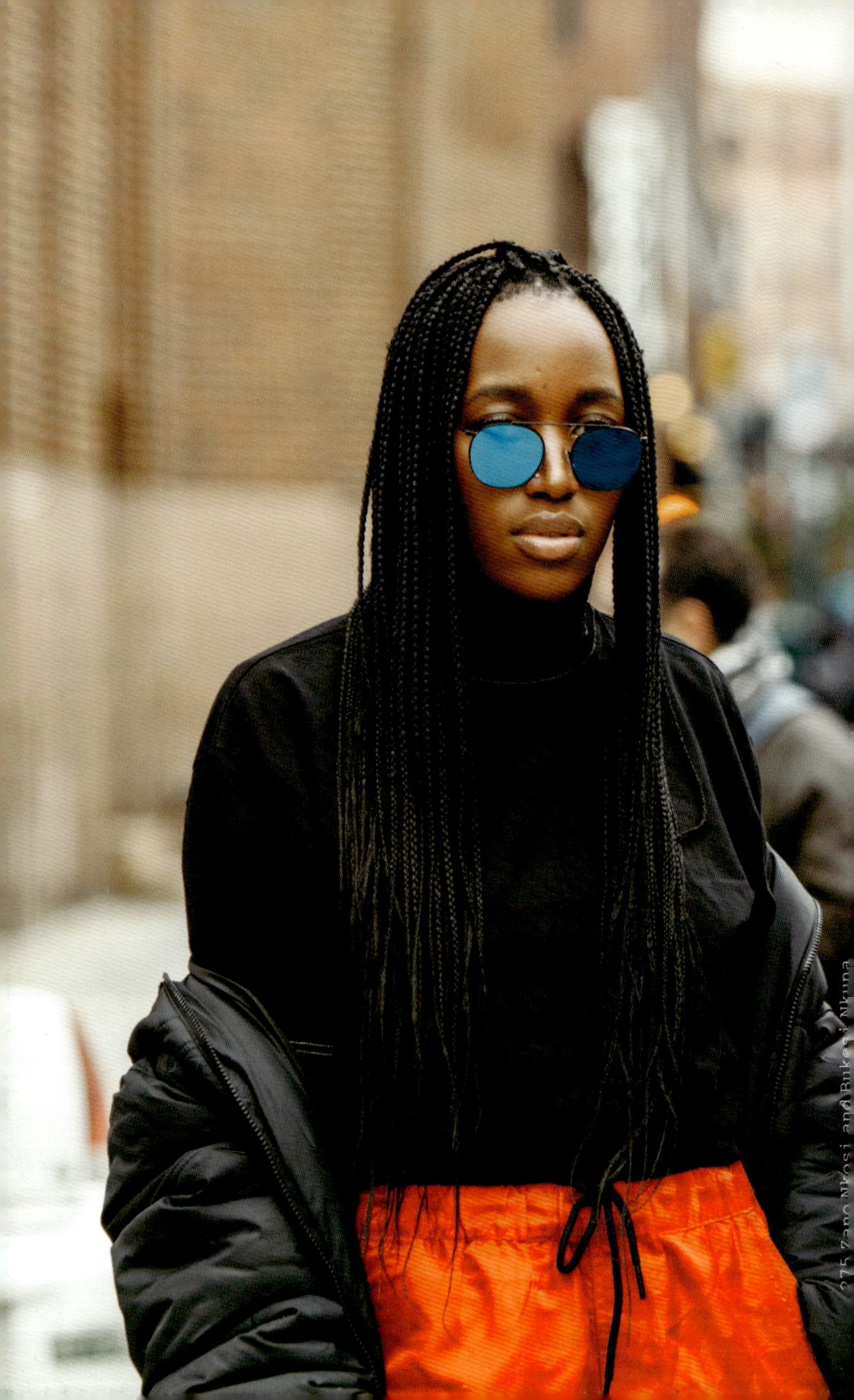

275 Zano Nkosi and Bukeqi Nkuna

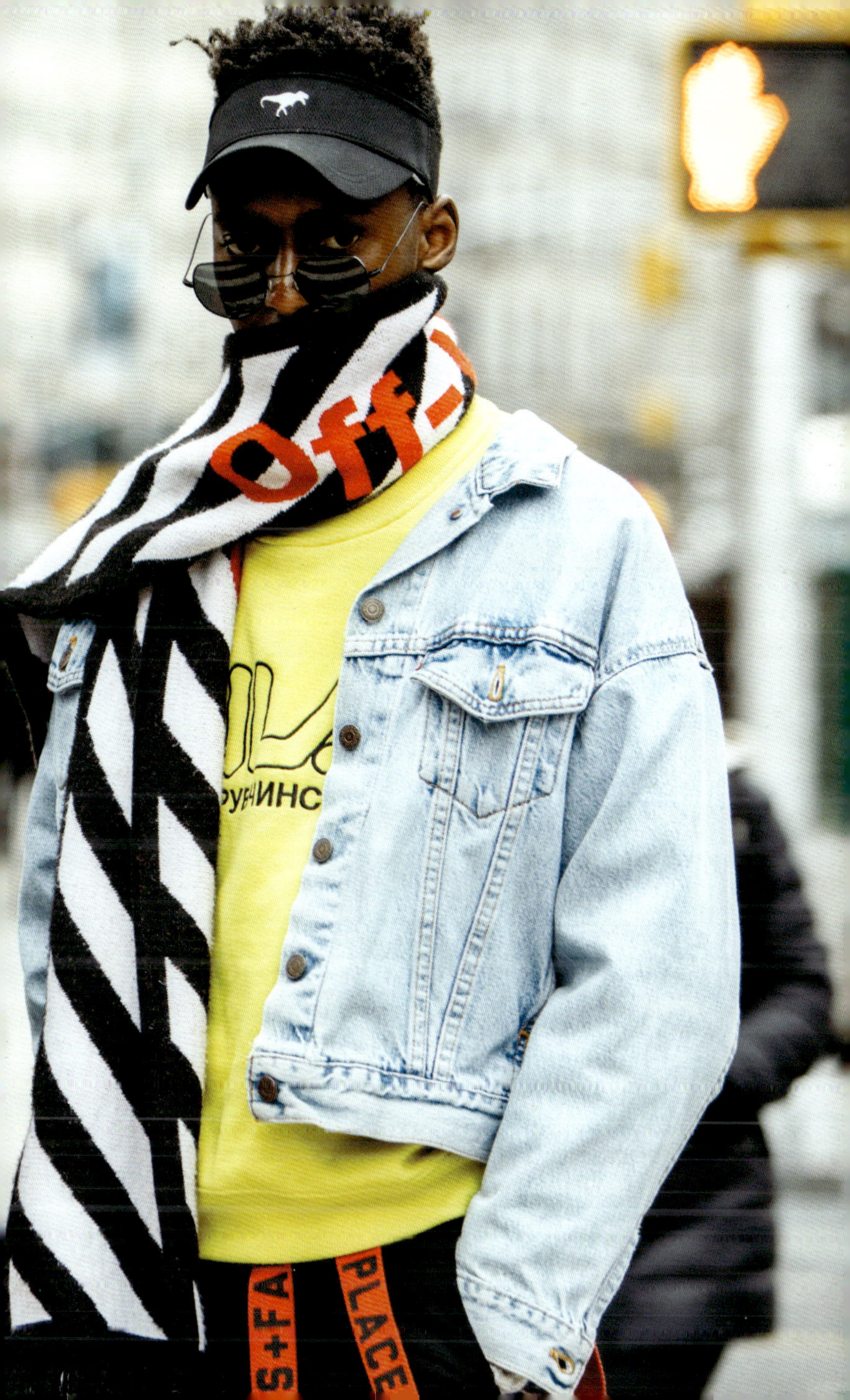
Off-
S+FA
PLACE

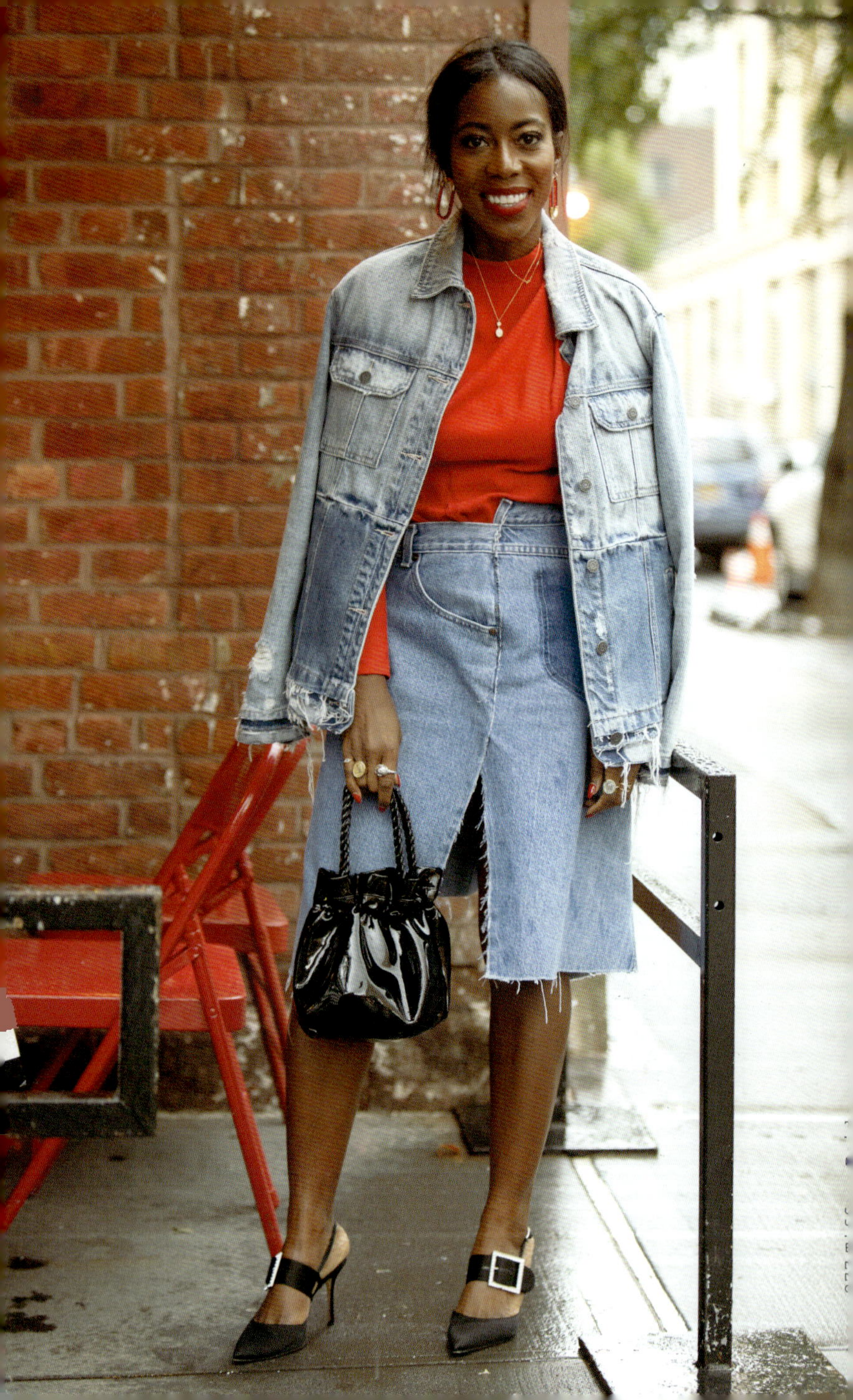

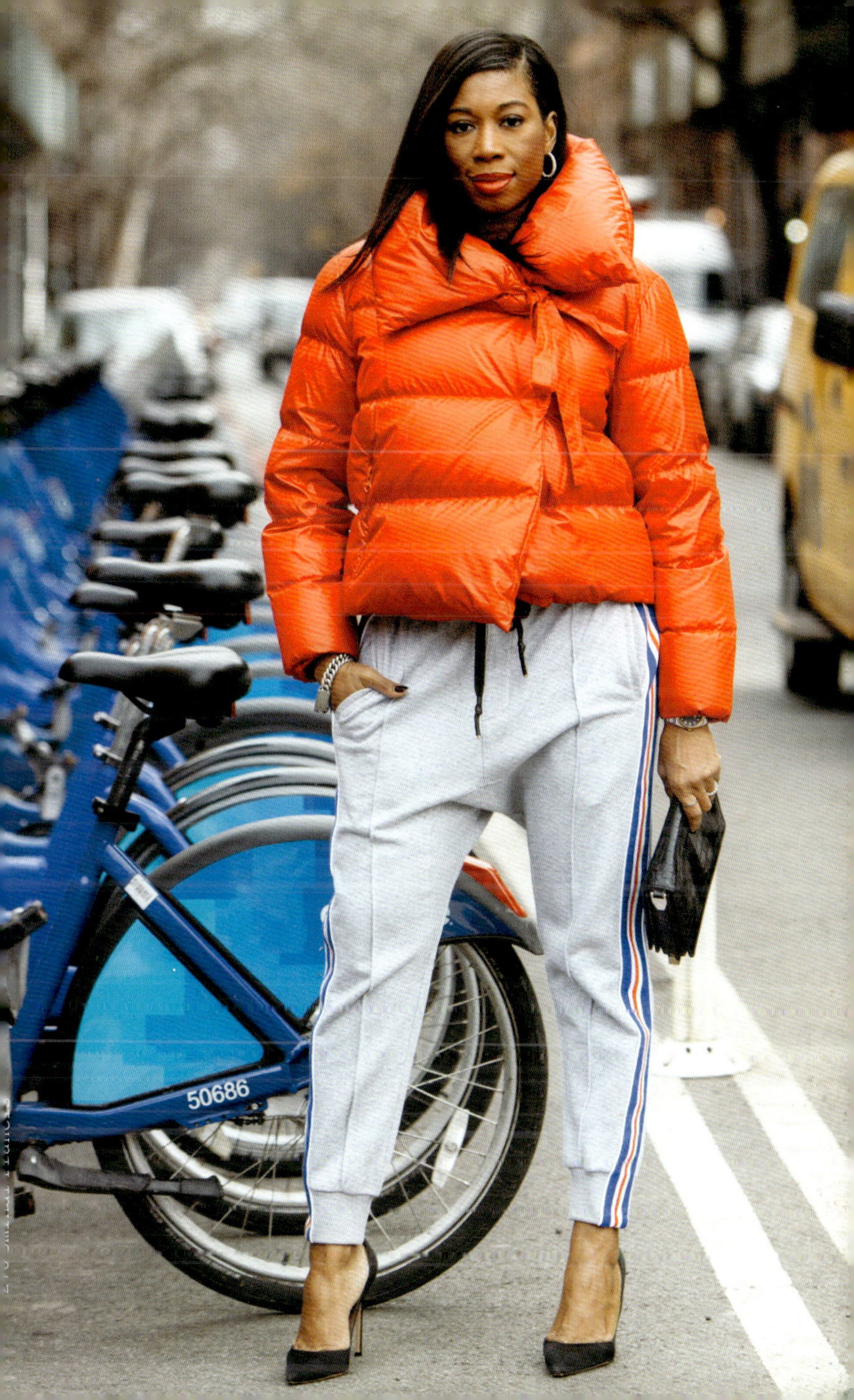
50686

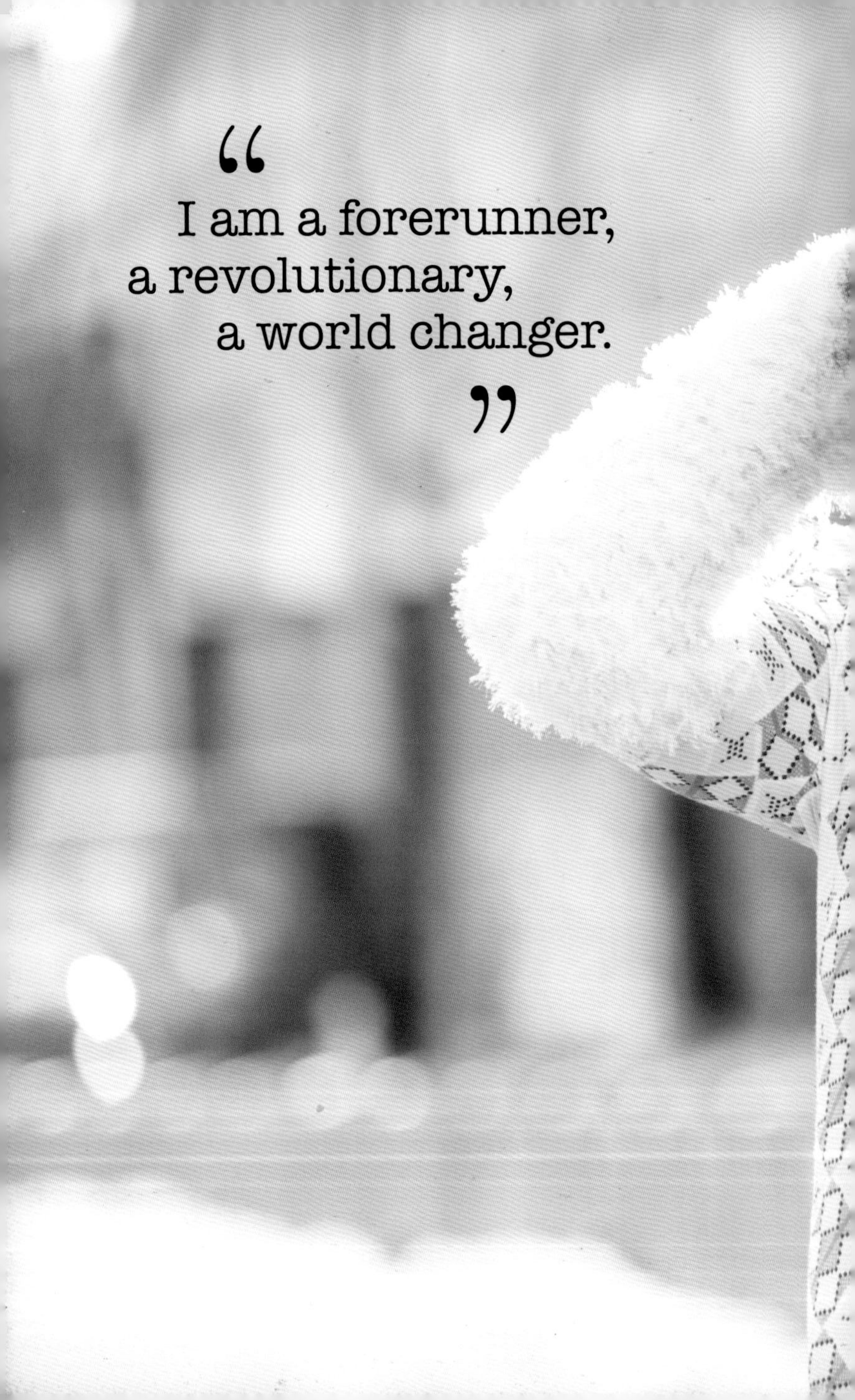

"I am a forerunner,
a revolutionary,
a world changer."

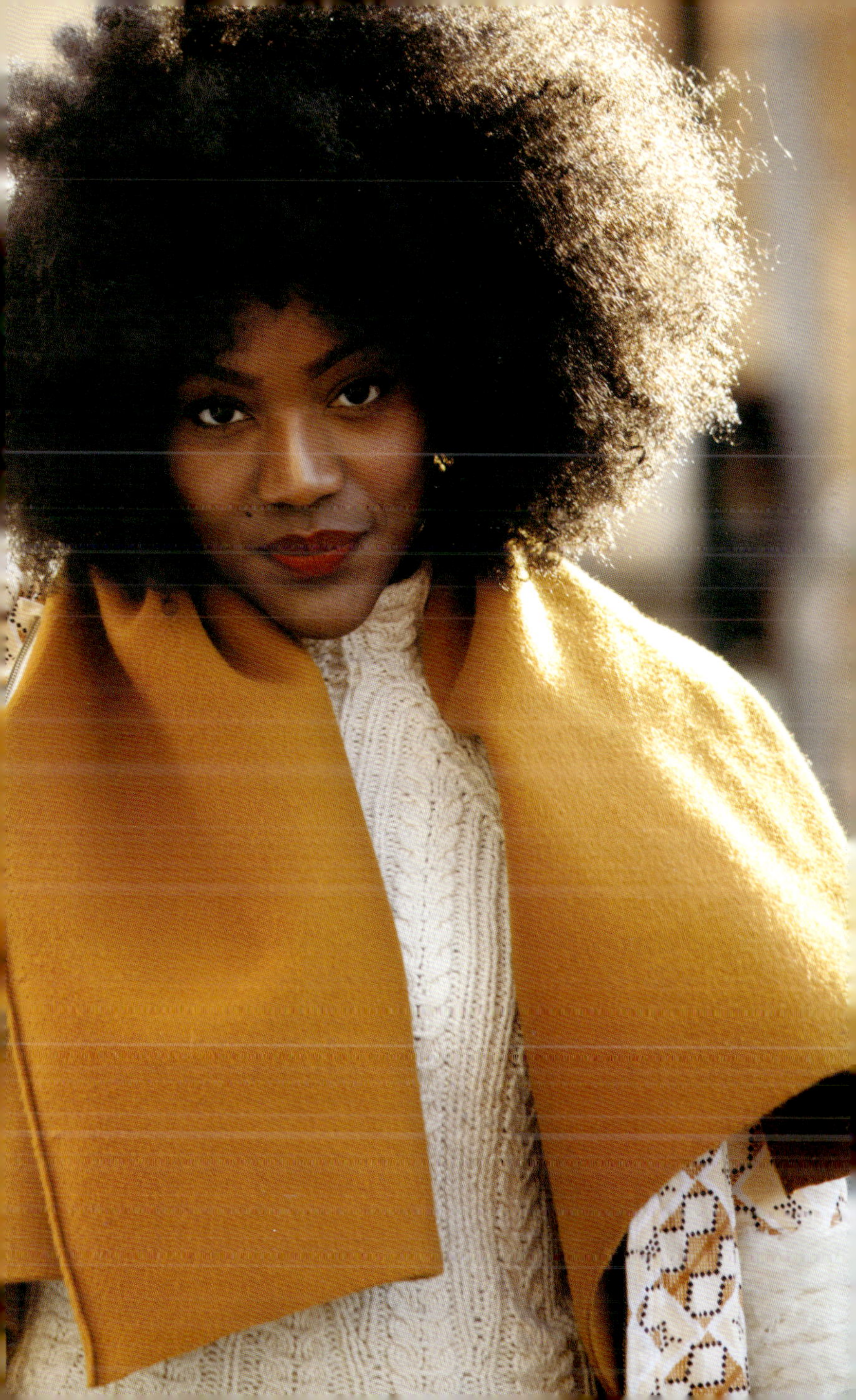

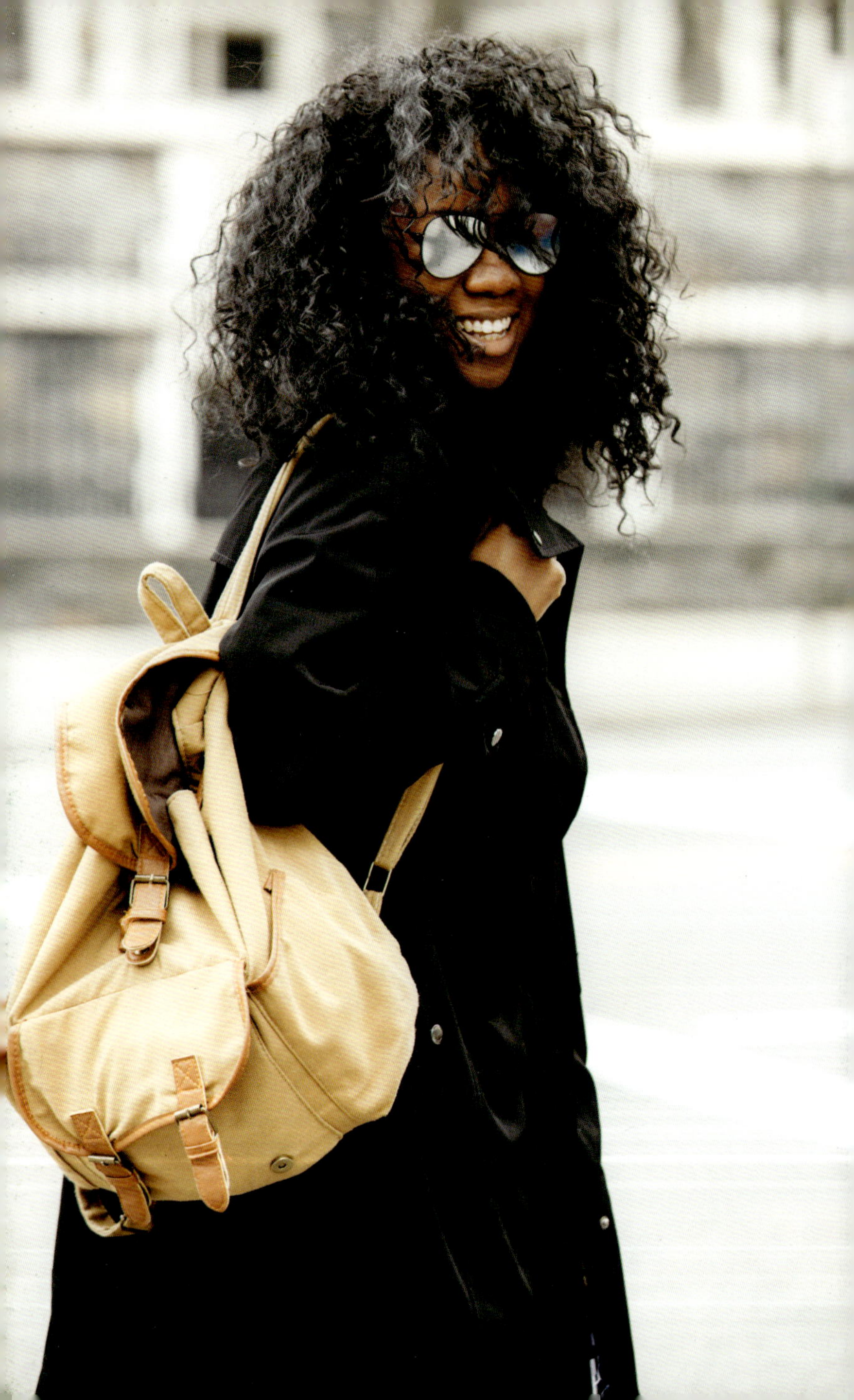

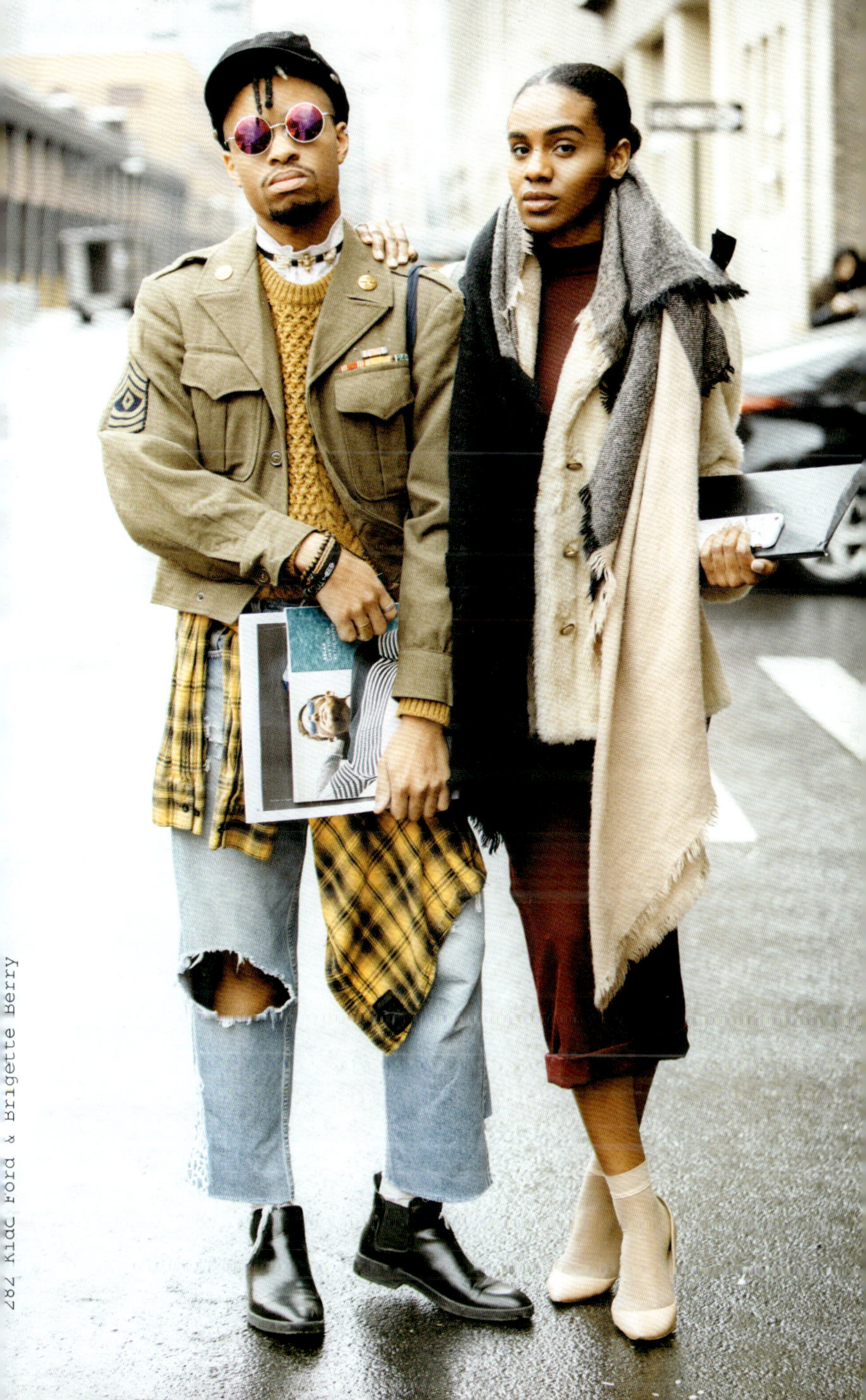

282 Kidd Ford & Brigette Berry

“I see the world as a vast network of art in which we are all connected and can embrace the openness of it.”

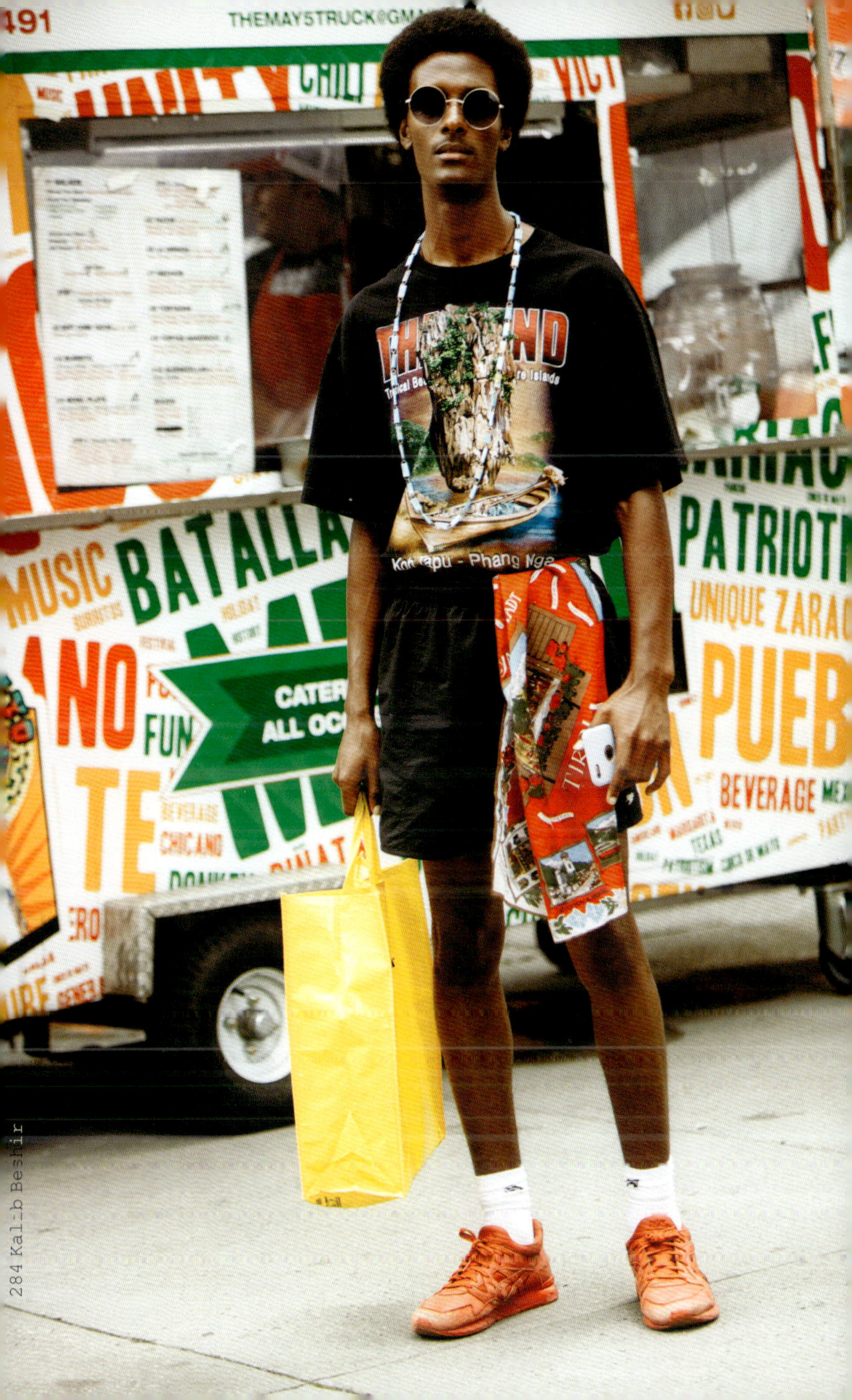

284 Kal-b Beshir

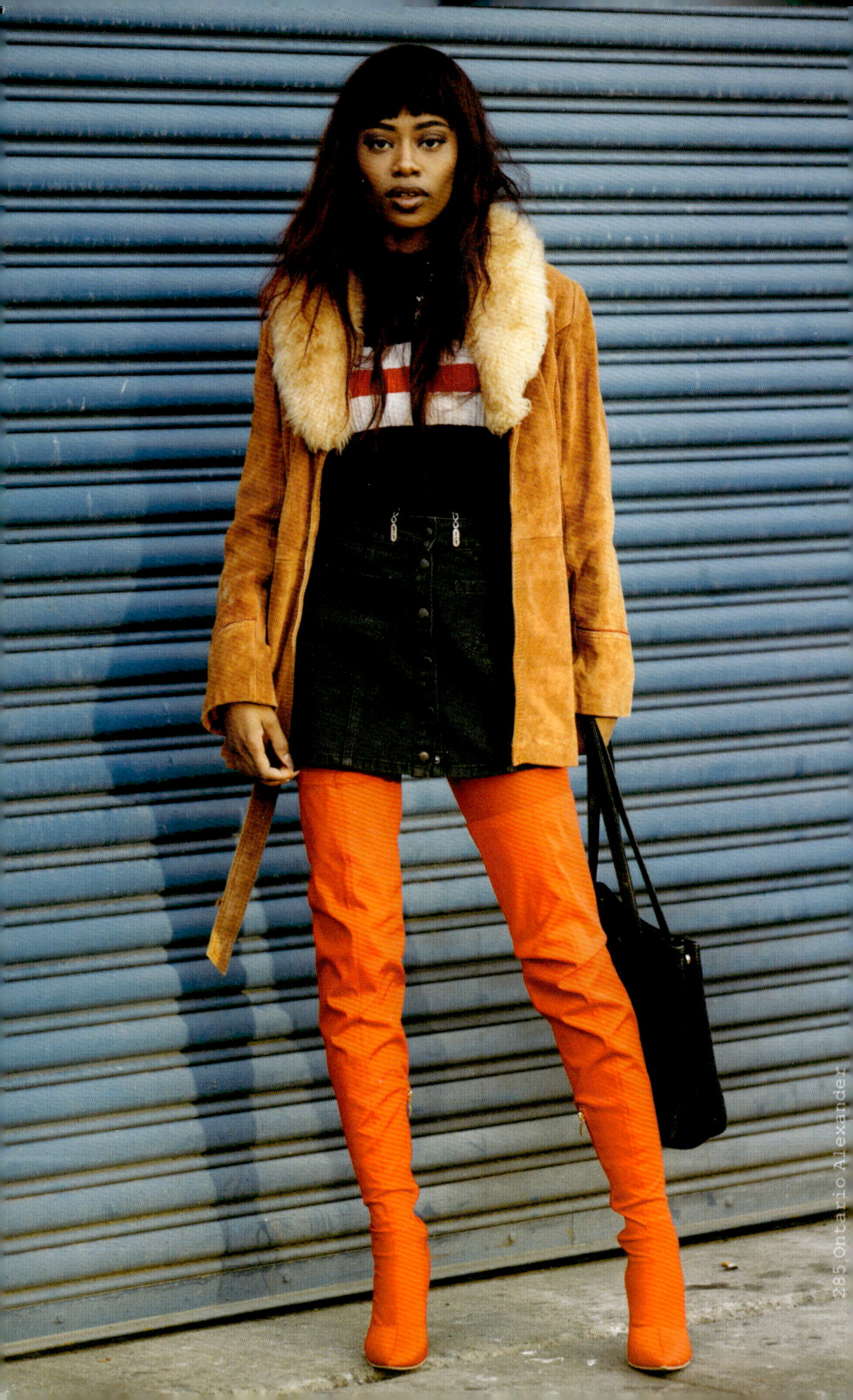

285 Ontario Alexander

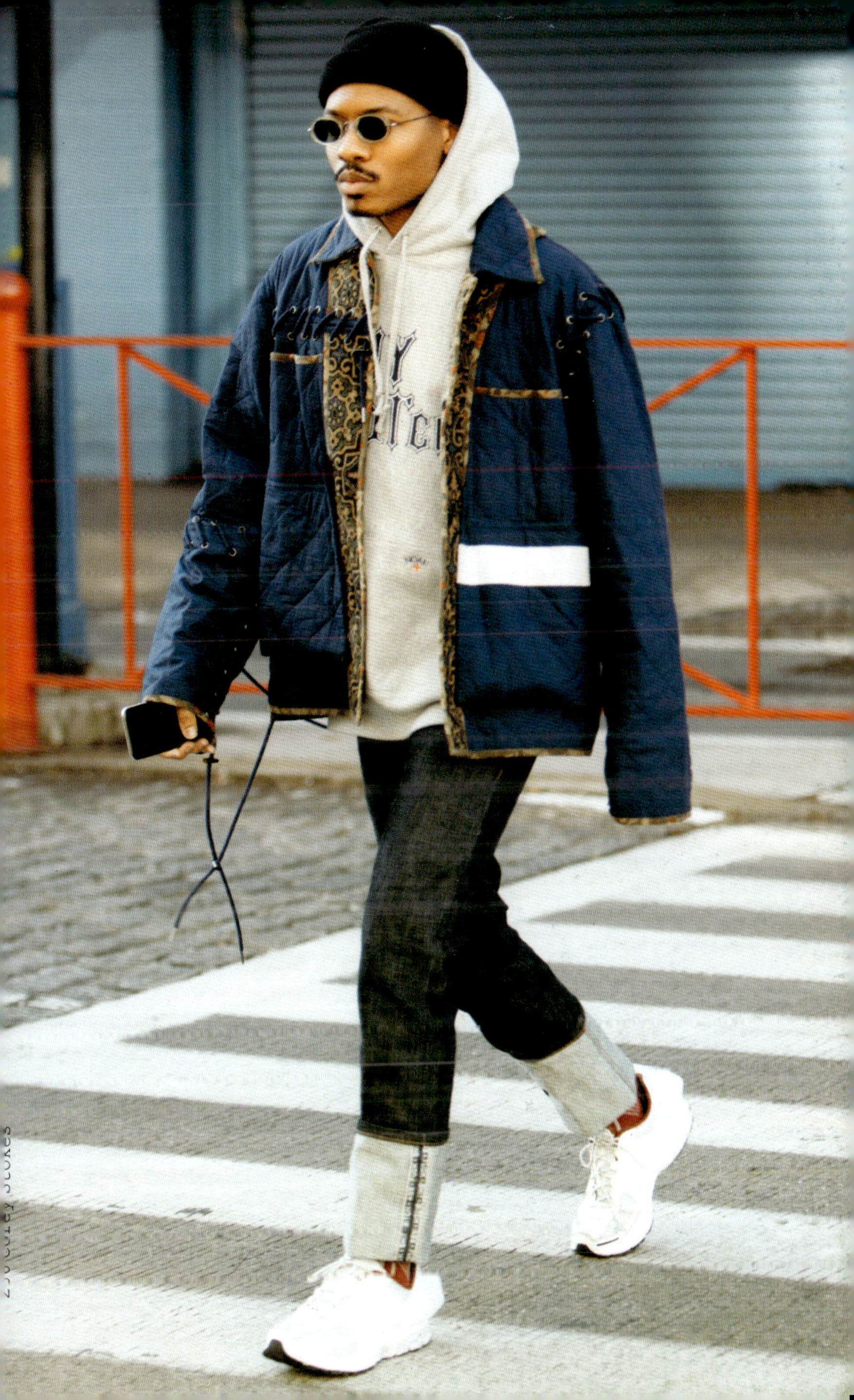

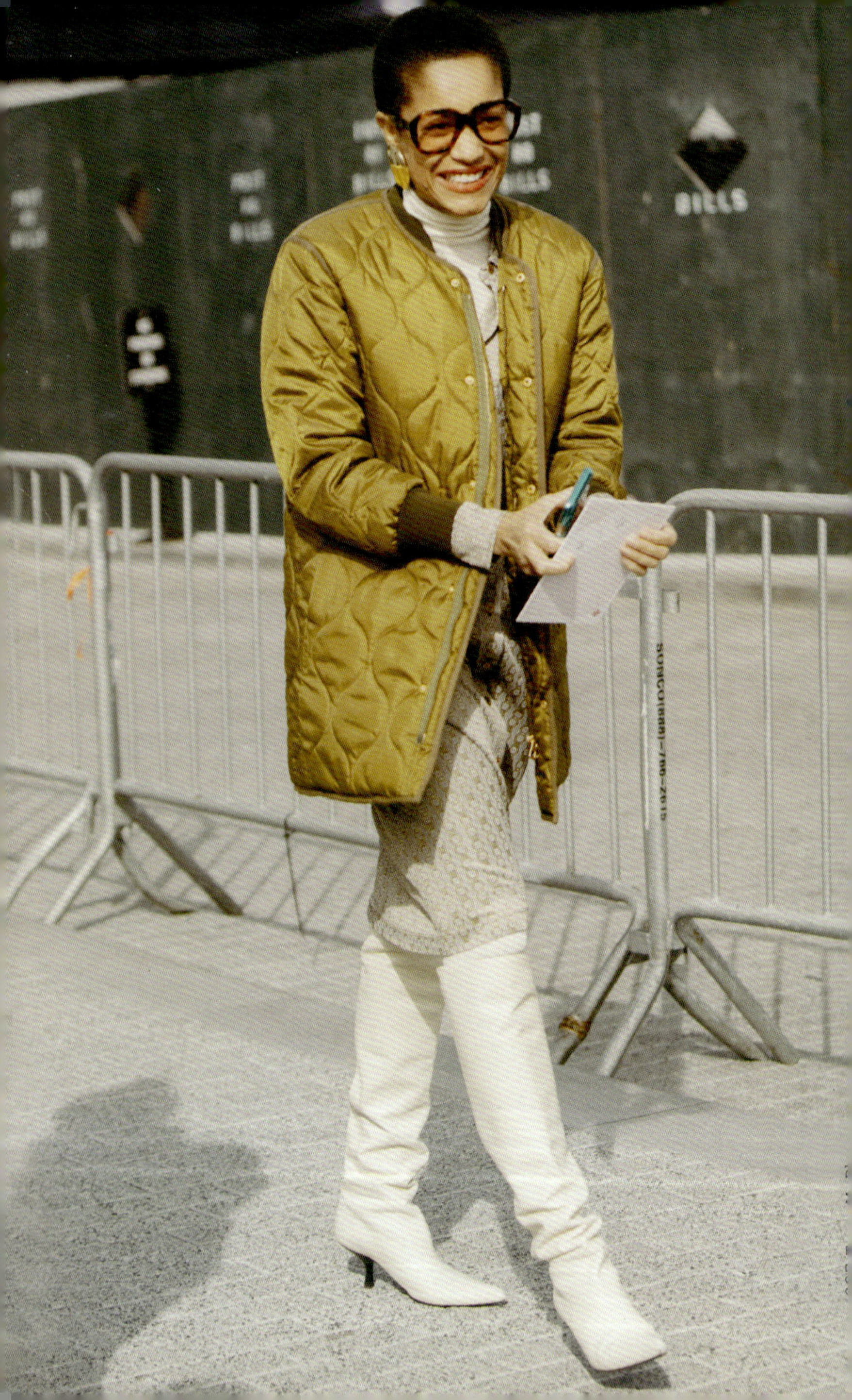
BILLS

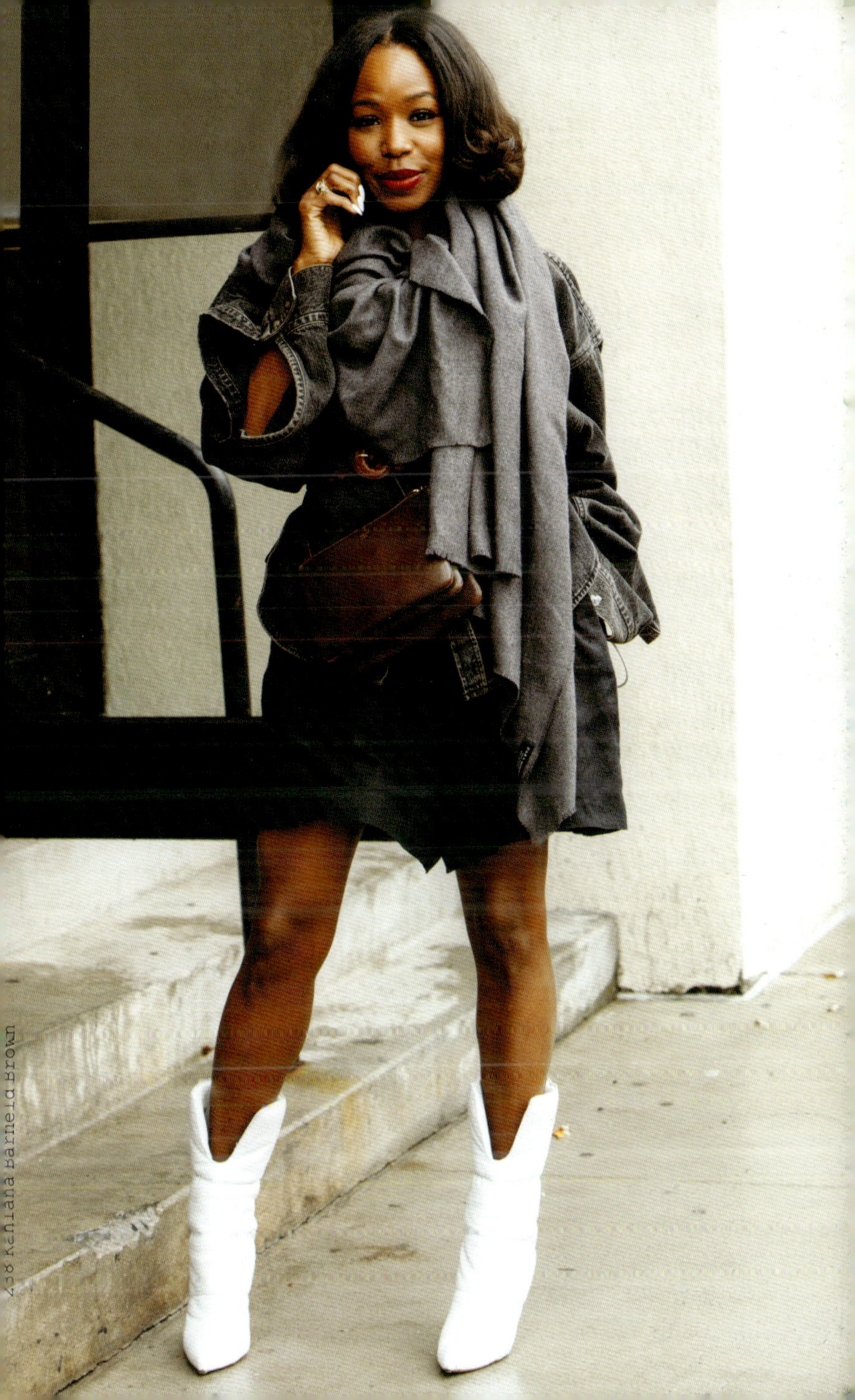

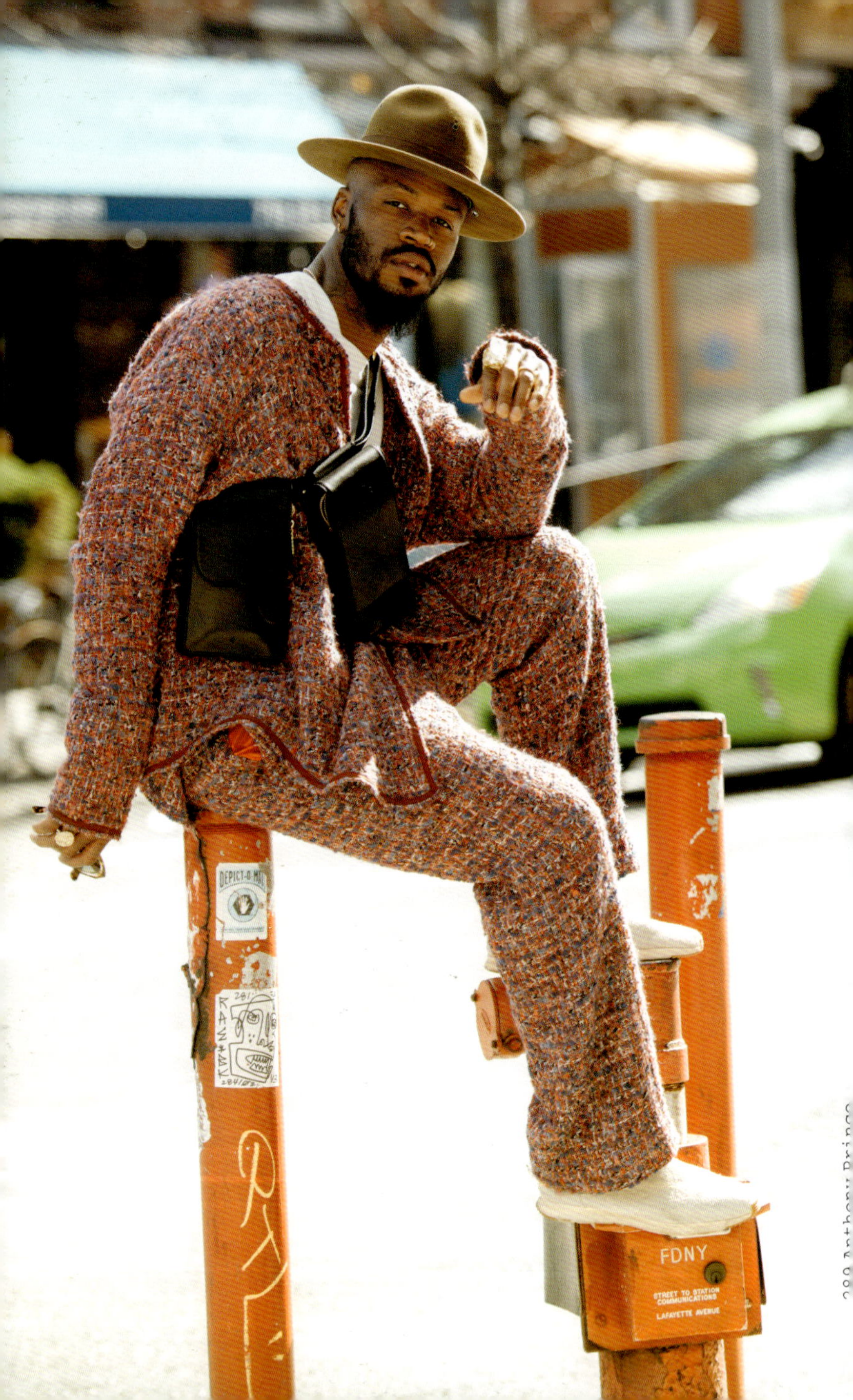

 Anthony Prince

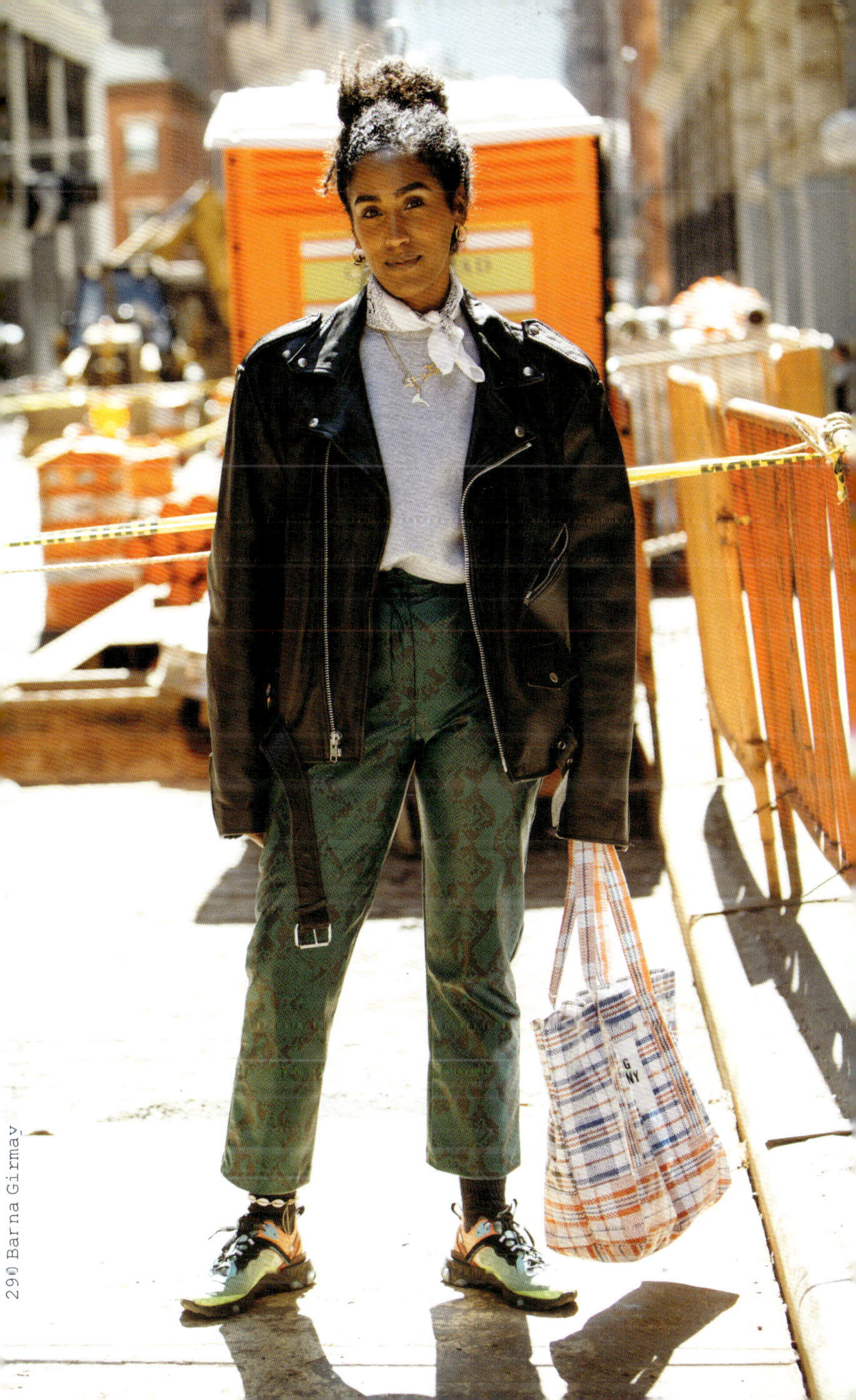

290 Barna Girmay

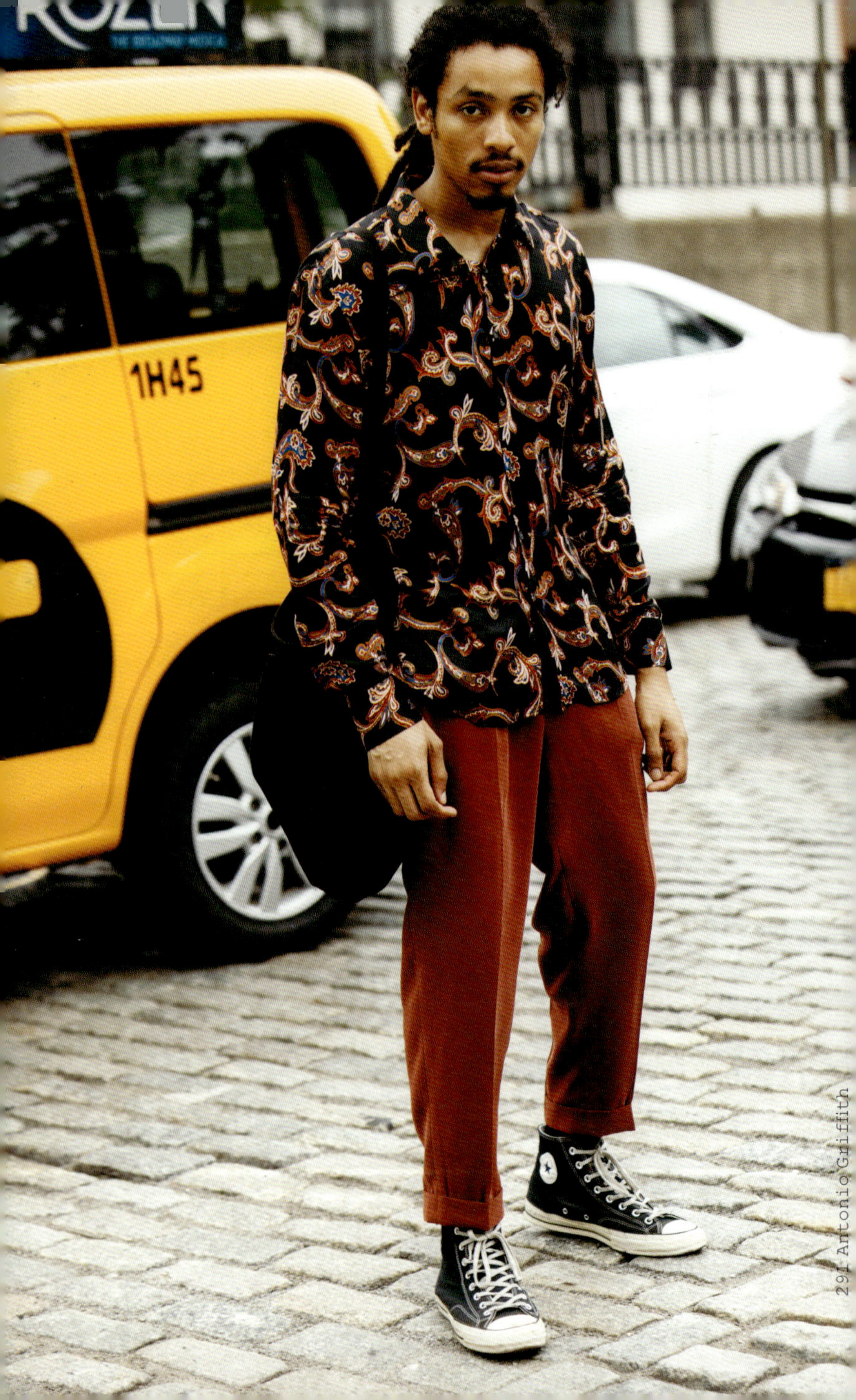

291 Antonio Griffith

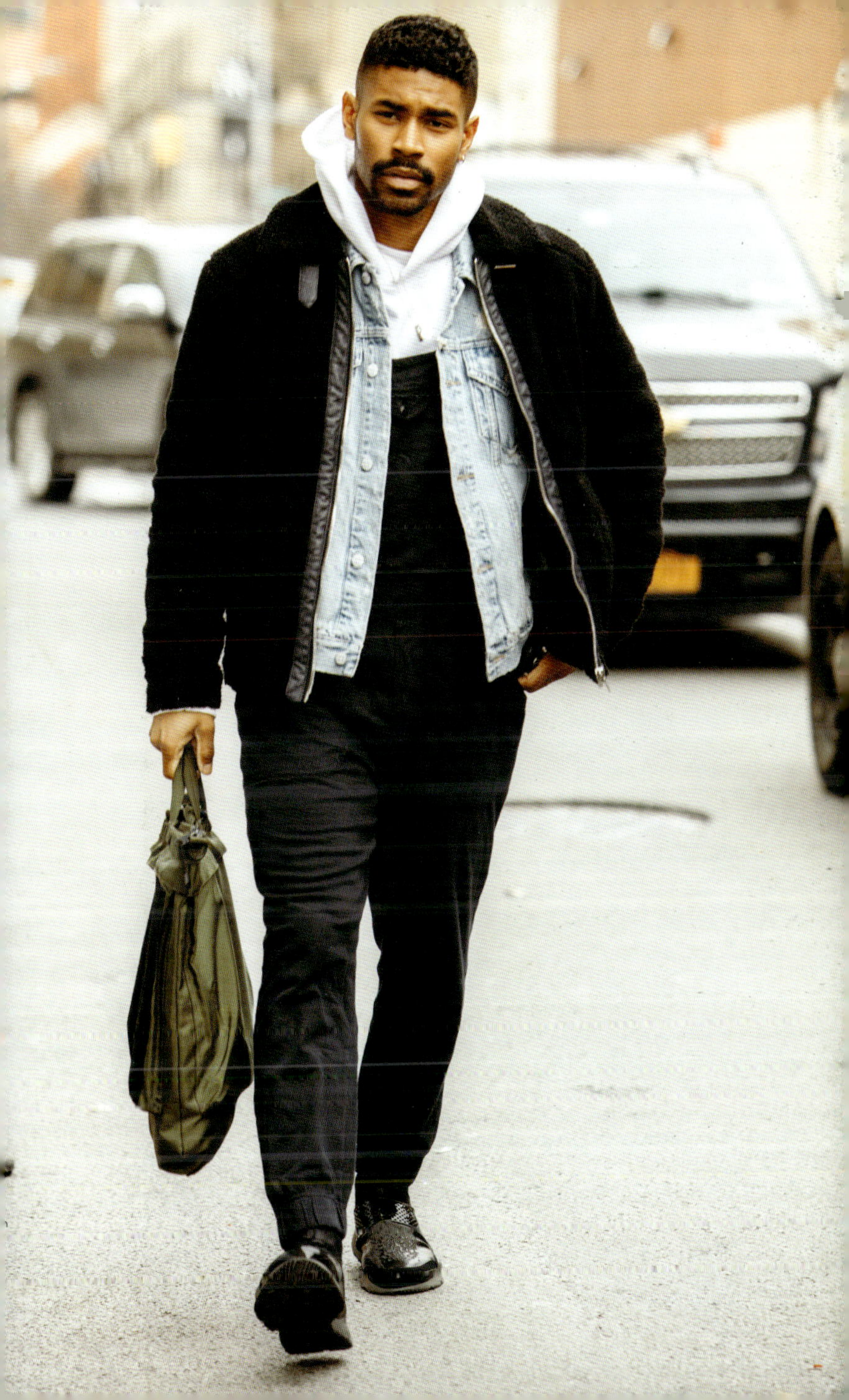

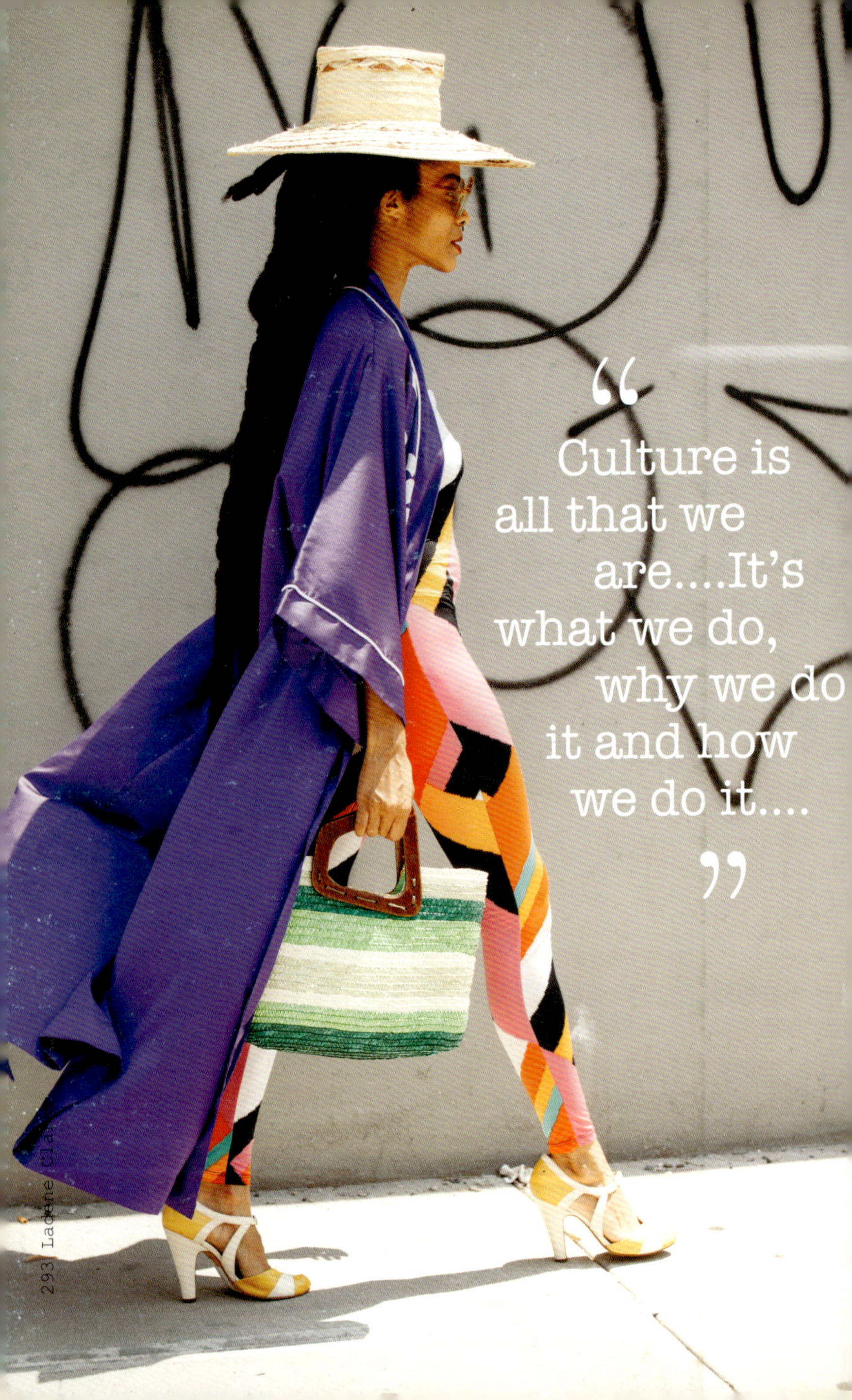
"Culture is all that we are....It's what we do, why we do it and how we do it...."